Multidisciplinary Perspectives on Literacy Research

Second Edition

LANGUAGE & SOCIAL PROCESSES
Judith Green, editor

Multidisciplinary Perspectives on Literacy Research

Second Edition

edited by

Richard Beach
University of Minnesota

Judith Green
University of California, Santa Barbara

Michael Kamil
Stanford University

Timothy Shanahan
University of Illinois

HAMPTON PRESS, INC.
CRESSKILL, NJ 07626

Printed in the United States of America

Multidisciplinary perspectives on literacy research / edited by Richard Beach ... [et al.]--2nd ed.
        p. cm. (Language and social processes)
    Includes bibliographic references and index.
    ISBN 1-57273-626-7 -- ISBN 1-57273-627-5
        1. Language arts--Research--Congresses. 2. Language arts--Research--Methodology--Congresses. 3. Applied linguistics--Research--Congresses. I. Beach, Richard. II. Series.

LB1576.M85 2005
428".0072--dc22

                                                        2005040301

Hampton Press, Inc.
23 Broadway
Cresskill, NJ 07626

Contents

Preface

The first edition of *Multidisciplinary Perspectives on Literacy Research* appeared in 1992. Since that time, a number of changes have occurred that are reflected in this revised, second edition, changes that reflect shifts in the prevailing disciplinary and theoretical perspectives shaping literacy research as well as the methodological approaches employed. In many ways, this second edition represents an entirely new collection; of the 17 chapters included in this volume, only 4 are revised versions of original chapters.

One of the major shifts is suggested by a change in the name of the professional organization sponsoring this collection, the National Conference on Research on Language and Literacy. The purpose of this conference is to (a) stimulate and encourage research in the teaching and learning of language and literacies; (b) synthesize, interpret, and publish significant research and compilations of research in the teaching and learning of language and literacies; (c) support research and special projects authorized by the executive committee; and, (d) recognize and reward outstanding achievements in the teaching and learning of language and literacies. (For more information about the conference, visit the conference Web site at http://education.nyu.edu/teachlearn/research/ncrll/.)

The name of the conference in 1992, at the time of the original edition, was the National Conference on Research on English. In 1995, members of the organization voted to change "English" to "Language and Literacy" given the fact that their research encompassed much more than what is typically associated with the field of "English." While the question, "What is English?" has been the subject of much debate for decades, the fact that the members changed the organization's name reflected a larger shift in how they conceptualize their work. They perceived the need to understand "English" as involving broader aspects of language learning and literacy practices associated with understanding and producing texts—one possible definition of "English." Given major disciplinary shifts in fields associated with "language" toward an increased interest in sociolinguistics, dialect studies, pragmatics, discourse-processing, and second-language learning in the 1980s and 1990s, research on language learning had focused increasingly on social and cultural aspects of language. Some of this shift was precipitated by the need to address the language learning issues of an increasingly diverse population of students related to reading and writing.

This broader conception of language learning, certainly reflected in chapter 13 in the first edition, is continued in the third section of this edition in chapters by Bloome, Gee, Hornberger, Dixon and Green, and Ivanic. These researchers focus on language uses in literacy events and contexts to perform a range of different social actions and practices, for example, building relationships, defining status/power hierarchies, including and excluding others, or defining identities.

Similarly, the inclusion of "Literacy" in the organization's name reflected a shift away from traditional skill-based, decoding models toward broader notions of literacy as reflected in interest in literacy practices and socio-cultural models of literacy learning. This broader conception of literacy learning frames researchers analysis of literacy as social practices employed in institutions and communities, learning mediated by various tools—language, narratives, genres, artifacts, images. Some of this expansion of notions of literacy reflects shifts toward increased uses of technology-based, digital literacies that have exploded in the past decade as reflected in uses of e-mail, chat, and web-based communication. It also reflects an increased interest in pedagogical aspects of critical literacy—as represented in the final section of the collection in chapters by Freebody and Mellor and Patterson. A critical literacy agenda, in turn, continually examines the meaning of institutional and technological shifts in literacy uses themselves, for example, the increasingly commodification of popular culture and media. A critical literacy agenda also suggests the need for educators to practice what they preach—to recognize that their theories of literacy learning are manifest in how they teach or interact with participants in research projects. As Jerome Harste (1992) noted in the forward to the first edition:

> Language research must be rooted in our envisionments of education and the role that our discipline (language and language education) plays in learning. I firmly believe that the way we teach and research language affects the kind of profession, as well as society, we create. What a new theory of language research changes says a lot about what they new theory of language research is and whether or not it has value. (p. xii)

The basic premise of the first and this new edition is that research on language and literacy requires multidisciplinary perspectives that draw from a range of different disciplines—psychology, sociology, history, anthropology, economics, linguistics, sociolinguistics, rhetoric, composition studies, literary criticism/studies, cultural studies, and so on. These various disciplinary perspectives are themselves continually evolving and overlapping, creating new, alternative subdisciplinary perspectives that challenge status quo disciplinary perspectives (Klein, 1996; Latour, 1987, 1999; Messer-Davidow, Shumway, & Sylvan, 1993). Shifts in these disciplinary perspectives or epistemological orientations foster new research methods whose uses are based on and are justified by their underlying disciplinary perspective. For example, the value of fieldnotes and extensive observations are justified by the anthropologists' beliefs in the need to "make the familiar strange and the strange familiar" in understanding a culture.

The chapters in first section, "Multiple Disciplinary Perspectives and Issues of Research Design" address these often philosophical and epistemological issues as to what constitutes a "disciplinary perspective," the value of adopting alternative perspectives, and implications for literacy research methods, issues reflected throughout this collection. One issue, for example, is the degree to which researchers interrogate the limitations of their own particular disciplinary perspective, particularly in relation to competing disciplinary perspectives. For example, whether or not cognitive psychologists examine the extent to which literacy practices are constituted by participation in social and cultural contexts is an issue addressed by John Hayes. Another issue has to do with the extent to which certain methodological approaches—descriptive/qualitative, experimental, ethnographic, case study, survey, and so on, are supported by particularly disciplinary perspectives. Although ethnographic analyses of literacy practices are more likely to be supported by sociocultural and critical literacy perspectives, are there other perspectives that may yield further insights into ethnographic data? For example, as Berkenkotter documents in her chapter, given the increasing uses of photographic and digital data, media studies or semiotics may provide useful insights into the meaning of images related to capturing cultural contexts. And, another issue has to do with the ongoing debate between proponents of a positivist, quantitative orientation valued within certain social science perspectives and a more descriptive, qualitative orientation valued in other social science perspectives regarding matters of validity, generalizability, and "scientific" merit, a debate addressed by George Hillocks. (We should add that George, former president of NCRLL when this project was launched, retired in Spring 2003 after a distinguished career as a literacy researcher at the University of Chicago, particularly in the area of composition research.)

One of the major disciplinary shifts in the past decade has been the increased influence of sociocultural or activity theory perspectives of learning on literacy research, the focus of the second section of this book. These perspectives draw on interdisciplinary perspectives of sociocultural psychological theories, sociology, language/literary theory, and rhetoric/genre theory, and, in particular the work of Vygotsky, Bakhtin, Leontev, Engestrom, Bourdieu, Habermas, and Latour, all of whom were interested in how participants learned various practices in social and institutional settings, a primary focus of this section. It is difficult to readily label each of these theorists as representative of a particular disciplinary perspective because they were each challenging traditional disciplinary practices to create new interdisciplinary perspectives.

Given this disciplinary shift, literacy researchers are much more likely to study how participants acquire literacy practices within the context of particular institutional settings outside of schools than was the case in the past. This is reflected in a sharp increase in what, in their chapter, Tusting and Barton describe as "community-based local literacy research." It has also meant an increased interest in intercultural or cross-cultural literacy research in which researchers examine the ability of participants to move within and across boundaries and borders of different social and cultural contexts. Any understanding of literacy practices in institutional settings requires perspectives from sociology, anthropology, economics (particularly neo-Marxist), political science, or cultural studies, perspectives that may not be familiar to literacy researchers.

To understand the influence of these disciplinary perspectives on literacy research methods, we asked individual contributors to formulate definitions and explications of the disciplinary/theoretical perspective(s) shaping their research. This included having them chart the evolution or history of their perspective(s) and reasons for this evolution, unpack assumptions regarding literacy and literacy learning underlying their perspective(s), and demonstrate how their perspective(s) shapes their own current research.

We should also note that given space limitations, we were not able to include some examples of particular disciplinary perspectives represented in the first volume. Therefore, we refer readers to chapters in the first volume for discussions of ethnomethodology/sociology (James Heap), literary/dialogic theory (Russell Hunt and Douglas Vipond, Joanne Golden), sociolinguistics (Jenny Cook-Gumperz and John Gumperz), cognitive processing (Arthur Graeser, Joseph Magliano, and Paul Tidwell), sociocultural learning theory (Luis Moll), and postmodern/poststructuralist perspectives (Linda Brodkey, Peter McLaren).

We hope that by illustrating how the researchers in this volume have drawn on these perspectives to inform their research, this volume will be useful for beginning literacy researchers as they work through the complex intersection of how disciplinary perspectives shape their own research questions and procedures. We also hope that some of the novel disciplinary perspectives contained in this volume will serve to foster new perspectives and procedures so that literacy researchers will continue to interrogate the theoretical limitations of their current research in order to break new ground in understanding the complexities of literacy learning.

REFERENCES

Harste, J. (1992). Foreword. In R. Beach, J. L. Green, M. L. Kamil, & T. Shanahan (Eds.), *Multidisciplinary perspectives on literacy research* (pp. ix-xiii). Urbana, IL: National Conference on Research in English/National Council of Teachers of English.

Klein, J. (1996). *Crossing boundaries: Knowledge, disciplinarities, and inter-disciplinarities.* Charlottesville: University Press of Virginia.

Latour, B. (1987). *Science in action: How to follow scientists and engineers through society.* Cambridge, MA: Harvard University Press.

Latour, B. (1999). *Pandora's hope: Essays on the reality of science studies.* Cambridge: Harvard University Press.

Messer-Davidow, E., Shumway, D., & Sylvan, D. (Eds.). *Knowledges: Historical and critical studies in disciplinarity.* Charlottesville: University of Virginia Press.

PART I

MULTIPLE DISCIPLINARY PERSPECTIVES AND ISSUES OF RESEARCH DESIGN

Timothy Shanahan
University of Illinois

Michael L. Kamil
Stanford University

INTRODUCTION

Policymakers and practitioners are interested in the products of research. Even a cursory glance at the emphasis on scientifically based research shows this to be true. However, they often have little patience for details about how the investigations were conducted, and usually want to focus on outcomes, findings, and conclusions. If for some reason they needed to read a research paper, they would likely cut right to the conclusion or summary section to find out the bottom line. That emphasis on outcomes is only natural for those trying to apply to practice and policy the knowledge gained from science, but as any scholar can attest, it often misses the real story. What we know is a function of how we know, and we have many ways of knowing—many ways of figuring out the ways of the world.

By contrast, the hurried scholar often jumps not to the conclusions section but to the methods section. Knowledge is not a unitary, tangible thing, waiting to be received. It has to be constructed. The most solid foundation for knowledge comes when we have an understanding of *both* what and how information and insights were constructed in a research study. Simply put, conclusions depend on the methods by which they are reached. It is important to understand that different methods may lead to different results.

The scholars writing in this volume expose and explain the methodological and theoretical vantages from which they conduct their studies of literacy and language. Each approach to conducting research obviously entails particular research methods and procedures, but, less obviously, these methods entail perspectives, theories, and beliefs all of which shape the "knowledge" that is created through them. These perspectives and theories often lead researchers to ask quite different questions about the same domain. In this section, we examine some of the implications of the research approaches drawn from cognitive psychology and community anthropology.

In this first section, the authors explore implications of the methodological choices that they make in their literacy research. The discussions of these implications show the lack of neutrality of our research methods; that is they reveal how particular methodological choices shape the questions to be asked, expand and narrow the focus of the investigators, and influence how the resulting findings are likely to be used by others.

Research methodology includes a plethora of techniques and procedures for collecting and analyzing empirical data and for reporting the results of the investigation. It should not be surprising that research methods shape our understandings, as these methods can differ even over fundamental points such as what constitutes data and what it means to know something. In turn, the understandings gleaned from research can shape future research methodologies. Research is a recursive process.

Researchers from different perspectives sometimes foolishly argue for the primacy of their particular approach to looking at the world. What they fail to realize is that different perspectives are valuable because they allow us to see things that we might not discern from another perspective. The underlying premise of this volume is that we will best understand literacy if we approach it from many points of observation, through many different lenses, but with a discerning understanding of how the method shapes the outcome. Through one lens a particular issue or phenomenon might be totally hidden from sight, while from another it becomes visible with crystal clarity.

The reading wars (Kamil, 1995; Stanovich, 1990) produced much acrimonious debate (e.g. Edelsky, 1990; McKenna, Robinson, & Miller, 1990) before they subsided. In that acrimonious debate, the two sides at times seemed as if they were deliberately trying to misunderstand each other. This debate, however, was largely academic and involved many details about research and conclusions that held little or no interest for many policymakers and practitioners. Each side was making exaggerated claims, based on its definition of research and methodology that were unacceptable or unintelligible to the other. As both Stanovich and Kamil pointed out, however, neither side should be able to make statements that do not translate into some phenomenon in each perspective, no matter how salient the phenomenon is.

What are these abstract ideas like in the real world? What is a perspective? We take this to mean a collection of ideas about what important phenomena go to make up the ability we call *literacy*. Perspectives are not always sharply defined, in contrast to theories, which are, or should be, worked out in some detail. Perspectives are often implicit statements about emphasizing one aspect or another in literacy. For example, a psychological perspective emphasizes individual literacy behaviors like decoding. A sociocultural perspective might emphasize the role of others in determining literacy practice. Still other perspectives might emphasize the role of gender or communities in the outcomes of literacy.

Disciplines are something else. They refer to organized bodies of knowledge about a particular topic. These are often thought of as content areas. Disciplines focus on a relatively narrow range of knowledge, allowing for different perspectives on important features of that knowledge. What counts as a discipline has been gradually broadened. Rather than the simple Aristotelian notion of discipline (e.g., rhetoric) we now have exotic disciplines like materials sciences. We count literacy as a discipline, a body of knowledge that is informed by many other disciplines: psychology, anthropology, sociology, literary criticism, and many others.

These definitions show clearly why we need multiple perspectives to make sense of all of the relevant knowledge and information that is relevant to literacy. Ultimately it is the combination of findings from a variety of perspectives that will converge to provide us with the clearest idea of what literacy means in our personal and public lives, and how best to extend the benefits of literacy to all. The first section of this book lays the groundwork for developing an understanding of the value of different perspectives and for considering how we can best accumulate knowledge across perspectives.

REFERENCES

Edelsky, C. (1990). Whose agenda is this anyway? A response to McKenna, Robinson, and Miller. *Educational Researcher, 19*, 7-11.

Kamil, M. L. (1995). Some alternatives to paradigm wars. *Journal of Reading Behavior, 27*, 243-261.

McKenna, M., Robinson, R., & Miller, J. (1990). Whole language: A research agenda for the nineties. *Educational Researcher, 19*, 3-6.

Stanovich, K. E. (1990). A call for an end to the paradigm wars in reading research. *Journal of Reading Behavior, 22*(3), 221-231.

1

Modes of Inquiry in Literacy Studies and Issues of Philosophy of Science

Timothy Shanahan
University of Illinois at Chicago

We spend much time telling teachers and potential teachers what we think we know about literacy and literacy education. Whether we advocate direct instruction or whole language or something in between, our affiliations, approaches, and recommendations are based to a great extent on our interpretations of empirical observations—our knowledge, if you will. This chapter takes a fundamentally different approach. Rather than dwelling on what I think we know and should do as literacy educators, I consider what it means to "know" about literacy at all. My intention is to focus on my own work, but to discuss that work with the idea of making evident my own biases and limitations (inquiry is a least in part a personal quest).

Through an examination of brief illustrations from my own work, I hope to pose questions about the epistemological assumptions underlying all research on literacy. These questions should help us to understand the similarities and differences in the various "perspectives" represented in this book—with regard to basic theoretical assumptions and empirical approach. It is, I believe, the answers to these questions that determine who we are *together* as scholars and whether or not we are involved in a *shared* enterprise of accumulating knowledge.

Most recently, I have been engaged in a number of research syntheses, usually conducted for public purposes at the request of various government or educational agencies. For instance, in the mid–1990s, the North

Central Regional Education Lab (NCREL) came to Rebecca Barr and me, wanting to know if the research showed that Reading Recovery© worked or not, as states were investing heavily in it and governors wanted to evaluate the wisdom of this policy (Shanahan & Barr, 1995). Later, I served on the National Reading Panel (NRP, 2000), a group convened at the request of the U.S. Congress to determine what works in reading instruction; a task undertaken with the hope of ending the divisive "reading wars." Currently, I am chairing similar panels on second language literacy and early and family literacy for the U.S. Department of Education and the National Institute for Literacy (NIFL), respectively.

These synthesis projects have given me a special vantage from which to consider the meaning of varied perspectives in literacy research. However, I also make reference to some of my own primary investigations into literacy here, such as my studies of reading-writing relationships.

One thing that is obvious is that there are many ways to categorize or divide an intellectual community into subgroups. The easiest way is topically. Some of us might study teacher decision making, others the psychological connections between reading and writing, and still others the social implications of language differences. A community of scholars can examine any of these topics, and the participants in that enterprise will tend to read and publish in certain journals, and participate at certain conferences. The members of another group—this one interested in another literacy topic—will tend to read different journals, attend different conferences, and intellectually hang out with a different crowd for the most part.

Topical distinctions are useful because none of us has the need or energy to know all aspects of literacy research. Metaphors and inquiry methods can be used across topical boundaries, but even with this not all information on literacy will have direct or immediate application to all other aspects of literacy. Topical organization increases efficiency of communication, and facilitates steady development of new knowledge on issues of particular interest to the group or groups working on the project.

NRP paid much attention to topical distinctions when it synthesized research. The Panel, for example, held public hearings at which more than 300 people testified—and virtually all of this testimony argued for attention to particular topics of study. NRP followed suit organizing its work around eight specific literacy topics (phonemic awareness, phonics, oral reading, methods for encouraging students to read, vocabulary, comprehension, teacher education, technology). The panel only reviewed research on these topics, omitting any study that did not focus on these issues. That meant that NRP had to screen through tens of thousands of literacy studies to find those on these topics. It is sometimes claimed that NRP reviewed more than 100,000 studies (it did not), and some go further, claiming that so few studies were ultimately reviewed (about 400) mainly because of the serious flaws in most reading research (again, not true). Actually, NRP set aside more studies due to topical differences than to any other criterion.

As useful—and even necessary—as such topical categories may be, they fail to tell the whole story of who we are and how our work together has meaning. This point can best be made through a consideration of a basic definition of *perspective*: "the interrelationships of proportionate significance of facts or information as considered from a particular point of view." Modes of inquiry—the methods that are used to conduct studies and investigations—are a second useful way of thinking about the literacy community (Lessnoff, 1974) because research methods help determine what our points of view will be, and inherent in these methods are the basic assumptions that we use to determine the proportionate significance of facts or information. Although the merit of dividing the field on the basis of inquiry methods might be debatable, it is apparent that inquiry communities do exist in literacy and we, whether rejecting or applauding such divisions, must understand their implications. Meehl (1989) goes so far as to suggest that social scientists cannot make satisfactory progress until they understand the philosophical issues of inquiry nearly as well as the philosopher of science.

Inquiry by its nature has an underlying epistemology or philosophy; a set of beliefs or assumptions about the nature of the world and how we might best go about understanding that world. When we conduct an ethnographic study or a quasi-experiment or any other kind of inquiry we are making implicit claims about what is interesting, how we learn, and the nature of reality. This brief chapter will raise a number of epistemological questions, drawn from the philosophy of science, about various modes of inquiry. The purpose of posing these questions is to enhance our understandings of the various perspectives represented in this collection and of the relations among them, and to consider whether these ways of knowing represent alternative approaches to the world, or alternative worlds.

EXISTENCE AND EPISTEMOLOGY

My own work tends to use experimental, quasi-experimental, and correlational-descriptive methods that have been appropriated from psychology (via agriculture) and economics—and I have tended to synthesize studies from these traditions as well. The meta-analytic procedures of synthesis that I favor are drawn from education or educational psychology—methods that have now been adopted in many other disciplines. Within such methodologies, I begin from the Cartesian premise that the universe, external to me, does exist. My own understanding of the universe is necessarily imperfect because of the limits of my own perceptual and intellectual apparatus, as well as my unique, and necessarily skewed individual perspective. Of course, it is possible to understand a great deal about one's world just by living (our grandmothers probably know or knew a great deal about how people think or the nature of language—witness the different definitions of the word empirical), but the scholar, according to my perspective, is unique *because* he or she tries to reach beyond the vision possible from a necessarily narrow individual vantage. It is these methods and procedures—the rules of conducting inquiry—that allow knowledge to accumulate and that are the very basis of constructivist notions. Science is formally constructivist. That is, science sets out to specify clearly what methods or operations are used to "construct" the results of its investigations.

In a study that I conducted of classroom authorship activities, I attempted to describe behaviors that actually existed—and that I believe existed separately from my ability to perceive them. (Yes, I do believe that the tree that falls unheard in the forest makes sound or has sound potential.) However, my belief in some corporal reality outside of my own being does not mean that I, or anyone, can perceive things accurately or meaningfully. For this study, I focused on behaviors and activities that I have a personal and ideological commitment to, so it is possible for anyone to upset or recast the meaning that I found by looking in a different manner or by recalibrating the categories. A major aspect of research is trying to convince others in our community that our imperfect perception was actually correct (a rhetorical function that requires the inquirer to not only "know," but to be convincing about what is known). The major purpose of the logical and empirical procedures of my epistemology is to minimize error and to attempt to overcome, or reach beyond, individual limits.

In my study, because I wanted to employ teacher self-observations, how could I be certain that they would recognize the activities of interest? One of the things that I did to increase the possibility of such accuracy was to design an instrument, on the basis of previous observations, that permitted accurate coding and that did not bias teachers toward emphasizing "authorship" during the study (listed categories did not include authorship choices alone, and all choices were presented as being equally desirable). Next, I trained teachers in the use of the instrument so that we would have equivalent definitions of behaviors. Finally, an assistant and I observed a sample of the recorded lessons to permit the computation of interrater reliabilities. Such procedures increased the possibility that we were not omitting actions that took place, nor were we inventing behaviors that did not exist (even if those same behaviors could be categorized or interpreted in other ways or even ignored in other investigations). That several of us were able to see the same phenomenon consistently gives me support for the fact that I am not suffering from wishful thinking, or just seeing what I wanted. (On the other hand, such procedures might lead me to neglect some less reliable actions that might be important, also. My approaches to accuracy and validity encourage me to notice the consistent and repeatable at the expense of the idiosyncratic and particular.)

Many of the empirical procedures that I employ (sampling, random assignment, interrater reliability, etc.) are meant to reduce the influence of my own biases and misperceptions. These methodologies are used to make my results more objective (i.e., less influenced by my subjectivity). Similarly, I look for these methodological protections in the work of others when I synthesize their studies to determine what we know collectively. Knowing specifically and thoroughly how the individual studies were done is essential to being able to trust the results and to synthesize or combine the results in any meaningful way. (More subjective work is of less value to me, because it is less evident how it can be weighed and combined.)

Not all research perspectives necessarily accept these fundamental premises. Do scholars who use the various research paradigms subscribe to the idea of the existence of a real and separate universe? And, if, according to a particular perspective, this autonomous universe does not exist, what kind of phenomenological devices are used to replace it? Do all research approaches accept that our role as scholars is to reach beyond the basic flaws in our ability to grasp the world or do they see the act of scholarship as one of creation, action, or ideology (the creation of possible worlds, rather than the accurate description of existing ones)? If an approach to inquiry does accept the need for rigorous procedures to overcome the personal limits of the individual scholar, then what procedures or other apparatus are believed to be necessary to minimize this personal influence or bias?

THE QUEST FOR TRUTH

Another critical idea in inquiry is that of the role of truth. Historically, and popularly, science has been seen as an attempt to describe the world in accurate, nonideological terms. "Truth," the holy grail of science, is accomplished, according to such views, when we are able to achieve this one-to-one correspondence between phenomenon and explanation. The strongest evidence of such correspondence is usually seen as the ability to make predictions on the basis of past events.

However, this simple, and simplistic, notion of truth no longer holds sway in our communities. What is seen to be true is now believed to have its basis less in a positivistic correspondence of this type, but on theory. Theoretical paradigms are used to guide our way of looking at the world, and they determine how we interpret what we see. Thus, truth-seeking is not a final determination of facts, but is, instead, an attempt to find correspondence between expectations and reality. In other words, there can be no final truth, except within particularly well-defined theoretical conditions.

In my study of authorship, there is only a weak correspondence between phenomenon and explanation. Although there was a significant correlation between authorship activities and critical reading (about 20% variance explanation when controlling for variables such as grade level), it is unknown whether my findings would transfer to other teachers if they used the types of authorship activities that I observed. Additional studies would be needed to make these findings convincing to the skeptical, or even to make me certain that what I had "seen" actually existed.

Nevertheless, my findings are consistent with theories of social interaction and social construction (Nystrand, 1990), as well as with other investigations of literacy (Rowe, 1989). This correspondence makes my findings more interesting to my colleagues, and it can deepen my ability to understand what I have seen. Because these findings fit into a theoretical explanation, and possibly enhance this explanation, I believe that I understand what I am seeing. As encouraging as this might be, these findings do not become "true" because of this theoretical correspondence (others in my community might have it wrong, too). Theory gives my findings meaning; it helps me to interpret what I see. But, in my tradition, I am required to see things that might not match with theory, too. I must array my observations in a manner that permits the rejection of theory, not just its acceptance (Popper, 1959). Whether the correspondence of phenomenon and explanation is evidence of truth or simply a rigorous rhetorical requirement of my discipline, my findings must be strengthened in this way if they are to contribute to our mosaic of "understanding."

How meaning arises from the experimental data that I synthesize may be somewhat easier to grasp because of the focus on well-accepted practical outcomes. A researcher hypothesizes that a relationship is likely to exist between some set of instructional actions (e.g., teaching a child to hear and manipulate the phonemes within words) and a particular educational outcome (e.g., early reading achievement). This is usually done on the basis of some theoretical notion of what it takes to learn to read (i.e., readers will need to learn the alphabetic system, alphabetics would be easier to grasp if students can hear the phonemes, some kids have trouble with this). Given this rudimentary theory, the researcher comes up with a plan for having these instructional actions carried out and analyzes the outcomes under certain conditions (i.e., with a pretest of reading, with a similar group of teachers and students serving as a control). If the results come out as predicted, that is promising, but it is not the whole game. Would the procedures work under other conditions, say with different kinds of children or teachers or tests? How long will the outcomes last? What if we intensified the instruction—or made it briefer? Eventually enough studies may be conducted to answer such questions that I would be willing to conclude—as the NRP did—that phonemic awareness instruction confers an early learning advantage on children. Meaning results from this convergent accumulation of related evidence under a set of conditions that widely obtain.

The movement of science away from notions of truth has had varied implications on the modes of inquiry. Is the conception of truth within a perspective something to be arrived at through a careful and thorough delineation of theory and evidence? Or, is it more consciously an act of rhetoric? That is, would truth better be defined as the accomplishment of social agreement among the participants in a scholarly community? Is inquiry seen as an activity that can increase our understanding of a real world, or is it more an activist pursuit in which we convince the community to move in particular ideological directions?

THE NATURE OF CONSTRUCTS AND OPERATIONALISM

The role of operationalism and construct definition in any mode of inquiry must be understood if we are to grasp the nature of what it is that researchers are trying to accomplish. Our ability to understand the universe is dependent on our ability to define constructs that summarize or describe phenomena and experience in valid, reliable, and useful ways. In the physical sciences, scholars have been able to define constructs that for most practical purposes have become "closed." That is, although there might be a number of ways of measuring something like temperature, these measures are widely accepted as alternatives rather than as different or separate constructs and the implications of heat or the movement of molecules within theories of thermodynamics are widely accepted no matter what the system of measurement (a construct such as temperature would generally be considered to be closed even though some relevant issues concerning that construct, such as absolute zero, have not been entirely resolved). In the social sciences and the humanities, because of the nature of the phenomena that we study, we have had a greater need to rely on "open constructs," that is constructs that are subject to major redefinitions on the basis of operationalism. A construct like intelligence is definable and measurable in many ways, each of which can lead to different normative and substantive conclusions about the nature of the human intellect.

Because of our reliance on open constructs, the role of operationalism in our modes of inquiry is especially important. In my own work, I had to devise a classroom activity diary that would permit notions of authorship to be seen. Of course, many investigators have sought to observe classroom instruction (Durkin, 1978-1979; Florio, 1979; Good & Brophy, 2000), but these have not typically arrived at the same categories that I used. To create my observation instrument, I relied on theoretical approaches to reading-writing relationships (Tierney & Shanahan, 1992); that is, I attempted to formulate variables that were consistent with various theories. It was no accident that I observed authorship and that so many classroom observation studies have ignored this in literacy. My measures are *constructs*. I constructed them to allow me to see particular types of outcomes and activities in the same classrooms. What if I had used a more thorough measure of critical reading—having students trying to recognize craft and rhetoric rather than seeking errors? The outcomes of studies do not just happen, but they are shaped by the measures that we construct.

What kinds of measures are used in the different approaches? How are such operations arrived at? How are the operations viewed within the inquiry community? Are they reified ("intelligence is what is measured by an IQ test") or are they discussed as being conditional? What must the researcher do to convince himself/herself of the validity and reliability or trustworthiness of the observations that result? Does the inquiry end with "findings" (something that existed that we discovered)? Are any constructs "closed," within a particular inquiry community?

THE NATURE OF DESCRIPTIVE LANGUAGE AND SCHOLARLY COMMUNICATION

Inquiry has a heuristic quality; that is, participation in it can lead to greater understanding on the part of the inquirer no matter what the tangible reportable results. However, formal inquiry, as participated in by professional scholars, carries with it a commitment to share outcomes with the community (however, we choose to define that community). This need for communication means that our perspectives are as rhetorical as they are empirical.

The requirement that we be able to share our insights requires that we develop or adopt a descriptive language. The language that is used for telling about our results/findings is necessarily open to misinterpretation. The demands of communication, and empirical rigor, require that we make an effort to use a descriptive language that interferes as little as possible with understanding. This means that we not only must clearly define our terms, but that our measures be described in some unambiguous manner that allows others to share in the outcomes of our efforts.

In my approach to inquiry, quantification is used to reduce ambiguity. It is not enough for me to say that I saw a positive relationship between authorship activities and critical reading. I must indicate how many observations were made (between 14 and 39 lessons were observed in each classroom), the frequency of the various authorship activities (authors were discussed in less than 10% of the lessons in which commercially published text was used, whereas they were discussed about 75% of the time that student-written text was used), and the specific degree of relationship and significance (the likelihood of chance occurrence, not the importance) of the relationship between these activities and the critical reading measure (if all teachers emphasized authorship to the same extent as the teachers who did this the most, and if these activities were causally linked to critical reading, then scores would improve by about 20%). Quantification does not make my observations true, and it does not necessarily make them accurate. However, quantification of this type does facilitate communication by allowing those who read my work to evaluate the importance of the magnitudes of relationship that I found or the frequency of observations that I reported.

Such quantification is highly desirable for research synthesis as well. Most of the newer techniques for synthesis make great use of meta-analytic procedures for combining the results of studies. These procedures allow for the strength of effects to be accounted for across studies and to weight these by the sample sizes. That way, if a study shows a strong impact of some teaching procedure, its results may be balanced by other studies that showed weaker results. Quantification within these studies is just one of the ways that replication (the repetition of the same study with consistent findings—a basic premise of reliability) can be facilitated. Exact language of all types is required in my research tradition.

Not all modes of inquiry rely on quantification—or even replication, however (Smith, 1983). Why not? Is it due to the nature of the phenomena being studied or to tradition of using other rhetorical devices for facilitating clear communication? If quantification is not used, how do researchers reduce ambiguity and miscommunication when describing phenomena? Does quantification, a tool for clear communication, ever lead to unnecessary confusion? Can its use be premature (Hunt & Vipond, 1992)? Under what circumstances would quantification be considered worthwhile in a particular mode of inquiry?

The literature has been rich with discussions of the comparative benefits or appropriateness of so-called quantitative and qualitative methods (Hayes, 1993). This terminology is unfortunate because it has confused the rhetorical and communication issues with the teleological or purposeful ones. It is, however, possible to use numbers as a descriptive language in both methods that have been called quantitative and those called qualitative. The issue of the value of statistics appears less one of summarizing information in numerical terms, and more one of the purpose of the investigation (to describe an individual event vs. to describe a general outcome, or more accurately, to describe an individual event relative to a set of normative probabilities).

THE TRANSPORTABILITY OR GENERALIZABILITY OF OUTCOMES

If we are a common literacy/language community that is separated by modes of inquiry, then we need to consider the relations between these approaches (Howe, 1985; Phillips, 1983). Approaches to inquiry necessarily have implications for the meaning of what we come to understand, and these implications can influence the generalizability or transportability of our findings. Can all results be synthesized? Are our perspectives equivalent in their ability to inform our decisions about policy, instruction, and research? What are the relations among the various modes of inquiry? Can they all result in equally informative rigorous outcomes, or are some perspectives more appropriate to the nature of the research questions being asked?

Again, my experience with NRP is pertinent. We were asked to determine public policy, so we limited our investigation to a consideration of what works. Basically, we set out to evaluate how well various instructional methods taught reading. To accomplish this, we had to make decisions about what constituted sufficient evidence that a program worked—that it "caused" children to do better in reading. Obviously, research studies can be flawed, and some can be flawed so seriously that they are impossible—or very, very difficult—to interpret. The Panel, not surprisingly, set aside such studies. But the more interesting—and knotty question—is whether all forms of research, if well executed, can inform this question of what works.

Recognizing the possibility that a positive research finding in this context could result in a national mandate, the panel was determined to establish the highest standard of evidence for making causal claims of this sort. Specifically, NRP required the use of experimental or quasi-experimental data for making such determinations. Experimental methods, while not being the only ones that we can learn from, are the *only* research methods that allow for this unambiguous attribution of causation because of their manipulation of an independent variable under well-described conditions.

The decision to only examine experimental data has been highly controversial in the research community, as many investigators who do not conduct experiments claim that this marginalizes their studies or implies that their approaches lack value. None, however, has come forward to argue that their research methodologies are as suitable for attributing causation as are experiments—at least within the range of problems under discussion.

During the NRP process, I argued for the inclusion of studies using other methodologies—in much the way that other fields, most notably medicine, use such findings. I agree with the approach the Panel took with regard to major determinations—to say that something worked there had to be sufficient numbers and quality of experimental studies showing a positive effect. However, once a determination on effectiveness is made (i.e., phonics instruction helps kids learn to read better), I thought it would be wise to examine other evidence about how phonics instruction works, how kids and teachers interpret it, and so on. Unfortunately, I did not get far with this argument. The reason? I simply could not find sufficient research data of this type to justify my position. That is, there simply were very few relevant studies using other methodologies on any of the topics under study. Certainly, useful case studies and ethnographies could be conducted in the context of vocabulary instruction or comprehension instruction, but such studies simply do not exist.

In my view, some inquiry approaches are right for particular problems and useless for others. But is this the case for all perspectives? Which questions or problems can be addressed from a particular mode of research? How would the different perspectives converge on a problem such as the role of author intentions in the interpretation of text in an informative manner? Are different perspectives able to pose the same questions, and how would the outcomes of such alternative approaches differ? And, if they proved unable to pose the same questions, what portions of the problem would each method best inform?

Are particular perspectives more useful at different points in epistemological time? Is a particular approach best when theory development is weak, or little is known about a phenomenon? Does appropriateness change as we learn more about a phenomenon? Are experimental techniques best reserved for a later stage of inquiry, when we have a clearer grasp of the phenomenon under study? Hunt and Vipond's (1992) early efforts seem an apt demonstration of the dangers of premature definition of experimental variables and conditions without adequate understanding of the phenomenon under study. Would the field be better served by studies such as Rowe's (1989) participant-observation approach to the meaning of authorship in the classroom early on, and by more intentional descriptive research approaches, such as mine, a bit later, and by rigorous experimental techniques still later? Rowe spent eight months observing the literacy interactions of 3- and 4-year-old children in order to describe patterns of how the children talked about literacy in general, and how they as authors specifically considered their audience's perspective.

If certain approaches to inquiry are more likely to lead to valid understanding, at least for some types of questions or at different points in time, then what of the findings/results of the other perspectives (Firestone,

1987)? Should we treat such outcomes as being generally valid? Only valid when supportable by our own perspectives? Or, are such findings "fruit from the poisoned tree," no more useful in a formal sense then our grandmother's homely intuitions? This issue is especially important when one considers the synthesis of results across studies.

Rowe's (1989) approach to the issue of authorship was quite different from my own, and people who are comfortable with the methods of either of us may be somewhat disquieted by the methods of the other. Although I have cited Rowe's work positively within my own, I am not altogether certain that this is fair, honest, or reasonable. If I do not feel confident in findings that are so reliant on the observational powers of a single individual (even one who is intelligent and well-schooled), then how can I use them when they are consistent with my own? If we had opposing conclusions, would I try to explain the discrepancy as I would with a study from my own empirical traditions, or would I use her methods as a whipping post for suggesting that my results were the correct ones? (This works both ways, of course. I have seen ethnographers who argue that their methods are the appropriate ones for studying human beings resort to experimental citations when the findings matched their own beliefs.)

How should the findings from alternative methodologies be considered? Are such findings used as evidence, or as points of departure? If we use findings across perspectives, as many of us try to do, is this testimony to our belief in the validity of those approaches, or is it evidence of our own lack of understanding of the ideological or political meanings of all approaches to inquiry? Do we bear a responsibility as scholars to consider the work from other perspectives and to bring those perspectives to our own work, or at least to make sure that differences in outcome be clearly understood?

THE NATURE AND ROLE OF THEORY USE AND CREATION

I once visited a local elementary school near the end of winter. Kindergarteners in the school had been working on a science experiment designed to show them the relevance of sunlight to plant growth. The children planted seeds in cups of soil and added water. They divided the group of seed cups in half, placing some in a dark closet and others along the sunny windowsill. When I was there the teacher was in some consternation. The seeds in the closet had sprouted over the weekend, and the ones in the sunlight were still dormant. She was hurriedly switching the cups before the buses arrived so that the children would get the "right" result.

My first, unstudied, reaction was that sunlight probably wasn't implicated in plant growth and that the only reason that any of us thought that it was is the result of the strong theories of our kindergarten teachers (who for thousands of years had switched the cups). On some reflection, I decided that the teacher, and I up to that point, had a rather imperfect notion of theory about the role of sunlight in plant growth and that our partial theory was misleading us into believing that somehow the children had failed to come up with the "right" results. (The students were actually studying seed germination, not plant growth; heat, not light, is the impetus of germination. If the March sun had provided as much heat as the dark closet, the results would likely have been different.)

Formal inquiry proceeds from a clearer theoretical stance. Theory tells us which phenomena are interesting, what variables and relations among variables are likely to be critical, and whether or not our empirical investigations have managed to arrive at the correct answer. In my own work, I am trying to make connections between normative social construction theory (one tenet of which is that the prototypical reader thinks about authors while they read) and social interaction theory (that holds that children learn through the communications that take place among us during shared events). I did not "discover" authorship like children discovering the cave art at Lascaux, but I went looking for it on the basis of the theories that I use. I am also theoretically compelled by a view of teaching as an intentional act. Teaching does not cause learning, but it increases the possibility of children constructing the types of skills, knowledge, and ability that we want them to have. I've selected my methods on the basis of these views (I suspect that Rowe is in sympathy with the first two theories, but that she would reject my focus on teachers' behaviors instead of children's and, thus, employs a very different methodology).

To understand inquiry, we need to understand the theories from which it proceeds and to which it tries to contribute. What is the nature of the theories that are used to conduct inquiry from these various approaches? What are some of the theoretical models that have been developed in each of these? How rigorous and specific are these theories in their ability to generate empirical predictions about phenomena? Is causation used as a construct?

Some of these approaches to literacy are quite new. How far are they in theory development? What is the relationship of theory to the results of empiricism? According to Popper (1959), the purpose of empiricism is to test, and ultimately, to falsify invalid theoretical positions. (If empirical inquiry were carried out simply to demonstrate our accuracy, there would be no need for inquiry at all; our theories would already contain the truth. Therefore, from my empirical tradition, theories must be tested with a realistic possibility of eventually rejecting my beliefs.) Is falsification seen as useful, necessary, or possible as a test of the validity of theories? What role does confirmation play in theory development? What would characterize progress in understanding within these modes of inquiry? Do the theories require the development of laws or general principals, or simply the identification of critical exemplars that prove the possibility or existence of a particular phenomenon? Is the goal actually just social agreement among researchers?

CONCLUSIONS

The questions posed throughout this chapter do not exhaust all of the issues that we must confront in order to have a full understanding of the various perspectives and their relations. However, thinking about these questions in relationship to each of the chapters presented in this volume, or in relation to one's own work, would be an effective start toward understanding the implications of these perspectives, and to increase our appreciation of the limits and possibilities of each. Only through such awareness and understanding will we move toward the creation of a field of literacy studies and ensure that our research outcomes, together, will have meaning.

It is obviously not incumbent on any of us to adopt a joint or shared perspective; such a homogenization is not likely to increase knowledge or to fuel the research enterprise. However, a research perspective is like a lens (Green, this volume). To use it properly, we must have a deep understanding of *both* what we hope to see and the nature of the glass through which we consider the world. Unless we understand what our colleagues are seeing and why their vision is often so different from our own, it is difficult to claim that we adequately grasp either the world or our particular lens.

REFERENCES

Durkin, D. (1978-1979). What classroom observations reveal about reading comprehension instruction. *Reading Research Quarterly, 14,* 481-533.

Firestone, W. A. (1987). Meaning in method: The rhetoric of quantitative and qualitative research. *Educational Researcher, 16*(7), 16-21.

Florio, S. (1979). The problem of dead letters: Social perspectives on the teaching of writing. *Elementary School Journal, 80,* 1-7.

Good, T. L., & Brophy, J. E. (2000). *Looking in classrooms* (8th ed.). New York: Harper & Row.

Hayes, J. R. (1993). Taking criticism seriously. *Research in the Teaching of English, 27,* 305–315.

Howe, K. R. (1985). Two dogmas of educational research. *Educational Researcher, 14*(8), 10–18.

Hunt, R., & Vipond, D. (1992). First, catch the rabbit: Methodological imperative and the dramatization of dialogic reading. In R. Beach, J. Green, M. Kamil, & T. Shanahan (Eds.), *Multidisciplinary perspectives on literacy research*. Urbana, IL: National Conference on Research in English/National Council of Teachers of English.

Lessnoff, M. (1974). *The structure of social science.* London: Allan & Unwin.

Meehl, P. (1989). What social scientists don't understand. In D. W. Fiske & R. A. Shweder (Eds.), *Metatheory in social science: Pluralisms and subjectivities* (pp. 315–338). Chicago, IL: University of Chicago Press.

National Reading Panel. (2000). *Teaching children to read: The report of the National Reading Panel.* Washington, DC: National Institute of Child Health and Development.

Nystrand, M. (1990). Sharing words: The effects of readers on developing writers. *Written Communication, 7,* 3–24.

Phillips, D. C. (1983). Postpositivistic educational thought. *Educational Researcher, 12*(5), 4–12.

Popper, K. (1959). *The logic of scientific discovery.* New York: Basic Books.

Rowe, D. W. (1989). Author/audience interaction in the preschool: The role of social interaction in literacy learning. *Journal of Reading Behavior, 21,* 311–350.

Shanahan, T., & Barr, R. (1995). Reading Recovery: An independent evaluation of the effects of an early instructional intervention for at risk learners. *Reading Research Quarterly, 30,* 958–996.

Smith, J. K. (1983). Quantitative versus qualitative research: An attempt to clarify the issue. *Educational Researcher, 12*(3), 6–13.

Tierney, R. J., & Shanahan, T. (1992). Research on the reading-writing relationship: Interactions, transactions, and outcomes. In R. Barr, M. L. Kamil, P. Mosenthal, & P. D. Pearson (Eds.), *Handbook of reading research* (Vol. 2, pp. 246–280). New York: Longman.

2

Some Issues Concerning Differences Among Perspectives in Literacy Research

Reconsidering the Issues After a Decade of Change

Michael L. Kamil
Stanford University

In the decade since the publication of the first edition of this volume (Beach, Green, Kamil, & Shanahan, 1992) the literacy landscape has changed dramatically. In place of the reading wars that were dominating the intellectual activities, we have arrived at a different place. The landscape in this new place has different terrain; several trends are clearly evident.

The most obvious trend is that we are engaged in large-scale attempts to synthesize what we know from research, how it is applicable, and what other research is needed. These attempts have altered the debate to focus on evidence, whether or not there is agreement about the utility of the syntheses. In 1992, the *Handbook of Reading Research* (Barr, Kamil, Mosenthal, & Pearson, 1991) was the most evident attempt at a comprehensive synthesis. Other attempts have followed: *Preventing Reading Difficulties* (Snow, Burns, & Griffith, 1998); *The Report of the National Reading Panel* (National Reading Panel, 2000); *Handbook of Reading Research* (Kamil, Mosenthal, Pearson, & Barr, 2000); and *Reading for Understanding* (RAND, 2002). Currently underway are other efforts at synthesizing research in areas other than those addressed in those mentioned. The *National Literacy Panel for Language Minority Children and Youth* (under the auspices of the Center for Applied Linguistics and SRI International) is examining research related to second-language and language-minority issues. Other panels are planned to examine research in other genres and other areas.

This is a very positive development because it has the potential to begin to allow literacy researchers and practitioners the opportunity to sort out what it is that is and is not known. It also creates the opportunity to implement those findings for which there is evidence and to research those promising elements that are yet to be shown effective. The composition of these review panels reflects a concern that multiple disciplines be represented.

A second trend is that the concerns of a decade ago are being replaced by new concerns. We are concerned about what evidence we need to have to be able to translate literacy research into practice. We are concerned about the accumulation of research that may or may not bear on the questions most in need of answers. This is related to the synthesis trend described previously. However, the intellectual discussion centers on the value of the syntheses and whether or not they will produce the desired outcomes, rather than on the value of a single perspective or methodology.

In the preface to the *Handbook of Reading Research*, two general themes are suggested that encompass the great changes in concerns for the field of reading research. First, the definition of reading has been broadened. As the authors state:

> Reading researchers began to draw from a variety of social-science disciplines—most noticeably, sociology and anthropology. In the process, reading took on social cultural and multicultural dimensions. Moreover, reading researchers began to interpret reading in terms of critical literacy theory as well as in terms of the politics of the times (thus uniting reading and political science). (Kamil et al., 2000, p. xi)

The second theme identified in the *Handbook* is that the reading research agenda has been substantially broadened. A third trend is that the field continues to develop new perspectives, new methodologies, and new foci. There is a temptation to suggest that this is a new or recent problem. It is not. We are simply continuing a trend that we can trace back to Aristotle.

It would be impossible to list all of the new perspectives that have arisen or have been pursued since 1992. The *Handbook of Reading Research* is a bellwether for these new trends. The third volume contains a great deal of material on new topics. A review of research on neural-level functions in the brain related to literacy was included for the first time.

Similarly, issues of media and technology were represented because of the impact on literacy.

The *Handbook* also moved in two new directions. The volume includes reviews from researchers outside of North America, clearly signaling a change is the acceptable perspectives on research. Additionally, there are reviews of research methodologies, pointing the way to those new methods and perspectives that have become commonplace since 1991. Among these "new" methodologies are reviews of historical research, teacher as researcher, narrative approaches, and sociocultural perspectives, to name only a few.

All of these trends have both affordances and costs. The affordances are that we have engaged in a different kind of discussion; the incivility of the "reading wars" has waned even if it has not disappeared. The field is far richer for these new influences, but the cost is that there is now a disturbing isolation that can be observed among various camps. Although few still believe that the reading wars will be won or lost by one side or the other, there is still an insularity that pervades reading research.

In what follows, some of the issues that were raised in the first edition of *Multidisciplinary Perspectives* (Kamil, 1992) are re-examined in light of current thinking.

DO WE NEED MULTIDISCIPLINARY PERSPECTIVES?

When one examines the history of science, it is clear that the number of disciplines has multiplied. As only one example, Stanford University offers graduate degrees in 63 academic departments or programs. At the undergraduate level, there are 51 majors listed (the last of which is "individually designed major"). Clearly, knowledge has been compartmentalized. As that knowledge becomes more specialized, it is the case that we divide knowledge into smaller chunks. When that happens, we run the risk of missing relevant knowledge from another, relevant discipline. It is *only* through the use of multidisciplinary perspectives that we can overcome the limitations imposed by the fractionation of knowledge.

There is a prevalent belief that science can be conducted as a dispassionate, objective, value-free endeavor. Beginning with Kuhn's (1962, 1970) work, a new realization has become apparent. Science involves choices among methodologies, problems, and interpretations. A researcher may be disposed to study some problems rather than others. Methodologies can be chosen arbitrarily or maintained out of habit. Interpretations of data and construction of theory are clearly colored by predispositions. In the following discussion, the word *perspective* has been used as a collective description of what a researcher believes, in the most global sense, about the domain to be studied. The term *perspective is* intended to be more inclusive than the notion of paradigm introduced by Kuhn. Although this discussion is framed in the context of literacy and literacy research, it might easily be generalized to other fields of study.

The simple answer to the question "Do we need multidisciplinary perspectives?" is yes. But we need to look more carefully at what such perspectives entail.

WHAT IS A LITERACY PERSPECTIVE?

Literacy research perspectives usually address the following issues:

1. The nature of reality as it relates to the acquisition, use, and instruction of literacy and literacy skills.
2. The nature, acquisition, and structure of general knowledge about literacy. These are general epistemological issues that relate to how individuals come to know about literacy.
3. The nature, acquisition, and structure of scientific knowledge and theory concerning literacy. These are different from the general epistemological issues; this set of issues relates specifically to the scientific enterprise rather than to common knowledge.
4. The consequences of individual differences (i.e., individual group descriptions) for literacy use, acquisition, and instruction.

In adopting a particular perspective, researchers need to select certain methods for studying literacy, choices limited by certain theoretical assumptions or lines of reasoning. It is impossible to avoid many consequences of adhering to a perspective, even if a researcher might want to avoid those consequences.

Consequently, an overriding concern is the identification of a perspective. What makes a perspective "cohere" as a unique entity? It is not a simple task to identify what a perspective must or should be. The following sections each deal with a different facet of perspectives related to the many variables that should be considered in formulating or arguing from a perspective. Often, there are questions rather than answers. The questions are useful in stimulating thinking about problems rather than implied solutions to them.

The incorporation of multiple disciplines allows for the merging and expansion of single perspectives, convergent on a set of research problems. It is a recognition that there are phenomena that lied outside a single discipline perspective at any given time in history. As noted previously, disciplines change and evolve over time. If multiple perspectives have explanatory utility, they may eventually become a single entity.

Level of Detail in Perspective

An important issue is the breadth of a perspective on literacy research. Does a research perspective have to encompass a broad range of phenomena? Or can it simply focus efforts on a smaller slice of reality? These questions lead into the difficult problem of complete versus partial determination of phenomena. That is, if an explanation includes all possible factors influencing an event or outcome, it is said to be fully determined. If the explanation does not include all those factors, it is incomplete, or partially determined. Literacy research perspectives seem compelled, on a theoretical basis, to focus on a full range of literacy phenomena. On a pragmatic basis, however, literacy research seems more effective when conducted on narrower ranges of phenomena. If it is more efficient to study these phenomena in smaller pieces; then each of the small pieces, when put together, should account for the broad range of events. This line of reasoning implies that no single perspective can take the position of excluding some phenomena without specifying some way of ultimately including them in the explanatory structure (or theoretical account) of the relevant domain.

It is certainly the case that the more multidisciplinary the perspective, the more likely the perspective is to avoid the trap of focusing on either too large or too small a piece of the literacy problem of interest. This is the true affordance of multidisciplinary perspectives.

Psychological Versus Social Components of Literacy

Is there a psychological "reality" to literacy phenomena that can be separated from social influences or social contexts? Can we determine whether literacy phenomena have psychological components that are different from the social/interpersonal components? Literacy seems inherently a social process. Except for writing notes to oneself, making entries in a diary, and similar activities, most literacy phenomena require the existence of another individual. Even in the cases of "private" communications, many social psychologists would argue that individuals act as if they were two different personas.

Language is a social "agreement" to use certain conventions for communication. Although much of language processing is certainly conducted at a psychological or cognitive level, there is an obvious need to include social causal factors in scientific explanations. Because many processes do take place at the psychological level, cognitive processes related to literacy seem heavily weighted on the side of the "private" world of an individual. We have accumulated ample evidence that neither the psychological nor the social aspects are sufficient in themselves for a complete description of literacy phenomena.

Perspectives must question whether it makes sense to study the psychological processes of literacy apart from the social components. Can it be done? Can some parts be studied and others not? If so, are the results obtained from a psychological perspective usable in instructional or other "social" contexts?

Although these questions may not have compelling theoretical answers in all perspectives, clearly there are researchers who pragmatically study literacy from a purely psychological or purely social framework. Such a course of action will lead to difficulty if researchers assume there is nothing more to be added—that the psychological or the social component is the only important source of scientific data in explanations of literacy. Certainly, the trend today is toward reconciling differences between them.

Compatibility Among Perspectives

Do the results from research with one perspective have to be compatible with results from other perspectives? Can they be at odds? Can they co-exist with small discrepancies? Related to this is *the question of whether a perspective can be a combination of different types of* research purposes, aims, perspectives, and the like. How similar (or related) do the various assumptions of a perspective have to be to represent a single, coherent perspective? This question has been addressed by Stanovich (1990, 1993) and Kamil (1995). They both believe it is imperative that the discussion of problems must be possible across boundaries of perspectives, or the value of the scientific endeavor is lost. Despite this, there is still a strong tendency of many researchers to cite only evidence from their own perspective.

What Should the Goals of a Perspective Be?

There is also a need to consider the uses of perspectives for scientific or political/policy/social ends. For example, the use of schema theory as a scientific theory can be easily questioned (Pascual-Leone, 1980), but it has been used to focus important energies and resources on reading research. So, schema theory serves an important function, even if it is not one that contributes directly or immediately to the acquisition of accurate scientific knowledge about literacy. Other perspectives can focus on educational exceptions to draw attention to and attempt to collect information on a class of problems that might otherwise be ignored. Current examples of similar phenomena are the role of metacognition in reading and learning to read and the use of technology as part of literacy instruction.

This idea requires a dual view of science and research. Science, at one level, is often assumed to be the dispassionate collection of knowledge about the world. At another level, science does make available different kinds of data that are useful for policy, social, and political purposes. Whether these are a priori or a posteriori functions of science is debatable. Scientific data can be used to justify policies that were going to be implemented anyway, or they can be used to create or rationalize policies to achieve desired ends. Perspectives often reflect the ends or goals of the research, and it is critical that anyone adhering to a perspective be aware of those ends.

Some research perspectives will have the additional problem of interfacing with policy perspectives. The degree to which research perspective goals match policy perspective goals will be important in determining which problems are studied, how much funding will be available, who will be supported in research efforts, and the ultimate sources of funds. It is important to be aware of the line where policy begins and science ends. Scientific data can also be affected by this interface between policy and research perspectives. Additionally, the application of research findings by policymakers may have consequences unintended or not considered by researchers. The manifestations of these issues have resulted in the broadening of literacy research agendas noted earlier (Kamil et al., 2000).

Although the preceding discussion does not resolve the question of defining or identifying perspectives, it raises major issues. By considering the questions posed, we can guide our use of the term *perspective* in a more productive manner. The following discussion of evaluating perspectives presupposes that we can establish criteria for identifying perspectives.

EVALUATION OF PERSPECTIVES

To evaluate perspectives, we have to ask about the utility of information and research derived from different perspectives. Is there differential utility of the information produced from different perspectives for research and scientific knowledge? Instruction and schooling? Policy? These are pragmatic criteria, not theoretical ones.

How can the utility of information be evaluated? Because this question is often bound to the assumptions of the paradigm, cross-perspective sensitivity issues are crucial in evaluating the utility of information. This suggests that there is an objective reality to which *all* perspectives can refer. This pragmatic assumption merely reflects the fact that most of what we do and believe in language and thought is held in common among most individuals. If we cannot explain what we do or find across different perspectives, we can have little or nothing in the way of usable, accumulated knowledge. Our very acts of speech and communication become futile. If we want to reflect how the world actually works, we need to take account of the fact that persons usually act as if there were an objective and mutually understandable reality undergirding all observable phenomena.

The criterion can be stated as a "test": If the results or implications of research or theory are not explainable so that anyone else can understand them, they are simply not useful.

CRITERIA FOR EVALUATION OF PERSPECTIVES

The following section was written for the first edition. It no longer serves the same function it did in 1992, when it was generally assumed that one or another perspective would "win" the "reading wars" (Kamil, 1995; Stanovich, 1990, 1993). It is retained here with some alteration because there are still some researchers who do not adhere to the principles.

We seem to be in a particularly disabling period of time in terms of justifying or systematizing our research efforts. We are, as a community, engaging in much research, but we seem to be fixated on data. We spend relatively little time determining what our data *really* mean. We need to spend more time dealing with the theoretical and less time at the empirical data level. If this requires closer examinations of the underlying assumptions and precise consequences of one's conclusions, so much the better. If this requires less data collection and more thoughtful reflection of the meaning, consistency, and explanatory value of data, so be it. Too often we examine such a small portion of what interests us that our conclusions cannot possibly be generalized to the larger domain, much less to the "real" world. And yet, almost every piece of literacy research comes complete with its "implications for instruction." This is a pernicious trend that, at best, undermines the credibility of the research effort. At worst, it leads to erroneous applications of practices that were only minimally, if at all, supported by a narrow research effort.

Some assumptions that underlie the following discussion are that there is an objective reality, that communication among and between researchers (and other persons) is possible, and that the ultimate goal of science and research is the production of knowledge. At base, this set of assumptions relies heavily on a scientific pragmatism: if we are to discover things about the world, those methods that do it more effectively and efficiently are in an urgent sense "better."

There are presently no formal criteria for what constitutes a perspective, as opposed to criteria for more formal entities like theories or hypotheses. This issue needs to be addressed urgently. Until it can be determined what makes a perspective an identifiable entity, little progress can be made in evaluating perspectives. Not only do we have to be able to identify what a perspective is, we have to be able to distinguish one from another, without reference to the advocates of the perspective stating "this is my perspective."

The following is a proposed set of evaluative criteria for perspectives. This proposal assumes that we can identify perspectives, despite the caveats in the preceding paragraphs. These are intended as a first approximation, to be refined when definitions of perspectives have been sharpened. This proposal deliberately sidesteps the complexities of that issue for now.

THE CRITERIA

Scope

A perspective is to be preferred if it comprehensively deals with the phenomena in its domain. Although a perspective does not have to deal with all phenomena in its domain, perspectives that have a larger scope are preferable to those with smaller scopes. A subcriterion is that perspectives should provide a complete account of the phenomena under study. If a perspective chooses to focus on one or a few aspects of a domain, that focus should not produce results that are contradictory to data collected on other aspects of the same domain. This last issue is related to the next criterion.

Consistency

If the perspective leads to an internal contradiction or an absurdity, it is flawed. In short, any time a perspective admits of contradictory data (without explaining or rejecting some of those data), it is invalid. This represents the criterion of internal consistency. If the perspective requires the invalidation of other data we know to be true, outside its domain, it is externally inconsistent. That is, any knowledge gained from a perspective must be consistent with what we have obtained from other perspectives, unless it can be demonstrated that one or the other piece of knowledge is somehow flawed. Moreover, a perspective must have a mechanism for resolving disagreements among observers on what the phenomena are. When observers disagree about a phenomenon, the perspective must specify a method or methods by which the dispute can be settled.

Scientific Utility

If the perspective leads to predictions, confirmable by research, it is useful. The more different, confirmable predictions a perspective yields, the more useful it is. If there are not conditions under which the perspective could be validated or invalidated, it lacks scientific utility. In that case, the perspective has become faith rather than science.

Simplicity

This is otherwise known as "Occam's Razor": Entities should not be multiplied unnecessarily. Simpler perspectives are always preferable. Perspectives that resort to complex explanations, require the creation of hypothetical constructs, or make reference to nonexistent or unobservable entities should be suspect. Although this is an extremely difficult criterion to apply, it is a necessary condition to prevent flawed perspectives from being shored up by the invention of complex or fanciful explanatory devices. This is related to the question of utility discussed earlier. The more complex, strained, or fanciful an explanation is, the less likely it is to be useful.

Distortion

If the perspective does not introduce distortions of the data, it is to be preferred. By implication, perspectives that introduce less distortion are preferred to those that introduce more. Although this introduces a notion of objectivity that may be rejected by some perspectives, it is important to know when and if a perspective systematically (or unsystematically) distorts reality. Without this criterion, the notion of resolving disagreements over observations or phenomena is futile.

Presumption

A perspective cannot assume itself as essential to the understanding of itself or of phenomena in its domain. If we do not make this assumption, we can never devise an independent criterion against which to measure progress in terms of the accumulation of knowledge.

Stimulation

A less formal evaluative criterion is that a perspective should stimulate research and the acquisition of knowledge. In this regard, some perspectives that might not meet the more formal evaluative criteria, described earlier, do prove useful. An illustrative case is the use of schema theory as an explanation of reading comprehension. Several paradoxes and internal contradictions are present in the various formulations of schema theory (Bereiter, 1985; Pascual-Leone, 1980). Yet, schema theory has certainly stimulated much reading research over the past two decades. Schema theory rates high on this criterion although it is low on others.

SUMMARY

Several criteria are presented as starting points to formulate evaluations of perspectives and the ultimate interpretation of research. It is argued that we need multidisciplinary perspectives in order to enrich our research, encompass a broader range of problems and solutions, and made our scientific knowledge more comprehensive. The several dimensions suggested here will allow for comparisons and contrasts among perspectives in important ways. Developmental work in refining perspectives should result in stronger, more coherent perspectives, and consequently, accelerated scientific progress. The reading research landscape has shifted dramatically in the past decade in what appears to be a positive direction. We hope this trend continues.

REFERENCES

Barr, R., Kamil, M., Mosenthal, P., & Pearson, P.D. (Eds.). (1991). *Handbook of reading research, Volume II*. New York: Longman.

Beach, R., Green, J., Kamil, M., & Shanahan, T., (Eds.). (1992). *Multidisciplinary perspectives on literacy research*. Champaign, IL: National Conference for Research on English.

Bereiter, C. (1985). Toward a solution of the learning paradox. *Review of Educational Research, 55,* 201-226.

Kamil, M. L. (1995). Some alternatives to paradigm wars. *Journal of Reading Behavior, 27,* 243-261.

Kamil, M., Mosenthal, P., Pearson, P. D., & Barr, R. (Eds.). (2000). *Handbook of reading research* (Vol. 3). Mahwah, NJ: Erlbaum.

Kuhn, T. (1962). *The structure of scientific revolutions*. Chicago: University of Chicago Press.

Kuhn, T. (1970). Logic of discovery or psychology of research? In I. Lakatos & A. Musgrave (Eds.), *Criticism and the growth of knowledge* (pp. 1-23). London: Cambridge University Press.

National Reading Panel. (2000). *Report of the National Reading Panel: Teaching children to read*. Bethesda, MD: National Institute of Child Health and Human Development.

Pascual-Leone, J. (1980). Constructive problems for constructive theories: The current relevance of Piaget's work and a critique of information-processing simulation psychology. In R. H. Kluwe & H. Spada (Eds.), *Developmental models of thinking* (pp. 263-296). New York: Academic Press.

RAND Reading Study Group. (2002). *Reading for understanding: Toward an R&D program in reading comprehension.* Santa Monica, CA: Rand.

Snow, C. E., Burns, M. S., & Griffin, P. C. (1998). *Preventing reading difficulties in young children.* Washington, DC: National Academy Press.

Stanovich, K. E. (1990). A call for an end to the paradigm wars in reading research. *Journal of Reading Behavior, 22*(3), 221-231.

Stanovich, K. E. (1993). Romance and reality. *Reading Teacher, 47*(4), 280-291.

Stanovich, K. E. (1998). Twenty-five years of research on the reading process: The grand synthesis and what it means for our field. *National Reading Conference Yearbook, 47*, 44-58.

3

Qualitative versus Quantitative Research

A False Dichotomy?

George Hillocks, Jr.
The University of Chicago

Researchers concerned with the nature and learning of literacy come from a wide variety of fields: literature, rhetoric, linguistics, testing and measurement, elementary and secondary education, anthropology, sociology, psychology, and various amalgams of each. Furthermore, researchers within any one of these fields are likely to see themselves as quite diverse in the way they approach problems of literacy. One of the major differences cutting across these fields is that between quantitative and qualitative research. In the mid-1960s, most research in literacy was quantitative. Researchers focused on problems that were accessible to quantitative measures. In writing, for example, especially after the publication of Hunt's (1965) important study, dozens of studies examined the characteristics of the written or spoken syntax of children and teenagers. Many more examined the effects of sentence combining in changing the syntactic features of their writing. Although these studies were useful and important at the time, there was a growing awareness that, despite their neat quantitative measures, they did not get at the heart of writing. Emig's (1971) study of the writing processes of high school students set a new goal for research: to understand the processes of writing through detailed case studies. Despite the very small sample and the untested methods and reporting, the study opened up possibilities for understanding literacy practice, learning, and teaching through qualitative methods that involved intensive examination of a few subjects in the context of classroom or out-of-school settings. Increasingly, researchers turned away from the quantitative to the qualitative arguing that quantitative research made use of methods that decontextualized learning and practice, that they posited an independent reality that they could only pretend to know, and that they presented constructions of reality as though they did represent reality. The tradition was derogated as "positivist." By the mid 1980s, the battle had become venomous. In 1990, for example, Egon Guba, calling himself a constructivist, claimed that "the positivist (and postpositivist) paradigms are badly flawed and must be entirely replaced" (p. 25). His colleague, Yvonna Lincoln (1990), made the same point: "Accommodation between paradigms is impossible" (p. 81). Such critics constructed the two paradigms as strictly dichotomous.

POSITIVISM VERSUS CONSTRUCTIVISM

The terms positivist and positivism were originally used to designate the philosophy of Rudolf Carnap and others who were known as "logical positivists" and who were concerned with the "logical analysis of scientific knowledge" and the nature of the statements making it up. (See the *Internet Encyclopedia of Philosophy*, entry for "logical positivism.") By definition, the term positivist is not applicable to most quantitative researchers. It is used as a term of derogation to suggest that quantitative researchers do not realize that all knowledge is the product of human minds and any statement about what is true or not true is merely a construction.

This distinction between positivist and constructivist divides us over questions such as what counts as research, what counts as evidence, and what the principles are by which we connect evidence to our claims. These differences are, I suspect, exacerbated by the political needs of researchers in newer fields, like the study of writing, to legitimize both their objects of study and their methodologies. In 1983, John K. Smith, in an article for *Educational Researcher*, outlined what he saw as the major polarities of the debate over research methods. The first is based on "the relationship of the investigator to what is investigated" (p. 6). According to Smith, those working in the empirical tradition of Comte, Mill, and Durkheim posit a reality outside themselves that can be examined in an unbiased fashion through the use of appropriate methods. Because they posit the independent reality, Smith called them realists—a more neutral term than positivist. Researchers in this tradition attempt to eliminate their own values, biases, preconceptions, and emotional involvements. Qualitative researchers in the tradition of Dilthey, Rickert, and Weber believe that because everything must be examined through the human mind and because knowledge is a product of human minds, any separation of the investigator from that which is investigated is impossible. Smith used the term idealist to designate researchers in this tradition, emphasizing their insistence on the role of the human mind in creating or shaping reality. According to Raymond Williams (1983), this is the original philosophical sense of the term—that "ideas are held to underlie or to form all reality."

A second set of polarities has to do with the nature of truth. According to Smith, realists judge a statement to be true if it "corresponds to an independently existing reality and false if it does not" (Smith, 1983, p. 9). For idealists, no concept of correspondence is acceptable. Because any one observer's understanding exists in that observer's mind, there is no outside referent against which to test a statement of reality. Truth then becomes a matter of agreement, reached through and justified by interpretation.

These ideas of truth imply different ideas of objectivity. For the realist, objectivity may be achieved through the use of methods that permit an unbiased examination of phenomena. These methods provide what amounts to public knowledge, knowledge that can be tested by others, assuming they have similar levels of skill and use comparable methods on comparable problems. On the other hand, idealists believe that, because any concept of reality is dependent on the mind of the observer, objectivity sought by realists is not possible. For the idealists, objectivity is "nothing more than social agreement; what is objectively so is what we agree is objectively so" (Smith, 1983, p. 10).

A fourth set of polarities has to do with the nature of goals of the two research traditions. According to Smith, the "ultimate goal of researchers in the empirical tradition is to develop laws that make prediction possible" (p. 11). Smith cited as an example of scientific law the statement that if a metal bar is heated, it will expand. In the social sciences, Smith pointed out, such absolute laws are not always possible. Qualitative researchers do not seek to establish such laws believing that the situatedness and contexts of what they study make such laws impossible. Smith said that idealists seek, not a set of overarching laws, but rather "interpretive understanding." The hermeneutic process that gives rise to such understanding demands that the investigator examine relationships among parts and the whole of the phenomenon under investigation, including the investigator's own values and interests.

DEALING WITH PROBABILITIES

I know of no social science that has developed or would pretend to develop absolute laws, such as Boyle's law, which concerns the compression and decompression of gases, that are always true under any conditions. Rather, the goals of all social science that I know about are statements of probability: If X occurs, then, to some greater or lesser degree, Y occurs. Aristotle recognized the enormous difference between the arguments involved in arriving at statements of probability and those in arriving at absolutes. He deals with the former in *The Art of Rhetoric* and the latter in *Posterior Analytics*. The major goal of statistical procedures is to arrive at estimates of probabilities. The product of the hermeneutic processes of qualitative investigations can be no more than what Aristotle would see as statements of probability.

ARE THE TWO RESEARCH TRADITIONS REALLY MUTUALLY EXCLUSIVE?

If we attend to the words of Guba and Lincoln, it would appear that investigators of one persuasion could never accept the methods or findings of those of the other. However, the distinction may not be as stark as it appears in recent bouts of polemics and in descriptions such as Smith's.

Are the two research traditions really mutually exclusive? We may attempt to answer this question in two ways. First, we might test the assumption that the traditions are mutually exclusive by taking them to their logical extremes. At one extreme, a realist would have to choose research problems on the basis of established laws. There would be no room for hypothesis development via interpretation and imagination. At the other extreme, idealists would not accept any correspondence between their ideas about speeding cars and the independently existing reality of speeding cars on a busy highway. Idealists at this extreme would have to convene a conference to reach some social agreement about when it is safe to cross the highway. The extreme, however, is not a viable position. Researchers who use quantitative methods must use the interpretive methods of qualitative researchers in at least four areas: problem finding, explaining the nature of what counts a data, and explaining particular cases in light of established knowledge and theory. When qualitative researchers present their observations, they must convince their audiences that their presentation is accurate and comprehensive. To meet this challenge, they explain their methods and present their observations and the contexts of those observations in meticulous detail. Even then, however, they are aware that, because reality is a construct of mind, the reality of one mind may differ from that of another. For one observer to become immersed in the culture observed, they know, does not make the resulting observations any more than the product of a single, fallible mind (witness the case of *Coming of Age in Samoa*). Therefore, the needs to explain procedures, to verify observations, and to cross check sources become as important for the qualitative as for the quantitative researcher, and the methods are quite similar.

Additionally, careful qualitative researchers understand the problems of extrapolating from a small sample, and so increase the sample size or limit their generalizations. In this, their concern is the same as that of quantitative researchers, though their methods of dealing with it may be different. If the two methodologies are inescapably linked in these ways, then making use of the linkages and allowing the methods to work together are likely to be advantageous for both.

Second, to examine the assumption of mutual exclusivity we can attempt to determine whether, in fact, the position described by Smith (1983) or by Heap (1992) accord with our own experience. Smith claimed that realists seek laws that make predictions possible and that idealists seek agreement reached through interpretive justification. In a sense, this distinction begs the question of how the two differ. Does it mean that anthropologists never expect their results to be replicated and don't care? It seems quite evident to me that they do. For example, Miller and Sperry (1988) examined, among other verbal phenomena, the onset of narratives in three 2-year-old girls from a working-class community. Later, they undertook further investigations in four other communities to determine whether narratives began in similar ways. These careful ethnographic studies clearly imply predictions (e.g., the onset of narratives about highly emotional occurrences are co-constructed with caregivers and that in different communities, they may be guided by different sets of values (see also Miller, Potts, Fung, Hoogstra, & Mintz, 1990). Miller et al. provided no probability statistics, but the predictive power and apparent intent of the work is, I think, uneniable. Prediction is simply approached in a different way.

Smith (1983) and Heap (1992) implied that realists or positivists seek certainty. Smith wrote of the development of laws. However, most so-called hard scientists, during the 20th century, learned to live with ambiguity (e.g., the Heisenberg principle in quantum mechanics). Often, in fields such as particle physics, quantum mechanics, and the measurement of chemical and thermodynamic constants, different experiments yield results that are statistically inconsistent. It is not unusual for reviewers of studies attempting to establish physical properties to eliminate 40% of the available studies to establish more reliable measurements (Hedges, 1987). When experiments yield significantly different results, interpretation becomes essential for positing possible explanations for the differences.

Heap (1992) wrote with certainty about the inabilities of realists to attain certainty. He cited the "frame problem" as an example to explain why. The frame problem derives from the possibility that a test taker may select an intended wrong answer as the correct one. This, Heap stated, means that "when a student gets thirty-three out of fifty items correct, there can be no certainty that the student's failure to answer correctly the remaining seventeen questions is evidence of a lack of the relevant skill.[1] He is, of course, quite right about what the results do not indicate. However, standardized tests do not claim that a particular score indicates the certain lack of particular skills. Instead, they claim that the number of correct responses is equivalent to some normatively determined level of response to reading material of that kind, expressed at some level of probability or with some margin of error. Such a claim is quite different from claiming that wrong answers indicate the certain absence of some particular skill.

Furthermore, the work of careful quantitative researchers is always reported in terms of probabilities, not certainties. Rhetoricians examining such things report that important features of scientific texts are the presence of "hedges" (Crismore & Farnsworth, 1990) and "modal qualifiers" (Butler, 1990), both means of avoiding statements of certainty and implying the necessity of interpreting results.

Both qualitative and quantitative researchers are empirical. Both are deeply concerned with representing what they observe as though those phenomena have status in some reality independent of the mind of the observer. An ethnographer of mother-child interactions would be very much concerned if another observer examining mother-child interactions in a comparable environment reported quite different kinds of interactions. The researcher would indubitably attempt to discover reasons for the discrepancies and would certainly not pass them off as simply the product of another mind that constructed reality in a different way. In the same way, when quantitative researchers in the physical and social sciences find different results coming from different experiments, they seek to understand the differences.

Although quantitative and qualitative research are not mutually exclusive, they can and do focus on different kinds of problems. For example, quantitative methods cannot deal directly with historical problems of cause and effect or the interpretation of unique social phenomena. On the other hand, qualitative researchers find it difficult, if not impossible, to represent the responses of large numbers of individuals to different kinds of stimuli (e.g., different methods of teaching or attitudes toward social conditions or political events). In the sense that the two sets of methods allow researchers to deal with problems of different dimensions in different contexts, they are complementary. However, the methods are more than complementary in the general sense of enabling researchers to deal with different kinds of problems. They enable researchers to bring different methodologies and insights to bear on the same problem—and this complementarity is possible without the metaperspective that Heap (1992) implied is necessary for complementarity, but argued is impossible. Heap stated, "there can be no single metaperspective that would allow us to judge and articulate the claims of all the disciplines that study literacy. There can be no such metaperspective because there is no single conception of science that each relevant discipline shares" (p. 35). Undoubtedly, Heap is right in saying that widely differing disciplines share no single conception of science. At the same time, however, no single conception of science is necessary for differing research methodologies to be used successfully in a complementary fashion.

Even within a single discipline, it is easily demonstrable that practitioners use quite different methodologies. Astronomers, for example, can specify methods for describing and measuring the motion of planets and comets around the sun. However, they cannot specify methods for inferring the existence and nature of gravity. In other words, astronomers use these two quite distinct methodologies (measurement and interpretation) in an entirely complementary fashion.

ARGUMENTS OF PROBABILITY AS SYNTHETIC AGENT

The finds or claims of different methodologies are synthesized by the use of argument. Although the methods used to derive different claims may be in conflict, the claims themselves are not—or at least not necessarily. A complex argument involves a series of claims, used in a variety of ways to support a major proposition—which is the point of the argument. The minor claims are of different types, by virtue of being based on different evidence tied to the claims by different kinds of warrants. For example, the proposition that Mr. Zee is guilty of speeding at 55 mph in a 35-mph zone is based on three different claims, each based on a different set of evidence tied to the claim by a different kind of warrant. The claim that Mr. Zee's car was traveling at 55 mph is based on the evidence of a radar reading. The radar reading in itself, however, does not mean that Mr. Zee was actually traveling at 55 mph. In addition, the argument requires information about the reliability of the radar reading, its margin of error, and so forth. The information about the radar instrument itself serves as a warrant that ties the evidence (the reading of 55 mph) to the claim that Mr. Zee was traveling at that speed. A second claim is that Mr. Zee was in a 35-mph zone at the time the reading was made. The evidence underlying this claim has to do with the actual boundaries of the 35-mph zone and the arresting officer's interpretation of the position of the speeding car in relation to the zone. The warrant which ties the evidence to the claim that Mr. Zee was in the 35-mph zone has to do with the veracity of the arresting officer. Finally, the claim that the speed limit was 35 mph is based on statutory evidence. The warrant tying the statutory evidence to the claim about the speed limit in a particular zone involves interpretations of the statutes, precedents, or both. Although each of these minor claims rest upon its own evidence and warrant, each different from the other, each claim plays a necessary but complementary part in the larger argument which results in a fine for Mr. Zee.

Furthermre, although the claims and their warrants are quite different, they are united in a system of argument that permits their integration. That is possible because researchers in disciplines outside mathematics and the hard sciences (e.g., physics), by necessity make arguments dealing with propositions that are probabilistic, not absolute. That is, they use a logic that is capable of entertaining premises that are not certain. In the social sciences, law, and the humanities, scholars use the kind of argument appropriate to the data they confront, data about which there are few absolutes. They are constrained to nonsyllogistic argument.

Following the ancient Greek philosophers, especially Aristotle, philosophy (read also science) was based on syllogistic arguments for many centuries. The conclusions of syllogisms were regarded as True, with a capital T. Syllogisms were the mechanisms for arriving at truth, statements that were absolute about the nature of things, the kind of truth that many think quantitative researchers seek. All of us have encountered such arguments in geometry and algebra. We solve equations with unknowns through axioms that tell us that equals subtracted from, added to, multiplied, or divided by equals are equal. Algebraic equations may be seen as syllogisms.

A verbal syllogism has a fixed structure, a major premise, a minor premise, and a conclusion.

> Socrates is a man.
> All men are mortal.
> Therefore, Socrates is mortal.

Toulmin (1958) called these arguments analytic syllogisms, analytic because the conclusion is already implicit in the premises. One characteristic of the valid syllogism is that it is tautological; one of the premises includes the information that the argument presents as a conclusion. In fact, Toulmin (1958) demonstrated that valid analytic syllogisms cannot tell us anything not already included in the premises. The validity of the syllogism depends upon the relationship between the premises, not the weight of the evidence brought to bear. The facts that Socrates is a man and that all men are mortal allow us to conclude that Socrates is mortal because he is a member of the group stipulated as mortal. The validity depends on the minor premise sharing a term with the major premise. In this kind of logic, the following is just as valid as the argument about Socrates: George is boy. All boys are unicorns. Therefore, George is a unicorn. Within a system that allows for all boys to be considered unicorns, the conclusion that George is also a unicorn is inescapable. It is this very characteristic of certainty within a system that allows for the certainty of mathematics and physics.

THE NECESSITY FOR ARGUMENTS OF PROBABILITY

Furthermore, Toulmin (1958) argued that the syllogism, although having received the lion's share of attention over the centuries, is not applicable to most of the arguments we make in practice.

We make claims about the future, and back them with reference to our experiences of how things have gone in the past. We make assertions about a man's feelings, or about his legal status, and back them by references to his utterances and gestures, or to his place of birth and to the statutes about nationality; we adopt moral positions, and pass aesthetic judgements, and declare support for scientific theories or political causes, in each case producing as grounds for our conclusion statements of quite other logical types than the conclusion itself. (pp. 124-125)

In *The Art of Rhetoric*, Aristotle (1991) would agree with Toulmin. Aristotle made it very clear that the his theory of rhetoric is specifically concerned with nonsyllogistic arguments, arguments in which the premises are not certain. He called these arguments enthymemes. He outlined three kinds: the forensic argument about specific facts, the epideictic argument about praise or blame (judgments), and deliberative arguments about policy. None of these develop from certain premises. All stem from statements of probability. Such arguments are at the heart of the social sciences and of literacy research, no matter what the tools we use to collect our evidence.

Toulmin (1958) called such arguments *substantive*. They cannot be made syllogistically. Their success is dependent on the force of the evidence presented, rather than on the formal relationships of the premises as in the syllogism. Toulmin (2001) argued that the speculative pursuit of knowledge has "played a central part in human culture for 2,500 years and more" covering the whole range of inquiry "from geometry and astronomy at one pole to autobiography and historical narrative at the other" (p. 14). Furthermore, he argued that "for more than two thousand years, all such activities were given equal consideration" (p. 15). After Descartes' use of geometry as the model for knowledge, that "equal consideration" began to dissipate with greater prestige going to sciences that attempted to emulate Euclidean geometry in the precision and consistency of their theories. According to Toulmin (2001), this ideal was also adopted by certain of the social sciences, most notably economics. In fields related to education, perhaps the work of B.F. Skinner best illustrates an attempt to achieve the ideal of geometric precision. But that work, except perhaps for aspects of behavioral modification, has been largely rejected by the psychological and educational communities as a theory that will bring an end to the consternation we face in education.

We cannot make use of the syllogistic arguments that underlie the kinds of arguments found in mathematics and the hard sciences. We must, as Toulmin (1958, 2001) might say, forge ahead with the reasoning processes of substantive argument, admitting in every case that absolute certainty is not possible. We work in areas in which probabilities must be our business. We must construct our representations of what we believe to be true, and, in the course of developing our arguments, lay bare our assumptions, methods, evidence, and warrants.

PUTTING THE QUALITATIVE AND QUANTITATIVE TOGETHER

At the same time, because we work with substantive arguments, we are able to draw together evidence of different kinds derived through the use of different methods. The claims derived from quite different research methods can be used in complementary ways to establish or disestablish propositions and theories. For example, considerable experimental evidence indicates that certain kinds of student-led small-group discussions (collaborative learning) can have a powerful impact on individual writing when the students work together in those discussions to solve problems parallel to those they will confront in their individual writing (Hillocks, 1986). Comparison of these results to those obtained through relatively unstructured response groups, individual conferences, or teacher lecture indicates that the structured small-group discussions are on the order of three to four times more effective than the other methods.

Although the evidence from these studies is quite strong for cognitive growth, and although the kind of cognitive growth can be inferred from the writing of students in the studies, the experimental trials provide virtually no information about how growth takes place. Research currently under way at the University of Chicago makes use of classroom observations and audiorecordings of classes and small-group discussions to examine the processes in small-group discussions that may be responsible for the change in students' thinking and writing. Preliminary examination of the data indicates that the processes strongly evident in certain types of student-led discussions recur in talk-aloud protocols when students are writing independently, and show up as results in independent writing. That is, the processes used in the small groups appear to be internalized for individual use, a probability that is supported by Vygotskian theory.

An ardent qualitative researcher might argue that we had no need for collecting any of the experimental data at all. Such a person might argue that the main study should have examined the situated student-led small-group discussions in the first place. Such is not the case, however. Most of the quantitative studies supply explicit enough discussions of the instructional methods in both the experimental and control treatments to allow reasonably strong inferences about the tested results. Additionally, across several studies the effect size of experimental treatments (vs. that of control treatments) is homogeneous, providing an unusually strong generalization about the effects of this kind of treatment (Hillocks, 1986). The study of small groups alone, although possibly capable of indicating the effective instruction, could not carry the weight of generalizations developed across large groups of students. Taken together, the two kinds of studies provide far richer and more convincing findings than could either alone.

Recently, I completed a study that set out to examine the impact of large scale testing of writing in state level assessments on the teaching of writing in five states (Hillocks, 2002). The design of the study was guided by assumptions from both qualitative and quantitative paradigms. How to collect data was an important concern. It seemed to me that in depth interviews with teachers and administrators would be extremely important. Questionnaires would not do the job. Earlier studies taught me that teachers would provide a wealth of detail in an extended interview and that I would be able to probe for more detail. Questionnaires seemed to be a different matter. Teachers however well intentioned were less likely to provide nearly as much detail in writing. The qualitative decision to use interviews raised the problem of sample size, a problem form the quantitative paradigm. I wanted a sample size as large as possible, but that would be restricted by the funds available (for which I am indebted to the Spencer Foundation). Having worked with and studied many classrooms over the four decades preceding the beginning of the study, I believed my perception of the existing reality of differences among schools was correct. (There is a positivist statement for you.) Visiting only one site in each state would very likely be disastrous. (I have subsequently seen a study that attempts to examine the impact of a writing assessment through interviews with teachers in a single school. The results do not allow generalizing about the assessment beyond the response of that single faculty, although the researcher does so with impunity.)

My decision was to stratify the sample using school districts of different types: two large urban, two suburban (one of middle and one of lower middle socioeconomical status), one small town and one rural. I assumed that this selection in each state would provide the kind of variety that would be helpful in interpreting results. This is clearly a quantitative plan. However, the study was essentially qualitative relying on the analysis of documents from states, school systems, and classrooms and interviews with many teachers and administrators at local and state levels. The conclusions about the impact of the assessments on instruction were developed largely by interpretation of the documents and interviews.

However, it seemed to me to be absolutely essential to quantify some findings to demonstrate the extent of the impact. Therefore, my assistants and I coded all teacher interviews for a large number of variables so that we could use descriptive statistics to help in interpreting the data. In Illinois, for example, teachers and administrators talked a lot about the importance of teaching the five-paragraph theme to increase test scores. I quoted many to demonstrate how the state writing assessment encouraged such teaching. I developed detailed analyses of the Illinois prompts, testing conditions, scoring criteria, and benchmark papers to show how the system gives rise to formulaic writing. All of this evidence is available through tools from the qualitative paradigm.

However, I turned to descriptive statistics derived from our coding of the teacher interviews for additional support. The descriptive statistics are simple counts, in this case converted to percentages, but definitely a tool from the quantitative paradigm. But they provide excellent support for the same contention supported by the qualitative evidence. In my opinion, they clinch the argument. In Illinois, more than 70% of teachers interviewed told us that they taught the five-paragraph theme, but in Kentucky, with a quite different assessment, only 6% mentioned it. In this case, the quantitative measure complements and supports the qualitatively derived claim that the assessment in Illinois promotes vacuous, formulaic writing. At the same time, the decision about what to count as an indication of interest in five-paragraph theme writing is a qualitative decision involving interpretation and the construction of the underlying idea of the five-paragraph theme. This is necessarily true of any phenomenon we identify on the basis of criteria in order to count. One might argue that all quantitative research must be based on interpretations of phenomenon to permit identification and counts.

On the other hand, counts are implicit in most good qualitative work. When an anthropologist generalizes about the practices in a culture, those generalizations are based on counts. That is the nature of generalizations. In *The Religion of Java*, for example, Clifford Geertz (1960), early in the text, set out to describe religious ceremonies of one "subvariant within the general Javanese religious system" (p. 5). As he began to describe the marriage ceremony, he commented on his method:

I shall describe the marriage ceremony in the fullest form in which it appears, but I shall include no practice not carried out on the occasion of at least one wedding I saw during the time I was in Modjokuto. It must be remembered not only that ceremonies for middle daughters are usually somewhat less elaborate, but also that various people omit various parts of the ceremony pretty much at will (p. 54).

A consciousness of numbers and counting is implied throughout that statement, even though specific numbers do not appear. The number observed is greater than one, each practice described must have been carried out in at least one wedding witnessed, and the range of practices within the wedding ceremony appears to vary widely from a minimum of going to the mosque to pronounce the Moslem Confession of Faith to an elaborate series of practices over 2 days, with certain events in some weddings taking place after an additional interval of 5 days. Geertz saw no reason to present these numbers and ranges in a formal way.

It is clear, however, that counts and necessity for counts lurk in the corners of qualitative research. They are as ubiquitous in qualitative research as are interpretations in quantitative research. If quantitative measures appear and can be used in tandem with qualitative interpretations, one has to wonder whether the distinction between the two paradigms is a real one.

That certain concerns and methods may be used profitably together does not obviate the contradictory assumptions about the existence and the nonexistence of an objective reality. But contradictory assumptions exist in the hard sciences, too. Some physicists, for example, have accepted a wave theory of light, whereas others accepted a particle theory. Certain experiments verified one theory, whereas other experiments verified the other. More recently, physicists have recognized that the two may be more appropriately seen as different explanations of the same phenomena, based on different assumptions underlying the experiments used to verify them.

Is it not possible that divergent assumptions about objective reality simply represent different metaphors about our relations to reality, and that both have validity under certain sets of conditions? It is useful to think of reality as objective, particularly when we deal with sensory experience that can be observed repeatedly under different conditions, even though we must allow and test for the failures of perception. We could not live our daily lives without this assumption. On the other hand, when our concerns involve chains of inference (as in research on language learning), then it is imperative to remember that our minds mediate reality, that even though two observers begin with quite similar sensory perceptions, their chains of inference may lead to quite divergent representations of their observations. In research on literacy it is important both to establish what appears to be objective and to interpret those facts—to give them meaning. Given those demands, we cannot in good conscience reject either set of assumptions or methods. We need both to accomplish the tasks before us. I have to conclude that the dichotomy between the qualitative and quantitative is a false one.

NOTE

1. Heap went on to say that "there is no way of calculating a margin of error" for such items. In fact, it is possible, using Rasch model analysis, which provides person and item measure, fit statistics, and standard errors for items. Rasch model analysis provides a means of identifying items of the kind to which Heap objected (Wright & Stone, 1979).

REFERENCES

Aristotle. (1991). *The art of rhetoric* (H. Lawson-Tancred, Trans.). New York: Penguin.

Butler, C. S. (1990). Qualifications in science: Modal meanings in scientific texts. In W. Nash (Ed.), *The writing scholar: Studies in academic discourse* (pp. 137-170). Newbury Park, CA: Sage.

Crismore, A., & Farnsworth, R. (1990). Metadiscourse in popular and professional science discourse. In W. Nash (Ed.), *The writing scholar: Studies in academic discourse* (pp. 118-136). Newbury Park, CA: Sage.

Emig, J. (1971). *The composing processes of twelfth graders.* Urbana, IL: National Council of Teachers of English.

Geertz, C. (1960). *The religion of Java.* Glencoe, IL: The Free Press.

Guba, E. G. (1990). The alternative paradigm dialog. In E.G. Guba (Ed.). *The paradigm dialog* (pp. 17-27) Newbury Park, CA: Sage.

Heap, J. (1992). Ethnomethodology and the possibility of a metaperspective on literacy research. In R. Beach, J. Green, M. Kamil, & T. Shanahan (Eds.), *Multidisciplinary perspectives on literacy research* (pp. 35-56). Urbana, IL: National Conference on Research on English/National Council of Teachers of English.

Hedges, L. V. (1987). How hard is hard science, how soft is soft science? The empirical cumulativeness of research. *Journal of the American Psychological Association, 42,* 443-455.

Hillocks, G. (1986). *Research on written composition: New directions for teaching.* Urbana, IL: National Council of Teachers of English.

Hillocks, G. (2002). *The testing trap: How state writing assessments control learning.* New York: Teachers College Press.

Hunt, K.W. (1965). *Grammatical structures written at three grade levels* (NCTE Research Report No. 3). Champaign, IL: National Council of Teachers of English.

Lincoln, Y.S. (1990). The making of a constructivist: A remembrance of transformations past. In E. G. Guba (Ed.), *The paradigm dialog* (pp. 67-87), Newbury Park, CA: Sage.

Miller, P. J., Potts, R., Fung, H., Hoogstra, L., & Mintz, J. (1990). Narrative practices and the social construction of self in childhood. *American Ethnologist, 17,* 292-311.

Miller, P. J., & Sperry, L. L. (1988). Early talk about the past: The origins of conversational stories of personal experience. *Journal of Child Language, 15,* 293-315.

Smith, J. K. (1983). Quantitative versus qualitative research: An attempt to clarify the issue. *Educational Researcher, 12*(3), 6-13.

Toulmin, S. (1958). *The uses of argument.* New York: Cambridge University Press.

Toulmin, S. (2001). *Return to reason.* Cambridge, MA: Harvard University Press.

Williams, R. (1983). *Key words: A vocabulary of culture and society.* New York: Oxford University Press.

Wright, B. D., & Stone, M. H. (1979). *Best test design.* Chicago: Mesa.

4

A Psychological Perspective on Literacy Studies

John R. Hayes
Carnegie Mellon University

What I describe here is my own perspective on literacy studies. It is a psychological perspective in that it focuses on the individual and emphasizes empirical methods, as do most psychologists. However, within psychology, my perspective is a specialized one. It falls fairly comfortably, with some divergences to be noted, within the current cognitive paradigm. In what follows, I explain how I came to adopt a cognitive perspective, describe what I have found useful about the cognitive perspective, and discuss the nature of paradigm change, and the interactions between paradigms in psychology.

HOW I BECAME A COGNITIVE PSYCHOLOGIST

As is true of many of my cognitively oriented colleagues, I came to psychology by way of the physical sciences. In high school, I was fascinated by physics. I was first hooked on the subject when I happened to read a brief history of atomic physics. The important thing, I think, was that the topic was presented not as a body of facts, but as a narrative about real people asking hard questions about nature and then struggling, sometimes against adversity, to answer them. Intrigued, I read biographies of Madame Curie, Galileo, Copernicus, and other scientists and began serious study of college physics texts. I had no doubt that my future lay in physics because I was having such a wonderful time building spectrographs and vacuum pumps in my cellar laboratory.

Everything about physics was magical to me. I expected to love physics even more in college, but a peculiar thing happened. It soon became clear to me that the professors at Harvard whom I so admired and whom I wanted to model myself after had no interest in involving undergraduates in research or even in talking to them very much. They were too busy earning their Nobel prizes. Until years later, I didn't really understand why my interest in physics faded and why I became fascinated instead with psychology. I'm sure that it had nothing to do with the subject matter. Rather, I'm convinced it was because I found psychology professors who were willing to let me get involved in doing psychology. I knew I had found a home when they let me have my own rat lab. Later reflection on the events that changed me from a physicist into a psychologist made me acutely aware of the important impact teachers can have on their students' lives simply by paying attention to them.

Harvard psychology at the time was dominated by Skinner and his radical behaviorism. I bought into it enthusiastically; I was happy to work with pigeons and rats because I accepted the behaviorist dictum that psychology is best pursued "bottom up." Behaviorists believed that you have to understand the simple things first: conditioning in rats and pigeons before language and learning in humans. Basic research questions were strongly favored over applied ones. I accepted all of these attitudes as truth and criticized Skinner's enemies, or as I saw it, "our enemies," for their fuzzy-headedness, for their mentalism (i.e., their tendency to explain behavior in terms of internal mental states), for their failure to define their concepts operationally; in short, for their failure to be hard-core behaviorists.

I carried my behaviorist enthusiasm with me when I went to graduate school at MIT, where I studied with George Miller and was able to take courses with Jerome Bruner and anthropologist John Whiting. And I carried that enthusiasm through to my thesis, a study of the motivation of preschool children for playing games. I started my thesis believing that I could account for children's enthusiasm for games in terms of Skinner's schedules of reinforcement. I designed games in which young children would be rewarded by viewing pictures, intended to entertain them, according to various schedules of reinforcement.

In one way, my results were consistent with the Skinnerian point of view. The children's interest in my games was related to the schedules of reinforcement roughly as I had predicted. In another way, though, my results were radically at odds with the Skinnerian point of view. The children were not treating my reinforcements, the pictures, in the way I expected. They weren't attending to them in the way that rats or pigeons in a Skinner box would snap up morsels of food. Actually, they hardly gave my pictures a glance. But they did have a lot of interest in discovering the rules of the game. What I found was that the children weren't being conditioned; they were enjoying a cognitive activity: problem solving.

My experience with the nursery school children made it clear to me that there were some very interesting phenomena that fell outside of the Behaviorist worldview. I began to look for a new, more inclusive psychology. This was 1955. 1 didn't have long to wait. The events that led to the birth of cognitive psychology were already under way.

One of these events was the publication of Chomsky's (1959) devastating critique of Skinner's (1957) book *Verbal Behavior*. Skinner had attempted to extend his conditioning studies with rats and pigeons to human language and had failed disastrously. Perhaps the behaviorists' bottom-up approach was not such a good idea.

Another event in the paradigm shift was the publication of George Miller's (1956) "The Magic Number Seven, Plus or Minus Two." This precedent-setting paper offered the first important cognitive model. The model was cognitive in that it explained memory in terms of unobserved mental structures and processes (a sort of mentalism the Skinnerians completely rejected). The paper was important because the limitations of short-term memory that Miller described constitute a bottleneck through which many human thought processes must pass.

The event with the most far-reaching effect, however, was Newell and Simon's (1972) powerful computer metaphor for thought. Oddly, the computer metaphor had the effect of encouraging psychologists to study human thought. The behaviorists believed that it was unscientific to talk about internal thought processes because they were not directly observable. Seeing that computer scientists discussed the internal information processes of their machines in respectable scientific ways, however, gave psychologists courage to disregard behaviorist strictures and consider parallel kinds of process descriptions for human thought.

HOW THE COGNITIVE PARADIGM HAS HELPED MY RESEARCH

Switching to the cognitive paradigm has helped my research in two critical ways:

1. It provided an environment in which I could escape the strictures of the Behaviorist paradigm.
2. It provided some very useful theoretical and observational tools.

I discuss each of these in turn.

Escaping From Behaviorism

For the behaviorists, learning was the psychological phenomenon of primary interest. In describing any behavior, the central question for them was "How was that learned?" For cognitive psychologists, that is still an interesting question but it is not the only question. Cognitive psychologists are interested in learning, but they are also interested in memory, perception, representation, decision making, language, problem solving, and creativity. My own research, which has concentrated on the last three topics, would not have been encouraged in behaviorist psychology departments.

Another aspect of the behaviorist perspective was a preference for simple things before complex ones. Simple tasks, especially those shared by rats and pigeons (such as conditioning and maze learning), were preferred to complex tasks performed primarily or exclusively by humans, such as problem solving and reading. Cognitive psychology is much more oriented to studying complex human tasks than is behaviorism. It is hard for me to imagine that my own interest in the study of writing would have been well received in a behaviorist department.

A final aspect of the behaviorist perspective is the Skinnerian refusal to discuss internal mental processes. Concepts such as thought, imagery, and memory were considered unscientific by Skinner because they were not directly observable. Cognitive psychologists, building on Newell and Simon's computer metaphor, saw internal mental processes as not substantially more mysterious than internal computer processes. Thus, they felt comfortable in considering memory and imagery as respectable phenomena. Indeed, the essence of the cognitive paradigm is the belief that much of what people do can be understood in terms of internal cognitive processes such as memories, images, and plans.

New Theoretical and Observational Tools

The cognitive paradigm provides two important tools to aid the researcher in investigating cognitive processes:

1. *Cognitive process models* that allow for systematic descriptions of interactions among cognitive processes and their relation to the individual's performance of an activity.
2. *Protocol analysis* that helps in the identification of the nature and sequence of cognitive processes involved in the performance of activities such as solving a problem or reading a sentence.

I have found these tools very useful for conducting research in the field of literacy. For example, the 1980 Hayes-Flower model of written composition is thoroughly cognitive in character. First, the model is a cognitive process model because it represents relations among cognitive processes and indicates how these processes are involved in the task of writing. Second, the underlying data for the model were derived through protocol analysis of writers in the act of composing. Third, the general structure of the model, that is, the top-level division of the model into task environment, memory, and cognitive processes is borrowed quite directly from Newell and Simon's (1972) cognitive architecture. The 1996 model (Hayes, 1996), which superceded the earlier model, is an updated cognitive process model designed to account the results of numerous studies carried out since 1980. Many of these studies made use of protocol data.

My colleagues and I have used protocol data and in constructing cognitive process models to describe a wide variety of literacy phenomena including paragraphing (Bond & Hayes, 1984), text generation (Kaufer, Hayes, & Flower, 1986), revision (Hayes, Flower, Schriver, Stratman, & Carey, 1987), and reading problems in low-literate children (Schriver & Hayes, 1998). Additionally, we used protocol analysis as a practical tool to improve the clarity of technical documents (Swaney, Janik, Bond, & Hayes, 1981). Of course, many other literacy researchers have used protocol analysis and cognitive modeling as well.

CHANGING PARADIGMS:
REVOLUTION OR REFOCUSING?

My work in the field of literacy clearly bears the imprint of the cognitive paradigm. But that does not tell the whole story. The way I approach literacy studies depends importantly on the cognitive paradigm, but it depends even more importantly on the psychological tradition generally. It is easy to dismiss earlier psychological paradigms as irrelevant to current thought, as paradigms that have been tried and found wanting. We dismiss the structuralists because we no longer believe that a psychology can be constructed entirely from subjective observation. We dismiss Gestalt Psychology because we find its visual metaphor for thought too narrow. We dismiss the behaviorists because their anti-mentalism and their focus on learning seem unnecessarily constraining. However, it is easy to overemphasize the radical nature of paradigm shifts. Paradigm shifts in psychology have caused extensive refocusing, but they have not been absolute. Although much is abandoned in a paradigm shift, much is also saved.

It is hard for us to stand back and see that much of our everyday practice as cognitive psychologists is actually borrowed from earlier psychologies. Our approach to problems, the familiar research methods we use, and the standards for argument we apply were honed by experimenters in research traditions that are no longer popular, that is, by behaviorists, structuralists, and Gestalt researchers. Practitioners of these earlier psychologies have faced the same sorts of problems that we now face. In their attempts to understand thought and behavior, they have assembled a rich body of observational methods and have established high standards for argument based on data. These methods for evaluating arguments have continued to be useful despite paradigm changes. The basic psychophysical methods and the reaction-time methods were invented by structuralist psychologists. Many of the standard experimental designs described by Campbell and Stanley (1963) and many of the statistical methods now in use were borrowed by behaviorist researchers from the agronomists who developed them for application to agricultural research. Standards for argument in psychology such as those described by Huck and Sandler (1979) have developed not just during the current paradigm, but throughout the history of psychology. We draw on these methods and these standards continually and unconsciously in our everyday research pursuits. Many of the literacy studies I have been involved in, for example, studies of voice (Hatch, Hill, & Hayes 1993), studies of revision (Wallace & Hayes, 1991), and studies of text generation (Chenoweth & Hayes, 2001) employ only experimental procedures borrowed from earlier traditions. Most of my studies that use protocol analysis also use these other procedures.

I propose to characterize the legacy of attitudes, methods, and standards for argument as *psychology's rhetorical tradition.* I call it rhetorical because it is centrally concerned with argument and persuasion. It is the framework that guides psychologists when they try to convince an audience of peers that their claims are plausible. It is used as a standard by which arguments are judged. Psychologists who do not meet the standard—by failing to recognize confounding variables, by omitting needed control groups, by using inappropriate statistical methods—are criticized or, more to the point, their arguments are rejected as unconvincing.

To be more specific about the content of the rhetorical tradition in psychology, I believe it includes at least the following:

- A belief that empirical observations can provide a very effective basis for assessing claims. As a consequence of my psychological training, I frequently find myself responding to claims by trying to imagine empirical observations that could support or refute them.

- A preference for measurement over narrative description. This preference distinguishes psychology from such as history and anthropolgy. Historically, psychologists have made use of both quantitative measures such as numbers of responses and response times and qualitative measures such as categorizations and rank orderings. Clearly, protocol analysis involves qualitative measurement.
- A well-developed set of methods for collecting and interpreting data. Although empirical methods are often popularly viewed as ways of proving assertions, they really have nothing to do with proof, as Mill (1877) has pointed out. Rather, they should be viewed as methods for convincing people of the plausibility of claims. Some of these methods are listed here:

  Reliability measures
  Replication
  Triangulation
  Randomization
  Counterbalancing
  Choice of study designs
  Control groups
  Statistical methods
  Hedging

- A well-developed set of sensitivities to factors that may invalidate empirically based arguments. These sensitivities require that researchers be alert to the myriad factors other than the hypothesized ones that can create patterns in their data. Some of these factors are listed in Table 4.1.

Table 4.1. Psychology's Rhetorical Tradition Emphasizes Sensitivity to Factors Found to Threaten the Acceptability of Empirical Arguments.

Reliability of Observations
- Unreliability within and between observers
- Systematic drift in accuracy (e.g., fatigue)

Effects of the Act of Observing on the Observed
- Observer bias in the treatment of the participants
- Observer bias in the perception of the results
- Participant responses to observation (e.g., the Hawthorne effect, the placebo effect)

Distortions in the Observing "Window"
- Sampling bias (applies to participants, materials, and contexts)
- Problems with self-report (e.g., telling the observers what they want to hear)
- Shared participant experience (e.g., the problem of using intact classes)

Unaccounted Changes in the Observed
- Maturation (e.g., changes in the participants due to age and experience)
- Order effects
- Testing effects (e.g., the second test is typically better than the first)
- Differential dropout rates for treatment and control groups
- Regression to the mean

Unwarranted Inferences from Observation
- Generalizing beyond studied context
- Inferring causation from correlation
- Generalizing from small samples (e.g., drawing negative conclusions from studies with low statistical power)
- Data fishing (e.g., drawing conclusion from unpredicted results)

PARADIGMATIC LEVELS VERSUS RHETORICAL LEVELS OF PSYCHOLOGICAL RESEARCH

If my view is correct, it would be appropriate to distinguish between two levels of description in discussing the history of psychology: a *paradigmatic* level and a *rhetorical* level. At the paradigmatic level of description, psychology might be seen as a sequence of mutually incompatible schools, each school replacing earlier ones in revolutionary paradigm shifts. With each shift, much of the content of the earlier paradigm is either reinterpreted or becomes irrelevant. Thus, in 1950, much psychological journal space was devoted to descriptions of animal experiments designed to test Hull's (1943) stimulus-response theory of learning. Since the shift from the behaviorist to the cognitive paradigm, this very large body of research is rarely referenced. It is seen as irrelevant to the new paradigm that is focused on research designed to test information-processing models of human thought. We should note, however, that the factual results of earlier paradigms are not necessarily lost, For example, although the behaviorist work on schedules of reinforcement is not of much interest to the cognitive psychologists, it has been employed by ethologists to account for such phenomena as optimal foraging by animals in the wild.

At the rhetorical level of description, psychology is a collection of argumentative practices that psychologists employ in the process of attempting to persuade the audience of the plausibility of psychological claims. These practices include experimental designs, statistical methods, and standards for argument. Rather than exhibiting revolutionary change, these practices appear to have evolved in a relatively continuous way over more than a century of psychological investigation. Each school of psychology, although rejecting the paradigms of other schools, seems to share quite freely in their argumentative practices. Thus, at the paradigmatic level, psychology appears to be a sequence of relatively disjoint programs, each emerging by revolutionary rejection of earlier programs, but at the rhetorical level, it appears to be a continuously evolving array of argumentative practices. The continuity of the rhetorical tradition is supported by a relatively stable system for transmitting the argumentative practices: required courses in statistics and experimental design, the apprenticeship of graduate students, and criticism by editors and peer reviewers of papers submitted for publication.

I view this rhetorical tradition, the legacy of methods and standards for argument, as the most valuable intellectual product of the psychological enterprise—more valuable, indeed, than any body of theory or fact. Each of the social and physical sciences as well as the fields of history, law, and journalism have parallel traditions of adherence to high standards for method and argument for interpreting observational data. In the field of literacy research, I feel that the factor that most sharply differentiates more effective from less effective researchers is their participation or nonparticipation in a strong rhetorical tradition for interpreting empirical results.

INTERACTIONS BETWEEN PERSPECTIVES

As this volume attests, multiple perspectives are currently active in literacy studies. Some focus on culture, others on language, and still others on power relations among groups. Although, there is no need that these perspectives be anything but complementary and mutually supportive, in fact, turf wars are not uncommon.

Some time ago, I was involved in a discussion that revealed a great deal to me about the interaction between competing perspectives. I had become involved in a project on creativity that was inspired by the work of Chase and Simon (1973). These authors estimated that chess players, by the time they reached the level of grand master, had learned approximately 50,000 chess patterns. For even the most precocious players, this learning required about 10 years of intensive practice. I wondered if a similar effect might be observed in creative activities such as musical composition or painting. So I set about examining the biographies of great composers to find out when they first became seriously involved in music and when they produced their most notable works. My question was, would the great composers of the last three centuries need years of practice before they began to produce the works for which they were famous?

To get advice about my research, I went to an experienced musicologist and explained my project to him. He was not impressed. He told me, in a nice way, that my study was not worth doing. The esthetic goals of musicians who composed in different centuries and in different artistic traditions were so diverse that there could be nothing in common among them. Therefore, no consistent results could be expected.

The musicologist's argument was certainly a reasonable one. However, I didn't agree with it. He came from a perspective emphasizing the importance of cultural and historical influences. I came from a perspective emphasizing the importance of practice. It is not surprising that he guessed that the effects of cultural differences would mask the effects of practice and that I guessed the opposite.

In fact, I found that of the 76 composers I studied 73 had had 10 or more years of practice before they wrote the works for which they became famous and the remaining 3 had either 8 or 9 years (Hayes, 1985). I found similar results for painters. Practice, then, clearly had an impact on creative performance even though cultural factors must surely have been operating as well.

My point here is not that one perspective won out over another. Indeed, I don't think that happened. Both the musicologist and I agreed that practice and cultural factors are important but we disagreed on their relative importance in a particular situation. Perhaps if I had broadened the range of cultural differences, say by including Middle-Eastern, African, and Asian music in my study, cultural factors might have had greater impact. The most important point, however, is this. If my study had failed to produce robust results, the musicologist's perspective would have helped me to interpret the outcome. I would have been alerted to the importance of cultural differences in such situations. Perspectives can be mutually supportive. When different perspectives overlap, each has the potential to enrich the other.

Unfortunately, although different perspectives can be mutually supportive, often they are not. Perspectives have a tendency to produce *paradigm zealots*, people who believe that there is one best way to approach a topic and that other approaches are simply wrong or, in extreme cases, evil. As I noted earlier, I was a paradigm zealot when I first took up the behaviorist cause. The result was that I closed myself off from the interesting stream of results that the social psychologists on campus were discovering. Unfortunately, the harm that paradigm zealots can cause is not limited to themselves. When such people occupy influential positions in granting agencies and journals, they can deny funding and publication to researchers who do not share their perspective.

PROBLEMS WITH THE COGNITIVE PARADIGM

Although I find the cognitive paradigm and the rhetorical tradition of psychology extremely useful for conducting studies in literacy, I feel that neither is perfectly attuned to the needs of the literacy researcher. The rhetorical tradition of psychology has placed heavy emphasis on experimentation and has seriously undervalued exploratory studies. Symptomatic of this undervaluation is Campbell and Stanley's (1963) dismissal of case-study research as being "of almost no scientific value" (p. 6). But surely the observations that give rise to hypotheses should be considered as important as the observations that we use to test them.

If an extraterrestrial were to land among us, we would certainly want to study it, even though it provided only a one-shot case study. Study of the case couldn't lead to any firm conclusions about extraterrestrial life in general, but it could provide some pretty interesting hypotheses. At the present state of literacy studies, exploration and hypothesis formation may be more important than hypothesis testing.

A major deficiency in the cognitive psychology paradigm for literacy researchers is its failure to address issues of motivation. Hilgard (1987) noted that with the advent of the cognitive paradigm there was a decline in attention to motivation. He attributed the decline in part to the fact that cognitive theories are not based in physiology and that the study of physiologically based drives has been a traditional source of interest in motivation. Whatever the reasons for the omission, cognitive psychology definitely has not focused on motivation. However, because motivation is of such urgent concern in the field of literacy, literacy researchers cannot afford to ignore it. I have attempted to sketch some of the functions of motivation in writing in my 1996 model (Hayes, 1996). Developing effective approaches for studying motivational issues must be a high priority for literacy research.

Strong rhetorical traditions for interpreting empirical results are extremely valuable tools for literacy researchers. Without such traditions, meaningful dialogue among researchers is difficult and progress toward the very important goals of the field is slow. Fostering strong rhetorical traditions requires effort. Graduate students can't be expected to absorb such traditions in a one-semester course. We have to provide them with substantial training and apprenticeship. Journals can help by insisting on reasonable standards of argument. With a strong rhetorical tradition attuned to the needs of literacy researchers, we might hope to make faster progress in understanding some of the urgent problems we face.

REFERENCES

Bond, S.J., & Hayes, J.R. (1984). Cues people use to paragraph text. *Research in the Teaching of English, 18,* 147-167.

Campbell, D.T., & Stanley, J.C. (1963). *Experimental and quasi-experimental designs for research.* Boston, MA: Houghton Mifflin.

Chase, W., & Simon, H.A. (1973). Perception in chess. *Cognitive Psychology, 4,* 55-81.

Chenoweth, N. A., & Hayes, J. R. (2001). Fluency in writing: Generating text in L1 and L2. *Written Communication, 18,* 80-98.

Chomsky, N. (1959). Review of verbal behavior, by Skinner. *Language, 35,* 26-58.

Hatch, J., Hill, C., & Hayes, J.R. (1993). When the messenger is the message: Readers' impressions of writers. *Written Communication, 10*(4), 569-598.

Hayes, J.R. (1985). Three problems in teaching general skills. In S. Chipman, J. Segal, & R. Glaser (Eds.), *Thinking and learning skills.* Hillsdale, NJ: Erlbaum.

Hayes, J.R. (1996). A new framework for understanding cognition and affect in writing. In C. M. Levy & S. Ransdell (Eds.), *The science of writing* (pp. 1-27). Mahwah, NJ: Erlbaum.

Hayes, J.R., & Flower, L. (1980). Identifying the organization of writing processes. In L. W. Gregg & E.R. Steinberg (Eds.), *Cognitive processes in writing: An interdisciplinary approach* (pp. 3–30). Hillsdale, NJ: Erlbaum.

Hayes, J.R., Flower, L., Schriver, K.A., Stratman, J.F., & Carey, L. (1987). Cognitive processes in revision. In S. Rosenberg (Ed.), *Advances in applied psycholinguistics: Vol. 2. Reading, writing, and language learning* (pp. 176-240). Cambridge, UK: Cambridge University Press.

Hilgard, E.R. (1987). *Psychology in America: A historical survey.* San Diego: Harcourt Brace Jovanovich.

Huck, S.W., & Sandler, H.M. (1979). *Rival hypotheses: Alternative interpretations of data based conclusions.* New York: Harper & Row.

Hull, C.L. (1943). *Principles of behavior.* New York: Appleton-Century-Crofts.

Kaufer, D., Hayes, J.R., & Flower, L.S. (1986). Composing written sentences. *Research in the Teaching of English, 20,* 121-140.

Mill, J.S. (1877). *A system of logic* (8th ed.). New York: Harper. (Original work published 1843)

Miller, G.A. (1956). The magic number seven, plus or minus two: Some limits on our capacity for processing information. *Psychological Review, 63,* 81-97.

Newell, A., & Simon, H.A. (1972). *Human problem solving.* Englewood Cliffs, NJ: Prentice-Hall.

Schriver, K.A., & Hayes, J.R. (1998, April). Making assessment tests fair for all students. Paper presented at the meeting of the American Educational Research Association, San Diego, CA.

Skinner, B.F. (1957). *Verbal behavior.* New York: Appleton-Century-Crofts.

Swaney, J.H., Janíc, C.J., Bond, S.J., & Hayes, J.R. (1981). *Editing for comprehension: Improving the process through reading protocols* (Tech. Rep. No. 14). Pittsburgh, PA: Communication Design Center, Carnegie Mellon University.

Wallace, D.L., & Hayes, J.R. (1991). Redefining revision for freshmen. *Research in the Teaching of English, 25,* 54-66.

PART II

SOCIOCULTURAL/ACTIVITY THEORY PERSPECTIVES ON LITERACY RESEARCH

Richard Beach
University of Minnesota

INTRODUCTION

One of the major developments in literacy research since the 1980s has been an analysis of acquiring literacy practices as tools for participating in social or cultural events. Employing qualitative and/or ethnographic methods, researchers have examined how literacy practices are constituted by various social practices necessary for constructing identities and community in various cultures. In doing so, they draw on sociocultural learning theory regarding how culturally constituted literacy practices and tools are acquired through participation in these cultures (Heath, 1983; Lee, 1993; Smagorinsky, 1995, 2002).

All of this requires a reconceptualization of static, artificially constructed notions of research contexts as containers in which various factors/variables may be controlled or manipulated. Studying contexts as containers fails to capture the ways in which context is constructed through and mediated by participants' uses of literacy practices and tools (Rex, Green, Dixon, 1998; Witte, 1992). As Engestrom (1996) noted:

> Contexts are neither containers for actions nor situationally-created experiential spaces. They are activity systems. An activity system integrates the subject, the object, and the instruments (material tools as well as signs and symbols) into a unified whole. (p. 67)

If learning and development occurs through participation in culture, then literacy researchers need to study contexts as constituted by participation in activity. As Green and Dixon (2002) noted, "what counts as context is signaled in participants' discourse and actions, what they hold each other accountable to and for, which they orient to, and how they take up and respond to what is occurring" (p. 105).

Rather than conduct research within often artificial laboratories or contrived events, researchers examine literacy practices as acquired through social participation with others in social or cultural events, attempting to understand how these practices are "situated" in these events. They focus on participants' *uses* of specific literacy practices as tools that help them achieve certain social or cultural objectives. Much of this work on situated uses of literacy was precipitated by early research by Scribner and Cole (1981) of the literacy acquisition of Vai's particular language use as well as research on Brazilian street children who in selling candy learn to make complicated math calculations as a tool to help them succeed in the work (Saxe, 1991).

A sociocultural perspective on literacy research focuses on how participants use literacy practices within the very contexts constructed through these uses. For example, a sociocultural perspective on reading highlights learners learning to read certain types of texts in certain ways as part of acquiring and engaging in certain social practices—ways of talking about, valuing, using, interpreting, or believing in texts (Gee, 1999). Researchers then identify these various social practices operating in social events such as keeping notes as part of an organization's meeting in order to maintain a written record of an organization's history (Barton & Hamilton, 1998; Barton, Hamilton, & Ivanic, 2000; Baynham & Prinsloo, 2001; Street, 2003).

Central to a sociocultural perspective on literacy learning is work of Lev Vygotsky (1978, 1986, 1987, 1997. For applications of Vygotsky's theories to literacy research, see Cazden, 1988; John-Steiner, 1997; Lee & Smagorinsky, 2000; Moll, 1990; Rogoff, 1990, 1995; Wells, 1999; Wertsch, 1981, 1985, 1991). As Vygotsky (1978) argued, learners acquire the uses of various tools through social interactions and collaboration with others that is then internalized as inner dialogue: "every function in cultural development appears twice: first, on the social level, and later on the individual level; first between people, and then inside . . . all the higher functions originate as actual relationships between individuals" (p. 46).

The idea of development as occurring through social interaction in which children internalize others' voices and discourses connects Vygotsky to Bakhtin's (1986) notion of identity as a dialogic process of appropriating and "double-voicing" others' language as they move through different activities or communities of practice (Vadeboncoeur & Portes, 2002). This suggests the value of examining literacy development in terms of acquiring social practices through participation in multiple or "layered" activities (Lave & Wenger, 1991; Prior, 1998; Rogoff, 1995; Wenger, 1998). For example, Rogoff identified three "planes" of growth: apprenticeship, guided practice, and participatory appropriation. Wenger identified a five different learning trajectories: peripheral, which lead to full community participation; inbound, in which newcomers are invested in the potential of full participation; insider, which involves construction of new forms of identities in response to new demands; boundary, which involve moving across and linking different communities; and outbound, which involve leaving a community to construct new, alternative positions, as when adolescents leave their home.

In chapter 5, Mahn and John-Steiner apply the seminal contributions of Vygotsky (1987, 1997) to the formulation of a sociocultural learning theory. They describe the ways in which Vygotsky charted how literacy development occurs through individuals' interrelationships with activity and worlds through language, thought, and literacy practices. They document how Vygotsky's analysis of the sociocultural nature of inner speech and verbal thinking mediates and is mediated by these individual-world interrelationships. This interactionist perspective, as they demonstrate, has shaped research on the processes of learning and development in composition and second-language learning. Their chapter also demonstrates the importance of Vygotsky's notion of the uses of various tools—language, signs, images, or texts that are used to achieve certain purposes or outcomes of activities.

In chapter 10, Tusting and Barton examine research on community-based local literacies. Based on their own extensive research on literacy practices in community contexts and organizations (Barton & Hamilton, 1998; Barton et al., 2000), they argue for the need for qualitative analyses of social interactions constituting various social practices. Participants assign certain meanings to social practices depending on how they function within particular communities. Analyzing these meanings for community-based social practices therefore entails extensive observations and interviews with participants as well as the various artifacts and documents that mediate uses of social practices within a community.

Rather than examine literacy practices as de-contextualized, autonomous skills or cognitive process, sociocultural researchers examine how practices, tools, genres, and artifacts mediate participation in activity and communities of practice. As Rogoff (1995) demonstrated, in engaging in the activity of selling Girl Scout cookies, Girl Scouts employ sales pitches to establish rapport with customers or charts or ledgers to organize information about cookie sales. Participants perceive the value and use of certain tools based on their understanding of the purposes they might serve to construct their identities, relationships, and values in some community of practice.

CULTURAL-HISTORICAL ACTIVITY THEORY

Consistent with Vygotsky's sociocultural learning theories, cultural-historical activity theory (CHAT) of learning (Engestrom, 1987/2001; Leont'ev, 1978, 1981) focuses on the historical and institutional nature of activity systems. (For further reading on activity theory, see Bazerman & Russell, 2003; Chaiklin, Hedegaard, & Jensen, 1999; Chaiklin & Lave, 1996; Cole, Engestrom, & Vasques, 1997; Engestrom, 1987/2001; Engestrom & Middleton, 1998; Engestrom, Miettinen, & Punamaki, 1999; Nardi, 1996; Russell & Bazerman, 1997). Current activity theorists also draw on a range of other disciplinary perspectives such as Latour's (1987; Latour & Woolgar, 1979) actor/network theory, Goffman's (1974, 1981) and Giddens (1984, 1993) sociological theories, Bourdieu's (1984, 1991) analysis of the relationship between "habitus" or "field" and agency, or Bahktin's (1981) notion of the "chronotope" as related to constructions of space and time (Leander, 2001; Prior, 1998).

One drawback in the shift in literacy research to study literacy practices in more "authentic," local contexts is the difficulty of extracting themes that apply across different events or systems in ways that move beyond the local (Brandt & Clinton, 2002). One of the arguments for adopting a CHAT perspective emanates from the need to move beyond literacy research that focuses only on immediate, local situations (Barton & Hamilton, 1998; Street, 2000). Although the meaning of literacy practices is certainly specific to particular, local contexts, the meaning of those practices are also constituted by larger historical and cultural forces. Thus, in their chapter on community-based literacy practices, Tusting and Barton examine how practices not only operate in specific communities, but also how those practices are shaped by and evolve over time due to larger historical and economic forces.

Activity theorists define learning as acquiring experience through participation in activity designed to fulfill a particular object or outcome as grounded in cultural and historical institutional traditions (Engestrom, 1987/2001; Leont'ev, 1981). Activity theorists define an activity as the intersection between agents attempting to achieve objects or outcomes through the uses of certain tools. The object or outcome often involves changing or improving an activity, creating a motive for achieving that object or outcome. Through such participation, participants acquire uses of various tools—language, images, genres, and so on, designed to achieve an object or outcome.

Adopting activity as the primary unit of analysis highlights the collective nature of activity and how the meaning of tool/language use is evident in collectivity. Leont'ev (1978) gave the example of a hunt in which the meaning of the tools employed by beaters beating the brush to scare the prey can only be understood by how these tools are being used in the activity of the hunt. Similarly, Wertsch (1998) cited the example of the fiberglass pole employed in pole vaulting. The pole has no meaning other than in its use in mediating the action of pole vaulting.

Tools, therefore, mediate agent-object relationships in collective activity. Understanding their function as mediating activity requires an understanding of their evolving functions in historical contexts. As Roth and Tobin (2002) note, tools have a cultural-historical origin, which determines the particular ways in which they "are used and the ways their structural properties are recognized as 'affordances.' The ensemble of mediated relations therefore provides a context for the object-oriented activity of the individual participant" (p. 114).

The classic Vygotskian triangle of the agent, object, and tool as mediating the agent-object relationships served as the basis for Engestrom's (1987/2001) formulation of the notion of the activity system constituted by rules, roles/division of labor, and community. Russell (1997) defined an activity system as, "any ongoing, object-directed, historically conditioned, dialectically structured, tool-mediated human interaction. Some examples

are a family, a religious organization, a school, a discipline, a research laboratory, and a profession" (p. 510). Analysis of activity involves three
dimensions driving activity: objects, outcome, and motive (Engestrom,
1987/2001; Leont'ev, 1978).

At the level of activity (as opposed to the level of actions/goals), objects
serve as "horizons" (Engestrom, 1999) driving an activity (for a discussion
of the complexity of the concept, "object," see Foot, 2002). The outcome is
the final product produced by participation in an activity. For example, a
possible outcome of participation in a political campaign is a candidate winning the campaign. Objects (promoting a candidate in the campaign as
"winnable") are transformed into outcomes (winning the campaign)
through tools (press releases, fundraisers, door knocks, speeches, mailings).
The motive to obtain or fulfill the object evolves from a tension between a
need state and the object, serving to energize the activity (Foot, 2002).

Activity involves involves multiple motives (Leont'ev, 1978), suggesting
that the concept of *activity* refers to both the overall, whole activity, as well
as a part of the whole. Prior and Shipka (2003) noted that activity involves
two types of activity:

> Activity[1], the whole, is concrete historical practice, the total, the
> union and disunion of all the things going on; it is what is happening.
> Activity[2] is the analytical plane that pulls out the collective and moti-
> vated as opposed to action and operational levels. Activity[2] points to
> durable human life projects, like getting food, establishing shelter, cre-
> ating social relations and institutions, providing for security, reproduc-
> tion (literal and social), play—all immensely transformed and compli-
> cated by the sociohistorical development of specific practices.
> (Consider the distance between gathering local plants to eat and the
> many networks of economic, political, technological and everyday
> activity that bring grapes from Chile to homes in the U.S. during win-
> ter.) Thus, when Leont'ev (1978) says that all activity is multimotiva-
> tional, it signifies that activity[1] always involves multiple, co-present
> activity[2]'s.

TENSIONS AND CONTRADICTIONS IN ACTIVITY SYSTEMS

Activity theorists presuppose that actions are realized through incomplete,
tentative intentions that stem from perceived contradictions operating in a
system (Engestrom, 1987/2001). A contradiction may include "differences
between what [people] believe they need to know in order to accomplish a
goal and what they do, in fact, know at any point in time" (Jonassen, 2000,

p. 94). When participants are engaged with a range of different systems, or even within a system, they may experience competing objects or outcomes, resulting in contradictions between these systems. Engestrom and Escalante (1996) demonstrated the failure of the tool uses of a "buddy kiosk" in a post office—an attempt to transform the post office into a more user-friendly experience as due to the incompability of the kiosk with the post office staff's ways of operating.

In their experience of different systems, participants experience various conflicts given the competing objects or outcomes of different systems (Russell, 1997). For example, in my own research (Beach, Lundell, & Jung, 2002), developmental college students are told that they lack requisite skills from their high school experience necessary for success in the university (through admissions policies), yet they perceive themselves as being successful in other systems. They may perceive their supportive small classes and advising as helping them succeed in their developmental program, but they may describe this experience as inconsistent with large, lecture-style instructional approaches employed in other units in what they perceive to be the "real university," units for which they are being prepared to enter in their developmental programs. All of these tensions create contradictions for students in their negotiations between different systems: high school, the developmental program, and the "real university."

Participants learn to use tools for coping with these tensions and contradictions endemic to different systems. For example, inner-city residents acquire uses of various tools for coping with often inept or unsupportive bureaucratic support systems (Cushman, 1998; Rogers, 2002). During high school, students acquire genres as tools for negotiating the borders and barriers between school, home, peer-group, and workplace worlds. Analysis of California high school students from lower socioeconomic homes found that some acquired genres that helped them bridge gaps between the middle-class culture of the high school and their home cultures of their homes (Phelan, Davidson, & Yu, 1998). Based on high school students' perceptions of participation in different worlds, Phelan et al. (1998) identified six different types of relationships between family-peer group and school worlds: "congruent worlds/smooth transitions; different worlds/border crossings managed; different worlds/border crossings difficult; different worlds/border crossings resisted; congruent worlds/border crossings resisted; different worlds/smooth transitions" (p. 16). When worlds are perceived as incongruent, students perceive these borders as insurmountable barriers between worlds, particularly when they assume they lack the social or cultural capital (Bourdieu, Passeron, & de Saint Martin, 1984) valued in academic worlds. It may also be the case that practices transfer successfully across different worlds when these worlds are congruent or overlapped (Dias, Freedman, Medway, & Pare, 1999; Phelan et al., 1998; Valdes, 1996).

In discussing the notion of "co-genesis" between activity systems, Prior (1998) argued that practices in activities and worlds often overlap with each other as intersecting layers that influence each other in complex ways. Drawing on Goffman's (1981) notion of multiple footings, he argued that participants engage in multiple activity footings across different "laminated" or "layered" activity systems. He posited the need for researchers to go beyond analysis of literacy practices in singular, bounded contexts to capture the complexity of participating in multiple contexts or systems. Analysis of an undergraduate student's writing in courses versus her college's public relations job reflected her ability to negotiate the competing, conflicting motives of these two activity systems (Ketter & Hunter, 2003).

Examining these tensions between different systems shifts the focus of analysis from individuals as "failures" to problematic aspects of the systems themselves as failing individuals. Such research was evident in Rogers (2002, 2003) analysis the nonalignment between a poor, nonmainstream mother and daughter and the daughter's special education program. Rogers' analysis of the discourses constituting the marginalizing institutional positioning of both mother (from her own previous schooling experience) and daughter implicates the limitations of these systems. And, Knobel's (1999) analysis of four early adolescents documents the richness of their uses of out-of-school literacy practices, particularly related to participation in media. Given the purposeful nature of learning those practices, school experiences acquired more meaning when those experiences were driven by purposes related to transforming status quo, "real-world" institutions (see also Beach & Myers, 2001). Similarly, Dyson (1997) documented the ways in which children's participation in popular culture provides them with tools for writing development. Studies of out-of-school or workplace literacies (Hull & Schultz, 2001, 2002), demonstrate that literacy practices employed in, for example, a computer factory, may or may not match practices in acquired in schools (Hull, 2000).

CHAT perspectives have also been applied to examining uses of technology tools as mediating agent-object relationships in learning in activity (Barah, Barnett, Yamagata-Lynch, Squire, & Keating, 2002; Jonassen, 2000; McKillop & Myers, 1999; Myers & Beach, 2001). Work in the field of "distributed cognition" (Hutchins, 1995) posits that certain practices associated with an activity become embodied or "distributed" in tools. For example, navigational instruments are used to capture what is known about navigating the seas. Given the idea of histories of practices embedded in tools, researchers examine how technology tools function to mediate activity. Vygotsky's (1978) notion of children's development as shaped by participation in zones of proximal development (ZPD) constructed by experienced peers or adults served as the basis for research on how technology tools can be used to create ZPDs. For example, in after-school computer-mediated projects designed as activity systems, participation in computer games and activities resulted in increased student engagement, participation, and learning within a community (Blanton, Greene, & Cole, 1999; Gutierrez, Baquedano-Lopez, Alverez, & Chiu, 1999). Geisler (2003) analyzed the ways in which the Palm™ technology as tool mediates both a cultural history or legacy of various cognitive and social resources operating in an activity with a developmental history of individuals with their own personal subjective experiences of everyday life to function in ways of organizing or what she describes as "databasing our lives."

The Inquiry Page Web site housed at the University of Illinois is designed to mediate professional development activity for educators and media specialists teaching successes and collective expertise (Bruce & Easley, 2000). Research on uses of professional development sites indicates the importance of the quality of social interaction in this online co-inquiry. For example, one study of a site designed to foster sharing of inquiry-instruction ideas by Indiana math and science teachers examined how the site was employed to achieve the object of more discussion/sharing about inquiry instruction, with the intended outcome being improved understanding of inquiry-based instruction (Barab, Schatz, & Scheckler, in press).

In chapter 6, Carol Lee and Arnetha Ball review the basic theoretical suppositions of a CHAT perspective. They then apply a CHAT perspective to analysis of reading and writing as cultural practices acquired within and outside of school settings. They document the ways in which acquiring various tools such as signifying serves to transform activity processes in which students and preservice teachers are engaged. Consistent with the CHAT focus on relationships between different activity systems, they demonstrate how, for example, high school students employing understanding of signifying serves as a tool to link everyday language use with interpreting symbolic meanings in literary texts. And, consistent with a CHAT focus on tensions and contradictions, they document how, in any classroom, there are contradictions between teachers' official goals versus students' unofficial goals that suggest the need to create new systems. They also examine how preservice teachers' perspectives on diversity shifted through uses of reflective writing as a mediating tool leading to transformation of perceptions of diversity in the classroom.

GENRE TOOLS IN ACTIVITY

Building on Miller's (1984) groundbreaking notion of genre as social action, current genre theorists examine how genres operate as tools in activity to construct identities and communities. These theorists also draw on Bakhtin's (1986) concept of "speech genres" as constituting creative, dialogic social interactions (Hunt, 1994), Burke's (1969) "new-rhetoric" theory of language as symbolic action (Giltrow, 2000), speech-act theory (Austin, 1962) notions of "uptake" (Freadman, 1994, 2002), Halliday's (1994) functional linguistic theory (Christie & Martin, 1997), Fairclough's (1992) notion of intertextuality (Schryer, 2000), and critical ethnography (Berkenkotter, this volume) as evident in Cintron's (1997) analysis of Chicago gang members' uses of graffiti.

Applying this revised notion of genre as social action, researchers focus on the typifications (Schutz & Luckmann, 1973) constituted by genre use in particular settings, typifications constituted by historical, institutional, and material systems, again, allowing researchers to move beyond studying just the local (Brandt & Clinton, 2002). Genres function to typify both motives and contexts, creating recognizable forms of predictable actions linked to other recognizable forms (Bazerman, 2000).

Consistent with CHAT notions of tool use, genres also function to mediate various types of connected texts and actions. Russell (2002) defined these links both in terms of "breadth"—the range of different, available genres or "genre sets" (Devitt, 1991), and "depth"—how genres mediate actions within an activity. He found, for example, that Kentucky teachers used a range of texts in portfolios to engage in the activity of fostering classroom learning, contributing to the state's writing assessment, and linking writing to "real-world" rhetorical contexts.

Consistent with the CHAT notion of tools as mediating transformations in status quo systems, genres also function to create "spaces" for experimenting with new, alternative practices and identities (Dias et al., 1999). For example, various documents were used in engineering projects as genres that fostered experimentation in those projects (Winsor, 1999)

Genre theorists are also interested in how genres reflect and perpetuate power hierarchies and ideology, as evident in the debate over teaching "genres of power" as entrées for underprivileged or outsider people into systems, genres which may, at the same time, perpetuate the inequalities within those systems (Dias & Pare, 2000).

These theoretical perspectives lead genre researchers to address the following questions as formulated by Coe, Lingard, and Teslenko (2002):

> What sorts or communication does genre encourage, what sort does it constrain against?
>
> Who can—and who cannot—use this genre? Does it empower some people while silencing others?
>
> Are its effects dysfunctional beyond their immediate context?
>
> What values and beliefs are instantiated with this set of practices?

What are the political and ethical implications of rhetorical situation constructed, persona embodied [cf., subject positioning], audience invoked and context of situation assumed by a particular genre? (pp. 6-7)

In chapter 7, Bazerman and Prior move beyond notions of genre as text or as rhetoric, to define genre as social action. Consistent with the multidisciplinary focus of this volume, they draw on a range of disciplinary perspectives—rhetoric, discourse, phenomenological sociology, speech act theory, anthropological and psychological studies of discourse practices, and sociology to define genres as highly dynamic, fluid, hybrid, and situated through their social and material uses in activity. They note how genres often function as "genre sets"—texts or utterances that stand in relationship to each other, for example, letters, memos, tax forms, or conversations associated with a "genre set" employed by tax accountants (Devitt, 1991). These "genre sets" intersect with various "genre systems" (see also Yates & Orlikowski, 2002) involved in productions and uses of texts—for example, a teacher's use of a syllabus, notes, assignments, lesson plans, exams, e-mails, written comments, and so on, as part of a course, a "genre system" that mediates participation in "layered" activity systems. They also examine how CHAT notions of disciplinarity problematize traditional notions of disciplines (Berkenkotter & Huckin, 1995) as bounded discourse communities, suggesting the need for layered relationships between different, continually evolving disciplines as domains of activity, a discussion relevant to the evolving multidisciplinary perspectives represented in this volume.

Chapter 8 (Berkekotter, with Thein), illustrates Bazerman and Prior's discussion of genre systems as mediating practices in institutional settings. The authors demonstrate how institutional settings such as classrooms or schools serve as systems that constitute the meaning of genre use in those systems, focusing on the ways in which various social genres organize students' physical practices in a preschool classroom and a high school institutional setting. (This chapter's use of photography as a tool for documenting the preschool classroom's practices demonstrates the increasing important of visual tools within critical ethnography research as itself an activity.) The familiar, ritual-like genres operating in the preschool classroom function to create spaces that literally position children to engage in "embodied learning" associated with not only learning science, but also acquiring "dispositions" (Bourdieu, 1991) constituting practices in a Montessori school. Observations of the high school's traditions associated with sports and a annual winter festival demonstrate the ways in which genres reflecting working-class community values serve to both exclude and include students based on race and class. Their analyses demonstrates the benefits of studying the uses of genres as constituted by larger community values.

VALUE STANCES IN ACTIVITY

Beach and Kalnin (chapter 9) examine the ways in which participants adopt value stances as constituted by discourses (Gee, 1996, this volume) and cultural models (Holland, Lachicotte, Skinner, & Cain, 2001) operating in systems. We define value stances as more than personal beliefs or attitudes, but rather as orientations, alignments, or "dispositions" (Bourdieu, 1991) associated with participation in activity systems, as illustrated by a senator's participation with political interest groups. As constituted by participation in activity, value stances assume four functions— they reflect participants' alignment with or orientation toward cultural models and discourses; they foster a need or desire for action; they involve participation in activity to change the norm or status quo; and they reflect conflicted allegiances with layered activities. We also argue that the volitional force driving literacy practices is related to the perceived need to transform status quo systems.

This chapter's focus on discourses and cultural models serves to bridge this second section of the book with the third section on linguistic, critical discourse, and micro-ethnographic analyses of literacy practices. The sociocultural disciplinary perspectives of the second section mesh with other disciplinary perspectives of the third section to create further new approaches for analyzing literacy practices in particular events or settings.

REFERENCES

Austin, J.L. (1962). *How to do things with words: The William James lectures delivered in Harvard University in 1955* (J. O. Urmson, Ed.). Oxford, UK: Claredon Press.

Bakhtin, M.M. (1981). *The dialogic imagination: Four essays* (M. Holquist, Ed.). Austin: University of Texas Press.

Bakhtin, M.M. (1986). *Speech genres and other late essays.* Austin: University of Texas Press.

Barah, S., Barnett, M., Yamagata-Lynch, L., Squire, K., & Keating, T. (2002). Using activity theory to understand the systematic tensions characterizing a technology-rich introductory astronomy course. *Mind, Culture, and Activity, 9*(2), 76-107.

Barab, S., Schatz, S., & Scheckler, R. (in press). Using Activity Theory to conceptualize online community and using online community to conceptualize theory. *Mind, Culture, and Activity.*

Barton, D., & Hamilton, M. (1998). *Local literacies: Reading and writing in one community.* New York: Routledge.

Barton, D., Hamilton, M., & Ivanic, R. (Eds.). (2000). *Situated literacies: Reading and writing in context.* New York: Routledge.

Baynham, M., & Prinsloo, M. (Eds.). (2001). New directions in literacy research: Policy, practice, and pedagogy. Special Issue: *Language and Education, 15*(2/3).

Bazerman, C. (2000). Singular utterances: Realizing local activities through typified forms in typified circumstances. In A. Trosberg (Ed.), *Analysing the discourses of professional genres* (pp. 25-40). Amsterdam: Benjamins.

Bazerman, C., & Russell, D. (Eds.). (2003). *Writing selves/writing society: Research from activity perspectives. Perspectives on writing.* Fort Collins, CO: The WAC Clearinghouse and Mind, Culture, and Activity.

Beach, R., Lundell, D., & Jung, H. (2002). Developmental college students' negotiation of social practices between peer, family, workplace, and university worlds. In J. Higbee & D. Lundell (Eds.), *Multiculturalism and developmental education*. Minneapolis: University of Minnesota, Center for Research in Developmental Education and Urban Literacy.

Beach, R., & Myers, J. (2001). *Inquiry-based English instruction: Engaging students in literature and life.* New York: Teachers College Press.

Beaufort, A. (1999). *Writing in the real world: Making the transition from school to work.* New York: Teachers College Press.

Berkenkotter, C., & Huckin, T. (1995). *Genre knowledge in disciplinary communication: Cognition/culture/power.* Hillsdale, NJ: Erlbaum.

Blanton, W.E., Greene, M.W., & Cole, M. (1999). Computer mediation for learning and play. *Journal of Adolescent & Adult Literacy, 43*(3), 272-278.

Bourdieu, P. (1984). *Distinction: A social critique of the judgment of taste.* Cambridge, MA: Harvard University Press.

Bourdieu, P. (1991). *Language and symbolic power* (J.B. Thompson, Ed.). Cambridge. MA: Harvard University Press.

Bourdieu, P., Passeron, J.C., & de Saint Martin, M. (1984). *Academic discourse: Linguistic misunderstanding and professorial power.* Stanford, CA: Stanford University Press.

Brandt, D., & Clinton, K. (2002). Limits of the local: Expanding perspectives on literacy as a social practice. *Journal of Literacy Research, 34*(2), 337-356.

Bruce, B. C., & Easley, J. A., Jr. (2000). Emerging communities of practice: Collaboration and communication in action research. *Educational Action Research, 8*(2), 243-259.

Burke, K. (1969). *A rhetoric of motives.* Berkeley: University of California Press.

Cazden, C. (1988). *Classroom discourse: The language of teaching and learning.* Portsmouth, NH: Heinemann.

Chaiklin, S., Hedegaard, M., & Jensen, U.J. (Eds.). (1999). *Activity theory and social practice: Cultural-historical approaches.* Aarhus, Denmark: Aarhus University Press.

Chaiklin, S., & Lave, J. (Eds.). (1996). *Understanding practice: Perspectives on activity and context.* New York: Cambridge University Press.

Christie, F., & Martin, J. R. (1997). *Genres and institutions: Social process in the workplace and school.* London: Cassell.

Cintron, R. (1997). *Angel's town: Chero ways, gang life, and the rhetorics of the everyday.* Boston. MA: Beacon Press.

Cole, M., Engeström, E., & Vasquez, O. (Eds.). (1997). *Mind, culture, and activity: Seminal papers from the laboratory of comparative human cognition*. New York: Cambridge University Press.

Coe, R., Lingard, L., & Teslenko, T. (Eds.). (2002). *The rhetoric and ideology of genre*. Cresskill, NJ: Hampton Press.

Cushman, E. (1998). *The struggle and the tools: Oral and literate strategies in an inner city community*. Albany: State University of New York Press.

Devitt, A. (1991). Intertextuality in tax accounting. In C. Bazerman & J. Paradis (Eds.), *Textual dynamics of the professions* (pp. 336-357). Madison: University of Wisconsin Press.

Dias, P., Freedman, A., Medway, P., & Pare, A. (1999). *Worlds apart: Acting and writing in academic and workplace settings*. Hillsdale, NJ: Erlbaum.

Dias, P., & Pare, A. (Eds.). (2000). *Transitions: Writing in academic and workplace settings*. Cresskill, NJ: Hampton Press.

Dyson, A. (1997). *Writing superheroes: Contemporary childhood, popular culture, and classroom literacy*. New York: Teachers College Press.

Engeström, Y. (2001). *Learning by expanding: An activity theoretical approach to developmental research*. Helsinki: Orienta-Konsultit. (Original work published 1987)

Engeström, Y. (1996). Work as a testbench of activity theory. In S. Chaitlin & J. Lave (Eds.), *Understanding practice: Perspectives on activity and context* (pp. 64-103). New York: Cambridge University Press.

Engeström, Y. (1999). Innovative learning in work teams: Analyzing cycles of knowledge creation in practice. In Y. Engeström, R. Miettinen, & R. Punamaki (Eds.), *Perspectives on activity theory* (pp. 377-404). New York: Cambridge University Press.

Engeström, Y., & Escalante, V. (1996). Mundane tool or object of affection? The rise and fall of the Postal Buddy. In B. Nardi (Ed.), *Context and consciousness: Activity theory and human-computer interaction* (pp. 325-374). Cambridge, MA: MIT Press.

Engeström, Y., & Middleton, D. (Eds.). (1998). *Cognition and communication at work*. New York: Cambridge University Press.

Engeström, Y., Miettinen, R., & Punamaki, R. (Eds.). (1999). *Perspectives on activity theory*. New York: Cambridge University Press.

Fairclough, N. (1992). *Discourse and social change*. Cambridge, UK: Polity Press.

Foot, K. (2002). Pursuing an evolving object: A case study in object formation and identification. *Mind, Culture, and Activity, 9*(2), 122-149.

Freadman, A. (1994). Anyone for tennis? In A. Freedman & P. Medway (Eds.), *Genre and the new rhetoric* (pp. 43-66). London: Taylor & Francis.

Freadman, A. (2002). Uptake. In R. Coe, L. Lingard, & T. Teslenko (Eds.), *The rhetoric and ideology of genre* (pp. 39-53). Cresskill, NJ: Hampton Press.

Freedman, A., & Medway, P. (Eds). (1994a). *Genre and the new rhetoric*. London, UK: Taylor & Francis.

Freedman, A., & Medway, P. (Eds.). (1994b). *Learning and teaching genre*. Portsmouth, NH: Heinemann.

Gee, J. P. (1996). *Social linguistics and literacies: Ideology in discourses*. New York: Falmer.

Gee, J. P. (1999). Critical issues: Reading and the new literacy studies: Reframing the National Academy of Sciences Report on Reading. *Journal of Literacy Research, 31*(3), 355–374

Geisler, C. (2003). When management becomes personal: An activity-theoretic analysis of Palm™ technologies. In C. Bazerman & D. Russell (Eds.), *Writing selves/Writing society: Research from activity perspectives. Perspectives on writing.* Fort Collins, CO: The WAC Clearinghouse and Mind, Culture, and Activity.

Giddens, A. (1984). *The constitution of society: Outline of the theory of structuration.* Berkeley: University of California Press.

Giddens, A. (1993). *The Giddens reader.* Stanford, CA: Stanford University Press.

Giltrow, J. (2000). Argument as a term in talk about student writing. In R. Andrews & S. Mitchell (Eds.), *Learning to argue in higher education* (pp. 129–145). Portsmouth, NH: Heinemann.

Goffman, I. (1974). *Frame analysis.* New York: Harper & Row.

Goffman, I. (1981). *Forms of talk.* Philadelphia: University of Pennsylvania Press.

Green, J., & Dixon, C. (2002). Context in literacy. In B. Guzzetti (Ed.), *Literacy in America: An encyclopedia of history, theory, and practice* (pp. 104-107). Santa Barbara, CA: ABC-CLIO.

Gutierrez, K., Baquedano-Lopez, P., Alverez, H. H., & Chiu, M. M. (1999). Building the culture of collaboration through hybrid language practices. *Theory into Practice, 38*(2), 286-303.

Halliday, M.A.K. (1994). *An introduction to functional grammar.* London, UK: Edward Arnold.

Heath, S. B. (1983). *Ways with words: Language, life and work in communities and classrooms.* New York: Cambridge University Press.

Holland, D., Lachicotte, W., Skinner, D., & Cain, C. (2001). *Identity and agency in cultural worlds.* Cambridge, MA: Harvard University Press.

Hull, G. (2000). Critical literacy at work. *Journal of Adolescent and Adult Literacy, 43*(1), 648-652.

Hull, G., & Schultz, K. (2001). Literacy and learning out of school: A review of theory and research. *Review of Educational Research, 71*(4), 575-611.

Hull, G., & Schultz, K. (Eds.). (2002). *School's out! Bridging out-of-school literacies with classroom practice.* New York: Teachers College Press.

Hunt, R. (1994). Traffic in genres, in classrooms and out. In A. Freedman & P. Medway (Eds.), *Genre and the new rhetoric* (pp. 211-230). Philadelphia: Taylor & Francis.

Hutchins, E. (1995). *Cognition in the wild.* Cambridge, MA: MIT Press.

John-Steiner, V. (1997). *Notebooks of the mind: Explorations of thinking.* New York: Oxford University Press.

Jonassen, D. H. (2000). Revisiting activity theory as a framework for designing student-centered learning environments. In D. H. Jonassen & S. M. Land (Eds.), *Theoretical foundations of learning environments* (pp. 89-122). Mahwah, NJ: Erlbaum.

Ketter, J., & Hunter, J. (2003). Creating a writer's identity on the boundaries of two communities of practice. In C. Bazerman, & D. Russell (Eds.), *Writing selves/writing society: Research from activity perspectives. Perspectives on writing.* Fort Collins, CO: The WAC Clearinghouse and Mind, Culture, and Activity.

Knobel, M. (1999). *Everyday literacies: Students, discourse, and social practice*. New York: Peter Lang.

Latour, B. (1987). *Science in action*. Cambridge, MA: Harvard University Press.

Latour, B., & Woolgar, S. (1979). *Laboratory life: The social construction of scientific facts*. London: Sage.

Lave, J., & Wenger, E. (1991). *Situated learning: Legitimate peripheral participation*. Cambridge, UK: Cambridge University Press.

Leander, K.M. (2001). "This is our freedom bus going home right now": Producing and hybridizing space-time contexts in pedagogical discourse. *Journal of Literacy Research, 33*(4), 637-680.

Lee, C. D. (1993). *Signifying as a scaffold for literary interpretation: The pedagogical implications of an African American discourse genre*. Urbana, IL: National Council of Teachers of English.

Lee, C. D., & Smagorinsky, P. (Eds.). (2000). *Vygotskian perspectives on literacy research: Constructing meaning through collabative inquiry*. New York: Cambridge University Press.

Leont'ev, A. N. (1978). *Activity, consciousness, and personality*. Englewood Cliffs, NJ: Prentice-Hall.

Leont'ev, A. N. (1981). *Problems of the development of the mind*. Moscow: Progress.

McKillop, A. M., & Myers, J. (1999). The pedagogical and electronic contexts of composing in hypermedia. In S. DeWitt & K. Strasma (Eds.), *Contexts, inter-texts, and hypertexts* (pp. 65-116). Cresskill, NJ: Hampton Press.

Miller, C. R. (1984). Genre as social action. *Quarterly Journal of Speech, 70*, 151-167.

Moll, L. (Ed.). (1990). *Vygotsky and education: Instructional implications and applications of sociohistorical psychology*. New York: Cambridge University Press.

Myers, G. (1990). *Writing biology: Texts in the social construction of scientific knowledge*. Madison: University of Wisconsin Press.

Myers, J., & Beach, R. (2001). Hypermedia authoring as critical literacy. *Journal of Adolescent & Adult Literacy, 44*(6), 538-546.

Nardi, B. (Ed.). (1996). *Context and consciousness: Activity theory and human-computer interaction*. Cambridge, MA: MIT Press.

Phelan, P., Davidson, A., & Yu, H. (1998). *Adolescents' worlds: Negotiating family, peers, and schools*. New York: Teachers College Press.

Prior, P. (1998). *Writing/disciplinarity: A sociohistorical account of literate activity in the academy*. Mahwah, NJ: Erlbaum.

Prior, P., & Shipka, J. (2003). Chronotopic lamination: Tracing the contours of literate activity. In C. Bazerman & D. Russell (Eds.), *Writing selves/writing society: Research from activity perspectives. Perspectives on writing*. Fort Collins, CO: The WAC Clearinghouse and Mind, Culture, and Activity.

Rex, L., Green, J., & Dixon, C. (1998). What counts when context counts: The uncommon "common" language of literacy research. *Journal of Literacy Research, 30*(3), 405-433.

Rogers, R. (2002). Between contexts: A critical discourse analysis of family literacy, discursive practices, and literate subjectivities. *Reading Research Quarterly, 37*(3), 248-277.

Rogers, R. (2003). *A critical discourse analysis of family literacy practices: Power in and out of print.* Mahwah, NJ: Erlbaum.

Rogoff, B. (1990). *Apprenticeship in thinking: Cognitive development in social context.* New York: Oxford University Press.

Rogoff, B. (1995). Observing sociocultural activity and three planes: Participatory appropriation, guided participation, and apprenticeship. In J. Wertsch, P. del Rio, & A. Alvarez (Eds.), *Sociocultural studies of mind* (pp. 139-164). New York: Cambridge University Press.

Roth, W., & Tobin, K. (2002). Redesigning as "urban" teacher education program: An activity theory perspective. *Mind, Culture, and Activity, 9*(2), 108-131.

Russell, D. (1997). Rethinking genre in school and society: An activity theory analysis. *Written Communication, 14*(4), 504-554.

Russell, D. (2002). The kind-ness of genre: An activity theory analysis of high school teachers' perception of genre in portfolio assessment across the curriculum. In R. Coe, L. Lingard, & T. Teslenko (Eds.), *The rhetoric and ideology of genre* (pp. 225-242). Cresskill, NJ: Hampton Press.

Russell, D., & Bazerman, C. (Eds.). (1997). The activity of writing, the writing of activity. Special issue: *Mind Culture and Activity, 4*(4).

Saxe, G. B. (1991). *Culture and cognitive development: Studies in mathematical understanding.* Hillsdale, NJ: Erlbaum.

Schryer, C. (2002). Walking a fine line: Writing "negative news" letters in an insurance company. *Journal of Business and Technical Communication, 14*(4), 445-497.

Schutz, A., & Luckmann. T. (1973). *The structures of the life-world.* Evanston, IL: Northwestern University Press.

Scribner, S., & Cole, M. (1981). *The psychology of literacy.* Cambridge, MA: Harvard University Press.

Smagorinsky, P. (1995). Constructing meaning in the disciplines: Reconceptualizing writing across the curriculum as composing across the curriculum. *American Journal of Education, 103*, 160-184.

Smagorinsky, P. (2002). Activity theory. In B. Guzzetti (Ed.), *Literacy in America: An encyclopedia of history, theory, and practice* (pp. 10 –13). Santa Barbara, CA: ABC-CLIO.

Street, B. (2000). Literacy events and literacy practices. In M. Martin-Jones & K. Jones (Eds.), *Multilingual comparative perspectives on research and practice* (pp. 17-29). New York: John Benjamin's.

Street, B. (2003). *Academic literacies across educational contexts.* Philadelphia: Caslon.

Swales, J. (1990). *Genre analysis: English in academic and research settings.* Cambridge, UK: Cambridge University Press.

Swales, J. (1998). *Other floors, other voices: A textography of a small university building.* Mahwah, NJ: Erlbaum.

Vadeboncoeur, J., & Portes, P. (2002). Students "at risk": Exploring identity from a sociocultural perspective. In D. M. McInerney & S. Van Etten (Eds.), *Research in sociocultural influences on motivation and learning* (Vol. 2, pp. 89-127). Greenwich, CT: Information Age Publishing.

Valdes, G. (1996). *Con respeto: Bridging the distances between culturally diverse families and schools.* New York: Teachers College Press.

Vygotsky, L. (1978). *Mind in society: The development of higher psychological processes* (M. Cole, V. John-Steiner, S. Scribner, & E. Souberman, eds.). Cambridge, MA: Harvard University Press.

Vygotsky, L. S. (1986). *Thought and language* (A. Kozulin, ed.). Cambridge, MA: Harvard University Press.

Vygotsky, L. S. (1987). *The collected works of L. S. Vygotsky: Vol. 1. Problems of general psychology.* New York: Plenum.

Vygotsky, L.S. (1997). *The collected works of L. S. Vygotsky: Vol. 3. Problems of the theory and history of psychology.* New York: Plenum.

Vygotsky, L.S. (1998). *Child psychology. The collected works of L. S. Vygotsky: Vol. 5. Problems of the theory and history of psychology.* New York: Plenum.

Wells, G. (1999). *Dialogic inquiry: Towards a sociocultural practice and theory of education.* New York: Cambridge University Press.

Wenger, E. (1988). *Communities of practice: Learning, meaning, and identity.* New York: Cambridge University Press.

Wertsch, J. V. (1981). *The concept of activity in Soviet psychology.* Armonk, NY: M. E. Sharpe.

Wertsch, J. V. (1985). *Vygotsky and the social formation of mind.* Cambridge, MA: Harvard University Press.

Wertsch, J. (1991). *Voices of the mind: A sociocultural approach to mediated action.* Cambridge, MA: Harvard University Press.

Wertsch, J. (1998). *Mind as action.* New York: Oxford University Press.

Wertsch, J., del Rio, P., & Alvarez, A. (1995). *Sociocultural studies of mind.* New York: Cambridge University Press.

Winsor, D. (1999). Genre and activity systems: The role of documentation in maintaining and changing engineering activity systems. *Written Communication, 16,* 200-224.

Witte, S. (1992). Context, text, intertext: Toward a constructivist semiotic of writing. *Written Communication, 9,* 237-308.

Yates, J., & Orlikowski, W. (2002). Genre systems: Chronos and kairos in communicative interaction. In R. Coe, L. Lingard, & T. Teslenko (Eds.), *The rhetoric and ideology of genre* (pp. 103-122). Cresskill, NJ: Hampton Press.

5

Vygotsky's Contribution to Literacy Research

Holbrook Mahn
University of New Mexico

Vera John-Steiner
University of New Mexico

Sociocultural researchers have made significant contributions to the study of literacy research relying on different aspects of Lev Vygotsky's work, including his writings on the cultural influence of social interaction in the development of the mind; on concept formation and its relationship to the zone of proximal development (ZDP); and on the interrelationship of language and thinking as exemplified in his studies on inner speech and verbal thinking (Clay, 1991; Emig, 1971; Gee, 1991, 1997, 2001; John-Steiner, Panofsky, & Smith, 1994; Lee & Smagorinsky, 2000; Moll, 1992; Scribner & Cole, 1981; Wells, 1999; Zebroski, 1994, etc.). These contributions have helped "study how readers and writers learn to adopt different stances or ways of knowing as constituted by social and cultural forces" (Beach, Green, Kamil, & Shanahan, 1992, p. 3)—a goal of the first edition of this volume. Sociocultural literacy research has helped capture the complexity of situated literacy activities (Gee, 1997; Harste, Woodward, & Burke, 1984) using Vygotsky's methodological approach to conceptualize literacy more broadly.

Most of Vygotsky's writing on literacy is embedded in his studies examining the origins and development of higher mental functions and their part in the development of consciousness (1987, 1997). In these studies, Vygotsky, in his analysis of the acquisition of language and written symbol systems, focused on the nature of *meaning* and the interrelationship between individuals and their sociocultural worlds. We examine the ways that Vygotsky's analysis of the relationship between language and thought, and, in particular, his examination of the nature of inner speech and verbal thinking, contribute to literacy research. We start with a brief overview of his methodological approach, through which he examined the origins of the phenomenon being studied and analyzed its development as a dynamic, changing process. He used this approach to explore the development of language and literacy for both the species and the individual.

After describing how Vygotsky's methodological approach helps inform literacy research, we examine interpretations and critiques of his work on writing. We conclude by showing the ways in which Vygotsky's work has influenced our studies of inner speech and verbal thinking in the writing processes of native speakers of English and second-language learners.

THEORETICAL PERSPECTIVES

The multidisciplinary perspectives on literacy research reflected in this volume represent an effort to construct an integrated, coherent theory. The complexity of doing so is evident when literacy is situated in sociocultural contexts and not just viewed as individual cognitive processing. It is further complicated when multiple literacies (New London Group, 1996) and discourses (Gee, 1991) are recognized and when new brain research on how people learn (National Research Council, 1999) is considered. This complexity demands a methodological approach that accomplishes the following:

- Situates literacy in concrete social, cultural, historical, and political, contexts/environments.
- Examines literacy as developmental, looking at its origins and the processes through which it has grown.
- Looks at the role of *meaning* in literacy activities.
- Looks at the relationships of language, thought, and literacy.
- Examines culture's profound role in the acquisition and use of literacy.
- Accounts for affective/emotional factors.
- Accounts for the development of higher mental processes in literacy activities.

The approach to the study of the mind that Vygotsky developed in the late 1920s and early 1930s in the Soviet Union provides a solid foundation for studying literacy's complexity. Vygotsky's analysis of the social sources and social situations of development and his dialectical methodological approach have been used to develop an interactionist approach to literacy (John-Steiner et al., 1994), which rests on the following four assumptions:

1. Language needs to be viewed in relation to its functions in social and family life.
2. Literacy and language acquisition are developmental processes that involve a dynamic interaction between the individual and the social.
3. Literacy activities need to be examined in their sociocultural context.
4. The investigation and analysis of literacy needs to focus on the processes of learning and development and not just the products.

We built on these assumptions and Vygotsky's analysis of inner speech and verbal thinking in our literacy research. By applying Vygotsky's analysis to situated literacy, we hope to contribute to the development of pedagogical approaches to teaching literacy that meet the needs of all students, including linguistically and culturally diverse students and those who struggle for whatever reason.

VYGOTSKY'S METHODOLOGICAL APPROACH

Vygotsky examined phenomena as dynamic, contextual, complex entities in a constant state of change and, in so doing, surmounted the dichotomies that have ruled Western thought since Descartes' time. Rather than isolating the mind from matter, Vygotsky approached the study of the mind by looking at its origins and development, by exploring interconnections with the physical world and social systems, and by examining the important role played by emotions in its development. He used this dialectical approach in developing his method.

> The search for method becomes one of the most important problems of the entire enterprise of understanding the uniquely human forms of psychological activity. In this case, the method is simultaneously prerequisite and product, the tool and the result of the study. (Vygotsky, 1978, p. 65)

In contrast to theories that depended on behaviorism or idealism, Vygotsky examined the ways that the increasingly complex *cultural* contexts into which children are born shape innate reflexes. He emphasized the

internalization of social activity and, in particular, the acquisition and internalization of language, which laid the foundation for a qualitative transformation into consciousness. Vygotsky (1997) described the "processes of
mastering external materials of cultural development and thinking: language, writing, arithmetic, drawing" (p. 14). Near the end of his life,
Vygotsky clarified the role he ascribed to *meaning* as the key to understanding these processes (Prawat, 2000; Wertsch, 2000; Yaroshevsky &
Gurgenidze, 1997). He recognized that he had not focused sufficiently on
meaning in the development of symbols and instead focused on the structure and mediational functions of language and other symbol systems. He
felt that his earlier works had focused too narrowly on the connections
between the sign and meaning and had not sufficiently examined how they
were distinct. Vygotsky died before he could fully explore the distinctions,
but his notes revealed the logic of his argument.

> Meaning is not the sum of all the psychological operations which stand
> behind the word. Meaning is something more specific—it is the internal
> structure of the sign operation. It is what is lying between the thought
> and the word. Meaning is not equal to the word, not equal to the
> thought. This disparity is revealed by the fact that their lines of devel-
> opment do not coincide. (Vygotsky, 1997, p. 133)

In this quote, Vygotsky foreshadowed many contemporary efforts that
study the developmental processes in meaning making—social interaction,
negotiation, dialogue, and socialized attention (Zukow-Goldring & Ferko,
1994). Vygotsky viewed meaning both as a structure and a process and felt
that it was necessary to look at the different phases of its construction to
discover the development of its inner structure. Because Vygotsky's analysis of *meaning* provides the foundation for our literacy research, we briefly
give an overview of its theoretical underpinnings.

To reveal the inner dynamics of meaning, Vygotsky (1987) examined
the unity of thought and language and its relationship to conceptual
thinking.

> The complex structure of this unity, the complex fluid connections and
> transitions among the separate planes of verbal thinking, arise only in
> process of development. The isolation of meaning from sound, the iso-
> lation of word from thing, and the isolation of thought from word are
> all necessary stages in the history of the development of concepts. (p.
> 284)

In this process of isolation or abstraction, "[t]he child learns to hear himself 'from outside' and to evaluate his speech from the viewpoint of others. He develops a removed, objectively social attitude to his speech activity; his consciousness develops" (Gal'perin, 1967, p. 29).

Through this process children bring their meanings into line with meanings in the adult world. Meaningful communication develops through the give and take and negotiation during which caretakers ascribe communicative intent to infant's verbalizations and gestures. The communication of meaning becomes the driving force for language and literacy acquisition; meaning develops through dialogue and social interaction. The subsequent internalization of meaning develops into and through inner speech and verbal thinking, which are central concepts for Vygotsky's analysis of literacy and writing, in particular. The unification of speaking and thinking in verbal thinking stimulates the growth of language, literacy, and creativity. This unity is essential to the development of consciousness and the higher mental processes that humans use to make meaning of their sociocultural worlds. This was a focal point of Vygotsky's studies and provides the foundation for our research.

Vygotsky's starting point for his study of the unity of thinking and speaking was an examination of newborns' perceptions of and interaction with the worlds into which they are born. He analyzed the social and cultural influences on the child's acquisition of language and literacy and studied the ways in which meaning is given to infant's sounds and gestures and promote dialogic communication. As the child's use of language begins to conform to commonly accepted and culturally appropriate usage, a qualitative change takes place through the internalization of speech and its unification with rapidly developing mental processes, leading to the development of verbal thinking and consciousness. Vygotsky's investigation focused on the role of meaning in this process and he used the development of written language to clarify it. This examination of the role of verbal thinking and inner speech in the development of written language provides a foundation for our literacy research.

ORAL AND WRITTEN SPEECH

To clarify this foundation, we examine Vygotsky's views on the relationship between oral and written language by looking at the seeming contradiction that Cazden (1996) and others find in two statements of his: "Research indicates that the development of written speech does not reproduce that of oral speech" (Vygotsky, 1987, p. 2) and "In the same way as children learn to speak, they should be able to learn to read and write"

(Vygotsky, 1978, p. 118). In this clarification, we hope to show that an incomplete understanding of Vygotsky's methodological approach can lead to contradictory interpretations. In order to explain the differences between written speech and oral speech, Vygotsky (1987) looked at the genesis, structure, and functions of both.

Vygotsky found the origins of writing in the child's gesture, play, scribbling, and drawing; for the species, Vygotsky found it in the auxiliary devices used to assist memory.

> [I]f humanity is thought to have begun with the use of fire, then the appearance of the written word must be considered to be the boundary separating lower from higher forms of human existence. Tying a knot for remembering also was one of the very first forms of the written word. This form played an enormous role in the history of culture, in the history of the development of writing. (Vygotsky, 1997, p. 50)

The prehistory of written language begins with the gesture, which, Vygotsky (1978) writes, "is the initial visual sign that contains the child's future writing as an acorn contains a future oak. Gestures, it has been correctly said, are writing in air, and written signs frequently are simply gestures that have been fixed" (p. 107). In the child's development, two other domains link gestures to the origins of written language—the first is scribbling and the dramatizations that often accompany it; the second is symbolic play, in which a child assigns meaning to an object through gesture. Vygotsky (1978) argues that the second-order symbolism used in make-believe play is "a major contributor to the development of written language—a system of second-order symbolism [initially]" (p. 110). Writing development continues as the child uses symbols in drawing. When the child begins to "draw speech," writing begins to develop as a first-order symbol system for the child. "The entire secret of teaching written language is to prepare and organize this natural transition appropriately. As soon as it is achieved, the child has mastered the principle of written language and then it remains only to perfect this method" (Vygotsky, 1978, p. 116).

Vygotsky compared the abstraction necessary for writing with language acquisition as children abstract from the concrete to the general. A word "dog" represents a particular dog and the attributes of that dog are generalized to all similar creatures that have four legs, fur, a tail, and so on. Through social interaction, the child begins to abstract from the concrete dog and to develop a concept of a dog so that the word "dog" applies to the species. In writing there is yet another level of abstraction—a child must abstract "from the sensual aspect of speech itself. He must move to abstracted speech, to speech that uses representations of words rather than the words themselves" (Vygotsky, 1987, p. 202). In writing Vygotsky additionally described the abstraction from the interlocutor who is present in conversational speech.

Vygotsky (1987) also looked at the different roles *motive* and *conscious awareness* play in the acquisition processes of written and oral speech. When children are writing, they are removed from the situations in which conversational speech occurs, and, therefore, must "act with more volition with written speech than with oral speech. . . . With written speech [they] must become consciously aware of the word's structure. [They] must partition it and voluntarily recreate it in written signs" (p. 203).

Vygotsky examined the structure and function of written speech in relationship to inner speech, and found that "Written speech is an entirely unique speech function. Its structure and mode of functioning are as different from those of oral speech as those of inner speech are from external speech" (p. 202). Vygotsky's analysis of the internalization of speech revealed the central role of social interaction in the process (Wertsch & Stone, 1985). Adults in verbal interaction with children help them regulate activity; for example, in doing a puzzle with children, adults will say, "The green one goes there, etc." Children appropriate that language to help solve the puzzle and use it even when no one else is around. Over time, children recognize that they do not need to articulate this regulatory speech and say it subvocally and, finally, internalize it as inner speech. In this meaning-making process, the previously distinct paths of development of language and thought become inextricably intertwined. For Vygotsky (1987), *meaning* results from and through the development of thinking and speech, yet it is distinct from both. His search for the ways in which meaning was connected to, yet distinct, from thought and language centered on inner speech and verbal thinking and the notion that "inner speech is an internal plane of verbal thinking which mediates the dynamic relationship between thought and word" (p. 279).

INNER SPEECH

Vygotsky (1987) pointed out that although external speech precedes the development of inner speech, written speech presupposes the existence of inner speech. The conscious awareness that a child must have to produce written speech has inner speech as its foundation. Vygotsky differentiated between written speech and inner speech on a number of levels, including the grammatical and syntactical. "Inner speech is maximally contracted, abbreviated, and telegraphic. Written speech is maximally expanded and formal, even more so than oral speech" (p. 204). The existence of a prior system—oral language—is an essential difference between the development of oral and written speech. He used the same distinction when examining the relationship between learning one's first and second language. A prior system already exists for the second language learner, that of the first language, which will shape the acquisition of the second.

Vygotsky cautioned, however, that the examination of the profound differences between written and oral speech and the acquisition processes of first and second languages should not obscure the fact that they are all aspects of a unified process of language development.

> All three of these processes, the learning of the native language, the learning of foreign languages, and the development of written speech interact with each other in complex ways. This reflects their mutual membership in a single class of genetic processes and the internal unity of these processes. (Vygotsky, 1987, p. 179)

Meaning-making is the unifying aspect of these processes and provides the rationale for Vygotsky's (1978) statement, "In the same way as children learn to speak, they should be able to learn to read and write" (p. 118). Vygotsky used dialectics to analyze the unification of distinct and often contradictory processes such as speaking and writing. In contrast to formal logic, which isolates speaking and writing from their contexts and examines them in isolation, dialectical logic captures the *process* behind their development, including the unification of the distinct processes of speaking and writing. Vygotsky analyzed this unification by tracing its development in relation to conceptual thinking.

CONCEPT FORMATION

Understanding Vygotsky's (1987) view of concept formation is key to unraveling his seemingly contradictory statements about the relationship between speaking and writing. Vygotsky described the formation of "spontaneous" or "everyday" concepts as children begin to acquire language through social interaction and make meaning of the worlds around them. He contrasted these concepts to "scientific" concepts or concepts within systems, to which the child is introduced on entering school.

> Only within a system can the concept acquire conscious awareness and a voluntary nature. Conscious awareness and the presence of a system are synonyms when we are speaking of [scientific] concepts, just as spontaneity, lack of conscious awareness, and the absence of a system are three different words for designating the nature of the child's [everyday] concept. (Vygotsky, 1987, pp. 191-192)

Vygotsky noted that before scientific concepts could emerge, there needed to be the "development of voluntary attention, logical memory, abstraction, comparison, and differentiation" (1987, p. 170). When scientific concepts do emerge, there is a "complete restructuring of the child's spontaneous concepts" (p. 236) with scientific concepts providing "the gate through which conscious awareness enters the domain of the child's concepts" (p. 193). He added, "the basic characteristic of [scientific concepts'] development is that they have their source in school instruction" (p. 214).

Vygotsky (1987) described the interfunctional reorganization in concept formation as a process in which scientific concepts grow downward from the domain of conscious awareness and volition "into the domain of the concrete, into the domain of personal experience" (p. 220), while everyday concepts, which begin in the concrete and empirical, "move toward the higher characteristics of concepts, toward conscious awareness and volition. The link between these two lines of development reflects their true natures. This is the link of the zone of proximal development and actual development" (p. 220). Vygotsky emphasized that everyday concepts and scientific concepts are connected by extremely complex relationships, and that "the links between the two processes and the tremendous influence they have on one another are possible because their development takes such different paths" (p. 220). Similar to his view of the relationship between oral and written speech, Vygotsky saw scientific and everyday concepts as "neither two entirely independent processes nor a single process. . . . [T]hey are two processes with complex relationships" (p. 201).

CONCEPTS AND FIRST- AND SECOND-LANGUAGE ACQUISITION

To further explain his theory of concept formation, Vygotsky compared the differences between scientific and everyday concepts and those between acquiring one's native language and a second language. Children learn their native languages and develop their everyday concepts without conscious awareness. In learning a second language in school, traditional approaches begin "with the alphabet, with reading and writing, with the conscious and intentional construction of phrases, with the definition of words or with the study of grammar" (Vygotsky, 1987, p. 221). He added that in this approach the child has to first master the complex characteristics of speech as opposed to the spontaneous free use of speech.

Just as is the case with written and oral speech, so too do first- and second-language acquisition processes "represent the development of two aspects of a single process, the development of two aspects of the process of verbal thinking. In foreign language learning, the external, sound and phrasal aspects of verbal thinking are the most prominent. In the development of scientific concepts, the semantic aspects of this process come to the fore" (pp. 222-223). Vygotsky added that in learning a second language, the word meanings that a student is acquiring are mediated by the meanings in the native language. Similarly, prior existing everyday concepts mediate relationships between scientific concepts and objects (Vygotsky, 1987). The role of concept formation in oral language acquisition and in the development of writing is central to understanding Vygotsky's influence on literacy research. Vygotsky's analysis of the ways in which inner speech and verbal thinking helps develop conceptual thinking, including literacy acquisition, provides a framework for our studies described here. Before doing so we clarify our understanding of this analysis by examining the contradictions raised in "Selective Traditions: Readings of Vygotsky in Writing Pedagogy" (Cazden, 1996) and the reasons for different interpretations and applications of Vygotsky's theory on writing.

INTERPRETATIONS AND APPLICATIONS OF VYGOTSKY'S WRITINGS

Cazden (1996) looked at the ways in which Vygotsky's work has been variously interpreted in literacy research and highlighted three aspects of his theoretical framework that have influenced writing education—inner speech, ZPD, and the relationships between development and instruction in concept formation. She identified theorists influenced by Vygotsky's work grouped around "three clusters of interpretations of Vygotsky's ideas: one centering on inner speech and implicit knowledge, the second on more explicit scaffolded assistance, and the third on cultural and political aspects of writing tasks" (p. 171). (Unless noted otherwise, page references in this section refer to Cazden, 1996.)

James Britton (1987) is offered pride of place in representing those who rely on Vygotsky's theory of inner speech to inform their teaching practice. Britton argued that as speech is internalized, it overcomes "the constraints of conventional public word meanings" and the child "begins to be capable of carrying out mental operations more subtle than anything he or she can put into words" (Cazden, 1996, p. 171). From this Britton argued against explicit teaching and advocated that "if the source of inner speech is the shared social activity of the child, then the classrooms must be language-rich communities" (p. 171). Cazden found another example of this first reading of Vygotsky in the work of Yetta Goodman and Kenneth Goodman (1979, 1990), who argued for a holistic approach to reading that focuses more on meaning-making than on discrete, isolated skill building.

James Moffett (1981) relied on a concept of inner speech developed from studying stream of consciousness writers such as Joyce, Woolf, Faulkner, and Eliot, but unlike Britton and the Goodmans, he offered a "more fully articulated instructional program" (p. 173), a characteristic of the second group identified by Cazden (1996). These writing educators focused more on Vygotsky's discussions of school learning and depended on "Bruner's construct of instructional scaffolds" (p. 174). Cazden referenced Langer and Applebee (1987), who wrote in *How Writing Shapes Thinking* that they drew on the work of both Vygotsky and Bruner "[who] see language learning as growing out of a communicative relationship where the adult helps the child understand as well as complete new tasks" (pp. 174-175).

Gunther Kress's (1993) use of the Australian-developed genre method of teaching writing, which advocates the explicit teaching of the genre rules or conventions, places him in the second group identified by Cazden. His argument that pedagogical approaches need to take into consideration issues of culture, conflict, and power places him in the third group. Deborah Hicks (1998) argued that the genre method of teaching does not adequately answer such questions as "How do children construct a voice in writing? How do teachers and other literacy educators provide scaffolding that will help young writers 'find' a voice, without denying the children the right to bring the 'ways with words' (Heath, 1983) of their communities to their classroom development as writers" (p. 28). Hicks focused on the students' responses to text not on their ability "to frame their texts in one fashion or another" (p. 33).

Tony Burgess (1993), reflecting the third group identified by Cazden, argued that the focus on conflict and power should be broader than that offered by representatives of the first group when they write of cultural and social influences on the child: "[T]his third reading adds . . . not simply the dimension of variation in language use and social power in societies heterogeneous in gender, culture, and class, but also how these dimensions of variation affect the individual thinker, learner, and writer" (Cazden, 1996, p. 179). Vygotsky has been criticized for not explicitly addressing the issue of power in his writing. This critique ignores the fact that Vygotsky based his theory on a well-developed and coherent social theory—historical materialism.

> We can anticipate that the basic features of the historical development of behavior in this domain will be directly dependent on the general laws that govern the historical development of human society. . . . In methodological terms [the central points in psychology] are extremely

difficult, but they are central to any analysis of human behavior. We
have attempted to address them on the foundations provided by dialectical and historical materialism. (Vygotsky, 1987, p. 120)

Vygotsky assumed a basic understanding of the central tenets of historical
materialism among his readers and also assumed a familiarity with the
dialectical method which underlay it.

Historical materialism examines which class has power and controls
social organization including the use of written language—historically used
to oppress the nonruling classes. Although literacy empowers individuals, it
is a mistake to conflate the power gained by individuals through literacy
with the power wielded by a state that has functioned historically to deny
those individuals access to literacy and social power. If literacy is viewed in
its sociocultural interconnections, it is clear that neither literacy nor pedagogical approaches are ideologically neutral. Historical materialism provided the foundation for Vygotsky's theories of language, thinking, and cultural development that started with the perspective that "the cultural development of behavior is closely linked to the historical or social development
of humanity" (Vygotsky, 1998, p. 168). The relationship of this development to natural processes is at the center of the different interpretations of
Vygotsky's work on literacy and their concomitant differing pedagogical
approaches.

LITERACY AS A NATURAL, SOCIAL PROCESS

A widely accepted interpretation of the relationship between speech and
writing is that because speech is primary, both ontogenetically and phylo-
genetically, and is an attribute of the human species, that it is natural,
whereas literacy, because it is secondary and does not exist species wide, is
not natural. This position is used to justify direct instruction of phonemic
awareness in the teaching of reading and of more traditional approaches to
teaching writing that focus on form and correctness. It is also used as the
theoretical underpinning for a view that meaning resides solely in the
autonomous text (Olson, 1977).

Vygotsky's analysis of the relationship between the elementary mental
functions and the higher mental functions helps clarify his position on natural and cultural influences on human development. He saw cultural influence as starting with the adult world's first soothing words after the trauma
of birth. Vygotsky (1997) looked at the "natural history of emergence of
signs from which speech was derived" (p. 133), and compared this with the
"history of the development of writing [which] begins with the appearance
of the first visual signs in the child" (p. 133). In both cases, the core is

meaning-making, and it is in this sense that Vygotsky wrote that children learn to read and write in the same way that they learn to speak.

The Vygotskian framework has focused our literacy research in a variety of different domains—second language writing, the development of semantic systems for bilinguals, the creative process, the generative nature of inner speech and verbal thinking for writers, and the role of dialogue and social interaction. In the next section, we report aspects of our literacy research that used Vygotsky's theoretical framework as a guide, drawing on his analysis of the role played by inner speech and verbal thinking in the meaning-making process in general, and on writing, in particular.

VYGOTSKY'S THEORETICAL INFLUENCE

The influence of Vygotsky's work on both of us has been profound—his theoretical framework has shaped our careers and research. In what follows we do not attempt to describe the breadth of his influence but rather focus on meaning, verbal thinking, and inner speech from a number of different perspectives. The concept of inner speech guided John-Steiner's work on the relationship between communicative intent and its realization for both beginning and proficient speakers (John-Steiner & Tatter, 1983) and novice and expert writers (Elasser & John-Steiner, 1977) of the native languages. John-Steiner's (1985) research on bilinguals explored the ways in which Vygotsky's key concepts of verbal thinking and inner speech helped explain speech production of bilingual speakers. In her study of inner speech writing in the diaries of Virginia Woolf, Henry Miller, Dostoevsky, and others, John-Steiner (1997) looked at the ways experienced and accomplished writers used *inner speech writing* to represent the meaning they were creating. These two studies provide the foundation for Mahn's (1997) research on the ways that second language learners reflect on their own use of inner speech and verbal thinking in learning to write in English.

BILINGUALS MAKING MEANING

In research on bilinguals, John-Steiner (1985) looked at the interfunctional connections between the semantic aspect of language and its production in bilingual speakers and writers.

> We see a dual process at work in the development competencies of the bilingual, namely the separation of two or more languages at the production level, with a concomitant process of unification at the level of verbal meaning and thought. (p. 365)

Although the different aspects of the meaning potential (Halliday, 1975) are initially realized in the first language, there is a process of unification at the level of verbal thinking and meaning-making and at the same time an increasing separation between the first and second languages to minimize interference errors in production. John-Steiner (1985) presented these ideas at the first international conference on the work of Vygotsky held in 1980 in Chicago, where there were a number of interpreters. Because the audience members were experiencing the unification of two languages in their translation at the level of meaning and had to separate them in their interpretive renditions, they readily appreciated John-Steiner's concept of unification and separation. This concept was further illuminated by an interpreter who demonstrated to John-Steiner a form of inner speech writing used by sequential interpreters who had developed their own symbol system to represent key concepts. Using these symbols helped prevent the realization of the concept in either the source language or the target language from becoming so dominant that it overshadowed an appropriate expression in the other language.

In *Notebooks of the Mind*, John-Steiner (1997) explored the use of inner speech writing by both novice and accomplished writers to help shape their future works. She found that the "inner language of thought differs from language used for communicative exchanges in its rapidity, in its condensed form, and its functions. . . . Verbal thinking is often condensed and metaphorical, akin, in some ways to poetry" (p. 139). She gave examples of inner speech writing from the notebooks and diaries of Virginia Woolf, Dostoevsky, and Henry Miller in which one encounters many passages of condensed planning of their major works—from plans for an entire chapter as in Woolf's notes on her biography of Roger Fry, to Dostoevsky or James using their notebooks to explore the development of characters, to Henry Miller's description of planning "the book of his life." "In emphasizing these telegrams of thought—the condensed idioms of inner speech—I have attempted to illustrate the broader issues confronting all artists and thinkers; namely, the way in which one transforms thought into communicable form" (John-Steiner, 1997, p. 128). These examples of inner speech writing illustrate the rapidity with which inner speech planning of major works takes place before the writer has the opportunity to develop and craft full-scale passages. They also provide confirmation of Vygotsky's notion that inner speech involves a planning role for language production, oral or written.

> An example of written thought was offered by Stephen Spender in his essay on "The Making of a Poem." In the essay, Spender quotes from one of his notebooks the line "A language of flesh and roses." He has multiple associations and memories attached to this highly condensed thought; they deal with a man-made world, and a language of sorts, which has gotten out of our control. (John-Steiner, 1997, p. 139)

For John-Steiner a central challenge in the work on creativity has been the tension between the intent and the realization. It is frequently difficult to get hold of the intent because we only see the different drafts of the increasingly finished work. What is interesting about inner speech writing is that it gets to the very beginning of the process, where the writer is first exploring the possibilities. In its abbreviated form, it also resembles inner speech dialogue—verbal communication during which there is maximal understanding between individuals.

THE GENERATIVE POWER OF INNER SPEECH

Rivers (1987) related Vygotsky's discussion of inner speech and language production to the notion of writing as discovery. "As the writer expands his inner speech, he becomes conscious of things of which he was not previously aware. In this way he can write more than he realizes" (p. 104). Zebroski (1994) quotes Luria (1969) on the reciprocal nature of writing and inner speech. "The functional and structural features of written speech have still another important feature; they "inevitably lead to a significant development of *inner speech*. Because it delays the direct appearance of speech connections, inhibits them, and increases requirements for the preliminary, internal preparation for the speech act, written speech produces a rich development of inner speech." (p. 166)

Mahn (1997) looked at the reciprocal nature of writing and inner speech through the eyes of second-language writers who reflected on the use of dialogue journals in learning to write in English. His study explored the interconnections of sociocultural theory and writing process pedagogy and examined the role of inner speech and verbal thinking in students' making meaning through writing. The goals of Mahn's study were to develop an approach to study the complexity of the writing processes of second language learners who are acquiring English literacy, and to present a means of representation that maintained the authenticity of the meaning-making process in situated literacy activities. We briefly describe his representation of data to provide a framework for the presentation of his students' perspectives on inner speech and verbal thinking in their writing processes.

THE REPRESENTATION OF DATA

Elliot Eisner (1997) presented a perspective on research that captures the motivation behind Mahn's study. Discussing the importance of researchers "engendering a sense of empathy for the lives of the people they wish us to know" (p. 8), Eisner argued that empathy may be an important aspect of understanding others and the situations they face. "Forms of representation that contribute to empathic participation in the lives of others are necessary for having one kind of access to their lives" (p. 8). In examining alternative ways to represent what we find, observe, absorb, and experience in our research, he described what constitutes research for him: "I will count as research reflective efforts to study the world and to create ways to share what we have learned about it" (p. 8). Eisner situated the issue of alternative forms of data representation "on the cutting edge of inquiry in research methodology" (p. 4) and underlined its importance "for illuminating the educational worlds we wish to understand" (p. 4). Kirsch (1997) argues that the thrust of alternative attempts to represent data has been to

> reflect the interactive, dialogic nature of writing and research processes, because they honor and preserve the voices of others. . . . [They] expose the multiple subject positions writers and readers often occupy, collapse boundaries between different genres of writing, and challenge traditional forms of academic discourse (such as single-voiced, seamless research reports). . . . [M]ulti-vocal texts disrupt the smooth, linear progression of argumentative and narrative forms of writing, thereby asking readers to confront multiple, at times conflicting, realities. (p. 193)

The second-language learners in Mahn's study who helped construct the multivocal text represented a wide cross-section of students from around the world; therefore, he tried to take into consideration the cultural aspects of their situated literacy activities. Zamel (1997) questioned the cultural insularity academia historically has adopted, which distorts the understanding and appreciation of other cultures.

> The ways in which we theorize and write about cultures may very well reflect as well as reproduce what Canagarajah (1996) sees as the tradition of academic work—with its "pretense of objectivity," its semblance of "accurate representation," and its tendency to codify and systematize what in reality are complex, contradictory phenomenon. (pp. 323-324)

The researcher's theoretical stance inevitably shapes the analysis and presentation of the large quantities of written and spoken text produced by participants in qualitative studies. In essence, the researcher is creating another text (Rosenblatt, 1978, 1988). When representing the students' texts, Mahn wanted to retain the dialogic character of their writing and to let the content dictate the form. An underlying premise in the use of dialogue journals is that they provide an almost amorphous form in which students can write whatever content suits them. Mahn attempted to maintain the free-flowing character of the dialogue journals in the presentation of the student writing and to use a format in which their voices dominated.

THE DRAMALOGUE

These considerations led to a presentation of the students' voices in a dialogue presented as a drama—a "dramalogue" as it combined dialogic aspects cast in a drama among many players. Mahn collected various texts the students produced—in dialogue journals, spontaneous quickwrites, interviews, and questionnaires—and arranged selected passages into the themes that evolved from the texts. He did not alter nor correct the students' texts, nor did he create texts for them in the dramalogue. In order to construct a frame for the student texts, to move the dramalogue forward by providing transitions, and to comment on the student texts, he created speaking roles for his dissertation committee members and for himself as instructor and researcher.

DIALOGUE JOURNALS

Mahn used a Vygotskian theoretical framework to help analyze the student texts, which were windows through which to view the students' perspectives on their own cognitive processes and to see the complexity of literacy activities. In this section we focus on student perspectives on the influence dialogue journals had on both their inner speech and verbal thinking and how that affected their composing processes. Students emphasized two distinct but interrelated themes—that a focus on correctness inhibited their thinking and writing processes and that the writing environment fostered by dialogue journals helped facilitate thinking, thus increasing fluent writing.

The way that a second language is learned will have an impact on access to inner speech and verbal thinking. Inner speech functions differently for children learning a second language naturally than it does for those learning a second language through traditional, grammatical approaches in school. The initial writing for many students in grammar-oriented classes is connected to written exercises. When they move on to other types of writing, there is often an overriding emphasis on correctness, which causes them to edit in their minds before writing (Jones, 1985). Mahn's study examined whether writing in dialogue journals helps students to subordinate the editing in their heads and to discover writing as a way to think and develop ideas. Students reported that dialogue journals helped them overcome the short-circuiting of thought that can occur if too much attention is paid to correctness (Perl, 1979)—and that dialogue journals helped them write ideas versus writing grammar (Shaughnessy, 1977).

If the conscious awareness of correctness that is a part of the latter approaches dominates, affective factors, including those that result from different cultural practices, may impede the internalization of English and disrupt verbal thinking. One student described the frustration she felt with her verbal thinking while writing in English as compared to her native Chinese.

> When I started writing in English, the level of ideas go downward as the problem of English. We have to choose simple word to express the abstract and beautiful feeling which appear in my Chinese thinking. It, of course, is impossible. The thinking level decreases and then the original mood and idea cannot continue. And I need to struggle with the sentences construction, the grammar, the tense, and the vocabulary. (Mahn, 1997, p. 229)

A number of students, who described this disruption in their thinking and/or composing processes, added that when writing in their dialogue journals without worrying about correctness, their ideas are both more accessible and easier to convey.

BLOCKING IN THE ELBOW

Students' descriptions of this process were often most insightful when there were blocks or obstacles somewhere along the path from verbal thinking to inner speech to external speech. They described the interruptions in the flow of their thoughts, caused in large part by focusing on correctness.

> I realized that journal really help me to write down my idea without any blocking into my elbow. When I have idea in my head and I start to make it go down my arm to the paper, if I think about grammar and structure. my idea blocks into my elbow and never goes to the paper. (Mahn, 1997, p. 254)

A problem in the move from verbal thinking to production of written speech arises because of the absence of an interlocutor—an essential contributor to the internalization of speech. An interlocutor in oral speech helps achieve intersubjective understanding through intonation, gesture, and creation of a meaningful context centered on communicative intent. In written speech, however, the absence of intersubjective understanding and meaningful communicative interaction can make production difficult and constrained. Pedagogical approaches that focus on errors in students' texts can diminish the intersubjective understanding and the motivation to communicate. This not only makes production more difficult, especially for second-language learners, but also impairs the internalization of speech, which is blocked by the emphasis on correctness. Abbreviation and predication, two essential transformations in the process, do not take place when verbal thinking concentrates on structure and form and the motivation to communicate is diminished.

In contrast, students reported that the meaningful communication in the dialogue journals promoted intersubjective understanding, which helped them overcome blockages in both the internalization and externalization processes. Through the interaction in the journals and by shifting the focus from form and structure to meaning, students reflected that they could use English inner speech more effectively. The spontaneity of writing in the dialogue journals helped them get their ideas down on paper without worrying about correctness at the point of production. "[T]he journals allowed me to expand my thoughts and get my massage across with out interrupting myself thinking about what words to use or what the correct grammer should be (all the things that can be done later)" (p. 223). "I still have a lot of mistakes, but now I can express my ideas clear" (p. 205). "Many times when writing a journal I did not have a clear ideas how to write or how to address a subject and as I write it became more easy to find the right words" (p. 241).

They also commented that their writing was facilitated because they were motivated to communicate ideas. With the focus on meaning, the students would get their ideas on paper and deal with the form and structure after the production rather than trying to work out the grammar in their heads before committing the thought to paper. "I wrote while thinking rather than formulating sentences in the mind" (p. 221). Students reported that too much attention to mechanical correctness while composing caused them to lose their ideas or not be able to convey them—they evanesced not into thought, but into thin air. "When I'm afraid of mistakes, I don't really write the ideas I have in mind" (p. 189). Students related that because of writing in their dialogue journals, they experienced an increased flow of ideas inward and outward once they decreased this attention to surface structure. With this increased flow, they also benefited from the generative aspect of verbal thinking. "With the journal you have one idea and start writing about it and everything else just comes up" (p. 221). "They seemed to help me focus on what I was writing in the sense that I let the words just flow and form by themselves" (p. 247). "The journals we did in our class were useful to me because it help me form my thoughts" (p. 232). "Journal helps me to have ideas flow and write them down instead of words sticking in my mind" (p. 191).

ANALYSIS THROUGH A VYGOTSKIAN LENS

Students described using dialogue journals to overcome obstacles in both the internalization and externalization processes and to expedite inner speech's function of facilitating "intellectual orientation, conscious awareness, the overcoming of difficulties and impediments, and imagination and thinking" (Vygotsky, 1987, p. 259). These functions of inner speech usually develop about the time a child turns 7, when the egocentric speech of early childhood is differentiated structurally and functionally from social speech: *"the isolation of speech for oneself and speech for others from a general, undifferentiated speech function* that fulfills both these tasks in early childhood" (Vygotsky, 1987, p. 261). This differentiation of speech functions leads to the internalization of speech for oneself—a process that plays a significant role in the production of external speech, both oral and written. Second-language learners repeat this process of differentiation of inner and external speech as they learn their second language. It is complicated, however, by the prior existence of a relationship between inner and external speech in their native language. The students' perspectives indicated that they had trouble both with internalization and externalization of speech. Vygotsky (1987) said that when the differentiation between internal and external speech is extensive, we "know our own phrase before we pronounce it" (p. 261) because verbal thinking has developed. It is the struggle to "know the phrase" that can provide a stumbling block for the second-language learners whose verbal thinking in their new language is complicated by the existence of inner speech and verbal thinking in their native language.

Vygotsky acknowledged the role that inner speech played in putting a thought into words. The movement in both directions is interrelated, but can be separated to analyze what causes blockages in both directions with second-language writers. The undeveloped second language prevents the effective use of inner speech and verbal thinking in that language when the focus is on correct semantics and syntax and not on meaning. When second-language learners are composing and they have to translate their verbal thinking from their native language, there is another step introduced—one that can be an obstacle to the expression of their ideas in a second language. Vygotsky used the concept of words evanescing into thought through changes in syntax and semantics in inner speech, but if these aspects are not developed in the second language, the movement from inner speech to verbal thinking in the target language and the movement from verbal thinking to written production in the second language is hard to accomplish. As John-Steiner (1985) pointed out the semantic aspect is often woven together in the two languages, but there has to be a separation in production. If meaning and comprehension are emphasized, the move from verbal thinking to written production in a second language is facilitated. The importance of focusing on meaning in literacy activities becomes more urgent when one considers the effort by the U.S. government to focus literacy instruction on skill building and not on meaning and comprehension.

CONCLUSION

The current push to reduce literacy to phonemic awareness and to fund only empirical research that displays scientific rigor excludes work such as that done by Vygotsky. However, Vygotsky's work provides the theoretical foundation for scientific inquiries into the complexity of literacy activities using a scientific approach. A number of articles and books have exposed the narrow view of literacy used in the National Reading Panel Report (2000), which has spawned legislation like No Child Left Behind (Allington, 2002; Coles, 2000; Garan, 2001, 2002; Yatvin, 2002). Unlike the National Reading Panel Report, which focused on a single aspect of the reading process, these studies emphasize the importance of meaning, comprehension, culture, and context when examining reading and writing processes.

Because Vygotsky's analysis of the relationship between meaning and inner speech and verbal thinking provides a scientific foundation for literacy research, we emphasized this aspect of his work in our research. Inner speech and verbal thinking are less accessible and, therefore, tend to be neglected in the analysis of written language. Our research has focused on the notion that the production of written language is governed by communicative intent and is linked to inner speech and verbal thinking. Our work has put meaning at the center and looked at ways in which meaning can be communicated through written language. Our motivation has been to contribute to the development of pedagogical approaches that meet the literacy needs of all students, and especially those who are learning to speak and write in a second language.

REFERENCES

Allington, R. (2002). *Big brother and the national reading curriculum: How ideology trumped evidence.* Portsmouth, NH: Heinemann.

Beach, R., Green, J.L., Kamil, M.L., & Shanahan, T. (1992). *Multidisciplinary perspectives on literacy research.* Urbana, IL: National Council of Teachers of English.

Britton, J. (1987). Vygotsky's contribution to pedagogical theory. *English in Education, 21,* 22-26.

Burgess, T. (1993). Reading Vygotsky: Notes from within English teaching. In H. Daniels (Ed.), *Charting the agenda: Educational activity after Vygotsky* (pp. 1-29). New York: Routledge.

Canagarajah, A.S. (1996). From critical research practice to critical research reporting. *TESOL Quarterly, 30*(2), 321-331.

Cazden, C. (1996). Selective traditions: Readings of Vygotsky in writing pedagogy. In D. Hicks (Ed.), *Discourse, learning and schooling* (pp. 165-185). Cambridge and New York: Cambridge University Press.

Clay, M. (1991). *Becoming literate: The construction of inner control.* Portsmouth, NH: Heinemann.

Coles, G. (2000). *Misreading reading: The bad science that hurts children.* Portsmouth, NH: Heinemann.

Eisner, E. (1997). The promise and perils of alternative forms of data representative. *Educational Researcher, 26*(6), 4-10.

Elsasser, N., & John-Steiner, V. (1977). An interactionist approach to advancing literacy. *Harvard Educational Review, 47*(3), 79-97.

Emig, J. (1971). *The composing processes of twelfth graders.* Urbana, IL: National Council of Teachers of English.

Gal'perin, P. I. (1967). On the notion of internalization. *Soviet Psychology, 5*(3), 28-33.

Garan, E. (2001) Beyond the smoke and mirrors: A critique of the National Reading Panel Report on phonics. *Phi Delta Kappan, 82*(7), 500-506.

Garan, E. (2002). *Resisting reading mandates: How to triumph with the truth.* Portsmouth, NH: Heinemann.

Gee, J. P. (1991). Socio-cultural approaches to literacy (literacies). *Annual Review of Applied Linguistics, 12,* 31-48.

Gee, J. P. (1997). Thinking, learning, and reading: The situated sociocultural mind. In D. Kirshner & J. A. Whitson (Eds.), *Situated cognition: Social, semiotic, and psychological perspectives* (pp. 235-259). Norwood, NJ: Erlbaum.

Gee, J. P. (2001). A sociocultural perspective on early literacy development. In S. B. Neuman & D. K. Dickinson (Eds.), *Handbook on research in early literacy* (pp. 30-42). New York: Guilford.

Goodman, K., & Goodman, Y. (1979). Learning to read is natural. In L. Resnick & P. Weaver (Eds.), *Theory and practice of early reading* (Vol. I, pp. 137-154). Hillsdale, NJ: Erlbaum.

Goodman, K., & Goodman, Y. (1990). Vygotsky in a whole-language perspective. In L. C. Moll (Ed.), *Vygotsky and education: Instructional implications of sociohistorical psychology* (pp. 223-251). New York: Cambridge University Press.

Halliday, M. (1975). *Learning how to mean.* London, UK: Edward Arnold.

Harste, J. C., Woodward, V. A., & Burke, C. L. (1984). *Language stories and literacy lessons.* Portsmouth, NH: Heinemann.

Heath, S. B. (1983). *Ways with words: Language, life, and work in classrooms and communities.* New York: Cambridge University Press.

Hicks, D. (1998). Narrative discourses as inner and outer word. *Language Arts, 75*(1), 28-34.

John-Steiner, V. (1985). The road to competence in an alien land: A Vygotskian perspective on bilingualism. In J.V. Wertsch (Ed.), *Culture, communication, and cognition: Vygotskian perspectives* (pp. 348-371). New York: Cambridge University Press.

John-Steiner, V. (1997). *Notebooks of the mind: Explorations of thinking* (2nd ed.). New York: Oxford University Press.

John-Steiner, V., Panofsky, C.P., & Smith, L.W. (1994). *Sociocultural approaches to language and literacy: An interactionist perspective.* New York: Cambridge University Press.

John-Steiner, V., & Tatter, P. (1983). An interactionist model of language development. In B. Bain (Ed.), *The sociogenesis of language and human conduct* (pp. 79-97). New York: Plenum Press.

Jones, S. (1985). Problems with monitor use in second language composing. In M. Rose (Ed.), *When a writer can't write* (pp. 96-118). New York: Guilford.

Kress, G. (1993). Genre as a social process. In B. Cope & M. Kalantzis (Eds.), *The power of literacy: A genre approach to teaching writing* (pp. 22-37). Philadelphia: Falmer.

Kirsch, G.E. (1997). Opinion: Multi-vocal texts and interpretive responsibility. *College English. 59*(2), 191-202.

Langer, J.A., & Applebee, A.N. (1987). *How writing shapes thinking: A study of teaching and learning.* Urbana, IL: National Council of Teachers of English.

Lee, C., & Smagorinsky, P. (2000). *Vygotskian perspectives on literacy research: Constructing meaning through collaborative inquiry.* New York: Cambridge University Press.

Luria, A.R. (1969). Speech development and the formation of mental processes. In M. Cole (Ed.), *A handbook of contemporary Soviet psychology* (pp. 121-162). New York: Basic Books.

Mahn, H. (1997). *Dialogue journals: Perspectives of second language learners in a Vygotskian theoretical framework.* Unpublished dissertation. University of New Mexico, Albuquerque.

Moffett, J. (1981). *Coming on center: English education in evolution.* Portsmouth, NH: Boynton/Cook.

Moll, L. C. (1992). Literacy research in community and classrooms: A sociocultural approach. In R. Beach, J. L. Green, M. L. Kamil, & T. Shanahan (Eds.), *Multidisciplinary perspectives on literacy research* (pp. 211-244). Urbana, IL: National Council of Teachers of English.

National Reading Panel. (2000). *Teaching children to read: An evidence-based assessment of the scientific research literature on reading and its implications for reading instruction.* Washington, DC: National Institute of Child Health and Human Development.

National Research Council. (1999). *How people learn: Brain, mind, experience, and school.* Washington, DC: National Academy Press.

New London Group. (1996). A pedagogy of multiliteracies: Designing social futures. *Harvard Educational Review, 66*(1), 60-92.

Olson, D. R. (1977). From utterance to text: The bias of language in speech and writing. *Harvard Educational Review, 47*(3), 257-281.

Perl, S. (1979). The composing processes of unskilled college writers. *Research in the Teaching of English, 13*, 317-336.

Prawat, R. S. (2000). Social constructivism and the process-content distinction as viewed by Vygotsky and the pragmatists. *Mind, Culture, and Activity, 6*(4), 255-273.

Rivers, W. J. (1987). *Problems in composition: A Vygotskian perspective.* Unpublished doctoral dissertation, University of Delaware, Newark.

Rosenblatt, L. (1978). *The reader, the text, and the poem: The transactional theory of the literary work.* Carbondale: Southern Illinois University Press.

Rosenblatt, L. M. (1988). *Writing and reading: The transactional theory.* Washington, DC: Educational Resources Information Center (ERIC Document Reproduction Service No. ED 292 062).

Scribner, S., & Cole, M. (1981). *The psychology of literacy.* Cambridge, MA: Harvard University Press.

Shaughnessy, M. P. (1977). *Errors & expectations: A guide for the teacher of basic writing.* New York: Oxford University Press.

Vygotsky, L. S. (1978). *Mind in society: The development of higher psychological processes.* Cambridge: Harvard University Press.

Vygotsky, L. S. (1987). *The collected works of L. S. Vygotsky: Vol. 1. Problems of general psychology.* New York: Plenum.

Vygotsky, L.S. (1997). The historical meaning of the crisis in psychology: A methodological investigation. In *The collected works of L. S. Vygotsky: Vol. 3. Problems of the theory and history of psychology* (pp. 233-343). New York: Plenum.

Vygotsky, L.S. (1998). *Child psychology. The collected works of L. S. Vygotsky: Vol. 5. Problems of the theory and history of psychology.* New York: Plenum.

Wells, G. (1999). *Dialogic inquiry: Toward a sociocultural practice and theory of education.* New York: Cambridge University Press.

Wertsch, J. V. (2000). Vygotsky's two minds on the nature of meaning In C. Lee & P. Smagorinsky (Eds.), *Vygotskian perspectives on literacy research: Constructing meaning through collaborative inquiry* (pp. 19-30). New York: Cambridge University Press.

Wertsch, J. V., & Stone, C. A. (1985). The concept of internalization in Vygotsky's account of the genesis of higher mental functions. In J. V. Wertsch (Ed.), *Culture, communication, and cognition: Vygotskian perspectives* (pp. 162-179). New York: Cambridge University Press.

Yaroshevsky, M. G., & Gurgenidze, G. S. (1997). Epilogue. In R. W. Reiber & J. Wollack (Eds.), *The collected works of L. S. Vygotsky: Vol. 3. Problems of theory and history of psychology* (pp. 345-369). New York: Plenum.

Yatvin, J. (2002). Babes in the woods: The wanderings of the National Reading Panel. *Phi Delta Kappan, 83*(5), 364-369.

Zamel, V. (1997). Toward a model of transculturation. *TESOL Quarterly, 31*(2), 341-352.

Zebroski, J. T. (1994). *Thinking through theory: Vygotskian perspectives on the teaching of writing.* Portsmouth, NH: Heinemann.

Zukow-Goldring, P., & Ferko, K. R. (1994). An ecological approach to the emergence of the lexicon: Socializing attention. In V. John-Steiner, C. P. Panofsky, & L. W. Smith (Eds.), *Sociocultural approaches to language and literacy : An interactionist perspective* (pp. 170-190). New York: Cambridge University Press.

6

"All That Glitters Ain't Gold"

CHAT as a Design and Analytical Tool in Literacy Research

Carol D. Lee
Northwestern University

Arnetha Ball
Stanford University

"All that glitters ain't gold" is an old African-American proverb (Smitherman, 2000). We use it as a metaphor for the role that Cultural historical activity theory (CHAT) can play in helping researchers filter through normative assumptions about literacy learning (i.e., the glitter) and to mine the rich complexity of literate practices constructed within low-income and ethnic minority communities.[1]

This chapter examines a perspective on the study of literacy practices and learning that focuses on the cultural contexts of cognition. Here, we explore its implications for reading and for writing as cultural practices. We attend explicitly to how this approach may be used to either examine links between cultural models and scripts constructed inside and outside of schools, the learning of formal academic constructs, and the use of cultural tools to transform activity processes.

CULTURE AND COGNITION

A turning point in the study of human cognition came as psychologists wrestled with two fundamental questions: Does knowledge reside only as internal mental structures in the minds of individuals, merely as neural synapses in individual brains? What are the roles that interactions with other people, material artifacts, and the ideas embedded in each play in the ability of people to plan and engage in problem solving? In the study of literacy practices, these questions were and are also linked to questions about the role of printed texts in the abilities of persons and social groups to engage in logical thought (Goody, 1968; Ong, 1982). The work of Scribner and Cole (1981) in the late 1970s in Liberia contributed greatly to a shift in the field's perspective on these two questions. Scribner and Cole went to Liberia to study the influences of (Western) school-based literacy practices on the ability of schooled and nonschooled Vai people to engage in syllogistic reasoning. The original assumption was that syllogistic reasoning represented the sine qua non representation of high intellect. Embedded in these early investigations were assumptions about IQ as a stable measure of individual mental functioning. Scribner and Cole made several important observations. First, the competencies demonstrated by the people depended on the particular social practices associated with one of three literacies. The Vai are one of the few cultures that have independently invented a phonetic writing system. This writing system has remained in active use for 150 years within the context of Vai traditional rural life. This Vai script, a syllabary of 200 characters with a common core of 20 to 40, is transmitted outside of any institutional setting and without the formation of a professional teacher group. Vai literacy coexists with two universal and institutionally power script—the Arabic script, used by Muslims and transmitted through Qur'anic schools, and the Roman script, used as the official script of political and economic institutions operating on a national scale and transmitted through English schools. Scribner and Cole estimated that approximately 28% of the adult Vai male population was was literate in one of the three scripts, the majority in the indigenous Vai script, the next largest group in Arabic and the smallest in English. Because each script involves a different orthography, completion of a different course of instruction and, in the cases of Arabic and English, use of a foreign language, multiliteracy was a significant accomplishment. Scribner and Cole found that individuals using the Vai script were just as capable of planning and problem solving as the users of the Arabic or English script. As a result of this study, researchers began to consider more seriously external structures that influence knowledge construction and the role of interaction in problem solving.

Other research not involving alphabetic literacy also included studies of the mathematical knowledge demonstrated by the Brazilian candy sellers (Nunes, Schliemann, & Carraher, 1993; Saxe, 1991) and the Liberian tailors (Lave, 1977), among others. These studies, which brought together disciplinary orientations from psychology and anthropology, were accompanied by a discovery among Western scholars of the works of Lev Vygotsky, Leont'ev, and Luria from the Russian School of Psychology. The evolution of these families of studies has come under the rubric of what is now called *sociocultural theory* (Cole, 1996; Rogoff, 1990; Wertsch, 1991). Sociocultural theory now embraces cognition, anthropology, linguistics and critical theory. Cole (1996) focused attention on the multiple dimensions of time and took a broader view on what he called cultural historical activity theory.

CHAT

CHAT calls on researchers to use practice or activity as the unit of analysis in the study of human functioning. Within any activity system are people who act as both individuals and as members of the community of practice, the artifacts they use as tools to problem solve, the rules that guide their behavior, the ways they divide up the work of the activity, and the overarching and emerging goals of the activity (Cole, 1996; Engeström, Miettinen, & Punamaki, 1999; Rogoff & Lave, 1984). Goals are often emergent and always negotiated, constrained, or made possible by the nature of tools available. Participation structures captured by the division of labor and the rules for how people interact are the medium through which negotiations around emergent goals occurs. This dynamic system is represented in Fig. 6.1. The artifacts people use in an activity system may be material (such as pencils, tape recorders, digital cameras) and/or conceptual (ideas such as what it means to write a narrative or read a satire) or may combine both concepts as well as materiality (computers, texts,). Literacy practices will almost always involve participation in an activity system, even if the practice simply involves an individual reading a book. Literate practices involving reading and writing occur in both school and nonschool settings (Barton, 1994; Heath, 1983). Literacy researchers try to understand the nature of these practices, the kinds of cognitions in which people engage as they participate in these practices, and the social and other interactional processes through which people learn to engage and sustain their engagement in these practices. Because such systems of literate practices are complex and dynamic, a major challenge for researchers is how to study dynamic systems, especially ones that involve open-ended symbolic systems of natural language, whether oral or print. CHAT perspectives offer fruitful resources for such investigations. Two CHAT perspectives in particular offer useful tools for our studies of literacy practices and learning; the concept of mediated action and Rogoff's three planes of analysis as lens for understanding mediated action.

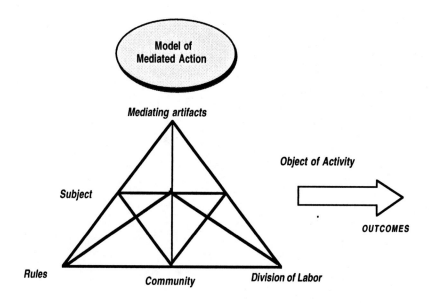

Figure 6.1.   An activity system.

Engeström et al. (1999) built on Leont'ev's (1981) earlier work on activity theory and offered a graphic heuristic to represent not only the key elements of an activity system, but also the interrelationships among these elements. The triangle depicted in Fig. 6.1 leads us to gather data on the subject(s) or people of interest, the larger community of people involved, the rules that inform how they act, the ways they divide up the work of the activity, the goals of the activity, and the artifacts the people use.

Perkins (1993) discussed this as a person-plus-unit of analysis, what the person brings from his or her own prior knowledge, experiences and goals, along with the enabling capacities that people, rules, roles, tools and ideas bring. The point here is that what enables people to accomplish both the goals of the practice (and their own emerging goals, particularly if these goals are consistent with the goals of the activity) are the *interactions* among all these elements. This construct is often labeled mediation or mediated action. According to Wertsch (1991), "mediation is best thought of as a process involving the potential of cultural tools to shape action, on the one hand, and the unique use of these tools, on the other" (p. 22). In Vygotsky's (1978) writings, the construct of mediation—especially semiotic mediation—played a central theoretical role. Vygotsky (1978) noted that "the central fact about our psychology of activity is the fact of mediation" (p. 166). It is "this idea that runs as the unifying and connecting lifeline throughout the works of Vygotsky, Leont'ev, Luria, and the other important representatives of the Soviet cultural-historical school" (Engeström et al., 1999, pp. 28-29).

Because our interests focus on a cultural orientation to literacy, we illustrate mediation through a speech genre. Bakhtin (1986) noted how speech genres invite speakers into a dialogic relationship with the past in the sense that these genres carry with them historically constituted roles, perspectives, and reified themes. At the same time, each new generation and each individual speaker imbue that speech genre with their own special meanings and uses. For example, in the African-American English speech community is a long-standing tradition of signifying. *Signifying* is a form of ritual insult that involves double entendre and a high use of figurative language (Mitchell-Kernan, 1981; Smitherman, 1977). Engaging in the act of signifying requires the interlocutors to recognize the socially accepted norms for rejecting a literal interpretation of a claim (i.e., "Your mama so skinny she could do the hoola hoop in a cheerio") and by analogical reasoning to reconstruct a metaphoric interpretation. To respond to a ritual insult, the respondent is constrained by the rules of the genre to construct a retort that (a) is not literally the truth, (b) is consistent with the tenor of the first metaphor (i.e., "Your mama so skinny Sally Struthers sends her food"), (c) is humorous, and (d) involves an original metaphor (Lee, 1993). When individuals are socialized into use of a speech genre, they learn, usually tacitly, the rules for reasoning within it. Thus, when one hears African-American English speakers signifying with one another, one is not witnessing simply individual displays of creativity (although that is certainly the case). The goal to insult with humor, the invocation of metaphor and hyperbole as tools to construct the humor, the rules for when and how to respond (including the cross-party talk of observers), and the division of labor among interlocutors—including third-party members—are all mediational resources that come with the speech genre.

Although Fig. 6.1 captures the elements of an activity system as outlined by Engeström, the triangle representation does not capture both the emergent nature of goals, including the fact that there are almost always competing and contradicting goals on the floor. The division of labor, the rules for interacting, and tools available for problem solving are what make possible the nature of negotiations through which competing goals are worked through. In classrooms, this can result in antisocial behaviors and disengagement by students if teachers design local classroom cultures that do not provide connections with students' prior knowledge and belief systems or that do not provide spaces for what sense students make of classroom work. Gutierrez, Rymes, and Larson (1995) accounted for such problems by distinguishing between the official script of the teacher, the unofficial script of students, and a space, which they call the third space, where these two are negotiated.

The issue of how mediated action occurs in an activity setting is an issue of consideration for researchers who draw on a CHAT perspective. In their investigations, however, focusing on all planes of analysis that correspond to the personal, interpersonal, and community processes can be daunting, both conceptually and methodologically. Rogoff (1995) described three planes of analysis that allow the researcher to zoom in on one plane of an activity system while keeping the others in the background. Rogoff defined these three planes as apprenticeship, guided practice, and participatory appropriation. Apprenticeship focuses on the routines, concepts, and artifacts that one inherits from the history of the practice into which one is entering. Guided practice focuses on the nature of the interaction and supports that individuals or groups of people experience from other people and artifacts that are part of the activity. Participatory appropriation refers to the efforts of the individual to make sense of and use the resources available to him or her in the activity. She emphasized the need to incorporate all three planes into sociocultural research, noting that "it is incomplete to focus only on the relation of individual development and social interaction without concern for the cultural activity in which personal and interpersonal actions take place . . . [or] to assume that development occurs in one plane and not the others . . . or that influence can be ascribed in one direction or another" (Rogoff, 1995, p. 141). Policy initiatives (at the classroom, school, district, state, or federal levels) intended to make schools more effective suffer from the assumption that creating explanations or responses on one plane is a sufficient leverage for change. On the apprenticeship plane, the policy response is academic standards. On the guided practice plane, the policy response is either scripted lessons or pedagogical strategies. On the individual plane, the policy response tends to be deficit explanations regarding students efforts and goals. This latter response often takes the form of punishment for the individual, such as mandatory grade retention. We argue that no one of these leverage points is sufficient for change because the person acting culturally, within school or without, is never engaged solely on one of these planes in isolation from the other.

RELEVANCE OF CHAT TO THE STUDY OF CULTURALLY RESPONSIVE LEARNING ENVIRONMENTS

As noted earlier, studies of literacy learning and routine literacy practices among Black and Brown populations, populations within the United States whose first language is other than English, and populations living in economically depressed conditions have been circumscribed by Western hegemonic intellectual traditions. Research in this tradition has argued that students from the populations described suffer from cultural deficits (Beretiter & Engelmann, 1966; Hernstein & Murray, 1994; Jensen, 1969) and that uses of languages and varieties of English that do not reflect what has come to be called *Standard English* have limited capacities for intellectual work. The weight of terms that are still used to describe such populations (*at risk, culturally diverse, marginalized, underachieving, underclass, students of color*) all inherently presume a racially White and economically middle or upper class standard against which all others are evaluated and presumed to be deficient. In contrast, there is a strong body of research, in areas such as sociolinguistics, that explores the richness, for example, of African-American English discourse practices (Ball, 1995c; Foster, 1987; Gilyard, 1991; Lee, 1993; Morgan, 1998; Rickford & Rickford, 1976) or of the multiple language resources to which speakers who are bilingual have access (Gutierrez, Baquedano-Lopez, & Tejeda, 1999; Mercado & Moll, 1997; Nieto, 2000; Reyes, 1991; Valdes, 1996). Many design experiments in culturally responsive curriculum and pedagogy for literacy learning have documented what it means to tap the array of language and conceptual resources that students from communities that have been defined as out of the "mainstream" bring to classrooms and other settings in which learning is an explicit goal (Au, 1980; Ball, 1995ba, 1995bc, 1999; Gutierrez et al., 1995; Lee, 1994, 1995a; Mahiri, 1998; Moll & Greenberg, 1990; Tharp & Gallimore, 1988).

The fundamental argument of CHAT, that to understand human goal-directed behavior one must attend to people's experiences over time, to the cultural contexts of their experiences, and to view practice as the fundamental unit of analysis inherently call for the kinds of analyses that the culturally responsive design experiments cited bring to bear. CHAT, including a broad family of frameworks (Cole, 1996; Greeno, 1997; Wertsch, del Rio, & Alvarez, 1995),[2] offers a number of concepts that serve as rich conceptual tools for understanding the culture of literacy practices. These concepts include cultural models and scripts, zone of proximal development (ZPD), and intersubjectivity within apprenticeship.

CULTURAL MODELS AND SCRIPTS

Cultural models (D'Andrade, 1987) are schemas that are shared within a cultural community, that serve as guides or filters through which experience is interpreted, and that guide people in their actions across a number of life activities. Cultural scripts (Cole, 1996; D'Andrade, 1990; Schank & Abelson, 1977) are schema for events that specify the people who are expected to participate, the roles they can play, the objects they would use, and the sequence of activities within the event that are appropriate. The culturally responsive design experiments just cited each use ethnographic methods to uncover cultural models and scripts that members of these target communities draw on as they engage in routine cultural practices. The object of the analyses generally have been to demonstrate ways that these cultural models and scripts are either taken up in service of literate practices; or ways in which they have come into conflict with traditional school practices, often with negative consequences for student learning.

ZONE OF PROXIMAL DEVELOPMENT

CHAT concepts put forward a dynamic view of learning, for our purposes, a dynamic view of the contexts in which literate practices emerge. Vygotsky's (1981) notion of a zone of ZPD goes against the grains of assumptions about IQ, and suggests that in order to help a learner appropriate new concepts, one must take into account what the learner already knows. The cultural orientation we advocate privileges the cultural funds of knowledge that learners bring to the learning of literate practices. Taking into consideration what the learner knows and values is a prerequisite for a state of intersubjectivity between the learner and the more knowledgeable other in a ZPD, where they share if not a common, at least a mutually negotiated set of expectations around the goal of their work together.

INTERSUBJECTIVITY WITHIN APPRENTICESHIP

A ZPD may be seen as an apprenticeship. The concept of an apprenticeship implies that routine practices have a history, and with that history comes a set of knowledge rich resources that have sustained the practice over time. Collins, Brown, and Holum (1991) referred to the specialized learning in schools as *cognitive apprenticeships*. Our interests are in exploring those knowledge-rich resources that sustain the apprenticeship. Bahktin (1986) added to our understanding of intersubjectivity by claiming that we speak with dialogical voices that are always in contact with the history of other perspectives on the topic. Our interests are in the dialogical relationships between school-based literacies and the out-of-school literacies of students and of teachers. Bahktin also brings forward the idea of social languages and genres, the idea that there are structures to ways we communicate that have historical force, that communicate status and social–power relationships in their invocation. In our research, these social languages often include uses of African-American English (Ball, 1992, 1995b, 1995c, 1999; Lee, 1997). We do not have space in the context of this chapter to fully explore these CHAT family concepts, but rather we wish to make the point that they are conceptual tools that fit squarely with a cultural orientation to understanding literacy practices. We demonstrate their uses in the two research programs we describe here. Our goal is to highlight the research methodologies employed and the ways that CHAT was used as both a conceptual as well as methodological tool in literacy research.

CULTURAL MODELING: USING CHAT IN THE STUDY OF RESPONSE TO LITERATURE

In this section, we describe one approach that involves both literacy curricula design and data analysis that draw on CHAT as a framework. Cultural Modeling is a framework for the design of learning environments that links forms of tacit knowledge that students bring from their home and community experiences with deep disciplinary knowledge (Lee, 1993, 1995a, 1995b, 2000). Lee's work with Cultural Modeling has focused on response to literature as the target literacy domain and the funds of knowledge that African-American adolescents develop as speakers of African-American Vernacular English (AAVE) and as participants in routine, culturally defined, out of school activities. When AAVE speakers engage in speech genres such as signifying (and related genres such as sounding, loud talking, playing the dozens, he-said/she-said), they routinely produce and interpret literary tropes—symbolism, irony, satire (Mitchell-Kernan, 1981; Rickford & Rickford, 1976; Smitherman, 1977). As noted earlier, these speech genres serve as mediational tools for problem solving in nonschool arenas. Cultural Modeling brings these community-based mediational tools as resources for discipline-specific academic goals. Rap culture certainly crosses many borders, but rap culture is clearly rooted in African-American youth culture (Kitwana, 2002). When adolescents engage in the process of interpreting the lyrics of rich rap lyrics, they are interpreting symbolism, irony, satire, and uses of unreliable narrators (Lee, 1993). In both communities of practice, these young people are employing strategies and habits of mind that are tacit. D'Andrade (1990) argued that cultural models are often tacit and people often are not able to explicitly describe these models or how they use them.

Design principles of Cultural Modeling call for a careful analysis of the target domain, in this case, response to literature, as well as a careful analysis of the funds of knowledge that students construct outside of school that may be relevant to the demands of the target domain. The Cultural Modeling Project has identified a set of generative concepts that constitute the domain of response to literature (Lee, 2001; Smith & Hillocks, 1988). These concepts are considered generative in the sense that they allow people to read with understanding a wide variety of texts: across national traditions (British literature, American literature, Russian literature, Ghanaian literature, etc.), genres (bildung roman, magical realism), and interpretive processes (processes for interpreting symbolism, irony, satire, etc.). Instruction based on Cultural Modeling principles involves (a) focusing on a generative concept and set of related strategies, (b) identifying a set of cultural data sets whose interpretation requires the student to engage the target concept and use appropriate strategies for tackling the target concept, and (c) selecting a series of canonical texts, each of which demands that the reader engage with the target concept. For example, a unit of instruction might focus on symbolism as a generative construct in the domain of response to literature. Symbolism is considered generative because if the reader can detect that a passage or stretch of text is not intended to be interpreted literally, but figuratively—that is, identify the category of interpretive problem that the text poses—and then draw on a set of flexible strategies for constructing a warrantable hypotheses as to a possible figurative meaning, the reader is empowered to tackle a wide variety of texts, from William Butler Yeats' "The Second Coming," to Alice Walker's "Everyday Use," to Chinua Achebe's *Things Fall Apart*, to Dostoyevsky's *Crime and Punishment*, to John Keats' "Ode on a Grecian Urn." A cultural data set in a unit on symbolism might include lyrics from a rap song, a stretch of signifying dialogue dialogue,[3] a scene from a television program or movie, an ad from a popular magazine. The criteria for the selection of a data set are that it must demand a sophisticated knowledge of the target construct—say symbolism (i.e., it must be challenging to make sense of); and that students must be very familiar with it already.

The design principles behind Cultural Modeling curricula involve creating an activity system within classrooms that provides novices with sustained guided practice over time in learning to identify categories of interpretive problems, in this case, in the study of literature. For example, while reading Shakespeare's Sonnet 18 that begins "How shall I compare thee to a summer's day," a reader needs to recognize that the lines "Rough winds do shake the darling buds of May" poses a particular kind of interpretive problem, namely symbolism, and that it is not merely a simple description. Norms for talk in Cultural Modeling classrooms during the modeling phase involve supporting students in making explicit and public the strategies they use, for example, to figure out that the allusions to a mask in the Fugees' lyrics "The Mask" are not intended to be literal, and to support their claims with evidence, both from the text and from their lived experiences. In Cultural Modeling, this kind of talk is called metacognitive instructional discourse (Lee, 1998). Such talk creates a participation structure that positions students and teachers as both experts and novices simultaneously, from the very beginning of instruction. The division of labor that follows from modeling through the examination of cultural data sets establishes norms that call on students to hypothesize, to construct arguments, to initiate ideas, to question one another; in other words, to begin to engage in the routines that characterize response to literature as a community of practice. Additionally, because cultural scripts and cultural models are so central to Cultural Modeling as a design framework, norms for talk in Cultural Modeling classrooms involve the sustaining of hybrid discourse spaces. Routine norms for talk in such classrooms are hybrid in the sense that the talk includes, for example, African-American English discourse norms (when the student population is African American) in pursuit of literary reasoning. From a Bahktinian perspective, two social languages interanimate and enter into dialogue with one another (Bahktin, 1986). Such discourse norms include use of overlapping, multiparty talk, a high use of gesture and rhythmic prosody, body language, and so on. In Cultural Modeling classrooms, with African-American students, Lee (1992, 1995a, 1995b, 2001) found that when students show high levels of engagement in literary problem solving, they are almost always simultaneously invoking African-American English discourse norms, in part, because the designed activity system creates a space for such talk.

As part of the Cultural Modeling Project, Carol Lee taught one high school English class each of the 3 years of the intervention. In the classroom dialogue presented here, a group of African-American high school seniors in Lee's class are discussing Toni Morrison's award winning novel *Beloved*. These are students whose levels of literary reasoning here would not be predicted by their standardized reading scores. However, because of the mediational supports provided through Cultural Modeling, their reasoning reflects sophisticated literary norms. In Line 1, Victor, without prompting by the teacher, has recognized a salient detail that serves as an indice of symbolism. It is a detail that Lee had not noticed. Both Lee and the class respond with an emotional and public "oooh," indicating that these literary norms are shared by the class. In Lines 3-5, in their own private side bar, two students revoice what Victor has said and clearly indicate in Line 3 engagement by their expression of a need to know what Victor had said. In Lines 2, 6, and 7, large numbers of students invoke the African-American discourse norm of multiparty overlapping talk. Victor further demonstrates the literary norms for making arguments that have been internalized as part of the culture of the classroom when in Line 7 Victor responds to the teacher's request that he explain his claim by going directly—without prompting—to the text as his supporting evidence. David has been trying all along to get into the dialogue and in Lines 12 and 14 makes intertextual links to the function of the symbol of the tree in other parts of the text. David's remark is not made in response to anything the teacher has said, but in response to Victor's observation. Even when the teacher, in Line 16, tries to close out this part of the discussion, one of the students

(Line 17) insists she still needs to continue the dialogue. This dialogue is characteristic of the levels of engagement, use of literary reasoning, and invocation of African-American discourse norms that occur in the Cultural Modeling classroom.

1. Victor: When it came out of the water she sat in on the tree all day and night resting her head on the trunk (inaudible).

2. Prof. Lee: Ooooh. Ahhhh. (the class says that at the same time.) Wow.

3. S2: What did he say?

4. S3: He put something under the tree.

5. S2: Beloved is a tree.

6. Prof. Lee: Victor (Students are all talking at the same time.) Hold up. Victor please explain that. That's powerful.

7. *[overlapping talk from other students]*

8. Victor: Let me find it exactly.

9. Prof. Lee: Alright Victor. Tell us the page.

10. Victor: (Opens his book and begins reading directly from the text,) Walk down to the water, lean against the mulberry tree all day and night. All day and all night she sat there with her head rested on the trunk --- (Inaudible) enough to crack the brim in her straw hat.

11. Prof. Lee: She's not only resting on a tree but she seemed to be abandoned on this tree Oooh this is good. Now, so alright David a little bit louder so everybody can hear you. Charles Johnson are you listening? David a little louder.

12. David: This book is connected to trees like tree is sweet home. Tree on her back, tree in her back yard.

13. Prof. Lee: Ahhh.

14. David: Tree on this, tree on that.

15. *[overlapping talk by other students in the class]*

16. Prof. Lee: Now don't you all have a worksheet on trees? (Students are laughing and talking all at the same time.) Okay hold up. You should have. (students are talking loudly.) Quiet. You should have, check in your folder if you don't have this worksheet with the picture of the tree, you don't have it raise your hand so I can give it to you.

17. S4: Dr. Lee, can I just say something real fast.

In addition to invoking CHAT as a framework for design, the Cultural Modeling framework also employs CHAT as a frame for analyzing data. Classrooms are complex interactional spaces. Goals are constantly being negotiated. Neither students nor teachers are passive recipients of district standards, of commercial textbooks, or of packaged curriculum. Goals are emergent. Teacher scripts and students' scripts often come into conflict— Gutierrez (Gutierrez et al., 1995) Gutierrez labeled these *counterscripts*. Different social languages come into contact with often unpredictable consequences. From a cultural perspective, many of the cultural scripts and cultural models that teachers and students construct from both their personal experiences and from the lived experiences over time of the multiple groups to which they belong also come into play in classrooms. Where these multiple sources of difference come into contact with one another is often seen by educational researchers and teachers as explanations for low levels of academic achievement for students—African-American, Latino/a, Native American, poor, speakers of other languages or language varieties than the so-called Standard English. From a Cultural Modeling perspective, these sources of differences are resources to be strategically and principally drawn on. Among the many challenges to researchers, then, is to study the complex cultural systems of classrooms in principled ways that are not reductionist. CHAT offers some useful ways to approach this problem.

In looking at a classroom as a local activity system, CHAT helps the researcher to identify the elements of the activity system about which she or he might collect data: data about the subject or subjects who are the focus, the forms of and uses of mediating artifacts, the division of labor among participants, the other members of the community engaged in the practice who may not be the explicit focus of the analysis, the rules that guide what participants do and how they go about doing what they do. Earlier approaches to studying classrooms employed a process-product paradigm, with the assumption that if assessment data from one point in time were collected and researchers back tracked into identifying the practices of teachers, the analysis could account for student achievement. Such approaches did not take into account the complex nature and negotiation of classrooms as activity systems. In many respects, the notion of best practice grows out of process-product approaches and inherently assumes a one-size-fits-all approach.

Also, a CHAT perspective on data analysis calls on researchers to take into account the multiple dimensions of time: studying classrooms across longer stretches of time, conducting micro-genetic analyses of how activity unfolds minute by minute, taking into account the developmental trajectories of students (i.e., middle schoolers, adolescents); looking for the influences of historical time on the nature of the activity (i.e., the intervention takes place in 2002 after a change in both the local district and national political leadership), and so on.

APPLICATION OF CHAT TO DATA ANALYSIS

We demonstrate with several examples how Cultural Modeling has used CHAT in data analysis. In one study, Lee and colleagues (Lee & Majors, 2000) examined the activity system of Cultural Modeling classrooms by asking what roles the students and teachers assume over time, what levels and models of literary reasoning emerged over time, and what in the unfolding of the activity system over time seemed to create the opportunities for learning. These questions are relevant ones from a CHAT perspective. Following the Engeström (1987) model, data was collected on students (interviews, their class assignments), the teacher[4] (lesson plans, reflective journals), mediating artifacts (the Cultural Modeling curriculum, artifacts routinely used such as graphic organizers, reflective journals, guiding questions, the cultural data sets and canonical texts, etc.), and the division of labor and rules for participation (videotapes of daily instruction across each year). Having collected such a large corpus of data, however, the challenge remained as to how to analyze the data in order to address the questions that were posed for the study.

The videotapes were the primary source of data for the analysis because they allowed the researcher to view the local activity system of the classroom as an entity in motion, rather than a fixed artifact.[5] The other data collected were used to ground observations in the video through a process of triangulation. When one gathers data across such a broad scope of time—in this case a full year of instruction—the researcher needs a grounded criteria by which to select data for more detailed analysis. The Santa Barbara Discourse Group (Green & Dixon, 1994) developed a useful approach for documenting classroom routines over long period of times. Based on the goals of the Cultural Modeling Project—that is, to apprentice novice readers into the ways of reasoning about literary texts that reflect response to literature as a community of practice—episodes of literary reasoning at each phase of the intervention designed provided the criteria for selection. The interest was in understanding how episodes of literary reasoning were interactionally constructed over time; and what differences, if any, were evident at the modeling phase, the scaffolding phase, and the phase of more fully independent participation. The researchers viewed repeatedly all of the videotapes by unit of instruction. For each tape, the initial unit of analysis was an instructional episode, defined by the goals of the activity. The goal of an instructional episode might be to take care of routines like attendance and collecting homework; to model a concept and/or set of strategies through analysis of a cultural data set; to examine an interpretive problem in a canonical work of literature; to discipline students, and so on. Because of the breadth of data collected, the next level of analysis focused on episodes of modeling from cultural data sets and examining interpretive problems in canonical texts. A time line was created to mark the dates of each class session and within that class session the kinds of instructional episodes. In order to analyze the quality of reasoning within such episodes, the researchers used Toulmin's (Toulmin, Rieke, & Janik, 1984) structure of argument and Kuhn's (1991) levels of evidence to categorize the quality of literary reasoning as high, medium, or low. The researchers could have stopped their analysis at that point if the primary interest had been in the products of student thought. However, because the interest was in the classroom as a cultural activity system, it was important to tackle the question of how these levels of literary reasoning were interactionally constructed over time, and what roles the cultural funds of knowledge of students and the teacher played in the process. In order to address these two questions, the researchers employed discourse analysis to understand the nature of interactions and their consequences for participants. From the perspective of Rogoff's three planes of analysis, the discourse analysis allowed the researchers to look at the nature of guided practice and participatory appropriation. The construct of apprenticeship—as defined in Rogoff's three planes of analysis—allowed the researchers to document the affordances and constraints that historical cultural practices provided as knowledge-rich resources.

Because it is a very broad methodology, it is important to describe in some detail how discourse analysis was useful in the analysis. Goffman's (1974) participation framework allowed researchers to identify roles that participants played in the construction of an argument within an episode. Michaels' (O'Connor & Michaels, 1993) notion of revoicing was expanded to look at the ways that particular intellectual roles were constructed for others by both the teacher and students. For example, when a student problematized a hypothesis put forward by another student, the problematizer created a condition of uncertainty that would prompt someone else (another student or the teacher) to examine either the evidence or the warrants for the evidence that underlies the original assertion. Phillips' (1983) participant framework allowed researchers to examine the social roles and power relationships that were constructed out of the roles participants came to play. For example, in the following example, students assume the role of teaching the teacher, when analyzing the meaning of the allusion to the golden child in the lyrics to "The Mask" by the Fugees:

T: What does he mean here, so
many fronts in his mouth I
thought he was the golden
child.

                        S 16, 17, 18: Gold teeth.

T: But...

16: That's like a big front anyway, cuz he got all this gold, all up in his mouth, and he just makin it his business to smile and let it be noticed.

T: But who is the golden child?

18: The golden child that little boy who...

16: Eddie Murphy played

17: In that movie (laugh)

T: So he's referring to something in a movie?

17: Yeah. (pause) You know how the golden child had all the power in the movie. (waits for a response) OK (laughs).

17: It was the movie. You ever seen the movie The Golden Child?

T: I'm listening.

16: Oh well that's... (laughs)

17: It was the movie where this little boy he had all the power. But I don't really think that he just directly referring to it. He just indirectly. Everybody know the Golden Child had all the power. But he said that he had all these fronts in his mouth and he's the Golden Child . . .

T: Umm, umm (no.)

16: Right, Golden Child, except you know he got gold teeth.

17: . . . He had all this gold in his mouth like he this Golden Child.

Accompanying the use of discourse analysis to examine episodes of literary reasoning was an analysis of how the artifacts being used within the discourse made certain opportunities possible. For example, because the students brought greater prior knowledge of the rap lyrics used as cultural data sets than the teacher, the power relationships (i.e., who could serve as sources of authoritative knowledge) in the construction of arguments were more equitable between teacher and students from the very beginning of instruction. The example just presented illustrates this. The norms for talk also came to function as mediating artifacts. When students became most intensely engaged in the literary problem solving, they immediately began to invoke AAVE discourse norms. They engaged in multiparty overlapping talk, often loud and characterized by a high use of prosody, gesture, and rhythmic tone. They used AAVE patterns such as narrative interspersion (Ball, 1992; Smitherman, 1977) to insert personal narratives in the middle of structured arguments in order to anchor the warrants on which their evidence was based. Lee (2001) argued that the cultural script that students shared about this form of talk provided forms of engagement that were meaningful to them, roles for them to play (the instigator in loud talking or marking) and forms of back channeling that sustained conversation across time (i.e., such as call and response). These uses of language as mediating artifacts or conventions were central to the activity system created in the Cultural Modeling classrooms. They served to link the local activity system of the classroom with broader levels of cultural contexts.

Finally, the researchers consciously sought to avoid the pitfall of selectively taking examples that support one's hypothesis as the qualitative data to be presented in the findings. Drawing again on the work of the Santa Barbara Discourse Group (Green & Dixon, 1994), the Cultural Modeling researchers developed graphs that represented the levels of literary argumentation across an entire unit of instruction. In this way, anyone can see the patterns in the data and examples that are chosen to be discussed can reasonably be argued to be representative and not idiosyncratic. The team graphed not only the level of literary reasoning within episodes, but also the levels of participation by students versus the teacher. This allowed the researchers to examine relationships between roles assumed by students, by teachers and the quality of argumentation. If the pattern had been that generally episodes of high literary reasoning were ones in which the teacher played the biggest role in moving the argument forward, and especially if this pattern persisted across time, then it could not be argued that the intervention in fact apprenticed the students to be able to engage in the practice without the teacher. In fact, among the most powerful findings of this research was the powerful role of students in constructing distributed arguments of literary reasoning. Because of the use of cultural data sets, students were able to engage in the practice with a high level of quality from the very beginning—a very different example of modeling from the traditional literature—and to then transfer those strategies that had heretofore been tacit to the examination of canonical literature.

The perspective of apprenticeship within CHAT allowed the researchers to document the role that cultural artifacts played. The intervention described focused explicitly on African-American cultural and language as mediational resources. The signifying dialogues, rap lyrics, rap videos, and film clips that were used as cultural data sets were ones with which the students were already very familiar. In their routine engagement with these cultural texts outside of school, these African-American adolescents invoke a literary aesthetic on uses of language. That is, what is important is not only the message or content, but equally important is the creative form that the language takes. This attitude toward language play has been heavily documented in the literature on African-American English, and other African and Africanized European languages (Morgan, 1993; Mufwene, Rickford, Bailey, & Baugh, 1998; Smitherman, 2000). This attitude toward language play is socialized within African communities from early childhood on and is reinforced through the music, the literature, and routine speech genres. The analysis of the discourse within the episodes of literary reasoning provided consistently strong evidence of the use of AAVE as a mode of communication and the aesthetic appreciation of language play as a tool for identifying stretches of text worth paying attention to.

There is still much research to be done investigating intersections among genres invoked in nonacademic settings and text based genres that are the focus of school subject matters. These out-of-school genres include rap and other forms of popular music, current spoken word traditions for poetry, speech genres within ethnically diverse speech communities, film and television medium, to name a few. It is clear that students who are not successful in school do problem solve with and through these popular genres in the social contexts of their family and peer networks. It is equally clear that literature, as one example, has always appropriated oral traditions. We believe that this orientation holds great promise for future literacy research.

LITERACIES UNLEASHED: USING CHAT IN THE STUDY OF REFLECTIVE WRITING AND TEACHER DEVELOPMENT

In this section, we describe one approach that involves the use of writing in the professional development of teachers. Literacies Unleashed provides a framework for the design of investigations of the transformative power of reflective writing as a tool for facilitating the development of teachers who are committed to using literacies in strategic ways to teach poor, underachieving and marginalized students, many of whom come from cultural and linguistic diversity backgrounds (Ball, 1992, 1999). Ball's (1998) work on Literacies Unleashed has focused on two themes: the writing of African-American students in formal and informal settings and the writing of teachers who are preparing to teach diverse student populations. This section reports on teachers' reflective writing as the target literacy domain that is a cultural tool used to mediate teachers' professional development. The premise of the research is that when teachers enter teacher education programs they bring with them preconceived notions about cultural and linguistic diversity. By engaging teachers in a carefully designed teacher education course as a local activity system, the teacher educator is able to broaden their perspectives on literacy and to facilitate their developing commitment to teach *all* students (Ball, 2000b). CHAT helps the researcher to identify the elements of the activity system on which she might collect data about the United States and South African teachers who are in the course, including the written artifacts produced by the teachers over time, audio- and videotapes of the dynamic discussions that challenge teachers' preconceived notions about literacies and about students, case studies of teaching experiences with diverse students, and the rules, other members of the community, and divisions of labor that support participation within the teacher education program and within the course (see Fig. 6.1). The reflective writing produced by the teachers were the primary source of data for this phase of the analysis because it allowed the researcher to document the teachers' changing perspectives on literacy and on teaching diverse students. The texts produced by the teachers over time provided insights concerning the teachers' thinking on these issues. Discourse and text analyses provided the researcher with a tool for exploring how teachers' developing commitment can be facilitated when intellectual activity is coupled with interactive participation in carefully designed classroom activities and for showing how those developing commitments are revealed in the teachers' developing discourse practices.

Ball's work draws on the work of Vygotsky (1978), Leont'ev (1981), and Luria (1981) to build a theoretical frame that helps to explain teachers' developing commitment and how those developing commitments are revealed in their oral and written discourses. Three central underlying themes of activity theory are important to this investigation: the idea that higher mental processes in individuals are originally found in social or external processes; the idea that mental processes can be understood only by understanding the tools and signs that mediate them; and the use of a developmental or genetic method of investigation in activity theory that allows us to see, describe, and explain the emergence and transformation of a psychological function (Wertsch, 1981, 1991). A very important theme for Vygotsky (1981) and other researchers in activity theory is that the higher intellectual processes are of central concern. In his investigations of higher intellectual processes, Vygotsky (1978) noted that the mechanism of individual developmental change is rooted in society and culture. He argued that there is an inherent relationship between external and internal activity, and that it is a developmental relationship in which the major issue is how external processes are transformed to create internal processes. Internalization is that process through which developing teachers move beyond the parroting of theory and practices toward internalization, reflection, and commitment (Ball, 2000c). In Leont'ev's (1981) words: "the process of internalization is not the (mere) transferal of an external activity to a preexisting, internal 'plane of consciousness': it is the process in which this plane is formed" (p. 57). According to Vygotsky, developmental functions move from the social to the psychological plane: "First it appears *between* people as an interpsychological category, and then *within* the [adult or] child as an intrapsychological category. This is equally true with regard to voluntary attention, logical memory, the formation of concepts, and the development of volition" (p. 163, italics added). Vygotsky's notion of internalization helps to explain the mechanisms that account for how teachers' perspectives on literacy and issues of diversity move from the interpsychological to the intrapsychological plane to become catalysts for developing commitment to teaching diverse students. This process of internalization can be facilitated and even transformed by engagement with meaningful theory and activities in teacher education programs coupled with the deep reflective activity that is prompted by writing.

A second critical theme in activity theory is the notion that human action is mediated by signs and tools—primarily psychological tools such as language. The facilitation of language used within a local activity system, then, is the predominant means by which people make sense or meaning. In this research, written reflections and dynamic oral discussions that the teachers engaged in throughout the course served this meaning making function as the teachers in this teacher education course used reflective writing, challenging discussions and literacy-based activities to confront issues of literacy and diversity in their own lives and in the teaching and learning of others. Ball proposed that, as teachers talked about and then wrote about the theory and their own authentic teaching activities in the presence of peers and supportive instructors, they would become metacognitively aware of the perceptions they brought into the course and that they would come to challenge their preconceived notions about teaching diverse student populations. Engagement in these activities allowed teachers to begin to stretch themselves to consider different perspectives and new possibilities for their future teaching. As they contemplated theoretical issues—new material, new concepts, new conditions—that related to teaching for diversity, as they engaged with these issues through writing, and as they struggled to implement these theoretical notions in their research and authentic teaching situations, they voiced their changing perspectives in the language they used in their daily journals, reflective essay writing and classroom discussions. According to Bakhtin (1981):

> . . . there is a struggle constantly being waged [within us] to overcome the official line, . . . a struggle against various kinds and degrees of

authority. In this process, our discourse . . . does not remain in an isolated and static condition. It gets drawn into the contact zone, and
develops as it is applied to new material, new conditions; as it enters
into interanimating relationships with new contexts. . . . More than
that, it enters into an intense interaction, a *struggle* with other internally persuasive discourse. Our ideological development is just such an
intense struggle within us for hegemony among various available verbal
and ideological points of view, approaches, directions and values. (see
pp. 345-346)

By analyzing the texts that the teachers produced, Ball was able to better
understand their mental processes (their changing perspectives and developing commitments and ideologies) as she better understood the tools and
signs (the language) they used to mediate them.

Finally, according to activity theory, the developmental or genetic
method of investigation allows us to see, describe, and explain the emergence of psychological function. Vygotsky felt that any phenomenon
could be captured through studying its origin and development. His insistence on using a developmental or genetic analysis when examining human
mental functions meant that, for him, the major route to understanding the
mind was to specify the origin of mental functions and the transformations
they have undergone as they develop. Thus, activity theory asks us to look
at what is uniquely human in behavior and to trace its emergence. The
uniquely human behavior that Ball investigates is the teachers' changing
perspectives concerning the teaching of culturally and linguistically diverse
students. She investigates that process by focusing on the written activities
that took place in the teacher education course and noting the emerging
discourse practices that develop as a result of the teachers' engagements in
that course—since the development of higher mental functions takes place
first on an external plane before they become internalized. Ball's investigation focused on the written activities of these teachers because, according
to Langer and Applebee (1987), the active nature of writing provides a
medium for a student's exploration and thinking through new relationships among ideas. Ball used writing as a tool to facilitate the teachers' con-
templation of new relationships among ideas and new possibilities for their
teaching. Langer and Applebee further noted that the role of writing in
thinking can be conceptualized as a medium that allows the writer to
retrieve, rethink, reorganize, revise, and reconceptualize their ideas over an
extended period. It has been found that writing about a topic fosters
thoughtful examination and further learning. Studies of learning and writing provide clear evidence that activities involving writing lead to better
learning than activities involving reading and studying alone; that different
types of writing activity lead students to focus on different kinds of information in different ways; and that writing leads to quantitatively and qual-

itatively different kinds of knowledge attainment (Anderson & Biddle, 1975; Michael & Maccoby, 1961; Newell, 1984; Scardamalia & Bereiter, 1985). Based on these findings, Ball recognized that, within our activity system, writing served as one of the artifacts teachers used as a tool to problem solve as they moved toward the overarching goal or object of the activity, becoming effective teachers with a commitment to teaching diverse student populations. Drawing on the developmental method used in activity theory, Ball observed the teachers' initial conceptions and their developing perspectives as psychological processes and she designed her investigation to focus on all of the course activities at both a social and a psychological or cognitive level. In doing so, she confirmed what, we must realize that, according to Scribner and Beach (1993) said: "that which is experienced socially is cognitively re-experienced in a newly reorganized form." Thus, she recommended that teacher education programs focus on providing activities that engage teachers at a social as well as a psychological or cognitive level. Writing is a tool that is well suited for accomplishing this goal.

Ball's research was designed to investigate how teachers move beyond surface-level engagements with theory and best practices in teacher education programs toward transformative engagements that lead them to take positions of reflective commitment that can guide them in their decisions to become effective teachers of culturally and linguistically diverse students. To address this question, she collected the written texts of more than 100 U.S. and South African teachers that she taught over a 3-year period. The written texts that she collected were written by these U.S. and South African teachers to reflect their developing perspectives on literacy and teaching during a course that she taught them. The data included the teachers' narrative essays of their own literacy experiences, journal entries, reflections they wrote in response to carefully selected course readings and course experiences, and transcripts of classroom discussions. Ball hypothesized that, as teachers write reflectively on important and challenging issues while they are being exposed to strategically designed readings and activities within a teacher education program, their perspectives on literacy and commitments to teaching diverse student populations would be affected in positive ways. The research was designed to explore how teachers' developing perspectives and commitments can be facilitated by particular classroom activities and how those developing perspectives and commitments are revealed in their written discourses.

Building on her previous research that provided teachers with a knowledge base and strategies for teaching students who speak nonprestige varieties of English (Ball, 1992, 1995a, 1995c, 19998, 2000a), this study investigates U.S. and South African teachers' changing perspectives on what it means for a person to be literate and reveals evidences of their developing commitment. These U.S. and South African teachers were exposed to a course that she designed to give them opportunities to consider the role and function of literacies in their lives and the lives of others and to consider how literacies could be used strategically to teach diverse students more effectively. The course introduced developing teachers to a range of theoretical frameworks and best practices that undergird effective teaching of diverse students, teaching experiences and the production of literacy case studies on diverse students, engaging in dynamic class discussions that challenged teachers preconceived notions about literacies and diverse students, and providing teachers a safe environment where they could question and reflectively write about their changing notions about literacy and its use in teaching all students more effectively. Of critical importance, these teachers were given frequent opportunities to engage in reflective writing activities as they engaged in the other carefully designed activities.

Of particular interest in this research are the transformations that occur in the teachers' written discourses over time as they engage in this well-designed activity system. The goal or object of this research was to investigate the transformative power of reflective writing as a tool for facilitating the development of teachers to become committed to using literacies in strategic ways to teach poor, underachieving, and marginalized students, many of whom come from cultural and linguistically diversity backgrounds. In their research, Scribner and Cole questioned the frailty of the evidence for generalizations about the cognitive consequences of writing. Within today's context of the demands of multiliteracies, Ball revisited and reframed their question to investigate the influence that writing—in conjunction with other activities—can have on teachers changing perspectives concerning diverse students and their desire to work with them. Some scholars have concerned themselves with theoretical conjectures on the cognitive consequences of writing. Vygotsky (1962) considered that writing involved a different set of psychological functions from oral speech. Greenfield (1968) suggested that written language in the schools is the basis for the development of "context-independent abstract thought"—the distinguishing feature of school-related intellectual skills. Scribner (1968) speculated that mastery of a written language system might underlie formal scientific operations of the type Piaget investigated. Olson (1975) argued that experience with written text may lead to a mode of thinking that derives generalizations about reality from purely linguistic, as contrasted to, empirical operations.

Ball proposed that the reflective writing that occurred within this activity system would serve to ignite thoughtful reflection about recreating their future classrooms to become spaces, for not only for tolerating the presence of cultural and linguistic diversity, but for validating and building on the language and literacy practices that students bring into the classroom.

When most of these teachers entered the course, they brought with them very limited perspectives about cultural and linguistic diversity, its relationship to literacy in our society, and its role in their classrooms. It was hoped that through engagements with strategically designed course readings and activities (activities that included challenging in-class discussions, adolescent case study projects, and teaching in diverse classrooms) coupled with sustained reflective writing experiences, teachers enrolled in the course would begin to give serious consideration to the possibility of using literacies in strategic ways to teach language-diverse students. By the end of the course, transformations had occurred in these teachers' perspectives about what it meant for a person to be literate and about ways they could build on students' home language and literacy patterns to more effectively teach content area materials to students from diverse backgrounds such that all students would have access to educational success. Indicators of these teachers' transformed perspectives were the changes in their discourses, the broadened definitions of literacies they wrote about in their journals, and the plans they made for using a range of language and literacy activities in their future classrooms. One student in the program wrote the following:

> I came into this course arrogant and self-assured. Critical thinking had always been my forte; it has been my natural disposition to try and search for deeper meaning and deeper truths. I began with my personal essay about "what I wanted to do for the rest of my life." And in this way I began the course, with a love for literature, arrogance from acquired knowledge, and hope for a glorious future. . . . Our class had engaging discussions on critical thinking, on critical reading, communicating with students, and lots of activities. And then I read an article that stated: "The life experience of teachers stem from their beliefs and belief structures . . . these belief structures strongly affect the literacy practices a teacher may use . . ." I began to ask lots of questions: Is this a sin? Is there an escape from such personal biases?
>
> And from then on, my arrogance began to deflate. I began to realize my potential role within these students' lines. I was introduced to things I had never even considered. What if my students cannot read? How will they internalize this lack of skill? Who will they become as adults? How can I change this? How can I become the teacher I want to be? I began trying to see through the student's eyes, trying to remember what it was like to be like them. The reading I have done for this class have elucidated cobwebs of half thoughts and have finished solutions that had begun in my head. . . . In this way my thinking has evolved, going down various allies of hypotheses, analyzing potential results, and choosing what to incorporate or not to incorporate from my new research into my future practice as a teacher. . . . And one would think that exposure to such future scenarios of "what if" and

"what to do next" would calm my anxieties. But . . . I am anxious about having been ignorant and insensitive to certain students. . . . I am afraid to make the wrong moves just as I am excited to make the right one. But in the end, I take my future position . . . as a privilege to have the opportunity to help mold the wet clay that will one day become fine art. . . . I do not see myself as an English teacher, but a teacher of life, an educator of human emotions, of human relationships, and human history. I believe the subject at question is not the literature but the many diverse students that I will be teaching. It is their minds that I am exploring and trying to expand.

This student came to the course with preconceived notions about literacy and diversity. Her engagement with the theory and activities that were planned for her in the course—including an online tutoring project, face-to-face mentoring activities, her own tutoring and peer-counseling activities, challenging classroom discussions, and an abundance of reflective writing activities—served as a catalyst that helped her to seriously consider the challenges of teaching diverse students. The course activities, which engage the teachers at a social as well as a psychological level, challenged her to seriously consider some important issues that are reflected in her developing discourse.

In his work on "psychological tools" or "mediating means," Vygotsky made his most extensive and concrete comments on mediation in connection with natural language, but his list of psychological tools also included "various systems for counting, mnemonic techniques, algebraic symbol systems, works of art, writing, schemes, diagrams, maps, and mechanical drawings, conventional signs" (Vygotsky, 1981, p. 137). Fundamental to his understanding of the role of mediational means was the assumption that "by being included in the structure of mental behavior, the psychological tool alters the entire flow and structure of mental functions. It does this by determining the structure of a new instrumental act" (Vygotsky, 1981, p. 137). In such a view, the introduction of a psychological tool such as writing in collaboration with other well-designed activities within an activity system leads to an important transformation or even a redefinition of that action. Vygotsky's line of reasoning is grounded in an analysis of how various influences come into contact and transform action. In the "instrumental act" of engagement with strategically designed activities that include reflective writing, discussions that challenge preconceived notions about language diversity, engagement with sound theory and teaching practices, and teaching activities with diverse students as part of a teacher education program, neither the individual nor the mediating means function in isolation, and if examined in isolation neither would provide adequate foundations for an account of the action that takes place—transformations in teachers attitudes concerning their work with diverse students.

Vygotsky's (1982a, 1982b, 1982c, 1983, 1984) thesis about the human mind postulates an object in transformation and suggests that methods adequate for studying this must themselves also constantly undergo transformation. From this perspective, CHAT systems and the complexes of symbolic mediation they incorporate are particularly well suited for this research. Building on Saussure, for whom signs are the formal means of correspondence between phonetic representation and representations of the world, we realize that teachers in teacher education programs internalize the knowledge they gain by engaging in meaningful ways with theory and best practices, teaching interactions with diverse students, and challenging discussions with their peers and others concerning literacies and diversity learners. As this new knowledge is taken up and internalized by teachers, this itself makes up a filter for their access to the world. As this human activity mediated by oral and written language develops and changes, the teachers' reflective written language also tends to change and becomes channeled into different forms of discourses. In her analysis of the written discourses of the teachers in the teacher education program, Ball noticed that the teachers' attitudes and perspectives toward language diversity were transformed over time. According to Bronckart (1995), discourses are the modalities for structuring language activity; they tell the world while acting within it (p. 81). . . . [I]ndividual discourses give situations of action a meaning and constitutes the most objective outline of the actual activity and interpretation of human action (p. 82). The discourse analysis that is used as an analytic lens in this research looks at the social context of production, the content of a vast body of oral and written texts produced by U.S. and South African teachers, and in-depth study of the linguistic units that appear in the texts. Activity theory has the conceptual and methodological potential to be a pathbreaker in studies that help us understand how the thoughtful introduction of new cultural tools into the activity systems of teacher education programs can inevitably transform it.

CONCLUSIONS

Although the research of Lee and Ball target different audiences, they share the goal of drawing on the cultural models that learners bring to the literate tasks and concepts they are learning. Both programs of research conceptualize cultural funds of knowledge constituted outside the academy as strategic resources for both teaching and learning. Because learning in any setting is always complex and dynamic, both researchers have found CHAT a useful tool for both design and analysis. Because literate practices are a common target for both programs of research and, the tools of literate practices serve as dialogic mediational artifacts, CHAT provides concepts and strategies for studying the transformations that occur for both teachers and students.

ENDNOTES

1. The Cultural Modeling Project reported in this chapter was funded by the Spencer Foundation and the McDonnell Foundation's Cognitive Studies in Education, Carol D. Lee, principal investigator. The Literacies Unleashed research reported in this chapter was funded by the Spencer Foundation, Arnetha F. Ball, principal investigator. Comments made in this chapter do not necessarily reflect the funding agencies.
2. The family of related frameworks includes cultural psychology, situated cognition, distributed cognition, sociocultural theory, and cultural-historical-activity theory. The distinctions among them are not relevant to our general argument.
3. Signifying is a genre of talk within African-American English that involves ritual insult and a high use of figurative language and double entendre.
4. As part of the Cultural Modeling intervention involving the entire English department of an urban high school, Carol Lee taught one high school English class each year. This citation references a class taught by Carol Lee.
5. We acknowledge that videotaping always involves perspective taking (Goldman-Segall, 1998).

REFERENCES

Anderson, R. C., & Biddle, B. W. (1975). On asking people questions about what they are reading. In G. Bower (Ed.), *The psychology of learning and motivation* (Vol. 9). New York: Academic Press.

Au, K. H. (1980). Participation structures in a reading lesson with Hawaiian children: Analysis of a culturally appropriate instructional event. *Anthropology and Education, 11*(2), 91-115.

Bakhtin, M. M. (1981). *The dialogic imagination: Four essays by M. M. Bakhtin* (M. Holquist, Ed.). Austin: University of Texas Press.

Bahktin, M. M. (1986). *Speech genres and other late essays.* Austin: University of Texas Press.

Ball, A. F. (1992). Cultural preferences and the expository writing of African-American adolescents. *Written Communication, 9*(4), 501-532.

Ball, A. F. (1995ba). Community based learning in an urban setting as a model for educational reform. *Applied Behavioral Science Review, 3*, 127-146.

Ball, A. F. (1995b). Investigating language, learning, and linguistic competence of African-American children: Torrey revisited. *Linguistics and Education, 7*(1), 23-46.

Ball, A. F. (1995c). Text design patterns in the writing of urban African-American students: Teaching to the strengths of students in multicultural settings. *Urban Education, 30*, 253-289.

Ball, A. F. (1998). *Literacies unleashed: Expanding community-based discourse practices and instilling a passion to write in urban at-risk youth and their teachers* (unpublished School of Education Project Report). Ann Arbor: University of Michigan.

Ball, A. F. (1999). Evaluating the writing of culturally and linguistically diverse students: The case of the African American Vernacular English speaker. In C. R. Cooper & L. Odell (Eds.), *Evaluating writing: The role of teachers' knowledge about text, learning, and culture* (pp. 225-248). Urbana, IL: National Council of Teachers of English Press.

Ball, A. F. (2000a). Empowering pedagogies that enhance the learning of multicultural students. *Teachers College Record, 102*(6), 1006-1034.

Ball, A. F. (2000b). Preparing teachers for diversity: Lessons learned from the U.S. and South Africa. *Teaching and Teacher Education, 16*, 491-509 (Special Issue on Preparing Teachers for Diversity).

Ball, A. F. (2000c). Preservice teachers' perspectives on literacy and its use in urban schools: A Vygotskian perspective on internal activity and teacher change. In C. Lee & P. Smagorinsky (Eds.), *Worlds of meaning: Vygotskian perspectives on literacy research* (pp. 314-359). Cambridge, MA: Cambridge University Press.

Bereiter, C., & Engelmann, S. (1966). *Teaching disadvantaged children in preschool*. Englewood Cliffs, NJ: Prentice-Hall.

Cole, M. (1996). *Cultural psychology, A once and future discipline*. Cambridge, MA: The Belknap Press of Harvard University Press.

Collins, A., Brown, J. S., & Holum, A. (1991, Winter). Cognitive apprenticeship: Making thinking visible. *American Educator*, 6-91.

D'Andrade, R. (1987). A folk model of the mind. D. Holland & N. Quinn (Eds.), *Cultural models in language and thought* (pp. 112-147). New York: Cambridge University Press.

D'Andrade, R. (1990). Some propositions about the relationship between culture and human cognition. In R. A. Shweder & G. Herdt (Eds.), *Cultural psychology: Essays on comparative human development*. New York: Cambridge University Press.

Engeström, Y., Miettinen, R., & Punamaki, R-L. (1999). *Perspectives on activity theory*. New York: Cambridge University Press.

Foster, M. (1987). *"It's Cookin' Now": An ethnographic study of a successful black teacher in an urban community college*. Unpublished doctoral dissertation, Harvard University, Cambridge, MA.

Gilyard, K. (1991). *Voices of the self: A study of language competence*. Detroit, MI: Wayne State University Press.

Goffman, E. (1974). *Frame analysis: An essay on the organization of experience.* New York: Harper & Row.

Goldman-Segall, R. (1998). *Points of viewing children's thinking: A digital ethnographer's journey.* Mahwah, NJ: Erlbaum.

Goody, J. (Ed.). (1968). *Literacy in traditional societies.* New York: Cambridge University Press.

Green, J. L., & Dixon, C. N. (1994). Talking knowledge into being: Discursive and social practices in classrooms. *Linguistics and Education, 5*(3 & 4), 231-239.

Greeno, J. G. (1997). Response: On claims that answer the wrong questions. *Educational Researcher, 26*(1), 5-17.

Gutierrez, K., Baquedano-Lopez, P., & Tejeda, C. (1999, April). *Rethinking diversity: Hybridity and hybrid language practices in the third space.* Paper presented at the annual meeting of the American Educational Research Association, Denver, CO.

Gutierrez, K., Rymes, B., & Larson, J. (1995). Script, counterscript, and underlife in the classroom: James Brown versus Brown v. Board of Education. *Harvard Educational Review, 65*(3), 445-471.

Heath, S. B. (1983). *Ways with words: Language, life and work in communities and classrooms.* New York: Cambridge University Press.

Hernstein R. J., & Murray, C. (1994). *The bell curve: Intelligence and class structure in American life.* New York: The Free Press.

Jensen, A. (1969). How much can we boost IQ and scholastic achievement. *Harvard Educational Review, 39,* 1-123.

Kitwana, B. (2002). *The hip hop generation: Young Blacks and the crisis in African American culture.* New York: BasicCivitas Books.

Kuhn, D. (1991). *The skills of argument.* New York: Cambridge University Press.

Langer, J. A., & Applebee, A. N. (1987). *How writing shapes thinking: A study of teaching and learning.* Urbana, IL: National Council of Teachers English.

Lave, J. (1977). Cognitive consequences of traditional apprenticeship training in West Africa. *Anthropology and Education Quarterly, 8,* 177-180.

Lee, C. D. (1993). *Signifying as a scaffold for literary interpretation: The pedagogical implications of an African American discourse genre* (Research Rep. Series). Urbana, IL: National Council of Teachers of English.

Lee, C. D. (1994). The complexities of African centered pedagogy. In M. Shujaa (Ed.), *Too much schooling, too little education: A paradox in African-American life* (pp. 295-318). Trenton, NJ: Africa World Press.

Lee, C. D. (1995a). A culturally based cognitive apprenticeship: Teaching African American high school students' skills in literary interpretation. *Reading Research Quarterly, 30*(4), 608-631.

Lee, C. D. (1995b). Signifying as a scaffold for literary interpretation. *Journal of Black Psychology, 21*(4), 357-381.

Lee, C. D. (1997). Bridging home and school literacies: A model of culturally responsive teaching. In J. Flood, S. B. Heath, & D. Lapp (Eds.), *A handbook for literacy educators: Research on teaching the communicative and visual arts* (pp. 330-341). New York: Macmillan.

Lee, C. D. (1998, April). *Supporting the development of interpretive communities through metacognitive instructional conversations in culturally diverse class-*

rooms. Paper presented at the annual conference of the American Educational Research Association, Nashville, TN.

Lee, C.D. (2000). Signifying in the zone of proximal development. In C.D. Lee & P. Smagorinsky (Eds.), *Vygotskian perspectives on literacy research: Constructing meaning through collaborative inquiry* (pp. 191-225). New York: Cambridge University Press.

Lee, C.D. (2001). Is October Brown Chinese: A cultural modeling activity system for underachieving students. *American Educational Research Journal, 38*(1), 97-142.

Lee, C.D., & Majors, Y.J. (2000, April). *Cultural modeling's response to Rogoff's challenge: Understanding apprenticeship, guided participation and participatory appropriation in a culturally responsive, subject matter specific context.* Paper presented at the annual meeting of the American Educational Research Association, New Orleans, LA.

Leont'ev, A.N. (1981). The problem of activity in psychology. In J.V. Wertsch (Ed.), *The concept of activity in Soviet psychology* (pp. 37-71). Armonk, NY: Sharpe.

Luria, A.R. (1981). *Language and cognition* (J.V. Wertsch, Ed.). New York: Wiley Intersciences.

Mahiri, J. (1998). *Shooting for excellence: African American and youth culture in new century schools.* New York: Teachers College Press and National Council of Teachers of English.

Mercado, C.I., & Moll, L.C. (1997). The study of funds of knowledge: Collaborative research in Latino homes. *CENTRO, Journal of the Center for Puerto Rican Studies, 9*(1), 27-42.

Michael, D.N., & Maccoby, N. (1961). Factors influencing the effects of student participation on verbal learning from films. In A. A. Lumsdaine (Ed.), *Student response in programmed instruction.* Washington, DC: National Academy of Sciences.

Mitchell-Kernan, C. (1981). Signifying, loud-talking and marking. In A. Dundes (Ed.), *Mother wit from the laughing barrel* (pp. 310-328). Englewood Cliffs, NJ: Prentice-Hall.

Moll, L., & Greenberg, J.B. (1990). Creating zones of possibilities: Combining social contexts for instruction. In L. Moll (Ed.), *Vygotsky and education: Instructional implications and applications of sociohistorical psychology* (pp. 319-348). New York: Cambridge University Press.

Morgan, M. (1993). The Africaness of counterlanguage among Afro-Americans. In S. Mufwene (Ed.), *Africanism in Afro-American language varieties.* Athens: University of Georgia Press.

Morgan, M. (1998). More than a mood or an attitude: Discourse and verbal genres in African American culture. In S.S. Mufwene, J.R. Rickford, & G. Bailey (Eds.), *African-American English: Structure, history, and use* (pp. 251-281). New York: Routledge.

Mufwene, S. (Ed.). (1993). *Africanisms in Afro-American language varieties.* Athens: The University of Georgia Press.

Mufwene, S.S., Rickford, J.R., Bailey, G., & Baugh, J. (1998). *African-American English: Structure, history, and use.* New York: Routledge.

Newell, G. (1984). Learning from writing in two content areas: A case study/protocol analysis of writing to learn. *Research in the Teaching of Learning, 18*(3), 265-287.

Nieto, S. (Ed.). (2000). *Puerto Rican students in U.S. schools.* Mahwah, NJ: Erlbaum.

Nunes, T., Schliemann, A. D., & Carraher, D. W. (1993). *Street mathematics and school mathematics.* New York: Cambridge University Press.

O'Connor, M. C., & Michaels, S. (1993). Aligning academic task and participation status through revoicing: Analysis of a classroom discourse strategy. *Anthropology and Education Quarterly, 24*(4), 318-335.

Ong, W. (1982). *Orality and literacy.* New York: Methuen.

Perkins, D. N. (1993). Person-plus: A distributed view of thinking and learning. In G. Salomon (Ed.), *Distributed cognitions: Psychological and educational considerations.* New York: Cambridge University Press.

Phillips, S. U. (1983). *The invisible culture: Communication in classroom and community on the Warm Springs Indian Reservation.* New York: Longman.

Reyes, M. (1991, April). *The "one size fits all" approach to literacy.* Paper presented at the annual conference of the American Educational Research Association, Chicago, IL.

Rickford, J., & Rickford, A. (1976). Cut-eye and suck teeth: African words and gestures in new world guise. *Journal of American Folklore, 89*(353), 194-309.

Rogoff, B. (1990). *Apprenticeship in thinking: Cognitive development in social context.* New York: Oxford University Press.

Rogoff, B. (1995). Observing sociocultural activity and three planes: Participatory appropriation, guided participation, and apprenticeship. In J. Wertsch, P. del Rio, & A. Alvarez (Eds.), *Sociocultural studies of mind* (pp. 139-164). New York: Cambridge University Press.

Rogoff, B., & Lave, J. (Eds.). (1984). *Everyday cognition: Its development in social context.* Cambridge, MA: Harvard University Press.

Saxe, G. (1991). *Culture and cognitive development: Studies in mathematical understanding.* Hillsdale, NJ: Erlbaum.

Scardamalia, M., & Bereiter, C. (1985). Development of dialectical processes in composition. In D. Olson, N. Torrance, & A. Hildyard (Eds.), *Literacy, language, and learning.* New York: Cambridge University Press.

Schank, R. C., & Abelson, R. P. (1977). *Scripts, plans, goals, and understanding: An inquiry into human knowledge structures.* Hillsdale, NJ: Erlbaum.

Scribner, S. (1968). *The cognitive consequences of literacy.* Unpublished manuscript. Reprinted in *The Quarterly Newsletter of the Laboratory of Comparative Human Cognition,* October 1992.

Scribner, S., & Beach, K. (1993). An activity theory approach to memory. *Applied Cognitive Psychology, 7*(3), 185-90.

Scribner, S., & Cole, M. (1981). *The psychology of literacy.* Cambridge, MA: Harvard University Press.

Smith, M., & Hillocks, G. (1988, October). Sensible sequencing: Developing knowledge about literature text by text. *English Journal,* 44-49.

Smitherman, G. (2000). *Talkin that talk: Language, culture and education in African America.* New York: Routledge.

Tharp, R., & Gallimore, R. (1988). *Rousing minds to life: Teaching, learning, and schooling in social context.* New York: Cambridge University Press.

Toulmin, S., Rieke, R., & Janik, A. (1984). *An introduction to reasoning.* New York: Macmillan.

Valdes, G. (1996). *Con respeto: Bridging the distances between culturally diverse families and schools.* New York: Teachers College Press.

Vygotsky, L. (1978). *Mind in society: The development of higher psychological processes* (M. Cole, V. John-Steiner, S. Scribner, & E. Souberman, eds.). Cambridge, MA: Harvard University Press.

Vygotsky, L. S. (1981). The genesis of higher mental functions. In J. Wertsch, *The concept of activity in Soviet psychology* (pp. 144-188). Armonk, NY: Sharpe.

Wertsch, J. V. (1981). *The concept of activity in Soviet psychology.* Armonk, NY: M. E. Sharpe.

Wertsch, J. (1991). *Voices of the mind: A sociocultural approach to mediated action.* Cambridge, MA: Harvard University Press.

Wertsch, J., del Rio, P., & Alvarez, A. (1995). *Sociocultural studies of mind.* New York: Cambridge University Press.

Zinchenko, P. I. (1981). Involuntary memory and the goal-directed nature of activity. In J. V. Wertsch (Ed.), *The concept of activity in Soviet psychology* (pp. 300-340). White Plains, NY: Sharpe. (Original work published 1962)

7

Participating in Emergent Socioliterate Worlds

Genre, Disciplinarity, Interdisciplinarity

Charles Bazerman
University of California, Santa Barbara

Paul Prior
University of Illinois, Urbana

This chapter presents a new view of literate interaction and the role of the texts that mediate such interactions. It is a view that places genre at a central nexus of discourse practices and that sees discourse practices as a key constituent of social practices. It is a view that has appeared in varied fields, including developmental psychology (e.g., Dore, 1989; P. Miller, Hengst, Alexander, & Sperry, 2000), speech pathology (Hengst & Miller, 1999), sociology (Bergmann & Luckmann, 1994; Devault & McCoy, 2001; Guenthner & Knoblauch, 1995; Luckmann 1986; D. Smith, 1990, 1998), and anthropology (e.g., Bauman, 1992; Duranti, 1994; Hanks, 1987, 2000). However, it has been particularly central to literacy researchers across varied contexts (e.g., Bazerman, 1988, 1994b, 1999a, 2000a, 2000b, 2001b, 2001c; Berkenkotter, 2001; Berkenkotter & Huckin, 1985; Berkenkotter & Ravatos, 1997; Besnier, 1995; Bhatia, 1993; Chapman, 1994, 1995; Dias, Freedman, Medway, & Pare, 1999; Freedman, Adams, & Smart, 1994; Freedman & Medway, 1994; Kamberelis, 1999, 2001: Kamberlis & Scott, 1992; C. Miller & Selzer, 1985; Prior, 1998; Russell, 1997; Schryer, 1993;

Swales, 1990, 1998; Winsor, 1999). As in any emergent view, there are substantial differences among the details of the various theorists and investigators, and even a single expositor's view will vary or be elaborated from one text to another. The version presented here represents only a view negotiated between the two authors for the current text, but should give some of the flavor of the enterprise. This view of genre has drawn deeply on several fields, especially linguistic anthropology, sociolinguistics, phenomenological sociology, and sociocultural psychology. However, the value of this perspective has arisen most clearly out of historical challenges facing two fields related to literacy education—second-language education and composition-rhetoric.

The role of language theory, research, and pedagogy in varied contexts of literacy education entered a period of creative tension in the 1970s. The rise of Chomskyan linguistics in the 1960s had fostered great interest in questions of language; however, Chomsky's theories had addressed national languages (like English) only in their most abstract and structural senses (Chomsky, 1965). Educators who sought to apply this new science of language to their classes and researchers who sought to understand language as it was being used in specific cultural contexts quickly ran up against the limits of such abstract, structuralist accounts of national languages. Responding to a complex of forces, second- and foreign-language educators began to turn their attention from describing and promoting general language competence to a concern for the specific varieties of language in use in specific situations, to exploring how the resources of language were organized to achieve certain social functions (like promising, requesting, asking for information) and express certain cultural notions (like expressing feelings, talking about time or politics). With accelerating globalization, special purpose language courses blossomed at all levels, not only courses in restricted language domains such as maritime English, but also in complex and open-ended disciplinary knowledge domains, like medical English and English for academic purposes (EAP).

During roughly the same period, the teaching of writing in U.S. higher education underwent an institutional and disciplinary resurgence. As a modern descendent of European traditions of rhetorical education, composition programs in U.S. colleges had assumed an ongoing responsibility toward instruction in academic writing throughout the 1900s, with a particular growth during the post-World War II expansion of the university population. In the late 1960s and early 1970s, the size and diversity of the student population in higher education increased, bringing urgency to instruction in writing and an increasing sense of professionalism to the task. A new discipline especially oriented to college writing instruction, mainly within English departments, drew on classical rhetoric, psychology, and linguistics to inform its practice, theory, and research. Early attention was focused on the textual characteristics of student writing (Shaughnessy, 1977), the rhetorical situations and purposes of academic writing functions carried out by writing in academic and professional settings (Bitzer, 1968; Booth, 1963; Corbett, 1965), and the characteristics of academic and other texts that identified them as good writing (Christensen, 1967; Shaughnessy, 1977).

In its initial phase, research and theory in composition moved from a language- and text-based approach concerned with sentence form and textual organization (current-traditional rhetoric) to a process approach allied with personal expression, cognitive processes, and literacy development. With cognitive psychology providing the initial theoretical and methodological framework for the study of process, the development of a strong research agenda on writing processes turned attention away from the form and functions of the written text and to an isolated, individual process (Flower & Hayes, 1981, 1984). Such studies also turned attention away form the social contexts within which texts operated, as researchers attempted to identify general characteristics of novice and expert writers (Flower & Hayes, 1981; Geisler, 1994). By the mid-1980s, however, social and critical approaches to literacy began to supplant studies of cognitive processes in laboratory settings (see Nystrand, Greene, & Weimelt, 1993). Critical approaches pointed to the complexly intertwined links of ideology, power, and identity with literate practices and values (Bartholomae, 1985; Berlin, 1987; Bizell, 1992; Lunsford, Moglen, & Slevin, 1990; Street, 1984), whereas social approaches began detailed examination of the varied processes and contexts of writing in naturalistic cultural settings schools, laboratories, workplaces, home, and community (e.g., Barton & Ivanic, 1991; Brodkey, 1987; Heath, 1983; Herrington, 1985, 1988; Michaels, 1987; C Miller & Selzer, 1985; Paradis, Dobrin, & Miller, 1985; Rymer, 1988; Taylor & Dorsey-Gaines, 1988). Pedagogically, cross-curricular language programs in colleges (especially the writing-across-the-curriculum movement in the United States) began to feel tensions between generic advice about style, organization, process, and discipline- and workplace-specific practices. Because of their dual orientation to preparing students for future workplaces and course work in technical and scientific disciplines, technical writing programs became particularly concerned about how literate practice was specific to particular forms of professional practice.

In both applied language studies and the teaching of writing,[1] general approaches to language and literacy education encountered an expanding domain of complexly differentiated language use in academic disciplines and the workplace. The historical emergence of this domain first became evident in the 18th century (Foucault, 1970; Hoskin, 1993; Hoskin & Macve, 1993; Luhmann 1983; A. Smith, 1976), but grew in intensity in the 20th century (Geisler, 1994; Pickering, 1993; Prior, 1998).[2] The closing decades of the 10th century, however, also brought blurring, cracking, and interpenetration of disciplinarity most often labeled interdisciplinarity (Geertz, 1983; Klein, 1990, 1993, 1996; Prior, 1997).

> The fracturing or fissioning of disciplines into new specialities has been the dominant pattern of knowledge growth in the twentieth century. Yet there have been more breakups and recombinations throughout the sciences over the past three decades than in the previous millenium. Moreover, innovative scholars increasingly cross the boundaries of formal disciplines. (Klein, 1993, p. 192)

Paradoxically, Klein pointed out, as knowledge and disciplinary formations become increasingly specialized, they are also attaining greater global reach and displaying relentless permeations and mixings at the boundaries "that separate one discipline from another (physics from chemistry, history from anthropology), disciplinary groupings (hard versus soft, pure versus applied), and larger institutional constructs (the university, industry, government, and society)" (p. 186).

The expansion of disciplinarity-interdisciplinarity and expertise was accompanied by changes in participation—not only the increased movement of varied social groups into systems of (higher) education but also internationalization of both education and disciplines. New workplaces were increasingly geographically dispersed (a trend now referred to as globalization), textually mediated, and enmeshed in a growing array of media technologies (Bazerman, 1999a; Bolter & Grusin, 1999; Hoskin & Macve, 1993; Orlikowski & Yates, 1994; Yates & Orlikowski, 1992). These developments called for theoretical and methodological tools that would be sensitive to the varieties of language used in specific sociocultural settings, that would address the many dimensions of difference as well as the broad commonalities of language in use. For literacy theory, research, and instruction, this need has most often been addressed since the 1980s through an exploration of genres and their situated use. Genre, in short, has become not merely a central site for recognition of disciplinary and other social difference, but a site where the sociohistorical effects of the expanding domains of disciplinarity are being registered.

Although genre may first have been viewed by many as simply conventional text types, as genres began to be examined more deeply they came to be seen as signaling much deeper multidimensional differences of situation, interaction, and meaning. This new understanding starts from the recognition that texts are as interactional and social in character as any utterance (e.g., Brandt, 1990). Mediation of the utterance in written form creates possibilities for interactional displacement across space and time as well as multiplication of sites of appearance. A single text may mediate numerous interactions at multiple sites and times. Of course, the potential durability, mobility, and seeming fixedness of the artifact does not necessarily stabilize the meaning and interaction. In fact, meaning and interaction may be even more problematic. Because human symbolic or linguistic sense-making seems to have evolved from coordination of co-presence—that is, creatures observing or otherwise sensing each other's presence and acting with that knowledge (see Carruthers & Chamberlain, 2000; Deacon, 1997; Goody, 1995), our sense-making from language seems deeply dependent on immediate social situations and social interaction. In literate interaction, immediate co-presence can be seen in the (not unusual) meetings of collaborative writers (e.g., Cross, 1994; Lunsford & Ede, 1990; Prior, 1998) and in joint social readings (e.g., Heath, 1983); indeed, much of contemporary writing pedagogy has sought to increase the sense of co-presence through collaborative groups, student response, and similar means. Nonetheless, the social interaction of writing typically happens across time and space, with participants and their contexts imaginatively evoked and projected by individuals writing and reading a mediating text and with no opportunity for immediate mutual alignment or correction. This interactive distance of texts intensifies the need for mutual alignment of participants through aligned histories of enculturation and education (Brandt, 1990; Prior, 1998).

The one-dimensional text, when interacting with the imagination and understanding of the reader or writer, must serve as a kind of holographic plate: It must be actively illuminated to project a three-dimensional image of a social world—one with authors, readers, social motives, and referential objects. The dead words, symbols, and spaces must somehow come alive to animate relationships, communicative situations, and meaningful messages. The text must do extraordinary work, within sets of social understandings, to create co-orientation and to support activity. Moreover, this holographic evocation of interaction is extremely fragile and unstable; it may readily collapse or may transform variously within the minds of different users. Texts that manage to create relatively congruent relations and meanings across multiple readers, and perhaps multiple authors, are remarkable accomplishments, even when the texts seem to be of the most pedestrian character. In fact, that texts can be seen to be so robustly ordinary, given the delicacy and tenuousness of written communication is something that needs to be accounted for. The account we provide argues that only part of the meaning resides in the particular qualities of the texts, while much sits within the sociohistorical genesis of the social, institutional, and material systems within which the texts, users, and interactions are bound together in regularized activities. Such binding involves the building up of typifications, and a key discursive face of typification is found in genre.

GENRE AS ORGANIZED SOCIAL ACTION

Genre has been explored in recent decades from three quite different perspectives: as text, as rhetoric, and as practice. Genre has been traditionally
defined primarily in terms of textual features, with a focus on language or
style (syntax and lexicon) and organization. Organization in this sense
operates in the interface of classical rhetorical categories of arrangement
and topic. The salutation of a letter, the methods section of an experimental
report, the description of an invention in a patent application—all represent
both textual space (where things go and in what order) and topical content.
From this perspective, the central questions rest not on what a genre is
(genres are taken as the starting point), but on how genres are textually
realized, especially through linguistic and organizational means (see
Halliday, 1985; Halliday & Martin, 1993; MacDonald, 1994).

The second approach, genre as rhetoric, stays focused on textual features, but reads those features as parts of a sociorhetorical situation (authorial intentions, socially elaborated purposes, contextual exigencies, intertextual resources) that are made visible in the space of the text. In this
approach, topics, arrangement, and other sequentially ordered features can
be viewed as providing psychological pathways to guide the thought and
emotions of the audience. This situated psychological view of genres has
roots in classical rhetoric and poetics. This perspective also begins with stable textual forms as a given; however, it pays serious attention to the relation of those texts to their contexts. This approach, for example, considers
ways a text signals who wrote it and shapes the ethos of the author(s) (e.g.,
Myers, 1990; Ulman, 1996), how the text addresses and invokes audiences
(e.g., Gragson & Selzer, 1993), how the text enters into a history of social
"conversations" (McCloskey, 1985; Swales, 1990) how it draws intertextually and interdiscursively on resources (e.g., Bazerman, 1993a, 2004), how it
reflects and responds to the ideologies of the time (e.g., Brown & Herndl,
1996; Katz & Miller, 1996), and how texts structure reader experiences (e.g.,
Bazerman, 1988; Charney, 1993).

The third approach considers textual practices as fundamental to
generic action (see Bazerman, 1988, 1994a, 1994b; Berkenkotter & Huckin,
1995; Hanks, 1987, 1996; Hengst & Miller, 1999; Kamberelis, 1999; Prior,
1998; Russell, 1997). This perspective sees genres as fundamentally dynamic, fluid, heterogeneous, and situated. The generic quality of a text may be
changed not only by the textual form but by processes of production,
reception, and distribution; relations to material, social, and intertextual
conditions; use within activity; or many other aspects of the situation and
activity mediated by the text (e.g., see Ball & Lee, this volume; Cole 1996;
Wertsch, 1998). Thus, writing an experimental report for a teacher to grade
in a chemistry class is different from submitting an experimental report to

a chemistry journal. A term paper on history is different from one on optical memories for computers. An article about primate behavior based on field research is different from an article on primate behavior based on laboratory study. This kind of sensitivity to local conditions, historical processes, and the differing perspectives of multiple participants obviously involves a theory that emphasizes the fragility, plasticity, and heterogeneity of speech genres. It also points to possibilities for the dialogic interpenetration of genres themselves. From this perspective, terms like *identity*, *genre*, and *situation* do not name distinct elements that can simply be combined like puzzle pieces to form the whole picture. Thinking again of the metaphor of a holograph, the piece (the text that has some generic characteristic) contains a partial fuzzy image of the whole. The text with its generic qualities is partly constituted by, among other things, the identities, situations, and acts of those participating in its reading or writing, while at the same time, those identities, situations, and acts are being partly constituted by the presence and force of the text and the textual practices it indexes. From this practice perspective, we start not with genres as stable objects, but with the process of making genres, which might better be referred to as genrification, generic activity (Berkenkotter & Huckin, 1995), or genring—following the model of Becker's (1988) notion of languaging.

The practice approach to genre we present here synthesizes six lines of influence:

1. Rhetoric oriented to content, purpose, and situation as well as form and style.
2. Theories of discourse as dialogic, situated, and heteroglossic.
3. Phenomenological sociology, which finds the emergent order of everday social activity resting on processes of typification and recognizability.
4. Speech act theory, which sees utterances going beyond conveying meaning to making things happen in the social world.
5. Anthropological and psychological studies of discourse practices as situated, distributed, and mediated.
6. Structurational sociology, which sees larger structuring of events and relations emerging interactionally from the local actions and attributions of participants.

These approaches locate linguistic and literate practice as continuous and coextensive with cognitive, social, and material practices. A focus on practice implies seeing individual practice as situated within, co-emerging with, and contributing to larger ensembles of social accomplishment and knowledge. The centrality of such larger social ensembles also suggests that genres are properly seen not as isolated types but as constitutive parts of multidimensional systems of activity (Bazerman, 1994b). Each of these influences is elaborated here.

Rhetoric as Motivated Invention and Strategic Language Choice

Where school rhetoric in the United States had become, and to some extent still is, reduced to current-traditional concerns for the arrangements/topics of a limited set of pedagogical genres (variations on the persuasive five-paragraph essay being the best exemplar of this tradition), a rhetorical resurgence that coalesced in the 1960s emphasized rhetorical situation, action, and purpose as well as a more complex view of topics and invention (Bitzer, 1968; Burke, 1945, 1950; Kinneavy, 1971; Perelman & Olbrechts-Tyteca, 1969). This resurgence also had the effect of encouraging the expansion of rhetorical analysis to a wider range of genres and functions (especially consideration of epistemic as well persuasive purposes). Rhetorical studies of inquiry and its presentation have focused attention on sciences and social sciences (Bazerman, 1988; Gusfield, 1996; McCloskey, 1985; Selzer, 1993), on diverse participants in environmental debates (e.g., Herndl & Brown, 1996), on workplace rhetorical practices (e.g., Bazerman, 1999a; C. Miller & Selzer, 1985), on the everyday rhetoric of street gangs (Cintron, 1997); even on that least privileged form, student writing (e.g., Bartholomae, 1985; Herrington, 1988). The range of rhetorical work is suggested by the contrasts among Bartholomae (1985), Miller and Selzer (1985), and Cintron (1997). Bartholomae read student placement essays, asking how they drew on commonplaces to construct a rhetorical position in an unfamiliar rhetorical situation. His readings examined the ways textual moves projected (effectively or not) not only the ethos of the writer but also the context itself, hence his argument that student writers must invent the university. Looking at the rhetoric of transportation engineers, Miller and Selzer (1985) also read texts (e.g., transit development plans) to identify topics, but supplemented their readings with ethnographic methods (interviewing). Their analysis highlighted the complex interaction of topics drawn from different domains (disciplinary, generic, and organizational), but also looked beyond language to other semiotic means, considering topographic maps, charts, diagrams, and mathematical analyses as central topics in these genres. Cintron (1997) undertook a long-term, intensive ethnography in a Latino/a community, especially to ask how members of the community constructed identities and sought respect under conditions of racism and alienation. Among other analyses, he explored the rhetoric of gang graffiti, examining ways that words, images, and text vectors (especially up and down directionality) were used to promote one group and challenge others. Each of these very different analyses of very different genres, however, shares the goals of expanding the domains of rhetorical analysis and pursuing complex readings of rhetorical action.

Dialogic Situatedness and Heterogeneity of Utterances

Voloshinov's critique of structural accounts of linguistics has provided a particularly provocative framework for rethinking text-centered approaches to genre. Voloshinov's approach to language and the genred forms it takes in situated use (echoed in Bakhtin) is grounded in a dialogic unit of analysis, the utterance.[3] Utterances build on prior utterances, forming chains in which "each utterance refutes, affirms, supplements, and relies on the others, presupposes them to be known, and somehow takes them into account" (Bakhtin, 1986, p. 91). Because these chains of utterances are not disembodied sentences or linguistic abstractions, but the situated talk or text of particular persons, they index personal, interpersonal, institutional, sociocultural, and material histories and are charged with affective overtones and motivational trajectories as well as semantic meanings. Utterances are also dialogically addressed, anticipating the responsive understanding of recipients, future utterances by others or the speaker herself, and future actions or events in the world. Finally, utterances are dialogic because they are co-constituted through the active understanding of recipients. The utterance is a process, a form of co-production, a circuit that is complete only when actively produced *and* actively received. For Voloshinov and Bakhtin, utterances are fundamentally historical phenomena. Speech genres then are genres of dialogic utterance.

> Language is realized in the form of individual concrete utterances (oral and written) by participants in the various areas of human activity. These utterances reflect the specific conditions and goals of each such area not only through their content (thematic) and linguistic style, that is the selection of lexical, phraseological, and grammatical resources of the language, but above all through their compositional structure. All three of these aspects—thematic content, style, and compositional structure—are inseparably linked to the whole of the utterance and are equally determined by the specific nature of the particular sphere of communication. Each separate utterance is individual, of course, but each sphere in which language is used develops its own relatively stable types of these utterances. These we may call speech genres. The wealth and diversity of speech genres are boundless because the various possibilities of human activity are inexhaustible, and because each sphere of activity contains an entire repertoire of speech genres that differentiate and grow as the particular sphere develops and becomes more complex. Special emphasis should be placed on the extreme heterogeneity of speech genres (oral and written). (Bakhtin, 1986, p. 60)

It is also critical to understand that Voloshinov, Bakhtin, and Medvedev strongly emphasized the power of content in constituting genre. They saw content as a consequence of people's situated engagements in spheres of social activity (a view most clearly articulated in Bakthin's notion of chronotopes). Volosinov, Medvedev, and Bakhtin all saw genres as ideological constructions fostering particular kinds of meanings (see also Beebe, 1994). Bakhtin and Medvedev (1978) talked of seeing reality with the eyes of genre and suggested that "human consciousness possesses a series of inner genres for seeing and conceptualizing reality" (p. 134). Although history produces patterns of form, meaning, and context recognizable as genres, Voloshinov, Medvedev, and Bakhtin argued that when we speak or write we produce individual utterances that are never reducible to the abstract types they echo and evoke. Genres emerge in the resonance of utterances with histories of prior utterances, recognizable as the same genre.

Genres as practiced then are "boundless" and display "extreme heterogeneity" because they are multiply determined. Bakhtin emphasized the capacity of genres to embed and play off of other genres in many ways. Recent research has begun to expand on and detail this recognition. Kamberelis (2001), for example, detailed the multiple domains of practices and discourses that are cobbled together in two children's joint authorship of a science report. Likewise, Dyson (1997) tracked the intricate and varied ways that mass media, community, and classroom events and discourse were deployed and indexed in children's storytelling. Prior (1994, 1998) noted the hybrid discourses and genres that were found in talk and text of graduate seminars and disciplinary work. Bazerman (1999a) examined such hybridity in Edison's notebooks. Hybridity can also occur in the multiple semiotic modes of the textual practice, potentially incorporating talk, text, bodily stance and gesture, the materiality and location of the text, graphics, mathematics, and other symbolic activity woven together in threads of interactional history (see Witte, 1992).[4]

Typification, Recognition, and Attunement

C. Miller (1984) integrated perspectives from speech communication and rhetoric with perspectives from phenomenological sociology to arrive at an understanding of "genres as typified rhetorical actions based in recurrent actions" (p. 159). Central to her theory were the notions of typificiation (Schutz & Luckmann, 1973) through recurrent action and of rhetorical situation (Bitzer, 1968) embodying recurring exigencies. Typification refers to social and intersubjective classifications of the complex lifeworld, whereas rhetorical situation points to discourse as motivated and responsive. C. Miller (1984) also stressed the dynamic, emergent character of rhetorical action and typification: "the new is made familiar through the recognition of relevant similarities; those similarities become constituted as a type" (pp. 156-57). These types then also shape our imaginable motives and sense of possible actions. We conceive and seek what we perceive genres empower us to do. Miller's seminal article, her account of genres as typified communicative practices that arise under the demands of recurrent sociorhetorical situations, has been central to subsequent accounts (e.g., Bazerman, 1988, 1994a, 1994b; Berkenkotter & Huckin, 1995; Swales, 1990). Bazerman (1988) located writing as "a fundamentally historical phenomena" (p. 318). He defined genre as "a sociopsychological category which we use to recognize and construct typified actions within typified situations. It is a way of creating order in the ever-fluid symbolic world" (p. 319). The phenomenological emphasis on the need to make sense of, to order activity in, a complex lifeworld also leads to a view of genre as multidimensional, fluid, and dynamic but socially and historically stabilized. As Schryer (1993) suggested, genres are "stabilized enough for now." Generic typification is seen as not only offering the individual resources to manage complexity in the lifeworld, but as contributing to the stabilization and, thus, (re)production of social institutions and communities.

Thus, the work of locating a text in a genre for readers and writers is a multidimensional and socially distributed act of classification. As Wittgenstein (1958) argued in his discussion of games, classifications are matters of family resemblance rather than formal logic. To generate a genre then, people have to align their words and actions recognizably to the genre, which also means aligning to others who will receive it *as* that genre, as a recognizable but flawed attempt at the genre, or as not the genre at all. Swales (1990) argued that family resemblance alone is too fertile a process (anything can resemble anything) without some constraints. Although he noted domains of activity (like eating) as one possible constraint, he focuses particularly on the cognitive notion of prototypicality, proposing communicative purpose as a privileged feature of prototypicality for genres. A sociological perspective suggests the *in situ* cognitive accomplishment of resemblances is socially and historically sedimented, especially through long-term typifying alignments of persons, practices, artifacts, institutions, and natural/social worlds in coordinated and historied systems of persons, practices, and texts.

Attunement to others is central to phenomemological sociology (Garfinkel, 1967; Luckmann, 1992). Although the actual material circumstances of the universe may exist apart from human consciousness, and although individual attention may wander far, only those aspects of material and social context that are indexed in the shared discourse and other actions of participants become relevant to the ongoing social activity. That is, only those things we somehow indicate to each other through gesture and embodied action, word, glance, or otherwise as immediately relevant and worth attending to is part of our shared interactional space. When I say, "Do you hear that bird?" or noticeably perk my ears to a distant sound, I have changed the world I am sharing with my interlocuter. Hanks (1990, 1996) took this indexical structuring of attention one step further by suggesting that the specific perception of objects attended to is further shaped by the interactional means used to index it. Where the inside of a house meets the outside, where private and personal find boundaries, how far there is from here, are all determined by cultural understandings invoked by gesture and words, interactionally. In a scientific article, the theories, prior literature, methods, objects and ideas mentioned and implied; the roles of author and reader; the specific experimental actions chronicled; the results reported; and interpretations offered all enter into the interactional space of shared attention. Further those objects are attended to in just the way that discipline characterizes those things, so that if color is characterized by wavelength as in physics or by hue and saturation as in descriptive archeology, it is those articulated aspects that are part of the discursive reality. Thus, as suggested by Bakhtin's (1981) concept of chronotope, a genre carries with it an expected world of objects, actors, actions, events, and atmospheres that one attends to in that space.

Utterance As Typified Speech Act and Social Fact

Genres can be seen not only as conveying recognizable meanings, but as carrying out recognizable acts. A letter can request, or complain, or mollify. A filled-in form can make application, comply with a regulation, or report on an event. An article can oppose or support, set out a new perspective or raise questions on an old, excite hopes or diffuse concerns. Austin (1962), following Wittgenstein's view of language as a move in a game, developed the idea that utterances accomplish things in the world, whether declaring a state of affairs, making a demand, committing oneself to a course of action, or asserting a truth. He further identified "felicity conditions" that must be met in order for the speech act to be successful. Searle (1969) continued the analysis of general speech act types and the general conditions of their success. Austin (1962), however, near the end of his analysis, suggested that ultimately the conditions of success depend on local situational and institutional histories and conditions: "The total speech act in the total speech situation is the *only actual* phenomenon which, in the last resort, we are engaging in elucidating" (p. 148).

Although Austin and Searle were concerned with short spoken utterances (of the length and character of "I bet you that . . ." and "I declare you guilty of the crime of . . ."), longer written texts can be understood as carrying out social actions as well, though some cautions and qualifications are necessary in carrying out the details of analysis (see Bazerman, 1994b). Genre then would provide means for typifying and recognizing action as much as textual form. From a sociocultural perspective we can see genres as mediators of social activities. It is the mediating artifact that gives shape to the activity and affords particular relations and accomplishments. Furthermore, the mediating artifact becomes part of the way people think in the situation and activity as they come to use and understand the artifact in particular ways and as they see the mediating artifact as an extension of their own action. As with all mediating artifacts that serve as tools for accomplishing participants' objects, although genres may suggest and support particular typical objectives, they can be used flexibly depending on each participant's personally framed objects (Cole, 1996; Wertsch, 1998).

In this mutual alignment achieved through the mediating artifact, speech acts are accomplished, for people come to some sense(s) of agreement on the meaning, interactional force, and consequences of actions. The acts accomplished by genred utterances in turn establish social facts of what has been accomplished as well as supporting social facts in the meanings, situations, and orientations.[5] Social facts are those things people believe to be true, and therefore bear on how they define a situation and act within it. The sociologist W. I. Thomas stated it so: "If [people] define situations as real, they are real in their consequences." Thus, the worlds successfully evoked and enacted in the genred utterances can become a kind of self-fulfilling prophecy (Merton, 1968) or deictic evocation and shaping of a life world (Hanks, 1990, 1996).

That documents create social facts is most easily seen in texts like contracts, applications and business orders. In such cases the text provides the basis for further action (e.g., job interviews will be scheduled and products will be shipped) and holds parties accountable for the commitments made in the text (e.g., that I will complete the contracted work or that I will accept delivery of the product ordered). However, less obviously behavioral statements can also be seen as acts and consequent social facts. As Austin and Searle both pointed out, assertions are also acts. Assertions do not necessarily need to be taken as true to be taken as a social fact that they have been asserted. If an appropriately credentialed member of a profession presents a controversial research paper to a professional audience, delivered in an appropriate form and forum, then people do not have to accept the claims as true for them to recognize that the claim was made. The intellectual landscape of that profession will have been changed to the extent that the author has gotten people to attend to that claim. Indeed if the statement is extremely controversial, then there will be many consequences and further acts from the social recognition that the person has made this claim. It may become very difficult for the controversialist to erase the opprobrium that comes from the social fact of being associated with such claims. It even may be the case that the author never hoped for agreement, but only wished to challenge current views and create a discussion. In that case, the author would have created exactly the desired social fact. Every text that is attended to or otherwise finds place on the discursive landscape can be said to create some kind(s) of social fact, even if it is only to leave an objection in the record. Of course, the textual act might not be recognized for every-thing the author would wish it to be, but then one can begin viewing the success of the text in terms of what conditions it would have to meet in order to carry out the desired act of the author. What new evidence or experiments would the author need to produce in order to stave off a par-ticular objection? On the other hand, what maneuver can the opponents make to undermine the apparent accomplishment of having an experiment accepted as valid and definitive for the theory in question?[6] These condi-tions that have to be met for an act to be successfully realized may be seen as forms of accountability. If a condition is not met—a legal document is not filed before a requisite deadline, confirming experimental evidence can-not be found for a chemical claim, a political claim does not resonate with the interests of the electorate—then the speech act will be called to account and fail. Of course, if the author can provide an additional account that puts the account back on the positive side of the ledger—a lawyer success-fully argues that an extension be granted on the deadline, the chemist con-vincingly describes the limitations of the experimental apparatus, the politi-cian appeals to nobler motives that bestir the electorate to rise above their interests—the speech act might still be retrieved (Bazerman 1997).

Practice as Situated, Distributed, and Mediated

Central is Hanks' (1996, 2000) notion of genres as situated (as in dialogic theories of utterance), indexical (see also Ochs', 1988, account of indexical socialization), and dispositional (through the multiple but mundane impacts of repeated engagements in some set of sociocultural scenes and practices). Sociocultural theories emphasize that learning/development is constant, that every interaction is part of a history of learning and development (not necessarily, of course, positive). Moreover, what is getting changed or rein-forced through interaction is multiple, not only the persons participating in the activity, but also the practices, the texts, institutions, and other artifacts. Following these theories, we suggest that genre, as an activity practice, must be understood as distributed among participants (Bazerman & Russell, 2003; Cole & Engestrom, 1993; Hutchins, 1995), mediated (Scribner, 1997; Vygotsky, 1978, 1987; Wertsch, 1991, 1998), and constantly emergent with-in configurations of people, tools, and forms of activity (Beach & Kalnin, this volume; Berkenkotter, this volume; Engestrom, 1993; Lave & Wenger, 1991; Lee & Ball, this volume; Rogoff, 1990).

Because of the central focus on tools (material and psychological or semiotic) as carriers and shapers of human consciousness (what del Rio and Alvarez, 1995, refer to as cultural architectures for mind and agency), sociocultural approaches pay particular attention to how tools, such as genre practices, are appropriated in situated interaction, how they mediate social activity, how they may work to resolve or exacerbate contradictions within and between activity systems, and how such tools are themselves formed, coming to have embedded within them as affordances traces of the sociohistorical conditions of their production and past use. It is critical to recognize that learning does not involve full internalization, that practices are distributed (see Wertsch's, 1998, discussion of mastery, also Prior, 1998). Thus, learning genres involves learning to act—with other people, artifacts, and environments, all of which are themselves in ongoing processes of change and development. In short, this practice perspective draws our attention to how genre practices are learned through, and transformed in, situated interaction.

Structuration: The Social Structure as Interactionally Emergent

Because our utterances commit us to actions, relations, and identities in specific situations as they are recognized and typified by ourselves and other participants, genred utterances are what Giddens (1984) called structurational of society. Each act recognizably made by any participant evokes, maintains, and (re)produces a recognizable structure of social relations and social life. It is only by each action carrying forward and perhaps modifying particular understandings of society and relations that social life is maintained and carried forward. Of course, people may recognize different things in the same action, and may even attend to quite different aspects of the situation; there may be struggle and/or negotiation of the character of the action and situation, or there may be degrees of misunderstanding, mismatch, and failure of interaction. Goffman (1983) was particularly eloquent on the fragility of what he called the interactional order. He was also incisive on how people establish, negotiate, and manipulate the definition and alignment of the situation, or what he called footing (Goffman, 1981).

But such fragility of the social fabric and communicative alignment calls to attention those means by which some degree of alignment is achieved and even robustly stable social arrangements are maintained. The social is neither created and governed by abstract entities (culture, social norms) nor reduced to only contingent local interaction, but must be understood as the concrete historical spread of practices across integrated networks. Giddens (1984) emphasized the ways local practices draw on patterns of practice from previous situations and ways they spread through space and time producing broader social structures and patterns. Although such processes are typically distributed across many social actors, some individuals or groups can attempt through mediating artifacts to gain control of the reproduced patterns of practice. Latour (1987, 1999), for example, discussed how modern global institutions gain power by becoming centers of calculation, through the control of inscriptional practices (the making and using of tables, diagrams, maps, lists, and other texts) that allow for institutional reach (see also Yates, 1989). The power of individuals in local situated action then can be radically enhanced by such structuration, by the presence of elements from, and by connection to, longer and wider chains of distributed activity. Genres are a nexus of such typifying understandings that are evoked within each act, allowing for reasonable congruent alignment among participants. The strength of that evocation will become clearer as we discuss below how genres fit within larger systems of genres and systems of activity.

FROM GENRE SETS TO ACTIVITY SYSTEMS

Genre Sets

Each new text draws on a history of utterances from which the genre has emerged and been maintained, such that texts can be identified and understood within a tradition of utterances of that type, or genre. Furthermore, specific situations, roles, activities, or social systems can be associated with a finite number of genres of texts or utterance that stand in relation to each that define the work and roles of the participants, and that are resources and points of reference within the interactional situation. Devitt (1991), in examining the writing of tax accountants, found that 13 named genres of letters and memoranda comprised the total regular work of these accountants. These she called a genre set. Devitt especially noted the intertextual links among these genres, the ways they formed sequences. She suggested that this set of genres, along with oral genres and the tax return forms themselves, formed the larger genre system or set of tax accountants. By extension we can see that any position or profession might be characterized by a distinctive genre set produced and received in the routine course of work.

Furthermore, Devitt found that each client or case the tax accountants worked with could be associated with and characterized by a file. These files defined the relevant information, unfolding events and contingencies, and outcomes bearing on all future actions in this case. Each new document in the file is intertextually linked to prior documents in the file. The concept of a file characterizing a case has been noted by a number of people working with institutional ands corporate discourse (Berkenkotter & Ravatos, 1997; Garfinkel, 1967; Yates, 1989); and the production of the file has been seen as highly consequential for how a client, events, or projects are treated.

Finally, Devitt noted that all genres of the tax accountants are explicitly or implicitly intertextually related to the tax laws and regulations, but each genre or document has a different functional relationship to the tax laws, regulations and precedents, as well as has a different characteristic mode of explicitly or implicitly referring to the tax documents. These several findings indicate that work is organized and carried forward through a structure of related genres, which are held accountable to each other in genre-specific ways (Bazerman 1988, 1997).

Genre Systems

Expanding Devitt's notion of genre set, Bazerman (1994b) articulated the structural relations among genres within a setting by defining a genre system as:

> the full set of genres that instantiate the participation of all parties. . . . This would be the full interaction, the full event, the set of social relations as it has been enacted. It embodies the full history of speech events as intertextual occurrences, but attending to the way that all the intertext is instantiated in generic form establishing the current act in relation to prior acts. (pp. 98-99)

A genre system is comprised of the several genre sets of people working together in an organized way plus the patterned relations in the production, flow, and use of these documents. So a genre system captures the regular sequences of how one genre follows on another in the typical communication flows of a group of people.

The genre set written by a teacher of a particular course, for example, might consist of a syllabus, assignment sheets, personal notes on readings, notes for giving lectures and lesson plans for other kinds of classes, exam questions, e-mail announcements to the class, replies to student individual e-mail queries and comments, comments and grades on student papers, and grade sheets at the end of the term. Students in the same course would have a somewhat different genre set: notes of what was said in lectures and class, notes on reading, clarifications on assignment sheets and syllabus, e-mail queries and comments to the professor and/or classmates, notes on library and data research for assignments, sketches and rough drafts and final copies of assignments, exam answers, letters requesting a grade change.

However, these two sets of genres are intimately related and flow in predictable sequence and writer–reader circulation patterns. The instructor is expected to distribute the syllabi on the first day and assignment sheets throughout the term. Students then ask questions about the expectation in class or via e-mail, and then write clarifications on the assignment sheets. In class and out, in talk and perhaps in e-mail, the teacher explains the assignment and answers students' questions. The assignment sheets in turn guide student work in collecting data, visiting the library, and developing their assignments. The pace of their work picks up as the assignment deadline approaches. Once assignments are handed in, the instructor comments on and grades them, then records the grades in a record book and returns the commented-on assignment to the student. Similarly the instructor prepares then delivers lectures and organizes class activities relevant to concepts the students are to write about; students are expected to take notes on readings beforehand; they then usually take notes on what the instructor says in class, then they study those notes on class and readings before the various quizzes and exams. Moreover, students often talk with other students, friends, and/or family members about the ideas and their texts. At some points in or before the semester, the instructor may also look at the lectures and assigned readings in order to write questions for quizzes and exams. The students take the exams and the teacher grades them. At the end of the term, the instructor calculates by some formula the sum of all the grades to produce the content of the grade sheet, which is submitted to the registrar to enter into an institutional system of genres.

Activity Systems

Engestrom (1987, 1990, 1993), drawing on Leont'ev (1981), extended the Vygotskyan view of object-oriented activity as mediated by tools and artifacts, to elaborate the organized ways the community, rules, and division of labor also mediate and organize activities. It is only one further step then to locate texts as mediating artifacts within activity systems, conditioned by the community, rules, and division of labor as well as by the objects of activity (see also Lee & Ball, this volume). Russell (1997) used the notion of activity system to specify the underlying notions of setting and activity that link participants and texts together in a genre system. From this perspective, genres are seen as tools that mediate the regularized activities of the system. Considering the example of cell biology, he used the flow of genres (and intertextual references) to map out the structured production of activity and to identify the relations among multiple interlinked activity systems (in classrooms, research laboratories, drug companies, government agencies, and people's everyday use of medicines). All three levels of characterization, from genre set through genre system to activity system point out that genres have regular places with larger social activity webs and further each instantiation of a genre invokes and (re)constitutes the larger systems it is participating in. Furthermore, they point to the specific intertextual relations that form the immediate situational grounds and resources of the utterance. A letter from one's insurance company announcing a change in coverage is not just an isolated event. It invokes correspondence and conversations one has had with the company and its representatives, policy documents, records concerning the covered items, discussions with family and friends about insurance, and perhaps newspaper or television advice genres. It also carries with it a relation to internal company records as well as relations to state and national laws, regulations, and court cases. When reviewing the letter, depending on the specific context and issue, the individual might immediately feel the weight of any and all of these domains of documents and discussions. Additionally, the specific intertextual references in the letter might bring to mind a particular local intertextual field identified as relevant and structured by the presentation in the letter.[7]

However, in considering the role of genred utterances within activity systems, we should avoid imputing homogeneous stability to the activity systems. Engestrom (1993) specifically rejected as such a reified reading of activity systems:

> An activity system is not a homogeneous entity. To the contrary, it is composed of a multitude of often disparate elements, voices, and viewpoints. This multiplicity can be understood in terms of historical layers. An activity system always contains sediments of earlier historical modes, as well as buds or shoots of its possible future. (p. 68)

Engestrom's (1987, 1993) model of activity systems emphasizes contradictions (internal and external) as well as heterogeneity. Applying this approach to a study of doctor-patient consultation in Finnish clinics, Engestrom (1993) identified contradictions and heterogeneity in the multiple voices or perspectives of the interactants, the layered presence of medical ideologies from different historical periods, and the ways consultations were structured by specific institutional legacies and linked to competing historical models of work. His analysis also highlighted the critical role of medical records. In this setting, they were a genre that served to mark and exacerbate the contradictions within and discoordinations between activity systems. For example, doctors routinely wrote telegraphic case notes (essentially to themselves) about patients whom they were unlikely to see again on subsequent visits. The result of this genre practice was a routine breakdown in continuity of care. (For an application of activity theory to composition research, see the online volume, Bazerman & Russell, 2003).

FROM DISCOURSE COMMUNITIES TO DISCIPLINARITY AND INTERDISCIPLINARITY

As we have been elaborating, genre is most usefully understood within a dynamic social theory of the nature of human activity. In a major and influential statement of genre theory, Swales (1990) argued that written genres depend on prototypical communicative purposes belonging to textual discourse communities (which he at the time distinguished from oral, face-to-face speech communities, see also Swales, 1998). In another major statement of genre theory, Berkenkotter and Huckin (1995) defined discourse community "ownership" of genres as a key dimension (with discourse communities here stretching across oral and textual modes). Although we find much of value in Swales' close analyses of linguistic and rhetorical features and share many key premises with Berkenkotter and Huckin's theoretical account, we see a different way of describing the grounding of genre in social activity. Quite simply, we have found structuralist notions of discourse communities inadequate to characterize the complex emergent, multiform, conflictual, and heterogenous character of human interchange and groupings. We have looked instead to more complex and differentiated characterizations of the groupings and forums within which discourses circulate and to the constantly emergent forms of activity realized through genred utterances, oral and textual (Bazerman, 1988, 1994b, 1999a; Prior, 1991, 1995, 1998).

As much (although certainly not all) of the work on discourse communities has emphasized disciplinary and professional discourses, in this section we focus on disciplinarity as an illustration of how practice and activity-oriented accounts may reconceive social formations from a concrete historical perspective. The combined legacy of everyday tropes for, and structuralist theories of, discourse and society has encouraged us to imagine disciplinary discourse communities as autonomous objects existing in detemporalized spaces, unified territories to be mapped, systems to be diagrammed, abstract rules and knowledge that govern action and are passed on to novices. However, research on disciplines (e.g., Becher, 1989; Crane, 1972; Foucault, 1972; Harding, 1991; Klein, 1990, 1993; Pickering, 1995; Prior, 1998) has routinely pointed to complex configurations and relationships as practitioners are situated by such factors as objects of study, methodologies (including use of instruments), theories, institutional sites, audiences, social identities, interpersonal and institutional relationships, and broader sociocultural discourses and ways of life. Disciplines in these accounts seem more like heterogeneous networks (Latour, 1987), displaying Wittgenstein's (1958) family resemblance, than stable social objects. Thus, it seems important to move from a discourse community notion of disciplines as unified social and/or cognitive spaces to a notion of *discipli-*

narity as the ongoing, mediated constitution of a kind of social network. Disciplinarity invokes the dynamic integration of the historical and the situated, the production of both knowledge and the social, the mature practice and the novice, the social representation of unity and the networked, dialogic hybridity of concrete activity.

From this perspective, we particularly want to emphasize that social life/structure, because it is fundamentally historical and concrete, is also deeply and routinely laminated (Prior, 1998). This notion of lamination was articulated by Goffman (1981) in his discussion of the ways participants manage multiple footings and is fundamental to Duranti and Goodwin's (1992) argument that multiple contexts or frames co-exist in social interactions, that they are best thought of as relatively foregrounded and backgrounded through dynamic and fluid contextualizations (rather than being thought of as a static stage where a common scene is enacted). Linking these notions to that of activity systems, we could say that multiple activity footings co-exist, are immanent, in any situation. When one activity system is foregrounded (e.g., school learning), other activity systems (e.g., of home, neighborhood, government, business) do not disappear. Lamination also points to perspective, the ways co-participants in an activity hold and coordinate differently configured activity footings (see e.g., Gutierrez, Rymes, & Larson, 1995; Holland & Reeves, 1994; Newman, Griffin, & Cole, 1989; Rommetveit, 1992). To take up again Russell's (1997) discussion of the genre system(s) and activity systems of a cell biology classroom, we argue that the institutional contextualizations of biology and the educational contextualizations of school as a site of social certification cannot be taken as given and shared, that the roles of teacher and student do not exhaust the footings on which participants operate in the classroom. One contextualization that matters would be sociocultural constructions of gender that are rooted in family, community, and public spheres of life. Feminist accounts of science (e.g., Haraway, 1989, 1991; Harding, 1991; Martin, 1994) offer examples of diverse ways that science has been gendered. More broadly, how participants are raced, gendered, and classed (how these social identities are performed and perceived) is always also present in the spaces of the discipline, the corporation, the government, and the classroom. And the histories of raced, gendered, and classed performances are sedimented into (embedded as affordances in) the texts, discourse practices, and activity systems associated with disciplinarity.

Lamination then suggests that disciplinarity is not a map of autonomous social spaces (here medicine, there physics, there art history), but a heterogeneous sphere of activity that partly constitutes other social domains of practice (those of family, government, community, entertainment, etc.), whereas those other domains simultaneously co-constitute disciplinarity. Of course, one of the challenges to seeing this heterogeneity is that bordering, idealizing, and spatializing what are in fact open, concrete, historical systems is a key representational practice of disciplinarity (see Fuller, 1993; Gieryn, 1999; Latour, 1993; Prior, 1998). It is this fundamental heterogeneity and lamination that most clearly distinguishes the notion of disciplinarity from that of disciplinary discourse community.[8] This heterogeneity and lamination also makes expected and mundane the interdisciplinarity, those multilayered permeations that Klein (1993) noted, and more broadly a whole range of intercontextual, interdiscursive blendings and blurrings.

If disciplinarity is understood as always under construction, though always with tools and in conditions that have been provided historically, then we need to account for practices of stabilization and change, for the production of foregrounded (and backgrounded) contextualizations and the management of laminated activity footings. At the core of this enterprise are developmental practices: how disciplines (re)produce themselves and participants over time, how novices are recruited and socialized into the evolving practice worlds of disciplines and how these newly socialized participants freshly perceive and novelly act to be part of the constant dynamic emergent reinvention of these fields. Thus, a practice view of disciplinary genres does not ask how novices acquire (or fail to acquire) the genres owned by some particular community of practice. Instead, it considers how generic activity is implicated in the ongoing (re)production of all the kinds of participants in the relevant spheres of activity, how disciplinarity/interdisciplinarity is produced as participants take up and use tools in situated activity, as they blend their multiple identities and manage multiple activity footings, and as they work to create some collective stabilized social formation and social representation of their practice through exclusions and inclusions, enculturation and enforcement, the foregrounding and suppression of contextualizations. In short, a study of genre activity in relation to disciplinarity dives into the dynamic, churning confluences of multiple streams of sociohistoric activity.

PROGRAMS OF RESEARCH

Up to this point in the chapter, the issues, outline, development and even phrasing of each sentence have been dialogically negotiated between the two co-authors as we have sent drafts and revisions back and forth. We hope a consistent, combined voice has developed. However, we have come to and used this perspective on genres and disciplinarity through separate lines of empirical inquiry and theorizing over the years. To give a flavor of what has drawn us to this view and the significance we find in it, the next two sections are devoted to separate narratives in the separate voices of the two co-authors. In these separate narratives you may find not only differences in history and application, but even differences in what this perspective means for us now. This heterogeneity we take as endemic to all disciplinary activity and self-exemplifying of the arguments we have been making. We also take as self-exemplifying the constant remaking of aims and projects, re-creating disciplinarity through the agency of each of the authors as well as through interdisciplinary encounters and integrations driven by the nature of our separate projects. After these personal excursions, we will reform the corporate voice to make a few concluding comments.

Bazerman—Epistemic Ways of the Communicative Life

My mother used to complain I had no discipline. Now I have far too many.

As an undergraduate I tasted many majors in sciences, social sciences, and humanities before settling on English literature in my senior year—my experience of that major was largely new critical, emphasizing close reading, but I caught some of the earliest waves of new historicism brought from the left coast by a new assistant professor. My graduate training in literature was strongly historical, but very rapid, so I did not feel the disciplining weight of graduate school for many years. Furthermore, I took 2 years out in the middle for inner-city elementary school teaching, redirecting my attention from literature to literacy. During this period I also became introduced to interpersonal psychology which helped me see the role of communication, interaction, and social surroundings in individual development (Bazerman 2001a, 2001d). I returned to graduate school to finish my dissertation on Renaissance occasional poetry—in that dissertation I had already focused on genre as it located texts both within ritual moments of a royal succession and within the class positions and decorums of the authors.

After completing my degree, I obtained a position to teach writing with special focus on open admissions at Baruch College in City University of New York. To this task and professional redefinition I brought the tools of close reading, historical and social consciousness, a 1960s-left-activist view of social change, an understanding of development and learning as interpersonal, and an elementary school teacher's view of the classroom as a place of learning activities. The very real and compelling task of teaching writing to underprepared students seemed to me to require I draw on all that I knew—including unpacking the skills I had gained in my own well-prepared and well-supported academic career (Bazerman, 1998). Those of my colleagues who took this teaching task serious also drew on the full range of skills, practices, and knowledges they each had uniquely available to themselves.

From my perspective, I soon defined the aim of my teaching as to make available the literacy skills that allowed academic success, and I quickly focused in on the skills that enabled one to search out, understand, evaluate, and use the writings and knowledge presented by others. What we now call intertextuality (Bazerman, 1993, 2004) seemed to me to be central to learning to take advantage of and participating within the knowledge environments of the university and the professional worlds that follow on university experience. But as I studied and taught the skills and practices of intertextuality, it became clear to me that the skills were differentially practiced and developed within specific genres assigned in university courses, with the research paper only being the most complex (and often vague and underdefined) example (Bazerman, 1995). Furthermore, I came to see that the textual practices and genres were differently distributed and organized in he different disciplines as taught. In order to understand the disciplinary practices as reflected in the classroom, I undertook to study the disciplinary practices as carried out on the professional level, assuming that there should be some (although not necessarily direct) relationship between the two. Thus, I was drawn ever more deeply from surface appearances of literate accomplishment into the socially organized intellectual and institutional worlds within which the texts were produced, evaluated, and used. I found that the worlds of publications in different disciplines were radically different on a number of variables—in the way they projected authorial and audience roles, the ways they understood and treated their objects of study, and the ways the positioned themselves to the literature. Each of these textual differences implied the difference of the material, social, and intertextual contexts within which the text resided. In the study "What Written Knowledge Does," I clearly was drawing on literary training in close reading and in situating texts within their sociohistoric context (Bazerman, 1981). I also started to draw on the sociology and history of science, which I began studying and participating in professionally, in order to understand that sociohistoric context (Bazerman, 1982).

Through investigating the history and development of the scientific experimental report, I found out not only that the genre was historically emergent and mutable, changed by local argumentative needs and circumstances, but that it was deeply embedded within the lives of the disciplines that used it. Experimental reports could not be understood apart from the material and social circumstances within which they appeared. In major ways they help constitute the social arrangements and material experiences of the disciplines which were constantly remaking the genre for their own purposes. The textual practices were of a co-emergent piece with the social, empirical, and theoretical practices and structures of the disciplines. Within this co-emergence and interdependence I found the answer to the puzzle of how humanly constructed texts arising in particular social and historical circumstances could be said to represent a material world that exists independently of our attention (Bazerman, 1988).

To further understand the emergent forms of life the textual and literate practice was part of and helped shape, I studied the work of two 18th-century thinkers who early in their careers wrote major works on rhetoric but later became known in other areas and who have been highly influential in giving shape to the modern world of knowledge and information: Joseph Priestley (Bazerman, 1991) and Adam Smith (Bazerman, 1993b). In both cases, I found their thinking as well as their recommendations for rhetoric part of an integrated view of human life and society, which integrated views also encompassed their later accomplishments in science and economics. I also found out that their own rhetorical practices throughout their careers were developments from their rhetorical theories and their more general views of how one might most fruitfully participate in society. I originally turned to Joseph Priestley to understand the origins of modern citation practices in science—for which his *History and Present State of Electricity*—seemed a crucial turning point. I found, however, a large millenarian democratic vision of how wise and successful living (including our practical knowledge of the material world) grows out of communal discussion that is respectful to the cumulative experience of humankind understood within changing historical conditions. In the case of Smith, I found his economics an outgrowth of his fundamental problem of social communication—again the democratic problem of how to create social order without the hierarchical domination of church or royalist state. The problem of social coordination and communication was made difficult by the differences of human perception, interests, and experience that led us to desire different ends and to vary in our basic terms of understanding. His solution was the creation of a system based on a least common denominator of exchange, through which all other values could be translated and negotiated—the economic marketplace. The role of the marketplace and finances in modern life is greatly illuminated once you can see it as a historically emergent activity system aimed at creating social order through homogeneous symbolic exchange among heterogeneous peoples. Its strengths and weaknesses as a communicative system and way of life stand out in much greater relief.

With some sense now of the historical emergence, genres, communicative practices, and symbolic forms of some of the more powerful systems in the modern world (science, academic disciplines, and capitalist marketplaces), I started to develop a sense of how literate practices have been coevolutionary with the complex systems of the modern world (Bazerman, 2000a). I also began to see more clearly how written genres started to take on certain robust mediating social roles, transforming face-to-face interactions into recognizable actions at a distance. I found evidence within the consistent pattern of genres emerging out of correspondence (which strongly identifies its social and temporal situation) that through genres we came to recognize new textualized spaces of social interaction that form the virtual worlds of institutions, information, and modernity (Bazerman, 1999b). The local moments we live are now complexly influenced and refigured by systems of law, government, knowledge and science, scriptural religions, literature and textual culture, finances, and other sociotextual systems.

But it is not sufficient to see these moments simply from the external systemic view. These moments only happen insofar as we participate in them, understand and interpret, make them come into being. Thus these emergent and changing systems must also be seen as the sites of individual action, individual cognition, social interaction, emergent social thinking and evolution, and self-formation. Our orientation to such moments, our ability to participate in them, the way in which we choose to participate, and the growth and learning that occurs as we act within the systematically organized moments, are all shaped by our understanding, experience and vision of this sociohistoric-communicative situation. My studies of Priestley and Smith revealed their rhetorical practices developed in tandem with their understandings of their worlds and their places within them. These moments then became sites of learning as these powerful authors learned to articulate their emergent vision to audiences they were emergently forming relationships with. My more recent study (Bazerman, 1999a), *The Languages of Edison's Light,* shows how Edison developed a system of incandescent light and power by strategically participating in the communicative systems of his time. The concrete work of invention is embedded within a complex of social communications and cooperations involving law, finances, marketplaces, corporations, journalism, consumers, and scientific and technical professions. Only by gaining presence, meaning and value for his inventive work in all these spheres could he bring light and power to material reality so that we can now plug into it in every wall.

This historical interactional view of how the social world works through communication embeds much of the social theory discussed in this article: the phenomenology of Schutz, ethnomethodology, and conversation analysis; the structurational sociology of Giddens and Bourdieu; the sociocultural psychology of Vygotsky and activity theory of Leont'ev; and the interpersonal psychiatry of Sullivan. If life does emerge complexly and multidimensionally, we need a very full set of interdisciplinary theoretical and analytical tools to get a sense of the whole without ignoring significant parts.

The complexity of communication within recognizable forms that act powerfully in the world presents very large educational challenges of great consequence. In learning to write, students are learning ways of being within specific ways of life, with all the knowledge and orientation that is part of competent participation in that world. Furthermore, in order to have motive to write and have felt communicative needs to generate new utterances, students need to gain a sense of their stakes and interests in being part of that particular communicative way of life. The success of writing across the curriculum depends on students engagement in the curriculum, though the positive commitment-forming act of writing can be an important part of building that engagement. My studies of classroom writing and my pedagogic (Bazerman, 1992, 1994a) and textbook writings have centered on student engagement with knowledge. *The Informed Writer* (Bazerman, 1995), *the Informed Reader* (Bazerman, 1989), and *Involved: Writing for College, Writing for our Self* (Bazerman, 1997) all are aimed at helping students identify their own interests and perspectives as they engage ever more deeply with the texts university life has to offer. How to get students to engage actively and intelligently with textually mediated knowledge is one of the central challenges of the information age. We need to make visible how information is not just an abstract commodity but a concrete rhetorical product of particular socially located communicative practices (Bazerman 2001b, 2001c) so students can learn to become agents within the informationalized world.

Prior—Making Genres, People, and Practices through Situated Activity

In the mid-1980s, I was teaching academic reading, writing, and conversation in an ESL program at the University of Wisconsin–Madison. Working with a very multicultural, multilingual, and multidisciplinary group of undergraduate and graduate students, I became increasingly interested in the question of what their academic needs were, what kinds of communicative competence, particularly in relation to writing they truly needed to be successful in their academic work. At that time, the literature in applied linguistics and writing studies typically analyzed published professional writing or surveyed the types of writing (e.g., long research papers or lab reports) that students did for classes. An interesting set of ideologically freighted assumptions seemed to exist about the nature of academic work that translated into pedagogical goals. For example, it was not unusual to hear English for academic purposes practitioners suggest that students needed to know how to listen, read, and write, but not necessarily to speak, that they could control a narrow field of academic discourse (say, biochemistry) with little need for broader cultural knowledge. These assumptions construed students at largely passive recipients of knowledge, academic work as rational and asocial, and disciplines as autonomous discourse communities. From my own experience and what I could see of my students' successes and problems, I had serious doubts about these representations of academic life.Returning to school to pursue a doctorate, I began in 1989 what turned out to be a series of three situated studies of writing in graduate seminars.

My research began with basic questions about academic writing tasks. I expected to find something like a very local and temporary discourse community, centered in a particular course and strongly influenced by the professor who set and responded to the tasks. However, I soon found my image of a unified writing task fracturing and multiplying as I traced ways the event structure of academic work (how writing tasks were cued, produced, and evaluated) interacted with participants' perspectives (their diverse evolving interpretations and goals) and with the lamination of activity (the multiple trajectories of personal, interpersonal, institutional, and sociocultural histories being relatively foregrounded or backgrounded by participants). I began to turn especially to the notion of speech genres to understand the intensely situated and dialogic character of talk and text in the seminars as well as to Vygotskyan accounts of learning and mediated activity to understand how such genres were involved in disciplinary enculturation (the formation of participants and the field). In retrospect, I would say that, through investigating the writing task, I came to seen the need to study the complex genre system(s) in and around the seminar in relation to the laminated activity systems that flowed together in participants' work.[9]

Theoretically, I concluded that writing was a problematic unit of analysis (see also Witte, 1992), suggesting in its place a notion of literate activity as situated, mediated, and dispersed:

> Usual representations of writing collapse time, isolate persons, and filter activity (e.g., "I wrote the paper over the weekend"). Actually, writing happens in moments that are richly equipped with tools (material and semiotic) and populated with others (past, present, and future). When seen as situated activity, writing does not stand alone as the discrete act of a writer, but emerges as a confluence of many streams of activity: reading, talking, observing, acting, making, thinking, and feeling as well as transcribing words on paper. (Prior, 1998, p xi)

The practical complexity of genre and activity systems came home to me most clearly in a case study of a student, Lilah, a first-year graduate student in an American Studies seminar. Lilah was the only one of about 90 graduate students participating in my studies who agreed to do a process log—and then actually did it. She produced a paper for the American Studies seminar that loosely resembled other students' texts, which were themselves quite diverse in length, topic, style, and organization. I had asked Lilah to keep her drafts and notes as well as to describe in her log entries her writing for the seminar and any reading, conversation, or other writing related to it. Although I had anticipated that other academic and nonacademic settings would be involved in her writing for *American Studies* and was interested in such connections, I was still asking essentially how these other things related to the focal writing task of the seminar. I had, in fact, tacitly accepted the privileged perspective of institutional production (a tendency de Certeau, 1984, described quite cogently), granting the seminar a fairly autonomous and dominant space on that official map. Lilah, on the other hand, did not respect the borders of the institutional territories she sometimes inhabited. In her log entries, she moved seamlessly not only from the research project for American Studies to papers she had written and was writing on Chicano ethnicity for immigration history seminars, but also to talk at home with her husband, TV programs and films, and various experiences—in the community, during her childhood, and from her days teaching high school (see Prior, 1997, 1998).

By beginning with the institutional space of the classroom, with the institutional identities of student and professor, and with the task as assigned by the professor, I was looking at literate activity through a screen that privileged the institution's perspective, that respected everyday categorizations of social worlds and the boundary work of discipline and school. To track the kind of complex historical trajectories that I saw most distinctly, but by no means exclusively, in Lilah's case, I needed a different methodological approach. I came to a strategy for *tracing voices in networks* that involves the following: (a) identifying the elements of a functional system of activity; (b) tracing the histories of some key elements, especially to recover the particular motives, goals, values, and practices interiorized in material and semiotic artifacts and practices as affordances; and (c) reanimating artifacts, treating them as participants with a voice in constituting contexts of activity.[10]

The intersection of following people where they go across activities with following the historical trajectories of artifacts, practices, and institutions that people are using has led me to a renewed concern for writing processes. Emig's (1971) seminal study of composing processes introduced the use of think-aloud protocols and the clinical writing tasks, research strategies that were taken up and developed at Carnegie Mellon by Flower, Hayes, and their students. However, there is a real distance between Emig's foundational work and the line of inquiry that emerged from Carnegie Mellon. Emig was much influenced by naturalistic accounts of literary authors. For example, in *Writers at Work* (Cowley, 1958), we are told of Hemingway waking early in the morning, standing at a reading board, writing in pencil on onionskin paper, and tracking his progress (words produced per day) on a chart on the wall, a chart that displayed some more productive days followed by blanks, as Hemingway pushed ahead one day so he could go fishing the next. While offering a systematic rendering of the microstructure of some composing processes, Flower and Hayes' models (e.g., 1981, 1984) represented a series of black box diagrams that reflected rational processes alone. The material, the social, the emotional and motivational, the historical, all of these disappeared from composing in those diagrams. By the middle of the 1980s, studies of writers writing began to be replaced by studies on the social contexts of writing. Phelps (1990) observed that writing researchers had been caught up in "textual and the psychologized rhetorics where abstractions like the fictive audience (textual representation) and the cognitive audience (mental representation) are more salient than the actual exchanges of talk and text by which people more or less publicly draft and negotiate textual meanings" (p. 158). Those more-or-less public exchanges became the writing process for me and other researchers (cf. Syverson, 1999). As I began to think through following writers wherever they went, I realized that part of this task meant reviving writing process research, finding ways to capture, theorize, analyze, and represent composing processes (inventional as well as transcriptional and textual trajectories) that were situated and dispersed. Currently, I am pursuing two studies along these lines.

In one research project, Jody Shipka, Gail Hawisher, and I have been asking people to share draft and final texts and to talk about the processes and contexts behind them, but also to draw images of their writing. These drawings have elicited accounts of the expected—of books, computers and desks, data from laboratories, but also of other elements often missing from process accounts, images of music, food, coffee, colleagues, walks, trips, showers, cats, kids, and many emotional upheavals. They point to specific historical events but also to the production of composing spaces, from ones as temporary as those achieved by cleaning a room and turning on a particular kind of music to ones so hardened that they involve the construction and furnishing of rooms and the cultivation of gardens.

In a second research project, I am in the early stages of tracing the voices in the networks for *IO* and its revision. *IO* is a web art object produced by Joseph Squier, a professor of art and design at the University of Illinois. Throughout his career, he has focused on the juxtaposition of words and images. Joseph is a photographer who has largely stopped taking photographs and become a recylcer of cultural images. His work is collecting and repurposing (or remediating in Bolter and Grusin's, 1999, terms). His office/workshop is full of images and old books he has collected, journals he has kept (mostly poetic fragments and thoughts), and the sophisticated computers, cameras, and programs he uses. Talking about the history of *IO* in an interview, Joseph explained:

> Um oh, 97 98 . . . I was reading a book called *Hamlet on the Holodeck* and Eliza was mentioned, so I went ah looking for it on the web and I found Eliza and I found a small repository of similar AI programs and I actually found one called Bob, and um, Bob was pretty stupid in that Bob didn't have an interesting vocabulary . . . but Bob was fascinating to me because Bob was written in Java and . . . the person who posted it had actually posted the raw code, so I could open that up and I could actually understand how it worked,

and once I made that recognition I realized that all I would have to do was switch out the vocabulary so Bob became *IO*. . . . *IO* is actually . . . a series of seven separate programs that interact with one another and they all do separate things. One just parses the words, one just checks the vocabulary list, another one actually decides how to construct the response, and one of these programs does nothing but um feed the output to the screen, and it um I always think of it as a typewriter program because basically what it does is it breaks the output into individual letters and then pauses a random amount of time before it delivers the next letter.

IO presents words written by Joseph in one space (in response to inputs from its vocabulary) and complexly overlaid images next to it. The words and images change, but those changes are not linked, in part because of conceptual hurdles but largely because he lacked the technology to make the links. After Joseph completed *IO*, a new tool (*Flash 5.0*) became available, and he realized that it put the linkage in his reach. For the first time, he chose to revise an art object rather than move on to the next project. Actually, to redo *IO*, he needed not only *Flash 5.0* but also a team of collaborators, including Nan Goggin, another professor in art and design, Christian Cherry, a professor in dance, and two student resident assistants, Tony and Uma. Together, they want to expand IO, so that the words and images are linked, so sound as well as images can be presented, and so that the program can become more interactive, as one observer remarked, to make an art project that learns.

What unites these research projects is a sense that genre systems must be understood as embodied, mediated, semiotically multimodal, and historically dispersed, that learning to write in genre and activity systems is truly about developing ways of being in the world—about embodied work and its material conditions, about attunement to and transformation of complex lifeworlds, and about sociohistoric trajectories of hybrid practices, artifacts, institutions, and persons. This research suggests that disciplinarity is richly laminated, full of the interdisciplinary and interdiscursive permeations Klein (1993) noted. I believe that following texts, practices, institutions, and people, the voices in the networks, will continue to push our theories of how people produce genres, how genres produce people, and how both are implicated in the constant unfolding of history.

AN APPROACH FOR LITERACY EDUCATION

We now return to the corporate voice for some final comments on the approach to literacy presented in this chapter and its implications for education. The view of genre as a mediator of complex sociocultural interactions embedded in experienced material worlds reflects the centrality of discourse socialization and participation as key to learning in schools and out of them. It points to the indexicality of utterance within participatory situations and the necessity to see writing not as an abstracted skill but as an embedded part of real epistemic and social activity. It prompts study of the social through studying discourse as historical practice—laminated, emergent, multimedia, and multimodal.

We do not intend to argue that studying genre alone is always best or even sufficient. Indeed, our theoretical accounts and our repeated use of the metaphor of holography render any such notion incoherent. Studying genre from this perspective requires that it be studied in relation to all salient aspects of the forms of life with which it may be associated. This approach calls for methods that will support rich contextualizations of discourse. Analysis of isolated texts (typically at the level of formal organization, style, or linguistic function) offers limited purchase on what students and other writers need to know and understand about genre in order to become competent communicators at any level. Because the view we offer here does not offer the opportunity for isolated studies of straightforwardly identifiable technical matters, it requires a more complex and contingent pedagogy. In viewing discourses and utterances as historical human action, this view not only shares the limits and strengths of other historical sciences (cf. Gould, 1989), but all the complexities endemic to sociology, anthropology, linguistics, and cognitive science as well as the unpredictable fecundity of the creative arts. Although those who would prefer research to tell only crisp, simplified stories and would desire simple monotonic pedagogies might find our approach unsatisfying, we find the richness exciting for it suggests how writing and other discursive practices are closely tied to human development, cognition, interaction, social formation, and culture.

In order to develop students' abilities to produce, understand, and use genres, a pedagogy must (a) (re)produce key elements of the systems of activity within which the genre has historically evolved and is now used (as advocated by Dewey and others who have espoused experiential and project based learning) and (b) acknowledge the dynamism of genre, not merely the transformability, and its role in creating both change and stabilization. Students or other novices need to see their work as not just conforming to the genre, but as carrying it forward, perhaps as challenging both its stabilized textual realizations and the stabilized forms of life they index. Students must understand themselves as participating purposefully within a rich, multi-dimensional communicative environment. For pedagogical purposes that environment may be made more immediate and visible than it is sometimes experienced in the worlds-at-a-distance mediated by literacy, but the pedagogical environments should never be stripped of the meaningful complexity of the communicative environments outside the classroom worlds.

Literacy education must attend not only the formal skills of encoding and decoding texts but also to the individualized processes of meaning making. One must also help students engage with the tools needed to understand, evaluate, and participate in the larger systems of social activity wherein the texts take on meaning and life. Students must become embedded within activities and develop the practices to make the holograph become fully dimensional, dynamic, and motivated. Some of the textually mediated systems within which literacy skills are important and need to be developed, are generally accessible to large parts of the population—say, the production and circulation of news, or consumer communication, or entertainment delivery or bureaucratic application and reporting. Some people, however, might not find these texts and activities widely practiced in their daily worlds, and even those familiar with such practices may have only partial knowledge of these systems, from the consumer side. Some of the textually mediated systems are less familiar and accessible—but these become particularly important in secondary and higher education when students are being introduced to wider worlds of possibility as well as the more focused worlds of professional, disciplinary, and other highly specialized activity with their characteristic genres, vocabularies, discourses, and patterns of document circulation and use.

Specialized discourses are highly consequential for life in the contemporary world. They are the symbolic environments within which information lives. For all of us to live in the information age we will need to learn how to make that information come alive. Those for whom the information remains dead will be the victims of the information age rather than its agents. Can we live on the holodeck without a robust holography?

ENDNOTES

1. The wall between applied linguistics and composition is often much higher than it needs to be. Internationally, much of the work of advanced literacy instruction that is done in the United States by compositionists is done by applied linguists. And within U.S. universities the work of applied linguistics in providing English as a second language (ESL) instruction and developing theory and research for that task is very close to the work of composition. Both are concerned with literacy instruction for young adults entering the university—and sometimes they are the exact same students (see Harklau, Losey, & Siegal, 1999). Yet the theories, traditions and practices of instruction on which they draw are often quite different. The conjunction of practical

concerns becomes even greater when looking at the education in specialized literacy skills for disciplines, professions, and workplaces — work that is considered Writing across the Curriculum/Writing in the Disciplines in composition and Language for Specific Purposes in the applied linguistic world. It is gratifying that in these areas there is a much greater conjunction of resources and mutual interest and that in fact a coordinated set of perspectives is developing. Starting from positions in these two separate fields, we have come to understandings of literate practices that are similar and that have been mutually informing and have come to teaching and research practices that are closely related. As such, they are indicative of others who have similar views, practices, and research at this conjunction.

2. Process approaches to literacy instruction also were developing in earlier grades; however, literacy instruction there did not grapple in the same way with disciplinary differences except perhaps in the case of Australian genre theory.

3. Voloshinov (1929/1973), most clearly in Marxism and the Philosophy of Language but also in his earlier work on Freud (1927/1976), set out the project of establishing an utterance-based linguistics — in contrast to the structural linguistics that has dominated since Saussure. In the 1929 volume, Voloshinov argued that speech genres and embedding in prior utterances (what Kristeva, 1980, later called intertextuality) were cornerstones of language use. Bakhtin and Medvedev (1929/1978) also described this utterance-centered view of genre as key to sociological poetics. Bakhtin, in the 1930s and after pursued genre and responsivity to other utterances in relation to the novel and other literary texts as forms of ideology and consciousness. Only in the 1950s did Bakhtin articulate a social theory of speech genres as situated utterances. His essay "The Problem of Speech Genres" was not published in Russian until 1979 and English until 1986, but it stands as the most detailed statement of the Russian circle's theories. Voloshinov's critique of structural linguistics has been echoed by many since, including Kristeva (1980), Todorov (1990), Harris (1981, 1987), and Hanks (1996).

4. The multiplicity of semiotic modes of inscription has led to suggestions for broader terms for genre. Taking up Witte's view in relation to their study of a student's drawings, Smagorinsky and Coppock (1994) proposed the term communication genre. Lemke (1998) suggested that many texts are best described as multimedia genres, using the example of typical science texts. Looking beyond the text to the contexts of production and reception, Prior (1998) suggested the term semiotic genres and more broadly yet, Lemke (1990) argued for a notion of activity genres. This last term echoes some of the earliest formulations

of dialogic theory, Voloshinov's (1929/1979) varied references to behavioral genres, behavioral speech genres, speech genres, and behavioral ideologies—perhaps summed up in his call for a study of "the very forms of semiotic communication in human behavior" (p. 20).

5. In practice, speech acts must be understood as complex. The social facts created may be unintended, multiple, even contradictory. What was intended as a claim in a professional setting may be taken up as a sign of mental illness or as a crime against the orthodox political or religious regime. Criteria for success are likewise complex. Austin (1962) discussed the many institutional felicity conditions that need to be aligned for a legal marriage to be achieved, but also conditions of sincerity on the part of bride and groom (another type of success). He called failures of the first sort misfires and of the second abuses. Consider, for example, if one party wishes to stage a deceptive wedding ceremony for some nefarious purpose; what is a success for that person is a misfire and an abuse from the perspective of the other party. See Bazerman (1994b) for a more extensive discussion of the need to rework speech act theory to take account of situatedness, particularity, and multiplicity of perspectives, as well as the complexity of longer utterances.

6. For further elaboration of this view of texts as creating social facts, see the concluding chapter of Bazerman (1999a). See also Latour's (1987; Latour & Woolgar, 1986) discussions of facticity in science.

7. Further empirical studies elaborating these perspectives are found in Bazerman and Paradis (1991), Russell and Bazerman (1997), Bazerman and Russell (2003), Dias et al. (1999), and Prior (1998).

8. Recently, other formulations like the community of practice (Lave & Wenger, 1991; Wenger, 1998), have partially eclipsed the notion of discourse communities, although Beaufort (1999) and Swales (1998) both argued explicitly for the continuing value of discourse community formulations. Like discourse community, the idea of a community of practice seems to function metaphorically more than technically, to have achieved a kind of instant allegiance. If it offers a salutary focus on learning as participation and on the dynamics of practice over time, it also continues to emphasize boundaries and shared knowledge. Wenger's (1998) definition also makes it clear that dense interpersonal interaction is criterial. The notion of disciplinarity shifts attention to processes rather than places: It is not concerned with distinguishing who and what is in from who and what are out (although it is interested in how such representations may be constructed by people). It asks, without a priori rules, in an empirical sense, how disciplinary activity is being achieved, with what resources, with what mix of participants, to what ends. See also Scollon's (2001) discussion of why he has now

rejected the notion of a community of practice as a fundamental construct in his approach to mediated discourse analysis. Finally, simply
shifting terminology and calling a social formation a community of
practice does not necessarily change structuralist assumptions. If the
community of practice is approached as homogeneous with respect to
practice (with variations limited to centrality of participation) and
tightly bounded (with little or no attention to lamination and heterogeneous networks), then key structuralist assumptions may have migrat-
ed to another terminological formulation. See Prior's (1998) discussion
of a similar migration in the development of notions of speech and discourse communities.

9. The details of my research and theory have been presented in a series of
reports (Prior, 1991, 1994, 1995, 1997) culminating in:
*Writing/Disciplinarity: A Sociohistoric Account of Literate Activity in
the Academy* (Prior, 1998). In approach and findings, my analyses in
many ways paralleled and echoed Michaels' (1987) study of the "writing system" in an elementary classroom.

10. Several sources particularly informed this approach. Hutchins' (1995)
notion of functional systems offered a key methodological and theoretical framework, especially when linked to Latour's (1987; 1999) strategy of following the actors and artifacts outward to widening heterogeneous networks of other times, places, and activities. The notion of
tracing voices was partly prompted by Griffin and her colleagues
(1993) analysis of the role of computer programs in educational settings, especially their suggestion that programs represented the frozen
voices of the programmers, voices that indexed those programmers'
own ideologies of education and technology. Finally, I drew on
Bazerman's (1988) Vygotskyan analysis of the co-evolution of scientific report genres and science, especially for his exploration of ways key
actors and events reshaped the genre and activity systems, highlighting
the personalization of the social through the sociogenesis of tools (see
also Prior, 2001).

REFERENCES

Austin, J. L. (1962). *How to do things with words.* Oxford, UK: Oxford University
    Press.
Bakhtin, M. (1981). *The dialogic imagination: Four essays by M. M. Bakhtin* (C.
    Emerson & M. Holquist, Trans.; M. Holquist, Ed.). Austin: University of Texas
    Press.
Bakhtin, M. (1986). *Speech genres and other late essays* (Vern W. McGee, Trans.).
    Austin: University of Texas Press.

Bakhtin, M.M., & Medvedev, P. (1978). *The formal method in literary scholarship* (A. Wehrle, Trans.). Baltimore, MD: The John Hopkins University Press. (Original work published 1929)

Bartholomae, D. (1985). Inventing the university. In M. Rose (Ed.), *When a writer can't write* (pp. 134-165). New York: Guilford.

Barton, D., & Ivanic, R. (Eds.). (1991). *Writing in the community*. Newbury Park, CA: Sage.

Bauman, R. (1992). Contextualization, tradition, and the dialogue of genres: Icelandic legends of the *kraftaskald*. In A. Duranti & C. Goodwin (Eds.), *Rethinking context: Language as an interactive phenomenon* (pp. 125-146). Cambridge, UK: Cambridge University Press.

Bazerman, C. (1981). What written knowledge does: Three examples of academic discourse. *Philosophy of the Social Sciences*, *11*(3), 361-88.

Bazerman, C. (1982). Scientific writing as a social act: A review of the literature of the sociology of science. In P. V. Anderson, J. Brockman, & C. R. Miller (Eds.), *New essays in technical and scientific communication: Research, theory, and practice* (pp. 156-184). Farmingdale, NY: Baywood

Bazerman, C. (1988). *Shaping written knowledge: The genre and activity of the experimental article in science*. Madison: University of Wisconsin Press.

Bazerman, C. (1989).*The informed reader: Contemporary issues in the disciplines*. Boston, MA: Houghton Mifflin.

Bazerman, C. (1991). How natural philosophers can cooperate: The literary technology of coordinated investigation in Joseph Priestley's *History and Present State of Electricity* (1767). In C. Bazerman & J. Paradis (Eds.), *Textual dynamics of the professions: Historical and contemporary studies of writing in professional communities*. (pp. 13-44). Madison: The University of Wisconsin Press.

Bazerman, C. (1992). From cultural criticism to disciplinary participation: Living with powerful words. In C. Moran & A. Herrington (Eds.), *Writing, teaching, and learning in the disciplines* (pp. 61-68). New York: Modern Language Association.

Bazerman, C. (1993a). Intertextual self-fashioning: Gould and Lewontin's representations of the literature. In J. Selzer (Ed.), *Understanding scientific prose* (pp. 20-41). Madison: University of Wisconsin Press.

Bazerman, C. (1993b). Money talks: Adam Smith's rhetorical project. In W. Henderson, T. Dudley-Evans, & R. Backhouse (Eds.), *Economics and language* (pp. 173-199). London, UK: Routledge.

Bazerman, C. (1994a). *Constructing experience*. Carbondale: Southern Illinois University Press.

Bazerman, C. (1994b). Systems of genres and the enactment of social intentions. In A. Freedman & P. Medway (Eds.), *Genre and the new rhetoric* (pp. 79-101). London, UK: Taylor & Francis.

Bazerman, C. (1995). *The informed writer* (5th ed.). Boston, MA: Houghton Mifflin.

Bazerman, C. (1997). *Involved: Writing for college, writing for your self*. Boston, MA: Houghton Mifflin.

Bazerman, C. (1998) Looking at writing; writing what I see. In T. Enos & D. Roen (Eds.), *Living rhetoric and composition* (pp. 15-24). Mahwah, NJ: Erlbaum.

Bazerman, C. (1999a). *The languages of Edison's light*. Cambridge, MA: MIT Press.

Bazerman, C. (1999b). Letters and the social grounding of differentiated genres. In D. Barton & N. Hall (Eds.), *Letter writing as a social practice* (pp. 15-30). Amsterdam: Benjamins.

Bazerman, C. (2000a). A rhetoric for literate society: The tension between expanding practices and restricted theories. In M. Goggin (Ed.), *Inventing a discipline* (pp. 5-28). Urbana, IL: National Council of Teachers of English.

Bazerman, C. (2000b). Singular utterances: Realizing local activities through typified forms in typified circumstances. In A. Trosberg (Ed.), *Analysing the discourses of professional genres* (pp. 25-40). Amsterdam: Benjamins.

Bazerman, C. (2001a). Anxiety in action. *Mind, Culture, and Activity, 8*, 174-186.

Bazerman, C. (2001b). Nuclear information: One rhetorical moment in the construction of the information age. *Written Communication, 18*, 259-295.

Bazerman, C. (2001c). Politically wired: The changing places of political participation in the age of the internet. In J. Yates & J. Van Maanen (Eds.), *IT and organizational transformation* (pp. 137-154). Thousand Oaks, CA: Sage.

Bazerman, C. (2001d). Writing as a development in interpersonal relations. *Journal for the Psychoanalysis of Culture & Society, 6*, 298-302.

Bazerman, C. (2004). Intertextuality: How texts rely on other texts. In C. Bazerman & P. Prior (Eds.), *What writing does and how it does it* (pp. 83-96). Mahwah NJ: Erlbaum.

Bazerman, C., & Paradis, J. (Eds.). (1991). *Textual dynamics of the professions: Historical and contemporary studies of writing in professional communities*. Madison: The University of Wisconsin Press.

Bazerman, C., & Russell, D. (Eds.). (2003). *Writing selves and societies: Research from activity perspectives*. Fort Collins, CO: The WAC Clearinghouse.

Beaufort, A. (1999). *Writing in the real world: Making the transition from school to work*. New York: Teachers College Press.

Becher, T. (1989). *Academic tribes and territories: Intellectual enquiry and the cultures of disciplines*. Stony Stratford, UK: Society for Research into Higher Education and Open University Press.

Becker, A.L. (1988). Language in particular: A lecture. In D. Tannen (Ed.), *Linguistics in context: Connecting observation and understanding* (pp. 17-35). Norwood, NJ: Ablex.

Beebe, T. (1994). *The ideology of genre: A comparative study of generic instability*. University Park: Pennsylvania State University Press.

Bergmann, J., & Luckmann, T. (1995). Reconstructive genres of everyday communication. In U. Quasthoff (Ed.), *Aspects of oral communication* (pp. 289-304). Berlin: Walter de Gruyter.

Berkenkotter, C. (2001). Genre systems at work: DSM-IV and rhetorical recontextualization in psychotherapeutic paperwork. *Written Communication, 18*, 326-349.

Berkenkotter, C., & Huckin, T. (1995). *Genre knowledge in disciplinary communication: Cognition/culture/power*. Hillsdale, NJ: Erlbaum.

Berkenkotter, C., & Ravatos, D. (1997). Genre as tool in the transmission of practice over time and across professional boundaries. *Mind, Culture, and Activity, 4*, 256-274.

Berlin, J. (1987). *Rhetoric and reality: Writing instruction in American colleges 1900-1985*. Carbondale: Southern Illinois University Press.

Besnier, N. (1995). *Literacy, emotion, and authority: Reading and writing on a Polynesian atoll*. London, UK: Cambridge University Press.

Bhatia, V. K. (1993). *Analyzing genre: Language use in professional settings*. Essex, UK: Longman.

Bitzer, L. (1968). The rhetorical situation. *Philosophy and Rhetoric, 1*, 1-14.

Bizell, P. (1992). *Academic discourse and critical consciousness*. Pittsburgh, PA: University of Pittsburgh Press.

Bolter, J.D., & Grusin, R. (1999). *Remediation: Understanding new media*. Cambridge, MA: MIT Press.

Booth, W. (1963). The rhetorical stance. *College Composition and Communication, 14*, 139-145.

Brandt, D. (1990). *Literacy as involvement: The acts of writers, readers and texts*. Carbondale: Southern Illinois University Press.

Brodkey, L. (1987). *Academic writing as social practice*. Philadelphia, PA: Temple University Press.

Brown, R., & Herndl, C. (1996). Beyond the realm of reason: Understanding the extreme environmental rhetoric of the John Birch Society. In C. Herndl & S. Brown (Eds.), *Green culture: Environmental rhetoric in contemporary America* (pp. 213-235). Madison: University of Wisconsin Press.

Burke, K. (1945). *A grammar of motives*. Berkeley: University of California Press.

Burke, K. (1950). *A rhetoric of motives*. Berkeley: University of California Press.

Carruthers, P., & Chamberlain, A. (2000). *Evolution and the human mind: Modularity, language, and meta-cognition*. Cambridge, UK: Cambridge University Press.

de Certeau, M. (1984). *The practice of everyday life* (S. Rendall, Trans.). Berkeley: University of California Press.

Chapman M. (1994). The emergence of genres: Some findings from an examination of first grade writing. *Written Communication, 11*, 348-380.

Chapman M. (1995). The sociocognitive construction of written genres in first grade. *Research in the Teaching of English, 29*, 164-192.

Charney, D. (1993). A study of rhetorical reading: How evolutionists read "The Spandrels of San Marco." In J. Selzer (Ed.), *Understanding scientific prose* (pp. 203-231). Madison: University of Wisconsin Press.

Chomsky, N. (1965). *Aspects of the theory of syntax*. Cambridge, MA: MIT Press.

Christensen, F. (1967). *Notes toward a new rhetoric*. New York: Harper & Row.

Cintron, R. (1997). *Angel's town: Chero ways, gang life, and the rhetorics of the everyday*. Boston, MA: Beacon Press.

Cole, M. (1996). *Cultural psychology: A once and future discipline*. Cambridge, MA: Harvard University Press.

Cole, M., & Engestrom, Y. (1993). A cultural-historical approach to distributed cognition. In G. Salomon (Ed.), *Distributed cognitions: Psychological and educational considerations* (pp. 1-46). Cambridge, UK: Cambridge University Press.

Corbett, E. P. J. (1965). *Classical rhetoric for the modern student*. New York: Cambridge University Press.

Cowley, M. (Ed.). (1958). *Writers at work, the Paris review interviews.* New York: Viking Press.

Crane, D. (1972). *Invisible colleges: Diffusion of knowledge in scientific communities.* Chicago: The University of Chicago Press.

Cross, G.A. (1994). *Collaboration and conflict: A contextual exploration of group writing and positive emphasis.* Cresskill, NJ: Hampton Press.

del Rio, P., & Alvarez, A. (1995). Tossing, praying, and reasoning: The changing architectures of mind and agency. In J. Wertsch, P. del Rio, & A. Alvarez (Eds.), *Sociocultural studies of mind* (pp. 215-247). Cambridge, UK: Cambridge University Press.

Deacon, T. (1997). *The symbolic species: The co-evolution of language and the brain.* New York: Norton.

De Vault, M. L., & McCoy, L. (2001). Institutional ethnography: Using interviews to investigate ruling relations. In J. F. Gubrium & J. A. Holstein (Eds.), *Handbook of interviewing.* Newbury Park, CA: Sage.

Devitt, A. (1991). Intertextuality in tax accounting: Generic, referential, and functional. In C. Bazerman & J. Paradis (Eds.), *Textual dynamics of the professions* (pp. 336-380). Madison: University of Wisconsin Press.

Dias, P., Freedman, A., Medway, P., & Pare, A. (1999). *Worlds apart: Acting and writing in academic and workplace contexts.* Mahwah, NJ: Erlbaum.

Dore, J. (1989). Monologue as reenvoicement of dialogue. In K. Nelson (Ed.), *Narratives from the crib* (pp. 231-260). Cambridge, MA: Harvard University Press.

Duranti, A. (1994). *From grammar to politics: Linguistic anthropology in a Western Samoan village.* Berkeley: University of California Press.

Duranti, A., & Goodwin, C. (Eds.). (1992). *Rethinking context: Language as an interactive phenomenon.* Cambridge, UK: Cambridge University Press.

Dyson, A. (1997). *Writing superheroes: Contemporary childhood, popular culture, and classroom literacy.* New York: Teachers College Press.

Emig, J. (1971). *The composing processes of twelfth graders.* Urbana, IL: National Council of Teachers of English.

Engestrom, Y. (1987). *Learning by expanding: An activity-theoretical approach to developmental research.* Helsinki: Orienta-Konsultit.

Engeststrom, Y. (1990). *Learning, working and imagining: Twelve studies in activity theory.* Helsinki: Orienta-Konsultit.

Engestrom, Y. (1993). Developmental studies of work as a testbench of activity theory: The case of primary care medical practice. In S. Chaiklin & J. Lave (Eds.), *Understanding practice: Perspectives on activity and context* (pp. 64-103). Cambridge, UK: Cambridge University Press.

Flower, L., & Hayes, J. (1981). A cognitive process theory of writing. *College Composition and Communication, 32,* 365-387.

Flower, L., & Hayes, J. (1984). Images, plans, and prose: The representation of meaning in writing. *Written Communication, 1,* 120-160.

Foucault, M. (1970). *The order of things; an archaeology of the human sciences.* New York: Vintage Books.

Foucault, M. (1972). *The archaeology of knowledge amd the discourse on language* (A. Sheridan Smith, Trans.). New York: Pantheon.

Freedman, A., Adams, C., & Smart, G. (1994). Wearing suits to class: Simulating genres and simulations as genre. *Written Communication, 11*, 193-226.

Freedman, A., & Medway, P. (Eds.). (1994). *Genre and the new rhetoric.* London, UK: Taylor & Francis.

Fuller, S. (1993). Disciplinary boundaries and the rhetoric of the social sciences. In E. Messer-Davidow, D. Shumway, & D. Sylvan (Eds.), *Knowledges: Historical and critical studies in disciplinarity* (pp. 125-149). Charlottesville: University of Virginia Press.

Garfinkel, H. (1967). *Studies in ethnomethodology.* Englewood Cliffs, NJ: Prentice-Hall.

Geertz, C. (1983). *Local knowledge: Further essays in interpretive anthropology.* New York: Basic Books.

Geisler, C. (1994). *Academic literacy and the nature of expertise: Reading, writing, and knowing in academic philosophy.* Hillsdale, NJ: Erlbaum.

Gieryn, T. F. (1999). *Cultural boundaries of science: Credibility on the line.* Chicago: University of Chicago Press.

Giddens, A. (1984). *The constitution of society: Outline of a theory of structuration.* Berkeley: University of California Press.

Goffman, E. (1981). *Forms of talk.* Philadelphia: University of Pennsylvania Press.

Goffman, E. (1983). The interaction order. *American Sociological Review, 48*, 1-17.

Goody, E. (1995). *Social intelligence and interaction: Expressions and implications of the social bias in human intelligence.* Cambridge, UK: Cambridge University Press.

Gould, S. (1989). *Wonderful life: The Burgess Shale and the nature of history.* New York: Norton.

Gragson, G., & Selzer, J. (1993). The reader in the text of "The Spandrels of San Marco." In J. Selzer (Ed.), *Understanding scientific prose* (pp. 180-202). Madison: University of Wisconsin Press.

Griffin, P., Belyaeva, A., Soldatova, G., & the Velikov-Hamburg Collective. (1993). Creating and reconstituting contexts for educational interactions, including a computer program. In E. Forman, N. Minick, & C. Stone (Eds.), *Contexts for learning: Sociocultural dynamics in children's development* (pp. 120-152). New York: Oxford University Press.

Guenthner, S., & Knoblauch H. (1995). Culturally patterned speaking practices: The analysis of communicative genres. *Pragmatics, 5*, 1-32.

Gusfield, J. (1996). *Contested meanings: The construction of alcohol problems.* Madison: University of Wisconsin Press.

Gutierrez, K., Rymes, B., & Larson, J. (1995). Script, counterscript, and underlife in the classroom: James Brown vs. *Brown v. Board of Education. Harvard Educational Review, 65*, 445-471.

Halliday, M. A. K. (1985). *An introduction to functional grammar.* Baltimore, MD: E. Arnold.

Halliday, M. A. K., & Martin, J. (1993). *Writing science: Literacy and discursive power.* London, UK: Falmer Press.

Hanks, W. (1987). Discourse genres in a theory of practice. *American Ethnologist, 14*, 668-692.

Hanks, W. (1990). *Referential practice.* Chicago: University of Chicago Press.

Hanks, W. (1996). *Language and communicative practices.* Boulder, CO: Westview.

Hanks, W. (2000). *Intertexts: Writings on language, utterance, and context.* Lanham, MD: Rowman & Littlefield.

Haraway, D. (1989). *Primate visions: Gender, race, and nature in the world of modern science.* New York: Routledge.

Haraway, D. (1991). *Simians, cyborgs, and women: The reinvention of nature.* New York: Routledge.

Harding, S. (1991). *Whose science? Whose knowledge? Thinking from women's lives.* Ithaca, NY: Cornell University Press.

Harklau, L., Losey, K., & Siegal, M. (Eds.). (1999). *Generation 1.5 meets college composition: Issues in teaching writing to U.S.-educated learners of ESL.* Mahwah, NJ: Erlbaum.

Harris, R. (1981). *The language myth.* New York: St. Martin's Press.

Harris, R. (1987). *Reading Saussure: A critical commentary on the cours de linguistique générale.* London: Duckworth.

Heath, S. B. (1983). *Ways with words: Language, life, and work in communities and classrooms.* Cambridge, UK: Cambridge University Press.

Hengst, J., & Miller, P. (1999). The heterogeneity of discourse genres: Implications for development. *World Englishes, 18,* 325-341.

Herndl, C., & Brown, S. (1996). *Green culture: Environmental rhetoric in contemporary America.* Madison: University of Wisconsin Press.

Herrington, A. (1985). Writing in academic settings: A study of the contexts for writing in two chemical engineering courses. *Research in the Teaching of English, 19,* 331-359.

Herrington, A. (1988). Teaching, writing and learning: A naturalistic study of writing in an undergraduate literature course. In D. A. Jolliffe (Ed.), *Advances in writing research, vol. 2: Writing in academic disciplines* (pp. 133-166). Norwood, NJ: Ablex.

Holland, D., & Reeves, J. (1994). Activity theory and the view from somewhere: Team perspectives on the intellectual work of programming. *Mind, Culture, and Activity, 1/2,* 8-24.

Hoskin, K. (1993). Education and the genesis of disciplinarity: The unexpected reversal. In E. Messer-Davidow, D. Shumway, & D. Sylvan (Eds.), *Knowledges: Historical and critical studies in disciplinarity* (pp. 271-304). Charlottesville: University of Virginia Press.

Hoskin, K., & Macve, R. (1993). Accounting as discipline: The overlooked supplement. In E. Messer-Davidow, D. Shumway, & D. Sylvan (Eds.), *Knowledges: Historical and critical studies in disciplinarity* (pp. 25-53). Charlottesville: University of Virginia Press.

Hutchins, E. (1995). *Cognition in the wild.* Cambridge, MA: MIT Press.

Kamberelis, G. (1999). Genre development and learning: Children writing stories, science reports, and poems. *Research in the Teaching of English, 33,* 403-460.

Kamberelis, G. (2001). Producing heteroglossic classroom (micro)cultures through hybrid discourse practice. *Linguistics and Education, 12,* 85-125.

Kamberelis, G., & Scott, K.D. (1992). Other people's voices: The coarticulation of texts and subjectivities. *Linguistics and Education, 4,* 359-403.

Katz, S., & Miller, C. (1996). The low level radioactive waste siting controversy in North Carolina: Toward a rhetorical model of risk communication. In C. Herndl & S. Brown (Eds.), *Green culture: Environmental rhetoric in contemporary America* (pp. 111-140). Madison: University of Wisconsin Press.

Kinneavy, J. (1971). *A theory of discourse: The aims of discourse.* Englewood Cliffs, NJ: Prentice-Hall.

Klein, J. (1990). *Interdisciplinarity: History, theory, and practice.* Detroit, MI: Wayne State University Press.

Klein, J. (1993). Blurring, cracking, and crossing: Permeation and the fracturing of discipline. In E. Messer-Davidow, D. Shumway, & D. Sylvan (Eds.), *Knowledges: Historical and critical studies in disciplinarity* (pp. 185-211). Charlottesville: University of Virginia Press.

Klein, J. (1996). *Crossing boundaries: Knowledge, disciplinarities, and interdisciplinarities.* Charlottesville: University Press of Virginia.

Kristeva, J. (1980). *Desire in language: A semiotic approach to literature and art.* New York: Columbia University Press.

Latour, B. (1987). *Science in action: How to follow scientists and engineers through society.* Cambridge, MA: Harvard University Press.

Latour, B. (1993). *We have never been modern.* Cambridge, MA: Harvard University Press.

Latour, B. (1999). *Pandora's hope: Essays on the reality of science studies.* Cambridge, MA: Harvard University Press.

Latour, B., & Woolgar, S. (1986). *Laboratory life: The social construction of scientific facts.* Princeton, NJ: Princeton University Press.

Lave, J., & Wenger, E. (1991). *Situated learning: Legitimate peripheral participation.* Cambridge, UK: Cambridge University Press.

Lemke, J. (1998). Multiplying meaning: Visual and verbal semiotics in scientific text. In J. R. Martin & R. Veel (Eds.), *Reading science: Critical and functional perspectives on discourses of science* (pp. 87-113). London, UK: Routledge.

Lemke, J. (1990). *Talking science: Language, learning, and values.* Norwood, NJ: Ablex.

Leont'ev, A.N. (1981). *Problems of the development of the mind.* Moscow: Progress.

Luckmann, T. (1986). Grundformen der gesellschaftlichen Vermittlung des Wissens: Kommunikative Gattungen [Basic forms of social mediation of knowledge: Communicative genres]. In *Koelner Zeitschrift fuer soziologie und Sozialpsychologie*, Sonderheft 27, 191-211.

Luckmann, T. (1992). On the communicative adjustment of perspectives, dialogue and communicative genres. In A. Wold (Ed.), *The dialogical alternative: Towards a theory of language and mind* (pp. 219-234). Oslo: Scandinavian University Press.

Luhmann, N. (1983). *The differentiation of society.* New York: Columbia University Press.

Lunsford, A., & Ede, L. (1990). *Singular texts/plural authors: Perspectives on collaborative writing.* Carbondale: Southern Illinois University Press.

Lunsford, A., Moglen, H., & Slevin, J. (Eds.). (1990). *The right to literacy.* New York: Modern Language Association.

MacDonald, S. P. (1994). *Professional academic writing in the humanities and social sciences.* Carbondale: Southern Illinois University Press.

Martin, E. (1994). *Flexible bodies: Tracking immunity in American culture from the days of polio to the age of AIDS.* Boston, MA: Beacon Press.

McCloskey, D. (1985). *The rhetoric of economics.* Madison: University of Wisconsin Press.

Merton, R. K. (1968). *Social theory and social structure.* New York: The Free Press.

Michaels, S. (1987). Text and context: A new approach to the study of classroom writing. *Discourse Processes, 10,* 321-346.

Miller, C.R. (1984). Genre as social action. *Quarterly Journal of Speech, 70,* 151-167.

Miller, C.R., & Selzer, J. (1985). Special topics of argument in engineering reports. In L. Odell & D. Goswami (Eds.), *Writing in nonacademic settings* (pp. 309-341). New York: Guilford.

Miller, P. J., Hengst, J. A., Alexander, K., & Sperry, L. L. (2000). Versions of personal storytelling/versions of experience: Genres as tools for creating alternate realities. In K. Rosengren, C. Johnson, & P. Harris (Eds.), *Imagining the impossible: The development of magical, scientific, and religious thinking in contemporary society* (pp. 212-246). Cambridge, UK: Cambridge University Press.

Myers, G. (1990). *Writing biology: Texts in the social construction of scientific knowledge.* Madison: University of Wisconsin Press.

Newman, D., Griffin, P., & Cole, M. (1989). *The construction zone.* Cambridge, MA: Cambridge University Press.

Nystrand, M., Greene, S., & Wiemelt, J. (1993). Where did composition studies come from? An intellectual history. *Written Communication, 10,* 267-333.

Ochs, E. (1988). *Culture and language development: Language acquisition and language socialization in a Samoan village.* Cambridge, MA: Cambridge University Press.

Orlikowski, W. J., & Yates, J. (1994). Genre repertoire: The structuring of communicative practices in organizations. *Administrative Science Quarterly, 39,* 541-574.

Paradis, J., Dobrin, D., & Miller, R. (1985). Writing at Exxon ITD: Notes on the writing environment of an R&D organization. In L. Odell & D. Goswami (Eds.), *Writing in nonacademic settings.* New York: Guilford.

Perelman, C., & Olbrechts-Tyteca, L. (1969). The new rhetoric (J. Wilkinson & P. Weaver, Trans.). Notre Dame, IN: University of Notre Dame Press.

Phelps, L. (1990). Audience and authorship: The disappearing boundary. In G. Kirsch & D. Roen (Eds.), *A sense of audience in written communication* (pp. 153-174). Newbury Park, CA: Sage.

Pickering, A. (1993). Anti-discipline or narratives of illusion. In E. Messer-Davidow, D. Shumway, & D. Sylvan (Eds.), *Knowledges: Historical and critical studies in disciplinarity* (pp. 103-122). Charlottesville: University of Virginia Press.

Pickering, A. (1995). *The mangle of practice: Time, agency, and science.* Chicago: University of Chicago Press.

Prior, P. (1991). Contextualizing writing and response in a graduate seminar. *Written Communication, 8,* 267-310.

Prior, P. (1994). Response, revision, disciplinarity: A microhistory of a dissertation prospectus in sociology. *Written Communication, 11,* 483-533.

Prior, P. (1995). Tracing authoritative and internally persuasive discourses: A case study of response, revision, and disciplinary enculturation. *Research in the Teaching of English, 29,* 288-325.

Prior, P. (1997). Literate activity and disciplinarity: The heterogeneous (re)production of American Studies around a graduate seminar. *Mind, Culture, Activity, 4,* 275-295.

Prior, P. (1998). *Writing/disciplinarity: A sociohistoric account of literate activity in the academy.* Mahwah, NJ: Erlbaum.

Prior, P. (2001). Voices in text, mind, and society: Sociohistoric accounts of discourse acquisition and use. *Journal of Second Language Writing, 10,* 55-81.

Rogoff, B. (1990). *Apprenticeship in thinking: Cognitive development in social context.* New York: Oxford University Press.

Rommetveit, R. (1992). Outlines of a dialogically based social-cognitive approach to human cognition and communication. In A. Wold (Ed.), *The dialogical alternative: Towards a theory of language and mind* (pp. 19-44). Oslo: Scandinavian University Press.

Russell, D. (1997). Rethinking genre in school and society: An activity theory analysis. *Written Communication, 14,* 504-554.

Russell, D., & Bazerman, C. (Eds.). (1997) *The activity of writing, the writing of activity* [Special issue]. *Mind Culture and Activity, 4,* 4.

Rymer, J. (1988). Scientific composing processes: How eminent scientists write journal articles. In D. A. Jolliffe (Ed.), *Advances in writing research, vol. 2: Writing in academic disciplines* (pp. 211-250). Norwood, NJ: Ablex.

Schutz, A., & Luckmann, T. (1973). *The structures of the life-world* (R. Zaner & H. Engelhardt, Trans.). Evanston, IL: Northwestern University Press.

Schryer, C. (1993). Records as genre. *Written Communication, 10,* 200-234.

Scollon, R. (2001). *Mediated discourse: The nexus of practice.* London, UK: Routledge.

Scribner, S. (1997). *Mind and social practice: Selected writings of Sylvia Scribner* (E. Tobach, R. Falmagne, M. Parlee, L. Martin, & A. Kapelman, Eds.). Cambridge, UK: Cambridge University Press.

Searle, J. R. (1969). *Speech acts: An essay in the philosophy of language.* London, UK: Cambridge University Press

Selzer, J. (Ed.). (1993). *Understanding scientific prose.* Madison: University of Wisconsin Press.

Shaughnessy, M. (1977). *Errors and expectations: A guide for the teacher of basic writing.* New York: Columbia University Press.

Smagorinsky, P., & Coppock, J. (1994). Cultural tools and the classroom context: An exploration of an artistic response to literature. *Written Communication, 11,* 283-310.

Smith, A. (1976). *An inquiry into the nature and causes of the wealth of nations* (R. H. Campbell & A. S. Skinner, Eds.). Oxford, UK: Clarendon Press.

Smith, D. (1990). *Texts, facts, and femininity: Exploring the relations of ruling.* London, UK: Routledge.

Smith, D. (1998). *Writing the social: Critique, theory, and investigations.* Toronto: University of Toronto Press.

Street, B. (1984). *Literacy in theory and practice*. Cambridge, UK: Cambridge University Press.

Swales, J. (1990). *Genre analysis: English in academic and research settings*. Cambridge, UK: Cambridge University Press.

Swales, J. (1998). *Other floors, other voices: A textography of a small university building*. Mahwah, NJ: Erlbaum.

Syverson, M. (1999). *The wealth of reality: An ecology of composition*. Carbondale: Southern Illinois University Press.

Taylor, D., & Dorsey-Gaines, C. (1988). *Growing up literate: Learning from inner-city families*. Portsmouth, NH: Heinemann.

Todorov, T. (1990). *Genres in discourse*. Cambridge, UK: Cambridge University Press.

Ulman, H. (1996). "Thinking like a mountain": Persona, ethos, and judgment in American nature writing. In C. Herndl & S. Brown (Eds.), *Green culture: Environmental rhetoric in contemporary America* (pp. 46-81). Madison: University of Wisconsin Press.

Voloshinov, V. N. (1976). *Freudianism: A Marxist critique* (I.R. Titunik, Trans.; I. R. Titunik & N. Bruss, Eds.). New York: Academic Press. (Original work published 1927)

Voloshinov, V.N. (1973). *Marxisim and the philosophy of language* (L. Matejka & I.R. Titunik, Trans.). Cambridge, MA: Harvard University Press. (Original work published 1929)

Vygtosky, L. (1978). *Mind in society: The development of higher psychological processes* (M. Cole, V. John-Steiner, S. Scribner, & E. Souberman, Eds.). Cambridge, MA: Harvard University Press.

Vygotksy, L. (1987). *Thinking and speech* (N. Minick, Ed. & Trans.). New York: Plenum.

Wenger, E. (1998). *Communities of practice: Learning, meaning, and identity*. Cambridge, UK: Cambridge University Press.

Wertsch, J. V. (1991). *Voices of the mind: A sociocultural approach to mediated action*. Cambridge, MA: Harvard University Press.

Wertsch, J.V. (1998). *Mind as action*. New York: Oxford University Press.

Winsor, D. (1999). Genre and activity systems: The role of documentation in maintaining and changing engineering activity systems. *Written Communication, 16,* 200-224.

Wittgenstein, L. (1958). *Philosophical investigations* (G.E.M. Anscombe, Trans.). Oxford, UK: Basil Blackwell.

Witte, S. (1992). Context, text, intertext: Toward a constructivist semiotic of writing. *Written Communication, 9,* 237-308.

Yates, J. (1989). *Control through communication: The rise of system in American management*. Baltimore, MD: Johns Hopkins University Press.

Yates, J., & Orlikowski, W. J. (1992). Genres of organizational communication: a structurational approach to studying communication and media. *Academy of Management Review, 17,* 299-326.

8

Settings, Speech Genres, and the Institutional Organization of Practices

**Carol Berkenkotter,
with Amanda Haertling Thein**
University of Minnesota

Over the past 18 years, I have combined ethnographic techniques such as participant-observation with discourse analyses of spoken and written institutional and professional genres. More recently, I have incorporated the perspective of critical ethnography into the field research courses I teach to graduate students in the Rhetoric Department at the University of Minnesota.[1] Field researchers using a critical ethnographic approach are concerned with the ways in which social structures and power relationships growing out of inequities in class, ethnicity, gender, or other sources of asymmetry are instantiated in every day practices. The focus here is on *practices* (a term with a long history in critical social science; see Turner, 1994) with the researcher's questions and data-gathering techniques foregrounding students or other participants' discourse practices, and in particular, their use of speech genres.

Discourse practices are not only linguistic; they also are semiotic. Thus, the ways in which people position their bodies, the arrangement of furniture to support their social interactions, as well as their context-sensitive language behaviors all play a role in how people, through their daily interactions, establish social roles, power relationships, or, conversely, how they resist and subvert the status quo, which of course is a power issue as well.

GENRE ANALYSIS IN THE CONTEXT
OF ETHNOGRAPHIC FIELDWORK

As a researcher, I work in the area in discourse studies known as *genre theory*, with the major analytical tool being genre analysis in the context of ethnographic fieldwork (and, more recently, historical archival research). Central to my approach to genre analysis is the view that speech genres aren't "out there;" rather, the concept of *genre* needs to be understood in terms of language users' recognition of what is appropriate at any given moment, in a particular setting or, in other words, *genre knowledge*. Genre knowledge is the tacit understandings of the "decorum" of the moment in response to the contextual cues of a particular setting.

In cultures or institutional settings that we do not understand, this knowledge may not be useful. For instance, recently my husband and I were in Venice for a week's holiday; the first few days we were clueless about what language behaviors were appropriate for the trattorias and cafes we found tucked away in every alley or beside the endless canals of the city. Certainly, our restaurant "scripts" for eating out in various kinds of establishments in the United States did not work in Venice. We found that there seemed to be a ratio between the location of the restaurant and the amount of time we waited for a waiter to show up (45 minutes in a small, dark trattoria near the Piazza de San Marco that our guidebook recommended), and that the people who serve you find it extremely rude when you ask for the check. After having been snubbed, ignored, or rebuffed by waiters, we learned to order by pointing to what we wanted in the menu in the sections on appetizers, pasta, fish or beef, salad, and, of course, wine. When, on the first day entering a trattoria, we attempted to order a pasta entrée for lunch, we found ourselves ignored for the better part of an hour, and then treated with great distain as our waiter explained that we could not order just one course in this establishment. Thus, in the course of a week of eating in cafes along the Grand Canal in various other spots, we gradually acquired the knowledge—mostly by watching Italians (and other Europeans) order—how to order "gracefully," without being gauche.

This view of cultural and context-sensitive genre knowledge as being at the center of genre analysis has marked much of my research over the last two decades. Specifically, I draw on five principles that Tom Huckin and I formulated several years ago and published in our book, *Genre Knowledge in Disciplinary Communication: Cognition/Culture/Power* (Berkenkotter & Huckin, 1995).

These five principles are as follows (for a detailed discussion and examples of this material, see Berkenkotter & Huckin, 1995, pp. 1-25):

1. **Dynamism:** Genres are dynamic rhetorical forms that are developed from actors' responses to recurrent situations and that serve to stabilize experience and give it coherence and meaning (see Bitzer, 1978; Miller, 1984). Genres change over time in response to their users' sociocognitive needs.

2. **Situatedness:** Our knowledge of genres is derived from and embedded in our participation in the communicative activities of daily and professional life. As such, genre knowledge is a form of "situated cognition," which continues to develop as we participate in the activities of the ambient culture.

3. **Form and Content:** Genre knowledge embraces both form and content, including a sense of what content is appropriate to a particular purpose, in a particular situation, at a particular point in time.

4. **Duality of Structure:** As we draw on genre rules to engage in professional activities, we *constitute* social structures (in professional, institutional, and organizational contexts) and simultaneously *reproduce* these structures.[2]

5. **Community Ownership:** Genre conventions signal a community or social grouping's norms, epistemology, ideology, and social ontology.

Since the publication of *Genre Knowledge* in the mid-1990s, many other books and articles have been published on genre theory and genre analysis, not only in my own field of rhetoric, but also in such disciplines as applied linguistics, sociology of knowledge, sociology of communication, literary theory, semiotics, anthropological linguistics, critical discourse analysis, pragmatics, and English as a second language (ESL). There have been two international conferences (in 1998 and 2001) that brought together genre theorists and researchers from these fields to identify major theoretical and methodological issues and concerns, and to discuss these issues and concerns from various disciplinary perspectives.[3]

Between 1995 and the present, my views on the functions of speech genres in institutional and professional discourse have shifted somewhat, specifically in relation to the unit of analysis. Many genre analysts in the mid- and late-1980s and early 1990s tended to focus on single genres (e.g., the scientific article). However, a convergence of factors—the growing influence of Bakhtin's ideas, in particular, intertextuality,[4] addressivity, and dialogicality; Fairclough's (1992) concept of intertextuality in the context of genre systems; and finally, Briggs and Bauman's (1992) literature review of the work in anthropological linguistics on the intertextuality of oral performances in various tribal settings—made it increasingly apparent to a number of American academics (including myself) that what had formerly appeared to be discrete genres were networked into larger chains of discourse (i.e., part of genre sets or systems; see e.g., Bazerman, 1994, 2000; Berkenkotter & Huckin, 1995; Devitt, 1991). In the mid-1990s, research I conducted with Doris Ravotas, a clinical psychologist, on psychotherapists' session notes and initial client evaluations (called "psychosocial assessments"; see Berkenkotter & Ravotas, 1997; Ravotas & Berkenkotter, 1998) required that we consider, not only one kind of text, or oral interaction, but the entire intertextual character of psychotherapists' oral interactions with clients, their session notes, and their client case histories. All of these oral and written texts were part of the "discursive system" of the particular mental health agency in northern Michigan where the therapists whose writing practices we studied, worked. Because we were examining therapists' session notes and reports as they functioned in the context of the entire system of texts in the mental health clinic (only a fraction of which we actually saw and analyzed), we needed to conceptualize these texts as part of larger chains of oral, written, and in some cases, electronic discourse.

These psychotherapy texts were not only intertextual (i.e., they referred to previous documents in a client's psychiatric record, and they were dependent on the diagnostic nomenclature and psychiatric classifications of the fourth edition of the *Diagnostic and Statistical Manual of Mental Disorders* [*DSM-IV*]), but they were also interdiscursive as well (i.e., they were constructed from the oral interaction between client and therapist during the initial psychotherapy session). This research on psychiatric case reports also led to another realization. As I became increasingly aware of the system of texts, codes, and oral and written interactions that constituted literate practices among professionals in the local mental health clinic, it also became clear that that therapists' practice of "writing up the case," and continuing to add more information to the psychiatric record during the course of the client's treatment, were practices that had historical antecedents. Moreover, these antecedents were enshrouded in the writing practices of asylum doctors (or "mad doctors," as they were called), as they recorded patient's cases in asylum casebooks in the 18th and 19th centuries.

These musings that led to several trips to various medical libraries' historical archives, set me to investigating the evolution of case history writing as a literate practice based on what is the quintessential practice in psychiatry, *taking the case*. In the process and over several years, I worked on a book on psychiatric case histories that examined the practice of reporting the case, with its cultural-historical roots in maintaining clinical records in the mental asylums in England and Europe in the 18th and 19th centuries, and slightly later in the United States in the 19th and 20th centuries.

All of this musing about taking the case and writing it up as an historically sedimented set of practices, led as well to my developing a second set of "core assumptions" for studying institutional and professional genres.

These assumptions, or "principles" as I called them are as follows:

1. **Genre systems play an intermediate role between institutional structural properties and individual communicative action** (cf. Miller, 1994; Swales, 1993). By the notion of "intermediate role," I mean, following Günthner and Knobauch (1995),

   > Communicative genres [and their repertoires] are not to be separated from the social structural features. They are links between subjective stocks of knowledge and the social structures of a community. Genres fulfill important functions with respect to coping with, transmission and traditionalization of intersubjective experience of the life-world. On the one hand they facilitate the transmission of knowledge by guiding the interactants' expectations about what is to be said. On the other hand they are the sediments of socially relevant communicative processes, as only those processes may be expected to be fixed into genres which are of some relevance to the social actors. (p. 6)

   From this perspective, genres and their systems can be said to instantiate—through actors' microlevel, situated practices—structures of social and institutional relations. Knowledge of these relations is tacit, imbricated in our symbolic systems and communicative genres—matters of practical knowledge and mutually held by members of a particular profession or discipline. As social/institutional relations across time and space are altered by technology and the changes in an institution's communicative budget, hybrid genres arise in relation to actors' microlevel activity. And here is where one's conceptual framework has to be multidimensional enough to be inclusive of:

   - actor + goal (object),
   - tools (including technology and symbolic systems) and their
   - affordances,[5]
   - constitutive rules,
   - traces of historical cultural practices (i.e., how these goals have been accomplished in the past).

2. **One of the central means for identifying texts in a genre system is their intertextual activity.** The texts that we see in a genre system are responsive to, refer to, index, or anticipate other texts. (*Text* here refers to both spoken and written, as well as electronically mediated discourse). As Fairclough (1992) suggested, "the concept of intertextuality points to the productivity of texts, to how texts can transform prior texts and restructure existing conventions (genres, discourses), to generate new ones" (p. 102).

Intertextuality, as described by Fairclough and others (Bazerman, 1994; Berkenkotter & Huckin, 1993, 1995; Bhatia, 1997; Bloome, this volume; Russell, 1997; Selzer, 1994), is a concept with considerable heuristic, or explanatory power because it provides an analytical framework for examining the relationship between diachronically or synchronically linked genres and systems of genres. The concept of intertextuality also enables us to see interrelationships between written and spoken activities in an organizational "communicative chain," as Gunnarsson (1997) proposed. Thus, in an engineering consulting firm, a proposal sent to a client is the outcome of many linked genres: oral, written, and electronically mediated (see Orlikowski & Yates, 1994; Yates, Orlikowski, & Okamura, 1999).

3. **The concept of genre systems enables the analyst to foreground the discursively salient component of human activity systems.** Researchers who study intertextually linked writing and/or speaking practices tend to focus either on what the actors are doing ("follow the actors"), such as the dyadic interactions of conversation analysis, or on the features and conventions of texts ("follow the texts"). With these analytical foci, however, it is easy to relegate to the background the many different kinds of contexts in which the situated activity we are studying is occurring, contexts such as the physical setting, material practices, and socioeconomic structures of the profession or organization, the history of its practices, the participants' background knowledge, the interpersonal relationships between the participants (e.g., doctor–patient, therapist–client, nurse–doctor), the co-texts, and so on (see Engeström, 1999). In fact, the very concept of *context* is itself problematic, as numerous commentators have observed (see Cole, 1996; Duranti & Goodwin, 1992; Engeström, 1993; Lave, 1988; Linell, 1998; Russell, 1997a; Tracy, 1998) . How do we study, analyze, describe, and theorize context?

UNDERSTANDING CONTEXT AS BEING MULTI-DIMENSIONAL, HISTORICALLY SEDIMENTED, CULTURAL, DIALOGICAL, DISCONTINUOUS, CONTRADICTORY, SOCIAL, AND IDEOLOGICAL REQUIRES A PARTICULAR KIND OF THEORETICAL LENS

To circumvent the problem of treating context either as "containers for actions or as situationally-created experiential spaces" (Engeström, 1993, p.

67), scholars and researchers in a number of disciplines have been using the multidimensional concept of *activity system* in place of context. (See, e.g., Cole, 1996; R. Engeström, 1985; Y. Engeström, 1987, 1993; Y. Engeström, Miettinen, & Punamäki, 1999; Lave & Wenger, 1991. For examples of North American writing researchers drawing on activity theory, see Bazerman, 1997; Berkenkotter & Ravotas 1997; Dias et al., 1998; Freedman & Smart, 1997; Prior, 1997; Russell, 1997; Winsor, 1999.)

Several works by Engeström—*Learning by Expanding: An Activity Theoretical Approach to Developmental Research* (1987), his chapter in the collection, *Understanding Practice* (1993), and more recently his edited collections, *Cognition and Communication at Work* (with David Middleton, 1998), and *Perspectives on Activity Theory* (with Reijo Miettinen and Raija-Leena Punamäki, 1999)—have been instrumental in introducing the concept of activity system to both researchers in the North American tradition of genre studies (Freedman & Medway, 1994; Hyon, 1996) and readers of educational research and theory (see also Cole & Engeström, 1993). Building on neo-Vygotskyan activity theory, Engeström (1993) observed the following:

> If we take a closer and prolonged look at any institution, we get a picture of a continuously constructed, collective activity system that is not reducible to series of sums of individual discrete actions, although human agency is necessarily realized in the form of actions [Leont'ev, 1978]. (p. 66)

From the perspective of activity theory, contexts should not be considered to be containers nor what Engeström called "situationally-created experiential spaces." Contexts are activity systems. "An activity system integrates the subject, the object, and the instruments (material tools as well as signs and symbols) into a unified whole. An activity system incorporates both the object-oriented productive aspect and the person-oriented communicative aspect of the human conduct. Production and communication are inseparable . . ." (Engeström, 1993, p. 67).

Underlying Engeström's conception of human activity is the view that communicative acts (what I would call speech genres) are part and parcel of the subsystems of production, distribution, exchange, and consumption (p. 67; see also Cole, 1996, for a discussion of these issues). In this respect, activity theory is a materialist theory. But it is not a deterministic theory in the sense that the life of an activity system is also discontinuous:

> Besides accumulation and incremental change, there are crises, upheavals and qualitative transformations . . . an activity system is not a homogeneous entity. To the contrary it is composed of a multitude of

> often disparate elements, voices and viewpoints. This multiplicity can
> be understood in terms of historical layers. An activity system always
> contains sediments of earlier historical modes. (Engeström, 1993, p. 68)

One way to observe the disparate elements, or dissonances within "activity settings" such as banks (Freedman & Smart, 1997), nursery school classrooms, high school classrooms, cafeterias, or pep rallies, is to examine the actors' (inhabiting those settings) constitutive interdiscursive and intertextual practices. By this I mean that the researcher, using some combination of ethnographic or case study techniques (e.g., participant–observation, semi-structured or unstructured "ethnographic" interviews, audio- or videotapes of oral interaction, photographs, artifact collection, etc.) seeks to identify the sorts of *multivoicedness* and *inner contradictions* existing within the institutional setting.

INSTITUTIONAL SETTINGS AS ACTIVITY SYSTEMS

The classroom is both institutional setting and activity system with its contextual cues, language, and bodily orientation, gestures, physical configuration of desks, animal cages, lab tables, overhead projectors, slide projectors, glass beakers, microscopes, blackboards, computers, and so forth. These are some of the tools, artifacts, and speech genres, and settings that are constitutive of the institutionalized practices that students of all ages come to learn, or, in some cases, to resist and ultimately reject. As sociologist Thomas Luckmann (1992), suggested:

> Institutionalized social interaction is more rigidly controlled with
> respect to means and has more clearly defined ends than other kinds of
> social interaction. This area of social life, therefore, tends to exhibit a
> low degree of tolerance for deviations from established procedure.
> Institutions organize the central functions of social life, such as produc-
> tion and distribution of the means of life, reproduction, the exercise of
> power and the construction of "meaning," that is, of legitimacy for the
> social order and of cognitive coherence for individual life in society.
> Institutions have a specific location in social space and time and they
> may, of course, also be seen as a specific aggregation of personnel. But
> essentially they are a "code" of action. (p. 221)

Central to this code of action are speech genres as they constitute the primary mediational means for organizing and communicating what Luckmann (1992) called the "central functions of social life," that is, as production and distribution of the means of life, reproduction, the exercise of power and the construction of "meaning." That is to say, speech genres serve to mediate practices in activity systems (i.e., institutions), as is seen here. There is as well, however, an undertheorized dimension to recent discussions of genres in activity systems and that is an examination of the ways in which institutional settings and the genres appearing in them are linked. Hence, the theoretical importance of Luckmann's perspective, specifically his notion that *institutional settings possess discursively organizing functions*, functions that are instantiated in what appear to be the most "common sense" (to native-speakers) and context-sensitive linguistic practices and behaviors.

SETTINGS AND INSTITUTIONALLY ORGANIZED SOCIAL PRACTICES

We now turn to some illustrative examples of institutionalized social interaction, to which Luckmann referred. These examples are particularly illustrative of how children's and adolescents' bodies are controlled through space and time in two quite different institutional settings: a preschool classroom and lunchroom in a Boulder, Colorado Montessori School and various settings in an urban high school in a large midwestern city. In the first of these settings, children "learn how to mean" in the context of tools and artifacts, genres, and contextual cues. In the second (in various high school activity settings, such as the school gymnasium where special events are held, the cafeteria, and the English classroom), the researcher's focus is on students "structuring" (and being structured by) these social spaces along the dimensions of inclusion and exclusion. We see that the organization of bodies in these spaces tacitly accomplishes social and political agendas through seemingly "everyday" activity. It is these everyday practices, and in "what everybody knows," that social structures are constituted and maintained.

Literacy as Embodied Practices:
Bear Walks Around the Sun Four Times in a Boulder Montessori School Classroom

It is in preschool settings that we can see most vividly how language and meaning are shaped by the physical positioning of children's bodies around tools and artifacts. In this respect, we can see how literate practices are quite literally embodied by young children as part of their enculturation into the practices of "doing school" (Dyson, 1984). I am suggesting here that school literacy and school discourses are first constituted through embodied practices in young children, in the course of their language socialization. The figures shown here depict a preschool literacy event in which children acquire a knowledge of scientific concepts through embodied activity and collective orientation to tools (including language) and artifacts.

First, a bit of background needs to be provided. The setting, a Montessori school classroom in Boulder, Colorado, is one of eight or nine Montessori nursery schools in this city. The children who attend are primarily White and middle class; however there are also a small number of Asian-American, African-American, and Hispanic children in this and other classrooms in the Montessori system. As is the case at many other institutions for preschool children, the school day is divided into units, beginning with outdoor play in the school's playground, a transition period for children between home and school. The children in the figures presented here have been recently been dropped off by their parents (Fig. 8.1).

The varieties of children's talk (i.e., their speech genres) are embedded in physical activities and mediated by the artifacts that are in the setting.

Thus, an observer is likely to hear snatches of conversations on the swing (see Fig. 8.2) or the utterances surrounding a child's swinging on monkey bars, laughter, and shouting (or crying) that accompanies a game that has been made up spontaneously. What's important to keep in mind is that language is embedded in activity, activity taking place in different settings, each of which is a semiotic context rich with cues for bodily and language behavior.

Figure 8.1.   Children on the playground

Figure 8.2. Children on the swing

Moving from the playground into each of two classrooms for preschoolers, one sees a setting designed for children's educational enrichment, filled with tools and artifacts to engage a child's curiosity; these include books, word games, puzzles, materials for painting and drawing, easels, paints, chalk, colored pencils, flat geometric shapes to draw with, other geometric shapes that are three dimensional, scissors, string, cutting paper, a cage with a guinea pig, and so on. But what is most salient to a casual observer are two concentric rings, each about 2 inches wide, made of bright blue tape affixed to the rug in each of the two classrooms I visited. What one also notices in these two classrooms are tools and artifacts of everyday living: hammers and nails, brooms, dish soap and towels, child-size kitchen sinks, and a number of other domestic tools and artifacts.

Children make the transition between outdoor and classroom activities by coming together in the circle to jointly participate in a beginning-of-school-day-activity. Often (but not always), it is some form of the activity that begins the school such as "morning news" or "sharing time."[6] Up to this point in the morning, most (although not all) children have been playing outside (weather permitting) running, swinging on bars, working at outside projects with sand, trucks, scoops, and shovels, or making up games, which frequently involve cooking of food (sand) in the latticed gazebo that sits in one corner of the play yard.

The joint activity that signals the ending of outdoor playtime and the beginning of class time does not begin until each child is seated in the outer blue ring. This is the physical configuration around which certain language and physical behaviors are organized. Children new to this setting are quickly oriented by the teacher and the assistant teachers to the kinds of talk and activity considered appropriate to sitting and participating in the circle. There are, in other words, conversational practices that the children learn to associate with sitting in the circle. Sitting in the circle at the beginning of the day helps "transition" the children from the spontaneous utterances of the playground to the more consciously organized and orchestrated (institutional) speech genres of the Montessori classroom (see Fig. 8.3).

Figures 8.4 through 8.7 depict an institutional activity sequence, "Bear's" fourth birthday celebration. This particular morning, Bear is the child who goes to the box containing the numbered squares and takes the one with the number 28 on it and sets it into the calendar. The clock on the wall shows school has begun: It is 9:10 a.m. in this Boulder Montessori classroom.

In Fig. 8.5, Bear's teacher, Joyce, is placing a candle in the shape of the sun in the center of the two rings (the inner one, which you can see), and she places rectangular cards with the names of months around the "sun." This is a ritual with which most of the children (except newcomers) are familiar, so they are pretty quiet as they look on.

Bear now begins his walk around the sun. He circles the lighted wax globe four times, once for each year of his life. This is an example of the kind of embodied activity that children in this Montessori school witness. Bear's activity here suggests a hybrid genre; Bear is celebrating his birthday with a set of rituals, but the birthday ritual is as well a science lesson because he is demonstrating the revolution of the earth around the sun.

There are two points that I wish to make with these photographs of a child's birthday celebration in this classroom. First, classrooms, like other institutional settings, are activity settings in which tools, artifacts, speech genres, and the setting are coconstitutive. Second, the literate practices in which we see the children engaged are embedded in the "work" and participation structures of the classroom.

In the lunchroom seen in Fig. 8.6, the tables are set for the birthday. The children's talk is more spontaneous in this setting, in contrast to the conversational circle; nevertheless, here as well the children are being socialized to perform a series of actions around which talk is organized.

Even in this less structured setting, the Montessori children are being socialized into the participation structures, or speech genres that are coconstitutive with busing their dishes

Figure 8.3.   Child changing the date of calendar

Figure 8.4.   Teacher putting candle in center of circle

Figure 8.5.   Bear circling the sun

Figure 8.6.   Empty lunch room with the tables set

Figure 8.7.   Children at the table eating, talking

Figure 8.8.   Children busing and washing dishes

What we have seen in Figs. 8.4 through 8.8 is an institutional activity sequence in which children are being socialized into literate practices, specifically those of formal schooling. Children who enter kindergarten not knowing how to "do school" begin their elementary school career in arrears (Dyson, 1984; Heath, 1983). Learning the oral and written genres of school is more than a matter of learning the surface conventions; this learning is very much embedded in the setting (e.g., outdoors vs. indoors); the activity occurring in the setting (e.g., catching balls, swinging on swings, sitting in the circle for a group activity like "morning news" or "show and tell"); and the objective(s) of that activity (e.g., science lesson cum birthday celebration). What is salient in these photographs is the extent to which the practices of school-based literacy are assimilated by 3- and 4-year-olds at the level of bodily orientation, or positioning in relation to artifacts and tools. In this regard, Bear's walk can be seen as a form of *embodied learning*, in that this ritual instantiates a formal scientific concept for Bear and his peers. If we foreground the ideological implications of Bear's movement as well as the other childrens' physical orientations once they move into the classroom, we can see how a child's "disposition/habitus" (Bourdieu, 1977, 1991) is constituted in and through everyday practices at Boulder Montessori (cf. Rex, 2002).

The children in these pictures are many years away from the disciplinary tasks and activities they will have to master as college students, but even at this early age they are beginning to acquire the concepts that will be needed for literate practices in a science curriculum. Their activities are semiotically heterogeneous, but we can see (even if we can't hear) the way in which talk is organized by and embedded in the various kinds of "work" in which the children are engaged.

Organization of Bodies in the Social Space: Scenes From an Urban High School

We now fast forward to a high school in a metropolitan setting to examine a school culture of inclusion and exclusion drawn on racial lines. (The material that follows is excerpted from an ethnographic narrative written by Amanda Haertling Thein, for the critical ethnography course mentioned at the beginning of this chapter.)

Thompson is a traditional working-class high school in an urban area of a large, midwestern city. Many students who attend Thompson have several generations of relatives who also attended the school and who still live in the neighborhood. Athletic events, particularly hockey games, are well attended by the community at large, not just by those with a direct connection to the school. Thompson's community involvement and athletic tradition prove to be key pieces to the puzzle of the workings of the school culture.

Physical Control of Students and Facilities.   A walk around any high school gives great insight into the culture of the school. At Thompson, what stands out first is the neatness and cleanliness of the facilities. The floors are spotless and the lockers are painted with what must be a fairly fresh coat of red paint. A glance into any classroom reveals clean desks in neat rows. There are no candy wrappers, soda containers, or empty bags of chips, nor are students seen eating in the hallways or classrooms. During lunch, three different groups of students can be seen going in and out of the cafeteria in a 90-minute period, students in each group carefully cleaning up after themselves. The minimal cleaning that needs to be done between groups is quickly taken care of by a team of custodians and cafeteria workers. Following the author's comment regarding the cleanliness of the facility, the assistant principal said, "This is what a real urban school is like. It's not *Dangerous Minds* around here."

In addition to the physical control of the facilities at Thompson, it is hard to miss the fact that the students are also kept very carefully in line. Again, the organization of the lunch period is a tell-tale sign of this control. Thompson has a closed campus, meaning that students are not allowed to leave campus during the day for lunch. Thompson is also on a block schedule, which means that there are only four class periods during the day. Most students do not have any free periods. Lunch takes place during the third period of the day. Students are divided into three sections, first, second and third lunch. Each of these sections goes to lunch during a predetermined part of third period. Each student is assigned a section along with the rest of his or her third period class. This schedule has important implications for controlling the actions of students. With very few free periods and no opportunity to leave campus, a school with this schedule is by nature much more in control of students' actions than a school with an open campus and seven or eight periods. Additionally, students have less freedom to plan their lunch periods with friends and also little opportunity to resist school social groupings because they must attend lunch with their third–period class and they must eat in the cafeteria.

Physical control over students is also noticeable in the fact that hallways are closely monitored. It is very rare to see students in the hallways except during passing periods. Students who leave class are expected to carry a pass from a teacher giving them permission to be in the halls. Additionally, students may not enter a class tardy without a pass from the desk at the entryway to the building, which tells the teacher the time that the student entered the building and shows that the student has signed up for a detention period. In the following section, a closer inspection of the workings of the school shows that physical control of the facilities and the students clearly affects many aspects of the school culture.

Physical Control in Maintaining School Traditions, and Social/Racial Hierarchies.   An examination of the "Winter-Fest" coronation ceremony can provide a framework for the way that physical control of the students and facilities of the school is carried out. "Winter-Fest" is a week in February when students prepare for the winter dance. It includes festivities throughout the week, dress-up days, and a ceremony at which the royalty for the dance are crowned. This ceremony is steeped in school tradition and is carefully managed by teachers and administrators.

The ceremony is held for several hours during the middle of the school day. Students are released from their classes in order to attend. Attempts to control the student body and the building during the coronation ceremony included a most striking incident in which the doors to the gymnasium, where the festivities were held, are guarded by ROTC students dressed in full regalia and carrying swords. Although they seemed to have little real authority to stop people from entering or sitting in the wrong place, they still evoke several strong images. First, they appear to be prison guards, keeping the inmates in line, but more importantly, because this is a coronation ceremony, they appear to be guarding the "royalty," in the manner of guards at the gates to a palace. This is interesting because, in fact, the integrity of the school tradition of crowning royalty is what they are protecting. The actual job of these ROTC students was to make sure that anyone entering the gymnasium was wearing a button. One teacher (Dan) explained how this process worked: He said that students did have to buy buttons to get in. He thought they cost $1. He also said that charging for the buttons serves two purposes. First, it is a fundraiser. Second, the students who don't like to attend pep assemblies are given a way out. Students who didn't attend stayed in selected classrooms throughout the building, watching videos. Dan also acknowledged that many students who did not want to attend the assembly simply left school, although this is against school rules. Further, he suggested that this was a way for administration to get kids to "self-weed the riff raff." And a way for students to resist: "I'm not going to buy your stupid button."
This attempt to guard who attends the coronation appeared successful. There was very little resistance on the part of the students in the audience to this traditional popularity contest. Any parent or outsider to the school walking into the gymnasium to watch this event might have assumed that this audience was the entire student body and that this student body was unified in support of the students being crowned as royalty. I noticed only one attempt at resistance on the part of small group of African-American students (although I'm not sure it was resistance, but perhaps a show of enthusiasm that was deemed inappropriate by the principal), which was quickly squelched by the principal:

> The principal sits near the podium. I can see that she is eyeing the students who are swaying and clapping. She signals to another teacher, who goes up to quiet the "disruptive" students. There are teachers "stationed" throughout the student sections to handle such situations.

The reality, according to Dan, is that many students at Thompson don't support such events that center around the mainstream "popular" students. However, these students are actually encouraged by the administration *not* to attend.

By and large, the students involved in the coronation ceremony are White, although there are a few students of color (see also Perry, 2001; Beach & Kalnin, this volume). For example, of the 20 to 25 girls involved, 3 were Asian, 3 were African American, and 1 was Latina. Looking into one classroom where some of the students who chose not to attend the ceremony are "kept" may provide some clues to who these resistant students are:

> I notice a dark classroom full of students watching a movie starring Bruce Willis. Apparently this is a group of students who chose not to go to go to the assembly. I notice several things about these students. First, the vast majority are students of color. Second, the two White students I notice (both female) are trying to do homework in the dark. Third, many students are sleeping, but no one is talking.

A possible explanation in studying these incidents is that because the school wants to maintain traditions and a sense of cohesiveness and control within the student body, they choose to exclude those students who may not hold these values. The African-American students who attended the ceremony but celebrated in a manner that was "inappropriate" are a perfect example of students operating with values that are not upheld by the school. Of course, this is not a simple issue. Some might say that it is humane to allow students who do not support pep assemblies to opt out of them. However, an argument could also be made that if the major events supported by the school were more inclusive, a larger diversity of students might choose to get involved. Traditions at Thompson were constructed through the values and norms of a primarily White student body and community. While vast demographic changes have occurred over the years, little has changed in these traditions—thus these traditions continue to privilege White students because they are the students who may most easily comply with the values that these traditions uphold. Additionally, in protecting the traditions of the school, the administration ultimately supports the norms and values of White students. As a result, it appears that students of color have been placed at the periphery of school culture, whereas White students occupy the positions of power.

In observations of the cafeteria during lunch periods I noticed a similar phenomenon. With very few exceptions, students clearly organize themselves into racial groups. According to one student, Ron, the most popular White students sit in the center of the cafeteria, whereas other racial and social groups sit on the periphery:

> I notice that Ron has come up above the cafeteria and is standing by me. I say hello. I ask him if he thinks there's a pattern to the way kids sit at lunch. He says yes without any hesitation. He says the popular kids sit in the middle and the "regular" kids sit together on the sides. He says the Asian students sit together, "unless you're cool," in which case you can sit in the middle. I ask him why the popular kids sit in the middle. He says it's because that's the middle of everything and that's where they've always been.

I noticed this same pattern in some classroom observations (in classes where students selected their own seats) as well.

> In the middle row of the class there are four White girls. In the row to the left of the middle row, there are two White girls in the front two seats. Next back there is an African-American girl, next are two Asian boys, and furthest to the back is an African American girl. The row to the right of the middle has another White girl in the front seat, followed by a White boy, Gina and Kayla (both White), another White girl and a White boy. The row closest to the door seats all Asian- and African-American students.

In this example, most of the White students sit in the three middle rows and in the front seat, whereas most of the students of color sit off to the sides or toward the back.

Also of note is the fact that basketball games are attended by a student population that is almost entirely African American (the African-American population of the school as a whole is 17%), despite the fact that the varsity team consists of seven African-American students, five White students, and one Latino student. It seems that because hockey has been claimed as the central school sport and is clearly dominated by mainstream, White, student culture (there was only one student of color on the team this year, a very popular Latino male), basketball has been left to the African-American segment of the student population as a consolation prize of sorts. Additionally, although basketball games are primarily attended by African-American students, there is still a sense that they are managed by White students because these students sell the tickets at the game, run the concession stand, and play in the band during the game.

In the examples of the classroom, the cafeteria, and the basketball game, it should be clear that there are many possible reasons why such segregation might occur. No simple answer exists as to how these patterns arose at this school. But regardless of how these patterns were set into motion, it is clear that although Thompson may be a very diverse school, there is evidence that students rarely interact between racial lines. So although White students at Thompson may see themselves as different from White students in suburban schools because of their physical proximity to students of color, they may actually have limited experience in dealing with issues of race. This lack of interaction between racial groups can be seen in classroom discourse at well.

In looking at student discussion it is clear that White students struggle to find "correct" or appropriate words to talk about race. An example is Katrina's (a White, female, senior) attempt to explain that many of her relatives have racist views because of their lack of interaction with people of color:[7]

KL (student):   =I thought of it as (.) almost like the whole (.) I thought about like, hh you know, the ^field ^trip? And like how we're going to go and IF SOMEONE FROM LIKE *PRAIRIE HILLS*, like they're (.) .hh so used to that (.), one whatever and then they came ^here? I think they'd kind of /freak /out (.) And that's what I think about fish and salt ^water? (.) you know the ones that can't survive /here=

DP (teacher):   =What do you think they'd freak out about? =Like I was trying to think=

KL: =Just (.) the whole= *diversity*, I mean =people= get *weird* about that like my *family* that lives out in like (.) out there and they

=(cough)=

live you know =like=, they go to like (.) just (.) basically *all* white schools and then

FS: =heh heh=

they're like "o:h, do you have (.) ^these ^people?" It's like, "Ye:ah, they're just like people like /us." They act like they're *not human* and I think they'd kind of like freak out if they /came /here. *That's what I =think*=

Several patterns arise here. First, Katrina struggles to find the right words to discuss race. She refers to race as "the whole diversity." She also avoids using any racialized words to describe people of color (cf. Bonilla-Silva's, 2001 discussion of "race-talk"). Rather she refers to "these people." Additionally, she makes reference to a metaphor that the whole class seems to rely on in discussing race (water is to fish as culture is to people), as well as using the views of her relatives as a means of anchoring her position as a nonracist.

It is possible that in keeping a sense of control over the facilities, the students, and the traditions of the school, the school community is resisting the cultural transformation that comes with shifting demographics in the community and the school since the late 1980s. Rather than becoming a place of true diversity, Thompson actually still thrives off of White culture and White traditions that have been in place for many years. Groups that are relatively new to the school have become peripheral factions rather than empowered and incorporated members of student culture. Therefore, when racial confusion and misunderstanding is observed in classroom discourse, the reason becomes clear. Thompson may be a demographically diverse school, but interaction among races is actually quite minimal.

Physical Control Manifested As Intellectual Control. The sense of physical control over students and facilities at Thompson in some cases manifests itself as intellectual control on the classroom level. On several occasions, I observed classrooms in which students seemed uncomfortable when given freedom to think critically and speak openly. A sense of calm and comfort returned when classrooms returned to a passive, teacher-directed environment.

In one case, I observed a teacher attempting to hold an open discussion on *The Catcher in the Rye*, in a regular level, 11th-grade English class. Although students seemed quite excited about the prospect of this discussion, they seemed to have very little experience with this type of intellectual and physical freedom to speak. Thus, the discussion was less than successful as the following excerpt shows:

> Soon there is a dialogue between Angie, in the back of the room, and James in the front of the room. They discuss whether having several conversation in your head (as Holden does) means you are crazy. Angie is arguing that it does not. Students quickly begin jumping into this debate, but the debate becomes a series of loud conversations between a few students—everyone is talking over each other. The teacher has to stop the dialogue. James then tries to talk again and then Angie tries. Each time they get started, students begin talking loudly

amongst themselves. The teacher lets it go on for a few seconds each time and then tries to regain control and calls on a student to speak.

After several attempts to make this discussion work, the teacher tries a different strategy:

> The teacher asks students to turn to a particular page in the book. He turns off the lights again and very softly asks everyone to help him by not talking and allowing him to talk about p. 38 for a few minutes. Students quickly become quiet, open their books, and turn their eyes to the teacher—they are quite willing to comply with his request. The mood clearly shifts in the classroom.

Although most students seemed excited to be involved in a class discussion, they were clearly much more comfortable with—and accustomed to—a teacher-directed classroom in which they passively took in information and in which the teacher had total control over the class.

On another occasion I observed a 12th-grade geometry class with 38 students. Initially, I found myself impressed with the teacher's ability to keep control of such a large group of students:

> Now the class is looking at page 120. The teacher has one student read aloud while he demonstrates this problem on the chalkboard. Everyone else seems to be listening and following along. There are students who don't appear to be interested, but they all have their books out and are not distracting others.

On closer examination, I realized that the ability of the teacher to control students' physical activities may not be purely positive because it may lead to a lack of intellectual activity on the part of students. Students in this class were not asked to do anything intellectual or even active. They were merely asked to open their books and be quiet. At this point, students could choose to passively accept the information being offered, or simply tune out. However, outwardly this class is in compliance with the values of the school as a whole.

As can be seen from Thein's observations, her focus is on activities and practices in contexts (i.e., the social semiotics of various activity settings at Thompson High School). The raw materials of these observations are frequently visual details described in her fieldnotes, and corroborated by material from student interviews and audiotaped recordings of oral interactions in the classroom. Her narrative is a good example of what small details can be noticed when students' everyday practices are interpreted within the framework of the setting. Many of Thein's inferences are tied to her positioning herself reflexively early in her narrative.[8] Students are "literate" semiotically, even if they don't participate in instructional discourse.

IMPLICATIONS

Studies of settings have importance for understanding the interrelationship between semiotics, speech genres, tool-use (i.e., tools functioning as mediational means), social practices, and institutional goals and objectives. This perspective has relevance as well for researchers' understanding of the subtle interrelation between the uses of space and artifacts in institutional settings, and the development of literate practices and their speech genres indigenous to particular institutional settings. My goal in this chapter (with Thein's generous contribution) has been to illustrate the power and influence of a setting's contextualization cues in shaping and affecting language users' linguistic practices and bodily orientations.

With the quick visit to the Boulder Montessori classroom, I attempted to show how the activity sequence that my photographs depicted was both birthday celebration and science lesson. In this kind of rich educational environment, the learning of scientific concepts can be a form of embodied learning for children as young as 3 and 4. It is also in the photos of Boulder Montessori classroom and lunchroom that one can see the role that tools, artifacts, speech genres and settings play in children's development of literate practices. The physical layout of this Montessori classroom with its conversational circles, tools, and artifacts helps us to more clearly understand the ways in which children learn how to construct meanings within a social (and socializing) space.

In her study of "Thompson High" with its tightly controlled flow of student movement outside of the classroom, Amanda Haertling Thein captures in her descriptions what Bourdieu (1980) referred to as "bodily hexis" (pp. 68-70), and illustrates how hexis is orchestrated (some would say regulated) by norms, values, and traditions prevalent in the community in response to demographic changes since the 1980s. In contrast to the smooth transitions the students appear to be making between class time, lunchtime, and social event time (the coronation of the Snow Day Queen and King), Thein describes how a seemingly "unstructured" deviation from the initiation/response/evaluation (IRE) pattern of instructional discourse—a group discussion—triggers the opening of multiple conversational floors, the resulting chaos leading to the teacher to resume monological discourse. Unlike the unsophisticated 3 to 5 year olds at Boulder Montessori School, the students at Thompson High know how to "do school," which includes for many students passively resisting mainstream rituals and celebrations of the demographic status quo before the community surrounding Thompson became multicultural.

My intention in this chapter has been to show how an ethnographic perspective can make more tangible concepts from genre theory and cultural–historical activity theory. Both the discursive and bodily practices in any setting (classrooms, lunchrooms, school yards, school assemblies, etc.) are part of a particular institution's semiotic system. An ethnographic gaze enables the researcher to focus on the *activity system* as the unit of analysis, and then to examine—in concert—settings, tools, actors, genres, and artifacts as the context for participants' meaning-making activities. A critical ethnographic perspective, I would further suggest, directs the observer's attention to the dissonances and conflicts, the disparate elements, voices and view points that are intrinsic to any activity system.

ENDNOTES

1. See Cintron (1997) and Barton and Hamilton (1998) for contrasting examples of critical ethnographies; for the epistemological assumptions informing a critical ethnographic approach in educational research, see Carspecken (1996).
2. Briefly, the concept of social structuration growing out of Gidden's (1983) theoretical work on the relationship between social structure and human action is that the two have a reciprocal relation to each other. Thus, rather than social structures existing somehow "outside" people's day-to-day activities, structure is constituted through human actions, often without people's discursive awareness.
3. The first of the three international conferences on genre theory and research was held in Montreal, in April 1992. The program chairs were Aviva Freedman and Peter Medway. A fourth genre conference was planned for summer 2004, to be held at the University of Cardiff in Wales.
4. Fairclough (1992) noted that that it was Kristiva (1966; rpt. 1986) who, in the late-1960s, coined the term *intertextuality* in bringing Bakhtin's "translinguistic" approach to an analysis of the relationship between texts. In the last 40 years, the concept has spread from literary theory and analysis to a number of other disciplines because of its explanatory richness. Basically the concept refers to the notion that all texts (oral, written, electronic) contain bits and pieces of prior discourse that index social, cultural, and historical contexts.
5. A number of activity theorists such as Rogoff (1990) and Cole (1996), have adopted Gibson's (1982) ecological theory that emphasizes the mutuality of environment and organism. A particular object, such as a

stick or chisel, has the potential to be grasped by particular animal, and conversely, that animal possesses the potential to grasp that object (Rogoff, 1990).

6. "Morning news" and "sharing time" are, as well, exemplars of what Bakhtin (1986) called primary speech genres, that is, speech events that are not in their execution separated in time or space from their representations as is, for example, dialogue in novels, novels being a secondary genre.

7. For Thein's transcription conventions, see the key in the appendix.

8. About her own background as observer, Thein noted:

> I bring with me years of attending suburban schools and 4 years of teaching in upper middle-class, predominantly White, suburban schools. It must be noted that the contrast between my previous school experiences and my observations of Thompson played a large part in what I initially noticed about Thompson. My analysis begins with what might seem like a minor descriptive point—the school is very clean and the students are well behaved. However, this point has become the key idea around which my analysis is constructed. Without my past experiences in suburban schools, where students were given a great amount of freedom and things were much less tidy, I may not have latched on to neatness of the physical environment as an organizing framework. In everything I see at Thompson, there is a piece of the suburban school student and teacher that I have been throughout my life.

APPENDIX:
CONVENTIONS FOR TRANSCRIPTION NOTATION*

(.)	Untimed pause (just hearable; < .2 sec.)
>fast<	"Less than" and "greater than" signs indicate talk that is noticeably faster
<slow>	or slower than the surrounding talk.
<u>under</u>	Underlining indicates emphasis.
. , ? !	Punctuation marks are used to mark speech delivery rather than grammar. A period indicates a stopping fall in tone; a comma indicates a continuing intonation; a question mark indicates a rising inflection; an exclamation point indicates an animated or emphatic tone.
end of line= =start of line	Equal signs indicate latching (no interval) between utterances.
( )	Unclear speech or noise
heh or hah	Indicate laughter
CAPITALS	Capital letters indicate talk that is noticeably louder than surrounding talk.
ho:me	A colon indicates an extension of the sound or syllable that it follows.
.hh	Audible inbreath
hh	Audible outbreath (sometimes associated with laughter).

The following conventions are also based on Wood and Kroger, but slightly altered.

^	Indicates marked rising shifts in intonation in the talk immediately following.
/	Indicates marked rising shifts in intonation in the talk immediately following.
[coughs]	Brackets enclose transcriber's descriptions of nonspeech sounds or other features of the talk [coughs] or [bell rings]
soft	Indicates talk that is noticeably more quiet than surrounding talk.

---

*From Wood and Kroger (2000).

REFERENCES

American Psychiatric Association. (1994). *Diagnostic and statistical manual of mental disorders* (4th ed.). Washington, DC: Author.

Bakhtin, M.D. (1986). *Speech genres and other late essays* (V.W. McGee, Trans.). Austin: University of Texas Press.

Barton, D., & Hamilton, M. (1998). *Local literacies: Reading and writing in one community.* London, UK: Routledge.

Bazerman, C. (1993). Intertextual self-fashioning: Gould and Lewontin's representation of the literature. In J. Selzer (Ed.), *Understanding scientific prose* (pp. 20-41). Madison: University of Wisconsin Press.

Bazerman, C. (1994). Systems of genres and the enactment of social intentions. In A. Freedman & P. Medway (Eds.), *Genre and the new rhetoric* (pp. 79-101). London, UK: Taylor & Francis.

Bazerman, C. (1997). Discursively structured activities. *Mind, Culture, and Activity, 4,* 296-308.

Bazerman, C., & Russell, D. (Eds.). (2003). *Writing selves and societies: Research from activity perspectives.* Fort Collins, CO: The WAC Clearinghouse.

Berkenkotter, C., & Huckin T. (1995). *Genre knowledge in disciplinary communication: Cognition/culture/power.* Hillsdale, NJ: Erlbaum.

Berkenkotter, C., & Ravotas, D. (1997). Genre as tool in the transmission of practice over time and across professional boundaries. *Mind, Culture, and Activity, 4,* 256-274.

Bhatia, V.K. (1997). The power and politics of genre. *World Englishes, 16,* 359-371.

Bitzer, L. (1968). The rhetorical situation. *Philosophy and Rhetoric, 1,* 1-14.

Bonilla-Silva, E. (2001). *White supremacy and racism in the post-civil rights era.* Boulder, CO: Lynne Rienner.

Bourdieu, P. (1980). *Logic of practice* (R. Nice, Trans.). Stanford, CA: Stanford University Press.

Briggs, C.L., & Bauman, R. (1992). Genre, intertextuality, and social power. *Journal of Linguistic Anthropology, 2,* 131-172.

Carspecken, P.F. (1996). *Critical ethnography in educational research: A theoretical and practical guide.* New York: Routledge.

Cintron, R. (1997). *Angels' town: Chero ways, gang life, and rhetorics of the everyday.* Boston, MA: Beacon Press.

Cole, M. (1996). *Cultural psychology: A once and future discipline.* Cambridge, MA: Harvard University Press.

Cole, M., & Engeström, Y. (1993). A socio-cultural approach to distributed cognition. In G. Salomon (Ed.), *Distributed cognitions: Psychological and educational considerations* (pp. 1-46). Cambridge, UK: Cambridge University Press.

Devitt, A. (1991). Intertextuality in tax accounting. In C. Bazerman & J. Paradis (Eds.), *Textual dynamics of the professions* (pp. 336-357). Madison: University of Wisconsin Press.

Dias, P., Freedman, A., Medway, P., & Pare, A. (1998). *Transitions: Writing in academic and workplace settings.* Cresskill, NJ: Hampton Press.

Duranti, A., & Goodwin, G. (1992). *Rethinking context: Language as an interactive phenomenon.* Cambridge, UK: Cambridge University Press.

Dyson, A.H. (1984). Learning to write/Learning to do school: Emergent writers' interpretation of school literacy tasks. *Research in the Teaching of English, 18,* 233-264.

Engeström, R. (1995). Voice as communicative action. *Mind, Culture, and Activity, 2,* 192-215.

Engeström, Y. (1987). *Learning by expanding: An activity–theoretical approach to developmental research.* Helsinki: Orienta-Konsultit Oy.

Engeström, Y. (1993). Developmental studies of work as a testbench of activity theory: The case of primary care medical practice. In S. Chaiklin & J. Lave (Eds.), *Understanding practice: Perspectives on activity and context* (pp. 64-103). Cambridge, UK: Cambridge University Press.

Engeström, Y., Miettinen, R., & Punamäki, R.L. (1999). *Perspectives on activity theory.* Cambridge, UK: Cambridge University Press.

Engestrom, Y., & Middleton, D. (1998). *Cognition and communication at work.* Cambridge, UK: Cambridge University Press.

Fairclough, N. (1992). *Discourse and social change.* London: Polity Press.

Freedman, A., & Medway, P. (Eds.). (1994). *Genre and the new rhetoric.* London, UK: Taylor & Francis.

Freedman, A., & Smart, G. (1997). Navigating the current of economic policy: Written genres and the distribution of cognitive work at a financial institution. *Mind, Culture, and Activity, 4,* 238-255.

Gibson, J. J. (1979). *The ecological approach to visual perception.* Boston, MA: Houghton-Mifflin.

Giddens, A. (1984). *The constitution of society: Outline of the theory of structuration.* Berkeley: University of California Press.

Gunnarsson, B. L. (1997). The writing process from a sociolinguistic viewpoint. *Written Communication, 2,* 139-188.

Günthner, S., & Knoblauch, H. (1995). Culturally patterned speaking practices: The analysis of communicative genres. *Pragmatics, 5*(1), 1-32.

Heath, S.B. (1983). *Ways with words: Language, life, and work in communities and classrooms.* Cambridge, UK: Cambridge University Press.

Hyon, S. (1996). Genre in three traditions: Implications for ESL. *TESOL Quarterly, 30,* 693-722.

Kristiva, J. (1986). Word, dialogue, and the novel. In R. Moi (Ed.), *The Kristiva reader* (pp. 34-61). Oxford, UK: Basil Blackwell.

Lave, J. (1988). *Cognition in practice: Mind, mathematics, and culture in everyday life.* Cambridge, UK: Cambridge University Press.

Lave, J., & Wenger, E. (1991). *Situated learning: Legitimate peripheral participation.* Cambridge, UK: Cambridge University Press.

Leont'ev, A.N. (1978). *Activity, consciousness, and personality* (M.J. Hall, Trans.). Englewood Cliffs, NJ: Prentice-Hall.

Linell, P. (1998). Discourse across boundaries: On recontextualizations and the blending of voices in professional discourse. *Text, 18,* 143-157.

Luckmann, T. (1992). On the communicative adjustment of perspective, dialogue, and communicative genres. In A.H. Wold (Ed.), *The dialogical alternative. Towards a theory of language and mind* (pp. 219-233). London, UK: Scandinavian University Press.

Miller, C.R. (1984). Genre as social action. *Quarterly Journal of Speech, 70*, 151-167.

Miller, C.R. (1994). Rhetorical community: The cultural basis of genre. In A. Freedman & P. Medway (Eds.), *Genre and the new rhetoric* (pp. 67-78). London, UK: Taylor & Francis.

Orlikowski, W.J., & Yates, J.A. (1994). Genre repertoire: The structuring of communicative practices in organizations. *Administrative Science Quarterly, 39*, 541-574.

Perry, P. (2001). *Shades of white: White kids and racial identities in high school.* Durham, NC: Duke University Press.

Prior, P. (1997). Literate activity and disciplinarity: The heterogeneous (re)production of American Studies around a graduate seminar. *Mind, Culture, and Activity, 4*, 275-295.

Ravotas, D., & Berkenkotter, C. (1998). Voices in the text: Varieties of reported speech in a psychotherapist's notes and initial assessments. *Text, 18*, 211-239.

Rex, L. (2002). Exploring orientation in remaking high school readers' literacies and identities. *Linguistics and Education, 13*(3), 271-302.

Rogoff. B. (1990). *Apprenticeship in thinking.* New York: Oxford University Press.

Russell, D. (1997). Rethinking genre in school and society: An activity theory analysis. *Written Communication, 14*, 504-554.

Selzer, J. (1993). Intertextuality and the writing process: An overview. In R. Spilka (Ed.), *Writing in the workplace: New research perspectives* (pp. 171-180). Carbondale: Southern Illinois University Press.

Swales, J. (1993). Genre and engagement. *Revue Belge de Philologie et d'Histoire, 71*, 687-698.

Tracy, K. (1998). Analyzing context: Framing the discussion. *Research on Language and Social Interaction, 31*, 1-28.

Turner, S. (1994). *The social theory of practices: Tradition, tacit knowledge, and presuppositions.* Chicago: The University of Chicago Press.

Winsor, D. (1999). Genre and activity systems: The role of documentation in maintaining and changing engineering activity systems. *Written Communication, 16*, 200-224.

Wood, L.A., & Kroger, R.O. (2000). *Doing discourse analysis: Models for studying action in talk and text.* Thousand Oaks, CA: Sage.

Yates, J.A., Orlikowski W.J., & Okamura, K. (1999). Explicit and implicit structuring of genres in electronic communication: Reinforcement and change of social interaction. *Organization Science, 10*, 83-103.

9

Studying Value Stances in Institutional Settings

Richard Beach
University of Minnesota

Julie Kalnin
University of Minnesota

After serving 12 years as a Republican senator from Vermont, on Thursday, May 24, 2001, Senator James Jeffords announced that he was leaving the Republican Party to become an Independent. His action was historical in that it resulted in the Democratic Party assuming control of the Senate in 2001. In his press conference statement, labeled as a "Declaration of Independence," Jeffords (2001a) stated the following:

> I became a Republican not because I was born into the party but because of the kind of fundamental principles that these and many other Republicans stood for: moderation, tolerance, and fiscal responsibility. Their party, our party, was the party of Lincoln.
>
> Increasingly, I find myself in disagreement with my party. I understand that many people are more conservative than I am, and they form the Republican Party. Given the changing nature of the national party, it has become a struggle for our leaders to deal with me, and for me to deal with them.
>
> Looking ahead, I can see more and more instances where I will disagree with the President on very fundamental issues: the issues of choice, the direction of the judiciary, tax and spending decisions, missile defense, energy and the environment, and a host of other issues, large and small.

The largest for me is education. I come from the state of Justin Smith Morrill, a U.S. Senator who gave America the land grant college system. His Republican Party stood for opportunity for all, for opening the doors of public school education to every American child. Now, for some, success seems to be measured by the number of students moved out of public schools.

In order to best represent my state of Vermont, my own conscience, and the principles I have stood for my whole life, I will leave the Republican Party and become an Independent.

I have changed my party label, but I have not changed my beliefs. Indeed, my decision is about affirming the principles that have shaped my career. I hope the people of Vermont will understand it. I hope, in time, that my colleagues will as well. I am confident that it is the right decision.

A conventional rhetorical analysis of this statement would focus on how Jeffords formulated his beliefs and attitudes associated with the projected persona of an "Independent" linked with the Democratic Party in an attempt to maintain the allegiances of his audience—Vermont voters.

In this chapter, we argue for the need for literacy researchers to also examine such texts in terms of how these texts both reflect and are motivated by allegiances to larger institutional cultural models and discourses. To do so, we draw on the notion of *value stance*. By value stance, we refer to those cultural models or discourses operating in certain institutional settings or activity systems that orient, position, or align participants in certain ways.[1]

Value stances are, therefore, more than individuals' beliefs and attitudes. In his theory of values, Thomas Green (1999) posited that individuals do not "have" certain values. Rather, values are endemic to activities or institutional worlds; they "are the forms that our relations assume in social life" (p. 131). As Green noted:

> Values are social structures. They are like institutions in as much as they require certain worldly assumptions in order to appear. These are not to be described as "the values persons have," but as the worldly conditions essential if persons everywhere are to enjoy certain social goods. (p. 140)

And, a leading moral philosopher, Alasdair MacIntyre (1985), argued that one's identity and moral orientation is constituted by experiences in a range of different institutions:

> We all approach our own circumstances as bearers of a particular social identity. I am someone's son or daughter, someone else's cousin or

uncle; I am a citizen of this or that city, a member of this or that guild or profession; I belong to this clan, that tribe, this nation. Hence, what is good for me has to be good for one who inhabits these roles. As such, I inherit from the past of my family, my city, my tribe, my nation, a variety of debts, inheritances, rightful expectations and obligations. These constitute the givens of my life, my moral starting point. This is in particular what gives my life its own moral particularity. (p. 220)

Participants in a larger activity adopt collective, shared value stances associated with mutually achieving the object or outcome of an activity. These collective, institutionalized value stances are inherent in and motivate uses of literacy practices or tools designed to achieve these objects or outcomes (Engestrom, 1987/2001). Jeffords' statement does more than express his own personal opinion or position. It reflects a larger value stance constituted by institutionalized activity of special education lobby groups, whose efforts—led by Jeffords—to require 40% of federal funding for mandated special education programs was rebuffed by the Republican majority in the Senate, one factor precipitating Jeffords' withdrawal from the Republican Party. As he explained in his book (Jeffords, 2001b), when his attempt to include such funding in the Senate's budget bill failed and when he was publicly chastised by a Republican colleague on the Senate floor for trying to push for such funding, his distance from his Republican colleagues only widened, creating a major ethical dilemma associated with his party affiliation and his value stance regarding special education funding.

Value stances also include a volitional component associated with a collective sense of the "motive" (Leont'ev, 1981) operating in an activity—the force leading to achieve an activity's object that orients uses of actions or tools in a certain manner. Jeffords' statement voiced value stances reflecting allegiances to the historical activity of the traditional Republican Party. He referred to the past traditions of the Republican Party as standing for "moderation, tolerance, and fiscal responsibility." Aligning himself with this past, historical system motivated him to reject what he perceived to be a current trend in the Party away from these beliefs.

Jeffords also cited Senator Morrill's commitment to the development of land-grant colleges, references reflecting a collective value stance associated with achieving the object of "opportunity for all, for opening the doors of public school education to every American child." Evoking this value stance provides further motivation to resists attempts to reduce educational funding.

All of this suggests the need for literacy researchers to examine how alignment with collective value stances operating in activity systems motivates actions or uses of literacy practices such as those employed in Jeffords' statement. In this chapter, we make five points about the uses of value stances in institutional settings. We argue that value stances:

1. Reflect or are constituted by cultural models and discourses.
2. Orient or motivate participants' uses of literacy practices in an activity.
3. Constitute identity construction around a sense of agency.
4. Align participants with the need to transform the status quo.
5. Reflect conflicted allegiances to competing value stances in different activity systems.

We then cite an example of the application of value stances in a study of high school students' responses to multicultural literature.

VALUE STANCES ARE CONSTITUTED BY CULTURAL MODELS AND DISCOURSES

Value stances reflect or are constituted by various cultural models or discourses that orient participants to adopt certain social practice in an institutional setting.

Cultural Models

Cultural models function to organize people's beliefs and choices based on achieving objects related to success, love, achievement, equality, work, or family relationships (D'Andrade & Strauss, 1992; Holland & Eisenhart, 1990; Holland, Lachicotte, Skinner, & Cain, 2001). Therefore, they constitute value stances that define hierarchical priorities in achieving certain objects in an activity system. These objects are linked to more specific schema, scripts, or knowledge associated with achieving that object, for example, a schema of focusing on "profits over people." As Gee (2001) noted:

> Cultural models tell people what is typical or normal from the perspective of a particular Discourse . . . [they] come out of and, in turn, inform the social practices in which people of a Discourse engage. Cultural models are stored in people's minds (by no means always consciously), though they are supplemented and instantiated in the objects, texts, and practices that are part and parcel of the Discourse. (p. 720)

For example, value stances reflect cultural models of schooling that orient students to adopt certain social practices in schools. Much of American schooling revolves around cultural models of "individualism" associated with middle-class values (Bellah, Madsen, Sullivan, Swidler, & Tipton,

1985). Within a middle-class value system, the individual is assumed to be capable of acting on his or her own without dependency on institutional support. Being a complete individual is equated with being independent from constraints or forces, whereas being an incomplete individual is equated with being dependent on institutions (Jung, 2001). Within schooling, lack of "self-discipline" is equated with an inability to "control one's self" and one's emotions. Emotional expression/outbursts are perceived as problematic and as needing to be controlled (Jung, 2001). Analysis focusing on students' social practices as simply a function of their own individual practices or motivation fails to capture the ways in which these practices are constituted by larger institutional systems.

Studying value stances, therefore, requires an understanding of the cultural models operating in different activities or institutions. For example, the cultural models constituting participation in the special education lobbying central to Jeffords's value stances contrasts considerably from those of conservatives in the Republican Party who are opposed to "big government" support and intervention in schooling. Fred Block (2002) described that conservative value stance as embodied in a narrative employed by conservatives beginning with Ronald Reagan in the 1980s:

> The United States was once a great nation with people who lived by a moral creed that that emphasized piety, hard work, thrift, sexual restraint and self-reliance, but there came a time in the 1960s when we abandoned those values. We came instead to rely on big government to solve our problems, to imagine that abortion, homosexuality and the pursuit of sexual pleasure were OK, and to believe that God had died and that religion should play no role in our public life. According to this narrative, only a systematic effort to restore the old values—to reduce the role of government, lower taxes, restore the central role of religion and piety in public life, and renew our commitment to sexual restraint and traditional morality—would make it possible for us to recapture our greatness as a people. (p. 20)

Researchers can examine literacy practices involved in political activity by focusing on how participants' value stances are constituted by such cultural models.

Discourses

Value stances are also constituted by discourses operating within activity systems. Discourses are ways of knowing or thinking based on, for example, scientific, legal, religious, sociological, economic, political, psychological orientations (Gee, 1996, this volume). Being a participant in an activity means adopting discourses constituting membership in that activity (Wenger, 1998). Members of an Alcoholics Anonymous (AA) community value certain practices such as the tradition of giving testimony about their progress in maintaining sobriety because those practices serve the larger object of maintaining their sobriety (Lave & Wenger, 1991). In their analysis of how language functions to define adolescents' membership in adolescent punk groups, Widdicombe and Wooffitt (1995) examined the ways in which these adolescents adopt *"positions in discourses* through which individuals are ascribed identities" (p. 51).

Critical discourse analysis typically identifies participants' uses of different discourses operating in institutional settings (Fairclough, 1992; Gee, 1996, this volume; Rogers, 2002). Based on her research on high school students' socialization into the culture of a college-prep class, Lesley Rex (2001, 2002) found that discourses function to orient and shape participation in activity. Teachers employ what Rex described as "orienting discourses" to position students as to what constitute appropriate social practices in this college-prep classroom culture. Her concept of "orienting discourses" is somewhat synonymous with our concept of value stance in focusing on discourses' role in mediating activity in an institution.

These value stances or "orienting discourses" are particularly evident in adolescents' adoption of social practices constituted by class discourses. In one study, upper middle-class female adolescents were highly judgmental of their peers' practices based on their perceived failure to adhere to institutional norms and expectations (Gee & Crawford, 1998). Adopting discourses of achievement and status oriented them toward continual scrutiny of their peers' practices as succeeding or failing to conform to group norms. In contrast, working-class female adolescents focused less on conforming to institutional norms and more on their own immediate interpersonal relationships, as reflected in their narrative accounts of conflicts and tensions in their relationships (Gee & Crawford, 1998).

In our own research on adolescents' value stances as evident in autobiographical writing and responses to literature (Beach, Kalnin, & Leer, 2001), we found that study participants drew on value stances constituted by discourses of belonging to or to establishing an identity within a peer or family world. In their autobiographies, students were reflecting on changes in their own lives that involved membership in or exclusion from a peer or family world. In belonging to a social world, they gained certain "dimensions of competence" (Wenger, 1998) through displaying their allegiances to that world. They also experienced exclusion or rejection, which led them to rethink their commitment to or membership in a world.

For example, one participant adopted a value stance constituted by discourses of competition and an eye-for-an-eye morality. He constructed himself as an aggressive, assertive kind of person who values his own individuality as separate from others. He adopted a somewhat authoritative, combative stance in his writing. In adopting these discourses, he contextualized social worlds in highly competitive terms in which people and characters are continually at odds with each other. At the same time, interpreting the text from this value stance, he had difficulty perceiving characters' plight in terms of larger institutional forces, as opposed to their own immediate, competitive relationships.

This suggests the need for literacy researchers to examine how different discourses associated with competing institutional allegiances shape the value stances operating in an activity. This approach is evident in Rebecca Rogers's (2002) ethnographic analysis of two African Americans, a mother and her special education daughter, coping with the disparities their value stances in the home versus the unsupportive school context. Applying the discourses of "Schooling," "Mothering," and the "Committee on Special Education," Rogers identified tensions "in which linguistic and institutional markers suggest the ways in which each discursive context insists on certain literate relationships and calls forth certain subjectivities" (p. 248). Although the mother exercised high levels of agency using literacy and social practices in the home context as constituted by a discourse of "Mothering," she had difficulty coping with the school and Committee on Special Education, whose discourses served to marginalize her.

VALUE STANCES ORIENT OR MOTIVATE PARTICIPANTS' USES OF LITERACY PRACTICES IN AN ACTIVITY

A second aspect of value stances is that they orient or motivate participants to employ various literacy practices as tools designed to achieve the object of an activity. Literacy researchers have recently posited the need to examine literacy practices as part of specific activities (Bazerman & Prior, this volume; Beach, 2000; Lee & Ball, this volume). In an activity theory approach to literacy research, researchers focus on literacy practices involved in participation in activity.

At the level of activity, activity systems are driven by joint, collective efforts to achieve certain objects or outcomes (Leont'ev, 1981). Specific actions such as Jeffords' "Declaration of Independence" are oriented to achieving certain objects or outcomes of an activity. Activity systems are comprised of tools, rules, roles, and sense of community—all are geared to fulfilling an object or outcome (Engestrom, 1987/2001). As noted in the introduction to Part II, in an activity system of a political campaign, participants are learning practices associated with achieving an object—winning an election, employing various tools—press releases, campaign ads, polling, door-knocking, and so on; adhering to certain rules or conventions associated with running a campaign—funding limits, ethical norms, and the like, and adopting different roles—such as manager, communications director, fund-raiser, speech writer. The transformed object—achieving victory in an election—becomes the motive driving participation in an election.

Activity theorists' concept of motive—the need or desire to achieve a certain object or outcome (Leont'ev, 1981)—is related to participants' value stances. Value stances are volitional in that, in social events (Bloome, this volume), they serve to orient or motivate participants to take action (Wenger, 1998). As a participant in the larger activity of support for special education funding, Jeffords adopted a value stance that spurred him on to take action. The various literacy practices that he and other special education advocates employed to challenge funding cuts are driven by the larger motive operating in the activity system of special education support and lobbying groups. Although participants in these systems may not be consciously aware of or may not be explicitly referencing this motive, it continually shapes and directs uses of practices of lobbying, formulating policy statements, conducting research, building coalitions, issuing statements, or formulating press releases.

This motive also shapes the ways in which participants read and interpret texts in terms of noting the level of commitment to or alignment with an activity's object. Readers define their purposes for reading texts based on a determination of an author's value stance related to their commitment to achieving an activity's object. This serves to redefine Hunt and Vipond's (1992) notion of point-driven reading stances discussed in the first volume in terms of inferring the "point" as constituted by larger objects or motives driving a readers' participation in activity systems (Beach, 2000). Readers' adopt a point-driven stance consistent with their value stances that shape their interpretation of an author's commitment to a motive operating in a system. A pro-special education reader responding to Jeffords' statement notes cues signaling his strong commitment to the need to maintain funding. The "point" of Jeffords' text for this reader is that Jeffords is not only on board with the activity, but also that his text can be used as part of a larger lobbying effort to bolster support for special education funding.

Analyzing how larger motive or motives operating in a system serves to motivate uses of specific literacy practices therefore requires attention to more than simply individual participants' sense of engagement or motivation (Vadeboncoeur & Portes, 2002). It also requires an analysis of the larger collective activity that provides varying degrees of engagement with that activity, for example, so-called "at-risk" adolescents' engagement in a multimedia production project in a high school literacy lab, a project itself that functioned to motivate students to display competences in a range of digital literacies (King & O'Brien, 2002). Given the propensity to place onus on individuals for their "lack of motivation" in acquiring literacy practices, it is important to shift the focus to determining aspects of larger activities themselves that serve to engage participants (Guthrie, 2004).

VALUE STANCES CONSTITUTE IDENTITY CONSTRUCTION AROUND A SENSE OF AGENCY

Through participation in activity, people develop a sense of agency that serves to define their identities or roles in activity. Identities are constructed as part of "figured worlds":

> a socially and culturally constructed realm of interpretation in which particular characters and actors are recognized, significance is assigned to certain acts, and particular outcomes are valued over others. Each is a simplified world, populated by a set of agents (in the world of romance: attractive women, boyfriends, lovers, fiancés) who engage in a limited range of meaningful acts of change of state (flirting with, falling in love with, dumping, having sex with) as moved by a certain set of forces (attractiveness, love, lust). (Holland, Lachicotte, Skinner, & Cain, 2001, p. 52)

Identities are constituted through participation in "figured worlds" as "figurative, narrativized, or dramatized" as part of a "story or drama, a 'standard plot' against which narratives of unusual events are told" (p. 53). Nepali women are constituted through a life-path narrative of obedience and devotion to husbands and the role of motherhood as part of the figured world of Hindi culture. People as newcomers to figured worlds are socialized to acquire certain practices through participation in these worlds (Scollon, 2001; Vadeboncoeur & Portes, 2002; Wenger, 1998), for example, new AA members acquire new identities as "reformed alcoholics" as mediated by testimonial narratives and practices of the AA figured world (Holland et al., 2001). Becoming a member of these figured worlds entails acquiring value stances operating in those worlds. These value stances are reflected in the dispositions or habitus (Bourdieu, 1977; Bourdieu & Passeron, 1990) operating in these worlds.

Constructing Identities Through Narrative

Participants acquire these dispositions through play or "imaginative fantasy" associated with rules of the game or drama operating in the world: "People may develop a 'sense' (in Bourdieu's term) of their worlds, an expertise in the use of cultural artifacts that may come to re-mediate their participation in them" (Holland et al., 2001, p. 137). In responding to narrative worlds, readers engage in the imaginative, vicarious play of being participants in such worlds.

Narrative analysis (Daiute & Lightfoot, 2004; Gee, 1996; Schank & Berman, 2002) can be used to define how identities are constructed in terms of protagonists'/tellers' agency—their relationships to institutional forces. Narratives also reflect what it means to be a certain kind of person with certain kinds of values consistent with the cultural models and discourses operating in a figured world. As Rymes (2001) noted "Through telling [stories], people are not creating a merely random identity, rather, they are actively narrating themselves relative to a moral ideal of what it is to be a good person" (p. 498).

Using what Staton Wortham (2001) defined as "interactional positioning," tellers portray themselves as being certain kinds of persons within particular settings or events. Wortham provided the example of a veteran AA member who provides testimonial narratives to novice members about their experience of "hitting bottom" and then, through following the AA regimen, restored their sense of self-worth. The meaning of his narrative is best understand in the context of a veteran convincing the novice of the value of sticking diligently to the AA regimen in order to define one's identity as an AA member.

Rather than assume that there is one defined, coherent self, Wortham argued that people construct particular identities or "dialogic selves" through narratives, identities that vary across different contexts or situations. Even within one certain context, people may adopt or enact different selves given their interactions with an audience or others they are "double-voicing." He cited the example of an interview with a female, Jane, by a graduate student-researcher. In the interview, Jane described her experience of taking a newborn to an adoption agency and deciding that, based on her own past experience of having been abandoned as a child by her own mother, she would rather keep her baby. Wortham described the different selves that this woman adopted in this interview:

> She first positions herself as passive and vulnerable, as a victim of traumatic early experiences whom the interviewer might want to console. But when the interviewer does not ratify this positioning, Jane repositions herself as a cooperative research subject. As the storytelling interaction continues, she slips into and out of a passive and vulnerable position relative to the interviewer. These cycles continue until, at the end, Jane positions herself as self-assertive with respect to the interviewer. Note that, because she is telling an autobiographical narrative, Jane has the opportunity to ventriloquate both others and herself. (p. 148)

In a study of Los Angeles Latino high school students' drop-out narratives, Betsy Rymes' (2001) documents how the students used narratives to project their "moral selves" in a positive light. The students' descriptions of why they dropped out of school often reflected their negative response to threats, violence, mistreatment, or boredom in a school. Through foregrounding aspects of the setting as leading to their reactions, the students defined a causal relationship between the negative contexts and their actions in ways that portray themselves in a positive light as necessary or justifiable responses to violent, threatening situations. She cited the example of Rosa, a student who described the event of a teacher chasing her down a school hallway and then holding her:

> Me and her started getting in a fight, and when I—when when when we—when we stopped fighting, they said a teacher's coming a teacher's coming so I ran you know. I was trying to get away eh—and he was chasing me. An' then, and so he wouldn't let go of my hand and I was telling him let go let go and he goes no your going with me an I was go get her, she—she started it and he wouldn't let me go—he wouldn't let me go so, heh heh, I don't know I got mad and I just hit him. That was why I didn't go to school cause I knew he was looking for me. (p. 31)

In this narrative, Rosa is establishing her identity around a sense of agency in resisting school authorities, resistance constructed through uses of such narratives to define a value stance of someone who believes that she has been mistreated. Through sharing such narratives with her peers, she engaged in collective activity resisting arbitrary school control. Thus, at the larger level of activity, narratives function to define and shape social and historical agendas and movements (Davis, 2002).

When participants are marginalized or demeaned from collective participation in an activity, they lose their sense of agency because they have little or no efficacy in that activity. Hicks (2001) cited the example of Jake, a young boy whom she followed from kindergarten through second grade. Jake enjoyed his experience of active, physical participation with woodworking and car racing valued by his father in the home, experiences that were often not available in his first-grade school setting. Jake did not do well on school-related reading and writing tasks. Yet, in his home setting, he employed literacies related to car racing or computer games that differ from the school's more decontextualized, essayist literacies. Moreover, as he moved into first and second grade, he became increasingly interested and involved in his father's woodworking business, something that served to further distinguish his interests with those promoted in school. Jake's negative reaction to school led him to define agency in terms of the kind of person who prefers practices outside of school. Because he lacked the agency to change the school system, he experienced higher levels of efficacy in his home setting.

Participants' value stances therefore reflect their sense of agency associated with their efficacy or responsibility to achieve the object of an activity (Holland et al., 2001). In some cases, given high levels of responsibility in an activity, participants adopt a positive value stance toward collective participation in an activity, participation that contributes to their sense of agency (Heath & McLaughlin, 1993). Being responsible for the success of a certain activity enhances one's sense of agency associated with increased efficacy in using tools in that activity.

VALUE STANCES ALIGN PARTICIPANTS WITH THE NEED TO TRANSFORM THE STATUS QUO

To cope with the conflicts and contradictions inherent in status quo activity, participants create new, alternative forms of activity that address these conflicts and contradictions. Engeström (1987/2001) noted that reflexivity in coping with contradictions leads to a recognition that traditional, familiar habits and practices are not working, requiring the development of new, alternative habits and practices, awareness associated with "'personal crises,' 'breaking away,' 'turning points,' or 'moments of revelation'" (p. 5). In the process, the old system evolves into the new, resulting in new value stances. One of Jeffords' short-term agendas was to put the Democrats in power so that his special education funding might receive a more favorable hearing. For Engestrom, addressing the contradictions inherent in the status quo systems lead to "the rise to actions anticipating the *created new* activity" (p. 16). Imagining this new, alternative activity provides a vision and motivating force for transformation by "transcending our time and space and creating new images of the world and ourselves" (Wenger, 1998, p. 176). Wenger argued that these acts of imagination are more than merely cognitive. They are also collectively constructed through mutual participation with others as a means of addressing shared problems and contradictions facing a group.

To illustrate the construction of new activity systems, Engeström cited the example of Huck Finn, who as a vagabond in a small, segregated town, is friends with both the middle-class Tom Sawyer, and also with the black slave Jim. He recognizes the contradiction here between "the private freedom of the individual vagabond and the public unfreedom prevailing in the vagabond's immediate culture context" (p. 11). In escaping on the raft with Jim, Huck faces another contradiction between having to lie to those pursuing escaped slaves in order to protect Jim, lying which goes against his tacit acceptance of slavery, but which reflects his moral obligation to support Jim's attempt to become free, creating a double bind. Having agonized over this double bind, Huck creates new activities in experiences with assisting the Grangerford daughter escape her family and, having assisted two crooks in stealing money, helping return the stolen money to the rightful owner. Engeström notes that through these actions, Huck is creating a new activity of "radical moral anarchism" involving "a deadly serious moral and existential struggle" (p. 14).

People adopt a positive value stance toward their participation in an activity because they value working to transform a system. In working in a political campaign, if they believe that a candidate will work to change campaign finance laws for instance, they perceive collective work on a campaign as worth their time and energy. In doing so, they value specific actions or practices associated with being a members of that campaign, given their desire for change. As Vasily Davydov (1999) noted:

> Actions as integral formations can be connected with nothing but needs based on desires, and the actions aimed at fulfilling certain tasks stem from motives. Motives in their turn are specific forms of needs in the case when a person has set himself a task and is undertaking certain actions to fulfill it. Thus motives are consistent with actions. (pp. 42-43)

The desire for change stems from a sense of dissatisfaction with or disidentification (Hodges, 1998) from the status quo, precipitating the need for transformation of the system (Davydov, 1999). The volitional nature of value stances reflects the fact that emotions play a key role in individuals' perceptions of the worth or value of transforming the object of an activity (Kupperman, 1999). Emotions function as "ways of seeing" (Solomon, 1976) and are "constitutive of acts of perceptions" (Vetlesen, 1994, p. 168) that actively orient participants' attention in certain ways. As Vetlessen noted, "emotions are active in disclosing a situation to us" by illuminating others' perceptions of a situation:

> Emotions make us attentive to the issue of how the *other* perceives the situation; emotions link our own perceptions of the situation to that of the other involved in it . . . to "see" suffering as *suffering* is already to have established an emotional bond between myself and the person I "see" suffering. (p. 166)

Emotions such as frustration, irritation, anger, or alienation lead to a desire for achieving new, potential systems. Having a desire for change is the motive for seeking to transform a system. Desires are also driven by certain needs—needs for popularity, recognition, status, power, and so on (Davydov, 1998), desires that are satisfied or fulfilled depending on whether or not one achieves certain objects (Wollheim, 1999).

Therefore, emotions create a value stance of moral responsiveness to or the need to be concerned about situation or event. Emotions shape perceptions of a situation "as laying a moral obligation on us, or as 'addressing' us, and, second, how we are the addressee of such an obligation by virtue of the kind of being we are—human subjects" (Vetlessen, 1994, p. 169).

The volitional, motivating force of value stances precipitate literacy practices of articulating "motivating reasons" (Kennett, 2001, p. 75) for actions consistent with one's desires to change the status quo. The motivating force behind literacy, as Freire and Macedo (1987) argued, is the desire for transformation of one's identity or agency through participation in transforming the system. And, articulation of reasons for change is bolstered through shared, collective deliberation in activity. Knowing that others' agree with the need for change serves to verify the validity of value stances as constituted by collective activity. Thus, one's individual desire for change becomes part of a larger activity driven by a collective desire for change.

VALUE STANCES REFLECT CONFLICTED ALLEGIANCES TO COMPETING VALUE STANCES IN DIFFERENT ACTIVITY SYSTEMS

Much of sociocultural literacy research draws on a community-of-practice model (Lave & Wenger, 1991) that examines ways in which participants acquire or display social practices associated with membership in a community of practice. In a critique of the community-of-practice model, Ron Scollon (2001) noted that focusing on issues of membership in bounded communities fails to account for the often complex, conflicting "nexus of practice" in which competing agendas and practices are at play in literacy events. These competing agendas and practices reflect participants' allegiances to multiple, competing communities systems. This suggests the need to study value stances as constituted by participation in highly conflicted or simultaneously "layered" systems (Prior, 1998; Prior & Skipka, 2003; Russell, 1997) given the alternative perspectives operating in any event or activity. Different perspectives, as Engeström (1999) noted, are "rooted in different communities and practices that continue to coexist within one and the same collective activity system" (p. 382). Studying activity as rife with competing, alternative value stances reflecting allegiances to competing worlds "serves as a hedge against simplified views of context that ignore the unsettled and conflicted relations between different positions and actors" (p. 382). In making his statement, Jeffords toed a fine line between his alliances and allegiances to his former Republican supporters, the new Congressional configuration, and the now hostile Bush administration.

Participants often become more aware of the status quo nature of value stances when confronted with these new, alternative value stances, creating what Elizabeth Ellsworth (1997) described as a "space of difference" that challenge "a single, fixed, locatable, decidable position" (p. 157). Recognizing their conflicted stances leads to reflexivity, defined by Donna Qualley (1997) as "a response triggered by a dialectical engagement with the other—an other idea, theory, person, culture, text, or even an other part of one's self, e.g., a past life" (p. 11). When faced with attempts by Republicans to limit special education funding, as the leading proponent of such funding, Jeffords was put on the spot—his value stances were challenged to the point that he was caught between remaining loyal to his party that was opposed to what he wanted and publicly challenging that party.

This suggests the need to examine how participants negotiate their competing alliances and allegiances to the different worlds of family, peer group, school, workplace, community organizations, and virtual Internet worlds they inhabit (Beach & Myers, 2001; Beach & Phinney, 1998; Phelan et al., 1998; Vadeboncoeur & Portes, 2002). This suggests the need to identify participants' perceptions of the points of incongruity between their worlds, how these incongruities affect learning, and strategies they employ to cope with these incongruities. Guerra (1998 described these negotiation strategies in terms of an "intercultural literacy" defined as "the ability to consciously and effectively move back and forth among as well as in and out of the discourse communities they belong to or will belong to" (p. 258).

This intercontextual model of negotiated value stances is particularly relevant for studying developmental or adult education in which students often experience incongruities between the discourses or cultural models of their family or peer cultures and academic cultures they are entering. In proposing a "social practices" model of developmental education, Linda Harklau (2001) posited the need to understand students' emic perspectives on distinct social practices acquired within different social worlds or microcultures. As part of their academic socialization, students learn that the same social practices are constituted and valued in different ways in these different worlds. For example, in her comparison of the same high school students' experiences in 12th grade and first-year college classes, students indicated that note-taking in high school was a highly structured and monitored practice, whereas in college it was assumed that students knew how to take notes (Harklau, 2001). In high school, the prevailing cultural model was one in which the teachers often assumed responsibility for students completing their work, whereas in college, students perceived themselves as being responsible for completing work. Learning to operate in these worlds involved learning to perceive valued social practices, for example, learning that sustained argument may be valued more in the university world than in a family or even a workplace world. These students are, therefore, positioned by competing voices and discourses constituting their value stances. "The self is a position from which meaning is made, a position that is 'addressed' by and 'answers' others and the 'world' (the physical and cultural environment). In answering (which is the stuff of existence), the self 'authors' the world—including itself and others" (Holland et al., 2001, p. 173).

In Beach's research on developmental college students' negotiation of practices across different worlds (Beach, Lundell, & Jung, 2002), these students' academic success often reflected their abilities to negotiate congruent and incongruent relationships between their developmental college program and their peer, family, workplace, community, university, and former high school worlds. These trajectories and negotiations were mediated by a variety of cultural models constituting valued practices, including models of independence, responsibility and autonomy, mobility, time management and self-discipline, and transition to adulthood. At the same time, participants' trajectories and ability to negotiate worlds varied considerably due to prior histories, cultural backgrounds, expectations, and past experiences with social and academic activities. Central to their success was their ability to negotiate between competing allegiances to their different worlds.

Similarly, dissertation writers in a large midwestern research university learned to negotiate the competing demands different activity systems: the graduate school, department, advisor, committee, employment, and potential job (Lundell & Beach, 2003). Although the graduate school and departments formulated one set of expectations, the advisor or committee articulated different expectations for completing the dissertation. Writers also experienced conflicting outcomes for the dissertation related to writing for an advisor or committee as opposed to positioning themselves for the job market, creating ambiguity related to their dissertation audience.

In negotiating the competing demands of different systems, participants learn that different systems are driven by different value stances. First-year college students learn that the value stances operating in the university differ from those of their high school worlds (Beach et al., 2002). Graduate students learn that the value stances operating in the job-market system differ from those of a dissertation committee (Lundell & Beach, 2003). From this experience, participants begin to recognize that value stances are not simply a function of individuals' beliefs and attitudes, but are constituted by larger institutional systems. Out of that awareness, they perceive language and literacy practices as voicing collective value stances associated with achieving objects and outcomes operating in certain systems. They also learn to orient themselves according to value stances operating in the systems they inhabit.

VALUE STANCES AND RESPONDING TO LITERATURE

We now turn to an illustration of how the concept of value stance can be applied to literacy research, in particular, research on response to literature. Recent application of activity theory to response to literature (Beach, 2000; Lee & Ball, this volume; Smagorinksy, 2001) posits that in responding to literature as participants in an activity system, readers interpret the meaning of characters' social practices as constituted by value stances reflecting institutional or cultural forces operating in literary texts. To make these interpretations, readers draw on value stances associated with lived-world institutions or cultures to construct or contextualize the fictional worlds of literature. In constructing historical contexts, readers draw on knowledge of activity systems—slavery, the plantation, the workplace, schooling, the church, the law, and so on, systems whose objects or outcomes, roles, rules, and history are mediated by cultural models and discourses.

Through the process of applying their value stances to constructing these fictional worlds as institutionalized systems, readers reflect on their value stances as constituted by their own institutional participation. David Bleich (1998) argued that readers experience a "reflexive ethnography": they are "reading literature as culturally heterogeneous, as comprehensive in its perceptions of its own society and its potential application to our societies" (p. 60), something Dennis Sumara (2002) described as "literary anthropology." For example, in responding to the novel *Kindred* by Octavio Butler (1979) that portrays characters moving between American culture of the 1970s and of 1830s in a slave plantation, readers infer the actions on the slave plantation as representing practices associated with a culture of slavery. In the novel, Dana, a 26-year-old African-American female living in California with her new White husband is suddenly transported back to the world of slavery. She saves Rufus, the son of a plantation owner, Weylin, from drowning, and builds a relationship with him each time she is transported back to the past, to the point that she fathers a daughter who is Dana's ancestor. When "the master," Mr. Weylin, issues a request to his slaves, that action is then interpreted as representing the practice of maintaining control and power over his slaves, a practice endemic to that culture.

To infer the meaning of characters' social practices, readers therefore need to contextualize these practices by constructing a cultural context constituting those practices (Beach & Myers, 2001). They do so by applying knowledge of discourses or cultural models specific to, for example, an institutional culture of slavery. Readers interpret Mr. Weylin's social practice of controlling slaves as consistent with a "habitus" (Bourdieu, 1977) as understood in terms of the cultural-historical context of the activity system of slavery—that "masters" during that period acquired and perpetuated practices as part of assuming the identity of being a "master." They apply a discourse of slavery and white racism to construct Mr. Weylin as the prototypical master/slave owner with beliefs and attitudes consistent with that role.

Responding to multicultural literature often creates a dialogic tension between readers' value stances associated with the activities of living in racially segregated or homogeneous worlds and those value stances portrayed in a text, creating a sense of "engaged resistance" (Möller & Allen, 2000). High school students respond with a highly individualized discourse of race that frames racial conflicts in terms of individual prejudices as opposed to a discourse of institutionalized racism and "whiteness" (Beach, 1997). Understanding the value stances readers bring to multicultural literature requires an understanding of different discourses of race identified by critical race theorists (Bonilla-Silva, 2001; Delgado & Stefancic, 2001). Bonilla-Silva noted that psychological discourses focus on individuals only as "racist"/"prejudiced," ignoring the ideological and institutional aspects of racism, as reflected in neoconservative framing of issues of welfare, housing, or poverty as an "individual" problem immune from institutional forces. He also noted that discourses of institutional racism, which posit that everything is "racist" is overly simplistic in that it fails to identity the root causes of racism.

In a move that is consistent with critical literacy theories, Bonilla-Silva (2001) proposed an alternative conception of racism as "racialized social systems" that function to place people in hierarchical social categories and that assign meanings to groups based on economic or political power in ways that serve to maintain and justify the social hierarchy. He also noted instances of how people adopt a "color-blind racism" through use of "racetalk" to avoid being labeled as "racist," as evident in statements such as "Everyone is equal, but . . ." or "I am not prejudice, but, . . ." in arguments such as "I didn't own slaves, so I'm not a racist," or in denials of structural nature of discrimination as reflected in critiques of affirmative action programs.

This critical race theory perspective highlights the role of language and discourses in the active construction of racist value stances constituting hierarchical systems. For example, discourses of "whiteness" serve to mediate and value certain practices such as controlling or exerting order/rationality against what is assumed to be disorder and irrationality. As Barnett (2000) noted, "discourses of 'whiteness' establish themselves as the norm through their reliance on particularly forms of 'rationality' . . . a term that highlights another attribute often credited to 'whiteness,' it's dependency on rules, order, and formal institutional structures" (p. 16). AnaLouise Keating (2000) described how discourses of "whiteness" shape readers' responses: 'Whiteness' operates as the unacknowledged standard against which all so-called 'minorities' are measured, racialized, and marked. Applied to theories of reading, this unmarked 'white' norm has become the framework, subtly compelling us to read ourselves, our texts, and our worlds from within a hidden 'whiteness'" (p. 58).

In using discourses of whiteness to construct value stances, people may resist the presupposition that they as individuals are engaged in racist practices, assuming that whiteness is an individual rather than an institutional discourse. However, one problematic aspect of analysis of whiteness is that students begin to assume that they are part of a new oppressed group (Barnett, 2000). Wiegman (1999) identified a number of different discourses of whiteness associated with the emerging field of whiteness studies, leading her to ask questions about whiteness studies:

> Why it has become so invested in figures of disadvantages whites, why it has been silent about the materiality of its own production in the academy, and why it emerges as a recognizable field in its own right— worthy now of a name that signifies off of and seems to form a symmetry with ethnic studies—at that point in its development when white scholars turn their critical gaze onto whiteness as an object of study. (p. 148)

The institutional nature of value stances related to race was reflected in an ethnographic study by Pamela Perry (2002) of White students' perceptions of their own identities and white culture from two different California high school schools: Valley Groves (VG) High School, a largely white, suburban school, and Clavey (C) High School, a highly diverse school with African Americans as the majority group. In these two schools, White students had totally different perceptions of their own cultural identities. VG students, who had little exposure to racial differences, adopted a race-neutral perspective, constructing White, Euro-American culture as the norm. Students of color in VG "rarely acted culturally different from the white students" (p. 122). Nor did they challenge the White students, so any potential challenge was neutralized. ("How the out-group defines itself has implication for how in-group members define themselves" [p. 123].) The Whites imposed their identities onto the students of color: "At VG, white youth and adults framed the race-neutral terms of discourse and students of color did not challenge that. With no clearly defined and assertive 'black,' 'Latino,' or 'Filipino' cultural identities, white students had no terms for defining 'white' cultural identity" (p. 124).

As was the case with the Winter Fest event at Thompson High School in Amanda Haertling Thein's analysis (Berkenkotter & Thein, this volume), the VG homecoming as an event or "a process," "privileged White perspectives as well as gender, sexuality, and class-based norms (all of which co-produce one another). As such, they contributed to the process of constituting and reconstituting what being white and American meant" (p. 41). Similarly, in the cultural context described by Perry that perpetuated the norm of white privilege, VG students ironically had no clear sense of their White identity; they were oblivious to their White privilege. White was therefore an "empty cultural category" that only served to define an "us/them" or "white/majority" versus "ethic/minority" distinction. And, "white students sense of group position was strongly influenced by neo-conservative articulation of the social position of Whites. Mainly, white students felt it was they, not people of color, who were the disadvantaged: they were stigmatized as 'racists' and discriminated against when seeking spots in college, scholarships, and jobs" (p. 151).

In contrast, in C, race was the "principle of social organization." White students at C had a clear sense of their White identity as "White." At C, "when whites tried to adopt practices associated with black identity, they had to do so 'naturally,' or be scoffed at." White C students who did not have a clear sense of their identity were "susceptible to self-hatred as a white person." "The informal culture of the school impressed on youth the importance of knowing your racial-ethnic background" (p. 91). However, despite their strong sense of identity, students lacked a clearly defined sense of ancestry or they dismissed their past family histories as irrelevant, what Perry described as "postcultural"—not believing that the past has any relevancy to the present.

White C students also were aware of differences within racial groups. They attended much more to in-group distinctions, often in terms of class origins, so that "mainstream" students who displayed middle class performances were contrasted with "alternative" students who challenged the mainstream norms. The tracking system "reinforced the dichotomies of good vs. bad, smart vs. 'bonehead,' controlled vs. rowdy, industrious vs. lazy, and white vs. black" (p. 52). White C students also conceived of culture in terms of "a type of currency that 'minorities' had and they, as whites, did not" (p. 101). They expressed resentment about affirmative action/scholarship.

In both schools, racial identification was often defined/manifested through cultural practices, dress, taste, body language, and speech. "Style, tastes, demeanor, and association had as much, if not more, power to define racial ascription as skin color or tradition" (p. 53). At VG, "clique affiliation deracialized youth; at C, it racialized youth; styles, tastes, and demeanor marked racial identity, including white identity" (p. 56).

All of this led to quite different value stances associated with race. In VG, racism was defined in terms of seeing racial differences or identifying racial difference. In C, racism was defined in terms of "history and consequences of White racial oppressions and inequality that white students well understood" (p. 65). Perry attributed this to the fact that students had taken a number of required social studies courses on oppressed groups. At C, there was a "dual awareness" of the history of white oppression and sociopolitical change, as reflected in a sense of helplessness in changing the system and guilt. White females at C experienced a negative stigma of being White and female; they often resorted to negative stereotypes of students of color. When they felt threatened by another group, they adopted more "conflictive, stereotypical, and defensive" stances. When they experienced a sense of equal status, they adopted more "porous, generous, and egalitarian" stances. These differences in value stances related to race were very much a function of institutional differences between the two high school cultures. However, as fish in water, the students in these two cultures may not have been aware of the degree to which their value stances are shaped by these institutional differences.

STUDENTS' LITERARY RESPONSES AS REFLECTING ALIGNMENTS TO VALUE STANCES IMPORTED FROM DIFFERENT WORLDS

In a study of high school students' responses to literature involving one of the authors (Beach, Haertling, Parks & Lensmire, 2003), the researchers examined the ways in which students formulate value stances through responses to multicultural literature. Participants included 14 Grade 11 and 12 high school students enrolled in a literature course for which they were receiving college credit. The course was taught by one of the researchers at Thompson High School, a diverse high school located in a working-class section of a large midwestern city (see also Berkenkotter & Thein, this volume, for a description of the school). This group of eight females and six males consisted of eight White, three Asian American, one Hispanic, and one student of African descent. Participants engaged in taped large- and small-group discussions for each of the texts read in the course (*House on Mango Street; Bless Me, Ultima; Kindred; Their Eyes Were Watching God; Obason; Smoke Signals* (film); *Woman Warrior; Love Medicine; Bastard Out of Carolina*; and *Yellow Raft in Blue Water*) and wrote journal entries and essays for each of these texts.

Previous research indicates that the literature teacher assumes an important role in creating a context in which students begin to interrogate value stances portrayed in literature and operating in their own social worlds, particularly when white students are confronted with challenges to their value stance of institutionalized white privilege (Blake, 1998; Fecho, 1998; Kumashiro, 2002; Smith & Strickland, 2001; Vinz, Gordon, Hamilton, LaMontagne, & Lundgren, 2000). Part of this challenge entails helping students recognize the very fact that systems are constituted by cultural or institutional forces (Lewis, 2000).

The analysis employed in this study illustrates our contention that understanding the value stances operating in a particular content, in this case, the literature classroom, requires an understanding of the value stances imported from the school, community, and peer-group "figured worlds" with which the students are aligned. The neighborhood surrounding Thompson High School has long been the home of European immigrant populations. Although the neighborhood has enjoyed groups from all parts of the globe, its primary background is tri-cultural with large communities of Italian, Scandinavian, and Polish immigrants. Although many of those communities have dispersed, long-time, family-owned Italian restaurants and aging Scandinavian and Polish community centers still attract an elderly weekend audience to polka nights or holiday gatherings. The vast majority of the neighborhood's long-time residents are connected with these populations and histories.

In addition to the affordable housing of the community, three different industries: a brewery, an iron works, and a chemical/mining factory drew the unskilled laborers to the neighborhood. As recently as the 1960s, neighborhood residents could complete high school and immediately find a "good" job. As one 1950s graduate of Thompson said of life after graduation in those days,

> You just walked out the front door [of the school], walked around back and across the tracks and down the street and you could get a job right off the bat; you graduate on Thursday, and Friday morning you could be working at a job. And they were well paying jobs within a few years, many of the kids got married and had families, could support a house and a car.

As with the rest of the country, the market for unskilled labor has rapidly diminished since the 1970s. Unemployment and lay-offs soared. Real estate values declined. Families in the larger homes began to subdivide and rent to multiple families of new immigrants.

The community then experienced a marked demographic shift with the immigration of African-American, Hispanic, and Vietnamese populations, as well as a large influx of Hmong refugees from the mountains of Laos. Additionally, changes in the district's enrollment policy allowed students from other neighborhoods to attend Thompson. These factors would be the impetus of change in the neighborhood's culture.

Thompson's current relationship with the surrounding community has become more ambiguous. With an increasingly diverse population, the school recognizes the need to adopt a more inclusive stance as a diverse cultural community. At the same time, although the school's hockey and football teams, made up largely White athletes, garner strong community support, sports populated primarily by students of color, such as basketball and soccer receive little to no community attention. The shift to a more inclusive stance creates strains in terms of alumni support, as evident in comments by the head of the alumni association. He explained the changes in his dealings with long-time supporters within the community.

> That is the thing. They [past graduates] think the neighborhood's went down. Their idea of the neighborhood's went down is they drive through once in a while and see some Black guys or some Hmong kids walking down the street. Well, that is different than actually knowing the Hmong kids, ya know. Like here at Thompson, I get to know most of them, and they're no different from anybody else's kids.

Despite these changes in the student population, however, it is clear that the White students at Thompson still remain systemically central in the culture of the school, reflecting the perpetuation of a status quo system mediated by a discourse of White privilege reflected in various traditions. The object of this system is to perpetuate and celebrate a sense of a fading past inconsistent with the realities of a diverse cultural population. This tradition was evident in the practices observed in an annual "Winter-Fest" coronation ceremony in 2002, which, as documented in the Berkenkotter & Thein chapter (this volume) attempt to foster the school tradition of White privilege through an emphasis on controlling every aspect of the event, reflecting a discourse of control constituted by the need for rules, order, and "rationality" (Barnett, 2000).

Another element of the school's traditions revolves around sports. The sports system's larger object is to foster a sense of school spirit associated with physical display of competence. This system is mediated by a discourse of competition and self-achievement that links the object of fostering school spirit with the identity of school athlete or jock. One student noted that the principal "likes sports players a lot cause she thinks they're like role models throughout the school." Interviews with school athletes reflected their adherence to this discourse of competitive self-achievement associated with the strong athletic tradition at Thompson. Athletes evoke narratives of hard work and training consistent with a discourse of competition. Being involved with sports serves as an extrinsic means for students to attain self-discipline. In order to participate in sports, students must maintain control of themselves both in school and outside of school. When one participant wrote an article for the school newspaper regarding athletes' use of alcohol, she was criticized by the school's athletic director for undermining the positive image of athletes in the school. Students involved in athletics at Thompson are not only supported on the field, but also in the positions of leadership at school. This intense support of athletes by the administration may be tied to the fact that these students exercise the physical self-control or self-discipline that is so valued by the school as a whole.

Another aspect of the school culture is the racial segregation within the school. Observations of the cafeteria during lunch periods offer further examples of social and racial stratification among students at Thompson (Tatum, 2003). With very few exceptions, students clearly organize themselves into racial groups. Basketball games are attended by a student population that are almost entirely African-American, despite the fact that the varsity team consists of 10 African American students, 4 white students, and 1 Latino student. The hockey team consists of overwhelmingly White students; attendance at hockey games consists primarily of Whites. Although basketball games are primarily attended by African-American students, there is still a sense that they are managed by White students because these students sell the tickets at the game, run the concession stand, and play in the band during the game.

Because the multicultural literature course was designed to offer college credit, the teacher attempted to create an alternative culture in the school that valued dialogic, intellectual exploration, and interrogation of the students' value stances that differed from the school culture constituted by cultural models and discourses of individual achievement/competition (Berkenkotter and Thein, this volume). This created some interesting tensions for some students in the course with competing allegiances to both the course and to the school culture. For example, as documented by Thein, the Winter Fest celebration for the popular White students reflected a tension between the mainstream, White "traditions" constituting the school culture versus the alternative cultures in the school associated with diversity that were challenging the mainstream culture, as illustrated by the fact that White students were the most prominent participants in the event and that, during the event, the school principal continually disciplined the students of color.

In course discussions, challenges to students' White privilege evoked a backlash from students whose stances were aligned with the mainstream school culture. As did the upper middle-class females in Gee and Crawford (1998), some of the White male students who were highly active in sports voiced the discourses of "control"/"self-discipline" in criticizing characters of color in the novels. In discussing *Love Medicine*, one White male student showed disdain for the action of the Native American characters in the novel, referring to them as "drunk, incest people." However, his response to poor, White characters in *Bastard Out of Carolina,* displaying similar behaviors, was more compassionate. In noting that while the characters in *Bastard Out of Carolina* may be "drunks," they were loyal to their families, making them worthy of respect in his eyes.

In discussions about issues of sexuality and rape in *Kindred* and *Love Medicine,* these students adopted a discourse of masculinity that served to exclude and silence some of the female students. This suggests that open disagreement between alternative value stances and voices fostered within a classroom culture may be undermined by the intrusion of allegiances to the larger school culture. One female student who identified more with value stances of worlds outside the school culture than with the school culture frequently challenged these male discourses, an example of how "dis-identification" (Hodges, 1998) from the mainstream culture results from identification with value stances outside of that world.

Students were continually negotiating value stances associated with their conflicted allegiances across different contexts. For example, a number of the males in the class were aligned to traditional male value stances associated with their participation in the strong traditions of sports in the school. This allegiance was reflected in their acts of male bonding in discussions in which they resisted challenges from female students and also voiced male characters' voicing of control/domination. These males also adopted discourses of whiteness as reflected in "new race talk" (Bonilla-Silva (2001) designed to avoid being perceived as racist.

Some of the students of color were reluctant to actively participate in discussions, reluctance that reflected the fact that while students of color constitute the majority in the school, they are rarely acknowledged or listened to by those with social power. Students also noted instances of "stereotype threats." One Asian-American student noted that White students experienced the invisible burden of a fear of being misunderstood as racists, whereas the students of color were fearful of being perceived as saying something primarily in terms of racial allegiance; they fear being seen as doctrinaire or narrow-minded. This student also noted that, given her outsider value stance, she had "learned how to read the other" [White students.] As she noted: "I'm used to being in a group of all Asian people. I'll be hearing the same thing because we see things the same. But to see what a white person has to say about certain issues, like racism . . . to see that it really does exist is as hard for them to confront it as for me."

During her participation in the course, she learned to realize the power of inbred institutional forces of privilege, to the point that she believes that even though she may challenge whites in the discussion, that it is unlikely that they would change their racist value stances:

> If I was to talk about it, how it happens at the Mall, I'm sure lots of
> kids would argue with me. Like a lot, like the majority of the class
> because they are all white. I wouldn't want to see that it isn't worth
> arguing over. I know I'm right. I know it is wrong and I wouldn't want
> to argue over it. They just have to realize it for themselves. I think if I
> were to criticize the white people, they would be really offended, even
> if the issue was wrong, like racism.

Students also drew on discourses of racism operating in their families, community, and school. In responding to explorations of issues of slavery in *Kindred,* some students argued that because they did not participate in past instances of racism, they should not face reverse discrimination evident (for them) in affirmative-action programs. Other students challenged this perspective, noting the need to recognize the influences of historical and institutional forces constituting characters' social practices. Some of the students began to examine their own perspectives related to issues of Whiteness, particularly in response to *Kindred* and *Love Medicine.* One student began to examine the contradictions of characters and in her life as someone who is stigmatized as both female and White (Perry, 2002).

One of the primary roles of the literature teacher is to socialize students into a literary community of practice (Edelsky, Smith, & Wolfe, 2002) through modeling of interpretive strategies and critical perspectives associated with being in a literature class. In his class, the teacher assumed a key role in helping students negotiate the contradictions between their allegiances to different lived-worlds. Because he explicitly described his own identity as constituted by his White, male, athletic, working-class background, he gained identification with some of the students in the class who began to value the worth of intellectual exploration. He also modeled ways of interrogating or constructively challenging others within the students' zone of proximal development, as well as providing support for expression of minority or alternative interpretations. His influence was increasingly evident in students' voicing notions of "subtext," "voices," and "culture," as well as their practice of citing textual evidence for their hypotheses. However, students of color noted ways in which they were excluded within the discussions by how issues of race were framed or ignored. The teacher's attention on interrogating White privilege served to focus on the lack of privilege, or "inferior" status of non-White students—leading to more overt discomfort for such students. Students of color were also fearful of being biased if they expressed racial solidarity with peers or characters of color.

Students had difficulty critiquing characters' practices as shaped by institutional forces because they frequently framed characters' practices as matters of personal morality, drawing on their discourse of individualism and competition. However, there were instances in which they analyzed practices as constituted by institutional forces. In responding to *Love Medicine*, they noted how the justice system often works against Native Americans. Or, in responding to *Bastard Out of Carolina*, they examined how the class system operating in a small, southern town served to limit the characters' sense of agency.

Overtime, some students did recognize how value stances reflect larger institutional forces, particularly in terms of recognizing how racism and sexism are constructed through language and discourses in both texts and their everyday lives (Bonilla-Silva, 2001). In discussing portrayals of racial conflict, they began to interrogate their value stances on Whiteness and race by attending to students of color's depiction of experiences of racism. For example, in her final focus group reflection, one White student noted how she changed her view on affirmative action programs, which she initially resented, because she became increasingly aware of how race and culture serves to disadvantage some groups "because of their race and their culture and how they grew up and all of the things that they had to deal with that I wouldn't being white." Another student noted:

> I just thought just because you were a minority you could just get along in life a little easier when it comes to school and stuff like that. Get scholarships and all that other good stuff. And then when we got into it a lot of it kind of changed my whole aspect on it like how look at that now. The way earlier hurdles and that sort of thing and where you come from and your family situation. So that changed me a lot.

Central to these changes was some students' increasing awareness of the contradictions in their own lives associated with competing allegiances to different worlds. Coping with these contradictions led them to recognize that their allegiances to peer group, family, school, sports, or community were constituted by larger institutional forces. For example, one White working-class female student became increasingly aware of how she was stigmatized by both discourses of gender and class. Based on discussions of characters coping with similar contradictions, she began to challenge some of the males' sexist notions of characters' actions as linked to their need for control. She noted that because she "sees things differently," she recognized how these males' value stances are constituted by institutions—by their participation in peer-group and sports activities.

The results of this study point to the value of helping students interpret alternative, conflicting value stances portrayed in literature as a means of challenging students' status quo perspectives and discourses. It also points to the role of the teacher in not only modeling and supporting ways of interrogating value stances, but—in keeping with the understanding that value stances are broadly constituted—without adopting a didactic agenda to attempt to change students' value stances. It also suggests that high school students have difficulty interrogating institutional discourses constituting characters' practices, but that some begin to examine the constructed nature of their own value stances. These changes in value stances are unlikely to occur from only responding to multicultural literature alone, or only from discussion with diverse peers, or only in responding to challenges from a teacher or peer, but rather from a combination of all three factors.

SUMMARY

In summary, we have argued that value stances are more than simply individuals' beliefs and attitudes; they are constituted by participation in activity systems mediated by cultural models and discourses. People frequently experience conflicted value stances given their allegiances to different systems, creating contradictions associated with problems in status quo systems. These value stances play an important subjective, volitional role through fostering literacy practices associated with challenging these status quo systems.

In responding to literature, readers apply their value stances to interpret characters' value stances as constituted by larger systems. As illustrated in the study of high school students' responses to multicultural literature, in sharing responses with peers, they challenge each other's stances, leading some of them to recognize the institutional nature of their stances. Beginning to understand that value stances are situated in broader, interacting systems, creates the opportunity for teachers and students to explore the social fabric of texts, and through this exploration, to gain new, transformative perspective on society.

ENDNOTE

1. We use the concept of *value stance* as opposed to valuing because there are instances of people adopting a negative stance—the fact that they may not value something. We also distinguish the concept of value stance from value judgment in that a value stance reflects a more consistent, basic value orientation, whereas a value judgment represents a more immediate act, an act that certainly reflects a value stance. And, we distinguish a value stance from a discourse (Gee, 1996) or cultural model (Holland & Eisenhart, 1990) in that a stance is a manifestation of a discourse or cultural model.

REFERENCES

Barnett, T. (2000). Reading "whiteness" in English studies. *College English, 63*(1), 9-37.

Beach, R. (1997). Students' resistance to engagement in responding to multicultural literature. In T. Rogers & A. Soter (Eds.), *Reading across cultures: Teaching literature in a diverse society* (pp. 69-94). New York: Teachers College Press.

Beach, R. (2000). Reading and responding at the level of activity. *Journal of Literacy Research, 32*(2), 237-251.

Beach, R., Haertling, A., Parks, D., & Lensmire, T. (2003, April). *High school students' responses to multicultural literature.* Paper presented at the annual meeting of the American Educational Research Association, Chicago.

Beach, R., Kalnin, J., & Leer, E. (2001, February). *High school students' negotiations of identities in responding to multicultural literature.* Paper presented at the meeting of the Assembly for Research, National Council of Teachers of English, Berkeley, CA.

Beach, R., Lundell, D., & Jung, H. (2002). Developmental college students' negotiation of social practices between peer, family, workplace, and university worlds. In J. Higbee & D. Lundell (Eds.), *Exploring urban literacy and developmental education.* Minneapolis: Center for Research on Developmental Education and Urban Literacy, University of Minnesota.

Beach, R., & Myers, J. (2001). *Inquiry-based English instruction: Engaging students in life and literature.* New York: Teachers College Press.

Beach, R., & Phinney, M. (1998). Framing literary text worlds through real-world social negotiations. *Linguistics and Education, 9*(2), 159-198.

Bellah, R., Madsen, R., Sullivan, W., Swidler, A., & Tipton, S. (1985). *Habits of the heart: Individualism and commitment in American life.* Berkeley: University of California Press.

Blake, B. (1998). "Critical" reader response in an urban classroom: Creating cultural texts to engage diverse readers. *Theory into Practice, 37,* 238-243.

Bleich, D. (1998). *Know and tell: A writing pedagogy of disclosure, genre, and membership.* Portsmouth, NH: Heinemann.

Block, F. (2002). The right's moral trouble. *The Nation, 275*(10), 20-22.

Bonilla-Silva, E. (2001). *White supremacy and racism in the post-civil rights era.* Boulder, CO: Lynne Rienner.

Bourdieu, P. (1977). *Outline of a theory of practice.* Cambridge, UK: Cambridge University Press.

Bourdieu, P., & Passeron, J. (1990). *Reproduction in education, society and culture* (2nd ed.). London, UK: Sage.

Butler, O. (1979). *Kindred.* Boston, MA: Beacon Press.

D'Andrade, R., & Strauss, C. (Eds.). (1992). *Human motives and cultural models.* New York: Cambridge University Press.

Daiute, C., & Lightfoot, C. (Eds.). (2004). *Narrative analysis: Studing the development of individuals in society.* Thousand Oaks, CA: Sage.

Davis, J. E. (Ed.). (2002). *Stories of change: Narrative and social movements.* Albany: SUNY Press.

Davydov, V. (1999). A new approach to the interpretation of activity structure and content. In S. Chaiklin, M. Hedegaard, & U. Jensen (Eds.), *Activity theory and social practice: Cultural-historical approaches* (pp. 39-50). Aarhus, Denmark: Aarhus University Press.

Delgado, R., & Stefancic, J. (2001). *Critical race theory: An introduction.* New York: New York University Press.

Edelsky, C., Smith, K., & Wolfe, P. (2002). A discourse on academic discourse. *Linguistics and Education, 12*(1), 1 – 38.

Ellsworth, E. (1997). *Teaching positions: Difference, pedagogy, and the power of address.* New York: Teachers College Press.

Engeström, Y. (1999). Innovative learning in work teams: Analyzing cycles of knowledge creation in practice. In Y. Engeström, R. Miettinen, & R. Punamaki (Eds.), *Perspectives on activity theory* (pp. 377-404). New York: Cambridge University Press.

Engestrom, Y. (2001). *Learning by expanding: An activity-theoretical approach to developmental research.* Helsinki: Orienta-Konsultit. (Original work published 1987)

Fairclough, N. (1992). *Discourse and social change.* London, UK: Polity Press.

Fecho, B. (1998). Crossing boundaries of race in a critical literacy classroom. In D. Alvermann, K. Hinchman, D. Moore, S. Phelps, & D. Waff (Eds.), *Reconceptualizing the literacies in adolescents' lives* (pp. 75-101). Mahwah. NJ: Erlbaum.

Freire, P., & Macedo, D. (1987). *Literacy: Reading the word and the world.* South Hadley, MA: Bergin & Garvey.

Gee, J. P. (1996). *Social linguistics and literacies: Ideology in discourses.* New York: Falmer.

Gee, J. P. (2001). Reading as situated language: A sociocognitive perspective. *Journal of Adolescent and Adult Literacy, 44*(8), 714-725.

Gee, J. P., & Crawford, V. (1998). Two kinds of teenagers: Language, identity, and social class. In D. Alvermann, K. Hinchman, D. Moore, S. Phelps, & D. Waff (Eds.), *Reconceptualizing the literacies in adolescents lives* (pp. 225-246). Mahwah, NJ: Erlbaum.

Green, T. F. (1999). *Voices: The educational formation of conscience.* Notre Dame, IN: University of Notre Dame Press.

Guerra, J. (1998). *Close to home: Oral and literate practices in a transnational Mexicano community.* New York: Teachers College Press.

Guthrie, J.T. (2004). Teaching for literacy engagement. *Journal of Literacy Research, 26*(1), 1-30.

Harklau, L. (2001). From high school to college: Student perspectives on literacy practices. *Journal of Literacy Research, 33*(1), 33-70.

Heath, S., & McLaughlin, M. (Eds.). (1993). *Identity and inner-city youth.* New York: Teachers College Press.

Hicks, D. (2001). Literacies and masculinities in the life of a young working-class boy. *Language Arts, 78*(3), 217-226.

Hodges, D. (1998). Participation as dis-identification with/in a community of practice. *Mind, Culture, and Activity, 5,* 272-290.

Holland, D., & Eisenhart, M. (1990). *Educated in romance: Women, achievement, and college culture.* Chicago: University of Chicago Press.

Holland, D., Lachicotte, W., Skinner, D., & Cain, C. (2001). *Identity and agency in cultural worlds*. Cambridge, MA: Harvard University Press.

Hunt, R., & Vipond, D. (1992). First, catch the rabbit: Methodological imperative and the dramatization of dialogic reading. In R. Beach, J. Green, M. Kamil, & T. Shanahan (Eds.), *Multidisciplinary perspectives on literacy research*. Urbana, IL: National Conference on Research in English/National Council of Teachers of English.

Jeffords, J. M. (2001a, May 24). *Declaration of independence*. Available Online: <http://www.senate.gov/~jeffords/524statement.html>.

Jeffords, J. M. (2001b). *My declaration of independence*. New York: Simon & Schuster.

Jung, H. (2001). *"Control yourself": Emotion and person in an American junior-high school*. Unpublished doctoral dissertation, University of Minnesota, Minneapolis, MN.

Keating, A. (2000). Reading's transformational potential. *Reader, 43*, 57-59.

Kennett, J. (2001). *Agency and responsibility: A common-sense moral psychology*. Oxford, UK: Clarendon Press.

King, J. R., & O'Brien, D. G. (2002). Adolescents' multiliteracies and their teachers' needs to know: Towarrd a digital détente. In D. Alvermann (Ed.), *Adolescents and literacies in a digital world* (pp. 40–50). New York: Peter Lang.

Kumashiro, K.K. (2002). Against repetition: Addressing resistance to anti-oppressive changes in the practices of learning, teaching, supervising, and researching. *Harvard Educational Review, 72*(1), 67-92.

Kupperman, J. (1999). *Value. . . . and what follows*. New York: Oxford University Press.

Lave, J., & Wenger, L. (1991). *Situated learning: Legitimate peripheral participation*. New York: Cambridge University Press.

Leont'ev, A. N. (1981). *Problems of the development of mind*. Moscow: Progress Publishers.

Lewis, C. (2000). Limits of identification: The personal, pleasurable, and the critical in reader response. *Journal of Literacy Research, 32*(2), 253-266.

Lundell, D., & Beach, R. (2003). Dissertation writers' negotiations with competing activity systems. In C. Bazerman & D. Russell (Eds.), *Writing selves/writing society: Research from activity perspectives*. Fort Collins, CO: The WAC Clearinghouse and Mind, Culture, and Activity.

MacIntyre, A. (1985). *After virtue*. London: Duckworth.

Möller, K. J., & Allen, J. (2000). Connecting, resisting and searching for safer places: Students respond to Mildred Taylor's *The Friendship. Journal of Literacy Research, 32*, 145-186.

Perry, P. (2002). *Shades of white: White kids and racial identities in high school*. Durham, NC: Duke University Press.

Phelan, P., Davidson, A., & Yu, H. (1998). *Adolescents' worlds: Negotiating family, peers, and school*. New York: Teachers College Press.

Prior, P. (1998). *Writing/disciplinarity: A sociohistorical account of literate activity in the academy*. Mahwah, NJ: Erlbaum.

Prior, P., & Skipka, J. (2003). Chronotopic lamination: Tracing the contours of literate activity. In C. Bazerman & D. Russell (Eds.), *Writing selves/writing soci-*

ety: Research from activity perspectives. Fort Collins, CO: The WAC Clearinghouse and Mind, Culture, and Activity.

Qualley, D. (1997). *Turns of thought: Teaching composition as reflexive inquiry.* Portsmouth, NH: Boynton/Cook.

Rex, L. (2001). The remaking of a high school reader. *Reading Research Quarterly, 36*(3), 288-314.

Rex, L. (2002). Exploring orientation in remaking high school readers' literacies and identities. *Linguistics and Education, 13*(3), 271-302.

Rogers, R. (2002). Between contexts: A critical discourse analysis of family literacy, discursive practices, and literate subjectivities. *Reading Research Quarterly, 37*(3), 248-277.

Russell, D. (1997). Rethinking genre in school and society: An activity theory analysis. *Written Communication, 14(4),* 504-554.

Rymes, B. (2001). *Conversational borderlands: Language and identity in an alternative urban high school.* New York: Teachers College Press.

Schank, R., & Berman, T. (2002). The pervasive role of stories in knowledge and action. In M. Green, J. Strange & T. Brock (Eds.), *Narrative impact: Social and cognitive* (pp. 287-313). Mahwah, NJ: Erlbaum.

Scollon, R. (2001). *Mediated discourse: The nexus of practice.* New York: Routledge.

Smagorinsky, P. (2001). If meaning is constructed, what is it made from? Toward a cultural theory of reading. *Review of Educational Research, 71,* 133-169.

Smith, M., & Strickland, D. (2001). Complements or conflicts: Conceptions of discussion and multicultural literature in a teacher-as-readers discussion group. *Journal of Literacy Research, 33*(1), 137-168.

Soloman, R. (1976). *The passions: The myth and nature of human emotions.* Garden City, NY: Doubleday.

Sumara, D. (2002). *Why reading literature in school still matters: Imagination, interpretation, insight.* New York: Teachers College Press.

Tatum, B. D. (2003). *Why are all the black kids sitting together in the cafeteria? And other conversations about race: A psychologist explains the development of racial identity* (rev. ed.). New York: Basic Books.

Taylor, C. (1989). *Sources of the self: The making of the modern identity.* Cambridge, MA: Harvard University Press.

Vadeboncoeur, J., & Portes, P. (2002). Students "at risk": Exploring identity from a sociocultural perspective. In D. McInerney & S. Van Etten (Eds.), *Sociocultural influences on motivation and learning* (pp. 89-128). Greenwich, CT: Information Age Publishing.

Vetlesen, A.R. (1994). *Perception, empathy, and judgement: An inquiry into the preconditions of moral performance.* University Park, PA: Pennsylvania State University Press.

Vinz, R., Gordon, E., Hamilton, G., LaMontagne, J., & Lundgren, B. (2000). *Becoming (other)wise: Enhancing critical reading perspectives.* Portland, ME: Calendar Islands.

Wenger, L. (1998). *Communities of practice.* New York: Cambridge University Press.

Widdicombe, S., & Wooffitt, R. (1995). *The language of youth subcultures: Social identity in action.* New York: Harvester Wheatsheaf.

Wiegman, R. (1999). Whiteness studies and the paradox of particularity. *Boundary 2, 26*(3), 115-150.

Wollheim, R. (1999). *On the emotions.* New Haven, CT: Yale University Press.

Wortham, S. (2001). *Narratives in action: A strategy for research and analysis.* New York: Teachers College Press.

10

Community-Based Local Literacies Research

Karin Tusting
Literacy Research Centre,
Lancaster University

David Barton
Literacy Research Centre,
Lancaster University

This chapter describes literacy research that steps outside the classroom and looks at literacy within the broader setting of the communities in which people live out their lives. We are using *community* here in its widest meaning, as signifying the multiple local social contexts within which people engage in all the different sorts of everyday activities that make up their existence, including home, work, family, friends, civic life, and so on. By stepping into these contexts and looking at the way reading and writing are part of people's everyday social activities, a different sort of understanding of literacy can be developed, which goes beyond looking at literacy as a thing in itself and enables us to see how literacy practices are integrated within people's broader lives, identities and purposes.

The chapter begins by briefly outlining the background and historical development of this approach, locating it within broader trends in philosophy and the social sciences. It then outlines the main features of the theory of literacy as a social practice, before describing some examples of literacy research in different communities that has been carried out from this perspective (Barton & Hamilton 1998; Barton, Hamilton, & Ivanic, 2000). Finally, some possibilities for the future development of community-based literacy studies are suggested.

HISTORY AND BACKGROUND

The community-based literacy research described here starts from an understanding of literacy as a social practice. Before 1980, the study of reading and writing took, for the most part, a cognitive perspective, which treated reading and writing as autonomous skills, best taught to children early in their school career, in separate, specialized institutions called "schools" or "classrooms." This is still a dominant account of literacy in much public and political discourse today. However, this model cannot tell us much about many common experiences of literacy and learning. How does it explain, for example, being shown how to fill in a tax return by a neighbor; being elected secretary of one's local neighborhood association and having to learn "on-the-hoof" how to take minutes of meetings; arriving at university with a clear schools-based idea of what "writing an essay" is supposed to mean and finding through a process of trial and error that something completely different is now required; or being taken to prison for the first time and having to work out how people are using literacy to communicate outside the constraints of the system?

To respond to questions of this nature, the situated approach to literacy that is presented here began to challenge the skills-based view. Instead of seeing literacy primarily as a measurable cognitive attribute of individuals, researchers began to look at how people actually use literacy in their everyday lives, understanding literacy as a "social practice," one among many of the social practices on which people draw every day in purposefully living their lives.

This move toward a recognition of the importance of the social world in understanding literacy was signaled by Stubbs' (1980) sociolinguistic approach. As early as 1981, Szwed called for an ethnographic approach to researching literacy. Later, Levine (1985) drew attention to the importance of the social context of literacy (1985), followed by Cook-Gumperz's (1986) analysis of literacy as a social construction. The relationship between "the word" and "the world," and the role of literacy in maintaining or challenging the state of that world, were analyzed by Freire and Macedo (1987).

At the same time, a more critical approach to literacy teaching was being developed from within adult education in South America, particularly in Brazil. Paolo Freire's (1970) critical approach to teaching literacy insists that literacy takes place within a social context. Freire was involved in teaching adults who were often among the least powerful and the most oppressed in his society, and he insisted on making plain the link between literacy problems and social inequality. He argued that literacy education must begin with an analysis of one's own position in society, which reflects on and critiques the inequalities of power related to this social structure. Literacy pedagogy can then become a liberating force that people can use to empower themselves, rather than a domesticating experience that aims to maintain the status quo. A Freirean approach to literacy teaching, therefore, begins from the situated experience of inequality in people's lives, and attempts to develop a critical understanding of these inequalities and how they can be addressed.

This more critical approach to literacy studies resonates with critical theory more generally, which aims to describe the (often hidden) inequalities in access to power and knowledge that constrain the possibilities open to people in their lives. Works such as Giroux (1983), Livingstone (1987), and Luke and Walton (1994) explore the implications of this critical approach for pedagogy in general, whereas Clark, Fairclough, Ivanic, and Martin-Jones (1990, 1991) called for the teaching of a critical awareness of the role of language in this social process. Gee's (1990) *Social Linguistics and Literacies: Ideology in Discourses* draws attention to the role of language in this process.

Three studies were particularly influential in the development of local and community-based literacy studies in the early 1980s. All three looked closely at particular societies, describing in detail how people in these societies used reading and writing in their everyday lives. Rather than trying to make universal generalizations by examining literacy in a laboratory using cognitive tests or through standardized questions in a large survey, these studies involved investigators spending a lot of time with different groups of people, examining and describing specific aspects of their lives and situations. By doing this detailed work, questions were raised about what "literacy" really means outside the laboratory or the classroom. It rapidly became clear that absolute definitions of literacy as merely a cognitive skill are misleading in terms of people's lived realities.

In a study published in 1981, psychologists Scribner and Cole described a detailed study of the literacies of the Vai in north west Liberia. Using a battery of cross-cultural psychological tests, coupled with interviews and observations of the community, they found there were three very different types of literacy associated with particular cultural traditions: Koranic, Western, and indigenous literacies. This study provided detailed descriptions of literacies being learned informally, outside the educational system, as well as in classrooms, and showed that different features were associated with the use of these literacies, depending on the context within which they were learned and used. They demonstrated clearly that literacy needs to be understood in the context of the social practices of which it is part.

From a different disciplinary perspective, the social anthropologist Street (1984) studied the lives of Islamic villagers in Iran. Comparing commercial and more traditional literacies, he found that the commercial literacies were tied up with oil development in the region, whereas the traditional literacies were not. He contrasts the "ideological" approach to literacy, recognizing that literacy varies from situation to situation and is dependent on ideology, with the dominant "autonomous" approach that defines literacy independently of its social contexts.

A third key work in the early 1980s was Heath's (1983) *Ways with Words*. Based on 7 years of ethnographic fieldwork in three Appalachian communities, Heath used ethnographic and sociolinguistic methods to provide detailed descriptions of reading and writing in the home and the community. Only after this did she look at school practices, and she was therefore able to analyze the relationship and the disjunctures between different communities' home literacies and school literacy practices. It was in this work that the key concept of a "literacy event" was introduced, that is, an event in which people use written texts in their everyday lives, thus defining literacy in terms of what people are doing, rather than as an individual attribute.

Since that time, similar conclusions have been reached by other detailed studies of literacy practices in homes and communities. Literacy practices in a variety of different "worlds" are presented in Hamilton, Barton, and Ivanic (1994). Community literacies have been studied in Australia (Breen and Louden, 1994) and South Africa (Prinsloo & Breier, 1996). The personal letter-writing practices of Pacific Islanders are examined in Besnier (1993). Wagner (1993) studied Arabic speakers in Morocco. American studies have often been of the literacies of minority communities, such as B. Moss (1994) and Reder (1987, 1994). Moll's (1994) work relates the school and community practices of Hispanics in the southwestern United States. Minority bilingual communities have also been studied in Britain (Baynham, 1993; Bhatt, Barton, Martin-Jones & Saxena, 1996; Gregory 1996; Martin-Jones & Jones, 2000; Saxena, 1994). Some researchers have focused on social institutions, such as literacy in religious groups (Fishman, 1988, 1991; Kapitzke, 1995) or in the workplace (Gee, Hull, & Lankshear, 1997; Gowen, 1992). A similar ethnographic approach has been taken by researchers investigating children's literacies at home and at school (Schieffelin & Gilmore, 1986; Solsken, 1993), and children's nonformal literacies (Camitta, 1993; Maybin, 1997; G. Moss, 1996). Denny Taylor (Taylor, 1983, 1996, 1997; Taylor & Dorsey-Gaines, 1988) produced a series of studies of literacy within families.

These detailed studies showed clearly that, rather than being an absolute skill that people either do or do not possess, the nature of literacy changes according to the contexts in which it is acquired and the purposes for which it is used. These studies of literacy mark an important shift from an individual internal cognitive paradigm for understanding literacy to a more social one. This can be understood as part of a broader shift toward developing more situated understandings of social phenomena within the social and psychological sciences.

BROADER THEORIES, EPISTEMOLOGICAL ASSUMPTIONS

Underlying this more social paradigm is a particular model of the world, which can be seen as part of a broader turn in many fields in the social sciences away from purely positivist understandings. The positivist approach starts from the premise that the world is governed by deterministic laws of cause and effect. Within this model, the job of the scientist is to observe and describe in an objective fashion events and phenomena in the world, and thereby to deduce what these deterministic laws consist of—often through applying variants of the experimental method—in order that we might predict and control future events. Anything that cannot be observed and measured objectively—such as people's thoughts, emotions or desires, or their knowledge about practices—is therefore not legitimate material for science and becomes irrelevant.

Changes in the view of literacy are part of broader developments, and this positivist understanding of the world has been critiqued from a variety of philosophical perspectives. It is worth outlining the fundamentals of this critique before turning to its effect on literacy research. The poststructuralist philosophers have challenged the very notion of an absolute "truth." Foucault's (1971, 1975, 1978) work examines the links between supposedly objective scientific perspectives on issues like madness, sexuality, and criminality. He showed clearly how "knowledge" has always been irrevocably intertwined with the power structures and interests of the producers of that knowledge and their place in society. He showed the role of discourses, that is, characteristic ways of talking and writing within particular societies or communities, in constructing particular perspectives, practices or states of affairs as "normal" and therefore unchallengeable, hiding the contingency of these perspectives and practices and their role in sustaining particular forms of social dominance and hierarchy. Lyotard (1984) challenged the very notion that any form of overarching "grand narrative" that could explain society might be possible, showing how such metanarratives, however neutral they might appear, always privilege particular points of view. Deconstructionist philosophers, following Derrida (1978), have shown how coherent-seeming narratives and explanations contain within themselves multiple possibilities and contradictions, this being inherent in the very nature of language as an open system, challenging the idea that it is even possible to produce any single, simple truth in linguistic form. Phenomenologists such as Husserl (1960), Heidegger (1978), and Merleau-Ponty (1962) demonstrated the importance of subjective experience and individually situated meaning-making in the process of making sense of the world, again challenging the premise of overarching explanatory frameworks offered by a positivist approach.

Within the philosophy of science, critical realism (associated with the philosopher Roy Bhaskar, 1978, 1989; Collier, 1994) and taken up within social science (Archer, 1995; Fairclough, Jessop, & Sayer, 2001; Sayer, 2000) and applied linguistics (Carter & Sealey, 2000; Sealey & Carter, 2001) also challenges the traditional models associated with positivist understandings of empirical research. The critical realist understanding of the world is that, although events in the social world clearly have causes, they cannot simply be explained in terms of the working of a single law. Rather, events are generated by the causal mechanisms that arise from the properties and powers of objects in the world. And they are always co-determined (i.e., caused by the interaction of multiple mechanisms). At the very least, the social world is emergent from the interaction of mechanisms at physical, chemical, biological, social, and psychological strata. And because any social event includes people who generate their own meanings, which you can never take account of fully, there are always going to be mechanisms involved in generating empirical reality which cannot be described or accounted for by the observer.

A social system is therefore always an open system, in that we can never account for all the causal factors generating any particular event. So the observation of series of events in the social world, looking for regularities that can serve as the basis for the deduction of the law governing the phenomena, is unlikely ever to be fruitful. It is not possible to simply abstract the relevant explanatory elements from this complex mix. This means that experimental studies, which try to understand the laws governing social phenomena (such as literacy acquisition) by controlling all variables save one, and looking for explanations in terms of this single factor, are unlikely to produce viable explanations—or even consistent results— because the systems within which they are being performed can never actually be closed in the way some physical or chemical systems can be in a laboratory.

So instead of seeking to find a simple explanation that can be abstracted across events in different contexts, the critical realist social scientist tries to understand the generative mechanisms that can cause events, by understanding the properties and powers of the objects under study in the world. Events are always emergent outcomes from particular contexts, generated by the interaction of the multiple powers and properties of the people, objects and structures within these contexts. Therefore, we are more likely to gain some understanding of what causes events in the world by immersing ourselves in the detail of those particular contexts and looking at the unique interactions of these people in this context, than by trying to abstract, generalise, and explain in terms of single factors across different contexts.

Sealey and Carter (2002) explain this by saying that rather than asking, "Does variable y cause result x?" the critical realist question would be, "What is it about variable y that can cause the result x, and in what contexts can it do so?" When applied to literacy research, this would imply that questions such as, "Is a particular pedagogy better or worse for literacy acquisition?" or "Does literacy cause economic growth?" or even "What is 'the' link between literacy and economic growth?" are really meaningless — at least, without the addition of "for which people, under which conditions, in which context."

These philosophical critiques have shown from different perspectives that any attempt to describe the social world in terms of simple cause-and-effect laws and detached, objective truth, while appealing in principle, is always going to be sabotaged by the complexity of the field being described and the irreducible meaning-making potential of the human beings under study. They also draw attention to the importance of the interests, agendas and power relations within which social scientific knowledge is developed. Social science is itself part of the social world it is describing, and the position and interests of researchers and disciplines inevitably influence what is being researched and described.

These critiques are one of the driving forces behind a general trend identified by Gee (2000) as the "social turn," of which local and community-based literacy studies are part. Gee listed 14 movements demonstrating this trend, but says there are more. His list included subdisciplines of linguistics in which a shift has been made from the study of linguistic systems to the way meaning is constructed in interaction, such as ethnomethodology, conversational analysis and interactional sociolinguistics (Schiffrin, 1994) and the ethnography of speaking (Gumperz, 1982; Hymes, 1974); subdisciplines of psychology, which have shifted from a behavioural or cognitive approach to taking a more social approach which foregrounds the role of meaning and interaction in explaining psychological phenomena, such as discursive psychology (Edwards & Potter, 1992), sociohistorical psychology (Wertsch, 1985, 1991, 1998), situated cognition (Lave & Wenger, 1991), activity theory (Engeström, 1990), and cognitive linguistics (Lakoff & Johnson 1980); science and technology studies, such as the sociology of scientific knowledge, which have studied the social processes underlying the construction of "objective" knowledge in the hard sciences

(Latour, 1987, 1991); and modern sociology, which, rather than focusing just on social structures, stresses the dialectical relationship between these and the ongoing processes of human thinking, acting and interaction which produce and reproduce them (Beck, Giddens, & Lash 1994; Giddens, 1984, 1987).

So, the approach to literacy being described here is part of a more general trend, a move toward focusing on the detail of social interaction, using qualitative rather than purely quantitative methods, in an attempt to capture the complexity of life as it is lived, rather than reducing it to some ostensibly simpler explanatory framework. It focuses on the role of social interaction in producing, reproducing, and changing the phenomenon under study. All of these approaches call on the researcher to experience and observe what is there, rather than ripping the phenomenon of interest out of context. They attend to the importance of language, communication, and meaning in the construction of social reality, and acknowledge that this meaning is not necessarily clear, but may be plural, and self-contradictory. This is the background to the development of local and community studies of literacy, which aim to describe reading and writing in people's everyday lives, explaining literacy in terms of social contexts and practices rather than as an autonomous skill, relating it to the opportunities, demands and constraints experienced by individuals, and describing the real complexities and contradictions in people's literacy lives.

LITERACY AS A SOCIAL PRACTICE

Building on the work just described, a particular theory of literacy has emerged, which sees literacy as a social practice. The main features of this social account of literacy are outlined in Barton (1994), Barton and Hamilton (1998), and Barton, Hamilton, & Ivanic (2000). It takes as its basic premise the notion that literacy needs to be seen as a set of social practices, which people use in literacy events. Literacy is located in interactions between people, rather than being a decontextualised cognitive skill—an activity, rather than merely an attribute. The direct implication of this view for research is that literacy is best studied by observing literacy events, that is to say social events that are mediated in some way by written texts.

Because literacy is located in interactions between people, and because interactions between people always occur in different social contexts, there are different literacies associated with different domains of life—that is to say, literacy is neither absolute nor universal. On a broader scale, literacy practices are situated in social relations, which are patterned by social institutions and power relations. This means that some literacies are more dominant, visible, and influential than others. "Vernacular" literacies—literacies associated with people's private, home and everyday lives, outside the domains of public power and influence—are often hidden. This account of literacy makes visible and valuable that which has previously often been unseen and ignored.

Given that literacy is part of the way people get on with their lives, literacy practices are purposeful, embedded in people's broader life goals and practices. Rather than looking at whether people do or do not possess literacy skills, in order to develop a full understanding of what literacy means in people's lives it is necessary to look at how they use literacy as part of the process of making sense of their lives and working toward achieving what they want, using the resources available to them.

As well as situating literacy in people's local contexts, this approach situates literacy in time, acknowledging its historically shaped nature. Current literacy events and practices are created out of the past, in an ongoing process of maintenance, development, and change. Literacy practices are therefore not absolute and fixed for all time, either for an individual or for a society. And often, these changes occur through processes of informal learning and sense-making, outside of a formal teaching situation. Therefore, research into literacy acquisition should not merely focus on classroom or school-based learning, but needs also to look beyond this to the way in which people acquire new practices in other domains, such as the home, the workplace and the neighborhood association.

IMPLICATIONS FOR RESEARCH

All of the above demonstrates the value of studying literacy as it happens, looking both at specific literacy events and at how these events are embedded in local social contexts. Therefore, literacy researchers need to be observing literacy events as they happen in people's lives, in particular times and places. The fact that different literacies are associated with different domains of life means that this detailed observation needs to be going on in a variety of settings, and also that findings from one setting cannot simply be generalized across contexts (as was made clear in the discussion of critical realism). The relationship between local literacy practices and broader social relations means that in addition to the detail of local observation, literacy research needs to extend its focus outward, using other methods such as drawing on historical research or social theory to produce an understanding of the broader situation within which the literacy events are happening. The importance of power relations in patterning literacy practices requires literacy researchers to develop an understanding of the processes of power in the society that they are studying, and to take a critical approach, in the sense of making visible power relationships that are often hidden.

This process of making visible is also necessary because of the hiddenness of nondominant, vernacular literacies. And because these vernacular literacies are hidden, literacy researchers studying them need to spend time developing relationships with people and gaining their trust, before these everyday literacy events can be observed and described—it cannot simply be a question of "parachuting in" and interviewing people as an unknown researcher. Part of the process of building up these relationships involves coming to understand what people's broader purposes and life goals are, and how literacy figures within these. It also involves getting to know people's histories and the histories of their communities, and how literacy practices have changed within these.

This sort of detailed, local study, involving the researcher spending time in particular communities, and using a variety of methods to get a rich and complex picture of people's social lives, is often called *ethnography*, although the goals of the literacy researcher are different from those of the anthropologist who uses ethnographic methods to produce a complete picture of a particular society. The researcher of local literacies employs a variety of qualitative (and some quantitative) methods to develop as complete a picture as possible of the multiform detail of complex contexts, and situates literacy practices within this.

Data collection methods may include some or all of the following: long-term observation of and participation in literacy events, which are documented using fieldnotes, audiotaping, and videotaping; formal and informal interviews and conversations, which might again be recorded in a variety of ways; the collection of texts and artifacts created within the community, as well as externally produced documents about the community where these exist; historical methods, including oral history interviews and working with archive material; it may involve methods such as questionnaires often associated with a more quantitative approach, but used here as one method among others to develop the picture; and some researchers are now working with information technology, using interactive Web sites, mailing lists, or chat rooms to interact with research participants and collect data.

A very important part of the research, implicit in what has already been written, is the need for a reflexive approach, particularly in respect to the ethical implications of the research. A critical approach to literacy, which challenges dominant simplifying voices, questions traditional assumptions, and makes power relations explicit is already an ethical stance in itself. But the ethical implications must also be considered carefully when research is being conducted. This approach sees participants not merely as subjects of the research but as people, who will make sense of the research process and results in their own way, and in whose lives the research will necessarily have an impact. The traditional understanding of the impact of research is that it is the dissemination of results that makes a difference, whereas the reflexive approach takes into account the significant effects produced by the research process itself. Therefore, the ethnographic researcher of literacy must constantly be aware of the potential effects, positive and negative, that the research may have. Obviously, professional guidelines and codes of practice need to be strictly adhered to. But when you are spending time getting to know people, building up relationships of mutual obligation, and stepping into normally private areas of their lives with them, your ethical obligations are not merely covered by the signing of a consent form. In-depth research of this kind requires high levels of awareness about the ethical impact of the research.

This sort of research usually generates a great deal of data of various kinds, and its analysis is not a straightforward or mechanical process. However, in the simplest terms, analysis of qualitative data of this kind means looking for patterns across the data. Often, the methodology involved in this is not made explicit, but Barton and Hamilton (1998) outlined a set of steps in the process.

The first step is finding a way to store the data—in filing cabinets, on a computer database, using qualitative research software, or as a list of word-processed files—or using a combination of storage appropriate for the sort of data that has been collected. (And inevitably there will also be data which cannot be stored, the researcher's synaesthetic memories of "being there," which, however detailed fieldnotes become, can never be fully captured in a written account—termed *headnotes* by Sanjek, 1990.) The categorizations developed for this storage are themselves an early stage of analysis.

The next stage involves the researchers familiarizing themselves with the data. Analysis of qualitative data requires lots of reading, re-reading, making notes, jotting down ideas about patterns, themes, exceptions to the rule, possible explanations, distinctive features—anything that comes to mind as being significant—a process called *memoing* in qualitative research. This might begin with spotting established themes, relating for instance to the particular research questions that motivated the project in the first place; but these established themes will be revisited, developed, and deepened through working with the data in this way.

This reading, re-reading, and memoing process will continue throughout work with the data. But there will also be a gradual process of selection of important parts of the data, and of a more systematic coding or categorization as particular themes emerge as being significant, and as the researchers compare these results to theoretical frameworks. Relationships between different codes and categories are constructed and tested, and checked for validity across different types of data. Depending on the research, different types of analysis might also be used, such as, for example, critical discourse analysis, particularly if the research has a significant interest in the relationship between language and power, or narrative analysis, if the research is interested in the stories that people tell about their literacy histories. The themes and focuses of the written-up research will emerge from this ongoing process of data analysis. And the writing, of a research report, article or book, is itself another stage of analysis, involving interpretation and selection.

COMMUNITY-BASED LITERACY RESEARCH

Moving away from theory now, to give an example of local and community-based literacy research, we outline the Literacy in the Community project presented in *Local Literacies: Reading and Writing in One Community* (Barton & Hamilton, 1998). This ethnographic research was conducted in one area of Lancaster, a small town in the northwest of England. The research began with semistructured interviews with participants in Adult Basic Education courses in Lancaster. These interviews gave insight into the experiences of people who defined themselves as having literacy difficulties. However, this only gave access to a small proportion of the community, and the research was interested in getting a picture of the literacy practices of the community as a whole, including those people who did not come to adult basic education classes.

The neighborhood research therefore began with a "street survey." After spending time travelling around the town, researchers selected one area ("Springside") with clearly defined geographical boundaries and a variety of inhabitants as the focus for the study. They knocked on the door of every fifth house until they had carried out 65 survey interviews, asking people about their ways of finding out about local information. This was used as a lead in to the topic of reading and writing.

One of the basic principles within this type of research is to know the sample well, in order to make theoretical sampling possible, and these initial interviews gave the researchers information about the sorts of people living in the area in order to be able to select particular individuals from the 65 for involvement in further research, in a theoretically motivated way. All of the case studies were to be of adults who had lived in the area for several years, had attended local schools and had left school at the minimum leaving age. Of those who fitted these criteria and were willing to participate further in the research, 12 households were selected for case studies. A range was chosen that was fairly representative of the residents in terms of gender, age, and ethnicity, and included people living in different types of family groups (single, couple, with family) and with different work statuses (working, retired, unemployed). At the same time, researchers were speaking to other key people in the neighborhood, such as workers at a local Housing Action Project.

The case study research was based on extended visits in people's homes, beginning with tape-recorded semi-structured interviews, which were followed up with less structured interviews exploring each individual's own interests and practices. A variety of other research methods were also used in the case studies: some people used maps to plot where they went on a regular basis, others kept letters or junk mail, two people kept diaries of their literacy practices, one couple recorded bed-time reading sessions with their daughter, one man was accompanied to the library and to his local café, and researchers met people at social events, in the pub and at meetings.

This data collection stage was followed by transcription and analysis of the data. Then the researchers returned to 10 people, five from the Springside studies and five from the Adult College interviews, more than a year later for a "collaborative ethnography" stage, to share parts of the data and analysis, to check the validity of the analysis against the way people made sense of their own lives, and to collect further data.

In addition to this case study work, researchers collected a wide range of contextual information about the area, to give a social and historical profile of the city and neighborhood. They also carried out interviews with people working in organizations with some relation to literacy, including schools and colleges, but also bookshops, libraries, greeting card shops, travel agents, post offices, the tourist information office, Citizen's Advice Bureau, and the Dyslexia Association, asking about the services provided, the literacies involved in attracting custom and dealing with the public, and the extent to which the organizations were aware of literacy difficulties. Researchers also documented local literacies in more informal and ad hoc ways, including taking lots of photographs of literacy artifacts like banners placed at a local traffic roundabout to announce birthdays. They carried out case studies of community groups and organizations, attended monthly residents' meetings and other meetings, and collected data for a case study with the Housing Action Project, with which they were in regular contact.

All these data were analyzed and written up using processes similar to those just described, in different ways depending on the type of data collected, moving from historical descriptions of the town as a whole, to detailed descriptions of the life of the area, through to case studies of several of the individuals that researchers worked with. The case studies in particular give insight into the fine details of literacy in people's lives.

Harry Graham was in his 60s. He made a clear distinction between "educated" and "uneducated" people, seeing himself as the latter. Educated people were associated with theoretical book-based learning, whereas uneducated people were associated with apprentice-based learning and more practical skills, which in some ways he valued more highly. He used a wide range of activities involving literacy to keep up with current affairs and study local history, and was particularly interested in reading factual material about the war. Shirley Bowker was active in the local community, both as a general advice-giver and a campaigner, using literacy to achieve her goals in this field. Her son had been diagnosed as being dyslexic, and she used literacy to pressure local authorities to provide him with the correct support. June Marsh was a woman without a particular interest in literacy, who used literacy on an everyday level to keep her household accounts, maintain relationships through sending cards, keep up with local news, and generally to live her life. Cliff Holt's "ruling passion" was leisure and pleasure. Literacy for him was closely related to his enjoyment of popular theater, comedy shows and music, and he wrote many letters to British celebrities such as Ken Dodd and Frankie Laine, often maintaining the correspondence over a period of years.

A wide range and diversity of literacies were encountered in people's homes. Some key themes and patterns were identified, which linked people's experiences: the gendering of home practices, particularly in gendered literacy networks and reading habits; the variety and importance of home numeracy practices, which are often integrated with literacy; and the significance of multilingual literacies in many of the homes in the area, which included a Gujarati-speaking community. The relationship between home literacies and the domain of education was examined in some detail, showing the importance of the home as a domain for learning both for adults and children, the interaction between the home and the school, and the importance of individuals' own relationships with education in their lives.

Education was not the only domain that overlapped with home in terms of literacy practices. All of the participants in the study were involved in some way with at least one self-organized local group or organization, and many had held officers' posts. To illustrate this in more depth, the researchers investigated two key literacy events at the local Allotment Association (communal gardens): the annual general meeting, and a campaign to defend the allotments against the loss of land for house building. They compared this to the Housing Action Project, an association with a very different relationship to the local community. Where the Allotment Association is a local organization, the Housing Action Project was initiated from outside the area, and its complex relationship between local and central organizations caused a variety of tensions and ambiguities, particularly within the local residents' association. This was reflected in the literacy practices involved in its work, for instance in the textual form of editorials written by Shirley Bowker for the residents' newsletter, which showed evidence of her attempts to balance multiple textual identities and subject positions.

This data shows the importance of people using reading and writing *in groups* to get things done, as one of a number of resources on which they draw. It is clear that literacy is significant in terms of local democratic participation, with these local groups underpinning political participation at the local level, and also offering ways in to more formal political organizations (although literacy can also be used in groups to control and undermine democratic participation). This view of literacy as a communal resource, rather than as an individual's particular skill, is therefore central both theoretically and in the data.

Literacy was used by people to make sense of events in their lives and resolve a variety of questions, such as those related to health, legal, and employment-related problems as well as issues around schooling. Often this involved confrontation with professional experts and specialized systems of knowledge, and people often drew on their networks for support and knowledge, thereby becoming expert in a particular domain and becoming a resource for other community members themselves. Literacy was also used for personal change and transformation, both within and outside education-related domains, for accessing information relating to people's interests, for asserting or creating personal identity, and for self-directed learning.

The research identified six key areas of everyday life where reading and writing were of particular importance: organizing life; personal communication; private leisure; documenting life; sense-making; and social participation. Importantly, these "vernacular literacies" are different from more dominant literacies. They are learned informally, and this learning is integrated with practical application and embedded in people's lives. More dominant and visible literacy practices are more formalized, more standardized, and defined in terms of the formal purposes of an institution, rather than people's own lives and purposes. Access to these dominant literacies is controlled through experts and teachers. Vernacular literacies are more likely to be voluntary and self-generated, and may also be a source of creativity, invention, and originality, giving rise to new practices. The research also brought to light the importance of social networks and relationships in these practices, with literacy being used for social communication, but also with people drawing on these social networks to help them with particular literacy requirements. But despite their importance for people's everyday lives, vernacular literacy practices frequently have a low cultural value. The book calls for more research into these vernacular literacies, and the diverse range of texts of everyday life on which they draw.

Local Literacies is an example of what can be achieved with a long-term, detailed, in-depth ethnographic study of one area. Commitment to research on the ground enabled the researchers to elaborate theoretical concepts, such as vernacular literacies and networks of literacies, which were grounded in empirical observations. They clarified the relationship between literacy practices and events, developed knowledge about the interaction between print and other literacies, and refined distinctions between different types of literacy, such as fact and fiction, or self-generated and imposed literacies. But the research is not only about developing theory. The detailed pen-portraits of particular individuals give insight into the role of literacy in people's lived realities that cannot simply be summarized in a few words.

Further examples of local and community literacy research can be found in the later edited volume *Situated Literacies* (Barton, Hamilton, & Ivanic 2000), which brings together a number of studies of reading and writing in a variety of different local contexts, informed by the same theoretical perspective outlined above. Many of the studies presented in this collection show how qualitative methods and detailed local studies can deepen a theoretical understanding of literacy. Wilson's work on prisons demonstrates the role of literacies in the struggle against institutionalization and "losing your mind," the importance of literacy in attempts to maintain an individual identity within a bureaucratic controlling institution, and the use of literacy to construct a "third space" between prison and Outside. This resistant use of literacy contrasts with Jones' work with bilingual Welsh farmers at an auction mart, where it is literacy that inscribes the people's lives into a transnational social order. She focuses on the process of filling in an "animal movement form," showing how the incorporation of individual farmers into the agricultural bureaucratic system is accomplished through a complex process of locally situated talk around texts.

Ormerod and Ivanic's study of children's school project work takes a social practice perspective on the materiality of projects, showing how the physical characteristics of these texts reflect attitudes, beliefs and approaches, are rooted in the children's experiences in and out of school, flow between different social and geographical domains, show the complexity and significance of the "physical dimension" to literacy learning, and demonstrate the ongoing processes of change in children's literacy lives.

De Pourbaix studies an electronic newsgroup of university language learners, exploring the features of these emergent literacy practices, mediated by new technologies, and how they changed over the life of the newsgroup. Pardoe studies students' writing within a Masters'-level environmental management course, drawing on his participant-observation to demonstrate how the unsuccessful features of students' essay writing identified by course tutors in fact arose from understandings which they had been exposed to during the course, and therefore offered insight into the ambiguities and tensions of the field within which they were working. Tusting's work on the role of literacy practices within a Catholic congregation shows how literacy is used to manage time in a variety of ways: how literacy artifacts are produced within a First Communion preparation class both as tangible evidence of commitment through showing investment of significant amounts of time, and to serve as a permanent historical record of a fleeting set of events; and how the parish bulletin is used to synchronize events in time, both locally within the parish community and globally in relation to the Catholic Church as a whole, thereby maintaining community identity. Hamilton's study of newspaper photographs and Pitt's analysis of television texts do not draw directly on ethnographic research in local communities, but both demonstrate how a social practice approach to literacy can inform the analysis of more mediated types of data.

THE FUTURE

In this chapter, we have painted a picture of an approach to literacy research that works from the ground up, seeking to describe the detail of people's literacy practices as they are situated within their local communities. It has highlighted the strengths of this approach, and its force as a critique of the account of literacy as an autonomous cognitive skill. It has situated the approach within a broader turn toward focusing on social practices in the social sciences, and outlined the characteristics of the theory of literacy on which the approach is based. Finally, it has outlined the implications of this theory for research, and given examples of different research projects that have put this approach into practice.

This approach to the study of literacy affords real possibilities for developing understandings of how reading and writing work in the world, and informing models of learning both within and outside classrooms. If we understand people's vernacular uses of literacy and how they are acquired and developed, this can be drawn on to show how vernacular literacies can support formal classroom-based learning, and how such formal learning can best respond to and contribute to people's lives outside the classroom.

The next challenge for the situated study of literacy in the community is to move forward with these detailed understandings. First, now that many in-depth studies of community literacy have been completed, it is time to look across them and assess the common patterns and trends, as well as the specific differences. This is emphatically not a call for researchers to look for general social "laws," or to develop a static picture of literacy. It is saying rather that, especially given the globalizing trends of the society within which we live, there are patterns identifiable across different particular situations, and the resonances across different locally situated studies of vernacular literacies can show the effects of broad social trends on literacy practices in the 21st century.

And second, this approach complements other approaches to literacy studies, including those outlined elsewhere in this volume. Analysis of texts and interactions using critical discourse analysis or conversational analysis can be used to deepen our insight into the linguistic processes involved in everyday literacy practices. An understanding of genre as organized social action can inform analysis of the texts drawn on in particular literacy practices. Broad national and cross-national surveys of literacy can offer another layer of context for situating the realities of people's practices on the ground, and local studies can inform the design of such larger scale research. The locally situated study of literacy in the community has an important role to play in the development of education, policy and understandings of the social world in the future.

ACKNOWLEDGMENTS

We are grateful to Rachel Hodge and the editors and reviewers of this volume for helpful comments.

REFERENCES

Archer, M. S. (1995). *Realist social theory: The morphogenetic approach.* Cambridge, UK: Cambridge University Press.

Barton, D. (1994). *Literacy: An introduction to the ecology of written language.* Oxford: Blackwell.

Barton, D., & Hamilton, M. (1998). *Local literacies: Reading and writing in one community.* London, UK & New York: Routledge.

Barton, D., Hamilton, M., & Ivanic, R. (Eds.). (2000). *Situated literacies: Reading and writing in context.* London, UK & New York: Routledge.

Baynham, M. (1993). Code switching and mode switching: Community interpreters and mediators of literacy. In B. Street (Ed.), *Cross-cultural approaches to literacy.* Cambridge, UK: Cambridge University Press.

Beck, U., Giddens, A., & Lash, S. (1994). *Reflexive modernization: Politics, traditions and aesthetics in the modern social order.* Stanford, CA: Stanford University Press.

Besnier, N. (1993). Literacy and feelings: The encoding of affect in Nukulaelae letters. In B. Street (Ed.), *Cross-cultural approaches to literacy* (pp. 62-86). Cambridge, UK: Cambridge University Press.

Bhaskar, R. (1978). *A realist theory of science.* London, UK: Verso.

Bhaskar, R. (1989). *The possibility of naturalism: A philosophical critique of the contemporary human sciences.* Hemel Hempstead, UK: Harvester Wheatsheaf.

Bhatt, A., Barton, D., Martin-Jones, M., & Saxena, M. (1996). *Multilingual literacy practices: Home, community and school* (Working Papers No. 80). Lancaster, UK: Lancaster University, Centre for Language in Social Life.

Breen, M., & Louden, W. (1994). *Literacy in its place: Literacy practices in urban and rural communities.* Western Australia: School of Language Education, Edith Cowan University.

Camitta, M. (1993). Vernacular writing: Varieties of writing among Philadelphia high school students. In B. Street (Ed.), *Cross-cultural approaches to literacy* (pp. 228-246). Cambridge, UK: Cambridge University Press.

Carter, B., & Sealey, A. (2000). Language, structure and agency: What can realist social theory offer to sociolinguistics? *Journal of Sociolinguistics, 4*(1), 3–20.

Clark, R., Fairclough, N., Ivanic, R., & Martin-Jones, M. (1990). Critical language awareness 1. *Language and Education, 4,* 249-260.

Clark, R., Fairclough, N., Ivanic, R., & Martin-Jones, M. (1991). Critical language awareness 2. *Language and Education, 5,* 41–53.

Collier, A. (1994). *Critical realism: An introduction to Roy Bhaskar's philosophy.* London, UK: Verso.

Cook-Gumperz, J. (1986). *The social construction of literacy.* Cambridge, UK: Cambridge University Press.

Derrida, J. (1978). *Writing and difference.* London, UK: Routledge & Kegan Paul.

Edwards, D., & Potter, J. (1992). *Discursive psychology.* London, UK: Sage.

Engeström, Y. (1990) *Learning, working and imagining: Twelve studies in activity theory.* Helsinki: Orienta-Konsultit.

Fairclough, N., Jessop, B., & Sayer, A. (2001, August). *Critical realism and semiosis.* Paper presented to the International Association for Critical Realism Annual Conference, Roskilde, Denmark.

Fishman, A. (1988). *Amish literacy: What and how it means.* Portsmouth, NH: Heinemann.

Fishman, A. (1991). Because this is who we are: Writing in the Amish community. In D. Barton & R. Ivanic (Eds.), *Writing in the community* (pp. 14-37). London, UK: Sage.

Foucault, M. (1971). *Madness and civilisation: A history of insanity in the age of reason.* London, UK: Tavistock.

Foucault, M. (1975). *Discipline and punish.* New York: Vintage Books.

Foucault, M. (1978). *The history of sexuality* (vol. 1). New York: Pantheon.

Freire, P. (1970). *Pedagogy of the oppressed.* New York: Continuum.

Freire, P., & Macedo, D. (1987). *Literacy: Reading the word and the world.* London, UK: Routledge.

Gee, J. (1990). *Social linguistics and literacies: Ideology in discourses.* London, UK: Falmer Press.

Gee, J. (2000). The new literacy studies: From "socially situated" to the work of the social. In D. Barton, R. Ivanic, & M. Hamilton (Eds.), *Situated literacies: Reading and writing in context* (pp. 180-196). London, UK & New York: Routledge.

Gee, J., Hull, G., & Lankshear, C. (1997). *The new work order: Behind the language of the new capitalism.* London, UK: Allen & Unwin.

Giddens, A. (1984). *The constitution of society: Outline of the theory of structuration.* Cambridge, UK: Polity Press.

Giddens, A. (1987). *Social theory and modern sociology.* Stanford, CA: Stanford University Press.

Giroux, H.A. (1983). *Theory and resistance in education.* London, UK: Heinemann.

Gowen, S. G. (1992). *The politics of workplace literacy: A case study.* New York: Teachers College Press.

Gregory, E. (1996). *Making sense of a new world: Learning to read in a second language.* London, UK: Paul Chapman.

Gumperz, J. J. (1982). *Discourse strategies.* Cambridge UK: Cambridge University Press.

Hamilton, M., Barton, D., & Ivanic, R. (Eds.). (1994). *Worlds of literacy.* Clevedon, UK: Multilingual Matters.

Heath, S.B. (1983). *Ways with words.* Cambridge, UK: Cambridge University Press.

Heidegger, M. (1978). *Basic writings: From "Being and Time," 1927, to "The Task of Thinking," 1964* (D. F. Krell, ed.). London, UK: Routledge & Kegan Paul.

Husserl, E. (1960). *Cartesian meditations: An introduction to phenomenology* (D. Cairns, Trans.). The Hague: Nijhoff. (Original work published 1929)

Hymes, D. (1974). *Foundations of sociolinguistics.* Philadelphia: University of Pennsylvania Press.

Kapitzke, C. (1995). *Literacy and religion: The textual politics and practice of Seventh-day Adventism.* Amsterdam: John Benjamins.

Lakoff, G., & Johnson, M. (1980). *Metaphors we live by.* Chicago: University of Chicago Press.

Latour, B. (1987). *Science in action.* Cambridge, MA: Harvard University Press.

Latour, B. (1991). *We have never been modern.* Cambridge, MA: Harvard University Press.

Lave, J., & Wenger, E. (1991). *Situated learning: Legitimate peripheral participation.* Cambridge, UK: Cambridge University Press.

Levine, K. (1985). *The social context of literacy.* London: Routledge & Kegan Paul.

Livingstone D.W. (Ed.). (1987). *Critical pedagogy and cultural power.* Toronto: Garamond Press.

Luke, A., & Walton, C. (1994). Teaching and assessing critical reading. In T. Tusen & T. Postelthwaite (Eds.), *International encyclopedia of education* (2nd ed., pp. 1194-1198). London, UK: Pergamon Press.

Lyotard, J. F. (1984). *The postmodern condition: A report on knowledge.* Manchester, UK: Manchester University Press.

Martin-Jones, M., & Jones, K. (Eds.). (2000). *Multilingual literacies: Reading and writing different worlds.* Amsterdam: John Benjamins.

Maybin, J. (1997). *Children's voices: The contribution of informal language practices to the negotiation of knowledge and identity amongst 10-12 year old school pupils.* Unpublished doctoral dissertation, Open University, Milton Keynes, UK.

Merleau-Ponty, M. (1962). *Phenomenology of perception.* London, UK: Routledge.

Moll, L. (1994). Mediating knowledge between homes and classrooms. In D. Keller-Cohen (Ed.), *Literacy: Interdisciplinary conversations* (pp. 385-410). Cresskill, NJ: Hampton Press.

Moss, B. J. (1994). *Literacy across communities.* Cresskill, NJ: Hampton Press.

Moss, G. (1996). *Negotiated literacies.* Unpublished doctoral dissertation, Open University, Milton Keynes, UK.

Prinsloo, M., & Breier, M. (1996). *The social uses of literacy: Theory and practice in contemporary South Africa.* Amsterdam: John Benjamins.

Reder, S. (1987). Comparative aspects of functional literacy development: Three ethnic American communities. In D. Wagner (Ed.), *The future of literacy in a changing world* (pp. 250-270). Oxford, UK: Pergamon Press.

Reder, S. (1994). Practice-engagement theory: A sociocultural approach to literacy across languages and cultures. In B. Ferdman, R. M. Weber, & A. G. Ramirez (Eds.), *Literacy across languages and cultures* (pp. 33-74). Albany: State University of New York Press.

Sanjek, R. (1990). *Fieldnotes: The making of anthropology.* Ithaca, NY: Cornell University Press.

Saxena, M. (1994). Literacies among Panjabis in Southall. In M. Hamilton et al. (Eds.), *Worlds of literacy* (pp. 195-214). Clevedon, Avon: Multilingual Matters.

Sayer, A. (2000). *Realism and social science.* London, UK: Sage.

Schieffelin, B., & Gilmore, P. (Eds.). (1986). *The acquisition of literacy: Ethnographic perspectives.* Norwood, NJ: Ablex.

Schiffrin, D. (1994). *Approaches to discourse.* Chicago: University of Chicago Press.

Scribner, S., & Cole, M. (1981). *The psychology of literacy.* Cambridge, MA: Harvard University Press.

Sealey, A., & Carter, B. (2001). Social categories and sociolinguistics: Applying a realist approach. *International Journal of the Sociology of Language, 152,* 1-19.

Sealey, A., & Carter, B. (2002, September). *How far can applied linguistic research establish "what works"?* Paper presented at the annual meeting of the British Association for Applied Linguistics, Cardiff University, Cardiff, Wales.

Solsken, J.W. (1993). *Literacy, gender and work in families and at school.* Norwood, NJ: Ablex.

Street, B. (1984). *Literacy in theory and practice.* Cambridge, UK: Cambridge University Press.

Stubbs, M. (1980). *Language and literacy: The sociolinguistics of reading and writing.* London, UK: Routledge & Kegan Paul.

Szwed, J. F. (1981). The ethnography of literacy. In M. F. Whiteman (Ed.), *Writing: The nature, development, and teaching of written communication.* Hillsdale, NJ: Erlbaum.

Taylor, D. (1983). *Family literacy.* London, UK: Heinemann Educational.

Taylor, D. (1996). *Toxic literacies: Exploring the injustices of bureaucratic texts.* Portsmouth, NH: Heinemann.

Taylor, D. (Ed.). (1997). *Many families, many literacies: An international declaration of principles.* Portsmouth, NH: Heinemann.

Taylor, D., & Dorsey-Gaines, C. (1988). *Growing up literate: Learning from inner-city families.* London, UK: Heinemann.

Wagner, D. A. (1993). *Literacy, culture and development: Becoming literate in Morocco.* Cambridge, UK: Cambridge University Press.

Wertsch, J. V. (1985). *Vygotsky and the social formation of mind.* Cambridge, MA: Harvard University Press.

Wertsch, J. V. (1991). *Voices of the mind: A sociocultural approach to mediated action.* Cambridge, MA: Harvard University Press.

Wertsch, J. V. (1998). *Mind as action.* Oxford, UK: Oxford University Press.

PART III

Linguistic and Discourse Analysis Perspectives on Language and Literacy Research

Judith Green
*University of California,
Santa Barbara*

INTRODUCTION

The past decade has seen an expansion of the methodological and intellectual dialogues across disciplines concerned with language studies in educational settings. One outcome of this expansion has been the publication of a range of cross-perspective volumes. Two directions are visible in these collections. First, there are collections, similar to the current and previous edition of this book, that invite researchers from different theoretical perspectives to write about what their perspective can address and how the work is undertaken. The juxtaposition of perspectives is left to the reader. This type of collection, like the current one in this section, is not designed to promote one perspective over the others or to show what each contributes to analysis of common data. Rather it is designed to make visible what each does with its own data, what theory and method relationships guide that work, how the work develops across time, and what is learned. An example of this approach can be found in the *Journal of Applied Linguistics* (Vol. 23, No. 2) and in edited collections focusing on a specific tradition (e.g., discourse analysis, Schiffrin, Tannen, & Hamilton, 2001; sociolinguistics, Coulmas, 1998; and language and ethnic identity, Fishman, 1999, etc.).

The second direction that has developed from the late 1980s to the present involves authors in examining the same data from different theoretical perspectives (e.g., *Discourse Processes*, Vol. 27, No. 2) or in examining data from a common data set (e.g., *Linguistics & Education*, Vol. 11, No. 4). This approach places an exploration of differences in analysis and interpretation of a common "bit of data" or data set in greater detail. It makes visible what can be learned about a particular literacy process or context from a particular perspective. Through examining the interpretations proposed from the analyses of common data, readers gain deeper insight into what difference the difference(s) in theories and methods make to our understandings of the phenomena under study (Green & Harker, 1988; Green & McClelland, 1999; Grimshaw, Burke, & Cicourel, 1994). These two directions focus on theory method relationships and make visible the tools, theories, and approaches available to those seeking to understand which might inform their own work.

The 1990s also saw an increase in synthesis work on the relationship between language and education. This work focuses on different questions, issues, groups, processes within and across groups and settings, as well as the language and literacy resources students bring to classrooms. In the previous edition, Jenny Cook-Gumperz and John Gumperz (1992) provided an illustration of this perspective in their historical look at the *Changing Views of Language in Education*. Their chapter is a good place to begin an exploration if one is new to this area or if one would like a base for contrasting information gained through syntheses.

In their chapter, they discussed the implications of the changing views of *Language in Education* for literacy research, exploring ways in which language has entered into studies in education over the past decades. They argued that, "Over the past twenty-five years, sociolinguists and educators have entered into a methodological and intellectual dialogue that has significantly changed both our views of language and our theories of how language enters into school learning processes" (p. 151). Their chapter is also important as a ground for the chapters in this edition, because many of the current authors build on one or more of the perspectives described in their chapter.

The new set of chapters in this edition provide new directions and important insights into the relationships between language and education, and the role and nature of language in education and its consequences for students and teachers and others.

The chapter authors represent a broad range of traditions, many of which were not present in the earlier edition. David Bloome is the only author in this section to be represented in both the first and second editions of this book (current writer excepted). In this edition, Bloome describes how the current work differs from the original conceptualization and why the change in conceptualization was needed. He argues that

> We built on then current directions in the study of language, literacy, and education across the disciplines of linguistics, anthropology, sociology, psychology, and others, that had rejected the distinction Saussure (1959) made between *langue* and *parole* and the distinction made in theoretical linguistics between competence and performance. Those multidisciplinary directions called for descriptions of language and literacy derived from the realities of how people actually use and make language in the events that make up their lives. We did not realize it at the time, but such a claim warranted more than a multidisciplinary approach. It required researchers to stand simultaneously in differing worlds, to move outside of academia, to seek an understanding of language and literacy from within all of the complex and conflicting worlds within which language and literacy events take place.

The journey he shares provides new directions and insights, not only into his argument, but also into ways of theorizing and studying complex processes and issues.

Critical linguistic perspectives are represented by work by James Gee on spoken discourse analysis and Roz Ivanic on written discourse analysis. Coming from two continents and two different intellectual traditions, these authors provide different ways of approaching critical linguistic research, even though their arguments have overlapping or compatible elements. Gee argues for a multiliteracies approach:

Literacy, in this view, is multiple: There are as many literacies as there are different ways in which written language is embedded in diverse social practices. Literacy is also, in this view, integrally connected to identity: the various social practices in which written language is embedded require one to recruit distinctive ways with both oral and written words, as well as ways of thinking, acting, and interacting, so as to take on particular socially situated identities. . . . From the perspective of critical discourse analysis, then, research on literacy is part of the study of social practices and identities at work in society (Gee, 1996). Thus, in this chapter, I concentrate on critical discourse analysis as a method of analyzing a wide variety of different types of spoken and written language within social practices.

In contrast to Gee's approach, which begins with a general perspective on discourse analysis and then moves to closer look at critical discourse analysis, Ivanic begins with a focused examination of one concept, inscription of the *writer's identity* in written artifacts from classrooms, rather than identity in a more general sense.

It [this chapter] focuses on the identity of the writer of a text, and specifically, the way in which the writer's identity is inscribed in the communicative resources on which he or she draws when writing. This perspective on literacy research is concerned specifically with the writer, the writer's sense of who he or she is, the act of writing, the linguistic and other semiotic characteristics of the texts writers produce, and the consequences for identity of these textual characteristics.

These two chapters, read together, provide a basis for understanding the differences in approach and what difference the differences makes in focus, understanding and methodology.

Two additional chapters contribute to this section. The Hornberger chapter provides a model that has been theoretically and empirically developed across a number of years and studies focusing on biliteracy. She argues that

Biliteracy can be defined as any and all instances in which communication occurs in two (or more) languages in or around writing. The continua model of biliteracy offers a framework in which to situate research, teaching, and language planning in linguistically diverse settings. The model uses the notion of intersecting and nested continua to demonstrate the multiple and complex interrelationships between bilingualism and literacy and the importance of the contexts, media, and content through which biliteracy develops. . . . In each case, I consider

> how the view of literacy in the continua model (a) reflects certain assumptions regarding literacy and literacy learning; (b) relates to other perspectives on literacy as well as to larger disciplinary perspectives; and (c) can be used in research and analysis of literacy practices.

This chapter demonstrates how research can be synthesized, can be used to conceptualize a complex process (i.e., biliteracy) and how model development is a continuing process that moves from empirical data to theoretical perspectives to help theorize a complex, yet everyday, process for certain groups of people.

The final chapter in this section is one that I co-authored with Carol Dixon, working collaboratively with data from her ethnographic research corpus from first grade. We take the reader on a journey to understanding, moving from the present, backward in time across a range of analyses to identify how students draw on spoken and written texts from previous moments in time within the classroom (and other settings) to read, interpret, and produce new texts, which in turn become resources for self and others in subsequent work.

> The purpose of our chapter is to demonstrate the need for historical and situational analyses and how these analyses can be undertaken through an integration of ethnographic and discourse analysis approaches. Central to this approach is a theoretical perspective on the social construction of knowledge and on events and knowledge within groups as intertextually and intercontextually tied across time.

The approach presented is one that has become known in the past decade as Interactional Ethnography.

MAKING VISIBLE WHAT IS BECOMING INVISIBLE IN EDUCATIONAL RESEARCH: AN ARGUMENT FOR WHY THIS VOLUME IS NECESSARY

One key place people new to an area search for information on theory and methods and what can be learned is in handbooks for a discipline. In the past decade, a number of new handbooks were developed in areas related to language and literacy. These handbooks include research approaches to language in education (Flood, Heath, & Lapp, 1997; Flood, Lapp, Jensen, & Squire, 2002). Focused on reaching those directly involved in literacy and language research both in and out of school settings, these volumes are invaluable sources of a broad range of work. Such handbooks are published intermittently, often with as much as 10 years between editions.

Another important source of synthesis papers is the *Review of Research in Education* (RRE) published annually by the American Educational Research Association. The *RRE* has published a growing number of pieces in which language played a central part (Dyson, 2000; Gee & Green, 1998; Hicks, 1999). This resource, like handbooks, often provides methodological work as well as syntheses of research generated by language and literacy researchers, making this body of research accessible to a broad audience. Given the increased understanding of the importance of understanding teaching and learning as shaping, and shaped by language processes and practices (Fairclough, 1990) represented in these volumes, the omission of a chapter in the fourth edition of the *Handbook of Research on Teaching* (Richardson, 2001) focused on classroom discourse and its consequences for students and teachers was unanticipated.

To understand why the omission of this chapter is important to consider, it is necessary to examine briefly the history of this volume and its impact. The *Handbook of Research on Teaching* is one of the oldest handbooks published by the American Educational Research Association and has had a major impact on defining directions in research, particularly research on classroom practices and processes. It pre-dates volumes that have a primary focus within a subject area: mathematics, literacy, science, communication arts, among others. This handbook has its origins in 1963 and builds the argument that there was little systematic research in classrooms. In the first two editions (Gage, 1963; Travers, 1973), the work on language and literacy (primarily reading) was limited to subject matter. However, in the third edition of this handbook (Wittrock, 1986), new perspectives that had emerged from sociolinguistics, psycholinguistics, and studies of child language in educational settings found representation in chapters on *Classroom Discourse* by Courtney Cazden (1986), in the chapter by Frederick Erickson (1986) on *Qualitative Research,* and in the chapter by Carolyn Evertson and Judith Green (1986) on *Observation as Theory and Method.* These chapters brought new conceptualizations of teaching and learning to the fore and new research directions, foci, and tools, that complemented and extended chapters on the subject matter.

Although, the fourth edition includes a broad range of chapters related to research on the teaching of reading (Barr, 2001), literature (Grossman, 2001), second languages (Hancock, 2001), and writing (Sperling & Freedman, 2001), what are missing are chapters on research methods and classroom discourse. In place of such chapters, are ones focusing the use of narrative (Gudmundsdottir, 2001); and race, ethnicity, and linguistic difference (Mercado, 2001). Although some readers might argue that the chapter on "teaching as dialogue" (Burbules & Bruce, 2001) represents work on classroom discourse, an analysis of this chapter indicates clearly a difference in orientation, literature cited, and research methodology. This chapter shifts the concept of dialogue to a philosophical view, rather than a one grounded in linguistics or discourse perspectives. This change marks a shift in how teaching, and its associated term, learning, is conceptualized. Gone is the view of teaching (and learning) as constituted in and through patterns of language use in the classroom (see Cazden, 1986, 2001; Green, 1983; Hull & Schwartz, 2002, for discussions of the historical evolution of this perspective). In its place is an approach to teaching that focuses on the use of dialogue, as an approach to teaching that is defined from a philosophical perspective (e.g., Socratic method).

This shift, and the omission of a focused chapter on spoken and written discourse in classrooms, makes the current volume particularly important. This volume, with its interdisciplinary approach and its international group of scholars, provides an important focus on language research in the area of literacy. The chapters in this section can be viewed as expanding work available in the handbooks and volumes within the field of language and literacy in education and as providing scholars interested in research approaches grounded in work on linguistics and discourse analysis with new directions. With this brief overview as background, we invite you to examine what each of the traditions provides, the historical roots that the authors present, and the types of work that these approaches and perspectives support.

REFERENCES

Barr, R. (2001). Research on the teaching of reading. In V. Richardson (Ed.), *Handbook of research on teaching* (4th ed., pp. 390-415). Washington, DC: American Educational Research Association.

Bloome, D., & Bailey, F. (1992). Studying language through events, particularity, and intertextuality. In R. Beach, J. Green, M. Kamil, & T. Shanahan (Eds.), *Multiple disciplinary perspectives on literacy research* (pp. 181-210). Urbana, IL: NCRE & NCTE.

Burbules, N., & Bruce, B. (2001). Theory and research on teaching as dialogue. In V. Richardson (Ed.), *Handbook of research on teaching* (4th ed., pp. 1002-1021). Washington, DC: American Educational Research Association.

Cazden, C. (1986). Classroom discourse. In M. Wittrock (Ed.), *Handbook of research on teaching* (3rd ed.). Washington, DC: American Educational Research Association.

Cazden, C. (2001). *Classroom discourse: The language of teaching and learning.* Portsmouth, NH: Heinemann. (Original work published 1988)

Cook-Gumperz, J., & Gumperz, J. (1992). Changing views of language in education: The implications of literacy research. In R. Beach, J. Green, M. Kamil, & T. Shanahan (Eds.), *Multiple disciplinary perspectives on literacy research* (pp. 151-180). Urbana, IL: NCRE & NCTE.

Coulmas, F. (Ed.). (1997). *The handbook of sociolinguistics.* Oxford: Blackwells.

Dyson, A. (2000). Transforming transfer: Unruly children, contrary texts, and the persistence of the pedagogical order. *Review of Research in Education, 24,* 141-171.

Erickson, F. (1986). Qualitative research. In M. Wittrock (Ed.), *The handbook of research on teaching* (3rd ed., pp. 119-161). New York: Macmillan.

Evertson, C., & Green, J. (1986). Observation as inquiry and method. In M. Wittrock (Ed.), *The handbook of research on teaching* (3rd ed., pp. 162-213). New York: Macmillan.

Fairclough, N. (1995). *Critical discourse analysis: The critical study of language.* London: Longman.

Fishman, J. (Ed.). (1999). *Handbook of language and ethnic identity.* Oxford: Oxford University Press

Flood, J., Heath, S. B., & Lapp, D. (Eds.) (1997). *Handbook for literacy educators: Research in the communicative and visual arts.* New York: Macmillan.

Flood, J., Jensen, J., Lapp, D., & Squire, J. (Eds.). (2002). *Handbook on teaching the English language arts* (pp. 205-225). New York: Macmillan.

Gage, N. (1963). *The handbook of research on teaching* (3rd ed.). Washington, DC: American Educational Research Association.

Gee, J.P. (1996). *Social linguistics and literacies: Ideologies in discourses* (2nd ed.). London: Taylor & Francis.

Gee, J., & Green, J. (1998). Discourse analysis, learning, and social practice: A methodological study. *Review of Research in Education, 23,* 119-169.

Green, J. (1983). Teaching as a linguistic process: A state of the art. In E. Gordon (Ed.), *Review of Research in Education, 10,* 151-252.

Green, J.L., & Harker, J.O. (Eds.). (1988). *Multiple perspective analyses of classroom discourse.* Norwood, NJ: Ablex.

Green, J., & McClelland, M. (1999). What difference does the difference make? Understanding difference across perspectives. *Discourse Processes, 27*(2), 393-406.

Grimshaw, A., Burke, P., & Cicourel, A. (Eds.). (1994). *What's going on here?: Complementary studies of professional talk,* Norwood, NJ: Ablex.

Grossman, P., (2001). Research on the teaching of literature: Finding a place. In V. Richardson (Ed.), *Handbook of research on teaching* (4th ed., pp. 390-415). Washington, DC: American Educational Research Association.

Gudmundsdottir, S. (2001). Narrative research on school practice. In V. Richardson (Ed.), *Handbook of research on teaching* (4th ed., pp. 226-240). Washington, DC: American Educational Research Association.

Hicks, D. (1996). Discourse, learning, and teaching. In M. Apple (Ed.), *Review of Research in Education, 21,* 49-98.

Hull, G., & Schultz, K. (2002). Literacy and learning out of school. *Review of Educational Research, 71*(4), 575-611.

Luke, A. (1996). Text and discourse in education: An introduction to critical discourse analysis. *Review of Research in Education, 21,* 3-48.

Mercado, C. (2001). The learner: Race, ethnicity and linguistic difference. In V. Richardson (Ed.), *Handbook of research on teaching* (4th ed., pp. 668-694). Washington, DC: American Educational Research Association.

Richardson, V. (Ed.). (2001). *Handbook of research on teaching* (4th ed.). Washington, DC: American Educational Research Association.

Schiffrin, D., Tannen, D., & Hamilton, H.E. (Eds.). (2001). *The handbook of discourse analysis*. Oxford: Blackwell.

Sperling, M., & Freedman, S. (2001). Research on writing. In V. Richardson (Ed.), *Handbook of research on teaching* (4th ed., pp. 370-389). Washington, DC: American Educational Research Association.

Travers, R. (1973). *Handbook of research on teaching* (2nd ed.). Washington, DC: American Educational Research Association.

Wittrock, M. (1986). *Handbook of research on teaching* (3rd ed.). Washington, DC: American Educational Research Association.

11

Introductions to Studying Language and Literacy, in Particular

David Bloome
The Ohio State University

The title of this chapter has changed from the original published in 1992. The original title was "Studying Language and Literacy Through Events, Particularity, and Intertextuality." In the original version, Francis Bailey and I laid out a multidisciplinary approach to the study of language and literacy based on a definition of language and literacy as actions taken by people in face-to-face events and other interactional events. We built on then current directions in the study of language, literacy, and education across the disciplines of linguistics, anthropology, sociology, psychology, and others, that had rejected the distinction Saussure (1959) made between *lange* and *parole* and the distinction made in Theoretical Linguistics between competence and performance. Those multidisciplinary directions called for descriptions of language and literacy derived from the realities of how people actually use and make language in the events that make up their lives. We did not realize it at the time, but such a claim warranted more than a multidisciplinary approach. It required researchers to stand simultaneously in differing worlds, to move outside of academia, to seek an understanding of language and literacy from within all of the complex and conflicting worlds within which language and literacy events take place.

In the original chapter, we noted that multidisciplinary inquiry was not new. Following Geertz (1983), we argued that what was new was a kind of "genre blurring" that had created a new research agenda that fundamentally changed the nature of inquiry. Rather than seeking universals, the new directions we described had an increasing emphasis on the particular: on what happens in a particular place, at a particular time, and with a particular set of people, engaged in a particular activity and event. What was important in such inquiry was describing the meaning of people's actions in *particular* events as they acted and reacted to each other as they created the event, the activity, who they were, social relationships, and connections to other events.

The emphasis on *particular* events in the original version and in the title of this version is an intertextual reference to a chapter titled "Language in Particular: A Lecture," by Alton Becker (1988). Becker, in his call for a humanistic linguistics, was not rejecting attention to structures or patterns but rather foregrounding what was particular about any use of language. Given Williams' (1977) statement that, "A definition of language is always a definition of people in the world " (p. 21), to reduce language and literacy to recurrent structures and patterns is to envision/conceptualize people as supplicants of social systems playing themselves out. To emphasize the particularity of language is to envision/conceptualize people as acting on the worlds in which they live. And, although it is always the case that people, both as individuals and collectively, must address the social systems in which they find themselves, one cannot simultaneously hold a view of people as acting on and in the worlds in which they live and hold a view of people as merely cogs in the machinery of a social system. To conceptualize people as acting on or in the worlds in which they live is to assign to them the possibility of efficacy with regard to change, stability, and resistance. It is also to hold them responsible for actions they take in support of the social, political and economic systems in which they live. To conceptualize people as merely cogs in a machine is to deny them the possibility of efficacious behavior and is to ignore the resistance and creativity that may be occurring in ways that lie below the surface of their participation in dominant social, political, and economic systems. None of which is to deny that people may find themselves in contexts that they cannot change and must accept nor is it the case that people always have the tools they need to be efficacious.

I use "Introductions" in the title of this chapter to signal two assumptions I make about the study of language and literacy. The first is that inquiry on language and literacy is defined in the doing and cannot be predetermined. As researchers capture and analyze a language or literacy event, they will be constantly challenging and revising the extant theoretics that provided the original methods and directions for their inquiry. Methodology in the study of language and literacy cannot be reduced to an algorithm or a given set of procedures to follow from beginning to end, as if different methodological approaches were merely the enactments of different grand narratives. Rather, as I view it, methodology must always be a reflective, critical, and recursive process in which researchers are attendant as much to the field and their location in it as to the events they are exploring. The enactment of any methodology must always include an under cutting of the grand narrative that defined it. Thus, all that methodological discussions can ever provide is an introduction, a point of departure for inquiry that turns both toward the object of that inquiry and toward itself.

The second assumption is that the study of language and literacy is inherently a multidisciplinary endeavor. It is not just that different disciplinary perspectives can be brought to the study of language and literacy, but rather that monolithic disciplinary frames distort the object of their inquiry—language and literacy—by absorbing that object within the disciplinary frame such that the inquiry becomes narcissistic. Monolithic disciplinary inquiry is incapable of seeing other than itself. The point of a multidisciplinary perspective, thus, is not the search for convergence among differing perspectives (as if convergence and divergence were not themselves constructions of an inquiry), but rather to keep the object of inquiry, language, and literacy, out there, strange, alien, unabsorbed.

Given these two assumptions, this chapter is organized as a series of "introductions" to the study of language and literacy, *in particular*. Those listed here are illustrative of research agendas that take seriously the ways in which people act on the worlds in which they live. They are not the only introductions that might be listed.

INTRODUCTION 1: EVENTS

Educational research, dominated by educational psychology, has predominately viewed the individual as the primary unit of analysis (McDermott & Hood, 1982). This is so even in many of the studies that explicitly employ other units of analysis such as the classroom, the task, the activity, the school, and so on. As Smith (1987) argued, it is the research framework that transforms a whole, with its structured relationships among people, into isolated units; individuals need to be seen as part of a whole. Regardless of what is the explicitly stated unit of analysis, the primary unit of analysis in educational research is the individual if the research is embedded in the discourse of individual achievement, individual action, development, and other individual outcomes (even if those individual outcomes are aggregated or described as contingent). The issue is made poignant in Moll's (1992; Moll & Greenberg, 1990) research on funds of knowledge. His research shows that research frameworks that view the individual as the locus of knowledge overlook the distribution of knowledge within a community to which all members of the community may have access. As a consequence of research frameworks that explicitly or implicitly hold the individual as the primary unit of analysis, some students and some people may be viewed as unknowledgeable or incapable although they have access to and can make use of a broad-based and diverse community knowledge fund and skill reservoir and thus are neither unknowledgeable nor unskilled. A research framework that takes an individual out of his or her community first distorts the individual, then studies the distorted individual, and then concludes the individual is distorted.

By emphasizing the event as the unit of analysis, people and their language are viewed as embedded in events, even though it is their actions and their use of language that constructs the event. By viewing the event as primary, people and language are defined as inherently social and other-oriented (Weber, 1968); meaning is located in the event rather than in people's heads (Geertz, 1973).

An event can be defined as a bounded series of actions and reactions that people take in response to each other at the level of face-to-face interaction. This does not mean that there has to be two or more people physically and proximally co-present in order for there to be an event. People are sometimes by themselves physically. However, whether with others or alone, a person is acting and reacting in response to other people, what they have done and what they will do. The task, in part, for the researcher interested in understanding the meaning of what people are doing is to identify the people context and the action context within which the acting and reacting is occurring (cf. Erickson & Shultz, 1977); that is, to identify the boundaries of the event. Stated simply, people act and react to each other. This seemingly simple notion needs to be discussed at greater length.

First, it is *people* who are acting and reacting to each other. It is not the individual who acts but a group of people who act. People are the context for each other (cf. Erickson & Shultz, 1977). Second, people *act and react* ("react" is used here similar to Bakhtin's, 1935/1981, and Volosinov's, 1929/1973, discussions of "response"). People react to actions immediately previous, to actions that occurred sometime earlier, and to sets, groups, and patterns of action. People also react to future actions. Any action, including a reaction, inherently includes within it a concept of consequence. Consequences presume future actions either by others or by oneself. As such, a "nonaction" can be a reaction. Third, the actions and reactions people take to each other are not necessarily linear. People may act together, and actions and reactions may occur simultaneously. Fourth, people may act and react to each other through sequences of actions and not just through individual actions. As an aside, it is important to note that the use of language is an action (cf. Volosinov, 1929/1973), it is something people do to each other, to themselves, and is part of the way that they act on the situations in which they find themselves. And fifth, meaning and significance are located in the actions and reactions people take to each other, not in abstracted or isolated psychological states. Inasmuch as there is no separation of people from events, there can be no separation between meaning, significance, and action. Which is not to say that people do not think about and reflect on the meaning and significance of actions and events, but rather to assert that such thinking and reflection are part of an event and are constituted by social relationships, language, and history. (An illustration of the use of these five theoretical constructs in an analysis of classroom language and literacy event can be found in Bloome et al., 2004.)

INTRODUCTION 2: MATERIAL

By *material*, I mean all those aspects of an event that can be experienced by the participants. This includes the physical setting (room, desks, chairs, etc.), where the event takes place, the artifacts (textbooks, handouts, pencils) manipulated by the participants during an event, the participants who construct the event (their bodies, their clothes, etc.), technology (including the hardware, electronic structures such as chat rooms, instant messanger, and hypertext links), and the behavior of the participants (e.g., how they act and react to each other, the utterances they make, etc.). Language also has a material basis. As Volosinov (1929/1973) argued:

> Every ideological sign is not only a reflection, a shadow of reality, but is also itself a material segment of that very reality. Every phenomenon functioning as an ideological sign has some kind of material embodiment, whether in sound, physical mass, color, movements of the body, or the like. In this sense, the reality of the sign is fully objective and lends itself to a unitary, monistic, objective method of study. A sign is a phenomenon of the external world. Both the sign itself and all the effects it produces (all those actions, reactions, and new signs it elicits in the surrounding social milieu) occur in outer experience. (p. 11)

From this point of view, language is a material response not only to what has been said or done before but also to what will be said or done in the future. Its material existence, however, depends on its ratification by others. An utterance that no one responds to (no ratification) loses its material existence and plays no role in the construction of an event. However, a nonratified utterance should not be confused with either a deliberate ignoring of an utterance, a negation of an utterance, or a nonratification of the meaning of the linguistic dimensions of an utterance (which nonetheless takes up space and time as occurs when people do not understand what someone has said but respond to the attempt).

What constitutes the material of an event? This question needs to be at or near the center of inquiries about events. It is answered similarly by the participants and the observing researchers. For both, the material of an event (and what it signifies) is given historically, created, made, and re-made, throughout the event.

INTRODUCTION 3: INTERTEXTUALITY

Intertextuality, simply defined, refers to the juxtaposition of texts. A reference in one text refers to another text; two or more texts share a common referent or are related because they are of the same genre or belong to the same setting; or, one text leads to another (as occurs when writing one letter leads to the writing of another or when the buying a theater ticket provides admission to a play). It is commonplace to view any text as indexing many others, imbued with the voices of many people and many past texts. Scholarship on intertextuality has tended to focus on written texts, but questions about intertextuality can include conversational texts, electronic texts, nonverbal texts (e.g., pictures, graphs, architecture), among others. In a classroom, the students may simultaneously have their textbooks open on their desks, be engaged in a conversation with the teacher, have maps hanging on the wall, and the teacher may be writing on the white board.

Intertextuality is something that teachers and students take for granted, so much so that they may not even realize that they are doing so. Thus, rather than ask if a particular classroom event involves intertextuality, it may be more appropriate to ask, "How does the event involve intertextuality?" and, "What stances do the teacher and students take toward intertextuality?" (cf. Beach & Anson, 1992).

I take the view that intertextuality is socially constructed (cf. Bloome & Egan-Robertson, 1993). That is, an intertextual connection is constructed by people in interaction with each other. In order to claim that an intertextual connection has been constructed, it must have been proposed, acknowledged, recognized, and have social consequence.

Given a view of intertextuality as socially constructed, questions can also be raised about the intertextual process, intertextual substance, and intertextual rights extant within any event. Intertextual process refers to *how* an intertextual connection was made (what forms of language were used, what patterns of response and reaction, etc.). Intertextual substance refers to the set of texts being juxtaposed, the levels at which they are being juxtaposed (e.g., lexical, syntactic pattern, textual structure, genre), and the meanings these texts holds for participants both as separate texts and as juxtaposed within a specific event. Intertextual rights refers to the distribution of privileges and constraints on the proposing, acknowledging, recognizing, and giving social consequence to intertextuality. It is not the case that in all events intertextual rights are distributed equally. By exploring the nature of intertextual processes, intertextual substance, and the distribution of intertextual rights, insights can be gained into the cultural ideology of the event (Bloome, 1993; Lemke, 1992; Shuart-Faris & Bloome, 2004).

Closely related to intertextuality is the construct of inter*context*uality (Heras, 1993; Lin, 1993). Part of the creation of any event involves the construction of relationships between the event and other events. Sometimes, such relationships are created overtly; for example, a teacher might say, "Today's lesson builds on what we did in reading group yesterday." Of course, merely proposing a relationship between one event and another does not in and of itself create a connection. For example, the students might not have heard what the teacher said, a fire drill might occur immediately after the utterance, or there might be no ongoing creation of connections (i.e., the connection is dropped). A connection among events has to be ratified by others. The participants have to acknowledge and recognize the connection, and the connection has to have social consequence.

With regard to intercontextual connections, one cannot assume that the social positioning and social identities that were extant in a referenced previous context will be reiterated in a current context. For example, if a social hierarchy existed in a previous context, intercontextual linkages do not necessarily mean that those social hierarchies will be reconstructed. Instead, one needs to examine how the intercontextual link is being used. It might be used by one or more people to reconstruct a particular set of social relationships but it might also be used to transform them. The key is in how people assign meaning and consequence to an intercontextual link.

Similar to the social construction of intertextuality, questions can be asked about intercontextual processes, intercontextual substance, and the distribution of intercontextual rights.

INTRODUCTION 4: HISTORY

Events do not occur in isolation from each other. What happens in one event—the meanings created, the social identities formed, the material goods given significance—influences other events. Historical influences can be seen in the construction of an event as constraining or limiting the options, meanings, language, and material goods that are available to the participants in an event. For example, in a classroom, teacher and students are constrained by the historical impetus that created the institution of their specific school with its concept of teacher and student roles, its specific views of knowledge and the acquisition of knowledge, and the specific historical/biographical experiences of the students and the teacher. On a smaller scale, within a classroom, any specific event is historically influenced by the events preceding on that same day or on previous days it (an intercontextuality socially constructed through the implicature of contiguity).

Historical relationships among events are established at many levels. Part of what is important in the study of events is unpacking the levels at which various events are historically related to each other. For example, two classroom events may be historically related because of their adjacency and proximity. Events that are not adjacent or proximal may be related because of direct reference (e.g., a statement made by the teacher and ratified by the students) or because they are similarly labeled (e.g., reading group, spelling test). However, events may be historically related even when they are not adjacent, proximal, directly referenced, or have the same label. For example, today's reading group may be related to last year's factory layoffs in part because of a reduction of school revenues resulting in a lack of material resources and larger reading groups, a change in attitude about the efficacy of school learning, and a change in children's and parents' attitudes about the security of nonprofessional jobs, producing an emphasis on reading group placement, articulated progress, and test scores.

Although it is not the case that history is deterministic, and although historical relationships, constraints, and limits are both materially related and socially constructed, it is the case that participants act and react within the context of the historical relationships they have constructed, and they must account for and react to those historical relationships. In order to understand the social dynamics of an event, researchers need to analyze those historical forces that have channeled specific people to a specific place at a specific time to accomplish a specific set of tasks. Such analysis requires a multidisciplinary blend of methods drawn from history, sociolinguistics, anthropology, among other disciplines.

INTRODUCTION 5: TIME

Despite its under theorizing, nearly every major theory related to language and literacy in classrooms—including developmental theories, learning theories, socialization theories, cultural transmission theories, and so on—either explicitly or implicitly invokes time as an important dimension. The case is similar in the social sciences in general.

> Not only does time seem to be a non-reflected aspect of social theory, it also lacks the multifacetedness displayed in thought, language, and the concomitant everyday life. Much like people in their everyday lives, social scientists take time largely for granted. Time is such an obvious factor in social science that it is almost invisible. (Adam, 1990, p. 3)

Teachers and students are constantly talking about time: "Be to class on time," "Finish your work on time," "When is the assignment due?" "Spend your time wisely," "Don't waste time," "This is not the time for that activity," and so on. Daily schedules are often written and displayed in classrooms. In middle and secondary schools, time is marked with bells. There is "passing time," "lunch time," "play time," "work time," "library time," and the like. There is the time of year marked by the seasons and report cards. Time can also be a "place" as in sending a student to "Time Out" for inappropriate behavior; similarly with detention, suspension, and expulsion. With regard to detention, time is defined as a quantity students have which is taken away from them for their transgressions; and as such, time becomes part of the moral code of schools and classrooms. The year as a unit of time comes into play with regard to concepts such as curriculum coverage, "passing" and "grade level." Students are grouped by their age in most schools, another time-based definition, and teachers may reprimand students for not acting their age.

Ball, Hull, Skelton, and Tudor (1984) argued that students (and perhaps teachers as well) in some classrooms may orient their behavior toward making it through the day. So much time has to be spent in the classroom, how to get through it without being painfully bored, embarrassed, having one's "face" or authority challenged or threatened, and how to put up with the physical challenge of sitting still for such an amount of time or not being able to relieve oneself until "bathroom time." Ball et al. suggested that one of the things that students may do to get through time in classrooms is to create diversions and resistance. Similarly, teachers and students need to get through their day in a way that "looks" like what "lessons" and "classrooms" are "supposed" to look like (Bloome, Puro, & Theodorou, 1987).

The examples just given suggest the ubiquitous nature of time in classroom education and that there are multiple definitions and social constructions of time. Time is a dimension that is used to define and evaluate students (e.g., Sally is a smart child, she gets the lesson quickly; John is not so bright as he takes a long time to get the lesson; Stephen is a good student he is always on time; Margaret is a bad student she never gets to class on time) and their parents (Walter's parents make time for him and find the time to come to school to talk with his teacher; Pamela's parents do not give her the time or attention she needs and they do not take time off work to come to school to talk with Pamela's teachers).

As the examples about "time" suggest, the concepts of time and space are intimately related, as Bakhtin's discussion of chronotopes illustrates. Chronotope was a concept that Bakhtin borrowed from Einstein's Theory of Relativity. Bakhtin (1935/1981) wrote:

> We will give the name chronotope (literally, "time space") to the intrinsic connectedness of temporal and spatial relationships that are artistically expressed in literature . . . [chronotope] expresses the inseparability of space and time. . . . In the literary artistic chronotope, spatial and temporal indicators are fused into one carefully thought-out, concrete whole. Time, as it were, thickens, takes on flesh, becomes artistically visible; likewise, space becomes charged and responsive to the movements of time, plot, and history. . . . [I]t is precisely the chronotope that defines genre and generic distinctions. . . . The chronotope as a formally constitutive category determines to a significant degree the image of man [sic] in literature as well. The image of man [sic] is always intrinsically chronotopic. (pp. 84-85)

Bakhtin analyzed chronotopes in various literary periods, showing how time and space are differently conceptualized and how the chronotope frames character development (or the lack of it), plot, and the meaning and significance of a novel. For example, Bakhtin analyzes the chronotope of Greek romances. In brief, the hero and heroine meet, fall in love, but are separated by events and have to go through a series of adventures and overcome obstacles to rejoin each other and marry. In this "adventure-time," as Bakhtin called it, although the hero and heroine may spend time in the adventure and travel different places

> it is simply days, nights, hours, moments clocked in a technical sense within the limits of each separate adventure. This time—adventure-time—highly intensified but undifferentiated—is not registered in the slightest way in the age of the heroes. . . . In this kind of time, nothing changes: the world remains as it was, the biographical life of the heroes does not change, their feelings do not change, people do not even age. (pp. 90-91)

Bakhtin's analysis of the chronotope of the Greek Romance highlights the power of a chronotope to frame human agency and the relationship of the individual to the world in which she or he lives.

> All moments of this infinite adventure-time are controlled by one force—chance. . . . In this time, persons are forever having things happen to them (they might even "happen" to win a kingdom). . . . But the

initiative in this time does not belong to human beings (p. 95). . . . In [adventure-time] there is no potential for evolution, for growth, for change. As a result of the action described in the novel, nothing in its world is destroyed, remade, changed or created anew. What we get is a mere affirmation of the identity between what had been at the begin- ning and what is at the end. Adventure time leaves no trace. (p. 110)

Because classrooms are not novels, Bakhtin's discussion of chronotopes cannot be directly applied. However, his discussion of chronotopes can be used as a starting point for raising questions about how time and space are conceptualized in classrooms language and literacy events. Similar to the way in which the action in a novel is set against a conception of time and space, the social and academic action in a classroom is also set against an underlying chronotope.

For example, perhaps in some classrooms the school day may be implic- itly conceptualized similar to "adventure-time," children and teachers leave their homes, have a series of adventures and overcome various obstacles in the classroom, and are reunited with their families essentially unchanged at the end of the school day. In other classrooms, time and space may be con- ceptualized as components of each individual's private life, internal to the person. The individual passes through time and space measured by how it affects and changes the student. Within such a conception of time and space, it is the internal world that evolves and changes, the external world— the social and political world, the classroom, the school—is untouched. In other classrooms, time and space may be implicitly conceptualized in terms of social action on the world outside the classroom (as in the projects described in Egan-Robertson & Bloome, 1998). Another way in which time and space might be conceptualized is as an attribute of the individual, with each student having so much time and space that they can exchange for other items of value, so that the passing of time and the use of space is not so much an arena within which to act but rather a commodity for exchange. (See Leander, 2001, for a detailed discussion of time and space relationships in classroom discourse.)

INTRODUCTION 6: PARTICULARITY

Much current social science and educational research has been concerned with discovering universals: Those rules, patterns, and generalizations that can be extracted from a phenomemon/a and shown to be operating in a wide array of situations. Consistent with the argument Francis Bailey and I made in the original version of this chapter, the argument here is for a dif- ferent agenda, an agenda concerned with the particular. Becker (1988) argued similarly with regard to the analysis of language in an event. He refused to allow the specific people involved in an event, their voices, their aesthetic uses of language, their specific social relationships and cultural accomplishments to get lost in the effort by researchers to describe a discourse or uncover universals of language. Becker wrote:

> [T]he variety of things we can do with language defeats cataloguing, except at the most general levels. And at those levels, the particularities that we're concerned with here [the conference at which Becker's paper was presented], the things that make you different from you and you different from you, these particularities wash out . . . If we are interested in those differences, if we're interested in getting across those differences to talk with another person, then those things which wash out at higher levels of generality are just the things we need and just the things we can't afford to wash out. (p. 28)

Shifting from Becker's concern with language to the more focused realm of classroom language and literacy events, consider a first grade classroom reading lesson in a new school in a southern city. The reading groups in the classroom are heterogenuously grouped in terms of reading level. The students are from a variety of ethnic, linguistic and economic communities that make up the catchment area for the school. Seven students and their teacher are sitting around a table, orally reading two lines each, in round-robin fashion. If they make a mistake, the teacher corrects them, they repeat the correction and continue. When they have finished reading the story, the teacher will ask questions, call on students to answer, and praise them when they give the correct answer. So far, what occurs in this reading lesson is similar to what has occurred in nearly every reading group lesson they have had this year. It is also what occurs in reading groups throughout their school and in many other schools and has occurred for many years. But, on this particular day, Stephen has a cold and has wiped his nose on his sleeve. Margaret is angry with Sarah for stealing her crayons. Beth is very interested in the story because this story is about a circus and her mother bought her a clown book yesterday and read it to her last night. Beth and Sarah are identical twins. Someone has written and drawn pictures in the margins of Walter's book, they have also colored in all the loops in all the letters on the first page of the story. Walter is turning the book side ways to examine the marginalia. The story was read by all of the other reading groups in this class months ago and they got to draw pictures about the circus first. The teacher is trying to get Patrick to participate in class more but Patrick has had enough of school, reading groups, and the teacher. Benjamin is happy the teacher picked him to read first because he never gets to read first and his favorite animal, the lion, is one of the words he gets to read. He reads it with a loud roar to which the teacher responds with a smirk, a raised eyebrow, and a stare. Benjamin does not roar the second time he comes to "lion" although he pauses slightly and looks up at the teacher mimicking her previous smirk. The teacher does not think that Benjamin is a good reader and thus she had always organized the round-robin reading so that he read later so that he could get used to the words and pick up a sense of the meaning of the passage to assist him in his oral performance, a technique she had learned in a professional development workshop. But she recently read an article that suggested letting students who are not good readers read first so that their anxiety would not build. Stephen, Margaret, Sarah, Patrick, and Beth are upset Benjamin got to read first because they all believe that they are better readers than Benjamin and they believe that the teacher usually picks the best reader to read first. Stephen has moved his chair closer to Patrick because they are friends. Laurietta has decided that she does not want to be called Laurie any more and is worried about how she will tell the teacher to call her Laurietta when her turn to read occurs. She is avoiding eye contact and trying to shrink in her chair. The teacher is tired and bored of the reading group routine, the round-robin reading, and the basal stories they have been reading and has decided to make this the last time they use the basal reader and round-robin reading.

All the nose wiping, crayon stealing, turn-taking, who's a good reader, marginalia, clown liking, lion roaring, last-time-round-robin-basal-story-reading, and so on, is part of the language of that reading group's face-to-face dynamics on that day. At one level what's going on in the reading group is similar to what goes on in most reading groups. But there is another level particular to that event on that day. It is not the same event as yesterday's reading group lesson or tomorrow's or as occurs in another classroom. Although it is the same room as yesterday and is similar to most other classrooms, today Robin is absent, Stephen has a cold, it is the first Friday in December, and Walter's book and those of other students have been altered. There are specific social relationships among the particular people in this event. Beth and Sarah are identical twins, Stephen forgot his handkerchief and is afraid to ask the teacher for permission to get the tissues. Some of the students are upset with each other, Benjamin, and the teacher. Patrick is ready to drop out. There are various and particular histories converging on this particular event: the history of this reading group in comparison to other reading groups in the classroom, the historical practices of this reading group in assigning social status and in defining who and what are a good reader, the history of the teacher teaching reading, the history of boredom that the teacher and Patrick share, the history of accountability for both teacher and students, and the history of national political debates about how to teach beginning reading. There are also various intertextual relationships converging on this particular event. The teacher has read some articles on the teaching of reading that are prompting a change, there are connections to what the teacher read and heard during her teacher education program, Beth has read a lot of books and stories about clowns and circuses, Benjamin has read a lot of books on lions, unknown people have written comments and drawn pictures in the margins of many of the books, the story is similar in structure and genre to many of the basal stories they have previously read, and so on. There is a tension in this particular event on this particular day between maintaining the status quo and change with regard to procedures and the social consequences of those procedures. There are also tensions between the twins who struggle with presenting themselves as a pair versus advocacy for themselves as individuals, between the students who want to read the story because it is about the circus and those who just want to get through the lesson, between the standardization of pedagogical practices and the independence of the new pedagogical practices the teacher wants to try, between "Laurietta" and "Laurie," between this reading group and the other reading groups with regard to the social significance of time and the story they are reading, and so on.

To "wash out" the things that make that reading group on that day particular, that is to separate out what is similar to other reading groups from what is particular in order to seek universals and generalizations, would make the particular reading group event unrecognizable to the participants, rob it of its depth of social interaction and language play, and distort it in ways that would make the study of such "washed-out" reading groups the study of distortion.

A concern for the particular inherently takes seriously what people do in the events that make up their everyday lives, refusing to homogenize the events of people's lives into a nameless and faceless set of general tendencies or rules. Consider the interviews of working people by Terkel (1972), observations of kindergarten children by Paley (1981), the sociological study of mothers by Smith (1987), the studies of Hispanic students by Sola and Bennett, (1985), the ethnographic studies of rural communities and classrooms by Heath (1983) and of families by Taylor (1983; Taylor & Dorsey-Gaines, 1994), the photographic and verbal record of white, tenant farmers in the south of the United States by Agee and Evans (1988), the linguistic memoir by Ilan Stavans (2001), and the written contributions of thousands of ordinary people in the United Kingdom to the Mass-Observation Archive (Sheridan, Street, & Bloome, 2000), among others. Although different in their disciplinary perspective and genre of writing, in these studies people and events unlikely to be featured in history books, *People* magazine, or television shows are highlighted and their importance asserted. To do this is a political act because so often in schools, in social policy, and in research, the voice, visibility, and situatedness of people and events go unacknowledged in research on classroom language and literacy, or worse, through an appeal to scientificism turned into a nonsequitor. It is a political act to foreground the particularities of the events of the lives of ordinary people, their historicalness, the particular material conditions in which they live, the specific contradictions to which they have to accommodate and respond, their agency (how they act on and in the historical circumstances in which they find themselves).

FINAL COMMENTS

In this chapter, I presented six "introductions" to studying classroom language and literacy, in particular. The six introductions are closely related; one implies and leads to the other and to other introductions not discussed here.

In the earlier version of this chapter, we had thought it possible for there to be a rapprochement between research on classroom language and literacy oriented to the universal and general and research orient to the particular. Perhaps it is still possible. But we were naïve not to recognize the power relation between two such orientations and the intrusion of the state into the relationship among orientations to research on classroom language and literacy. It is not just the exertion of control by the state over classroom language and literacy practices and events that contextualizes discussions of the particular and the universal/general in educational research, but the creation of a research discourse that homogenizes people and defines them in terms of a narrow set of dimensions. The study of classroom language and literacy, *in particular,* by contrast, provides an expansive and heteroglossic rhetorics for describing the events of people's lives.

Each of the introductions here is an implicit critique of the sort of approach to researching classroom language and literacy events that begins with a grand theory and uses the events of people's lives as illustrations for the theory. At a minimum, the richness of the events of people's lives creates a dialectic between the particularities of those events and the grand theories imported by researchers, politicians, and others. Attention to that dialectic can provide researchers and the people involved in their studies a critique of those grand theories and of the broader cultural and political ideologies promulgated by dominant social institutions.

REFERENCES

Adam, B. (1990). *Time and social theory.* Philadelphia, PA: Temple University Press.

Agee, J., & Evans, W. (1988). *Let us now praise famous men.* New York: Houghton Mifflin.

Bakhtin, M. (1981). Discourse in the novel. In M. Holquist (Ed.), *The dialogic imagination* (C. Emerson, Trans.). Austin: University of Texas Press. (Original work published 1935)

Ball, S., Hull, R., Skelton, M., & Tudor, R. (1984). The tyranny of the "devil's mill": Time and task at school. In S. Delamont (Ed.), *Readings on interaction in the classroom* (pp. 41-57). London, UK: Methuen.

Beach, R., & Anson, C. (1992). Stance and intertextuality in written discourse. *Linguistics and Education, 4* (3-4), 335-357.

Becker, A. (1988) Language in particular: A lecture. In D. Tannen (Ed.), *Linguistics in context* (pp. 17-35). Norwood, NJ: Ablex.

Bloome, D. (1993). The social construction of intertextuality and the boundaries of school literacy. *Changing English, 1*(1), 168-178.

Bloome, D., & Bailey, F. (1992). Studying language and literacy through events, particularity, and intertextuality. In R. Beach, J. Green, M. Kamil, & T. Shanahan (Eds.), *Multiple disciplinary approaches to researching language and literacy* (pp. 181-210). Urbana, IL: National Conference on Research in English/National Council of Teachers of English.

Bloome, D., Carter, S., Christian, M., Otto, S., & Shuart-Faris, N. (2004). *Discourse analysis and the study of classroom language and literacy events—a microethnographic perspective.* Mahwah, NJ: Erlbaum.

Bloome, D., & Egan-Robertson, A. (1993). The social construction of intertextuality and classroom reading and writing. *Reading Research Quarterly, 28*(4), 303-333.

Bloome, D., Puro, P., & Theodorou, E. (1989). Procedural display and classroom lessons. *Curriculum Inquiry, 19*(3), 265-291.

Egan-Robertson, A., & Bloome, D. (Eds.). (1998). *Students as researchers of culture and language in their own communities.* Cresskill, NJ: Hampton Press.

Erickson, F., & Shultz, J. (1977). When is a context? *Newsletter of the Laboratory for Comparative Human Cognition, 1*(2), 5-12.

Geertz, C. (1973). *The interpretation of culture.* New York: Basic Books.

Geertz, C. (1983). *Local knowledge: Further essays in interpretive anthropology.* New York: Basic Books.

Heath, S. (1983). *Ways with words.* New York: Cambridge University Press.

Heras, A. I. (1993). The construction of understanding in a sixth grade bilingual classroom. *Linguistics and Education, 5*(3&4), 275-300.

Leander, K. (2001). "This is our freedom bus going home right now." Producing and hybridizing space-time contexts in pedagogical discourse. *Journal of Literacy Research, 33*(4), 637-679.

Lemke, J. (1992). Intertextuality and educational research. *Linguistics and Education, 4*(3-4), 257-267.

Lin, L. (1993). Language of and in the classroom: Constructing the patterns of social life. *Linguistics and Education, 5*(3-4), 367-410.

McDermott, R., & Hood, L. (1982). Institutional psychology and the ethnography of schooling. In P. Gilmore & A. Glatthorn (Eds.), *Children in and out of school* (pp. 232-249). Washington, DC: Center for Applied Linguistics.

Moll, L. C. (1992). Literacy research in community and classrooms: A sociocultural approach. In R. Beach, J. L. Green, M. L. Kamil, & T. Shanahan (Eds.), *Multidisciplinary perspectives on literacy research* (pp. 211-244). Urbana, IL: National Conference on Research in English/National Council of Teachers of English.

Moll, L., & Greenberg, J. (1990). Creating zones of possibilities: Combining social contexts for instruction. In L. Moll (Ed.), *Vygotsky and education: Instructional implications and applications of sociohistorical psychology*. New York: Cambridge University Press.

Paley, V. (1981). *Wally's stories.* Cambridge, MA: Harvard University Press.

Saussure, F. de. (1959). *Course in general linguistics* (C. Bally & A. Sechehaye, Eds., A. Reidlinger, W. Baskin, Trans.). New York: Philosphical Library. (Original work published 1915)

Sheridan, D., Street, B., & Bloome, D. (2000). *Writing ourselves: Mass-observation and literacy practices.* Cresskill, NJ: Hampton Press.

Shuart-Faris, N., & Bloome, D. (Eds.). (2004). *Intertextuality and research on classroom education.* Greenwich, CT: IAP.

Smith, D. (1987). *The everyday world as problematic: A feminist sociology.* Boston, MA: Northeastern University Press.

Sola, M., & Bennett, A. T. (1985). The struggle for voice: Narrative, literacy and consciousness in an East Harlem school. *Journal of Education, 167*(1), 88-110.

Stavans, I. (2001). *On borrowed words: A memoir of language.* New York: Viking.

Taylor, D. (1983). *Family literacy.* Portsmouth, NH: Heinemann.

Taylor, D., & Dorsey-Gaines, C. (1994). *Growing up literate.* Portsmouth, NH: Heinemann.

Terkel, S. (1972). *Working.* New York: Ballantine.

Volosinov, V. (1973). *Marxism and the philosophy of language* (L. Matejka & I. Titunik, Trans.). Cambridge, MA: Harvard University Press. (Original work published 1929)

Weber, M. (1968). *Economy and society.* New York: Bedminster.

Williams, R. (1977). *Marxism and literature.* Oxford, UK: Oxford University Press.

12

Critical Discourse Analysis

James Paul Gee
University of Wisconsin-Madison

In this chapter I first discuss features common to many approaches to discourse analysis, at least those with one foot in the field of linguistics, before moving on to what is distinctive about critical discourse analysis. I then discuss two specific approaches to critical discourse analysis, namely Norman Fairclough's (1992, 1995) work and my own work (Gee, 1996, 1999a). I close on some brief considerations of the implications of critical discourse analysis for research on literacy and work in education more generally.

Some work in critical discourse analysis (e.g., Fairclough's) is not primarily interested in either literacy or education. Other work (e.g., my own), although it is interested in literacy and education, looks at literacy quite broadly. Literacy, on this view, is multiple: There are as many literacies as there are different ways in which written language is embedded in diverse social practices. Literacy is also, on this view, integrally connected to identity: The various social practices in which written language is embedded require one to recruit distinctive ways with both oral and written words, as well as ways of thinking, acting, and interacting, so as to take on particular socially situated identities (e.g., being a first-grade reader of a certain sort, a scientist of a certain sort, or a neo-liberal politician of a certain sort, etc.). From the perspective of critical discourse analysis, then, research on literacy is part of the study of social practices and identities at work in society (Gee, 1996). Thus, in this chapter, I concentrate on critical discourse analysis as a method of analyzing a wide variety of different types of spoken and written language within social practices.

DISCOURSE ANALYSIS

Discourse analysis of any type (Jaworski & Coupland, 1999; van Dijk, 1997a, 1997b) undertakes two related tasks, although some approaches emphasize one more than the other. One task is the study of correlations between form (structure) and function (meaning) in language (or other semiotic systems). Let's call this the form-function task. The other task is the study of interactions between language and context. Let's call this the language-context task. Though the two tasks are related, we will discuss them in turn.

The Form–Function Task

Specific structures or forms in a language are used as tools to carry out certain functions (i.e., to express certain meanings). For example, consider the Sentence labeled 1 (adapted from Gagnon, 1987, p. 65):

1. Though they were both narrowly confined to the privileged classes, the Whig and Tory parties represented different factions

This sentence is made up of two clauses, an independent (or main) clause ("the Whig and Tory parties represented different factions") and a dependent clause ("Though they were both narrowly confined to the privileged classes"—the conjunction "though" here marks this clause as subordinated to, dependent on, the following independent clause). These are statements about form. An independent clause has as one of its functions that it expresses an assertion, that is, it expresses a claim that the speaker/writer is making. A dependent clause has as one of its functions that it expresses information that is not asserted, but, rather, assumed or taken-for-granted. These are statements about function (meaning).

Normally, in English, dependent clauses follow independent clauses—thus, Sentence 1 might more normally appear as: "The Whig and Tory parties represented different factions, though they were both narrowly confined to the privileged classes." In this section, the dependent clause has been *fronted* (placed in front of the whole sentence). This is a statement about form. Such fronting has as one of its functions that the information in the clause is *thematized* (Halliday, 1994), that is, the information is treated as a launching off point or thematically important context from which to consider the claim in the following dependent clause. This is a statement about function.

To sum up, in respect to form–functioning mapping, one can say that Sentence 1 renders its dependent clause ("Though they were both narrowly confined to the privileged classes") a taken-for-granted, assumed, unargued for, although important (thematized) context from which to consider and, perhaps, argue over the main claim in the independent clause ("the Whig and Tory parties represented different factions"). The dependent clause is, one might say, a concession (other historians might prefer to make this concession the main asserted point and, thus, would use a different grammar).

All approaches to discourse analysis, in their consideration of form, go beyond grammatical structures as traditionally construed (which are restricted to relationships within sentences) to consider structures or patterns across sentences. For example, consider the following two sentences (adapted from Gagnon, 1987, p. 71):

2. The age of popular democracy lay far ahead. But the principle of representative government was already secure, as was the rule of law, which promised to protect all citizens from arbitrary authority of any kind.

The first sentence has the subject "the age of popular democracy," the second has the subject "the principle of representative government." The subject position (a form) in a declarative sentence is a grammatical structure that expresses the "topic" (a function) of the sentence in the sense of naming the entity about which a claim is being made and in terms of which the claim should be disputed. The conjunction "but" beginning the second sentence is a form that sets up a contrast in meaning (a function) between these two topics, making it clear that, for the author, a government could be representative without representing all the people in a country (which constitutes "popular democracy"). Here we see how patterns of form (structure) across sentences, and not just within sentences, relate to functions (meanings).

At a fundamental level, all types of discourse analysis involve form–function matching. Of course, different approaches to discourse analysis have different viewpoints on how to talk about form and function. For instance, some approaches have an expanded notion of form in which not only grammatical and cross-sentence patterns are considered, but, also, things like pausing, repetitions, repairs, eye gaze, speech rate, and timing of turn-taking (Ochs, Schegloff, & Thompson, 1997). Each of these latter are, in turn, related to various functions they serve in interaction.

Furthermore, different approaches to discourse analysis have different views about how to explicate what it means to say that form *correlates* with function. One perspective with which I am sympathetic would explicate this idea as follows: A particular form, thanks to a history of repeated and partially routine interaction among a group or groups of people, comes to function so as to allow listeners/readers reliably to "guess" that a particular sort of meaning is being expressed, although there need be no certainty about the matter and speakers/writers can "break rules" and innovate new forms and functions.

However, the meanings with which forms are correlated are rather general (meanings like "assertion," "taken-for-granted information," "contrast," etc.). In reality, they represent only the *meaning potential* or *range* of a form or structure. The more specific or situated meanings that a form or structure carries in a given context of use must be figured out by an engagement with our next task, the language-context task.

The Language-Context Task

What we have talked about so far is sometimes called *utterance-type meaning* (Levinson, 2000). That is, there are certain types of forms in a language like English (words, morphemes, phrases, and sentences) and they are associated with certain types of functions or meanings, what I previously called "meaning potentials." However, when we actually utter or write a sentence it also has what has sometimes been called an utterance-token meaning or what I call a *situated meaning*. Situated meanings arise because particular language forms take on specific or situated meanings in specific contexts.

Context refers to an ever-widening set of factors that accompany language in use. These include the material setting, the people present (and what they know and believe), the language that comes before and after a given utterance, the social relationships of the people involved, and their ethnic, gendered, and sexual identities, as well as cultural, historical, and institutional factors. Most contemporary approaches to discourse analysis assumes a *reflexive* view of the relationship between language and context. Reflexive here means that, at one and the same time, an utterance influences what we take the context to be and context influences what we take the utterance to mean.

For example, a form like "How areya?" ("how-question," reduced form of "you," combination of "are" and "ya") tends to signal a context that is informal and where the interlocutors are of fairly equal status. At the same time, we use such words (and they have, thus, the power of signaling this sort of context) because we take ourselves to be in such a context. Words and context mutually interact over time.

Another example, at the level of a single word now: The word "coffee" is an arbitrary form (other languages use different sounding words for coffee) that correlates with meanings having to do with the substance coffee (this is its meaning potential). At a more specific level, we have to use context to determine what the word means in any situated way. In one context, "coffee" means a brown liquid, in another context it means grains of a certain sort, in another it means berries of a certain sort, and it means other things in other contexts (e.g., a certain flavor).

To see a further example of situated meanings at work, consider Sentence 1 again ("Though they were both narrowly confined to the privileged classes, the Whig and Tory parties represented different factions"). Previously, I said that an independent clause represents an assertion (a claim that something is true). But this general form–function correlation can mean different things at a specific level in actual contexts of use, and can, indeed, even be mitigated or undercut altogether.

For example, in one context, say between two like-minded historians, the claim that the Whig and Tory parities represented different factions may just be taken as a reminder of a "fact" they both agree on. On the other hand, between two quite diverse historians, the same claim may be taken as a challenge (despite YOUR claim that shared class interests mean no real difference in political parties, the Whig and Tory parties in 17th-century England were really different). And, of course, on stage as part of a drama, the claim about the Whig and Tory parties is not even a "real" assertion, but a "pretend" one.

Furthermore, the words "privileged," "contending," and "factions" will take on different specific meanings in different contexts. For example, in one context, "privileged" might mean "rich," whereas in another context it might mean "educated," "cultured," "politically connected," "born into a family with high status," or some combination of each.

The form–function task and the language-context task are fundamental to any form of discourse analysis. However, they do not render an approach to discourse analysis "critical." So now we turn to what constitutes critical discourse analysis.

CRITICAL DISCOURSE ANALYSIS

Some forms of discourse analysis add a third task to the two discussed so far. They study, as well, the ways in which form–function correlations (Task 1) and language-context interactions (Task 2) are associated with social practices (Task 3). It is here where critical approaches to discourse analysis diverge from noncritical approaches. Noncritical approaches (e.g., see Pomerantz & Fehr, 1997) tend to treat social practices solely in terms of patterns of social interaction (e.g., how people use language to "pull off" a job interview). Critical approaches (e.g., Chouliaraki & Fairclough, 1999; Fairclough, 1992, 1995; Gee, 1999a; Luke, 1995; van Dijk, 1993; Wodak, 1996), however, go further and treat social practices in terms of their implications for things like status, solidarity, social goods, and power (e.g., how language in a job interview functions as a gate-keeping device allowing some sorts of people access and denying it to others). In fact, critical discourse analysis argues that language in use is always part and parcel of, and partially constitutive of, specific social practices.

Social practices are (partially) routine activities through which people carry out (partially) shared goals based on (partially) shared (conscious or unconscious) knowledge of the various roles or positions people can fill within these activities. Practices are embedded within practices. So, one session of a graduate seminar is a social practice, so is the whole seminar course. Some practices are more routinized than others, which may be more open-ended and fluid. The world is full of social practices: a medical exam; eating in a fancy restaurant; exercising in a health club; engaging in a gang drive by shooting; a police interrogation; a direct instruction reading lesson in a first-grade classroom; an election; giving a political speech; applying for a prestigious college; trading Pokemon cards, and so on through an endless list.

Social practices always involve people in relationships where either status or solidarity or both are at stake (Milroy, 1995). They always have implications for the distribution of social goods, whereby "social goods" means anything that people in a society or culture consider worth having or not losing. One way in which we can define "politics" is to say that politics involves any social relationships in which things like status, solidarity, or other social goods are potentially at stake. In this sense of politics, social practices are inherently and inextricably political. Because critical discourse analysis argues that language in use is always part and parcel of, and partially constitutive of, one or more specific social practices, language in use is, thus, itself inherently and inextricably political.

NORMAN FAIRCLOUGH AND CRITICAL DISCOURSE ANALYSIS (CDA)

One of the best known and distinctive approaches to critical discourse analysis is the work of Fairclough (1992, 1995). Fairclough's work is often referred to as "Critical Discourse Analysis" (with the words capitalized) or "CDA" for short. CDA views language as a mode of action in terms of which people act on the world and on each other. The term *discourse*, as a count term (in phrases like: "the discourse of neo-liberal economics" or "radical feminist discourses of sexuality versus patriarchal discourses of sexuality") is used for distinctive way of using language to construe the material and social world from a particular perspective (Fairclough, 1992).

Fairclough's CDA attempts to integrate together three separate forms of analysis:

1. Analysis of spoken or written *language texts*.
2. Analysis of *discourse practice* (i.e., processes of text production, distribution, and consumption).
3. Analysis of discursive events as instances of *social practice*.

Each of these are related, because texts are embedded in discourse practices and, in turn, discourse practices are embedded in or part of specific social practices that involve more than language. I discuss each of these types of analyses in turn.

Analysis of Spoken or Written Texts

For the first form of analysis—analysis of spoken or written texts—CDA uses a modified Hallidayian approach to how form is related to function in language (Halliday, 1994). The grammar of any (oral or written) text simultaneously carries out four functions (the relational and identity functions discussed here are closely related and together are called "the interpersonal function" by Halliday).

The first function is the *ideational (or experiential) function*. Here grammar *represents* experience and the world (content, message, information). For example, consider: "Terrorists assaulted the village" versus "Freedom fighters liberated the village." In the first, the world contains terrorists who assault villages. In the second, the world contains freedom fighters who liberate villages. The very same people and village may be being talked about in either case. Texts in their ideational function constitute systems of knowledge and belief (i.e., what we take to be in the world and how we take things in the world to be related to each other).

The second function is the *relational function*. Here grammar functions to enact and allow for the negotiation of social relationships. For example, by choosing "hornworms" as the subject in "Hornworms might vary a lot in how well they grow," and by choosing the modal "might," as well as other choices I have made, I have set up the possibility of a social interaction in which we discuss, in a relatively informal way, hornworms from a rather tentative perspective. If I had said instead, "Hornworm growth exhibits a significant amount of variation," I would have set up the possibility of a social interaction in which we discuss, in a relatively formal and specialist way, a measurable trait of hornworms ("hornworm growth") from the point of view of a rather definitive and scientific-like claim. Texts in their relational function constitute systems of social relationships.

The third function is the *identity function.* Here grammar functions to set up specific and diverse social identities. For example, in a traditional medical interview, an utterance from the doctor like: "Now, what seems to be wrong?" is an invitation for a list of symptoms given without a lot of personal information and opinions from the patient. Such language forms, coupled with an impersonal list of symptoms from the patient, help set up a distinctive doctor and patient identity. However, there are more contemporary forms of medicine where doctors attempt to mitigate these more traditional identities, perhaps by saying something like: "Tell me how you're feeling?" and later asking the patient his or her own opinion about treatment. Texts in their identity function constitute types of social subjects or specific socially situated identities.

The fourth function is the *textual function.* Here grammar serves to foreground and background information and to tie parts of a text together into a coherent whole, as well as tie texts to situational contexts (e.g., through situational deixis). For example, consider the following text (adapted from Martin, Matthiessen, & Painter 1997): "*For one thousand years,* whales have been of commercial interest. *About 1000 AD,* whaling started with the Basques. *Over the next few centuries,* a large variety of different whale species were widely hunted" (p. 6). The temporal modifiers (italics) at the beginning of each sentence in this text tie each sentence back to the preceding one and tie all the sentences together in terms of a temporal framework. Furthermore, by placing a temporal modifier in front of each sentence, the text thematizes temporal sequence as the perspective from which we view whaling. Texts in their textual function constitute, along with other features of texts and social interactions, what counts as coherence.

Second Form of Analysis: Analysis of Discourse Practice

The second form of analysis—the analysis of discourse practice—involves studying how texts are produced, distributed, and consumed. Although CDA sometimes does study how texts are produced and circulated as material objects, more often analyses center on the resources a text offers for interpretation (its meaning potential) and the ways in which these resources are or can be recruited by interpreters in specific contexts (situated meanings).

The analysis of discourse practice involves four tools or analytic lenses. The first tool is an analysis of *force*. Force (which is part of the relational meaning of a text) is what a sentence or larger part of a text is being used to do socially, what "speech act" it is being used to perform (e.g., give an order, ask a question, threaten, promise, etc.). Here CDA treats context and force as reflexively related, that is, as mutually constitutive of each other. To know what the force of an utterance is, the interpreter must arrive at an interpretation of what the context is. At the same time, the interpreter's judgments about the force of an utterance guides the interpreter in terms of what he or she makes of the context. For example, an utterance like "Your hair looks nice" may be taken as a compliment in some contexts and as sexual harassment in others, though such remarks, in tandem with other things being said and done, help partly to define a context as friendly banter or "coming on" to a colleague.

The second tool for studying discourse practice is an analysis of *coherence*. Coherence is partly a textual feature tied to the textual function, but it is also a property of actual interpretations interpreters give to texts. Texts "make sense" to people because they draw on both interpretive principles associated with the social groups to which they belong and interpretive principles associated with the conventions used to produce and understand particular types of texts, genres, and discourses. Interpreters come to take these linkages (between interpretations and social groups and conventions) as natural and normal. Interpreters who can engage in such "natural" productions and interpretations come to be seen as "competent." For example, a CDA analyst could study where and to whom a dialogue like: "She's giving up her job Wednesday. She's pregnant" (Fairclough, 1992, p. 84) makes coherent sense (because they accept the assumption that women give up work when they are pregnant) and where and to whom it does not.

The third tool for studying discourse practice is an analysis of *intertextuality*. "Intertextuality is basically the property texts have of being full of snatches of other texts, which may be explicitly demarcated or merged in, and which the text may assimilate, contradict, ironically echo, and so forth" (Fairclough 1992, p. 84). For example, consider the following text, a part of the Oakland, California, School Board's official proposal to support "Ebonics" in its schools:

> Whereas, numerous validated scholarly studies demonstrate that African American students as part of their culture and history as African people possess and utilize a language described in various scholarly approaches as "Ebonics" (literally Black sounds) or pan African Communication behaviors or African Systems; and. . . .
> Whereas, the Federal Bilingual Education Act (20 USC 1402 et seq.)

mandates that local educational agencies "build their capacities to establish, implement and sustain programs of instruction for children and youth of limited English proficiency,"

The terms *Ebonics, Black sounds, Pan African Communication behaviors,* and *African Systems* are all terms taken from and strongly associated with texts from one very specific type of linguistics (one carried out largely by scholars of African or African-American descent with a strong Black Nationalist orientation), although after Oakland's decision, some of these terms spread into wider use (terms like *African-American Vernacular English* were originally more widely used in linguistics; see Baugh, 2000). On the other hand, the quote from the Federal Bilingual Education Act imports into this text material from texts of a quite different sort, namely legislation. These two types of texts, here melded, had not before come into such close contact.

The fourth tool for studying discourse practice is an analysis of *interdiscursivity.* Interdiscursivity extends intertextuality by a consideration of how one and the same text can mix not just snippets of different texts, but different discourses and/or genres (i.e., different styles of language). The Oakland example already does this, but so does the following text which is taken from the warning on an aspirin bottle (Gee, 1996):

Warnings: *Children and teenagers should not use this medication for chicken pox or flu symptoms before a doctor is consulted about Reye Syndrome, a rare but serious illness reported to be associated with aspirin.* Keep this and all drugs out of the reach of children. In case of accidental overdose, seek professional assistance or contact a poison control center immediately. As with any drug, if you are pregnant or nursing a baby, seek the advice of a health professional before using this product.

The italic section beginning this text (which is actually underlined on the bottle and which is a newer part of the warning) is in a legalistic discourse, probably triggered by suits against the aspiring company. The rest of the warning (the older section) is in a more paternalistic official discourse, the discourse of a authoritatively knowledgeable company that "cares" (note the vague and more general language, the general references to children, mothers, and babies, and the multiple references to the medical profession, none of which involve anything so specific as "doctor").

When studying discourse practice through the tools of force, coherence, intertextuality, and interdiscursivity, CDA draws on a crucial overarching concept taken from Foucault (1981), namely the notion of an "order of discourse." An order of discourse refers to "the ordered set of discursive practices associated with a particular social domain or institution . . . and the boundaries and relationships between them" (Fairclough, 1995, p. 12).

For example, as an academic, I can draw on a variety of different ways of using oral and written language (different types of texts, different genres, different activities with language), for instance, lectures, discussions, research publications, committee reports, and so forth. Traditionally, business people have drawn on a different order of discourse containing different sorts of oral and written text types and ways with words. However, it is common today to see some elements of the business order of discourse get imported into the academic one, as colleges and universities operate more like entrepreneurial enterprises in the so-called "new economy."

For example, the University of Wisconsin at Stevens Point (1996) puts out a document that is called an "Annual Report," which constitutes the college's "accountability report" and fulfills a part of a state mandated recommendation to communicate "its performance to stockholders" (p. 3) (note there are, in reality, no stockholders for the University of Wisconsin at Stevens Point, perhaps they meant "stakeholders"). Here a discursive practice from business has immigrated into the academic order of discourse and, in the act, changed it.

As speakers and writers draw on elements within the various orders of discourse to which they have access, they create texts that always combine repetition and creativity. All texts are sites of tensions between what Bakhtin (1986) called centripetal pressures (the pressure to follow norms and conventions and to repeat what has been done in the past) and centrifugal pressures (the pressure to transform norms and conventions and do new things under the specific and almost always partly novel circumstances in which we actually find ourselves).

The tension between repetition and creation, centripetal, and centrifugal pressures, manifests itself in varying degrees of homogeneity of textual forms and meanings (where there is a consistent construction of relations between text producer and audience) or heterogeneity of textual forms and meanings (where there is an inconsistent construction of relations between text producer and audience). The heterogeneities of texts code social contradictions. It is this property of texts that makes them such sensitive indicators of sociocultural processes and change. CDA argues that the homogeneities/heterogeneities of texts can be shown through intertextual and interdiscursive analysis of the links between a text in a given discourse and other texts, text types, and discourses (Fairclough, 1995).

Analysis of Social Practice

The third form of analysis in CDA—the analysis of social practice—treats language (and discourse practice) as but one aspect of social practices.

Social practices often involve economic, political, cultural, and ideological aspects without any of these being reducible to language *per se*. Furthermore, language can be caught up in social practices in a variety of different ways. So here we have to take a more ethnographic approach and look at texts and discourse practice as they are recruited within specific social practices in their full array of social, cultural, and institutional contexts. CDA is particularly interested in how language is used within social practices to reproduce and sometimes to transform relationships of power in a society.

In its study of social practices, CDA draws on two key notions. The first is the notion of *ideology*. Ideologies are constructions of reality (the physical world, social relations, social identities) that are built into various dimensions of the forms ormeanings of discursive practices. Ideologies contribute to the production, reproduction, or transformation of relations of power and domination in society. The ideologies embedded in discursive practices are most effective when they become naturalized and achieve the status of "common sense" (Fairclough, 1992, p. 87). In claiming that a discursive event works ideologically, the analyst is not claiming that it is false. Rather, the analyst is claiming that the discursive event is working within specific social practices to help reproduce relations of power in society (Fairclough, 1995).

One example of ideology at work within a social practice is the traditional doctor–patient interview. Here both parties use language in ways that ultimately underwrite an ideological viewpoint that the doctor, and not the patient, is an expert in regard to the patient's body, that the patient's viewpoints and feelings are subjective and not really relevant, and that the patient is not really an agent in his or her own treatment and cure (Fairclough, 1995). Such a viewpoint helps reproduce the traditional (and, until recently, taken-for-granted) relations of power and status between doctors and patients.

The second notion is *hegemony*, a notion taken from the work of Antonio Gramsci (1971): Hegemony is the process through which one economically powerful class in a society gains ascent to its power, norms, and values, not through force, but by using ideologies to encourage less powerful classes of people to accept their power, norms, and values as "normal" or "natural." Hegemony is never achieved more than partially and temporarily. It is always an "unstable equilibrium" with multiple points of tension and open to challenge (Fairclough, 1992, p. 92).

One good example of hegemony at work is the way in which, in the language and interactions associated with a good many different social practices, Americans take for a granted a "success model" in terms of which "anyone can make it if they just work hard enough" (D'Andrade, 1984). This model hides or effaces the fact that people with economic and educational resources can much more easily act on this model than those with far fewer such resources. Thus, it makes it look as if more advantaged people "deserve" their success and less advantaged people "deserve" their lower spots in society. Although Fairclough did not overtly refer to work on such "cultural models," they are one good way to get at the workings of ideology and hegemony in language and I discuss them further.

Any approach to discourse analysis works better for some issues than it does for others. Thus, it is often advisable to use a variety of different (although ultimately compatible) approaches, varying one's tools as one takes up different questions. Fairclough's approach is but one approach, although a widely used one, and I discuss another approach here. Fairclough's approach, at least so far, has been most often applied to the analysis of (often written) texts (e.g., ads) and the ways in which they are situated in larger contexts (e.g., changes in the global economy). He has dealt less often with the interactional features of talk and with more micro-level features of context (e.g., the interactional goals and self presentation people produce and negotiate in the flow of moment-by-moment talk and interaction).

Another Style of Critical Discourse Analysis

My own work (Gee, 1996, 1999a) represents another approach to critical discourse analysis. Although it draws on many of the same themes as Fairclough's work, it primarily appeals to four analytic tools: social languages, situated meanings, cultural models, and Discourses (with a capital "D"). I take up each of these devices in turn.

Social Languages

A social language is a way of using language so as to enact a particular socially situated identity (i.e., to be a specific socially meaningful "kind of person"). For example, there are ways of speaking like a (specific type of) doctor, street-gang member, postmodern literary critic, football fanatic, neoliberal economist, working-class male, adaptationist biologist, and so on, through an endless array of identities. Often, of course, we can recognize a particular socially situated "kind of person" through his or her use of a given social language without ourselves actually being able to enact that kind of person.

In no way do I wish to imply that enacting and recognizing *kinds of people* (Hacking, 1986; Hicks, 2000) is a matter of people falling into rigid kinds. Enacting and recognizing kinds of people is all about negotiating, guessing, and revising guesses about kinds of people; it is all about contesting and resisting being positioned as a certain kind of person. Thus, too, there are often no strict boundaries to social languages.

Consider how different social languages are used in the text below taken from an interview with a White upper middle-class middle-school student attending an elite suburban public school (for further discussion of teenagers and social class, see Gee, 1999a; Gee, Allen, & Clinton 2001; Gee & Crawford, 1998):

> *Interviewer: Why do you think there are relatively few Hispanic and African-American doctors?*
>
> . . . well, they're probably discriminated against, but, but its not really as bad as—as people think it is, or that it once was. **Because, uh, I was watching this thing on TV about this guy that's trying to**—How colleges and and some schools have made a limit on how many white students they can have there, and a limit—and they've increased the limits on how many Black and Hispanic students they have to have. **So, a bunch of white people are getting**—even if they have better grades than the Black or Hispanic student, the Black or Hispanic student gets in because they're Black or Hispanic so. **So, I think that that kinda plays an effect into it.**

Note how this young man code switches between a vernacular social language (which appears in bold) and, in terms of word choice and syntax, a more formal, school-based sort of social language (which appears unbold). The more formal, school-based social language distances the speaker from the issue being discussed, making his interest in the issue sound more "rational" and dispassionate. However, in the interview with this young man it became clear that affirmative action was something he feared might stand in the way of his being able to use his high-level school credentials and accomplishments for attending an elite college and attaining a successful life. The more formal and distanced social language, thus, may being used to mask his very personal interests and concerns (which break through in his use of the more vernacular style of language).

Situated Meanings

Within social languages, words do not have general meanings (the sorts of things we find in dictionaries). Rather, they have meanings that are specific and situated in the actual contexts of their use. Words, phrases, and utterances in use act as "clues" or "cues" that guide active construction of meaning in context. For example, consider the following text taken from an interview with a white Female college anthropology professor:

But I think um, that um, basically that the lives of people of color are irrelevant to the society anymore. Um, they're not needed for the economy because we have the third world to run away into for cheap labor. Um, and I think that, that the leadership, this country really doesn't care if they shoot each other off in the ghettos. Um, and, and so they let drugs into the ghettos, and they, um, they, let people shoot themselves, shoot each other.

This academic appears here to be using the phrase "people of color" with the situated meaning of "primarily poor African-American people," because of the way in which she moves so smoothly from "people of color" through "they" to "ghettos," a term usually used with a situated meaning having to do with poor African Americans. Such a situated meaning for "people of color" helps to perpetuate a view that multicultural diversity in our society is primarily a matter of Black and White and that African Americans are primarily associated with poverty.

Cultural Models

The situated meanings of words and phrases within specific social languages trigger specific cultural models in terms of which speakers (writers) and listeners (readers) give meaning to texts. Cultural models (Strauss & Quinn, 1997) are everyday "theories" (i.e., storylines, images, schemas, metaphors, and models) about the world. Cultural models tell people what is "typical" or "normal" (not universally, but from the perspective of a particular Discourse—see the next section). Cultural models are not static (they change and are adapted to different contexts, Gee, 1992) and they are not purely mental (but distributed across and embedded in socioculturally defined groups of people and their texts and practices).

People sometimes pick up cultural models overtly by being told or having read them. More often they pick them up as "found" items in the midst of practice in a particular domain (often inside particular institutions), whether this be romance, doing literacy in school, raising children, playing computer games, going to a doctor, or engaging in Alcoholics Anonymous sessions, or what have you (also Holland, Lachicotte, Skinner, & Cain, 1998). People more adept at the domain pass on cultural models through shared stories, practices, and procedures that get newcomers to pay attention to salient features of prototypical cases in the domain, the ones that best reflect the cultural models in a domain. In turn, cultural models get reinforced and relatively ritualized as they are used in repeated practice. The models and allegiance to the models also become an important bonding cement within the social groups associated with a given domain of practice.

To see cultural models at work, consider the following text taken from an interview with a white working-class middle-school student:

> *Interviewer: . . . Is there racism [in society]?*
>
> . . . like colored people I don't, I don't like. I don't like Spanish people most of 'em, but I like, I like some of 'em. Because like if you, it seems with them, like they get all the welfare and stuff. Well, well white people get it too and everything but, I just—And then they think they're bad and they're like—They should speak English too, just like stuff like that.

This student's text appears, on first view, overtly contradictory because it seems to say that the student doesn't like "Spanish people" because they get welfare, while conceding that White people do too. Discourse analysis applies a "principle of charity" in terms of which we assume people do not overtly contradict themselves, unless, after much analysis, the matter is proven otherwise (see Gee, 1996, especially Chap. 1, for the moral basis of this notion, and, for a related notion, Davidson, 2001). One cultural model that this student may hold that would make his text less contradictory is this: People who take aid from society (like welfare) should speak English and be appreciative (which he thinks White people do and "Spanish people" don't). Certainly, this is a pervasive model in some segments of our society (including among certain politicians).

Discourses

A person cannot enact a particular kind of person all by themselves and by using only language. A *Discourse* (with a capital "D"—I use "discourse" with a lower case "d" to mean language in use) is a distinctive way of using language *integrated* with "other stuff" so as to enact a particular type of (however negotiable and contestable) socially situated identity (type of person).

What is this "other stuff"? It is distinctive ways of thinking, being, acting, interacting, believing, knowing, feeling, valuing, dressing, and using one's body. It is also distinctive ways of using various symbols, images, objects, artifacts, tools, technologies, times, places and spaces. Think of what it takes to "be/do" a "tough-guy detective" (in the Philip Marlowe mode, say), a traditional Catholic nun, or a Gen-X e-entrepreneur in the "New Economy" (magazines like *Fortune* regularly discuss the details of this latter Discourse).

Discourses are always defined in relationship to other Discourses. For example, the Discourse of Los Angelos African-American teenage gang members exists and has changed through history in reciprocal relations with the Discourse of Los Angelos policemen, as well as a good many other related civic, community, and church related Discourses. So, too, the Discourse of neo-Darwinian biologists exists and has changed through history in reciprocal relations with various religious Discourses, including the Discourse of American creationists (which only really started in the 1950s).

For example, consider the following text from an interview with a White middle school teacher who teaches poor and working-class middle-school children in the same town as the college anthropology professor discussed earlier. Compare the two texts to each other:

> *Interviewer: . . . would you ever tie that into like present power relations or just individual experiences of racism in their lives or something like that?*

> Uh I talk about housing. We talk about the we talk about a lot of the low income things, I said "Hey wait a minute," I said, "Do you think the city's gonna take care of an area that you don't take care of yourself?"

Space does not allow me to do justice to all the elements involved in the Discourses out of which the college professor and teacher are speaking. Let me, then, consider just one example of how language relates to or aligns with nonlanguage stuff in this case. Although they are both talking about power and racism, the middle school teacher's text aligns her with her *local* area and her specific classroom (she actually mimics herself talking to her students), whereas the college professor's text aligns her with the *national-global* world. Indeed, it turns out that the interviewer co-constructs this alignment, always forming her questions and responses to the teacher and professor so as to assume and invite these orientations, orientations that neither interviewee ever rejects or attempts to break out of.

Both the middle school teacher and the college professor are, of course, speaking out of "professional" Discourses. However, the middle school teacher enacts her expertise in terms of a colloquial ("everyday") social language and in terms of the actual dialogues and procedures of her day-to-day work. Thus, her "expertise" is aligned not only with the local, but with the "everyday" and with her specific actions as a teacher. The professor enacts her expertise in a specialist, noncolloquial language and in terms of distanced viewpoints, not in terms of the actual dialogues and procedures of her day-to-day work.

We can note, too, that the teacher's Discourse is aligned with the local and colloquial, in part, because of the ways it is currently, and has been historically, positioned in terms of status and power in relation to the professor's Discourse and in relation to other Discourses, such as those of professors in schools of education (which mediate between noneducational specialist Discourses and the multiple Discourses of teachers and schools). This is not to say, by any means, that one or other of these Discourses is always and everywhere the more (or less) politically powerful one.

To see that power can run in both directions, one need only look at the current stance of many neo-liberal politicians (e.g., George W. Bush). On the one hand, such politicians tend to privilege certain specialist Discourses (e.g., in testing and reading instruction) over teacher Discourses in determining curricula, pedagogy, and accountability. On the other hand, they tend to consider academic Discourses like that of our college professor as elitist viewpoints in relation to the "everyday" and "populist" wisdom of colloquial language and cultural models (e.g., models that hold that anyone can "make it" if they just behave "correctly," Frank 2000).

Like Fairclough's approach, my approach is one of several and works better for some issues than others. My approach has been applied to both written and oral texts and is concerned with both situated "identity work" that goes on moment by moment in interaction and the larger cultural and institutional contexts in which language is used. Furthermore, my approach has been fairly extensively applied to issues germane to schools, schooling, and education, including issues to do with cultural differences in classrooms and home/community-school differences. At the same time, my approach (like Fairclough's) has not been much applied to conversational data in which speakers take relatively short turns at talk. There is, in fact, little critical work on conversational data, where work in the tradition of conversational analysis (CA; see Psathas, 1995, for an overview) has stressed how social order is produced and reproduced moment-by-moment in turns at talk, but has stressed political, cultural, and ideological issues much less. Work in so-called "Discursive Psychology" (Edwards & Potter, 1992), inspired, in part by CA, does begin to touch on critical issues, although not in any way as directly as does Fairclough's work and my own work (see Gee, 1999b, for a critique).

CRITICAL DISCOURSE ANALYSIS, LITERACY, AND EDUCATION

Although a good deal of work in CDA does not deal with education directly, CDA has inherent implications for teaching and learning language and literacy in and out of schools. Work on CDA argues that the meaning of any piece of language (or any other sign system, for that matter) is always situated within specific genres and styles of language (or other sign systems), specific social practices, and specific orders of discourse or Discourses. Furthermore, when language is so situated it always involves enacting and recognizing specific socially situated identities. Humans are always enacting and recognizing particular social and cultural "kinds of people," whether this be a "gifted and talented" first grader, a special education student, an "at-risk" learner, a liberal humanist, an ardent radical feminist, a cutting-edge nuclear physicist, or the like.

Such identities (such kinds) always have implications for what counts as "normal," "appropriate," or "natural" here and now in social interaction. Foe example, there are ways to be a "normal" or "appropriate" student in a scripted instruction classroom and ways to be a non-normal or inappropriate student in such a classroom. Such ways of being and doing are never separable from the teaching and learning that is going on. Furthermore, issues of access and equity are always at stake, as well, in terms of who gets to take on which socially situated identities and who does not. In this sense—in the sense in which issues of the distribution of "social goods" are at stake (issues about what is "normal" or "natural" or who gets what benefits)—language-in-use is always and everywhere "political."

From this perspective, the first implication of CDA for education is that what children learn in school is never general or generic ("phonics," "language," "literacy," "English," "science"). Rather, it is a specific set of social practices recruiting specific ways with words, actions, and interactions replete with specific sorts of identities and political implications. CDA encourages teachers and learners to view school in terms of multiple and specific Discourses—that is, for example, in terms of what counts as being–doing science here and now in this classroom; what sorts of identities are being recruited; enacted, and recognized; who is included and excluded; and the ways in which these identities do or not resonate with other identities these learners take on in other parts of their lives.

Often in school just what Discourse is at stake—just what the rules of being and doing are supposed to be, for example, in school science or language arts—is confused and obscure. But clarity here is a matter not just of good pedagogy, but of social justice, as well. When such matters are left confused and obscure—or where the ties to Discourses outside school are confused or remote—children from homes where there are strong and clear views about what science or literature is (for example), and why they are important, are privileged and other children are not.

The following is a simple example of what I am talking about: Students in an elementary classroom have been discussing the question "What makes rust?" To help answer this question, the children have placed a number of metal and nonmetal objects in water to examine whether and what "gets rusty." In the following segment, the children have taken a metal bottle cap and plastic plate out of the water. The metal cap had been sitting on the plastic plate. The cap has become rusty from being in the water, whereas the plastic plate has rust on it that has fallen off the metal cap and onto the plate. In the following exchange, two children are discussing the cap and plate (material in brackets is mine, meant to clarify what the children appear to mean, given the whole transcript, which is not reprinted here):

Elizabeth: Why these marks here [on the plastic plate]?

Jill: Because the rust comes off the things and it goes on to there and it stays

Philip: And the rust gots nowhere to go so it goes on the plate

Jill: But if we didn't put the metal things on there [on the plate] it wouldn't be all rusty

Philip: And if we didn't put the water on there [on the metal bottle cap] it wouldn't be all rusty

Jill points out that rust comes off rusty metal things like the bottle cap and leaves marks on other things, like the plastic plate the bottle cap was sitting on. She later points out that if the rusty metal bottle cap had not been placed on the plastic plate, then the plate would not be "all rusty." Philip formulates his last contribution as a direct "copy" of Jill's immediately preceding contribution, pointing out that if water had no been placed on the metal bottle cap, then it would not be "all rusty".

This whole segment is typical of everyday language, and, in fact, reflects both the strength and weakness of such language. In everyday language, when we are trying to make sense of a problematic situation, we use patterns and associations, repetitions and parallelism, what might loosely be called "poetic" devices, to construct (or, as here, to co-construct) a senseful (sense making) design. This is a feature that much everyday talk shares with poetry, myth, and storytelling, regardless of what "genre" it is in formally. Far from meaning to denigrate this approach to sense making, I have elsewhere celebrated it (e.g., Gee 1991) and have no doubt that it has given rise to some of human beings "deepest" insights into the human condition. But it is not how the Discourses of the physical sciences operate; in fact, historically, while these Discourses most certainly grew out of this method of sense making, they developed partly in overt opposition to it (Bazerman, 1988).

Everyday language allows for juxtapositions of images and themes in the creation of patterns (like "it wouldn't be all rusty"), and, as I have just said, this is very often an extremely powerful device in its own right. But, from the perspective of scientific Discourse, it can create a symmetry that is misleading and which obscures important "underlying" differences (e.g., the underlying "reality" behind "a plastic plate that is all rusty" and the one behind "a metal cap that is all rusty"). Unfortunately, in science it is often this "underlying" level that is crucial.

The children's everyday language obliterates what is a crucial distinction and it obliterates the "underlying mechanisms" (here cause and effect) that are the heart and soul of physical science. Jill and Philip's parallel constructions above—in particular, their uses of "all rusty" and "if we didn't put . . . on, it wouldn't be . . ."—obscure the fact that these two linguistic devices here mean (or could mean) two very different things. Rusty metal things "cause" things like plastic plates to "be all rusty" (namely, by physical contact) in a quite different way that water "causes" metal things to "be all rusty" (namely, by a chemical reaction).

Furthermore, the plastic plate and the metal bottle cap are "all rusty" in two crucially different senses—that is, crucial for scientific Discourse, although not necessarily for everyday Discourse, that is content to pattern them together through the phrase "all rusty." In Jill's statement, "all rusty" means (or could mean) "covered in rust," whereas in Philip's statement it means (or could mean) "a surface which has become rusted." In other words, the distinction between "having rust" (a state) and "having rusted" (a process) is obliterated.

It is typical of everyday language that it tends to obscure the details of causal, or other systematic, relationships among things in favor of rather general and vague relations, like "all rusty" or "put on." Everyday language, in creating patterns and associations, is less careful about differences and underlying systematic relations, although these are crucial to science. Again, I do not intend to denigrate everyday language. The very weaknesses I am pointing to here are, in other contexts, sources of great power and strength. Everyday language is much better, in fact, than the language of science in making integrative connections across domains (e.g., light as a psychosocial -physical element in which we bathe).

The issues here, then, are these: What are the "rules" of the Discourse at play in this classroom? What ways of thinking, being, acting, interacting, and speaking are being recruited? What sorts of situated identities as thinkers, doers, speakers, and knowers of a certain sort are children being encouraged to enact and recognize? What are the connections between this "in school" Discourse and Discourses (like physical science) outside of school?

If the teacher is intending to build a "science-like" Discourse on "everyday" language, perhaps to encourage children, make ties to their out of school lives, and to empower them to think of themselves as inquirers, then we still must ask whether children who come to the classroom already understanding the difference between "accidentally covered with rust" and "caused to be rusty" (and, in turn, the difference between coincidental and causal relationships) are advantaged by this practice as against children who do not come already to classroom knowing these matters. The everyday language the children are using obscures a difference that is important to science. Children who do not already know the difference and do not already know that science cares more about causal relationships than it does about coincidental ones will not learn it from this sort of talk. Furthermore, it so happens in this case that the teacher will not intervene, because she happens to believe that teacher talk simply disempowers children's thinking. The point is not to take sides here, but to argue that teachers and learners need to reflect on and achieve clarity about such matters—matters about the social languages and Discourses at play in the classroom, as well as cultural models about teaching, learning, and science—matters that are inherent to a CDA view of language and interaction.

A second important implication of CDA for education is that efficacious literacy is always, and for everyone, "critical literacy" in a specific sense of that term. A deep understanding of any language or literacy practice is always an understanding of how language is specifically situated with specific Discourses. Knowing—consciously and at a meta-level—how situated meanings, social languages, cultural models, and Discourses work within a given Discourse (e.g., what counts here and how in a classroom as science) and comparatively across Discourses (e.g., how this compares to how social studies or literature works here and now in the same classroom) is, in my view, the most effective and efficacious form of knowledge one can gain in school.

This is so for two reasons. First, in our fast-changing times—thanks to modern media, science, technology, and the global economy—knowledge as "facts" goes quickly out of data (Gee, Hull, & Lankshear, 1996). On the other hand, understanding, comparatively and contrastively, how Discourses work in society is a form of critical understanding of systems that does not go out of date and leaves the learner prepared to understand new systems and the ever present transformations of old systems that are the stuff of our contemporary world. Second, for learners who come to school without mainstream "cultural capital"—that is, without the sorts of social and class backgrounds that more privileged learners bring to school—understanding how language and meaning work politically to include and exclude, to normalize some people and practices and marginalize others, and how social practices and Discourses can be transformed, is a crucial matter of social protection.

Here, again, let me give but a brief example. Roger Lewontin's (1991) little book *Biology as Ideology* is a gold mine of examples of what happens when we juxtapose one Discourse (in this case, biology) to other Discourses. For instance, from the point of view of medical science it is a truism that the cause of tuberculosis is the tubercle bacillus. But tuberculosis was a very common disease in the sweatshops and factories of the 19th century, whereas it was much less common among rural people and in the upper classes. So, why don't we conclude that the cause of tuberculosis is unregulated industrial capitalism? In fact, in light of the history of health and disease in modern Europe, that explanation makes good sense. An examination of the causes of death, first systematically recorded in the 1830s in Britain and a bit later in North America, show that most people did, indeed, die of infectious diseases. As the 19th century progressed, however, the death rate from all these diseases continuously decreased:

> Smallpox was dealt with by a medical advance, but one that could hardly be claimed by modern medicine, since smallpox vaccine was discovered in the eighteenth century and already was quite widely used by the early part of the nineteenth. The death rates of the major killers like bronchitis, pneumonia, and tuberculosis fell regularly during the nineteenth century, with no obvious cause. There was no observable effect on the death rate after the germ theory of disease was announced in 1876 by Robert Koch. The death rate from these infectious diseases simply continued to decline as if Koch had never lived. By the time chemical therapy was introduced for tuberculosis in the earlier part of this century, more than 90 percent of the decrease in the death rate from that disease had already occurred. (Lewontin, 1991, pp. 43-44)

It was not modern sanitation or less crowding in cities that led to the progressive reductions in the death rate, since the major killers in the 19th century were respiratory and not water borne, and parts of our cities are as crowded today as they were in the 1850s. More likely, the reduction in death from infectious diseases is due to general improvement in nutrition related to an increase in the real wage in "developed countries": "In countries like Brazil today, infant mortality rises and falls with decreases and increases in the minimum wage" (Lewontin, 1991, p. 44).

Thinking in terms of causal statements like "the tubercle bacillus causes tuberculosis", which medical and biological Discourses encourage us to do, cuts off meaning before it gets social and political. What Lewontin did here is widening the frame within which we look at a perfectly "natural" and "obvious" claim from biology. He juxtaposed the way the Discourse of medicine or biology looks a claim with how other Discourses (e.g., a Discourse of public health or a sociopolitical Discourse about capitalism) would look at the claim.

Another illuminating example that Lewontin gives is the way in which biologists talk about genes "self-replicating." Yet, genes cannot make themselves (any more than a blueprint can make a house). Genes are made by a complex machinery of proteins that uses the genes as models for more genes. It is not the genes that are self-replicating, it is the entire organism as complex system. Isolating genes as "master molecules", and effacing the "manufacturing machinery" of proteins that actually carry out the work of making other proteins and genes themselves, is "another unconscious ideological commitment, one that places brains above brawn, mental work as superior to mere physical work, information as higher than action" (p. 48). In fact, in this case, biology-internal talk about genes also leads to a good deal of misunderstanding about genes on the part of people who have actually studied biology.

Such work takes a meta-view of a Discourse, looking at how it functions in the universe of Discourses to create ideological meanings and not just at how meaning looks from strictly within the Discourse itself. Although one certainly wants to gain knowledge of how form and function work in biology, one also wants to gain knowledge of how form and function work in biology in relation to the universe of Discourses in a society, including other scientific and non-scientific Discourses. Only then can we understand how form and function within Discourses are always political (relevant to values and beliefs about the distribution of "goods" in society). Only then can people who have historically been disadvantaged by school-based Discourses come to master them without being "colonized" by them.

REFERENCES

Bakhtin, M. M. (1986). *Speech genres and other late essays.* Austin: University of Texas Press.

Baugh, J. (2000). *Beyond ebonics: Linguistic pride and racial prejudice.* Oxford, UK: Oxford University Press.

Bazerman, C. (1988). *Shaping written knowledge.* Madison: University of Wisconsin Press.

Chouliaraki, L., & Fairclough, N. (1999). *Discourse in late modernity.* Edinburgh, UK: Edinburgh University Press.

D'Andrade, R. (1984). Cultural meaning systems. In R. A. Shweder & R. A. LeVine (Eds.), *Culture theory: Essays on mind, self, and emotion* (pp. 88-119). Cambridge, UK: Cambridge University Press.

Davidson, D. (2001). *Inquiries into truth and interpretation: Philosophical essays* (2nd ed.). Oxford, UK: Oxford University Press.

Edwards, D., & Potter, J. (1992). *Discursive psychology.* London, UK: Sage.

Fairclough, N. (1992). *Discourse and social change.* Cambridge, UK: Polity Press.

Fairclough, N. (1995). *Critical discourse analysis.* London, UK: Longman.

Foucault, M. (1981). *History of sexuality (Vol. 1).* Harmondsworth, UK: Penguin.

Frank, T. (2000). *One market under God: Extreme capitalism, market populism, and the end of economic democracy.* New York: Doubleday.

Gagnon, P. (1987). *Democracy's untold story: What world history textbooks neglect.* Washington, DC: American Federation of Teachers.

Gee, J. P. (1991). Memory and myth: A perspective on narrative. In A. McCabe and C. Peterson (Eds.), *Developing narrative structure* (pp. 1-25). Hillsdale, NJ: Erlbaum.

Gee, J. P. (1992). *The social mind: Language, ideology, and social practice.* New York: Bergin & Garvey.

Gee, J. P. (1996). *Social linguistics and literacies: Ideology in discourses* (2nd ed.). London: Taylor & Francis.

Gee, J. P. (1999a). *An introduction to discourse analysis: Theory and method.* London: Routledge.

Gee, J. P. (1999b). Mind and society: A response to Derek Edwards' "Emotion Discourse." *Culture and Psychology, 5,* 305-312.

Gee, J. P., Allen A-R, & Clinton, K. (2001). Language, class, and identity: Teenagers fashioning themselves through language, *Linguistics and Education, 12,* 175-194.

Gee, J. P., & Crawford, V. (1998). Two kinds of teenagers: Language, identity, and social class. In D. Alverman, K. Hinchman, D. Moore, S. Phelps, & D. Waff (Eds.), *Reconceptualizing the literacies in adolescents' lives* (pp. 225-245). Mahwah, NJ: Erlbaum.

Gee, J. P., Hull, G., & Lankshear, C. (1996). *The new work order: Behind the language of the new capitalism.* Boulder, CO: Westview.

Gramsci, A. (1971). *Selections from the prison notebooks.* London: Lawrence & Wishart.

Hacking, I. (1986). Making up people. In T. C. Heller, M. Sosna, & D. E. Wellbery (Eds.), *Reconstructing individualism: Autonomy, individuality, and the self in Western thought* (pp. 222-236). Stanford, CA: Stanford University Press.

Halliday, M. A. K. (1994). *An introduction to functional grammar* (2nd ed.). London: Edward Arnold.

Hicks, D. (2000). Self and other in Bakhtin's early philosophical essays: Prelude to a theory of prose consciousness. *Mind, Culture, and Activity, 7,* 227-242.

Holland, D., Lachicotte, W., Skinner, D., & Cain, C. (1998). *Identity and agency in cultural worlds.* Cambridge, MA: Harvard University Press.

Jaworski, A., & Coupland, N. (Eds.). (1999). *The discourse reader.* London: Routledge.

Levinson, S. C. (2000). *Presumptive meanings: The theory of generalized conversational implicature.* Cambridge, MA: MIT Press.

Lewontin, R. C. (1991). *Biology as ideology: The doctrine of DNA.* New York: Harper.

Luke, A. (1995). Text and discourse in education: An introduction to critical discourse analysis. In M. W. Apple (Ed.), *Review of research in education* (Vol. 21, pp. 3-48). Washington, DC: AERA.

Martin, J. R., Matthiessen, C., & Painter, C. (1997). *Working with functional grammar.* London: Arnold.

Milroy, L. (1995). *Language and social networks* (2nd ed.). Oxford, UK: Blackwell.

Ochs, E., Schegloff, E. A., & Thompson, S. A. (Eds.). (1997). *Interaction and grammar.* Cambridge, UK: Cambridge University Press.

Psathas, G. (1995). *Conversation analysis.* Thousand Oaks, CA: Sage

Pomerantz, A., & Fehr, B. J. (1997). Conversation analysis: An approach to the study of social action as sense making practices. In T. A. van Dijk (Ed.),

Discourse as social interaction: Discourse studies 2: A multidisciplinary introduc-tion (pp. 64-91). London: Sage.

Strauss, C., & Quinn, N. (1997). *A cognitive theory of cultural meaning.* Cambridge, UK: Cambridge University Press.

University of Wisconsin-Stevens Point. (1996). *Annual report 1996.* Stevens Point: Author.

van Dijk, T. A. (1993). Principles of critical discourse analysis. *Discourse and Society, 4*(2), 249-283.

van Dijk, T.A. (Ed.). (1997a). *Discourse as social interaction: Discourse studies 2: A multidisciplinary introduction.* London: Sage.

van Dijk, T.A. (Ed.). (1997b). *Discourse as structure and process: Discourses studies 1: A multidisciplinary introduction.* London: Sage.

Wodak, R. (1996). *Disorders of discourse.* London: Longman.

13

Biliteracy*

Nancy H. Hornberger
University of Pennsylvania

INTRODUCTION

Biliteracy can be defined as "any and all instances in which communication occurs in two (or more) languages in or around writing" (Hornberger, 1990, p. 213), a definition that follows from Heath's definition of literacy events as "occasions in which written language is integral to the nature of participants' interactions and their interpretive processes and strategies" (Heath, 1982, p. 50; 1983). Unlike Heath's definition, which focuses on the literacy event, my definition of biliteracy refers to instances, a term encompassing events, but also biliterate actors, interactions, practices, activities, programs, situations, societies, sites, worlds, and so on (Hornberger, 2000; Hornberger & Skilton-Sylvester, 2000). Also, unlike Heath's definition, and because biliteracy addresses the conjunction between bilingualism and literacy, the above definition refers explicitly to the use of two or more language varieties.[1] As in Heath's definition, however, the centrality of communication in and around writing, via processes and strategies of interaction and interpretation, is key to defining and understanding biliteracy.

*Portions of this chapter, including the three figures, are reprinted from earlier publications, with permission and grateful acknowledgement: Nancy H. Hornberger (2000) published by John Benjamins in Philadelphia; and Nancy H. Hornberger and Ellen Skilton-Sylvester (2000) published by Multilingual Matters in Clevedon, UK.

Among early references to biliteracy are K. Goodman, Goodman, and Flores' (1979) use of the term in a report on issues of reading in bilingual education; and Lado, Hanson, and D'Emilio (1980), who argued for and demonstrated the value of preschool biliteracy in their Spanish Education Development Center Preschool Reading Project involving 50 children ages 3 to 5 from low-income families in Washington, DC. In early papers, the meaning of the term biliteracy was often left implicit or assumed. For example, Genesee (1980) used the term in the title and concluding paragraph of his article, but not in the main body of the text, which reports results of a survey focusing on second language reading habits of adolescent immersion students in Montreal. Similarly, Cummins (1981) used biliteracy in his title, but referred within to "bilingualism and the acquisition of literacy skills"; nevertheless, his was clearly a plea for attention to biliteracy, ending with the statement that "real equality of educational opportunity will result only from programs that attempt to optimize minority children's potential by continuing to promote literacy skills in both L1 and L2" (Cummins, 1981, p. 142). Valdés (1983) likewise made a plea for greater attention to biliteracy, and specifically for language planning to develop the use of written Spanish language in Hispanic communities; she too did not define biliteracy, instead assuming a meaning roughly along the lines of "reading (and writing) in two languages (or in a second language)."

Niyekawa (1983), on the other hand, in a paper calling for more studies on children's biliteracy acquisition in two structurally and orthographically unrelated languages such as one European and one Asian language, explicitly defined biliteracy as "an advanced state of bilingualism where the person can not only speak two languages fluently but also read and write these two languages" (p. 98), excluding from her definition not only those who are less than fluent but also those who are biliterate but not bilingual; her definition is thus considerably more strict than mine in disallowing "lopsided" bilingual or biliterate instances. Fishman's definition of biliteracy as "the mastery of reading in particular, and also of writing, in two (or more) languages" (Fishman, Riedler-Berger, & Steele, 1985, p. 377, perhaps a reprinting of Fishman, 1980, cited by Spolsky, 1981) is, like Niyekawa's, more specific than mine, in that it focuses on mastery; yet it shares with mine a perspective encompassing not just the use of two languages, but of two (or more) languages (or language varieties).

The original impetus for my 1989 review of literature relating to biliteracy was an ethnographic research project initiated in Philadelphia in 1987, the Literacy in Two Languages project (see later). In search of a framework to underpin that research and finding very little scholarly work attending explicitly to biliteracy (the conjunction of bilingualism and literacy), I looked instead to its component parts (i.e., the literatures on bilingualism and the teaching of second/foreign languages and the literatures on literacy and the teaching of reading/writing). These fields represent vast amounts of literature, a relatively small but increasing proportion of which explicitly addresses the overlap areas. A common ground in these literatures is that although we often characterize dimensions of bilingualism and literacy in terms of polar opposites such as first (L1) versus second languages (L2), monolingual versus bilingual individuals, or oral versus literate societies, in each case those opposites represent only theoretical endpoints on what is in reality a continuum of features (cf. Kelly, 1969, p. 5). Furthermore, when we consider biliteracy as the conjunction of literacy and bilingualism—and the dynamic interaction between them—it becomes clear that these continua are interrelated dimensions of one highly complex whole; and that in fact it is in the dynamic, rapidly changing and sometimes contested spaces along and across the intersecting continua that most biliteracy use and learning occur. These insights became the basis for the continua of biliteracy model that I proposed in 1989 and that has since informed my own and my students' research in Philadelphia, as well as students' and colleagues' research nationally and internationally (Hornberger, 2003). This chapter introduces the continua model, and the ethnographic research project which gave rise to it, considers the component parts of the model in relation to other areas of literacy research supporting and informing it, and concludes with a few comments on unanswered questions about the model and about biliteracy itself.

CONTINUA OF BILITERACY MODEL

The continua model of biliteracy, proposed in Hornberger (1989a) and revised in Hornberger and Skilton-Sylvester (2000), offers a framework in which to situate research, teaching, and language planning in linguistically diverse settings. The model uses the notion of intersecting and nested continua to demonstrate the multiple and complex interrelationships between bilingualism and literacy and the importance of the contexts, media, and content through which biliteracy develops. The notion of continuum is intended to convey that although one can identify (and name) points on the continuum, those points are not finite, static, or discrete. There are infinitely many points on the continuum; any single point is inevitably and inextricably related to all other points; and all the points have more in common than not with each other.

Specifically, the continua model depicts the development of biliteracy along intersecting L1-L2, receptive-productive, and oral-written language skills continua; through the medium of two (or more) languages and literacies whose linguistic structures vary from similar to dissimilar, whose scripts range from convergent to divergent, and to which the developing biliterate individual's exposure varies from simultaneous to successive; in contexts that encompass micro to macro levels and are characterized by varying mixes along the monolingual-bilingual and oral-literate continua; and (as revised in Hornberger & Skilton-Sylvester, 2000) with content that ranges from majority to minority perspectives and experiences, literary to vernacular styles and genres, and decontextualized to contextualized language texts (Skilton-Sylvester, 1997).

Figures 13.1 and 13. 2 schematically represent the framework by depicting both the nested and intersecting nature of the continua, whereas Fig. 13.3 summarizes all 12 continua (four nested sets of three intersecting continua each). It is worth noting that Figs. 13.1 and 13.2 are not intended to represent the continua model per se, but are meant rather as aids to visualization of the relationships among the continua. Figure 13.1 depicts the continua as a series of nested boxes representing contexts, media, content, and development of biliteracy respectively, whereas Fig. 13.2 shows that each box is a cluster of its three intersecting continua. Not only is the three dimensionality of any one set of three intersecting continua representative of the interrelatedness of those three constituent continua, but it should be emphasized that the interrelationships extend across the four sets of continua as well; hence the nesting of the three-dimensional spaces. Finally, the two-way arrows represent the infinity and fluidity of movement along each of the continua; the three-dimensional boxes must also be visualized as infinitely expanding and contracting spaces, not bounded boxes as in the diagram.[2]

The notion of continuum conveys that all points on a particular continuum are interrelated, and the intersecting and nested relationships among the continua convey that all points across the continua are also interrelated. The model suggests that the more their learning contexts and contexts of use allow learners and users to draw from across the whole of each and every continuum, the greater are the chances for their full biliterate development and expression (Hornberger, 1989a, p. 289). Implicit in that suggestion is a recognition that there has usually *not* been attention to all points and that movement along the continua and across the intersections may well be contested. In educational policy and practice regarding biliteracy, there tends to be an implicit privileging of one end of the continua over the other such that one end of each continuum is associated with more power than the other (e.g., written development over oral development); there is a need to contest the traditional power weighting by paying attention to, granting agency to, and making space for actors and practices at what have traditionally been the less powerful ends of the continua (Hornberger & Skilton-Sylvester, 2000). Fig. 13.3 depicts one common alignment of power relationships along the continua, but is not intended to suggest that this is the only alignment found in all multilingual settings around the world.

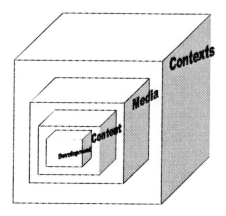

Figure 13.1. **Nested relationships among the continua of biliteracy.**

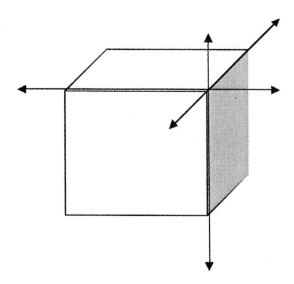

Figure 13.2. **Intersecting relationships among the continua of biliteracy.**

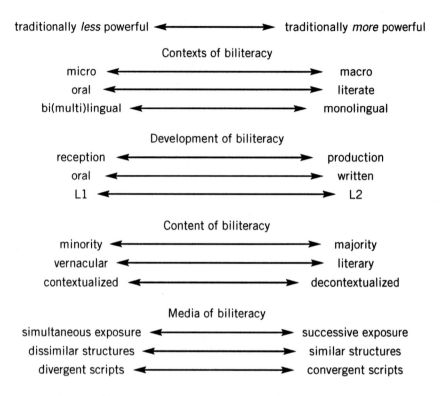

traditionally *less* powerful ⟵————————⟶ traditionally *more* powerful

Contexts of biliteracy

micro ⟵————————⟶	macro
oral ⟵————————⟶	literate
bi(multi)lingual ⟵————————⟶	monolingual

Development of biliteracy

reception ⟵————————⟶	production
oral ⟵————————⟶	written
L1 ⟵————————⟶	L2

Content of biliteracy

minority ⟵————————⟶	majority
vernacular ⟵————————⟶	literary
contextualized ⟵————————⟶	decontextualized

Media of biliteracy

simultaneous exposure ⟵————————⟶	successive exposure
dissimilar structures ⟵————————⟶	similar structures
divergent scripts ⟵————————⟶	convergent scripts

Figure 13.3.   Power relations in the continua of biliteracy.

LITERACY IN TWO LANGUAGES: SITUATING THE CONTINUA OF BILITERACY

The initial impetus for formulating the continua of biliteracy model was the "Literacy in Two Languages" project, a long-term comparative, ethnographic research project in two language minority communities of Philadelphia. Through participant observation, interviewing, and document collection in school and community settings in the Puerto Rican community of North Philadelphia and the Cambodian community of West Philadelphia, the study sought to understand biliteracy attitudes and practices in classroom and community, and their fit with local, state, and national policies and programs addressing them. Although the research questions for the project had already been formulated before the model was developed, the continua model proved useful in analyzing the data and drawing conclusions from the research; and by the same token, the ongoing research continually informed the evolving model.

For example, an early paper from this project (Hornberger, 1992) showed how biliteracy contexts for Puerto Rican and Cambodian students in Philadelphia in the 1980s were framed and constrained by national policies that emphasized english acquisition at the expense of minority language maintenance (e.g., the proposed English Language Amendment to the constitution, the 1984 and 1988 renewals of the Bilingual Education Act of 1968, and the Immigration Reform and Control Act of 1986), by an educational system that used minority languages only to embed the more powerful English literacy, and by the assimilative "charm" of English, which pulled students' biliterate development toward English. For the United States to achieve its goals of education for all, I argued, policy, curriculum, and community language and literacy use would have to change in ways that would encourage, rather than inhibit, biliterate individuals' drawing on all points of the continua for their full biliterate development.

Also as part of the Literacy in Two Languages project, Joel Hardman and I reported on our study of adult *biliteracy development* in programs for Puerto Ricans and Cambodians in Philadelphia, making an argument for the inadequacy of an autonomous, cognitive skills-based view of literacy with its emphasis on a single, standardized schooled literacy in the L2 and for the benefits of a complementary ideological, cultural practice view (Hornberger & Hardman, 1994). In an ESL literacy class for Cambodian adults, Hardman found evidence of a cultural practice approach in student-directed social learning strategies including prompting, collaboration and use of Khmer (the L1) to answer questions, talk with other students, and take notes; he further observed that students were most comfortable with repeating, copying and reading aloud, activities which as he pointed out use both receptive and productive skills (and oral-written ones too, in the case of reading aloud) (Hornberger & Hardman, 1994). These findings gave direct evidence of the space for learners to use their L1, oral, and receptive skills in a cultural practice approach to biliteracy teaching and learning.

I, too, found that in a bilingual GED program run by Philadelphia's ASPIRA (a nonprofit Puerto Rican education-advocacy organization originally established in 1961 in New York City), which focused on mastery of the discrete skills needed to pass the GED exam, the program embedded this "autonomous" literacy as cultural practice at every level in ways that gave space to the learners' Spanish language, Puerto Rican cultural identity, and "right to speak" (Norton Peirce, 1995), that is, in ways that recognized the minority, vernacular, contextualized ends of the *content* continua as well as the L1, oral, receptive ends of the *development* continua. For example, the program explicitly taught Puerto Rican culture and cultural awareness to both the Spanish-dominant and English-dominant groups, offered opportunities for students to act in solidarity with other Latin Americans, connected the students to a network of ASPIRA-sponsored organizations and programs that support the Puerto Rican community, drew on the Puerto Rican community to support students' development, allowed the students to accommodate the highly individualized competency-based program to the more collaborative learning approach they seemed to prefer, and acknowledged and addressed tensions between the Spanish-dominant Puerto-Rican born and English-dominant Philadelphia-born groups. One evidence of the success of this approach in creating a context where students' expressions were voiced and heard came in the very lively election campaign for class officers and ASPIRA Club Board representatives, including a several-verse rap song in Spanish spontaneously composed by a group of students (Hornberger & Hardman, 1994).

It was in a related, spin-off of the "Literacy in Two Languages" project, specifically her own dissertation study of literacy, identity, and educational policy among Cambodian women and girls in Philadelphia, that Ellen Skilton-Sylvester found it necessary to supplement the model with the continua of *biliteracy content* described earlier. Examples from Skilton-Sylvester's research include one 11th-grade high school student named Ty, who upon encountering Maxine Hong Kingston's *Woman Warrior* for the first time, asked, "Is she the only Asian writer?" The reading of this text fell at the minority (and literary) end of the content continua and, as such, opened a door for Ty to be a part of literary discourse in a new way (Skilton-Sylvester, 1997). Another young woman, Nan, was a proficient vernacular writer (writing letters, plays for friends and family members to perform, etc.) who was nevertheless often framed as a "non-writer" in schooling contexts, where the role of performance in vernacular writing was rarely evident. Soka, a student in an adult education class, undertook to write a letter to her former teacher (contextualized content that had meaning to her as a person), and in the process revealed to her current teacher a very complex understanding of the structure of personal letters (even though her English skills were relatively limited) (Skilton-Sylvester, 1997). Skilton-Sylvester concluded that if students' whole contextualized texts, with all of their imperfections, could be used as a starting point, meaning would be insured and students could intrinsically see the links between decontextualized and contextualized language and between the literary and the vernacular. If minority texts could be chosen as a part of the literary content of the classroom, links could also be made between the content students bring with them to school and the content they encounter at the school door.

When we turned our attention to the *media of biliteracy* in two-way bilingual programs in the Puerto Rican community, we found that faculty and staff continually faced challenging media-related decisions with regard to, for example: (a) placement of students in English-dominant and Spanish-dominant streams; (b) distribution of English and Spanish in the program structure and the classroom; and (c) the co-existence of various standard and nonstandard varieties of English and Spanish and the implications of this for instruction and assessment. In terms of the continua, the first two issues relate to the question of simultaneous versus successive exposure to (or acquisition) of the languages /literacies, and the last touches on the matter of language varieties' structures and scripts.

Whereas the programs tended to continually run aground in attempting to assign students to English-dominant and Spanish-dominant streams (consistent with a 2-way program) (Hornberger, 1991), the continua model helped us to understand that English-dominant and Spanish-dominant could not be self-evident categories, given the myriad constellations of language use, ability, and exposure present in a community where ongoing circular migration from Puerto Rico to Philadelphia and back is a fact of life for nearly everyone to one degree or another. The fact is that most Puerto Rican children do not grow up with just one (dominant or only) mother tongue and then acquire the second language in school, but rather that they are constantly crossing back and forth between both languages and the meanings and identities they convey (cf. Rampton's, 1995, notions of expertise, affiliation, and inheritance).

Students arriving (and re-arriving) at school with widely different constellations of biliterate expertise, affiliations, and inheritances pose a complex challenge, in terms of program structure and classroom interaction, to schools seeking to develop a two-way bilingual program that builds on both languages for all students (e.g., Hornberger & Micheau, 1993). A study of how one fourth/fifth grade homeroom teacher at Potter Thomas created successful learning contexts for her students' biliterate development—specifically how she built students' interaction with text—highlighted how she "allows small-group peer interaction to occur spontaneously and a-systematically as a natural outgrowth of shared cultural values, emphasizes her students' community-based prior knowledge, and seeks to help her students to 'connect and transfer' strategies across languages" (Hornberger, 1990, p. 227). Retrospectively, it appears that this teacher had in fact found ways to build on the biliterate affiliations, inheritances, and expertise that her students brought with them to school. Such an approach made a strength rather than a weakness out of students' crisscrossed, simultaneous (rather than successive) acquisition of two languages literacies.

A third *media*-related challenge on which the continua model helped shed light is the co-existence of standard and nonstandard varieties of English and Spanish in the school community's repertoire, and the implications of these for instruction and assessment. Although our earlier field-work had taken note in passing of the existence of Puerto Rican, Cuban, and other Latin American varieties of Spanish, and of school standard and African-American varieties of English all in use within one school (cf. Zentella, 1997, on the repertoire of Spanish and English varieties on New York City's *el bloque*), the focus in terms of the continua of biliterate media had been more on the relative similarities and convergences between the two languages (Spanish and English) and their writing systems as potential resources for transfer of literacy from one to the other, rather than on dissimilarities and divergences across varieties *within* the two languages that might impede literacy development even in one. The continua model helped us understand that the latter require our attention just as much as the former.

To pose a (partially) hypothetical example: a school with a 2-way program serving Puerto Rican children in Philadelphia decided, after many years of English-language standardized testing, to inaugurate Spanish-language standardized testing as well, in an effort to obtain a more representative picture of their students' biliterate accomplishments. The only trouble was that the only standardized testing materials available reflected Mexican, not Puerto Rican, language varieties and identities and, thus, hardly promised to render a truer picture of the Puerto Rican students' expertise. Similarly, another school elected to develop portfolio assessment in Spanish and called in an English-language expert on the subject, who was in turn stymied by the discovery that the teachers in the school, who spoke varieties of Puerto Rican, Cuban, and other Latin American Spanishes, could not agree on the "correct" form of Spanish to use. These are the kinds of contested spaces on which the continua model seeks to shed light.

Research in the "Literacy in Two Languages" project is ongoing and we continue to test the limits and potential of the continua model; I comment on ongoing research in the conclusion of this chapter. Here, we will look more closely at the model and at related research supporting and informing it. The following sections take up each of the four sets of continua—contexts, development, content, and media—in relation to assumptions and perspectives in related areas of literacy research. In each case, I attempt to show how the view of literacy in the continua model (a) reflects certain assumptions regarding literacy and literacy learning, (b) relates to other perspectives on literacy as well as to larger disciplinary perspectives, and (c) can be used in research and analysis of literacy practices. For convenience, I present the links between particular units of analysis, disciplinary perspectives and portions of the continua model in discrete and linear fashion, but it should be borne in mind that in fact the whole model is informed by all of the perspectives discussed.

CONTEXTS OF BILITERACY:
LITERACY EVENTS, INTERACTIONS, AND
IDEOLOGIES

The continua model of biliteracy posits that contexts influence biliteracy development and use at every level from two-person interaction (micro) to societal and global relations of power (macro) and that they comprise a mix of oral-to-literate, monolingual-to-multilingual varieties of language and literacy. Literacy practices are usually embedded in oral language use (Heath, 1982); furthermore, in some speech communities, oral discourse patterns in one language variety may constitute barriers to literacy in another (Leap, 1991). Multilingual speakers switch languages according to the context of situation; monolingual speakers may switch styles or dialects in much the same way (Hymes, 1972a). Any instance of biliteracy would need to be considered in light of such dimensions of context.

Assumptions within this model about the centrality of context in understanding biliteracy acquisition and use are directly attributable to the sociolinguistic and linguistic anthropological perspectives and research traditions that inform the continua model. An interest in context as an important factor in all aspects of language use dates back at least to the 1960s and the beginnings of sociolinguistics, linguistic anthropology, and the ethnography of communication (Fishman, 1970; Hymes, 1968; Pride & Holmes, 1972); and is evident in literacy research today in such concepts as *literacy event* and *literacy interaction*.

Sociolinguistics broke new ground in the 1960s by moving the analysis of language beyond a focus on structure to one on language use in social context. Rather than study homogeneous languages, sociolinguists (particularly those in the linguistic anthropological tradition) took up the study of speech communities and their verbal repertoires, described in terms of speech (or, more broadly, communicative) domains, situations, events, and acts. In his introduction to the 1964 special publication of the *American Anthropologist* on the ethnography of communication, Hymes proposed the following:

> [The ethnography of communication] must take as context a community, investigating its communicative habits as a whole, so that any given use of channel and code takes its place as but part of the resources upon which the members of the community draw. . . . The starting point is the ethnographic analysis of the communicative habits of a community in their totality, determining what count as communicative events, and as their components. . . . The communicative event thus is central. (Hymes, 1964, pp. 3, 13)

Building from communicative theory and work by Roman Jakobson, Hymes suggested an array of components that might serve as a heuristic for the ethnographic study of communicative events, where such events refer to activities, or aspects of activities, that are directly governed by rules or norms for the use of language. This array of components he later formulated into the mnemonic SPEAKING (Setting, Participants, Ends, Act, Key, Instrumentalities, Norms, Genres; Hymes, 1974a). Analysis of biliteracy events, from this perspective, then, involves describing the range of ways in which people "do" literacy in two (or more) language varieties and scripts, in terms of participants, settings, topics, purposes, norms, genres, and the like.

The notion of interaction has also come into literacy studies via sociolinguistic and linguistic anthropological work, primarily that of Gumperz, who in turn built on work by sociologist Erving Goffman on face-to-face interaction. "The key to Gumperz's sociolinguistics of verbal communication is a view of language as a socially and culturally constructed symbol system that is used in ways that reflect macrolevel social meanings (e.g., group identity, status differences) but also create microlevel social meanings (i.e., what one is saying and doing at a particular moment in time)" (Schiffrin, 1996, p. 315). This work, referred to as interactional sociolinguistics, investigates how contextualization cues, that is "signalling mechanisms such as intonation, speech rhythm, and choice among lexical, phonetic, and syntactic options" (Gumperz, 1982, p. 16), relate what is said to participants' background knowledge, enabling them to make situated inferences about their interlocutors' meaning. A biliteracy interaction, from this perspective, would be a face-to-face interaction involving a piece of writing and two or more language varieties and scripts, a notion closely related to biliteracy event in that the focus is on the "doing" of biliteracy, but with perhaps greater emphasis on the evolution of the interaction in real time and on *how* it creates and reflects micro- and macrolevel social meanings.

Biliteracy events and interactions are among the units of analysis for researching biliteracy acquisition and use *in context*. As suggested by the foregoing, it is important to emphasize that context comprises not only setting, topic, and participants, but also communicative purposes, social meanings, and underlying norms and ideologies. At the macrolevel, the purposes and meanings that spoken and written language express are affected by global and societal sociopolitical, socioeconomic, sociocultural, sociopsychological, and sociolinguistic statuses and processes; at the microlevel, oral and literate, monolingual and multilingual interaction in specific institutional, neighborhood, home, and family contexts plays a role in defining the communicative purposes and social meanings of spoken and written language choice as well. Policies of tolerance or intolerance toward multiple languages or language varieties, attitudes which stereotype biliterate individuals' or groups' linguistic and cultural difference and those that don't, and ideologies of assimilationism or pluralism all exert powerful influences on biliteracy development and use (cf. González & Arnot-Hopfler, 2003; Hornberger, 2002).

DEVELOPMENT OF BILITERACY: LITERACY PRACTICES, ACTIVITIES, AND LEARNING

The continua model posits that the development of biliteracy may start at any point on any of three intersecting continua of L1-L2, oral-to-written, and receptive-to-productive language and literacy skills, uses, and practices; that biliteracy learning may proceed in any direction along those intersecting continua; and that it may do so by backtracking, spurting, or criss-crossing just as readily as by steadily progressing in linear fashion. Second-language learners need not only comprehensible input, but also opportunities to produce comprehensible output (Pica, Holliday, Lewis, & Morganthaler, 1989; Swain, 1985). Biliterate learners not only learn to read and write through heavy reliance on oral language, but also have been observed to learn to read by writing and to write by reading (Goodman & Goodman, 1983; Hudelson, 1984), to spell words in the L2 based on the L1 sound system (Edelsky, 1986), and to read their second language beyond the level of their L2 speaking knowledge (Moll & Díaz, 1985). There is, in fact, an infinite potential for transfer of skills across any of the three continua, but, by the same token, understanding or predicting transfer is elusive if not impossible, precisely because the three continua are interrelated and furthermore nested within all the other continua.

In the ethnography of communication, communicative competence is understood as situated within communicative events (Hymes, 1972b, p. 282; Hornberger, 1989b, p. 217). Consistent with this view, the development of biliteracy in individuals occurs along the continua in direct response to the contextual demands placed on these individuals. "The environmental press that requires the successful interactant to use distinct subsets of linguistic and sociolinguistic knowledge can change from moment to moment in face-to-face interaction, and from one discourse unit to another in a written text with which ego is confronted. . . . Interaction with others in producing these diverse verbal and written texts constitutes practice in language use" (Erickson, 1991, p. 342). Assumptions within the continua model about the development of biliteracy in relation to contextual demands placed on biliterate learners have much in common with assumptions and perspectives about literacy and learning deriving from cross-cultural psychology, sociocultural theory, and social and cultural anthropology. Literacy practices and activities, as units of analysis with roots in these disciplines, provide conceptual tools for describing and understanding biliteracy development in context.

Cross-cultural psychologists Scribner and Cole (1981) are generally credited with introducing the term *literacy practices*, based on their ethnographic work among the Vai in Liberia. They came to see "literacy as a set of socially organized practices," arguing that "literacy is not simply learning how to read and write a particular script but applying this knowledge for specific purposes in specific contexts of use" (p. 236). "Cultural groups are said to have specific literacy practices in the same sense they are said to have specific religious practices, house-building practices, medicinal practices, and so forth" (Reder, 1994, p. 36). The notion of practices, in this sense, appears to have its roots in the traditional ethnographies of cultural anthropology; but as developed in literacy studies, it also gains sustenance from more recent "anthropological and sociological theorizing" about social practice, beginning from Bourdieu's (1977) *Outline of a Theory of Practice* (Lave & Wenger, 1991, p. 50).

Street (1984), who used and developed the concept of *literacy practices* in his ethnographic work in Iran, defined literacy practices as the "broader cultural conception of particular ways of thinking about and doing reading and writing in cultural contexts" (Street, 2000b, p. 22). In this usage, the term literacy practices appears to encompass what sociolinguists often refer to as "language uses and attitudes"—or more specifically, uses of and attitudes toward language and literacy (i.e., not only the observable uses but also the underlying norms, values, and conventions associated with those uses). In the New Literacy Studies, Street, Barton, and others distinguish between literacy events and literacy practices, characterizing the former as a descriptive category of observable occurrences and the latter as the cultural meanings behind them. In this view, bedtime story reading in U.S. middle-class homes (Heath, 1982), for example, is a literacy event (a parent/caregiver and child at home reading a book together at bedtime) undergirded by a set of literacy practices (story-reading conventions, attitudes toward books and literacy, expectations about parent-child relationships, etc.). "Literacy events are the particular activities where reading and writing have a role; literacy practices are the general cultural ways of using reading and writing which people draw upon in a literacy event" (Barton, 1994a, p. viii).

These are perhaps useful distinctions, although as noted earlier, the original sociolinguistic formulations of communicative event include explicit attention not only to the observable uses of language and literacy, but also to attitudes, norms, values, ideologies, and conventions underlying them (i.e., practices). Hymes' (1974b) phrase "ways of speaking" and

Heath's (1983) "ways with words" capture this dimension. Reder, for example, viewed literacy events and practices as not so much different in kind, as in frequency: "Literacy events are culturally patterned into recurring units, which Scribner and Cole (1981) have termed literacy practices" (Reder, 1994, p. 36).

In conventional usage, practice (as a noun) carries connotations of both frequent doing and learning by doing. Combining these notions with the previously mentioned connotations of customary ways of doing (from traditional anthropology) and uses and attitudes (from the New Literacy Studies), we can understand biliteracy practices, then, as the day-to-day, minute-to-minute, contextually situated uses of and attitudes toward two or more languages and literacies, that cumulatively add up to the ways of communicating within a particular speech community, classroom, family, society, program, or other socially constructed institution or interaction. These practices, in turn, support biliteracy learning along the continua of L1-to-L2, oral-to-written, and receptive-to-productive language and literacy skills.

Although practice carries connotations of learning, the salient meaning of activity, in conventional usage, is that of the active doing of a specific action. In recent years, however, activity has taken on special meanings more closely linked to the learning connotation, in association with work in psychology, and in particular sociocultural theory and activity theory building on the writings of Soviet psychologist Vygotsky (Wertsch, 1981, 1991). In Vygotsky's approach to mental functioning,

> jointly undertaken goal-oriented activity was primary. At any time, a culture is constituted by the systems of social activity that have developed historically through the use and improvements of tools and practices to mediate humans' action and interaction in the world. Each individual enters the world with a biologically given potential; but the development of a full human being is dependent on the "appropriation," or taking over, of the tools and practices already in use in the culture. Vygotsky focused specifically on the development of what he called the higher mental functions, such as voluntary memory and reasoning. These functions, he argued, are mediated by the use of semiotic tools, chief among which is language. Individual intellectual development is thus to be understood, in large part, in terms of the appropriation of the ways in which language is used in social interaction in the context of joint activity. (Measures, Quell, & Wells, 1997, pp. 21-22)

Based on these understandings and assumptions, a focus on biliteracy activities implies attention to the ways in which engagement in biliteracy events, interactions, and practices enables participants to appropriate the ways of speaking and writing already in use in the multiple cultures in which they participate. The continua model argues for biliteracy pedagogies that support L1, oral, and receptive biliteracy activities and practices as well as L2, written, and productive ones, thereby providing space for biliterate learners to appropriate the widest possible range of communicative resources; there is need for more research documenting these kinds of biliteracy activities and practices in classrooms and out of them.

CONTENT OF BILITERACY: IDENTITIES, GENRES, AND DISCOURSES

The continua model posits that *what* (content) biliterate learners and users read and write is as important as *how* (development), *where* (context) or *when and by what means* (media) they do so. Whereas schooling traditionally privileges majority, literary, and decontextualized contents, the continua model argues for greater curricular attention to minority, vernacular, and contextualized whole language texts. Minority texts include those by minority authors, written from minority perspectives; vernacular ways of reading and writing include notes, poems, plays, and stories written at home or in other everyday nonschool contexts; contextualized whole-language texts are those read and written in the context of biliteracy events, interactions, practices, and activities of the biliterate learners' everyday lives.

Assumptions within the continua model about the importance of incorporating minority identities and perspectives, vernacular genres and styles, and contextualized texts in biliteracy learning contexts parallel other developments in literacy research which emphasize content, including the funds of knowledge project, the New Literacy studies, and work on multilingual literacies. All of these are in turn underpinned by critical perspectives on language and literacy.

Critical approaches such as critical discourse analysis (Fairclough, 1995; Norton, 1997), critical language awareness (Clark, Fairclough, Ivanic, & Martin-Jones, 1990, 1991), critical literacy (Lankshear, 1997), critical ethnography (May, 1997), and critical pedagogy (Goldstein, 1997) all demand attention to communicative content. Lankshear (1997) suggested that "two essential elements of any and all critical practice . . . [are] the element of evaluation or judgement . . . and the requirement of knowing closely . . . that which is being evaluated" (Lankshear, 1997, p. 43). To think critically about language, discourse, or literacy, one must first know it closely; that is, one must pay attention to what it is—its content. In terms of literacy, Lankshear specified three possible contents, or "potential objects of critique: . . . literacies per se, . . . particular texts, [and] . . . wider social practices, arrangements, relations, allocations, procedures, etc." (Lankshear, 1997, p. 44). These he, in turn, related to discourse and Discourse, in Gee's sense (1990), where discourse with a lower case "d" refers to the language components of Discourse with a capital "D," which refers to social practices or ways of being in the world.

By drawing attention to minority (as well as majority) identities and perspectives and to vernacular (as well as literary) genres and styles in texts available to biliterate learners, the continua model attends to the ways in which discourses make up the Discourses, or possible ways of being in the world, available (or unavailable) to these learners. Available Discourses are multiple, indeed innumerable: "e.g. gangs, academic disciplines, bar gatherings, ethnic groups, friendship networks, types of men, women, gays, children, students, classrooms, workers, workplaces, etc." (Gee, cited in Lankshear, 1997, p. xv). Yet, they are not equally available to all; rather they are ordered hierarchically within the politics of daily life (Lankshear, 1997, p. 39). The continua model highlights the importance of whole contextualized texts/discourses that allow learners to draw on and express minority identities/perspectives and vernacular genres/styles as communicative resources.

In a similar vein, Moll and colleagues argued that "community funds of knowledge" (sometimes called household funds of knowledge or local funds of knowledge) are a resource that can and should be drawn on in schooling for language minority populations. They defined funds of knowledge as "those historically accumulated and culturally developed bodies of knowledge and skills essential for household or individual functioning and well-being" (Moll & González, 1994, p. 443) and emphasize that "becoming literate means taking full advantage of social and cultural resources in the service of academic goals" (Moll & González, 1994, p. 441). The centerpiece of their work is collaboration with teachers in conducting household research, because, as they put it, "it is one thing to identify resources but quite another to use them fruitfully in classrooms" (Moll & González, 1994, p. 441). In the words of one teacher collaborator, "the teacher mediates by creating curricula that reflect both the standard curriculum and the themes, languages, and culture of students' lives . . . when teachers incorporate household funds of knowledge into the curriculum and use dialogic teaching methods, students are liberated to direct their own learning" (Floyd-Tenery, 1995, p. 12).

The New Literacy Studies (NLS; Street, 1993, 1995, 2000a) have similarly drawn attention to minority, vernacular, and contextualized literacy practices and their role as communicative resources in the construction of social identities, through accumulating documentation of "multiple literacies"—the multiple social and cultural constructions of literacy in practice.

Street (1993) criticized what he called the autonomous model of literacy, a model that conceives of literacy as a uniform set of techniques and ascribes direct cognitive and social benefits to the acquisition of these skills; he suggested instead an ideological model, wherein literacies are seen as multiple and socially constructed. NLS researchers have produced a growing body of work on reading and writing as social practices embedded in particular historical and cultural contexts; and their work has explicitly pointed out that literacies may be implicated in operations of social power, as well as in the formation of identities and subjectivities (Collins, 1995, p. 81). Among the multiple literacies described in the NLS are *vernacular literacies*—literacy practices associated with culture which is neither elite nor institutional (Camitta, 1993; Shuman, 1993; Street, 1993); *local literacies*—literacy practices closely connected with local and regional identities (Barton, 1994b; Barton & Hamilton, 1998; Street, 1994); *indigenous literacies*—literacy development and practices in indigenous languages and contexts (Hornberger, 1996); *everyday literacies*—adolescent students' literacy practices in their everyday lives (Knobel, 1999); and *multilingual literacies*—literacy practices of multilingual individuals and groups (Martin-Jones & Jones, 2000).

This last notion, multilingual literacies, is of particular interest here because of its great resonance with the notion of biliteracy (Hornberger, 2000); both formulations take the view that multiple languages and literacies, and the cultural practices and views of the world in which they are embedded, are resources on which individuals and groups may draw as they "take on different identities in different domains of their lives" (Martin-Jones & Jones, 2000, p. 1). Their volume provides richly detailed accounts and analyses of, for example, a minority group member who, as an act of resistance, refuses to become literate because acquisition of majority-culture literacy requires the adoption of some of the cultural behaviors and values of the majority group (Blackledge, 2000); or how the interactions between a young Welsh farmer and a delegate of the Ministry of Agriculture Fisheries and Food (as they fill out an Animal Movement form) reflect a hybrid combination of elements of bureaucratic and farmworld discourses in Welsh and English (Jones, 2000). Martin-Jones and Jones tell us that one of the reasons they chose the term multilingual for the title of their book was to focus attention on the multiple ways people draw on and combine the codes in their communicative repertoires to make meaning as they negotiate and display cultural identities and social relationships; in the same way, the continua of biliteracy focuses attention on the use of codes as meaning-making and identity-constructing resources for the expression of majority-to-minority identities and perspectives, literary-to-vernacular genres and styles, and decontextualized-to-contextualized texts and discourses.

MEDIA OF BILITERACY:
MULTILITERACIES, MEDIATION, AND HYBRIDITY

Biliteracy is about communication in two (or more) languages in or around writing, and those languages and scripts (i.e., the media through which biliteracy is learned and used) are crucial. Media, in the continua of biliteracy model, refer to the actual communicative repertoires (i.e., the language varieties and scripts through which multilingual literacies are expressed), and the sequences or configurations in which they are acquired and used. The model defines these in terms of the linguistic structures of the languages involved (on a continuum from similar to dissimilar), their orthographic scripts (from convergent to divergent), and the sequence of exposure to or acquisition of the languages/literacies (ranging from simultaneous to successive).

In constructing the continua of media along these lines, the model built directly on research findings that increasingly pointed to recognitions such as the following: that type and degree of bilingualism (e.g., simultaneous vs. successive) have more to do with patterns of language use than with age of acquisition; that the L1 need not be fully developed before introduction of the L2, as long as it is not abandoned as a consequence of that introduction; that there are many possible mixes of L1-L2 literacy development (Hornberger, 1989a), that is, multiple paths of acquisition and varying degrees of expertise (cf. Martin-Jones & Jones, 2000); and that popular assumptions about greater structural dissimilarity between language varieties or higher divergence between scripts as inhibiting factors in biliteracy learning are not necessarily borne out in experience (Hornberger, 1989a).

Assumptions within the model about diversity of language varieties and scripts, multiple paths and varying degrees of expertise in the learning and use of communicative repertoire are consistent not only with the research findings just sketched, but also with the theoretical stance of the ethnography of communication, recent work on multimodal expression and multiliteracies, and sociocultural and constructivist approaches. The media component in the continua model is roughly equivalent to Hymes' (1974) notion of Instrumentalities in the SPEAKING heuristic, including both code and channel. Hymes' "code" refers to language varieties, dialects, styles, whereas "channel" includes written, as well as oral, telegraphic, and other communicative modes. Saville-Troike (1989) elaborated this into a grid made up of the intersection of vocal and nonvocal channels with verbal and nonverbal codes; hence the instrumental alternatives or *media* of communication include such communicative modes as paralinguistic and prosodic features (vocal, nonverbal), silence, kinesics, and proxemics (nonvocal, nonverbal), and written and sign languages (nonvocal, verbal), as well as spoken language (vocal, verbal). Similarly, the New London Group

(1996; Cope & Kalantzis, 2000) used the term multiliteracies to refer to the multiple communications channels and media in our changing world (and to the increasing saliency of cultural and linguistic diversity in literacy learning and use). The concept of multiliteracies, in this sense, extends literacy beyond reading and writing to other domains, such as the visual, audio, spatial, and behavioral.

Consistent with both the ethnography of communication and the New London Group conceptions, consideration of the media of biliteracy, entails attention not just to different languages, but also to different dialects, styles, discourses, and different communicative modes including technological ones, as they are acquired and used not in a dichotomized sequence but more often in criss-crossed, hybrid mixes. To maximize biliteracy development (within practices and activities), such considerations must be accommodated in every feature of learning contexts (e.g., events and interactions) and content (e.g., discourses, genres, identities).

None of this is meant to suggest that incorporating multiple varieties, scripts, communicative modes, and criss-crossed paths of acquisition and use proceeds unproblematically in schools or other biliteracy learning contexts. Indeed, given that biliteracy implies the intersection of biliterate learners' multiple literacy worlds in particular literacy sites (cf. Hornberger, 2000), some implicit conflict in norms, practices, and identities is inevitable. I mentioned earlier that sociolinguistics as it emerged in the 1960s shifted our analytical focus in the study of language from language structure to language use, and our unit of study from linguistic code to communicative event; a more recent shift is toward a focus on locating linguistic and literacy practices as parts of larger systems of social inequality (Gal, 1989), taking contexts of cross-cultural or intercultural communication as units of study, "for instance, speakers in institutions who do not share interpretative rules; local populations of speakers viewed in relation to the policies or discourses of states; and contrasting groups of speakers differentially located within a political economic region" (p. 349). It is precisely in these contexts of cross-cultural or intercultural communication, where "notions of group membership and community can no longer be accepted as fixed characteristics and well-defined totalities" (M. Rampton, 1992, p. 54), that relationships among differing language and literacy practices are most evident (in the same way that sociolinguistic norms of interaction are most salient when they are breached and the existence of speech situations and events is most observable at their boundaries, cf. Hymes, 1968, 1972a; Saville-Troike, 1989).

The shift in research focus to studying biliteracy practices as parts of systems of social inequality and to choosing sites of cross-cultural interaction as units of study bring notions of mediation and hybridity to the fore. The role of literacy mediator (Reder, 1987) is a recurring one as, for example, local people negotiate with "outsiders," government bureaucracies, or other national or globalizing agencies, and their languages and literacies. Hybridity, a notion derived from the work of Russian philosopher Bakhtin (1981), and captured succinctly as "the productive tension between official and unofficial discourse" (Cahnmann, 2001), is evidenced by children mixing, blending, and recasting literacy practices from home and school to unique new patterns and forms (as documented, e.g., in East London by Gregory & Williams, 2000), or by teacher's and students' acceptance and encouragement of multiple languages and registers, unauthorized side-talk, movement, spontaneous interaction and collaboration (as seen in the second- and third-grade two-way Spanish immersion classroom in Los Angeles studied by Gutiérrez, Baquedano-López, & Tejeda, 1999). In the latter case, Gutiérrez and co-authors used activity theory and Vygotsky's zones of proximal development as frames for closely analyzing one 6-week learning event, and to show how the participants in this classroom reorganize the activity and incorporate local knowledge, thereby creating "third spaces in which alternative and competing discourses and positionings transform conflict and difference into rich zones of collaboration and learning" (Gutiérrez et al., 1999).

Work of the Santa Barbara Classroom Discourse Group (Castanheira et al., 2001; Floriani et al., 1995; Green & Dixon, 1993) provides similarly detailed insights into the situated, constructed, and consequential nature of learning in linguistically diverse classrooms (Green & Dixon, 1998). Drawing on a series of linked ethnographic studies focusing on inquiry-oriented teaching across content areas in third through sixth-grade bilingual classrooms, this work offers rich documentation of literacy learning realized through discourse in all its myriad, mediated, and hybrid forms. Mediation and hybridity are useful, indeed essential, constructs in understanding the role of multiple varieties, scripts, communicative modes, and criss-crossed paths of acquisition and use (media), in biliteracy practices and activities (development), interactions and events (context), identities, discourses, and genres (content).

As the above discussion makes clear, the Continua model and its four component parts—context, development, media, and content—though originally situated in a specific ethnographic research project in Philadelphia, relate to a wide range of research areas and findings. As such, the model continues to inform and be informed by ongoing research around the world.

BEYOND THE CONTINUA

Beyond Philadelphia, the continua model has been applied in a range of contexts and to a variety of issues in the United States and internationally, including interpretation of language minority student voices in Arkansas (Lincoln, 2003), analysis of biliteracy development among Latino youth in New York City (Mercado, 2003), bilingual teacher preparation in the U.S. southwest (Pérez, Flores, & Strecker, 2003), bilingual education in India (Basu, 2003), multilingual classroom teaching in South Africa (Bloch & Alexander, 2003), and language planning and the Welsh National Curriculum in Wales (Baker, 2003). Its usefulness in a variety of contexts and for a range of purposes is testimony to a certain versatility, enabled perhaps by its complexity. That same complexity has been one of the drawbacks of the model as well; it is a difficult framework to grasp intuitively and has proven resistant to easy representation. Similarly, existing representations of the continua model (e.g. Figs. 13.1, 13.2, 13.3) are sometimes misinterpreted as conveying a static, bounded, dichotomized view rather than the fluid, flexible, and infinitely expanding model intended. Those who struggle with the framework long enough to grasp the dynamic nature of the intersecting and nested continua, however, eventually conclude that its complexity is also perhaps its greatest virtue, in that the phenomena it intends to represent are complex and too easily reified by over-simplification.

There remain unanswered questions about the continua model. It has proven useful in ethnographic research, but has yet to be tested as a basis for experimental or survey research. Likewise, it originated as a descriptive framework, but has evolved toward predictive and explanatory uses. One researcher looking at the policies behind Korean-English two-way immersion programs in the United States has suggested that the continua model "provides descriptive power to describe the details of the policies, predictive power to anticipate language-acquisition policy outcomes, and explanatory power to elucidate why certain outcomes are anticipated" (Jeon, 2003, p. 138). Such claims need further exploration through continuing research in a wide range of settings and circumstances.

More importantly, basic questions about biliteracy remain unanswered or partially answered. Questions like: Who becomes biliterate and where, when, how, and why do they do so? How can biliteracy best be acquired, nurtured, maintained, and promoted? What is the role of the family, the home, the school, the community, and the wider society in biliteracy acquisition and use? It is my hope that the continua model can contribute to answering some of these questions more fully than they have been answered up to now.

ENDNOTE

1. I use the expanded term *language varieties* to denote that the phenomena of bilingualism and biliteracy may exist not only across different lan-

guages, but also across different dialects of the same language, or different language varieties of whatever kind.

2. Other possible visualizations of the model that I have considered or that have been suggested to me include: a twelve-edged box with the four clusters of continua intersecting at each of the four corners; a bucket of paint with multiple colors mixed in different proportions; a set of refracting lenses lined up one behind the other; a sphere with all the continua intersecting in the middle, or an anchor attached to a rope of twelve intertwining strands. The point is not to try to pin down the model with one visual representation, but to use a variety of visual representations as ways of thinking about the complex relationships among the continua.

REFERENCES

Baker, C. (2003). Biliteracy and transliteracy in Wales: Language planning and the Welsh National Curriculum. In N. H. Hornberger (Ed.), *Continua of biliteracy: An ecological framework for educational policy, research, and practice in multilingual settings* (pp. 71-90). Clevedon, UK: Multilingual Matters.

Bakhtin, M. (1981). *The dialogic imagination*. Austin: University of Texas Press.

Barton, D. (1994a). Literacy practices and literacy events. In M. Hamilton, D. Barton, & R. Ivanic (Eds.), *Worlds of literacy* (pp. vii-x). Clevedon, UK: Multilingual Matters.

Barton, D. (1994b). Sustaining local literacies. *Language and Education, 8*(1&2).

Barton, D., & Hamilton, M. (1998). *Local literacies*. London: Routledge.

Basu, V. (2003). "Be quick of eye and slow of tongue": An analysis of two bilingual schools in New Delhi. In N. H. Hornberger (Ed.), *Continua of biliteracy: An ecological framework for educational policy, research, and practice in multilingual settings* (pp. 291-311). Clevedon, UK: Multilingual Matters.

Blackledge, A. (2000). Power relations and the social construction of "literacy" and "illiteracy": The experience of Bangladeshi women in Birmingham. In M. Martin-Jones & K. Jones (Eds.), *Multilingual literacies: Reading and writing different worlds* (pp. 55-69). Philadelphia: John Benjamins.

Bloch, C., & Alexander, N. (2003). A luta continua: The relevance of the continua of biliteracy to South African multilingual schools. In N. H. Hornberger (Ed.), *Continua of biliteracy: An ecological framework for educational policy, research, and practice in multilingual settings* (pp. 91-121). Clevedon, UK: Multilingual Matters.

Bourdieu, P. (1977). *Outline of a theory of practice*. Cambridge: Cambridge University Press.

Cahnmann, M. (2001). *Shifting metaphors: Of war and reimagination in the bilingual classroom*. Unpublished doctoral thesis, University of Pennsylvania, Philadelphia.

Camitta, M. (1993). Vernacular writing: Varieties of literacy among Philadelphia high school students. In B. Street (Ed.), *Cross-cultural approaches to literacy* (pp. 228-246). New York: Cambridge University Press.

Castanheira, M. L., Crawford, T., Green J. L., & Dixon, C. N. (2001). Interactional ethnography: An approach to studying the social construction of literate practices. *Linguistics and Education, 11*(4), 353-400.

Clark, R., Fairclough, N., Ivanic, R., & Martin-Jones, M. (1990). Critical language awareness part I: A critical review of three current approaches to language awareness. *Language and Education, 4*(4), 249-260.

Clark, R., Fairclough, N., Ivanic, R., & Martin-Jones, M. (1991). Critical language awareness Part II: Towards critical alternatives. *Language and Education, 5*(1), 41-54.

Collins, J. (1995). Literacy and literacies. *Annual Review of Anthropology, 24,* 75-93.

Cope, B., & Kalantzis, M. (Eds.). (2000). *Multiliteracies: Literacy learning and the design of social futures.* London: Routledge.

Cummins, J. (1981). Biliteracy, language proficiency, and educational programs. In J. Edwards (Ed.), *The social psychology of reading* (pp. 131-146). Silver Spring, MD: Institute of Modern Languages.

Edelsky, C. (1986). *Writing in a bilingual program: Había una Vez.* Norwood, NJ: Ablex.

Erickson, F. (1991). Advantages and disadvantages of qualitative research design on foreign language research. In B. F. Freed (Ed.), *Foreign language acquisition research and the classroom* (pp. 338-353). Lexington, MA: D. C. Heath.

Fairclough, N. (1995). *Critical discourse analysis: The critical study of language.* London, UK: Longman.

Fishman, J. A. (1970). *Sociolinguistics: A brief introduction.* Rowley, MA: Newbury House.

Fishman, J. A. (1971). The sociology of language: An interdisciplinary social science approach to language in society. *Advances in the Sociology of Language, 1,* 217-258.

Fishman, J. A. (1980). *Ethnocultural dimensions in the acquisition and retention of biliteracy.* Paper presented at the Mina Shaughnessy Memorial Conference.

Fishman, J. A., Riedler-Berger, C., & Steele, J. M. (1985). Ethnocultural dimensions in the acquisition and retention of biliteracy: A comparative ethnography of four New York City schools. In J. A. Fishman (Ed.), *The rise and fall of the ethnic revival* (pp. 377-383). Berlin, New York, Amsterdam: Mouton.

Floriani, A., Heras, A. I., Franquiz, M., Yeager, B., Jennings, L. B., Green, J. L., & Dixon, C. N. (1995). Two languages, one community: An examination of educational opportunities. In R. F. Macías & R. G. G. Ramos (Eds.), *Changing schools for changing students: An anthology of research on language minorities, schools, & society* (pp. 63-106). Santa Barbara, CA: Linguistic Minority Research Institute.

Floyd-Tenery, M. (1995). Teacher as mediator. *Practicing Anthropology, 17*(3), 10-12.

Gal, S. (1989). Language and political economy. *Annual Review of Anthropology, 18,* 345-367.

Gee, J. P. (1990). *Social linguistics and literacies: Ideology in discourses.* London: Falmer Press.

Genesee, F. (1980). Bilingualism and biliteracy: A study of cross-cultural contact in a bilingual community. In J. R. Edwards (Ed.), *The social psychology of reading.* Silver Spring, MD: Institute of Modern Languages.

Goldstein, T. (1997). Language research methods and critical pedagogy. In N. H. Hornberger & D. Corson (Eds.), *Research methods in language and education* (pp. 67-77). Dordrecht: Kluwer Academic Publishers.

González , N., & Arnot-Hopffer, E. (2003). Voices of the children: Language and literacy ideologies in a dual-language immersion program. In S. Wortham & B. Rymes (Eds.), *The linguistic anthropology of education* (pp. 213-243). Westport, CT: Greenwood Press.

Goodman, K., & Goodman, Y. (1983). Reading and writing relationships: Pragmatic functions. *Language Arts, 60*(5), 590-599.

Goodman, K., Goodman, Y., & Flores, B. (1979). *Reading in the bilingual classroom: Literacy and biliteracy* (ERIC Doc No. ED 181 725 ed.). Arlington, VA: NCBE.

Green, J. L., & Dixon, C. N. (Eds.). (1993). Talking knowledge into being: Discursive and social practices in classrooms. *Linguistics and Education, 5*(3&4).

Green, J. L., & Dixon, C. N. (1998). *Ethnographics and sociolinguistics: Mutually informing theories.* Unpublished manuscript.

Gregory, E., & Williams, A. (2000). Work or play? "Unofficial" literacies in the lives of two East London communities. In M. Martin-Jones & K. Jones (Eds.), *Multilingual literacies: Reading and writing different worlds* (pp. 37-54). Philadelphia, PA: John Benjamins.

Gumperz, J. J. (1982). *Discourse strategies.* Cambridge: Cambridge University Press.

Gutiérrez, K. D., Baquedano-López, P., & Tejeda, C. (1999). Rethinking diversity: Hybridity and hybrid language practices in the third space. *Mind, Culture, and Activity: An International Journal, 6*(4), 286-303.

Heath, S. B. (1982). What no bedtime story means: Narrative skills at home and school. *Language in Society, 11*(1), 49-76.

Heath, S. B. (1983). *Ways with words: Language, life and work in communities and classrooms.* Cambridge, UK: Cambridge University Press.

Hornberger, N. H. (1989a). Continua of biliteracy. *Review of Educational Research, 59*(3), 271-296.

Hornberger, N. H. (1989b). Trámites and transportes: The acquisition of second language communicative competence for one speech event in Puno, Peru. *Applied Linguistics, 10*(2), 214-230.

Hornberger, N. H. (1990). Creating successful learning contexts for bilingual literacy. *Teachers College Record, 92*(2), 212-229.

Hornberger, N. H. (1991). Extending enrichment bilingual education: Revisiting typologies and redirecting policy. In O. Garcia (Ed.), *Bilingual education Focusschrift in honor of Joshua A. Fishman on the occasion of his 65th birthday* (pp. 215-234). Philadelphia: John Benjamins Publishers.

Hornberger, N. H. (1992). Biliteracy contexts, continua, and contrasts: Policy and curriculum for Cambodian and Puerto Rican students in Philadelphia. *Education and Urban Society, 24*(2), 196-211.

Hornberger, N. H. (Ed.). (1996). *Indigenous literacies in the Americas: Language planning from the bottom up.* Berlin: Mouton.

Hornberger, N. H. (2000). Afterword: Multilingual literacies, literacy practices, and the continua of biliteracy. In M. Martin-Jones & K. Jones (Eds.), *Multilingual literacies: Reading and writing different worlds* (pp. 353-367). Philadelphia, PA: John Benjamins.

Hornberger, N. H. (2002). Multilingual language policies and the continua of biliteracy: An ecological approach. *Language Policy, 1*(1), 27-51.

Hornberger, N. H. (Ed.) (2003). *Continua of biliteracy: An ecological framework for educational policy, research, and practice in multilingual settings.* Clevedon, UK: Multilingual Matters.

Hornberger, N. H., & Hardman, J. (1994). Literacy as cultural practice and cognitive skill: Biliteracy in a Cambodian adult ESL class and a Puerto Rican GED program. In D. Spener (Ed.), *Adult biliteracy in the United States* (pp. 147-169). Washington DC: Center for Applied Linguistics.

Hornberger, N. H., & Micheau, C. (1993). "Getting far enough to like it": Biliteracy in the middle school. *Peabody Journal of Education, 69*(1), 30-53.

Hornberger, N. H., & Skilton-Sylvester, E. (2000). Revisiting the continua of biliteracy: International and critical perspectives. *Language and Education: An International Journal, 14*(2), 96-122.

Hudelson, S. (1984). Kan Yu Ret an Rayt en Ingles: Children become literate in English as a second language. *TESOL Quarterly, 18*(2), 221-238.

Hymes, D. H. (1964). Introduction: Toward ethnographies of communication. *American Anthropologist, 66*(6), 1-34.

Hymes, D. H. (1968). The ethnography of speaking. In J. A. Fishman (Ed.), *Readings in the sociology of language* (pp. 99-138). The Hague: Mouton.

Hymes, D. H. (1972a). Models of the interaction of language and social life. In J. Gumperz & D. Hymes (Eds.), *Directions in sociolinguistics: The ethnography of communication* (pp. 35-71). New York: Holt, Rinehart, & Winston.

Hymes, D. H. (1972b). On communicative competence. In J. B. Pride & J. Holmes (Eds.), *Sociolinguistics: Selected readings* (pp. 269-293). Harmondsworth: Penguin Books.

Hymes, D. H. (1974a). *Foundations in sociolinguistics: An ethnographic approach.* Philadelphia: University of Pennsylvania Press.

Hymes, D. H. (1974b). Ways of speaking. In R. Bauman & J. Sherzer (Eds.), *Explorations in the ethnography of speaking* (pp. 433-451). New York: Cambridge University Press.

Jeon, M. (2003). Searching for a comprehensive rationale for two-way immersion. In N. H. Hornberger (Ed.), *Continua of biliteracy: An ecological framework for educational policy, research, and practice in multilingual settings* (pp. 122-144). Clevedon, UK: Multilingual Matters.

Jones, K. (2000). Texts, mediation and social relations in a bureaucratised world. In M. Martin-Jones & K. Jones (Eds.), *Multilingual literacies: Reading and writing different worlds* (pp. 209-228). Philadelphia, PA: John Benjamins.

Kelly, L. G. (1969). *The description and measurement of bilingualism: An international seminar.* Toronto: University of Toronto Press.

Knobel, M. (1999). *Everyday literacies: Students, discourse, and social practice.* New York: Peter Lang.

Lado, R., Hanson, I., & D'Emilio, T. (1980). Biliteracy for bilingual children by Grade 1: The SED Center Preschool Reading Project, Phase 1. In J. Alatis (Ed.), *Current issues in bilingual education* (pp. 162-167). Washington, DC: Georgetown University Press.

Lankshear, C. (1997). *Changing literacies.* Philadelphia, PA: Open University Press.

Lave, J., & Wenger, E. (1991). *Situated learning: Legitimate peripheral participation.* Cambridge, UK: Cambridge University Press.

Leap, W. L. (1991). Pathways and barriers to Indian language literacy-building on the Northern Ute reservation. *Anthropology and Education Quarterly, 22*(1), 21-41.

Lincoln, F. (2003). Language education planning and policy in Middle America: Students' voices. In N. H. Hornberger (Ed.), *Continua of biliteracy: An ecological framework for educational policy, research, and practice in multilingual settings* (pp. 147-165). Clevedon, UK: Multilingual Matters.

Martin-Jones, M., & Jones, K. (Eds.). (2000). *Multilingual literacies: Reading and writing different worlds.* Philadelphia, PA: John Benjamins.

May, S. A. (1997). Critical ethnography. In N. H. Hornberger & D. Corson (Eds.), *Research methods in language and education* (pp. 197-206). Dordrecht: Kluwer Academic Publishers.

Measures, E., Quell, C., & Wells, G. (1997). A sociocultural perspective on classroom discourse. In B. Davies & D. Corson (Eds.), *Oral discourse and education* (pp. 21-29). Dordrecht: Kluwer Academic Publishers.

Mercado, C. (2003). Biliteracy development among Latino youth in New York City communities: An unexploited potential. In N. H. Hornberger (Ed.), *Continua of biliteracy: An ecological framework for educational policy, research, and practice in multilingual settings* (pp. 166-186). Clevedon, UK: Multilingual Matters.

Moll, L., & Díaz, S. (1985). Ethnographic pedagogy: Promoting effective bilingual instruction. In E.E. Garcia & R. V. Padilla (Eds.), *Advances in bilingual education research* (pp. 127-149). Tucson: University of Arizona Press.

Moll, L., & González, N. (1994). Lessons from research with language-minority children. *Journal of Reading Behavior, 26*(4), 439-456.

New London Group [Cazden, C., Cope, B., Fairclough, N., Gee, J., Kalantzis, M., Kress, G., Luke, A., Luke, C., Michaels, S., & Nakata, M.] (1996). A pedagogy of multiliteracies: Designing social futures. *Harvard Educational Review, 66*(1), 60 -92.

Niyekawa, A. M. (1983). Biliteracy acquisition and its sociocultural effects. In M. C. Chang (Ed.), *Asian-and Pacific-American perspectives in bilingual education* (pp. 97-119). New York: Teachers College Press.

Norton, B. (1997). Critical discourse research. In N. H. Hornberger & D. Corson (Eds.), *Research methods in language and education* (pp. 207-216). Dordrecht: Kluwer Academic Publishers.

Norton Peirce, B. (1995). Social identity, investment, and language learning. *TESOL Quarterly, 29*(1), 9-31.

Pérez, B., Flores, B., & Strecker, S. (2003). Biliteracy teacher education in the US Southwest. In N. H. Hornberger (Ed.), *Continua of biliteracy: An ecological framework for educational policy, research, and practice in multilingual settings* (pp. 207-231). Clevedon, UK: Multilingual Matters.

Pica, T., Holliday, L., Lewis, N., & Morgenthaler, L. (1989). Comprehensible output as an outcome of linguistic demands on the learner. *Studies in Second Language Acquisition, 11*, 63-90.

Pride, J. B., & Holmes, J. (1972). *Sociolinguistics: Selected readings.* Harmondsworth, UK: Penguin.

Rampton, M. B. H. (1992). Scope for empowerment in sociolinguistics? In D. Cameron, E. Frazer, P. Harvey, M. B. H. Rampton, & K. Richardson (Eds.), *Researching language: Issues of power and method* (pp. 29-64). London: Routledge.

Rampton, B. (1995). *Crossing: Language and ethnicity among adolescents.* London: Longman.

Reder, S. M. (1987). Comparative aspects of functional literacy development: Three ethnic American communities. In D. Wagner (Ed.), *Future of literacy in a changing world* (pp. 250-270). New York: Pergamon.

Reder, S. (1994). Practice-engagement theory: A sociocultural approach to literacy across languages and cultures. In B. M. Ferdman, R. Weber, & A. G. Ramirez (Eds.), *Literacy across languages and cultures* (pp. 33-74). Albany: SUNY Press.

Saville-Troike, M. (1989). *The ethnography of communication: An introduction* (2nd ed.). New York: Basil Blackwell.

Schiffrin, D. (1996). Interactional sociolinguistics. In S. L. McKay & N. H. Hornberger (Eds.), *Sociolinguistics and language teaching* (pp. 307-328). New York: Cambridge University Press.

Scribner, S., & Cole, M. (1981). *The psychology of literacy.* Cambridge, MA: Harvard University Press.

Shuman, A. (1993). Collaborative writing: Appropriating power or reproducing authority? In B. Street (Ed.), *Cross-cultural approaches to literacy* (pp. 247-271). New York: Cambridge University Press.

Skilton-Sylvester, E. (1997). *Inside, outside, and in-between: Identities, literacies, and educational policies in the lives of Cambodian women and girls in Philadelphia.* Unpublished doctoral dissertation., University of Pennsylvania, Philadelphia.

Spolsky, B. (1981). Bilingualism and biliteracy. *Canadian Modern Language Review, 37*(3), 475-485.

Street, B. (1984). *Literacy in theory and practice.* New York: Cambridge University Press.

Street, B. V. (Ed.). (1993). *Cross-cultural approaches to literacy.* Cambridge, UK: Cambridge University Press.

Street, B. V. (1994). What is meant by local literacies? *Language and Education, 8*(1&2), 9-17.

Street, B. V. (1995). *Social literacies: Critical approaches to literacy in development, ethnography, and education.* London: Longman.

Street, B. V. (Ed.). (2000a). *Literacy and development: Ethnographic perspectives.* London: Routledge.

Street, B. V. (2000b). Literacy events and literacy practices: Theory and practice in the New Literacy Studies. In M. Martin-Jones & K. Jones (Eds.), *Multilingual literacies: Reading and writing different worlds* (pp. 17-29). Philadelphia, PA: John Benjamins.

Swain, M. (1985). Communicative competence: Some roles of comprehensible input and comprehensible output in its development. In S. Gass & C. Madden (Eds.), *Input in second language acquisition* (pp. 235-253). Rowley, MA: Newbury House.

Szwed, J. F. (1981). The ethnography of literacy. In M. F. Whiteman (Ed.), *Writing: The nature, development, and teaching of written communication* (Vol. 1, pp. 13-23). Hillsdale, NJ: Erlbaum.

Valdés, G. (1983). Planning for biliteracy. In L. Elías-Olivares (Ed.), *Spanish in the US setting: Beyond the southwest* (pp. 259-262). National Clearinghouse for Bilingual Education.

Wertsch, J. (Ed.). (1981). *The concept of activity in Soviet Psychology.* Armonk, NY: Sharpe.

Wertsch, J. V. (1991). *Voices of the mind: A sociocultural approach to mediated action.* Cambridge, MA: Harvard University Press.

Zentella, A. C. (1997). *Growing up bilingual: Puerto Rican children in New York.* Malden, MA: Blackwell.

14

Studying the Discursive Construction of Texts in Classrooms Through Interactional Ethnography

Carol Dixon
Judith Green
University of California, Santa Barbara
with members of Santa Barbara Classroom Discourse Group
and Lois Brandts, El Camino Elementary School, Goleta California[1]

Dear Thomas

We know you have snow. We have sun. Our school is called Hollister. We know you are from Montana. We are learning about rainforests. What are you learning? We do not have rattlesnakes. I am six years old.

Love,

Lauren

In this chapter we present an approach to identifying *traces of discourse and experiential resources* on which Lauren drew in producing this text. This approach demonstrates the need for historical and situational analyses and how these analyses can be undertaken through an integration of ethnographic and discourse analysis approaches. Central to this approach is a theoretical perspective on the social construction of knowledge and on events and knowledge within groups as intertextually and intercontextually tied across time. The past two decades have seen a shift in focus of research on the social construction of knowledge in educational settings. At first, educational researchers sought to construct arguments *that knowledge was socially constructed*, drawing on extant theories across diverse fields, including Vygotsky (Reiber & Carton, 1987), Wallon (Voyat, 1984), and Piaget (1924/2001) in psychology; Gumperz and Hymes (1972/1986) in sociolinguistics; and Garfinkel (1984) and Berger and Luckmann (1966) in sociology. (See Bloome & Bailey, 1992; Cook-Gumperz & Gumperz, 1992; Heap, 1992; Moll, 1992, in the first edition of this volume for additional sources.) These initial arguments have led to the development of a growing body of theoretical work and to the acceptance of the concept that knowledge as socially constructed, is an a priori assumption (Heap, 1995). Educational researchers working within this perspective continue to extend what is meant by this premise, while turning to questions of *how social construction is accomplished* and *how such construction influences* the access students have to academic knowledge and to participation in subsequent social and academic situations. Scholars seek research perspectives that will enable them to examine the complexity of everyday life in and through which knowledge is constructed. This shift has also led to the development of a broad range of theoretical perspectives. It also resulted in exploration of additional traditions that can inform understandings of how knowledge is constructed and how it becomes consequential for students in classrooms across years of schooling (see chapters by Beach, Bloome, Freebody, Hornberger, Ivanic, Mahn & John-Steiner, in this volume, for examples).

For work within our research community, the Santa Barbara Classroom Discourse Group, this has meant identifying a coherent set of theoretical perspectives that frame our study of "text" construction and interpretation, an orienting framework that we have labeled *Interactional Ethnography* (Castanheira, Crawford, Green, & Dixon, 2000; Putney, Green, Dixon, Durán, & Yeager, 2000; Rex, Green, & Dixon, 1997; Rex & McEachen, 1999). This framework brings together theoretical constructs on the study of culture, communication, social interactions, and the social construction of knowledge, classroom life, and literacy, among others. These constructs provide a systematic and theoretically driven approach, a logic of inquiry, to entering the world of a social group and to examining what members need to know, produce, predict, and act to participate in socially appropriate ways (Birdwhistell, 1977; Heath, 1982; Spradley, 1980). In other words, such constructs provide a means of locating and identifying emic or insider knowledge necessary to engage in the events of everyday life within the group. This is achieved without breaking the social norms and expectations, roles and relationships, or rights and obligations that define members' knowledge and practices (Green, Dixon, & Zaharlick, 2002).

The Interactional Ethnographic framework provides a way of viewing Lauren's text, and other texts produced in classrooms, as historically and situationally constructed artifacts. From this perspective, Lauren can be viewed as the "author" of her text, but the words, practices of text construction, and content of the text that Lauren chose to include were not "her words, practices or content" alone. They were *words, practices, and content* that had been made available to her in the events of classroom life (Bloome, 1985a, 1985b, 1987; Cazden, 1988; Cazden, John, & Hymes, 1972; Edwards & Mercer, 1987; Edwards & Westgate, 1994; Gee & Green, 1998; Green & Harker, 1988; Green & Wallat, 1981; Guzzetti & Hynd, 1998; Hicks, 1995; Lemke, 1990; Mehan, 1979).[2] As such, the words, practices, and content were embued with the history of the group in which Lauren was a member (Bakhtin, 1986; Fairclough, 1993). For as Ivanic (1994, 1997) argued, to construct this text, Lauren chose among the discourses available to her, and in making these choices, she inscribed more than a simple message. She was constructing her identity as a writer, her understandings of the activity in which she was engaged, and her memberships in this and other communities. In other words, as Bakhtin (1986) and, more recently, Fairclough (1993) and others (e.g., Barthes, 1975; Bloome & Egan-Robertson, 1993; Kristeva, 1986) argued, a text contains traces of other historical meanings and texts on which writers (speakers) draw to construct the present text.

The Interactional Ethnographic approach to the exploration of knowledge construction in classroom settings provides a set of theoretical constructs and related principles of analysis for examining traces in the texts of classroom life, how students take up and use these texts (oral, written, and visual) as resources in accomplishing new tasks, and how these texts are *talked (acted) into being collectively and individually.* Two questions guided our analysis of Lauren's text recorded on a videotape:

1. What was immediately available prior to her production of the text that shaped her construction and presentation of this text to the group?
2. What traces of earlier texts (those across time and events) are visible in the current text?

These questions provided a means of exploring what students and the teacher jointly constructed and what cultural knowledge they developed through their sustaining interactions across time and events. Our task as researchers was to apply our theoretical lens and methodological approach to identify and understand the norms and expectations, roles and relationships, and rights and obligations of membership. We examined the social and cultural practices on which members drew to guide their work together to construct the opportunities for learning afforded members of this class community. As part of this exploration, we demonstrate the potential of this approach for studying issues of identity formulation, construction of content knowledge, and the development of academic practices. In demonstrating this approach, we also describe further advances in the last decade in theoretical understandings that guide work within the Santa Barbara Classroom Discourse Group on the social construction of knowledge, community and principles of practice in classrooms.[3]

FRAMING THE ARGUMENTS: THE DISCURSIVE CONSTRUCTION OF TEXTS

Our orienting framework is based on a set of constructs derived from our ongoing ethnographic research studies in K–12 classrooms since 1990. This research examines the local construction of culture, communication, knowledge, and social interaction in classrooms, and draws on theoretical perspectives from other bodies of work and from other programs of research. This framework consists of a set of constructs forming a logic of inquiry that guides us in making informed decisions about what data to collect, how, when, where, under what conditions, and for what purposes. This logic of inquiry orients us to particular analytic traditions we then use to frame our questions and undertake our analyses. The first set of constructs is related to the collective construction of everyday life in a classroom:

- Members of a class jointly construct patterned ways of acting, interacting, perceiving, and interpreting everyday life (Santa Barbara Classroom Discourse Group, 1992a).
- These patterned ways become cultural practices and processes that members use as resources for participating in and constructing the everyday events of life within their group (Putney et al., 2000).
- Through these processes and practices, members develop a history of activity, practice and content as well as a language of the classroom that becomes common knowledge, and thus, a material resource for members of the class (Bazerman & Prior, this volume; Engestrom, 1987; Lee & Ball, this volume; Lin, 1993; Santa Barbara Classroom Discourse Group 1992a, 1992b).
- Over time, such patterns and practices become ordinary and invisible to members unless a norm or expectation is broken or a member acts in unexpected ways—that is, an explicit or implicit frame clash occurs (Gumperz & Tannen, 1979; Mehan, 1979).

- When an overt or public frame clash occurs, members signal to each other the expected norms and expectations, their intentions, and their interpretations and repairs may be undertaken (Santa Barbara Classroom Discourse Group, 1992b).
- When a frame clash is on a tacit level, members may or may not view it as a difference in interpretation, understanding, or knowledge of the expected processes, content or practices. Thus, they may fail to repair or renegotiate with other(s) or may assess the participation of others negatively.
- The patterns and practices of life within a group are never fixed but are always being (re)formulated and (re)negotiated between individuals and the group as they work collectively to construct the content, context, meanings, and events of everyday life necessary to meet individual and collective goals (Putney et al., 2000).

These constructs form a basis for understanding the dynamic and developing nature of *collective life* within a classroom and the interrelationships between individual and collective development (Souza Lima, 1995).[4] In classrooms knowledge that is constructed is local knowledge (Geertz, 1983) and common knowledge at the same time (Edwards & Mercer, 1987). From this perspective, in each classroom situated definitions of what it means to be a reader, a writer, a historian, a peer, a teacher, a student, a group, an artist, a scientist and/or a mathematician are constructed within and across events of everyday life (e.g., Baker, 2001; Brilliant-Mills, 1993; Floriani, 1993; Heras, 1993; Kelly & Crawford, 1997; Lin, 1993; Putney et al., 2000, Yeager, Floriani, & Green, 1998). Additionally, members shape what counts as appropriate roles and relationships, content, and topics for talking and writing. The constructed topics and relationships then, in turn, define ways of writing or reading together (Bloome, 1985a, 1985b; Bloome & Egan-Robertson, 1993; Cochran-Smith, 1984; Floriani, 1993) along with what counts as text (Golden, 1988, 1990; Kelly, Crawford, & Green, 2001; Rex et al., 1997; Tuyay, Floriani, Yeager, Dixon, & Green, 1995), as disciplinary content (Brilliant-Mills, 1993; Kelly & Crawford, 1996; Lemke, 1990; Rex & McEachen, 1999), as curriculum (Chandler, 1992; Christie, 1995; Weade, 1992), and as opportunities for learning (Tuyay, Jennings, & Dixon, 1995). In other words, the patterns of life in a classroom are not fixed. They are constantly in a process of coming into being through the actions and interactions among members.

The previous discussion focused on constructs that frame development and activity within a group or collective. They also provide a framework for understanding "context" as produced through interactions and as shaping a text that guides an individual's actions within the group (Duranti & Goodwin, 1992; Erickson & Shultz, 1981). To frame further the relation-

ships between individual and collective activity and development, we draw
on a series of premises derived primarily from work on discourse analysis
and interactional sociolinguistics (see Gee & Green, 1998; Hicks, 1995, for
a summary of related work). This body of work argues the following:

- Members of a group act in concerted ways.
- Through these actions and interactions, members construct a referential system and discourse conventions that individuals may and
  do appropriate both to participate in and to contribute to the construction of the group activities as well as to accomplish their own
  purposes.
- Through their choice of language, discourse conventions, and
  actions, individuals within a group signal to each other their understandings of the norms and expectations of the group.
- As members interact they also signal to each other how they have
  elected to take up a position within the group as well as how they
  are attempting to position others or how they respond to the
  attempts at positioning by others.
- Through these interactions, members constitute the phases of activity, which, in turn, shape what participants then construct in subsequent activity. This process is recursive in that the text participants
  are constructing is also shaped by and shapes the actions and interactions among members (as well as the evolving text itself).

This set of constructs adds to our framework ways of understanding
how individuals, through their communication, contribute to the development of the group, and how, in turn, the group's actions and communications contribute to the construction of what individuals do, how they do it,
and what they say within the group. Viewed in this way, language is of a
group. Individual action is shaped by and shapes what counts as language,
communication, and action as well as what language is used. Thus, we speak
of the individual-within-the-collective, not of an independent being, and of
the class-as-a-collectivity, not merely a physical collection of individuals.[5]
To further explicate how we understand this complex and dynamic relationship between individual and collective, we consider the ways in which
the discourse of the classroom can be viewed as a particular type of conversation (Green & Wallat, 1979, 1981). Drawing on work in sociolinguistics
and discourse analysis, we see conversations as goal-directed, as dynamic,
and as collaborative. According to Grice (1975), to have a conversation,
partners must cooperate as well as act with felicity.
This is particularly true of instructional conversations in classrooms
where students are expected to respond to teacher's questions or to allow
others turns within the group (Christie, 1995; Green & Wallat, 1981; Lin,

1993; Rex et al., 1997). Additionally, Gumperz (1986) argued that members of a group bring linguistic, social, and cultural presuppositions on which they rely in new situations to guide their own inferences and actions, and their understandings of those of others. Furthermore, the actions and communications of the teacher, as a member of the classroom, are shaped by the responses (verbal and nonverbal) of the students, just as those of the student are shaped by the teacher's (and other students and participants) verbal and nonverbal actions and responses.

As Bakhtin (1986) argued, people do not speak and listeners merely listen. From this perspective, speakers take into consideration what they know and understand about listeners. They speak in light of their interpretations of the other. Hearers also listen with a presumed understanding of speakers. Such understandings may include presuppositions about common knowledge that members have, may be based on roles and relationships that are appropriate within this situation, as well as draw on social, linguistic, cultural, and contextual presuppositions among others.

A parallel to this process can be drawn for writing in classroom settings. In a classroom, a writer constructs a text within a context that is produced in and through the communication and actions between teacher and students or among students (Floriani, 1993; Putney et al., 2000; Tuyay, Jennings, & Dixon, 1995). The talk that precedes and surrounds a text becomes a resource that writers use when developing their texts. Additionally, as the writers construct their texts, they draw on inferences about the task, on the prior history they have with similar tasks, and on their interpretation of expected outcomes, as well as on the shared history of prior events, actions, content, and cultural practices they have jointly constructed over time with others in the class community (Bloome & Egan-Robertson, 1993). Viewed in this way, a written text is both locally produced and historically shaped through the choices and actions of the author(s). (See McHoul, 1978, for a similar argument on reading as a production of text.)

The importance of understanding the situated and historical nature of texts can be found in Bakhtin's (1986) argument:

> Sooner or later what is heard and actively understood will find its response in the subsequent speech or behavior of the listener. In most cases, genres of complex cultural communication are intended precisely for this kind of actively responsive understanding with delayed action. Everything that we have said here also pertains to written and read speech, with the appropriate adjustments and additions. (p. 60)

His argument that most genres of *complex cultural communication* are meant for delayed response is central to understanding student performance in the classroom and is a primary focus of our analysis of Lauren's letter. In this chapter, we are using the concept of genres in complex ways.[6]

The constructs presented in this section often began as theoretical issues to be examined but have since become part of the logic of inquiry guiding our research within and across classrooms. For as Heap (1995) asserts, once constructs are identified within the ethnographic data, they become a form of *a priori claims* in subsequent studies about the social accomplishment and consequences of everyday life in classrooms.

METHODOLOGICAL ISSUES AND APPROACH

Our analytic goal is to understand Lauren's text as members of her classroom might, and to offer evidence from the patterns and practices of everyday life within the group that supports or challenges our interpretations. To accomplish this task and to answer the questions just posed, we engaged in a process of backward and forward mapping across time and events (Tuyay et al., 1995). Backward and forward mapping, as we are using these terms, involves a process of tracing intertextual (Bloome & Egan-Robertson, 1993; Fairclough, 1993; Kristeva, 1986) and intercontextual relationships (Floriani, 1993) among events. The difference in these two constructs is found in their focus. Intertextuality examines the links among texts produced by various members of a classroom community. Intercontextuality refers to the links among cultural practices that members develop and use to shape the text being constructed. From this perspective, we view "context" as being "with text"—as in Spanish, contexto (Santa Barbara Classroom Discourse Group, 1995; for a broader discussion of context that informs our work see Duranti & Goodwin, 1992). Thus, intercontextuality refers to the cultural processes and practices members use to construct and interpret texts within and across events (Floriani, 1993). Analysis of intercontextuality, therefore, focuses on identifying those processes and practices members draw on from one context to another to construct the events and texts of everyday life.

To identify an intertextual or intercontextual relationship we adapt the following criteria proposed by Bloome and his colleagues (Bloome & Bailey, 1992; Bloome & Egan-Robertson, 1993):

1. It (the text or the contextual practice) is proposed by members of the class community in the event being constructed.
2. It is interactionally accomplished, recognized, and acknowledged through actions or talk of participants within the local event being constructed.

3. It is socially significant to the actors and/or actions of actors within the event being constructed.

As Bloome and Egan-Robertson (1993) argued, these criteria provide a means of distinguishing between texts that are merely juxtaposed by researchers for their own purposes and those that are used as linked resources by members. By applying these criteria as we engaged in a process of forward and backward mapping from Lauren's text, we were able to identify events that formed the historical context and guided our analysis of intertextual and intercontextual resources Lauren drew on to construct her text.

Our approach began by locating a key speech event (Gumperz, 1986; see also Bloome, this volume) within the classroom in which a written text was being talked into being (i.e., Lauren's letter). Once the event and the text within the event were located, we then identified other events across days, weeks, and months that were part of the cycle of activity[7] in which Lauren's text was constructed and/or played a significant role. In the case of Lauren's letter, this cycle was referred to in class as the "Artifact Box." A cycle of activity is a series of linked events that collectively provide a means of achieving a goal within the classroom (Green & Meyer, 1991; Tuyay et al., 1995). Figure 14.1 provides a graphic representation of the major events constituting the Artifact Box cycle of activity and locates them within the timeline of the school year.

Once the cycle of activity was identified, we then examined those events that preceded or followed the key event for intertextual and intercontextual ties. In this way, we were able to locate links within and across this cycle of activity and related cycles and to examine which practices and processes were precursors to or supports for the text being analyzed. Figure 14.1 provides an overview of the events identified within the Artifact Box cycle of activity.

After identifying events of the cycle, we then returned to the day on which Lauren's letter was produced and constructed two types of representations of the events of that day: event maps with differing levels of detail, and transcripts of classroom discourse (see Green & Wallat, 1981). An event map represents the phases of activity constructed by participants as they work interactively to accomplish their goals for the event under construction (Green & Meyer, 1991). An event map is constructed by observing how time was spent, with whom, on what, for what purpose, when, where, and under what conditions (Green & Meyer, 1991; Green & Wallat, 1979; Green, Weade, & Graham, 1988; Santa Barbara Classroom Discourse Group, 1992a, 1992b). The level of specificity of information on an event map reflects the purpose for which the map was constructed (e.g., timelines, exploration of organizational patterns by activity, and identifica-

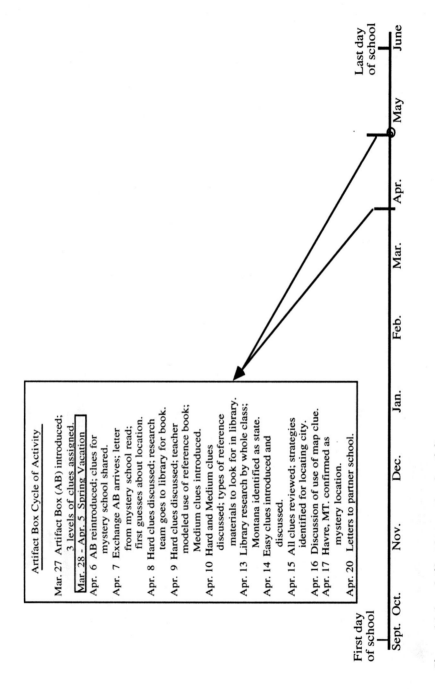

Artifact Box Cycle of Activity

Mar. 27 Artifact Box (AB) introduced;
        3 levels of clues assigned.
Mar. 28 - Apr. 5 Spring Vacation
Apr. 6 AB reintroduced; clues for
        mystery school shared.
Apr. 7 Exchange AB arrives; letter
        from mystery school read;
        first guesses about location.
Apr. 8 Hard clues discussed; research
        team goes to library for book.
Apr. 9 Hard clues discussed; teacher
        modeled use of reference book;
        Medium clues introduced.
Apr. 10 Hard and Medium clues
         discussed; types of reference
         materials to look for in library.
Apr. 13 Library research by whole class;
         Montana identified as state.
Apr. 14 Easy clues introduced and
         discussed.
Apr. 15 All clues reviewed; strategies
         identified for locating city.
Apr. 16 Discussion of use of map clue.
Apr. 17 Havre, MT. confirmed as
         mystery location.
Apr. 20 Letters to partner school.

First day
of school

Sept. Oct.   Nov.   Dec.   Jan.   Feb.   Mar.   Apr.   May   June

Last day
of school

Figure 14.1.   Artifact box cycle of activity.

358

tion of the range of practices and texts constructed within and across evolving events; Castanheira et al., 2000). Event maps, therefore, provide a macro-level (re)presentation of the range of activity that constitute an event or series of events.

The second type of (re)presentation constructed was a transcript of the moment-by-moment interactions among members of the collective as they acted in concerted ways to accomplish jointly the instructional goals of the activity among participants. This transcript was constructed using the discourse analysis approach developed by Green and her colleagues (Castanheira et al., 2000; Green & Wallat, 1979, 1981). The level of transcription in this paper focuses on the representation of talk in message, action, and turn units to explore what the teacher shapes for students as appropriate and expected actions. The talk is then presented graphically in columns (one or more) to reflect both the verbal and nonverbal actions among participants (e.g., teacher recording of talk in written form on blackboard; see Ochs, 1979).

These two types of representations constitute a researcher-constructed text that was then combined with videotape records, fieldnotes, and artifacts to develop our interpretations of the observed patterns of activity among members. Additionally, we returned to video records and other artifacts throughout this process to identify those texts and contexts that met the criteria for intertextuality and intercontextuality presented previously. Through this complex and interactive process the texture, and ebb and flow of life was maintained in ways not available in two dimensional texts. This analysis provided a basis for identifying the cultural practices Lauren drew on to construct her text.

TALKING TEXTS INTO BEING IN FIRST GRADE: AN ANALYSIS OF LETTER WRITING IN THE ARTIFACT BOX CYCLE OF ACTIVITY

The analyses in this section are presented as a series of *progressive disclosures* that move backward and then forward from the moment of Lauren's reading/presentation of her text to her classmates. Through these analyses we make visible intertextual and intercontextual ties constituting the body of local knowledge that members of the class and we, as researchers, needed to consider to understand what Lauren wrote. The analyses represent the interactive and responsive nature of ethnographic research and constitute the logic of inquiry of the analysis (Green et al., 2002). These analyses involved examining to whom she was writing, why she was writing on this day, why she included particular topics and linguistic forms in her letter, and why she adopted this particular format for letter writing. It also included examination of prior and past texts on which Lauren drew to construct her letter. Central to this particular phase of analysis is the examination of how a dialogic relationship (Bakhtin, 1986) between Lauren and the developing class texts was constructed and constituted in and through these events.

To explore the relationships between and among the actors we begin our analysis with a *frame grab*[8] from the video (Fig. 14.2) to make visible the physical space and the position of Lauren and the teacher. This frame grab provides a visual representation of the relationship and positions between the two key actors, and is used to contextualize the transcript of Lauren's text. In this figure, we see both Lauren and the teacher who was standing behind Lauren providing support for her as she reads her text. The coordinated actions of the two actors show that Lauren was the primary speaker/conversation partner for members of the class. The teacher, when she interacted with the class, did so to support Lauren's performance. From this angle of analysis, the two formed a whole, with Lauren oriented to her classmates and the letter, and the teacher oriented to Lauren. Thus, the members in the audience-position of this conversation could perceive Lauren and the teacher as forming an *"other."* The coordinated action provided information, that in this class, support for participation in a dialogic situation, and performance was not a test of individual ability. Examination of the videotape showed that this positioning of student and teacher was common across all letter readers on this day. Furthermore, analysis of the ethnographic records showed that this coordination of action was common for anyone sitting in the author's chair.[9] Reader position, therefore, was constituted by *student and teacher together as reader.*

The transcript accompanying the frame grab (Fig. 14.2) represents the *text that was talked into being* through Lauren's reading of her text to the class with the teacher's support; it does not represent the *text as written.* The written text itself was unavailable for copying because it was sent to Thomas on the day she read it to the class. However, both Lauren's text and the teacher's actions are available to us as they were to members of the class, through Lauren's oral rendition and what was visible. The text is presented in a message unit transcript to reflect the intonational contours of Lauren's rendering of her text. The teacher's actions are presented in a separate column that represents what the teacher did as Lauren read. Thus, this transcript represents their joint production of the reading of this text. We made no assumption that this was a "letter" at this point in our analysis.

Central to this analysis, then, is a view of Lauren not as an individual but as a part of a partnership that produced the reading of the text to the

Figure 14.2. Lauren reading her text.

dear thomas (pause)

we know you have snow (pause)

we have sun (pause)

our school is called hollister (pause)

we know you are from montana (pause)

we are learning about rainforests (pause)

what are you learning (said in a rising intonation)

we do not have rattle snakes (pause)

i am six years old (pause)

love (pause)

lauren (pause)

Teacher stands behind L with hands on top of chair, leaning forward so that she can see L's text.

Teacher follows L's reading of text, smiling and nodding as L reads

Teacher points to text as L reads the word rainforests

Teacher moves back to the original position with hands on top of chair, leaning forward to see the text

When L finishes the teacher compliments L on her reading

class. Furthermore, we see the lack of overt comments by students in the class as indicating that they understood this type of practice, and that by not asking questions or talking, they were cooperating in the production of the text. Even though they are not visually present in this *frame grab* or verbally present in the transcript, they were participants in this event (Lin, 1993). Their participation was also signaled by the positioning of the author's chair and the physical orientation of Lauren and the teacher.

To understand how Lauren came to be in the author's chair (emic/insider term) reading this particular text, we examined the teacher talk to students that preceded this observed moment, which in turn, led to the need to consider additional events and interactions within and across days. Figure 14.3 provides two interrelated event maps. The first map, labeled *Time and Events,* represents the classroom events of the whole day (6 hours). This map, with its level of detail (information) represents how time was spent by the students and their teacher throughout the entire day. The second map focuses on one specific event, entitled *Artifact Box Letters* and presents the subevents constituting this activity *(Time and Sub-Events).* As indicated in this map, there were nine subevents that preceded the subevent, *Writing Letters to Artifact Box Partners,* through which Lauren's text was produced/accomplished, recognized, acknowledged and became socially significant (i.e., criteria for intertextuality; Bloome & Egan-Robertson, 1993). The lines linking the two maps represent the *part–whole relationship* between these two levels of representation of time, space and activity. These events and subevents were identified by locating teacher talk and student actions that preceded and followed Lauren's presentation of her text to the class.[10] The maps enable us to show the *larger context* of the event within the classroom and its relationship to the locally produced rendering of the text to the group.

Through this analysis, we identified Lauren's presentation to the class as a phase of activity (reading her letter) within a larger subevent (reading of all letters), which was, in turn, part of an event (Artifact Box Letters), which itself was part of that particular school day. The nine subevents preceding the text-rendering began with the teacher's introduction to the "*lesson*" and then moved through a series of activities that included differential actions by members of the class: dictating, recording, listening, and revising as a class; individually selecting a particular person to write to; writing a letter; and sharing the written text with the class.

Analysis also showed that dictating, recording, listening, and revising were recursive activities on that day, which were used to generate two different bodies of information, that students could draw on when writing their letters. (These bodies of information are addressed in a separate analysis that follows.) Although how this information would be used and why it was being generated was evident when we examined intertextual and inter

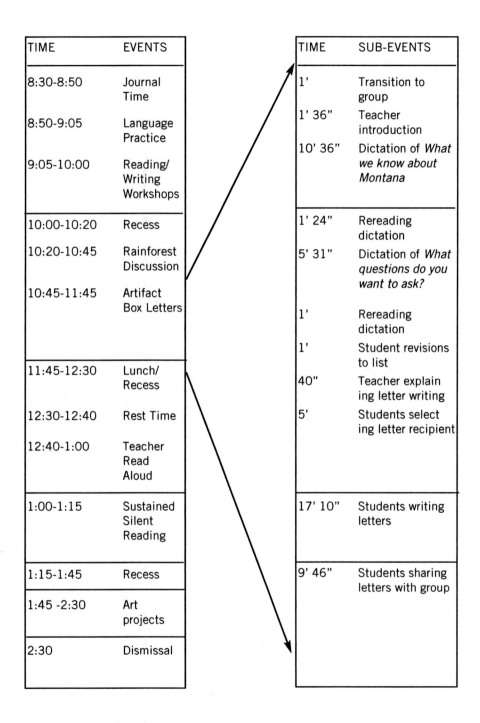

TIME	EVENTS
8:30-8:50	Journal Time
8:50-9:05	Language Practice
9:05-10:00	Reading/ Writing Workshops
10:00-10:20	Recess
10:20-10:45	Rainforest Discussion
10:45-11:45	Artifact Box Letters
11:45-12:30	Lunch/ Recess
12:30-12:40	Rest Time
12:40-1:00	Teacher Read Aloud
1:00-1:15	Sustained Silent Reading
1:15-1:45	Recess
1:45 -2:30	Art projects
2:30	Dismissal

TIME	SUB-EVENTS
1'	Transition to group
1' 36"	Teacher introduction
10' 36"	Dictation of *What we know about Montana*
1' 24"	Rereading dictation
5' 31"	Dictation of *What questions do you want to ask?*
1'	Rereading dictation
1'	Student revisions to list
40"	Teacher explaining letter writing
5'	Students selecting letter recipient
17' 10"	Students writing letters
9' 46"	Students sharing letters with group

Figure 14.3. Time and event maps.

contextual ties across these subevents, in the moments in which they were being generated, how they would be used was not visible to us or to the students. Thus, the teacher can be viewed as using a form of progressive disclosure of information to develop a common focus and set of resources for subsequent work (Putney et al., 2000; Rex et al., 1997).

To explore how progressive disclosure was accomplished and how it gained its social significance, we undertook a new level of analysis that involved constructing a message unit transcript of the entire Artifact Box Letter event (1 hour in duration). We then used this transcript as we viewed the tape several times to identify contextualization cues that would help us to understand just what type of text was being produced. For example, as indicated in Fig. 14.2, Lauren began her rendering using the words, *dear thomas*, a conventionalized opening for a letter, and concluded her presentation by the use of the conventionalized closing, *love Lauren*. Furthermore, on the basis of lexical markers and references (the teacher's words), and by listening to the contextualization cues[11] represented in the talk (Gumperz & Behrens, 1993; Gumperz & Herasimchuk, 1973), we identified this text as an authentic letter that would be sent to someone outside of this classroom, not merely as a classroom task (see Mehan, 1979).[12]

Although the genre was evident, what we were unable to understand was why she was "reading" a written letter to the class, how this letter came to be written, why it was written to *thomas*, who *thomas* was, why she included information about her school and about Montana, and why she asked Thomas a question. To examine these questions, we continued our analysis by moving backward in time looking for stretches of talk and speech events (Gumperz, 1986) that were indexical of the text rendered by Lauren. Through this approach, we identified sequences of talk in which direct references were made to the letter writing activity or related content represented in Lauren's rendering within the different subevents represented in Fig. 14.3.

IDENTIFYING SOURCES OF INFLUENCE ON LAUREN'S TEXT

Table 14.1 represents the first transcript segment,[13] identified through backward mapping, in which the *expectations for what to include in the task of letter writing* were made explicit, reformulating what was to occur both in the letter and in the subevents in which students were engaged. This segment occurred in the sub-event (Fig. 14.3) entitled, *Teacher Directions*, which preceded the subevent entitled *Selecting Letter Partner*.

TABLE 14.1   Transcript Segment of First Reference to Letter Writing

Scene: *This sequence of activity was identified in a subevent called* Teacher Directions *in Fig. 14.2, subevent map. Prior to this sequence, the students were sitting on the floor in the front of the room in a semi-circle. This sequence marked a change in topic and activity but not a change in physical space or orientation of the group. In time, this occurred approximately 23 minutes (and two subevents) prior to Lauren's text rendering.*

LINE	TEACHER	STUDENTS	COMMENTS
154	you're going to be writing a letter		
155	to one of the kids in the class		
156	I'm going to put their names on the board		
157	and let you pick out		
158	cause there's more of you		
159	and I want to make sure		
160	every single kid in that class gets a letter		
161	I'll put their names up on the board		
162	and you'll decide		
163	remember our letters		
164	to the other first graders		
165	we started out with dear comma		
166	and then we indented		
167	what I want you to do		on green board
168	is tell them three things about yourself		she writes the
169	and ask them two questions		number three
170	tell them three things about us		things about
171	ask them two questions		ourselves and
			two questions

Analysis of talk in this subevent showed that the teacher reformulated[14] and redirected student attention from generating information about what they knew and might use in the letter (subevents prior to this) to the task of writing the letter. We selected this segment because it is the first time that we identified *direct reference* to the actual expected content of the letter.

Thus, the backward mapping[15] process led us through and across two previous subevents with their situated focus and purpose to the one that showed how the teacher initiated the frame for the actual writing of the letter. In this way we identified a particular type of *intertextual and intercontextual ties—referentially explicit ties.* These ties are one form of a *trace* that members of this group made explicitly visible to each other by their invocation.

As indicated in this transcript segment, the teacher initiated this activity with a direct statement, "you're going to be writing a letter to one of the kids in the class" (154-155). She then proceeded to describe (in less than 40 seconds)[16] what writing a letter meant and what cultural knowledge was needed to do this task. To identify the task parameters and cultural knowledge, we examined the actions and the topics she named. Analysis of actions showed that she shaped future action and signaled intercontextual information that would be needed in this task. The future actions that they would take included: *writing a letter* (154-155, action unit 1),[17] *selecting names for a letter recipient* (157 and 161-162, action units 2 and 3, respectively), *reminding them to use prior information in structuring their letters* (163-166, action unit 4), and *telling them about yourself, and/or about us, and asking them questions* (168, 170; and 169 and 171, respectively, action unit 5). As indicated in this transcript, these statements about future actions that students were to take up created a set of parameters within which the writing of the letters was to take place. This analysis showed *Letter Writing* as a purposeful task that was embedded in a larger cycle of activity, which students' actions indicated that they understood. One way of viewing *Letter Writing* across the cycle of activity is to see it in Bazerman and Prior's (this volume) argument that letter writing can be viewed as both a genre and a genre tool. The social genres dimension has been discussed previously. However, it can also be viewed as a genre tool, which functions to help students learn not only how to write the genre, but also how to use it for individual as well as collective purposes.

From the transcript and videotape record, it was not possible to understand who the following people were: *one of the kids in the class* (155), *their names* (156 and 161), *every single kid in that class* (160), *and the other first graders* (164). What we could tell was what was expected of the letter writers and that the letter writers appeared to understand these referents. To readdress our lack of understanding, we engaged in a three-step process. The first step was to continue the backward mapping process for the immediate task to identify who the *kids in that class* were and what their names were (this analysis is presented in a later section). The second step was necessitated by the first analysis because there was no further reference to *the other first graders.* It was clear from the first analysis that they were not the ones to receive the current letters, leading us to question *what was being referenced, not just who was being referenced,* by the teacher's invocation of the other first graders. This question required that we examine the larger ethnographic record to locate information that would identify who *the other first graders* were and to assess what was being invoked by referring to this group. Fieldnote records in January provided the information about the group and about previous work with letter writing. This analysis was important in two ways. First, it signaled an intercontextual relationship between the letter writing activity they were about to do and an earlier one. Second, the content of the teacher's talk referenced the practices of writing that they were to use in the current letters—*conventions for creating openings* (165) *and indenting* (166). Thus, specific types of prior intercontextual knowledge were signaled as needed, and prior knowledge as a resource was signaled as appropriate, along with the repertoires for actions that were part of this knowledge.

Following the analysis of fieldnotes, we returned to our examination of the transcript segment in Table 14.1 (Step 3) and contrasted the content of that segment with observed actions of Lauren and others who rendered their letters to the class. Lauren's letter showed that she partially followed the teacher's directions. Differences in what the teacher stated as requirements and those we observed as content of the letters led to further exploration. Lauren (and other students) had used the format of letter opening *(dear xxx)* requested by the teacher. However, they went beyond the stated expectations to include a conventional closing *(love xxx)*. The inclusion of additional elements across all letters showed that the students had made an intercontextual tie by drawing on knowledge beyond this setting and using cultural practices that they had previously had an opportunity to learn. Thus, the teacher's talk served to initiate what students were going to do. It did not, however, define or limit what they actually did, as illustrated by the inclusion of additional conventions for letter writing.

Further analysis showed that the dynamic and negotiated nature of life in this classroom was visible not only in the use of conventions, but also in the content of the letter. Analysis of the video record provided further information that helped to contextualize the sources of influence on Lauren's production of the letter. This analysis showed that as the teacher talked about her expectations, she also wrote on the green board. In her talk she provided two sets of information that can be viewed as editing and not repetition of information. In Line 168, she stated that they should tell "three things about yourself." In Line 170, she stated that they should include "three things about us." At the same time, she wrote on the green board—3 things and 2 questions. Although the spoken and written texts can be seen as providing explicit information about ways of structuring the letters, these two texts differ in what was suggested, creating potential ambiguity in the task. However, subsequent analysis showed that students did not raise questions about the difference in *the referent to yourself vs us*;

rather, their letters showed that they took this opportunity to reformulate the task in their own ways by including both types of information, and in some cases by including more than the stated expectation—tell three things about yourself and three things about us.

Analysis of Lauren's letter showed that she chose to write four things about "us" (*we have sun; our school is called Hollister; we are learning about rainforests;* and *we do not have rattlesnakes*) and wrote one thing about herself (*I am 6 years old*). Additionally, she asked one question of Thomas (*what are you learning?*). When her text was compared with the teacher's oral text, we found that Lauren had taken up both topics formulated by the teacher (self and school) and the request to include questions, but she redefined the specifics of the task (i.e., the number of items for each type of information).

A discussion with the teacher following our analysis indicated that she intended to have students write three *telling statements*. However, the way in which she formulated the task left space for students to choose among possible options the information that they would include in their letters. This conversation and her observed actions across time led to the understanding that her directions were not intended to be literal directions, but rather were to serve as guides and boundaries for the content. Analysis of other students' letters showed a similar pattern of reformulation. That the choices made were appropriate was visible in the fact that the teacher mailed the letters that day, without further revision. This analysis showed that the talk that the teacher engaged in at the on-set of this activity provided boundaries for what the students did, the knowledge of letter writing conventions they used, and the range of content that each student included. It did not, however, lead to one right way of doing letters. The talk, therefore, provided a framework for students' actions and a formulation of the task that was taken up, interpreted and reformulated in appropriate ways by the students.

WHAT DO WE KNOW ABOUT MONTANA?

By moving between the different textual records, we were able to identify ties between events and practices and to create an interpretation of the referents in the text that can be seen as approximating insider knowledge. Furthermore, this analysis showed why historical knowledge was needed to interpret what was occurring in the class and why Lauren's letter was constructed in the way it was. In this section, we examine two additional types of referents whose meaning was not clear to us as analysts. Even with this level of backward mapping, the references to Montana, including the discussion of rattlesnakes, and reference to what they were learning were not visible to us, even though students and teacher in the class appeared to understand. Additionally, as she composed her letter, Lauren used this contrast between Montana and the location of her school. Lauren's contrast was not requested by the teacher, and therefore, we wanted to identify sources of influence that were available to Lauren that could explain why she might have used this approach to writing. To understand how this content came to be included, we engaged in further backward mapping to earlier subevents.

The next transcript segment identified (Table 14.2) occurred in the subevent entitled, *What We Know About Montana*. This subevent occurred approximately 19 minutes prior to the *Teacher Directions* subevent.

As indicated in this transcript segment, the teacher asked students to think about *what they know about Montana* and *those clues*. Her request acted as a transition into this subevent and signaled the types of information they needed to use to respond to this request (i.e., they needed to think about *those clues*). The students' actions (i.e., the lack of comment or questions) showed that they understood both why *Montana* was being discussed and what the teacher meant by *those clues*. In response to this request, the teacher and students engaged in a chain of actions that included *students dictating information, teacher recording student information on the board, teacher reading back the recorded information*, and *teacher commenting about student information*.

The information that the students dictated in response to this request and the teacher's comments on what they dictated are represented in Table 14.3.

As indicated in this table, the students provided information and the teacher accepted this information, representing the information in an abbreviated form while providing commentary on this information at particular points in time. Students offered nine bits of information and the teacher commented on seven of the nine. Analysis of the student comments showed evidence of claims about what they knew (i.e., statements beginning with *we know* . . .) as well as statements of fact (i.e., statements beginning with *the* _____, *they* _____, or *their* _____). The difference in these

TABLE 14.2 Transcript Segment 2: Referencing Montana

LINE	TEACHER
071	all right what do we know
072	what do we know about montana now
073	think about those clues

TABLE 14.3   What We Know Dictation

TEXT DICTATED BY STUDENTS	TEACHER COMMENTS WHILE READING DICTATED TEXT BACK TO STUDENTS
What do we know about Montana?	
1. The name of the town is Havre.	
2. We know they are cowboys and farmers and Air Force kids.	we found that out right in the beginning because they told us
3. They have gold mines.	they sent us that clue
4. Their state tree is the Ponderosa Pine.	that clue helped
5. We know that part of Montana is in song the Rockie Mountains.	we learned that from the state
6. The little map clue helped us a lot.	
7. We know they have a shortage of rain.	because the soil in the soil it said much needed rain
8. We know where rattlesnakes come from.	and we know some come from Montana so that fit with the others
9. The state is Montana.	actually we know a lot more than this, but this is just getting an idea

two forms of offering information is not treated as a difference by the teacher. Rather, her commentary on the information provided by the students served as a meta-narrative that made visible to students (and researchers alike) where and when she saw this information as being made available. To identify the meaning of clues, we examined the larger ethnographic record. This analysis showed that they had worked with clues sent to them earlier in the Artifact Box cycle of activity (from April 7 to April 17; see Fig. 14.1). Additionally, this analysis showed that they used library resources with the help of the librarian and the teacher to gain other information (e.g., state song and atlases). Furthermore, as indicated in Table 14.3, the teacher reminded the students that this list was not all inclusive of what they knew. She did this by telling them two things that they *"know a lot more than this,"* and that they were *"just getting an idea."* This approach by the teacher signaled to the students that they could go further on their own and could provide additional information in their letters.

When the information contained in this table was juxtaposed with Lauren's text, it confirmed our previous interpretation that students were able to reformulate the task by adding their own interpretations and understandings. In her letter Lauren claimed that *we know you are from montana* and *we do not have rattlesnakes.* The contrast of these two texts (the letter and the dictated information) showed that Lauren adapted *ideas* from the dictated text to include in her letter. In other words, the talk about the dictated text helped *talk her letter into being.* It also showed that Lauren went beyond the dictated text, confirming the teacher's claim that the students knew more than what was being said and/or recorded during the dictation. One way to view Lauren's actions is to see them as inscribing a rhetorical shift, from reproducing or merely taking up traces from the class texts, to composing her own text intended to create a "social connection" with Thomas, the recipient of her letter. The expansion of the text beyond traces suggests that Lauren envisions the possibility that Thomas might respond. This interpretation, when taken in the context of prior letter exchanges in this cycle of activity, becomes possible. It is supported by the fact that the classes have already exchanged class letters to initiate the activity; however, this was the first time that individuals were writing to another person from that classroom. However, it is not possible to know whether Lauren actually expected Thomas to write. We do know that she knew that the letters would be sent.

The analysis to this point showed possible sources of influence that shaped what *Lauren* chose to include in her letter. In the next analysis, we examine the sources of influence on the question that Lauren asked. To examine this issue, we were required to identify another subevent. This analysis involved moving forward in time from the subevent entitled *What We Know About Montana* to examine the subevent *What We Want to Know.* Table 14.4, transcript Segment 3 provides the needed information about how the teacher initiated the subevent focusing on question asking. This sequence of activity occurred two minutes after the *What we know about Montana* subevent represented in Table 14.3.

In this subevent, the teacher redirected students' attention from *thinking about what they knew about Montana* to a new chain of activity focusing on *asking questions.* She directed students to *"think of a question that you might want to ask these kids"* (Lines 100-101). She then established the conditions for asking the question, indicating that they did not have to confine their questions to *any of this clue business.* In this way, and through her next comments about personal information, she signaled to the students that they had a choice in what to ask and where the information to be included in the question could come from. These actions further supported our interpretation offered previously about the appropriateness of student reformulation of content within the parameters of the task of letter writing.

TABLE 14.4 Transcript Segment 3: Asking Questions

LINE	TEACHER
100	think of a question
101	you might want to ask these kids
102	now you don't have to confine
103	your questions to any of this clue business
104	maybe there's something personal
105	you want to ask these guys

Table 14.5 provides a summary of the questions the students asked and the teacher's commentary on these questions. As indicated in Table 14.5, the first two questions were not personal ones. That is, in these two questions, the students drew on prior knowledge about the Artifact Box and lottery tickets to ask questions (i.e., *Where did the Sharps buy the lottery ticket? How long did it take to make the artifact box?*). The teacher's meta-narrative and her actions provided information about whether these questions were ones that she wanted them to use. After the first question she made a comment about the content of the question, using a discourse approach similar to the one in Table 14.3 making connections to prior knowledge. After the second question, she indicated that it was a *really good question because it will help me next year to know that we did ours in about a month*. Once again, she provided a rationale for why this question would be helpful, not merely stating a positive acceptance. What occurred next, however, reminded students of the original expectation for question asking (see Table 14.6.). This action interrupted the direction that the students were taking and provided space for them to *reformulate* what was being asked of them—to go beyond asking questions about the Artifact Box to ask questions about the other students and their lives and school.

Returning to Table 14.5, in questions three through six, the students took up the personal focus suggested by the teacher and began to ask questions about *the kids* just like them who would receive these letters. In this shift in focus we also see a shift in register. Students moved from the register related to the information and inquiry processes of the Artifact Box to language more reflective of everyday talk among students in and out of the classroom.

In juxtaposing this text with Lauren's again, we see that Lauren's statement, "*We know you have snow*" can be linked to the teacher's meta-narra-

TABLE 14.5.   Questions to Ask Dictation

DICTATED TEXT	TEACHER COMMENTS WHILE READING DICTATED TEXT BACK TO STUDENTS
What questions do you want to ask?	
1. Where did the Sharps buy the lottery ticket?	that's those people who won 47 million
2. How long did it take to make the Artifact Box?	that's a really good question because it'll help me for next year to know we did ours in about a month
3. What do you sometimes do at school?	you know do they have play ground like we do
4. What do you do for P.E.?	if they have snow in the winter what do they do for P.E.
5. Where do you get your lunch?	maybe they all have to bring their lunch
6. Do they have art?	

TABLE 14.6.   Transcript Segment 4: Reformulating the Direction of the Questions

LINE	TEACHER
113	hey guys you don't have to confine yourselves to the Artifact Box
114	these are little kids just like you
115	don't you want to ask them about something
116	like where they play or what they do or
117	how many movies they have
118	I don't know
119	what their class school is like
120	it's real different

tive comments *"if they have snow in winter, what do they do for P.E.?"* Thus, once again, we see how the talk about the dictated text became a resource that Lauren used in composing her letter. In other words, once again, we see how the content of Lauren's written text was talked into being at an earlier time and how it became a text that she used in a later subevent, thus making an intertextual tie *between prior written texts and her own personal text.*

Although we gained additional information from this analysis about the students to whom Lauren and her peers were writing and sources of influence on the content included in their letters to these students, we still did not know about the *"clues"* nor did we have explicit information about who these students were and what the Artifact Box was. To explore these questions we once again used a backward mapping approach to locate additional information to add texture and understanding to our interpretation of the relationships among these oral and written texts. The final transcript segment that we will examine, Transcript Segment 5 (Table 14.7), was identified at the beginning of the Artifact Box Letters event.

YOU'RE GOING TO WRITE A LETTER

The following transcript initiated a change from a discussion of rainforests, the event immediately preceeding the Artifact Box Letters event, to a focus on letter writing in the Artifact Box Letters event.

In Transcript Segment 5, the teacher began by foreshadowing what the new activity will include, *"right now you're going to write a letter to."* In this segment, the identity of the "to" was not audible. However, her next

Table 14.7.   Transcript Segment 5: You're Going to Write A Letter

LINE	TEACHER	COMMENTS
001	right now you're going to write a letter to	
002	< >	
003	all right I kept thinking about those kids	
004	want to talk about the Artifact Box	
005	I kept thinking all weekend	
006	about those kids in Havre	writing Havre on board
007	they pronounce it hay-ver	
008	havre montana	
009	39 kids	
0010	in a little one room school house	

statement (Line 003) suggested that the recipients were *"those kids."* This statement shifted time from present to past as she indicated that she had been thinking about "those kids," making them the possible recipients of the letters. Her subsequent comments confirmed this interpretation. In the following comments, she provided contextual information about where those kids were located and how the name of their town was pronounced. Thus, in this transcript segment she provided contextual information to help students understand the meaning of *"you're going to write a letter to."*

Although the teacher had provided a range of cues, only students who shared a common history with her understood who "those kids" were and what the Artifact Box was. We, researchers and readers of the transcripts, still did not have sufficient information to know what the Artifact Box was or what the clues previously mentioned had to do with the box. To examine these issues we had to consider information available in the fuller ethnographic record of this class, a record that began on the first day of school and continued through out the year. Analysis of this record led to the identification of the cycle of activity (Green & Meyer, 1991) known as the Artifact Box (represented previously as Fig. 14.1) and other cycles of activity related to it.

By backward and forward mapping from this point in time, we found that the letter writing was the last phase of the activity within the larger cycle of activity that began the day prior to the Spring Break. This cycle of activity consisted of a series of events and subevents over a 3-week period of time. The cycle began when the teacher announced to the class that they would do the Artifact Box activity and that they had to prepare their own artifact box to send to their "mystery partners." She then described the activity to them and assigned clues to different students that were to be worked on with their parents over the Spring Break. Analysis of the ethnographic records of life within her class provided a basis for identifying the range of events that constituted the larger cycle of activity, just as it had done for the event called Artifact Box Letter Writing. In this way, we were able to identify the broader context that shaped the local history of the teacher and students and that served as resources for students in understanding what the teacher references meant.

To develop a broader understanding of the reference to *"those clues,"* we revisited the videotape data, records of interviews, and fieldnote records. Through this analysis we were able to construct a summary statement of this activity in general and to create a context for understanding the reference to *"those clues."*

The Artifact Box cycle of activity was the result of an Artifact Box exchange arranged by the teacher through the Artifact Box Exchange

> *Network. The teacher located this Network in a professional journal. She indicated that a teacher who wished to participate in an Artifact Box exchange had to contact the Network and they (the Network) arranged a pairing with a partner "mystery" class. Each class prepared sets of hard, medium and easy clues, following directions provided by the Network. The clues were intended to provide information about their location without giving the actual place name. Once a class had prepared the clues about their own location, they placed them in their "Artifact Box" and sent it to the Network. The Network, in turn, forwarded the box to the partner school. When a class received their exchange box, they worked with the clues provided by their mystery partner, attempting to identify the location of the mystery class.* (based on ethnographic records between March 27 and April 20)

As indicated in this summary, only part of the information was available to the students in and through their interactions with each other, the Artifact Box, the teacher, and the students in the other school. What was not available to students, but was necessary for us as researchers, was the origin of this activity and how the exchange of texts and artifacts was accomplished. Without this information our understanding of how Lauren's text was talked into being would have been incomplete. Through the interviews and discussions with the teacher, what became evident was that the teacher's decision to participate in the Artifact Box Exchange Network led to the onset of the cycle, which led to the talking into being of the texts that influenced Lauren's letter. Furthermore, as the summary analysis made visible, the prepared materials the teacher received also contributed to what would become Lauren's text. Thus, the ethnographic information was necessary to understand the overlapping contexts, resources, purposes, and goals of various members of this local group.

From the perspective of the students, the discursive processes and practices through which they shaped and reshaped the cycle became key sources of information and resources across time. Analysis of the ethnographic record showed that the students did not have access to how the teacher acquired the Artifact Box or why she engaged them in this activity. From the teacher's perspective, it was not necessary for the students to have this information even through this information about the Artifact Box was important for her actions because it shaped her actions, just as her discourse and actions with the students were important in guiding and shaping the group's actions. Both types of information were necessary for us in order to obtain a fuller understanding of this observed cycle of activity.

The ethnographic record provided information about the multilayered nature of the context for Lauren's text. The complex set of data allowed us to understand how it came to be talked into being on the day observed. Additionally, the ethnographic analysis showed the multiple texts that were intertextually and intercontextually tied to Lauren's text. It also showed how these texts were talked into being, shaping over time a local history, a set of discourse processes and practices associated with the events and subevents through which this cycle of activity was constituted, and how a local language of the Artifact Box cycle was constructed by members of the class.

IDENTIFYING INTERCONTEXTUALLY TIED CYCLES OF ACTIVITY AS RESOURCES FOR LAUREN'S LETTER

We conclude this discussion of our analysis of Lauren's text with the description of one additional analysis. During the forward and backward mapping activity, we identified a series of intercontextually tied, intersecting cycles of activity that were also related to the texts of the Artifact Box cycle as signaled in the teacher's references and student actions. One of these intersecting cycles was particularly relevant to our understanding of what cultural knowledge was visible in Lauren's text. This cycle is the Letter Genre cycle of activity that occurred across the entire school year. Figure 14.4 provides a graphic representation of these intersecting cycles. Given that each involved work across time and events, we represent them as two intersecting timelines.

To demonstrate how these intercontextual ties were signaled, we revisit briefly Table 14.1, Transcript Segment 1, in which the teacher asked students to *"remember our letters* (163) *to the other first graders"* (164). As discussed previously she told them that *"we started out with dear comma* (165) *and then we indented"* (166). In making these statements, she signaled to the students that they had cultural resources available to them that they could bring to the current task of writing to their Artifact Box partners. Her discourse showed the importance of using historical intertextual and intercontextual knowledge in the local task. Kristeva (1986) referred to this type of historical knowledge as *vertical intertextuality* in contrast to the *horizontal intertextuality* that characterizes intertextuality occurring in the local exchange.

As indicated in Fig. 14.4, the Letter Writing cycle of activity involved students in reading and writing a wide variety of letters from a number of people both within and outside of the class. Thus, the knowledge of how to write letters, who to write to, what to include, how the form of the letter was to be constructed, and what counted as content for a given letter was a dynamically constructed process in which new cycles of activity and new events provided opportunities for students to use, explore, and expand their cultural repertoires for action and for understanding the letter writing

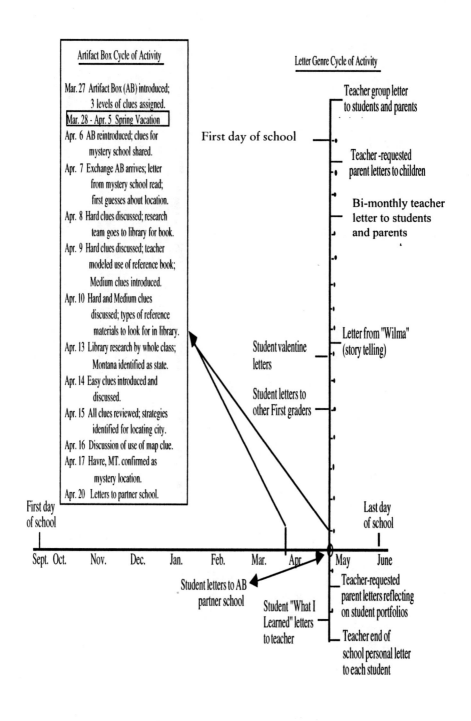

Figure 14.4. Intersecting cycles of activity: Artifact box and letter writing.

genre. As indicated in this figure, one of these letter wrting events occurred prior to the official start of school (the letter to the students and parents), and many of them preceeded the use of letter writing in the Artifact Box cycle of activity. Additional analysis that we have undertaken but will not present also showed intertextual ties of letter writing with other cycles of activity, including the *Author's Chair* cycle of activity and one entitled *Students as Detectives*. These intersecting cycles of activity and the inter-contextual and intertextual ties constitute a type of consequential progression of knowledge about content and practices needed to participate in the Artifact Box cycle of activity, making historicity a key analytic issue to develop emic understandings of texts, actions and discourses of the classroom (Bakhtin, 1986).

A second dimension of the analysis was to identify direct references in Lauren's text and to tie them to spoken discourse that was identified through the progressive disclosure. As the progressive disclosure of the sources of influence on Lauren's letter demonstrated, to understand this individual student's performance and the text that she presented to the class, we needed to move between levels of analysis and to shift our angle of vision from the collective to the individual repeatedly. To illustrate what this analysis enabled us to understand, we present one final representation of the influences on Lauren's letter. Figure 14.5 provides a graphic representation of the sources of influence on Lauren's text related to spoken discourse.

The information represented in this figure focuses on the hour-long event that surrounded Lauren's rendering of her text to the class. What is labeled *adopted or adapted* in this figure were textual dimensions of her letter that could be tied directly to what occurred during this hour-long event. Each of the textual dimensions that could be identified as having a direct intertextual or intercontextual tie to the discourse and actions in a particular transcript segment is indicated by a circle (for those adopted) or a rectangle (for those adapted). However, as indicated, some parts of the letter were not possible to tie directly to talk or actions within the discourse (spoken or written) that occurred during this hour. These textual dimensions are indicated by non-bracketed print (e.g., sun, learning about rainforests, learning, and love Lauren). For these, we needed the larger ethnographic record from the first days of school.

These textual dimensions demonstrate the agency that Lauren took in writing her text. They do not, however, lead to a claim of individual knowledge separate from what happened in this class. Such a claim would require extensive analysis of all classroom texts, which is well beyond the scope of this chapter. Without the multiple analyses framed within the Interactional Ethnographic approach, we would not have been able to achieve the level of emic understanding or to make visible the ways in which the words and

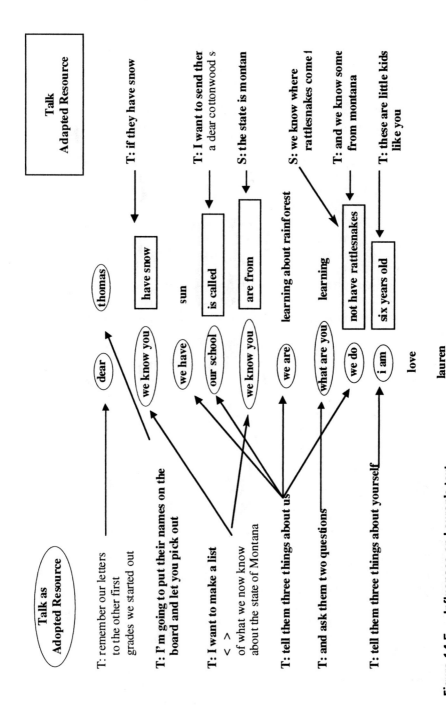

Figure 14.5. Influences on Lauren's text.

actions of the class were historically tied across time and events and served as resources for individuals within the collective as they participated in and produced work through the events of daily life.

In this chapter we have demonstrated why it is important to consider individual actions in relationship to the group, to explore the patterns of actions and events constructed by the group, and to contrast local moments with previous ones as well as ones that will follow. In other words, we have demonstrated the importance of understanding life in classrooms and performance of individuals as intertextually and intercontextually tied, and historical texts as resources that members adapt and adopt as they formulate and reformulate what they are doing in the events being constructed (cf. Bakhtin, 1986; Bloome & Bailey, 1992; Putney et al., 2000). Finally, these analyses demonstrated how the events in classrooms are part of a progression of types of knowledge that are consequential for students, both collectively and individually.

Although we have directed our discussion to researchers, a reviewer raised the question—What does such research provide teachers? One way to answer this is to refer readers to a journal in which Lauren's teacher and her colleagues in the South Coast Writing Project have written about the impact of our perspective on their work with students. In the journal *Primary Voices* (1999), this group of teachers demonstrated how this approach guided their own research. In our research community, the Santa Barbara Classroom Discourse Group, the teachers have also written collaboratively with the researchers about their work with students in their classrooms. (A list of these citations can be obtained from the following Web site: http://www.education.ucsb.edu/socialjustice under the *Classroom Research* heading.) Writings about the usefulness of ethnography and discourse analysis to teachers is growing. A full discussion of this topic, however, is beyond the scope of this chapter. Readers interested in this issue may want to begin by reading an international collection edited by Egan-Robertson and Bloome (1998) on how teachers are using ethnography and linguistic analyses with students.

ENDNOTES

1. Research for this project was supported by grants from the California Writing Project and The Spencer Foundation. The authors would like to thank Maria de Fatima Gomes, Federal University of Minas Gerais, and Audra Skukauskaite, University of California, Santa Barbara, for their editorial comments.

2. The citations in the text represent collections of work and reviews published in English, primarily in the United States. They represent historical and current work from a range of perspectives, including discourse analysis, ethnomethodology, sociolinguistics, sociocultural, anthropological, and sociological perspectives. In the past two decades, a number of journals across disciplines have begun publishing articles focusing on the social construction of knowledge and the situated nature of such knowledge (e.g., *American Educational Research Journal, Human Development, Journal of Classroom Interaction, Journal of Literacy Research, Language and Education, Journal of Research in Mathematics Education, Journal of Research in Science Teaching, Journal of Teaching of Physical Educa*tion, *Linguistics in Education, Mind, Culture & Cognition, Reading Research Quarterly, Research in the Teaching of English, Review of Research in Education*, among others). This growing list shows the rich base of work on classroom discourse, processes, and practices and the cross-disciplinary base of this body of work. In non-English-speaking countries, there are parallel bodies of work, often not available in English (e.g., Argentina, Brazil, Finland, France, Italy, Japan, Mexico, Russia, Spain, Sweden, Switzerland, Taiwan, The Netherlands, among others).

3. The Santa Barbara Classroom Discourse Group is a research community composed of university-based and classroom-based (teachers and students), ethnographic researchers, who work interactively across settings, questions, and times to identify and understand theory-in-practice and theories-of-practice of members of a classroom, or other institutional context. Members have published an extensive body of work nationally and internationally; a comprehensive bibliography of published materials is available on request from dixon@education .ucsb.edu.

4. The conceptualization of collective life in classrooms is discussed from different theoretical traditions. We view these traditions as providing different angles of vision on, and explanations of, a common phenomena, in this case collective life. Richard Beach, in reviewing this chapter, raised the issue of the similarity to (and possible explanatory power of) activity theory, while noting the possible difference between activity theory and the work of interactional ethnography. In exploring the possible relationship between our perspective and that of activity theory and other authors, he argued "The concept of collective life could be tied to the concept of activity system—of the classroom as constituted by an institutional history as a system. At the same time—and here's maybe where interactional ethnography or micro-ethnographic perspectives assume a different perspective—you are arguing for an understanding of the 'local,' unique features of a particular class setting that

both references the prototypical system and also resists that system through playing out its own unique version of practices whose meaning[s] are unique to particular relationships in particular time/space." Although this explanation is a possible one given what members of the class signal to each other, our theoretical stance is to *not assume the existence of the system* a priori but to see what members do and *how a local system is constituted* in and through their day-to-day interactions. In this way, we view the production of a local or particular system as the work of students and teachers who are constructing their community, not merely the result of a historical system or merely resistance to that system. In this we are closer to ethnomethodologists who see social life as the work of members of a community (Heap, 1991; Mehan, 1979). Following the work of Corsaro (Gaskin, Miller, & Corsaro, 1992) on socialization and Bloome (Bloome & Bailey, 1991; Bloome & Egan-Roberston, 1993) on interextuality and historicity, we see society and its systems as constantly being constructed, not merely reproduced. To see any action as a resistance to another, we need to see evidence that members of the group are signaling resistance to each other. In other words, we need to understand the complex relationships between collective development and individuals-within-the-collective. In recent work, we have identified issues of macro–micro system relationships that move beyond resistance frameworks to show ways in which intersecting systems support and at other times constrain what is possible to be constructed within a particular classroom (Dixon, Green, Yeager, Baker, & Franquíz, 2000). Thus, we have elected to use interactional ethnography with its theoretical framework as our *orienting theory*, and we see activity theory as a potential resource for an *explanatory theory* in cases when our data support the theoretical arguments of that theory.

5. For a related, yet theoretically different point of view on this issue, see Bazerman and Prior (this volume) and Lee and Ball (this volume.)

6. For an extended discussion of genres see Bazerman and Prior (this volume). They distinguish among three types of genres as social action, as rhetorical, and as textual. At first reading, we see the use of genres in this chapter as crossing the three types; however, further detailed analysis of Bazerman and Prior is necessary to expand our arguments. This is a promising future analysis but was not our goal for the present chapter.

7. The Artifact Box cycle of activity was the result of an Artifact Box exchange arranged by the teacher through the Artifact Box Exchange Network. The teacher located this network in a professional journal. A teacher who wishes to participate in an Artifact Box exchange contacts the network and they arrange a pairing with a partner "mystery" class.

The full description of Artifact Box process is described in a later section of this chapter. For more information about the Artifact Box Exchange Network see http://www.tased.edu.au/tasonline/tag /aaegt7/hogana.htm

8. A *frame grab* is a tool that enables us to pause a video of an ongoing event and to select one moment in time to capture a still photgraph. The photograph then provides a pause in the action to examine the physical orientations of those visible within the frame grab moment. Frame grabs can be obtained using a quicktime movie system or other form of linking video to the computer. In our case, we used the C-video program that allows us to capture video data and to take a *frame* and import it directly into an MS Word document. However, Microsoft picture objects (in power point) can be used when a CD-ROM with video segments on it exists.

9. *Author's chair* is an emic term used by the teacher to refer to the chair in which students took up the position as *author,* while addressing the whole group.

10. Lauren's reading of this text to the class constitutes a key speech event (see Gumperz, 1986) for this analysis in that it serves as a pivotal event for subsequent analysis.

11. Contextualization cues include pitch, stress, pause, juncture, proxemics, kinesics, and eye gaze. They are paralinguistic features that co-occur with spoken words that provide information on the meaning communicated and interpreted (Gumperz, 1992).

12. In his article, "What time is it Denise?", Mehan argued that many class assignments are not "authentic" but serve an instructional purpose. For example, the question, What time is it Denise? is asked in classrooms to get the student to give the time of a clock in a lesson, not to ask for actual time.

13. Given that this transcript represents only a small segment of the whole, we have elected to refer to these bits of transcription as transcript segments rather than transcripts (as many others do), which might lead the reader to assume that we ignored the full context of this bit of talk. This practice maintains the part-whole relationship between particular moments and the larger event being constructed (i.e., the resources constructed by the group that members had available to use in the key event).

14. Vygotsky (Rieber & Carton, 1987) spoke about the interactions between and among people as formulating knowledge that is then reformulated by the individuals as they internalize the information. We use this construct to describe what occurs between people and how across time information from one moment in time becomes reformulated in new contexts. Thus, this formulation–reformulation process con-

stitutes a dynamic and socially significant form of intertextuality and intercontextuality (Putney et al., 2000).

15. Backward mapping is a concept used in explorations of historical relationships between and among texts in both the discourse world (Green et al., 2002) and the policy analysis world (Chrispeels, 1997). It refers to moving backwards in time from the object of interest to explore the roots of this object (e.g., event). It moves from the object (e.g., key event) backward to the next instance that is closest temporally, which in turn, leads to additional analyses, each temporally related but more distant from the original key event.. In this way, the roots of the event are identified and the actions leading to the production of the event are located. This approach enables a systematic exploration of historicity (Bakhtin, 1986) and horizontal and vertical intertextuality (Fairclough, 1993; Kristeva, 1986). What is identified through this is a type of consequential progression (Putney et al., 2000).

16. The briefness of this time was significant to us in that we saw this as an indication that the teacher assumed shared knowledge of the actions of letter writing. The lack of questions by the students also suggested that they too shared an understanding of this reference.

17. *Action units* refer to clusters of tied message units (minimal bursts of speech, bits of talk) that constitute an action by the speaker. On the transcript they are indicated by spaces between groups of messages. The action unit is defined by observing and listening to the contextualization cues and by identifying shifts in the types of information being presented. An action unit can include more than one message to create options among actions. For example, in action unit 2 and 5, the teacher as speaker is taking one action that entails multiple actions or decisions by the students as listeners, who will need this information to do a subsequent task.

REFERENCES

Baker, W.D. (2001). *Artists in the making: An ethnographic investigation of discourse and literate practices as disciplinary processes in a high school advanced placement studio art classroom.* Unpublished doctoral dissertation, University of California at Santa Barbara.

Bakhtin, M.M. (1986). *Speech genres and other late essays.* Austin: University of Texas Press.

Barthes, R. (1975). *The pleasure of the text* (R. Miller, Trans.). New York: Hill & Wang.

Berger, P., & Luckmann, T. (1966). *The social construction of reality.* Garden City, NY: Doubleday.

Birdwhistell, R. (1977). Some discussion of ethnography, theory, and method. In J. Brockman (Ed.), *About Bateson: Essays on Gregory Bateson* (pp. 103-144). New York: E.P. Dutton.

Bloome, D. (Ed.). (1985a). *Classrooms and literacy*. Norwood, NJ: Ablex.

Bloome, D. (Ed.). (1985b). Reading as a social process. *Language Arts, 62*(4), 134-142.

Bloome, D. (Ed.). (1987). *Literacy and schooling*. Norwood, NJ: Ablex.

Bloome, D., & Bailey, F. (1992). Studying language through events, particularity, and intertextuality. In R. Beach, J. Green, M. Kamil, & T. Shanahan (Eds.), *Multiple disciplinary perspectives on literacy research* (pp. 181-210). Urbana, IL: NCRE & NCTE.

Bloome, D., & Egan-Robertson, A. (1993). The social construction of intertextuality in classroom reading and writing lessons. *Reading Research Quarterly, 28*(4), 304-334.

Brilliant-Mills, H. (1993) Becoming a mathematician: Building a situated definition of mathematics. *Linguistics and Education, 5*(3&4), 301-334.

Castenheira, M.L., Crawford, T., Dixon, C., & Green, J. (2000). Interactional ethnography: An approach to studying the social construction of literate practices. Special issue of *Linguistics and Education: Analyzing the Discourse Demands of the Curriculum, 11* (4), 353-400.

Cazden, C. (1988). *Classroom discourse: The language of teaching and learning*. Portsmouth, NH: Heinemann

Cazden, C., John, V. & Hymes, D. (Eds.). (1972). *Functions of language in the classroom*. New York: Teachers College Press.

Chandler, S. (1992). Learning for what purpose? Questions when viewing classroom learning from a socio-cultural curriculum perspective. In H. Marshall (Ed.), *Redefining student learning: Roots of educational restructuring* (pp. 33-58). Norwood, NJ: Ablex.

Chrispeels, J. H. (1997). Educational policy implementation in a shifting political climate: The California experience. *The American Educational Research Journal, 34*(3), 453-481.

Christie, F. (1995). Pedagogic discourse in the primary school. *Linguistics and Education, 7*, 221-242.

Cochran-Smith, M. (1984). *The making of a reader*. Norwood, NJ: Ablex.

Cook-Gumperz, J., & Gumperz, J. (1992). Changing views of language in education: The implications of literacy research. In R. Beach, J. Green, M. Kamil, & T. Shanahan (Eds.), *Multiple disciplinary perspectives on literacy research* (pp. 151-180). Urbana, IL: NCRE & NCTE.

Dixon, C., Green, J., Yeager, B., Baker, D., & Franquiz, M. (2000). "I used to know that": What happens when reform gets through the classroom door. *Bilingual Education Research Journal, 24*(1&2), 113-126.

Duranti, A., & Goodwin, C. (1992). *Rethinking context*. New York: Cambridge University Press.

Edwards, A. D., & Mercer, N. (1987). *Common knowledge: The development of understanding in the classroom*. New York: Falmer.

Edwards, A. D., & Westgate, D. P. G. (1994). *Investigating classroom talk* (2nd ed.). London, UK: Falmer.

Egan–Robertson, A., & Bloome, D. (Eds.). (1998). *Students as researchers of language and culture in their classrooms*. Cresskill, NJ: Hampton Press.

Engestrom, Y. (1987). *Learning by expanding: An activity-theoretical approach to developmental research*. Helsinki: Orienta-Konsultit.

Erickson, F., & Shultz, J. (1981). When is a context? Some issues and methods in the analysis of social competence. In J. L. Green & C. Wallat (Eds.), *Ethnography and language in educational settings* (pp. 147-150). Norwood, NJ: Ablex.

Fairclough, N. (1993). Discourse and text: Linguistic and intertextual analysis within discourse analysis. *Discourse and Society, 3*(2), 193-218.

Floriani, A. (1993). Negotiating what counts: Roles and relationships, content and meaning, texts and context. *Linguistics and Education, 5*(3&4), 241-274.

Garfinkel, H. (1984). *Studies in ethnomethodology*. New York: Blackwell.

Gaskin, S., Miller, P. J., & Corsaro, W. A. (Eds.). (1992). *Theoretical and methodological perspectives in the interpretive study of children* (Vol. 58). San Francisco, CA: Jossey-Bass.

Gee, J., & Green, J. (1998). Discourse ANALYSIS, learning, and social practice: A methodological study. *Review of Research in Education, 23*, 119-169.

Geertz, C. (1983). *Local knowledge: Further essays in interpretive anthropology*. New York: Basic Books.

Golden, J. (1988). The construction of a literary text in a story reading lesson. In J. Green & J. Harker (Eds.), *Multiple perspective analyses of classroom discourse* (pp. 71-106). Norwood, NJ: Ablex.

Golden, J. (1990). *The narrative symbol in childhood literature: Explorations in the construction of texts*. New York: Mouton de Gruyter.

Green, J., Dixon, C., & Zaharlick, A. (2002). Ethnography as a logic of inquiry. In J. Flood, J. Jensen, D. Lapp & J. Squire (Eds.), *Handbook for methods of research on English language arts teaching* (pp. 201-224). Hillsdale, NJ: Erlbaum.

Green, J.L., & Harker, J.O. (Eds.). (1988). *Multiple perspective analyses of classroom discourse*. Norwood, NJ: Ablex.

Green, J. L., & Meyer, L. A. (1991). The embeddedness of reading in classroom life. In C. Baker & A. Luke (Eds.), *Towards a critical sociology of reading pedagogy* (pp. 141-160). Philadelphia: John Benjamins.

Green, J.L., & Wallat, C. (1979). What is an instructional context? An exploratory analysis of conversational shifts across time. In O. Garnica & M. King (Eds.), *Language, children, and society* (pp. 159-174). New York: Pergamon.

Green, J.L., & Wallat, C. (1981). Mapping instructional converstations—A sociolinguistic ethnography. In J. Green & C. Wallat (Eds.), *Ethnography and languages in educational settings* (pp. 161-195). Norwood, NJ:Ablex.

Green, J., Weade, R., & Graham, K. (1988). Lesson construction and student participation. In J. Green & J. Harker (Eds.), *Multiple perspective analyses of classroom discourse* (pp. 11-48). Norwood, NJ: Ablex.

Grice, H. (1975). Logic and conversation. In *Syntax and Semantics* (pp. 41-58). New York: Academic Press.

Gumperz, J. (1986). Interactive sociolinguistics on the study of schooling. In J. Cook-Gumperz (Ed.), *The social construction of literacy* (pp. 45-68). New York: Cambridge University Press.

Gumperz, J. (1992). Contextualization and understanding. In A. Duranti & C. Goodwin (Eds.), *Rethinking context: Language as an interactive phenomenon* (pp. 229-252). New York: Cambridge University Press.

Gumperz, J.J., & Behrens, N. (1993). Transcribing conversational exchanges. In J. A. Edwards & M. D. Lampert (Eds.), *Talking data: Transcription and coding in discourse research* (pp. 91-121). Hillsdale, NJ: Erlbaum.

Gumperz, J., & Herasimchuk, E. (1973). The conversational analysis of social meaning: A study of classroom interaction. In R. Shuy (Ed.), *Sociolinguistics: Current trends and prospects* (Monograph Series on Language and Linguistics, 23rd Annual Round Table Vol. 25). Washington, DC: Georgetown University Press.

Gumperz, J.J., & Hymes, D. (Eds.). (1986). *Directions in sociolinguistics: The ethnography of communication*. New York: Blackwell. (Original work published 1972)

Gumperz, J.J., & Tannen, D. (1979). Individual and social differences in language use. In C. Fillmore, D. Kempler, & W. Wang (Eds.), *Individual differences in language ability* (pp. 305-325). New York: Academic Press.

Guzzetti, B., & Hynd, C. (Eds.). (1998). *Perspectives on conceptual change: Multiple ways to understand knowing and learning in a complex world*. Mahwah, NJ: Erlbaum.

Heap, J. (1991). A situated perspective on what counts as reading. In C. Baker & A. Luke (Eds.), *Towards a critical sociology of reading pedagogy* (pp. 103-139). Philadelphia: John Benjamins.

Heap, J. (1992). Ethnomethodology and the possibility of a metaperspective on literacy research. In R. Beach, J. Green, M. Kamil, & T. Shanahan (Eds.), *Multiple disciplinary perspectives on literacy research* (pp. 35-56). Urbana, IL: NCRE & NCTE.

Heap, J.L. (1995). The status of claims in "qualitative" research. *Curriculum Inquiry, 25*(3), 271-291.

Heath, S.B. (1982). Ethnography in education: Defining the essentials. In P. Gillmore & A.A. Glatthorn (Eds.), *Children in and out of school: Ethnography and education* (pp. 35-55). Washington, DC: Center for Applied Linguistics.

Heras, A.I. (1993) The construction of understanding in a sixth grade bilingual classroom. *Linguistics and Education, 5*(3&4), 275-299.

Hicks, D. (1995). Discourse, learning, and teaching. In M. Apple (Ed.), *Review of research in education* (pp. 49-95). Washington, DC: AERA.

Ivanic, R. (1994). I is for interpersonal: Discoursal construction of writer identities and the teaching of writing. *Linguistics and Education, 6*, 3-15.

Ivanic, R. (1997). *Writing and identity: The discoursal construction of identity in academic writing*. Amsterdam: John Benjamins.

Kelly, G., & Crawford, T. (1996). Students' interactions with computer representations: Analysis of discourse in laboratory groups. *Journal of Research in Science Teaching, 33*(7), 693-707.

Kelly, G. J., & Crawford, T. (1997). An ethnographic investigation of the discourse processes of school science. *Science Education, 81*(5), 533-559

Kelly, G., Crawford, T., & Green, J. (2001). Common task and uncommon knowledge: Dissenting voices in the discursive construction of physics across small laboratory groups. *Linguistics and Education, Special Issue on Language and Cognition, 12*(2), 135-174.

Kristeva, J. (1986). Word, dialogue, and novel. In T. Moi (Ed.), *The Kristeva reader* (pp. 34-61). Oxford, UK: Basil Blackwell.

Lemke, J. (1990). *Talking science: Language, learning and values.* Norwood, NJ: Ablex.

Lin, L. (1993). Language of and in the classroom: Constructing the patterns of social life. *Linguistics and Education, 5*(3&4), 367-409.

McHoul, A. (1978). The organization of turns at formal talk in the classroom. *Language in Society, 7,* 183-213

Mehan, H. (1979). *Learning lessons.* Cambridge, MA: Harvard University Press.

Moll, L.C. (1992). Literacy research in community and classrooms: A sociocultural approach. In R. Beach, J. Green, M. Kamil, & T. Shanahan (Eds.), *Multiple disciplinary perspectives on literacy research* (pp. 211-244). Urbana, IL: NCRE & NCTE.

Ochs, E. (1979). Transcription as theory. In E. Ochs & B.B. Schefflin (Eds.), *Developmental pragmatics* (pp. 43-72). New York: Academic Press.

Piaget, J. (2003). *The language and thought of the child.* London: Routledge. (Original work published 1924)

Putney, L., Green, J., Dixon, C., Durán, R., & Yeager, B. (2000). Consequential progressions: Exploring collective-individual development in a bilingual classroom. In P. Smagorinsky & C. Lee (Eds.), *Constructing meaning through collaborative inquiry: Vygotskian perspectives on literacy research* (pp. 86-126). Cambridge, UK: Cambridge University Press.

Rex, L., Green, J., & Dixon, C. (1997). Making a case from evidence: Constructing opportunities for learning academic literacy practices. *Interpretations: Journal of the English Teachers Association of Western Australia, 30*(2), 78-104.

Rex, L., & McEachen, D. (1999). "If anything is odd, inappropriate, confusing, or boring, it's probably important": The emergence of inclusive academic literacy through English classroom discussion practices. *Research in the Teaching of English, 34*(1), 65-127.

Rieber, R.W., & Carton, A. S. (1987). *The collected works of L. S. Vygotsky.* New York: Plenum Press.

Santa Barbara Classroom Discourse Group. (1992a). Constructing literacy in classrooms: Literate action as social accomplishment. In H. Marshall (Ed.), *Redefining student learning: Roots of educational change* (pp. 119-150). Norwood, NJ: Ablex.

Santa Barbara Classroom Discourse Group. (1992b). Do you see what we see? The referential and intertextual nature of classroom life. *Journal of Classroom Interaction. 27*(2), 29-36.

Santa Barbara Classroom Discourse Group. (1995). Two languages, one community: An examination of educational possibilities. In R. Macias & R. Garcia (Eds.), *Changing schools for changing students: An anthology of research on language minorities.* Linguistic Minority Research Institute 1994 Anthology.

Souza Lima, E. (1995). Culture revisited: Vygotsky's ideas in Brazil. *Anthropology & Education Quarterly, 26*(4), 443-457.

Spradley, J. (1980). *Participant observation.* New York: Holt, Rinehart & Winston.

Tuyay, S., Floriani, A., Yeager, B., Dixon, C., & Green, J. (1995). Constructing an integrated, inquiry-oriented approach in classrooms: A cross-case analysis of social, literate, and academic practice. *Journal of Classroom Interaction, 30*(2), 1-15.

Tuyay, S., Jennings, L., & Dixon, C. (1995) Classroom discourse and opportunities to learn: An ethnographic study of knowledge construction in a bilingual third grade classroom. *Discourse Processes, 19*(1), 75-110.

Vygotsky, L. S. (1987). The collected works of L. S. Vygotsky. In R. W. Rieber & A. S. Carton (Eds.), *Vol. 1: Problems of general psychology.* New York: Plenum.

Voyat, G. (1984). *The world of Henri Wallon.* Norwood, NJ: Aronson.

Weade, G. (1992). Locating learning in the times and spaces of teaching. In H. H. Marshall (Ed.), *Redefining student learning: Roots of educational change* (pp. 87-118). Norwood, NJ: Ablex.

Yeager, B., Floriani, A., & Green, J. (1998). Learning to see learning in the classroom: Developing an ethnographic perspective. In D. Bloome & A. Egan-Robertson (Eds.), *Students as researchers of language and culture in their classrooms* (pp. 115-139). Cresskill, NJ: Hampton Press.

15

The Discoursal Construction of Writer Identity

Roz Ivanic
Lancester University

This chapter is about a very specific aspect of literacy, yet it is, I think, an essential factor to take into account in literacy research. It focuses on the identity of the writer of a text, and specifically, the way in which the writer's identity is inscribed in the communicative resources on which he or she draws when writing. This perspective on literacy research is concerned specifically with the writer, the writer's sense of who he or she is, the act of writing, the linguistic and other semiotic characteristics of the texts writers produce, and the consequences for identity of these textual characteristics. Although it does not focus on reading events, these ways of understanding writer identity are relevant also to the study of reading, because readers "read off" messages about the writer from the text. Although it does not specifically incorporate detailed study of the social practices, contexts, and interactions in which literacy events are situated, it complements such approaches.

I have chosen to use the term *identity* in this chapter and elsewhere because it is a readily understandable everyday word, referring to an individual's sense of who he or she is. I take seriously people's lived experience of having an identity, and of being unique, and I make this lived experience of individuals the starting point for my research. However, there is also a danger in the term *identity* because it is sometimes interpreted as something that is individual, unitary, and uniform, rather than social, multiple, open to contestation, and changing over time. It is, therefore, important also to look beyond people's experience of who they are, to acknowledge the social factors that accompany and reinterpret biological and personality factors, and to see *identity* as situated in social interaction and in social context (see also Gee, this volume, for the use of the term *socially situated identity*). By describing people's identities as *discoursally constructed* by the communicative resources on which they draw, I emphasize the role of social factors in the formation of identities: who a person "is" depends on who he or she *can be* in his or her social context, and is always constructed in relation to the identities of others. The idea of the discoursal construction of identity accounts for the heterogeneity and fluidity of identities. Some theorists prefer the term *subjectivity* to draw attention to the social constructedness of identities (see, e.g., Kamberelis & Scott, 1992; Kress, 1996; Scott, 2000). However, I have chosen to hold on to the term *identity* for the reasons just given, and because it does not have the connotations of passivity associated with the word *subjectivity*. Some researchers also use the term *subjectivity* to refer to more subjective personal uses of language, to contrast with objective and impersonal uses, which is not the meaning I discuss here. Thus, I use the term *identity* to mean the same as *subjectivity* as used by the researchers just mentioned, but making people's experience of being someone my starting point, rather than making social explanations of identity my starting point. (For a more detailed discussion of this issue of terminology, see Ivanic, 1998.)

Most of what I present in this chapter could easily be applied also to speaker identity. I am particularly interested, however, in developing an argument about writer identity because writing is so often regarded as *impersonal*. In my view, writing is almost as personal as speaking, and positions writers in just the same way as speaking does. But it does lack the phonetic characteristics of regional varieties that are perhaps the most salient linguistic resources that people feel construct their identity when they are speaking.

The chapter consists of four sections. The first outlines the theoretical origins of the idea of the discoursal construction of identity. The second explains what I mean by the discoursal construction of writer identity, presenting a model consisting of four dimensions of writer identity, all of which are discoursally constructed. The third takes up three issues that I have found are necessary to address when undertaking research on the discoursal construction of writer identity, and extending the concept. The fourth outlines the two main research projects I have undertaken within this perspective, showing what can and cannot be illuminated with this approach.

THE IDEA OF THE DISCOURSAL CONSTRUCTION OF IDENTITY

The Fundamental Concept of Self-Representation

This perspective originated in the work of the sociologist Erving Goffman (1959), who drew attention to the key role of interaction in the social construction of identity: the way in which identity is not located in a solitary individual, but constructed through social relationships between two or more people. Goffman studied the behavior of members of a small Shetland Isles community, and noted that they conveyed messages about themselves to each other in subtle ways. A particular movement, gesture, or facial expression would be read as signifying that a person was, for example, friendly, annoyed, or arrogant. He commented on the way in which people could, to some extent, control these self-representations, behaving in ways that made them seem to have particular characteristics that were not strictly true of them. He also observed that people could inadvertently convey messages about themselves, not realizing how their behavior would be interpreted. He pointed out that the meanings of these signals were culture-specific: it was only people who were well-established members of this small community who interpreted the behaviors they observed as conveying particular messages, and hence islanders could only use these strategies to portray themselves in the light they wished to other members of the same community. He employed the metaphor of the theater to explain the representation of self, distinguishing the "performer" from the "character" he or she presented. His work has been criticized for reducing "identity" to a set of guiles and strategies for self-representation, for a somewhat mono-lithic view of culture and community in which there are no conflicts of values and beliefs, and for disregarding the workings of privilege and power in the social construction of identity. However, these criticisms do not, in my view, reduce the usefulness of his central insight about the way in which people construct messages about themselves through their behavior in interaction with others.

Roger Cherry (1988), working in the field of rhetoric and composition studies, was the first to pick up this idea and apply it to written language. He observed that writing is a very specific type of social behavior that can convey messages about the writer in the same way as physical movements and gestures do. He noted that the selection of particular words and structures could portray a writer in a specific way, quite differently from the way in which he or she would be constructed by the selection of other words and structures. He made interesting connections with work such as that of Lisa Ede (1984) on the way in which the reader is portrayed in a text, pointing out that although numerous studies have begun to explore the complexity of audience representation, no corresponding literature on self-representation in writing has yet emerged (Cherry, 1988, p. 252). The main claim of Cherry's article is that there is a need to distinguish two dimensions of self-representation in written discourse, what he called *ethos* and *persona*. Cherry equated ethos with the qualities of the writer him- or herself, and persona with the social role the writer was adopting. Although this is an interesting distinction, I have found it difficult to maintain, and Cherry himself did not pursue the implications of it beyond this article. His main contribution was to draw attention to the way in which Goffman's insights could be applied to written language: insights that I developed in my own work.

In my work on writing and identity (Ivanic, 1998), I was mainly concerned with the way in which writers often experience a "crisis of identity" when entering a new discourse community such as the academic discourse community. This caused me to focus my attention on problems with self-representation, clashes between different ways of representing oneself in writing, and the sense of inadequacy that writers frequently experienced when trying to undertake a new type of writing. Therefore, I took up the idea of self-representation from Goffman and Cherry, but looked also for ways of theorizing diversity, conflict, and issues of power inherent in self-representation in writing. Specifically, I took concepts and insights from Critical Discourse Analysis (CDA; see also Freebody, this volume) as the broader framing for understanding the way in which a writer's identity is discoursally constructed as he or she writes.

The Connections with Critical Discourse Analysis

CDA theorists such as Norman Fairclough (1989, 1992, 1995), Gunther Kress (1989, 1996), and James Gee (1996, 1999) take a social constructionist approach to language rather than a social interactionist approach. (For a discussion of the comparison and interplay between social interactionist and social constructionist theories of written language, see Nystrand, 1989.) This shifts the focus from individuals and specific acts of communication in their immediate social context to the more abstract linguistic resources — the socially available ways of communicating — which are drawn on in those specific acts of communication. This adds several extra dimensions to the idea of "self-representation" originating in the work of Goffman.

A Social Constructionist Approach.   The key insight of CDA is that it is necessary to look beyond the immediate context of social interaction to the broader social context consisting of conflicting views of the world, of patterns of privileging among them (see Wertsch, 1991, for the idea of patterns of privileging), and of unequal relations of power. In this view, the broader social context shapes, or constructs, and is constructed by the language people use. That is, people do not write as individuals, creating meanings from their own heads, but they draw on resources that are socially available to them, using language in ways that are culturally recognizable in their social context. This was hinted at by Goffman (1959), who he pointed out that people "incorporate and exemplify the officially accredited values of the society" (p. 31). Goffman did not develop this aspect of his theory, whereas CDA theorists make this their central focus. CDA theorists emphasize, however, that there is no one predetermined set of values and beliefs on which people draw: There are several socially available possibilities in any context of culture, although some have more status, and hence there will be pressure to conform to those. An important question in CDA concerns whose interests are being served by the maintenance of particular norms and conventions for language use. A key tenet of CDA is that each language user can in principle challenge the norms and conventions, and so contribute to contestation and eventually to social and discoursal change.

The Concept of Interdiscursivity in This Theoretical Perspective. Critical discourse analysts focus their attention on the linguistic resources that are available to people as they use language: That is, ways of using language that are available to be drawn on in specific social contexts. They assert that these resources are imbued with ways of seeing the world, values, beliefs, social roles, relationships and power relations. Fairclough and Kress referred to these resources as *discourses* and *genres*: Discourses are patterned ways of using language that carry with them particular worldviews, values, and beliefs; genres are patterned ways of using language that are associated with particular social roles in particular social contexts, involving particular social actions aimed at achieving particular social purposes. In this view, any instance of actual language use draws simultaneously on one or more discourse and on one or more genre. Gee used the term *social languages* in a way that does not distinguish between ways of seeing the world and social situations. One of the aims of many CDA practitioners is to study instances of language use—that is, one or more texts—in order to identify the linguistic resources that are in circulation, the views of the world that are inscribed in them, and whose interests are being served by their reproduction.

Interdiscursivity means the practice of drawing on one or more of these linguistic resources, along with the social and ideological meanings inscribed in them, in any specific act of communication. Interdiscursivity is in principle different from practices that involve reproducing a specific text such as quotation or plagiarism, but many theorists use the term *intertextuality* as an umbrella term for both these types of practice. Interdiscursivity is not something people choose whether or not to engage in: All acts of communication are, by nature, interdiscursive. The study of interdiscursivity also draws attention to the way in which each actual use of language is likely to draw on more than one set of linguistic resources, mixing them in novel and motivated ways to suit the immediate purposes of participants. Thus, interdiscursivity is more likely to be heterogeneous than homogeneous. This tendency toward heterogeneous interdiscursivity explains how each use of language can be unique, can contribute toward bringing new linguistic resources into circulation, and can play a small part in contesting the status quo.

A fundamental tenet of CDA is that it is in the interests of particular groups to maintain some discourses (views of the world) and genres (social relations among participants in social interaction) at the expense of others, and thus every communicative act is part of a struggle for supremacy not just among ways of using language, but among associated ways of viewing the world and relations of power. Kress and Gee, in particular, emphasized the way in which participating in discourses and genres through interdiscursivity has consequences for identity (or *subjectivity* as Kress and others prefer to call it), so that using language in a particular way can result in seeming to be a particular kind of person, with particular ways of viewing the world, and entering into particular relationships with others.

Inequality of Access to Discourses and Inequality of Entitlement Rights. One of the ways in which power and discrimination operate is through unequal access to the linguistic resources that are circulating in any social context; that is, the range of linguistic resources on which to draw interdiscursively may not include the resources that are most highly valued in their society. People have differential access to, and place differential value on linguistic resources, depending on the lives they lead. For example, a university lecturer's life may not lead him or her to value participation in gambling events, thus, he or she may not take any opportunity to encounter or learn how to enter into the sorts of discourses and social roles that are highly valued in gambling contexts. This does not disadvantage this individual because gambling discourse is not highly privileged in the culture in which he or she lives. People are disadvantaged, however, when their lives do not lead them to value participation in classroom events, and when they have not had opportunities prior to schooling to encounter or learn how to enter into the sorts of discourses and social roles that are highly valued at school. It is important to emphasize that participation in classroom events has no intrinsic value, it is just that it is highly valued by people with power in industrialized societies: People who do not value or participate in classroom discourse may be well able to learn and understand a great deal within discourses associated with other contexts, but they do not have, and often do not desire, access to socially ratified "schooling" discourses.

Associated with inequality of access is the unequal distribution of "entitlement rights" (see Bloome & Egan-Robertson, 1993). Depending on their life histories and sense of social status in particular contexts, people feel they have the right to participate in certain discourses and not in others; to take up certain roles in social interaction, and not others. Thus, someone who is a lecturer at a university is likely to have a sense of entitlement to participate in the discourses of academia and speak as an authority, and may have a sense of entitlement to write and speak as an authority in other settings too, but may be somewhat more hesitant in the context of a gambling event.

In terms of social, political, and educational policy, CDA theorists emphasize that there are two responses to these inequalities. One is to attempt to increase the opportunities for access and people's sense of entitlement, but this type of response reproduces the status quo, and is doomed to failure unless there are broader social and political changes to support it. A more radical response is to recognize the value of alternative discourses that people bring with them to socially ratified institutions such as schooling from their own contexts, discourses in which they do have a sense of entitlement, and to work to change the patterns of privileging in the social context in order to value those discourses as highly as others.

I find that these ideas add important dimensions to a theory of the discoursal construction of identity in writing. They place self-representation through written language in the context of the broader significance of the linguistic resources the writer draws on, and of the workings of power in the struggle over discourses. (For more detailed discussion and illustration of some aspects of these approaches, see Gee, this volume.)

DIMENSIONS OF WRITER IDENTITY

I have developed a diagram for thinking about writer identity that attempts to incorporate the most useful insights from these theoretical perspectives (see Clark & Ivanic 1997; Ivanic, 1994, 1998, for earlier stages in this development). In this diagram (see Fig. 15.1), which I call the "clover-leaf diagram," the first element to note is that all dimensions of writer identity come into being and operate within the context of socially available possibilities for self-hood: Resources for, and constraints on, who a person can be. This outer surround to the four dimensions of writer identity draws attention to the way in which the construction of "identity" is always a social, and not an individual undertaking, and to the way in which communicative resources (among other social patternings) shape individuals and their actions, and are also shaped by them, as explained in CDA.

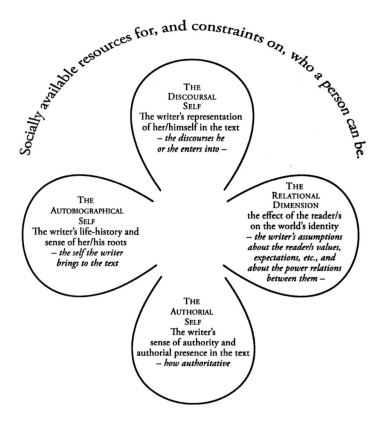

Figure 15.1.   Dimensions of writer identity.

Within the clover leaf, the four dimensions can be read chronologically from left to right: the autobiographical self is everything (shaped as it is by the socially available possibilities) that a writer brings to an act of writing. The discoursal self and the authorial self are aspects of the writer's identity that are constructed (from the socially available possibilities) at the very moment of writing. The relational dimension is the way in which, at the moment of writing, a writer conceives of the reader(s) who will be constructing an impression of the writer (from the socially available resources on which they are able to draw) as they read what has been written. These dimensions are not hermetically sealed from one another, but are all interrelated, as is represented by the open, interconnecting center of the clover leaf.

The autobiographical self takes up the idea of access and entitlement rights, drawing attention to the way in which a writer will embark on an act of writing having a unique history of encounters with different ways of using language, and a sense of which ones they desire to and are entitled to engage in themselves. Thus, the linguistic resources writers bring with them to an act of writing, shaped as they are by social opportunities and constraints on those writers' lives, are one dimension of their identity as a writer.

The discoursal self is what Goffman and Cherry called *self-representation*, referring specifically to self-representation through discourse (spoken or written). It is important to distinguish the discoursal self as a dimension of writing from writing about oneself as a topic, which can occasionally be included as part of the content of some types of writing. The discoursal self refers not to writing about oneself, but to the depiction of self that the writer constructs through the way in which he or she draws on socially available possibilities for self-hood in the act of writing—possibilities that are shaped by the writer's autobiographical self. The identity that is discoursally constructed in this way is typically multiple, changing from moment to moment, from clause to clause. The discoursally constructed self is not independent, but shaped in relation to others: through a process of alignment with some social groups and distancing from other social groups.

This act of self-representation is, in most cases, unconscious: Writers are not usually explicitly aware of the ways in which their deployment of communicative resources may be portraying them, and are sometimes rather daunted if this issue is raised to consciousness, although some also find awareness of self-representation in writing can help to overcome writer's block. It is also possible for a writer to consciously manipulate the way in which he or she is represented in writing by choosing to draw on particular resources in preference to others, but this tactic may or may not have the effect the writer intended. This depiction exists in a vacuum at the moment of writing, for it is not activated until it is taken up by a reader. (See Clayton, 2000; Hayes, Shriver, Hill, & Hatch, 1992, for research into readers' responses to the construction of the writer.)

When two or more people collaborate on a piece of writing, the different discourses, and hence the different positionings (discoursal selves) that each brings to the task become apparent. Joint authors often have to negotiate and compromise over how they are representing themselves, or (when it becomes impossible to agree!) to signal explicitly who owns which subject positions in the heterogeneous text. In Clark & Ivanic (1997), we faced these decisions and made an explicit statement about them in the introduction.

The authorial self is a dimension of writer identity that is only indirectly entailed by the theoretical perspectives I have mentioned so far, but refers to a factor that has been the object of a good deal of writing theory and research (Berkenkotter & Huckin, 1995; Kaufer & Geisler, 1989; Lillis, 1997), and in my view needs to be taken into account in a theory of writer identity. It is concerned with what many researchers and practitioners call the writer's voice, in the sense of the strength with which the writer comes over as the author of the text, what the writer has to say, and the writer's own opinions. This is a large part of what people (usually teachers) are referring to when they say things like "you can really hear the writer's own voice in that piece of writing." This dimension is a subcategory of the discoursal self: One of the aspects of self that writers construct discoursally is their authorship and authoritativeness, but it is more than that. It refers also to a sense of oneself as author: a sense that depends to a large extent on a writer's autobiographical self, and their assessment of the social relationship existing between them and their reader(s). This sense of self as author is what drives the process of meaning-making in writing, and it can be the basis for critical action toward social and discoursal change of the sort proposed in CDA. This aspect can be strengthened through joint or multiple authorship, and/or when writing is part of collective action involving wider community or group participation.

The relational dimension is a dimension I have not included in previous publications on writing and identity, but more recent theory and research, and formal and informal discussions with colleagues have convinced me that it needs to be included (see, e.g., Barat, 1999; Lillis, 2001, 2003). It refers to the effects that readers have on a writer's identity: the way in which writers anticipate their readers' values and beliefs, take account of the power relations between themselves and their readers, and construct their representation of self accordingly. This aspect of identity is at the heart of Goffman's account of self-representation, and I think it needs to be included explicitly in the dimensions of writer identity. The relational dimension also comes into operation at a later point in time, when readers interact with what the writer has written. At that moment the writer's identity is (re)constructed discoursally, as the reader reads off an impression of the writer from the text. I could go so far as to say that there is no such thing as "writer identity" until this moment of up-take—as I mentioned before, the writer's representation of self exists in a vacuum until then. However, I think this interpretation would lose the understanding that, at the moment of writing, the writer is actually being someone, whether or not that identity is ultimately taken up by another.

At the moment of writing, these four dimensions of writer identity are all in play simultaneously, interacting with each other. All aspects are shaped by the broader social context: By what I have called the socially available possibilities for self-hood. These resources construct the identity of, or position a writer each time he or she draws on them, building up for that writer a sense of who they are both at the moment of writing and cumulatively, over time. Each act of writing in turn contributes to shaping the constellation of resources available for the construction of identity for that writer in the future and, in so far that the writing is read, also to the constellation of resources that are socially available for the construction of identity for others. I have proposed this multidimensional model in order to attempt to take account of many different elements that contribute to the construction of identity, and many different aspects of that process of construction.

UNDERTAKING RESEARCH ON THE DISCOURSAL CONSTRUCTION OF IDENTITY

Researching the discoursal construction of identity requires the researcher to employ a variety of analytical frameworks and to engage with other perspectives on literacy. In the first research project I conducted within this framework on academic literacy (see Ivanic, 1998, and below), I focused mainly on the discoursal self as previously described. This involved close analysis of written texts in order to make claims about the sorts of representations of self the writers were constructing in relation to available linguistic resources. Therefore, I needed tools for analyzing texts, which I discuss in the section on Halliday's Systemic-Functional Grammar. More recently, it has become clear that the concept of the discoursal construction of identity can be extended beyond the consequences for identity of linguistic characteristics of texts to include the visual and material characteristics of texts, and to include the social practices in which writers engage when they write. Finally, in all my work I have been concerned with the pedagogic implications of the idea of the discoursal construction of identity (see Freebody, this volume). In this section, I take up each of these issues in turn.

Tools for Analysing Texts

Following Fairclough (1989), I treat the text that is produced by the writer as the central object of study in my research. In order to make observations about how linguistic resources position writers, it is necessary to have a powerful way of describing the linguistic characteristics of the texts they write. I have found that formal grammars are inadequate to this task because they are only able to generate observations about accuracy, correctness, and style. Functional grammars provide a very different perspective, because they link form to meaning, and these are what I have used in my research. So far I have used Michael Halliday's systemic-functional grammar, and in the future I intend also to work with Theo van Leeuwen's recasting of this, which in my view offers even greater insights into the discourses that writers enter into through the linguistic resources on which they draw. In this section, I give a brief overview and comparison of these two analytical tools for linguistic texts.

Halliday's Systemic-Functional Grammar. Halliday (1967, 1994) made two fundamental observations about linguistic resources that make his grammar especially useful when studying the discoursal construction of identity. First, he observed that linguistic resources are systemic, meaning that they can all be linked to a system of alternatives, with each alternative carrying a significant meaning in contrast to another. Halliday referred to these alternatives as choices, but I avoid this word because it suggests conscious selection among alternatives, rather than socially constructed selection. Halliday's second key observation is that not only lexical items but also grammatical constructions carry meaning. So, if someone uses transitive verbs such as carry (as I did in the previous sentence) and the person who does the carrying (the actor) and the object that is carried are both abstract noun phrases (as are the words "grammatical constructions" and "meaning" in the previous sentence), the grammar itself links the writing to a social setting in which abstractions act on each other—a social setting such as the academic community. Thus, Halliday showed how grammar is meaningful, or functional, and socially situated. He referred to language as a social semiotic (Halliday, 1978) in order to emphasize this point. These sorts of insights provided a grammar that allowed me to suggest things like, "because this writer used these particular grammatical features at this point, he or she was potentially being socially constructed in a particular way—as holding particular views of the world, and as taking up a particular position in relation to the reader(s)."

In his *Introduction to Functional Grammar,* Halliday (1994) set out some of this system of alternatives that he called *functional grammar.* He presented these as three systems which operate simultaneously: a system of grammatical alternatives for representing the world, one for conducting the exchange between speaker and listener/writer and reader, and one for constructing the message. Thus, he claimed that language simultaneously performs these three metafunctions, which means that any utterance, sentence, or clause can be analyzed in three ways, and I have suggested that language is consequently positioning the writer in these three ways. So a writer is discoursally constructed as viewing the world in a particular way, as being in a particular type of relationship with the reader(s), and as taking a particular approach to the act of communication itself (see Ivanic & Camps, 2001, for this argument).

Halliday's functional grammar is an extremely revealing tool for researching the discoursal construction of identity, and I continue to use many aspects of it. Recently, however, I have found van Leeuwen's approach particularly well suited to studying the discoursal construction of identity, and I have begun to incorporate it into my research.

Van Leeuwen's Theory of Representation.   Van Leeuwen's method of analysis is also concerned with the relationship between meaning and form (van Leeuwen, 1993, 1995, 1996, van Leeuwen & Wodak 1999), but he approached it from the opposite direction from Halliday. Instead of starting from alternative ways of using language, and identifying what sorts of meanings they carry, van Leeuwen started with social reality, identified its different components and contrasting ways of representing them, and only then mapped out possible linguistic realizations of these contrasts. So, for example, social actors (i.e., human participants) are one component of any social practice. Van Leeuwen (1996) made a broad distinction between representing human actors in a personal (e.g., "managers") or an impersonal way (e.g., "the management"), and then made a broad distinction between personal representations that name people (e.g., "John Simpson"), and those that categorize them (e.g., "students"). These broad distinctions, and finer ones that he offered too, provide a way of analyzing a text so as to show directly the relationship between its linguistic characteristics and their social implications, and hence the consequences for the discoursal construction of the identity of the writer. So, for example, an analyst can note that a group of texts have a tendency toward personal, named references to members of the business community in a town and impersonal references to homeless people in the same town, whereas another group of texts has opposite tendencies. The analyst might go on to suggest that this difference signals differences between the authors of these texts in their ways of thinking about people, and hence different degrees of social responsibility. Van Leeuwen's theory of representation is not yet published as a complete analytical framework, but his publications so far (see earlier) cover several elements of social reality and also elements that are added in the process of representation. These give a researcher extremely useful guidelines for this form of analysis.

Extensions of the Concept of the Discoursal Construction of Identity

In this section I discuss how identity is constructed by more than just language. In my research on the discoursal construction of identity in academic writing, I focused only on the way in which the linguistic aspects of texts construct identities for their writers. It soon became clear that this was a somewhat limited view of writing, and was missing other ways in which writers' identities are constructed. First, I am now making connections with the recent multimodal turn in the study of communication, paying attention to the way in which visual and material aspects of written texts construct identities for their makers. These other semiotic resources position their users just as much as written language does. Second, ethnographers of literacy (Bazerman & Prior, Tusting & Barton, Berkenkotter, this volume) have drawn attention to the fact that the selection of semiotic resources is only one among many social practices in which a writer engages. Engaging in the social practices that surround the writing of texts positions writers just as much as their selection of semiotic resources does. In this section, I explain a set of three terms, increasing in the scope of what they refer to. The term I have used so far, *linguistic resources*, can be broadened to *semiotic resources* in order to encompass also visual and material resources, and this in turn can broadened again to *communicative resources* to encompass not just semiotic practices but also other types of social practice involved in writing.

Applying the Idea of the Discoursal Construction of Identity to the "Wrighting" of Multimodal Texts.

The point has recently been cogently made that written texts are not only linguistic but also visual and material (Bruce, 2003; Cope & Kalantzis, 2000; Kress 1996, 2001; Kress & van Leeuwen 1996, 2001). This focus on the multimodality of texts affects CDA by showing that the socially available resources that are drawn on in the process of text-making are semiotic resources, not just linguistic resources, and that resources in all semiotic modes carry with them views of the world and power relations between producers and interpreters of meanings. The multimodality of meaning-making entails also that there is an interaction among modes: it is not just a question of the social significance of each individual sign system that is being drawn on, but also of the "intersemiotic" ensemble of several systems operating simultaneously. In order to emphasize the difference between this perspective and the more narrowly focused linguistic approach to writing, I have adopted the term *wrighting* to capture the idea that *wrighters* are creating and shaping their messages using other resources beyond linguistic ones, just as a wheelwright creates and shapes a wheel from many component materials.

Kress and van Leeuwen (1996) and van Leeuwen (1998) presented visual and material semiotic resources as systems of alternatives that differ according their meaning-carrying potential, in the same way as Halliday claimed that linguistic resources are systemic and functional. For example, they make a distinction between *static* or *conceptual* representation on the one hand, and *dynamic* or *narrative* representation on the other. Conceptual representation shows the generalized, universal characteristics of static objects or people, whereas narrative representation shows the more individual characteristics of specific objects or people involved in some activity. They associate this distinction, and the many others that they set out, with very different worldviews. Researchers who take a multimodal perspective on the discoursal construction of identity pay attention to the ways in which visual and material resources position wrighters just as much as linguistic resources do. Kress (1996) developed this argument and recent work by Glynda Hull (2001) extended it also to apply to the wrighting of digital videos that involve animation and movement as well as visual representation.

Incorporating a Broader Understanding of Literacy Practices. Work in the New Literacy Studies and other ethnographic approaches to literacy focus not so much on written text as on the purposes and practices that surround the making and using of written texts (Bazerman & Prior, Tusting & Barton, Berkenkotter, this volume; Barton, 1994, Barton & Hamilton, 1998; Barton, Hamilton, & Ivanic, 2000; Ivanic, 1998). A key insight of this perspective on literacy is that reading and writing are not done for their own sake, but are always serving purposes in people's lives and are shaped by the social context in which they are situated. In my view it would be extremely interesting and possible to extend the concept of the discoursal construction of identity to apply not only to the way in which a person's identity is constructed by the multimodal semiotic resources on which they draw, but also to the way identity is constructed by the literacy practices in which people participate. This is a bigger leap than the one toward treating texts as multimodal, and perhaps over-stretches the meaning of "discourse" to mean, as Gee (1996) and others suggested, not just ways of composing texts, but whole ways of being, thinking and acting in the world. Thus, identity is constructed, not just by the semiotic resources on which people draw, and the worldviews and power relations inscribed in them, but also by all the practices associated with multimodal communicative acts. The resources that are being drawn on are not just linguistic, not just semiotic, but more broadly communicative.

The Discoursal Construction of Identity in a Critical Approach to Literacy Education

The idea that writer, or "wrighter," identity is discoursally constructed in the ways outlined so far is not in itself located in education. It is relevant to writing in all settings, and research on the discoursal construction of writer identity can be conducted in relation to all types of writing. However, my interest in it, and the motivation to understand the relationship between writing and identity, originated in a pedagogic context: I wanted to understand the sense of identity crisis that many students experience when undertaking academic writing. Although my research has not specifically investigated ways of incorporating these understandings into critical pedagogy, I believe, and with my colleague Romy Clark have frequently suggested, that they lie at the heart of critical awareness-raising about language in academic and other settings (see especially Clark 1992; Clark & Ivanic, 1991, 1997, 1998, 1999; Ivanic 1995, 1998).

I have claimed that the way in which writers are positioned by the discoursal characteristics of their writing is the mechanism whereby they are coopted into particular ways of viewing the world, and that it should be one of the responsibilities of literacy educators to provide opportunities for students to gain understanding of how this happens. By focusing on the consequences for their own identities of using language (and other communicative resources) in particular ways, educators can raise students' awareness about the ideological nature of discourse. The benefits to students of this are, first, to take control over the discourses in which they are participating and the aspects of their identities (their views of the world, their relative authoritativeness, the relationship with the reader) that are thus being constructed; second, to recognize when it is issues of identity rather than issues of content that are blocking their writing; and third, to see the possibility of playing an active role in contributing to the circulation of some discourses as opposed to others. A particularly successful site for critical awareness raising of this sort is collaborative writing. As mentioned earlier, writing collaboratively involves decisions about what to say and how to say it, and each writer recognizes that the other's preferences do not always match their own. It is thus an opportunity for student writers to become aware of the discourses, and hence subject positions into which they are entering through the wordings they use.

USING THE NOTION OF "THE DISCOURSAL CONSTRUCTION OF IDENTITY" IN LITERACY RESEARCH: MY PERSONAL JOURNEY AS A RESEARCHER

Writer Identity in Academic Writing

In this research (Ivanic, 1998), I worked with eight mature students (i.e., students entering full-time higher education between the ages of 25 and 54). I met each of these eight people between two and six times, first to talk about their experience of academic writing more generally, and later to focus on one particular written assignment for one of their undergraduate courses. These eight people acted as co-researchers with me, investigating the characteristics of their own writing, the origins of these characteristics in their own life experience, their sense of how they were positioned by these characteristics, their sense of the influence of the reader on the way in which they presented themselves, and their sense of allegiance to the identities that were constructed in this way. My contribution to this joint knowledge-making process was to ask the right questions, and to share insights arising from linguistic analysis of their texts; theirs was to explore in depth and share with me their experience, perceptions, reactions and feelings. For many of my co-researchers, the research process was also a learning opportunity, and they said that they had learned a lot about academic writing through participating in the project.

The data collected in this way consisted of a complete written text by each of my co-researchers, along with at least two tape-recorded interviews: one about their lives and experiences of writing, and one or more about the text itself. In this research I had not yet made the move to broaden out my definition of *discourse*, and focused exclusively on the linguistic resources on which the writers were drawing. I started my analysis by looking particularly at parts of the texts which my co-researchers themselves had picked out as significant, and using Halliday's (1994) *Functional Grammar* to identify linguistic characteristics of these sections. One of the main findings at this stage was that all the students' texts were discoursally heterogeneous, and hence constructed multiple identities for their writers. For example, compare the following two extracts from John's essay for a course on Medical Ethics:

Example 1
Even though AIDS is a devastating illness that we don't have a cure for, it does not present any new problems in terms of confidentiality. What it does do is to take problems that already exist and enlarge them. AIDS achieves this by a number of routes. One, the virus is transmitted mainly (at the moment) by activity that is seen to deviate from a societal norm, e.g., unsafe gay sex and intravenous drug use.

Example 2
If gay men are having to visit lovers in hospital how will the hospital adapt to men wanting to show affection to each other? After all, the main weapon we have against AIDS at the moment is support and understanding.

In both these examples, I noted some constructions that sound more like spoken interaction: "*What it does do is,*" . . . the use of a question, "*After all.*" In Example 1 many nouns refer to aspects of illness: *AIDS, the virus, illness,* whereas in Example 2 many of the nouns refer to people: *gay men, lovers, men,* and the second use of *hospital,* meaning "the staff of the hospital." Even though John referred to real people in Example 2, he referred to them as categories—types of person—rather than as individuals, thus remaining within academic discourse rather than other, more personal discourses. In Example 1 the abstract nouns refer mainly to processes: *cure, problems, confidentiality, activity, norm, sex, use,* whereas in Example 2, the abstract nouns refer to feelings: *affection, support, and understanding.* In both samples, the word *we* is used, but in Example 1, it seems to mean "people in general," and in Example 2 it seems to carry the additional meaning of "me and people like me." In both examples, there are verbs that describe states of affairs: *is, have, exist,* which are common in academic writing. In Example 1 the other verbs refer to processes in which illness and abstract processes act on each other, including two passive constructions: *is transmitted, is seen to deviate,* whereas in Example 2, the other verbs are about active processes involving humans: *having to visit, wanting to show.* Both examples contain metaphors: in Example 1 the word *route* is what one might call an academic metaphor, making it possible to talk about generalized and abstract processes; in Example 2, the word *weapon* is what one might call an emotive metaphor, increasing the power of the message.

The claim I made was that John was positioned differently by the discourses on which he was drawing in these two parts of his text. In the first, his identity was discoursally constructed as relatively objective, impersonal, concerned with the abstractions and social processes of academic study, viewing the topic of AIDS in a technical, analytic way. In the second, his identity was constructed as relatively involved, concerned with the realities of human experience, viewing the topic of AIDS in a politically committed, campaigning way.

Detailed studies of samples like these led me to work on some particular linguistic features more systematically: those that positioned the writers within academia, those that positioned them in other domains of life, those that positioned them as espousing particular disciplinary values and beliefs, those that positioned them as relatively authoritative or relatively self-effacing. This constituted an analysis of the discoursal self and the authorial self for each writer. Because I also had the taped interviews with the writers about the texts I was analyzing, I was then able to find their accounts of when and where in their life histories they had encountered some of these particular ways of using language—that is, to explore the autobiographical self dimension of their discoursally constructed identities. Finally, I immersed myself more thoroughly in the interviews, and identified themes concerning both the influence of the reader on the way in which each writer's identity was discoursally constructed (the relational dimension), and the writers' sense of ownership of the identities that were discoursally constructed in their texts.

I developed the diagram presented in Fig. 15.1 through a cyclical process while engaged in this research. That is, I did not first develop the theory and then apply it; rather, I assembled some of the elements of the theory and based my research design on these. My interest in dimensions of writer identity drove my data collection, but it was only at the stage of data analysis, and during subsequent discussions with colleagues that the details presented in Fig. 15.1 fell into place. Since then, together with David Camps, I have applied the idea of the discoursal construction of writer identity to samples of academic writing by six Mexican postgraduate students (Ivanic & Camps, 2001). In this research, we elaborated on my earlier study of identity in academic writing by studying students writing in a second language, by distinguishing three types of positioning based on Halliday's three metafunctions of language (see earlier), and by using van Leeuwen's Theory of Representation for one of the detailed analyses. In these ways, the development of theory and the conducting of research were inextricably intertwined.

"Wrighter" Identity in Children's Multimodal Meaning-Making

In my current research I am incorporating the additional perspectives I mentioned in the section on "Extensions of the concept of the discoursal construction of identity," looking at how multimodal semiotic resources position wrighters of multimodal texts, and how the literacy practices in which they engage also position them, with a much broader interpretation of discoursal construction than in the academic writing research. In this research, my colleagues and I[1] collected five sets of project work produced by a group of 37 children, between the ages of 8 and 11 in one class in a primary school in the north west of England in the period 1994 through 1997. The work was the outcome of inquiry-based learning in which the children researched topics of their own choice. We collected these texts and mounted most of them in the form of digital scans on the Web site www.ling.lancs.ac.uk/lever/index.htm. In addition, we interviewed many of the children about the literacy practices associated with constructing the texts, and have analyzed the material properties of the texts as artifacts (Ormerod & Ivanic, 2000) and as means of communication (Ormerod & Ivanic, 2002).

The analysis in which I am currently engaged involves looking not only at the language, as in my study of writer identity in academic writing, but also at the visual and material characteristics of the texts, and using analytical techniques developed by Kress and van Leeuwen (1996) and van Leeuwen (1998) to reveal the ways in which these characteristics position the children. So, for example, two boys produced a page in a project about spiders that consisted of four images, each associated with short written texts, as shown in Fig. 15.2 (for descriptions of analysis, see www.ling.lancs.ac.uk/lever/projects/51/xt51/xt5102.htm).

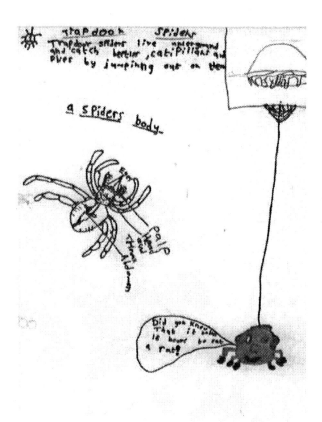

Figure 15.2.   A page from a project about spiders by Jim and Ryan, aged 9.

The first image, in the top left-hand corner of the page, is a schematic spider drawn in black felt-tipped pen with the number 1 inside its body: Jim is drawing on the practice, which is common in many books produced for children, of using a system of logos to decorate page numbers. He is showing an interest in the graphic presentation of his work, and in attracting the attention of his readers.

The second image, also drawn by Jim, is of a very different type: it s a realistic drawing of a trapdoor spider in its den underground, drawn in soft pencil, with several indistinct lines where the first attempt was erased. This image is boxed off with pencil lines in the top right-hand corner. In this image, Jim is presenting knowledge of spiders as something experienced in the real world, in which precise visual detail is relevant.

At the top of the page is a centered, underlined heading *Trapdoor Spiders*. Written beneath this heading, and between the page number to the left and the frame of the drawing on the right, are the words: *Trapdoor spiders live underground and catch beetles, caterpillars and flies by jumping out on them.* (For the original graphological features, see Fig. 15.2.) Here, Jim is writing as a scientist, using generic terms to refer to his objects of study, and present tense verbs to refer to universal truth regarding the repeated actions of this species.

The third drawing has an underlined title *a spider's body*, and is placed almost half-way down the page, slightly to the left. Jim employs yet another visual discourse: It is a diagram of a spider drawn in strong black felt-tipped pen, viewed from above, which he labels with the parts of a spider's body. This is what Kress and van Leeuwen (1996) called *conceptual representation*: showing the characteristics of phenomena in the world, rather than their actions. Like the sentence, it is a discourse in which scientific knowledge is presented in terms of unquestionable facts, with no reference to the processes of observation and research (as noted by van Leeuwen 1995).

The fourth drawing is by Ryan. It is a spider's web suspended from the frame of Jim's pencil drawing, with a single thread leading down to the bottom right-hand corner of the page, where a bright green cartoon-character spider with white eyes, red nose, and black mouth faces the reader, and has a speech bubble coming from it saying: *Did you know that it takes 16 hours to eat a rat!* In producing this image, Ryan is entering into yet another discourse: one in which individual, unrealistic fictional creatures are presented as speaking directly to the reader. Ryan's identity is constructed here as self-assured enough to play with knowledge, treating information as something to enjoy in small, humorous "sound-bites."

Each image and associated piece of text positions the boys differently, with different views of the world and relationships between them, their subject matter, and their readers. The page overall positions the boys as eclectic in their idea of what counts as knowledge—very much in the idiom of many current information books for children, which present information in visually complex double-spread pages, drawing on, juxtaposing, and overlaying many different verbal and visual discourses (for discussion of this trend see Moss, 2001, 2002). Among the many literacy practices associated with the production of this page, of particular note is the way in which the two boys worked on it together, one boy building on the contribution of the other. They not only draw on but also make a contribution to the communicative landscape by reproducing and thus helping to sustain this visually and verbally heterogeneous form of knowledge-making. This particular instance of making and connecting meanings reinforces some discoursal and generic trends rather than others, and will have its own small impact on the range of resources available to everyone who sees it. (For further discussion of this page, see Ivanic, 1999, and of other, similar pages, see Ivanic, in press).

CONCLUSION

In this chapter I started by discussing ways of referring to *identity*, and the issues surrounding this terminology. I pointed out the limitations of a view of identity as something inherent in the individual and unchanging over time and space. The chapter builds on the now well-established view that people's identities are constructed by the possibilities for selfhood that are socially available to them in their cultural context. This view of identity recognizes that, on the one hand, there is not complete freedom for people to be whatever type of person they choose to be, and on the other hand that people are not limited by simplistic stereotypes. People's identities are shaped by their life-histories, they are multiple, they are constructed in interaction, they take their shape from the subject positions available in each social context, and vary from context to context. Although this is a general view of the social construction of identity, in this chapter I have applied it specifically to writing, and the way in which identity is constructed through the discoursal resources on which writers draw.

I explained the origins of the idea of the discoursal construction of writer identity in Goffman's theory of the representation of self, Cherry's application of this to writing, and CDA. I presented an analysis of writer identity as constituted by four dimensions: the autobiographical self, the discoursal self, the authorial self, and the relational dimension, all constructed in the context of socially available resources for, and constraints on, who a person can be. I proposed that socially available resources for the construction of writer identity include not only linguistic resources but also other semiotic resources, particularly visual and material resources, and also communicative resources more broadly conceived, to include the literacy practices in which writers engage as they write. I indicated the sorts of analytical frameworks that can be drawn on in research aimed at analyzing how specific texts and acts of writing position their writers, or "wrighters." Finally, I outlined two research projects in which I have investigated the discoursal construction of writer identity, the first concerned with the linguistic resources that are drawn on in academic writing, the second concerned also with multimodal resources and literacy practices in which children engage in inquiry-based learning, and I gave examples of these sorts of analyses.

Further research in this field can develop in several directions. Although such research is not limited to educational settings it is, in my view, particularly well suited to collaborative investigations involving students and teachers together in simultaneous processes of researching and learning. First, more research is needed into the discourses which are circulating in the social contexts of students' lives, both inside and outside school. This would focus particularly on the outer circle of Fig. 15.1: the socially available possibilities for self-hood, and on the autobiographical self: the experiences of different discourses and genres that writers bring with them to writing. This type of research would be particularly well suited to participant-research methodologies, in which students and teachers work together to understand the sources of particular ways with words in students' experience, and to discuss the views of the world which are inscribed in these ways with words, and whose interests are served by them. Secondly, more research is needed into the moment-by-moment decision making of writers as they engage in different kinds of writing: why they choose particular expressions and constructions, and how they anticipate the reader's reaction. This would focus particularly on the discoursal self, the authorial self, and the relational dimension, in the context of available communicative resources. Again, this would be a form of research in which students and teachers work together to uncover processes which had previously remained invisible. Third, more research is needed into the reading of discoursally constructed identity: the impressions readers form of the values, beliefs, social role and authoritativeness of the writers whose writing they read. Such research needs to include contexts in which writing is read by someone other than a teacher—contexts where writing has a social purpose, and is not just produced in order to be assessed. Such research would focus on the relational dimension and the way in which discoursally constructed identities are taken up in the act of reading. And finally, research is urgently needed into classroom practice that aims at raising critical awareness of the way in which writers are positioned by the discourses and genres on which they draw. Such research would involve keeping records of teachers' attempts to implement such curricular innovations, and documenting the perspectives of all participants.

The primary goal of research on the discoursal construction of writer identity is to throw light on the ways in which writers are positioned by their acts of writing, both in terms of the worldviews in which they participate and in terms of the social relations into which they enter. Such research inevitably has political and pedagogical implications, since awareness of these processes can put writers in control of their self-representations, and can give them the power to contribute to the socially available resources for the construction of their own and others' identities in the future. Students and teachers can thus become more critically aware of their social responsibilities as writers and as readers—responsibilities to write in ways which build an equitable and inclusive social future for all.

ENDNOTE

1. The research was conducted by Roz Ivanic, Fiona Ormerod, Tony McEnery and Nick Smith and funded by The Leverhulme Trust. When I use "we" instead of "I" in this chapter, I am referring to the work of two or more members of the research team.

REFERENCES

Barton, D. (1994). *Literacy: An introduction to the ecology of written language.* Oxford, UK: Blackwell.

Barton, D., & Hamilton, M. (1998). *Local literacies: Reading and writing in one community.* London: Routledge.

Barton, D., Hamilton, M., & Ivanic, R. (Eds.). (2000). *Situated literacies: Reading and writing in context.* London: Routledge.

Berkenkotter, C., & Huckin, T. (1995). *Genre knowledge in disciplinary communication: Cognition /culture /power.* Hillsdale, NJ: Erlbaum.

Bloome, D., & Egan-Robertson, A. (1993). The social construction of intertextuality in classroom reading and writing lessons. *Reading Research Quarterly, 28*(4), 305-333.

Bruce, B. C. (Ed.). (2003). *Literacy in the information age: Inquiries into meaning making with new technologies.* Newark, DE: International Reading Association.

Cherry, R. (1988). *Ethos* versus persona: Self-representation in written discourse. *Written Communication, 5*(3), 251-276.

Clark, R. (1992). Principles and practice of CLA in the classroom. In N. Fairclough (Ed.), *Critical language awareness* (pp. 117-140). London: Longman.

Clark, R., & Ivanic, R. (1991). Consciousness-raising about the writing process. In P. Garrett & C. James (Eds.), *Language awareness in the classroom* (pp. 168-185). London: Longman.

Clark, R., & Ivanic, R. (1997). *The politics of writing.* London: Routledge.

Clark, R., & Ivanic, R. (1998). Critical discourse analysis and educational change. In L. van Lier & D. Corson (Eds.), *The encyclopedia of language and education, Vo. 6: Knowledge about language* (pp. 217-228). Dordrecht: Kluwer.

Clark, R., & Ivanic, R. (1999). Guest editors, and introduction: Raising critical awareness of language: A curriculum aim for the new millennium. *Language Awareness: Special Issue: Critical Language Awareness, 8* (2), 63-70.

Clayton, E. (2000). *Writing the writer, reading the writer. The discoursal construction of writer identity: An investigation with ten writers and the readers of their "work experience" letters.* Unpublished master's thesis, Department of Linguistics and Modern English Language, Lancaster University, Lancaster, UK.

Cope, B., & Kalantzis, M. (Eds.). (2000). *Multiliteracies: Literacy learning and the design of social futures.* New York: Routledge.

Ede, L. (1984). Audience: An introduction to research. *College Composition and Communication, 35,* 140-154.

Fairclough, N. (1989). *Language and power.* London: Longman.

Fairclough, N. (1992). *Discourse and social change.* Cambridge: Polity Press.

Fairclough, N. (1995). *Critical discourse analysis.* London: Longman.

Gee, J.P. (1996). *Social linguistics and literacies: Ideology in discourses.* London: Taylor & Francis.

Gee, J.P. (1999). *An introduction to discourse analysis: Theory and method.* London: Routledge.

Goffman, E. (1969). *The presentation of self in everyday life.* London: Allen Lane, The Penguin Press.

Halliday, M.A.K. (1967). *Language, society and the noun.* London: University College.

Halliday, M.A.K. (1978). *Language as social semiotic: The social interpretation of language and meaning.* London: Arnold.

Halliday, M.A.K. (1994). *An introduction to functional grammar.* London: Arnold.

Hayes, J., Shriver, K., Hill, C., & Hatch, J. (1992). Assessing the message and the messenger. *The Quarterly of the National Writing Project and the Center for the Study of Writing and Literacy, 14*(2), 15-17.

Hull, G. (2001, November). *Fashioning selves through multiple media: An exploration of digital literacies and digital divides.* Paper presented at the International Literacy Conference, Literacy and Language in Global and Local Settings, Cape Town, South Africa.

Ivanic, R. (1994). I is for interpersonal: Discoursal construction of writer identities and the teaching of writing. *Linguistics and Education, 6*(1), 3-15.

Ivanic, R. (1995). Writer identity. *Prospect: The Australian Journal of TESOL, 10*(1), 8-31.

Ivanic, R. (1998). *Writing and identity: The discoursal construction of identity in academic writing.* Amsterdam: John Benjamins.

Ivanic, R. (1999). Literacies and epistemologies in primary English. In C. Leung & A. Tosi (Eds.), *Rethinking language education* (pp. 139-152). London: Centre for Information on Language Teaching.

Ivanic, R. (in press) Intertextual practices in the construction of multimodal texts in inquiry-based learning. In N. Shuart-Faris & D. Bloome (Eds.), *Intertextuality and literacy in classrooms: Directions in educational research.* Westport, CT: Greenwood.

Ivanic, R., & Camps, D. (2001). I am how I sound: Voice as self-representation in L2 writing. *Journal of Second Language Writing Special Issue: Voice, 10*(1), 1-31.

Kamberelis, G., & Scott, K. (1992). Other people's voices: The coarticulation of texts and subjectivities. *Linguistics and Education: Special Issue: Intertextuality, 4* (3-4), 359-404

Kaufer, D., & Geisler, C. (1989). Novelty in academic writing. *Written Communication, 6*(3), 286-311.

Kress, G. (1989). *Linguistic processes in sociocultural practice.* Oxford, UK: Oxford University Press.

Kress, G. (1996). Representational resources and the production of subjectivity. In C.R. Caldas-Coulthard & M. Coulthard (Eds.), *Texts and practices: Readings in critical discourse analysis* (pp. 15-31). London: Routledge.

Kress, G. (2001). "You've just got to learn how to see": Curriculum subjects, young people and schooled engagement with the world. *Linguistics and Education, 11*(4), 401-415.

Kress, G., & van Leeuwen, T. (1996). *Reading images: The grammar of visual design.* London: Routledge.

Kress, G., & van Leeuwen, T. (2001). *Multimodal discourse: The modes and media of contemporary communication.* London: Arnold.

Lillis, T. (1997). New voices in academia? The regulative nature of academic writing conventions. *Language and Education, 11*(3), 182-199.

Lillis, T. (2001). *Student writing: Access, regulation and desire.* London: Routledge.

Lillis, T. (2003). Student writing as "academic literacies": Drawing on Bakhtin to move from critique to design. *Language and Education, 17*(3), 192-207.

Ormerod, F., & Ivanic, R. (2000). Texts in practices: Interpreting the physical characteristics of children's project work. In D. Barton, M. Hamilton, & R. Ivanic (Eds.), *Situated literacies: Reading and writing in context* (pp. 91-107). London: Routledge.

Ormerod, F., & Ivanic, R. (2002). Materiality in children's meaning-making practices. *Journal of Visual Communication, 1*(1), 65-91.

Moss, G. (2001). To work or play? Junior age non-fiction as objects of design. *Reading: Literacy and Language, 24*(3), 106-110.

Moss, G. (2002). Explicit pedagogy. In M. Barrs & S. Pidgeon (Eds.), *Boys' writing,* (pp. 54-60). London: Centre for Language in Primary Education.

Nystrand, M. (1989). A social-interactive model of writing. *Written Communication, 6*(1), 66-85.

Scott, M. (1999). Agency and subjectivity in student writing. In C. Jones, J. Turner, & B. Street (Eds.), *Students writing in the university: Cultural and epistemological issues* (pp. 171-192). Amsterdam: Benjamins.

van Leeuwen, T. (1993). Genre and field in critical discourse analysis: A synopsis. *Discourse in Society, 4*(2), 193-223.

van Leeuwen, T. (1995). Representing social action. *Discourse and Society, 6*(1), 81-106.

van Leeuwen, T. (1996). The representation of social actors in discourse. In C. Caldas-Coulthard & M. Coulthard (Eds.), *Texts and practices: Readings in critical discourse analysis* (pp. 32-70). London: Routledge.

van Leeuwen, T., & Wodak, R. (1999). Legitimizing immigration control: A discourse-historical analyis. *Discourse Studies, 1*(1), 83-118.

van Leeuwen, T. (1998). It was just like magic: A multi-modal analysis of children's writing. *Linguistics and Education, 10*(3), 273-305.

Wertsch, J. (1991). *Voices of the mind.* Hemel Hempstead, UK: Harvester Wheatsheaf.

PART IV

CRITICAL LITERACY AND LITERACY RESEARCH

Richard Beach
University of Minnesota

INTRODUCTION

This final section is devoted to chapters by Peter Freebody and Mellor and Patterson, who address the relationship between critical literacy and literacy research. (For useful collections or summaries of critical literacy, see Comber & Simpson, 2001; Cushman, Kintgen, Kroll, & Rose, 2001; Freebody, Muspratt, & Dwyer, 2001; Lankshear & McLaren, 1993; Muspratt, Luke, & Freebody, 1997; Yagelski, 2000). Researchers adopting a critical literacy orientation focus on the ways in which different literacies as social and cultural practices are constituted, valued, and promoted through different institutions. Rather than perceive literacy as simply a matter of individual skill acquisition, these researchers examine how institutions function to foster literacy development. As Peter McLaren (1992) noted in the first *Multidisciplinary Perspectives* volume, "a critical literacy is . . . one in which the personal is always understood as social, and the social is always historicized to reveal how the subject has been produced in particular" (p. 334).

In his chapter, Freebody defines critical literacy as a project that is particularly concerned with the pedagogical aspects of literacy learning related to social change and transformation of status quo systems, a topic consistent with the activity theory perspectives of the second section. A central goal of the critical literacy project, as illustrated in both the Freebody and the Mellor and Patterson chapters, is to not only foster students' critical analysis of how language and texts constitute ideological perspectives and stances, but also to change institutions and students' ways of thinking about those institutions.

Underlying critical literacy research on instruction is a critical pedagogy approach is a commitment to addressing issues of social justice with the goal of helping students learn to address social justice issues (Giroux, 1994, 1997; hooks, 1994; Shor & Pari, 1999.) (For applications of critical pedagogy related to literacy, see Allen, 1999; Edelsky, 1999; Fine & Weis, 2003; Fleischer & Schaafsma, 1998.) Critical pedagogy theory draws on Dewey's (1916/1966) notions of democratic forms of schooling and on Freire's (1970, 1973, 1985; Freire & Macado, 1987; Torres & Morrow, 2002) pedagogical methods of interrogating and reconstituting institutional forces that serve as barriers to change in the status quo. As Edelsky (1999) noted, "Studying systems—how they work and to what end—focusing on systems of influence, systems of culture, systems of gender relations . . . being critical means questioning against the frame of system, seeing individuals as always within systems, as perpetuating or resisting systems. Being noncritical . . . means seeing individuals as outside of . . . [and] separate from systems and therefore separate from culture and history" (p. 28). Attempts to reduce Freire's pedagogy to instrumental methods contradict the focus on problem-posing education as revolutionary (Macedo & Freire, 2001).

Critical pedagogy approaches have been particularly relevant for research on adult literacy practices (Hull, 1999; Martin & Fisher, 1999; Purcell-Gates & Waterman, 2000). Researchers have also examined how participation in community-based/service-learning projects often leads to shifts in agency and ways of thinking associated with contributing to inter-cultural literacy practices and entertaining alternative cultural perspectives (Fleisher & Schaafsma, 1998; Flower, 2002; Flower, Long, & Higgins, 2000).

However, in many current contexts, literacy teachers have difficulty employing or incorporating critical literacy perspectives into their teaching given lack of training, their own predilection, or the need to adhere to a test-driven curriculum. In an analysis of two literature teachers uses of whole-group literature discussion in two separate classes, Love (2000) found that one subscribed to a skill-based approach and the other, a reader-response approach. Although they were successful in fostering student participation in the discussions, students in neither class adopted their own critical stances because they were largely conforming to their teacher's preferred responses.

MULTIDISCIPLINARY PERSPECTIVES RELATED TO THE CRITICAL LITERACY PROJECT

A critical literacy project is informed by a range of different disciplinary perspectives, each of which provides critical literacy researchers with particular theoretical perspectives and research tools. For Allan Luke (2003), Bourdieu's (1984, 1991) notion of cultural capital as "dispositions" acquired in a social-class-based "habitus" occurs within larger institutional contexts beyond simply schooling and/or in conjunction with school. He posits the need to examine how all segments of society are responsible for providing students with equal access to various forms of capital associated with fostering literacy development:

> Fixing pedagogy one way or another might be necessary but is never sufficient for such a difference to be made. The consequences of litera-cy—and its ever present radical potential for altering life pathways and inequitable access to discourse, knowledge, and power—depend at least in part on the availability of other kinds of capital—social, economic, and symbolic, both within the school and across other social fields. (p. 139)

Luke argues for broadening the focus of literacy research to examine larger socioeconomic forces constituting literacy practices, power, language, and cultural capital:

> This work documents and describes how language, discourse, and literacy are media For the construction and negotiation of identity and power in all of their dynamic forms (e.g. sociocultural, economic, libidinal) and in relation to local collocations of social class, race, and gender. It has also begun to broaden its focus beyond schools and other educational institutions to examine the new and volatile life pathways to and through social fields (both informal and formal, community and corporate, traditional and modern) in relation to economic globalization and its new, oscillating formations of capital, discourse, and power. Such studies work both at the microethnographic level, examining institutional sites and relations, and via a macrosociological analysis, tracing globalized flows of language, discourse, texts, and power. These include (a) studies of diversity and multilingualism in worksplaces and other social institutions, which have begun to document new patterns of textual and identity work, the impacts of new technologies, and emergent power relations . . . and (g) studies of national and regional, local and "glocal" cultural and linguistic, social, and economic response to the hegemony of world-language English (e.g., Pennycook, 1996, 1998). (p. 134)

Sociolinguistics/Sociocultural Perspectives

Critical literacy theorists who adopt a sociolinguistic perspective have analyzed the influence of various "language ideologies" associated with the "English-Only" movement on the curtailment of bilingual/English as a second language programs (Gonzalez & Melis, 2000; Gutiérrez, Asato, Pacheco et al., 2002; Gutiérrez, Asato, Santos, & Gotanda, 2002; Krashen, 1999). As noted in the previous introductions, literacy researchers draw on sociolinguistic and sociocultural perspectives to examine how cultural practices are shaped by ideological orientations. In the first volume, Luis Moll (1992) posited the need for researchers to engage in ethnographic analyses of the rich "funds of knowledge" and language practices inherent in the everyday cultural practices in Hispanic communities that are often marginalized in schools. In a study of Mexican immigrants in a border town, Guadalupe Valdes (1996) found that the parents' family-oriented values often conflicted with those of educators, resulting in the alienation of parents from school participation. In an analysis of Chicago Mexican immigrant females' narrative and letter writing practices, Guerra (1998) identified complex rhetorical strategies in their literacy practices. And, in her analysis of poor women's literacy practices, Ellen Cushman (1998) documented how these women acquired literacy practices for coping with bureaucratic social service institutions. All of this research demonstrates the limitations of diminishing and marginalizing the literacy practices of presumably underprivileged people.

Historical Perspectives

Historical analyses documenting the influences of institutions such as libraries, families, schools, book clubs, organizations, publishing, newspapers, and so on, on the development of literacy practices provides tools for researchers to examine the influences of contemporary institutional forces (Eldred & Mortensen, 2002; Gere, 1997; Houston, 2002; Manguel, 1996). In her study of U.S. families' adaptation of literacy practices from the late 1800s to the 1980s, Deborah Brandt (2001) found that families learned to acquire and adopt new literacy practices to cope with changes in workplace and home social practices. In his study of the texts read by the British working classes, Jonathan Rose (2001) examined how texts influenced their social and political perceptions, as well as how reading served as a form of self-education.

Sociological/Economic Perspectives

One primary focus of the critical literacy project is a focus on the social inequities constituted by hierarchical power relationships in society. This perspective draws on the work Bourdieu's (1984, 1991) analysis of the distribution of "cultural capital" in society as related to class hierarchies (Guillory, 1993; Swartz, 1997). It also draws on Antonio Gramsci's (1971) analysis of hegemonic ideologies permeating society and Jurgen Habermas' (1973, 1984) theory of rationality as a form of "communicative action" based on the need to attain agreement with others as applied to instances of dominating forms of science or technology. This critique of the limitations of totalizing claims is also inherent in the feminist poststructuralist work of Donna Haraway (1988). Fredic Jameson (1972), a major neo-Marxist critic, employed dialectical criticism to examine the historical conditions that produce various uses of categories constituting ideological perspectives. This orientation is evident in studies of the influence of class differences on literacy development that identify different types of literacies valued in contexts defined according to class (Fine & Weis, 1998; Gee & Crawford, 1998; Hemphill, 1999).

Critical literacy researchers also draw on current economic analyses of "fast-track capitalism" and the globalization of the world economy that entails the use of a whole range of literacies associated with participation in marketplace production and consumption (Gee, Hull, & Lankshear 1996). In this context, a focus on "quality assurance," quantifiable, performance outcomes and the commercialization/privatization of social or governmental services emphasizes efficiency, speed, and "bottom-line" accountability which shapes notions of which literacies are valued and by whom in a "new capitalist" economy (Fairclough, 2003).

Poststructuralist Perspectives

A poststructuralist perspective draws on Jacques Derrida's (1976, 1979) deconstruction theory of language meaning based on the free play of signifiers and the on slippery nature of language categories. It also draws on Foucault's (1972, 1977) analysis of language as mediating institutional power. As Hagood (2002) noted, poststructuralist theories of subjectivity highlight how readers adopt a range of shifting, multiple positions, particularly in terms of different gender identities (Davies, 1993; Fuss, 1989; Walkerdine, 1980; Weedon, 1997) as well as how writers adopt different identities (Fecho, 2002). In the first volume, Linda Brodkey (1992) noted that poststructuralist theory provides her with three perspectives for analysis of language use and discourses:

1. The "notion of multiple and interdependent discourses means that the cultural hegemony in democratic societies . . . is contingent upon the struggle for domination among discourses" (p. 308).
2. "Each discourse offers not only a world view but an array of subject positions . . . as representing people in terms ranging from mostly satisfying or positive to mostly unsatisfying or negative" (p. 309).
3. "Some humans consistently fare worse than others across discourses, for some are commonly represented as diminished or objectified human subjects" (p. 309).

Feminist linguists such as Deborah Cameron (1995, 2000) examine the limitations of binary gender categories that presuppose certain linguistic patterns associated with "male" versus "female." A study of adolescents' after-school book-club discussions (Alvermann, Young, Green, & Wiseman, 1999) found that participants frequently challenged essentialist gender categories. By surfacing the tensions between competing stances toward gender and class, the students in this study began to interrogate value assumptions associated with perceived gender categories.

Postmodern Perspectives

Postmodern theory challenges the modernist's beliefs or "master narratives" associated with "progress," "truth," "human improvement," "high art," "science," "technology"—the assumption that these "narratives" will lead humans to a greater sense of happiness and fulfillment. Postmodern perspectives are evident in much of contemporary art, film, architecture, fiction, and music, through the use of a pastiche of different styles, parodying of narrative structures, interrogating representations of "reality," and examining the fragmentation and commodification of experience (Real, 1996). Postmodern perspectives meshed with contemporary rhetorical theory are also evident in composition studies of the cultural complexity of texts and contexts in lieu of expressionist or process models of composing (Brodkey, 1996; Clark & Ivanic, 1997; Goleman, 1995; Olson & Dobrin, 1994).

One limitation of a postmodern perspective is that as the "cultural logic of capitalism" it reifies a consumeristic culture (Jameson, 1991). In the first volume, Peter McLaren (1992) argued that a postmodern perspective failed to "recognize diverse paradigms," "develop a critical language of public life" (p. 323), "recognize feminist perspectives" (p. 324), and "recognize the reader as a historical entity" (p. 326). The later failure relates to Mellor and Patterson's critique of reader-response theory's focus on individual subjectivity, which, as McLaren argued, "ignores the way in which textual authority is linked to larger economies of power and privilege in the wider social order . . . [which] sidesteps collective participation in social transformation" (p. 328).

Critical Race Theory/Postcolonial Literary Critical Perspectives

Another important set of disciplinary perspectives emanates from critical race theory/postcolonial literary criticism that examines racism as an institutional, socially-constructed process in which categories and hierarchies privilege certain groups (Bonilla Silva, 2001; Delgado & Stefancic, 2001; Kumashiro, 2002; Trainor, 2002), leading them to interrogate characters' and peers' uses of language categories for constructing identity differences (McGinley & Kamberelis, 1996). For example, discourses of "Whiteness" are often used in literacy practices of controlling or exerting order/rationality against what is assumed to be disorder and irrationality associated with the "other" (Barnett, 2000). In one study, parents' and teachers' color-blind race talk in one school district masked the realities of racialized practices that influenced students (Lewis, 2001).

Postcolonial literary critical theory critiques colonial or imperialist representations of the third world or previously colonialized parts of the world as "non-Western" (i.e., as "backward," "uncivilized," "mysterious," "undeveloped," "primitive," and "dangerous"). In his study of "Orientalism," Edward Said (1978) demonstrated how "Orientalism" was a racist and sexist discourse for a superior European perception of the Orient as exotic, mysterious, erotic, different, and non-White or "other."

Media Studies Perspectives

Literacy researchers draw on media studies perspectives to example how media texts employ "modes of address" (Ellsworth, 1997) to position readers or viewers to adopt certain desired responses consistent with certain stances. Stuart Hall (1997) described three alternative positions readers or viewers may assume relative to the text: *dominant-hegemonic readings* in which audiences simply accept what Bakhtin (1981) described as "externally authoritative discourses" or stances because they lack their own "internally persuasive discourse"—a sense of their own agency to challenge dominant stances; *negotiated reading* in which audiences negotiate or struggle with the dominant stance; and *oppositional reading* in which audiences resist, challenge, disagree with, or reject the dominant stance. This does not mean that audiences are assumed to be simply as naïve, cultural dupes; rather, researchers examine how they adopt roles as active, productive agents in co-creating or subverting media texts in the "mediascape" (Abercrombie & Longhurst, 1998; C. Luke, 2002; Seiter, 1999; Storey, 1996).

This research draws on the work on de Certeau (1984), who distinguished between the media producers' uses of strategies, and the consumers, who employ bricolage-like tactics to cope with and subvert the producers' power. Consistent with the New London "new literacy" perspective on the value of multiliteracies (Cope & Kalantzis, 2000), it focuses on literacy practices associated with issues of design, as well as uses of various digital/computer literacies—computer chat, web design, gaming, digital video production, and so on—particularly by adolescents, who devote considerable time to engaging in these literacies (Alvermann, 2002; Harris & Alexander, 1998). Literacy researchers examining students' uses of digital/media literacies have focused on how they are used as tools to adopt critical stances. Part of studying these uses of such tools includes drawing on "users' insight about their own approaches to learning, on their theories about what counts as literacy, and on the strategies they enact for attempting to use contemporary literacy" (Hagood, Stevens, & Reinking, 2002, p. 83).

Feminist media-study researchers examine how female adolescents constructed gendered identities through responses to and construction of media texts (Alvermann, Moon, & Hagood, 1999; Finders, 1997; C. Luke, 1996). Pre-adolescent females constructed their responses to a romance novel around categories of "good" versus "bad" girl defined within the historical context of patriarchic discourse (Enciso, 1998). The females in this study collectively created their own subject position for dealing with the contradictions or double-binds associated with being both good and bad girls in school. This research also examines how, even within gender groups, adolescent females respond in ways that serve to socially exclude others students perceived to have less power (Finders, 1997). Knobel and Lankshear (2002) found that adolescent females employ zines "as vibrant, volatile, thriving social practices that describe deep currents and concerns within youth culture" (p. 172).

A critical literacy project also focuses on issues of control and ownership of media tools employed to engage in various literacies. The increased concentration of media outlets by a small number of media conglomerate giants has resulted in the commercialisation of the media and the diminution of alternative ideological perspectives, particularly perspectives critical of corporate/governmental policy control (Chomsky, 2001; McChesney, 2004).

In his chapter, Peter Freebody describes various elements of the critical literacy project as serving both the Deweyian democratic agenda of providing equal access to texts to all people, as well as the Frierian agenda of transforming the status quo that privileges some literacy practices over others to the detriment of certain segments of society. He focuses on the various ways in which texts and interactional practices are used to socialize students to adopt certain ideological stances relative to interrogating status quo systems. He cites the examine of previous research on how wealth and poverty of "less developed countries" are represented in high school economics textbooks to demonstrate that young readers are provided with highly limited perspectives and misrepresentations of poverty in these countries. He argues that critical literacy approaches need to not only interrogate these representations as framed by economic and ideological agendas producing these texts, but to also help students address and employ literacy practices as constituted by power relations.

Freebody's chapter serves as a useful precursor to the Mellor and Patterson chapter in that they posit the need "to alter the use of the text and to teach specific ways of looking (reading) that produce particular readings. The aim is to construct the reader as a social agent with particular capacities—such as that of producing feminist or anti-racist or plural or critical readings of a text." Their chapter provides an historical review of the strengths and limitations of basic approaches to teaching literature during this century: "Heritage," "New Critical," "Personal Growth," "Poststructuralist English," and "Critical Literacy." One of the limitations of the "Personal Growth" approach associated with reader-response peda- gogies is that although it served to promote students' expression of the experiences with texts, students were often not aware of how they were constructing their readings, so that they could not account for differences in their interpretations. By focusing on a contrastive analysis of critics and students' interpretations themselves as texts, students may then become aware of the ways in which these readings are constituted by ideological and discourse perspectives. However, Mellor and Patterson note the limita- tion of even a "Poststructuralist English" as not necessarily fulfilling a social justice agenda leading to social change. Focusing only on students "own readings" of texts may not necessarily lead them to change their ways of reading or thinking. They perceive the need to also change the practices operating in the institutional norms of schooling in ways that serve this social justice function. And, they posit the need to examine the practices of the English curriculum itself as a "construction," analysis that raises ques- tions posed by Moon (2001) regarding the need for inclusion of more "empirical information" in the English curriculum.

Given their call for historical analysis of literacy curriculum develop- ment, it is useful to contextualize the literature pedagogy developed by Mellor and Patterson, and their colleagues, as well as the Chalkface/NCTE textbook series, in the larger political context of the development of the Queensland State Literacy Strategy curriculum framework (C. Luke, 2002; C. Luke, Freebody, & Land, 2000). That curriculum framework, designed to address an economic context characterized by the need for multi-litera- cies requires for participation of what Luke describes as a "semiotic econo- my" (C. Luke et al., 2002, p. 188) requiring uses of "coding," "semantic," "pragmatic," and "critical" literacy practices. However, implementing such a curriculum remains a challenge. Surveys of teachers cited by Luke found strong support for a critical literacy agenda, but no clear sense of how to implement such as agenda. Research on teachers' literature instruction demonstrates difficulty in adopting critical literacy approaches given adher- ence to more familiar instructional models (Love, 2000).

REFERENCES

Abercrombie, N., & Longhurst, B. (1998). *Audiences: A sociological theory of per- formance and imagination.* Thousand Oaks, CA: Sage.
Allen, J. (Ed.). (1999). *Class actions: Literacy education for a democratic society.* New York: Teachers College Press.

Alvermann, D. (Ed.). (2002). *Adolescents and literacies in a digital world.* New York: Peter Lang.

Alvermann, D., Moon, J., & Hagood, M. (1999). *Popular culture in the classroom: Teaching and researching critical media literacy.* Newark, DE: International Reading Association.

Alvermann, D., Young, J., Green, C., & Wiseman, J. (1999). Adolescents' perceptions and and negotiations of literacy practices in afterschool read and talk clubs. *American Educational Research Journal, 36,* 221-264.

Bakhtin, M. (1981). *The dialogic imagination: Four essays.* Austin: University of Texas Press.

Barnett, T. (2000). Reading "whiteness" in English studies. *College English, 63*(1), 9-37.

Bonilla-Silva, E. (2001). *White supremacy and racism in the post-civil rights era.* Boulder, CO: Lynne Rienner.

Bourdieu, P. (1984). *Distinction: A social critique of the judgment of taste.* Cambridge, UK: Cambridge University Press.

Bourdieu, P. (1991). *Language and symbolic power.* Cambridge, MA: Harvard University Press.

Brandt, D. (2001). *Literacy in American lives.* New York: Cambridge University Press,

Brodkey, L. (1992). Articulating poststructuralist theory in research on literacy. In R.Beach, J. Green, M. Kamil, & T. Shanahan (Eds.), *Multidisciplinary perpsectives on literacy research* (pp. 294-318). Urbana, IL: National Conference on Research on English/National Council of Teachers of English.

Brodley, L. (1996). *Writing permitted in designated areas only.* Minneapolis: University of Minnesota Press.

Cameron, D. (1995). *Verbal hygiene.* New York: Routledge.

Cameron, D. (2000). *Good to talk: Living and working in a communication culture.* Thousand Oaks, CA: Sage.

Chomsky, N. (2001). *Propaganda and the public mind.* Cambridge, MA: South End Press.

Clark, R., & Ivanic, R. (1997). *The politics of writing.* New York: Routledge.

Comber, B., & Simpson, A. (Eds.). (2001). *Negotiating critical literacies in classrooms.* Mahwah, NJ: Erlbaum.

Cope, B., & Kalantzis, M. (Eds.). (2000). *Multiliteracies: Literacy learning and the design of social futures.* New York: Routledge.

Cushman, E. (1998). *The struggle and the tools: Oral and literate strategies in an inner-city community.* Albany: SUNY Press.

Cushman, E., Kintgen, E., Kroll, B., & Rose, M. (Eds.). (2001). *Literacy: A critical sourcebook.* Boston, MA: Bedford/St. Martin's.

Davies, B. (1993). *Shards of glass.* Cresskill, NJ: Hampton Press.

de Certeau, M. (1984). *The practice of everyday life.* Berkeley: University of California Press.

Delgado, R., & Stefancic, J. (Eds.). (2001). *Critical race theory: An introduction.* New York: New York University Press.

Derrida, J. (1976). *On grammatology.* Baltimore, MD: Johns Hopkins University Press.

Derrida, J. (1979). *Spurs: Nietzsche's styles.* Chicago: University of Chicago Press.

Dewey, J. (1966). *Democracy and education.* New York: The Free Press. (Original work published 1916)

Edelsky, C. (1999). *Making justice our project: Teachers working toward critical whole language practice.* Urbana, IL: National Council of Teachers of English.

Edelsky, C., Smith, K., & Wolfe, W. (2002). A discourse on academic discourse. *Linguistics and Education, 12*(1), 1–38.

Eldred, J.C., & Mortensen, P. (2002). *Imagining rhetoric: Composing women of the early United States.* Pittsburgh, PA: University of Pittsburgh Press

Ellsworth, E. (1997). *Teaching positions: Difference, pedagogy, and the power of address.* New York: Teachers College Press.

Enciso, P. (1998). Good/bad girls read together: Pre-adolescent girls' co-authorship of feminine subject positions during a shared reading event. *English Education, 30*, 44-62.

Fairclough, N. (2003). *Analyzing discourse: Textual analysis for social research.* New York: Routledge.

Fecho, B. (1998). Crossing boundaries of race in a critical literacy classroom. In D. Alvermann, K. Hinchman, D. Moore, S. Phelps, & D. Waff (Eds.), *Reconceptualizing the literacies in adolescents' lives* (pp. 75-101). Mahwah. NJ: Erlbaum.

Fecho, B. (2002). Madaz publications: Polyphonic identity and existential literacy transactions. *Harvard Educational Review, 72*(1), 93-119.

Finders, M. (1997). *Just girls.* New York: Teachers College Press.

Fine, M., & Weis, L. (1998). *The unknown city: The lives of poor and working-class young adults.* Boston, MA: Beacon Press.

Fine, M., & Weis, L. (2003). *Silenced voices and extraordinary conversations: Re-imagining schools.* New York: Teachers College Press.

Fleischer, C., & Schaafsma, D. (Eds.). (1998). *Literacy and democracy: Teacher research and composition studies in pursuit of habitable spaces.* Urbana, IL: National Council of Teachers of English.

Flower, L. (2002). Intercultural inquiry and the transformation of service. *College English, 65*(2), 181-201

Flower, L., Long, E., & Higgins, L. (2000). *Learning to rival: A literate practice for intercultural inquiry.* Mahwah: NJ: Erlbaum.

Foucault, M. (1972). *Archaeology of knowledge.* New York:Random House.

Foucault, M. (1977). *Discipline and punish: The birth of the prison.* New York: Pantheon.

Freebody, P., Muspratt, S., & Dwyer, D. (Eds.). (2001). *Difference, silence, and cultural practice: Studies in critical literacy.* Cresskill, NJ: Hampton Press.

Freire, P. (1970). *Pedagogy of the oppressed.* New York: Seabury.

Freire, P. (1973). *Education for critical consciousness.* New York: Seabury.

Freire, P. (1985). *The politics of education.* Westport, CT: Greenwood.

Freire, P., & Macedo, D. (1987). *Literacy: Reading the word & the world.* South Hadley, MA: Bergin & Garvey.

Fuss, D. (1989). *Essentially speaking: Feminism, nature and difference.* New York: Routledge.

Gee, J. P., & Crawford, V. (1998). Two kinds of teenagers: Language, identity, and social class. In D. Alvermann, K. Hinchman, D. Moore, S. Phelps, & D. Waff (Eds.), *Reconceptualizing the literacies in adolescents lives* (pp. 225-246). Mahwah, NJ: Erlbaum.

Gee, J.P., Hull, G., & Lankshear, C. (1996). *The new work order: Behind the language of the new capitalism.* Boulder, CO: Westview Press.

Gere, A.R. (1997). *Intimate practices: Literacy and cultural work in U.S. women's clubs, 1880-1920.* Urbana: University of Illinois Press.

Giroux, H. (1994). *Disturbing pleasures: Learning popular culture.* New York: Routledge.

Giroux, H. (1997). *Pedagogy and the politics of hope: Theory, culture, and schooling.* Boulder, CO: Westview Press.

Goleman, J. (1995). *Working theory: Critical composition studies for students and teachers.* Westport, CT: Bergin & Garvey.

Gonzalez, R. D., & Melis, I. (Eds.). (2000). *Language ideologies: Critical perspectives on the Official English movement.* Mahwah, NJ: Erlbaum.

Gramsci, A. (1971). *Selections from the prison notebooks of Antonio Gramsci* (Q. Hoare & G. Smith, Eds. & Trans.). New York: International Publishers.

Guerra, J. (1998). *Close to home: Oral and literate practices in a transnational Mexicano community.* New York: Teachers College Press.

Guillory, J. (1993). *Cultural capital: The problem of literacy canon formation.* Chicago: University of Chicago Press.

Gutierrez, K., Asato, J., Pacheco, M., Moll, L., Olson, K., Horng, E., Ruiz, R., Garcia., E., & McCarty, M. (2002). "Sounding American": The consequences of new reforms on English language learners. *Reading Research Quarterly, 37*(3), 328-343.

Gutiérrez, K., Asato, J., Santos, M., & Gotanda, N. (2002). Backlash pedagogy: Language and culture and the politics of reform. *The Review of Education, Pedagogy, and Cultural Studies, 24*(4), 335-351.

Habermas, J. (1973). *Theory and practice.* Boston: Beacon Press.

Habermas, J. (1984). *The theory of communicative action.* Boston: Beacon Press.

Hagood, M.C. (2002). Subjectivity. In B. Guzzetti (Ed.), *Literacy in America: An encyclopedia of history, theory, and practice* (pp. 632-637). Santa Barbara, CA: ABC-CLIO.

Hagood, M.C., Stevens, L.P., & Reinking, D. (2002). What do THEY have to teach us? Talkin' 'cross generations. In D. Alvermann (Ed.), *Adolescents and literacies in a digital world* (pp. 68-83). New York: Peter Lang.

Hall, S. (1997). *Representation: Cultural representations and signifying practices* (pp. 337-387). Thousand Oaks, CA: Sage.

Haraway, D. (1988). Situated knowledge: The science question in feminism as a site of discourse on the privilege of partial perspective. *Feminist Studies, 14*(3), 575-99.

Harrington, C.L., & Bielby, D. (1995). *Soap fans: Pursuing pleasure and making meaning in everyday life.* Philadelphia, PA: Temple University Press.

Harris, C., & Alexander, A. (Eds.). (1998). *Theorizing fandom: Fans, subculture and identity.* Cresskill, NJ: Hampton Press.

Hemphill, L. (1999). Narrative style, social class, and response to poetry. *Research in the Teaching of English, 33*(3), 275-302.

hooks, b. (1994). *Teaching to transgress: Education as the practice of freedom*. New York: Routledge.

Houston, R.A. (2002). *Literacy in early modern Europe: Culture and education 1500-1800*. New York: Longman.

Hull, G. (Ed.). (1999). *Changing work, changing workers: Critical perspectives on language, literacy, and skills*. Albany: SUNY Press.

Jameson, F. (1972). *The prison house of language*. Princeton, NJ: Princeton University Press

Jameson, F. (1991). *Postmodernism, or the cultural logic of late capitalism*. Durham, NC: Duke University Press.

Knobel, M., & Lankshear, C. (2002). Cut, paste, publish: The production and consumption of zines. In D. Alvermann (Ed.), *Adolescents and literacies in a digital world* (pp. 164-185). New York: Peter Lang.

Krashen, S. (1999). *Condemned without a trial: Bogus arguments against bilingual education*. Portsmouth, NH: Heinemann.

Kumashiro, K.K. (2002). Against repetition: Addressing resistance to anti-oppressive changes in the practices of learning, teaching, supervising, and researching. *Harvard Educational Review, 72*(1), 67-92.

Lankshear, C., & McLaren, P. (Eds.). (1993). *Critical literacy: Politics, praxis, and the postmodern*. Albany: SUNY Press.

Lewis, A. E. (2001). There is no "race" in the schoolyear: Color-blind ideology in an (almost) all-white school. *American Educational Research Journal, 38*(4), 781-811.

Love, K. (2000). The construction of moral subjectivities in talk around text in secondary English. *Linguistics and Education, 11*(3), 213-249.

Luke, A. (2002). What happens to literacies old and new when they're turned into policies. In D. Alvermann (Ed.), *Adolescents and literacies in a digital world* (pp. 186-204). New York: Peter Lang.

Luke, A. (2003). Literacy and the other: A sociological approach to literacy research and policy in multilingual societies. *Reading Research Quarterly, 38*(1), 132-141.

Luke, C. (Ed.). (1996). *Feminisms and pedagogies of everyday life*. Albany: SUNY Press.

Luke, C. (2002). Re-crafting media and ICT literacies. In D. Alverman (Ed.), *Adolescents and literacies in a digital world* (pp. 132-146). New York: Peter Lang.

Macedo, D., & Freire, A. M. A. (2001). (Mis)understanding Paulo Freire. In V. Richardson (Ed.), *Handbook of research on teaching* (4th ed., pp. 106-110). Washington, DC: American Educational Research Association.

Manguel, A. (1996). *A history of reading*. New York: Penguin.

Martin, L., & Fisher, J. (Eds.). (1999). *The welfare-to-word challenge for adult literacy educators*. San Francisco: Jossey-Bass.

McChesney, R. (2004). *The problem of the media: U.S. communication politics in the twenty-first century*. New York: Monthly Review Press.

McGinley, W., & Kamberelis, G. (1996). Maniac Magee and Ragtime Tumpie: Children negotiating self and world through reading and writing. *Research in the Teaching of English, 30*(1), 75-113.

McLaren, P. (1992). Literacy research and the postmodern turn: Cautions from the margins. In R. Beach, J. Green, M. Kamil, & T. Shanahan (Eds.), *Multidisciplinary perspectives on literacy research* (pp. 319-339). Urbana, IL: National Conference on Research on English/National Council of Teachers of English.

Moll, L. (1992). Literacy research in community and classrooms. In R. Beach, J. Green, M. Kamil, & T. Shanahan (Eds.), *Multidisciplinary perspectives on literacy research* (pp. 211-244). Urbana, IL: National Conference on Research on English/National Council of Teachers of English.

Moon, B. (2001). "The text is out there": History, research and *The X Files*. *English in Australia, 138,* 5–16.

Muspratt, S., Luke, A., & Freebody, P. (Eds.). (1997). *Constructing critical literacies: Teaching and learning textual practice.* Cresskill, NJ: Hampton Press.

Olson, G., & Dobrin, S. (Eds.). (1994). *Composition theory for the postmodern classroom.* Albany: SUNY Press.

Pennycook, A. (1996). *The cultural politics of English as an international language.* London: Longman.

Pennycook, A. (1998). *English and the discourses of colonialism.* New York: Routledge.

Purcell-Gates, V., & Waterman, R. (2000). *Now we read, we see, we speak: Portrait of literacy development in an adult Freirean-based class.* Mahwah, NJ: Erlbram.

Real, M. (1996). *Exploring media culture: A guide.* Thousand Oaks, CA: Sage.

Rose, J. (2001). *The intellectual life of the British working classes.* New Haven, CT: Yale University Press.

Said, E. (1978). *Orientalism.* New York: Penguin.

Seiter, E. (1999). *Television and new media audiences.* Oxford, UK: Clarendon Press.

Shor, I., & Pari, C. (Eds.). (1999). *Critical literacy in action.* Portsmouth, NH: Heinemann.

Storey, J. (1996). *Cultural studies and the study of popular culture.* Athens: University of Georgia Press.

Swartz, D. (1997). *Culture & power: The sociology of Pierre Bourdieu.* Chicago: University of Chicago Press.

Torres, C., & Morrow, R. (2002). *Reading Freire & Habermas; Critical pedagogy and transformative social change.* New York: Teachers College Press.

Trainor, J. S. (2002). Critical pedagogy's "other": Constructions of whiteness in education for social change. *College Composition and Communication, 53*(4), 631-650.

Valdes, G. (1996). *Con respeto: Bridging the distances between culturally diverse families and school: An ethnographic portrait.* New York: Teachers College Press.

Walkerdine, V. (1990). *Schoolgirl fictions.* London:Verso.

Weedon, C. (1997). *Feminist practice and poststructuralist theory* (2nd ed.). Philadelphia: Taylor & Francis.

Yagelski, R. (2000). *Literacy matters: Writing and reading the social self.* New York: Teachers College Press.

16

Critical Literacy

Peter Freebody
Griffith University

Put most simply, the term *critical literacy* refers to the application of critical theories, developed within a range of paradigms and disciplines, to the study of what, why, how, and when we read and write. So far so good, except that a referral notion of meaning does not get us very far. We know that words do not perform their meanings simply by joining together and pointing to things in the world; we need to consider the interchanges between the contextual and textual conditions in which words play if we wish to gather their meanings. When we do that, we can see that the term *critical literacy* may be on the brink of exhaustion or dissipation, playing in too many positions in too many games.

Rather than as a knowable entity, we can consider *critical literacy* as a term indicating a project that covers a range of studies, theoretical procedures, and disciplines. We can ask the general questions: "What is the Critical Literacy Project and what are its goals?" Considering these questions allows us to view points of both similarity and distinctiveness among various approaches. We find a rough, imperfect alignment between the focus and methods of study on the one hand, and, on the other, the disciplines that have developed these approaches:

- Linguists have generally taken the text as a semiotically structured object to be the prime unit of focus of critical literacy.
- Sociologists have generally focussed on how language uses signal the operation of social formations such as race, gender, and class,

and how these formations in turn give shape to how we read, write, look, talk, and listen.
- Anthropologists have taken cultural practices, and the ways that different literate representations implicated variously afford these, as the most productive analytic focus.

Each of these disciplines construes "literacy" and enacts a "critical" approach to that construct in distinctive ways (Janks, 2000). For example, the following versions of the project depend on the particular theoretical premises and procedures that define each of these informing disciplines:

- The Critical Literacy Project is about giving all individuals, groups, and communities access to the texts that are powerful in a society through enhancing their knowledge of how these texts are constructed, and how such texts can be deconstructed and linguistically transformed (e.g., Lemke, 1995; Martin, 1992).
- The Critical Literacy Project is about transforming the sociopolitical processes that act to make some texts more powerful than others, by mainstreaming and giving privilege to minority and marginalized texts, for example, indigenous/native texts, feminized texts (e.g., Clark & Ivanic, 1997; Lee, 1996; Threadgold, 2001).
- The Critical Literacy Project is about transforming education, the major arena through which members of a society learn not only what texts and textual practices are valued and dominant, but also the more fundamental fact that there is a hierarchy of textual forms and practices to begin with. That is, what is critical is developing the practical understanding that people are educated to become variously the objects and subjects (both the topics of and the readers and writers) of a selected tradition of representing reality in public and official forms (e.g., Graff, 2001; Lankshear & Lawler, 1987; Smith, 1999).

Researchers and educators from a variety of disciplines have worked with each of these ideas, sometimes in combination, but we can usually determine whether texts, social structures, or cultural practices constitute the prime focus of the work. Each of these approaches, using a variety of analytic techniques, takes it that, when a person engages in a literacy event, that person is at the same time activating a version of their personal subjectivity that is engaged in a public project—the family, the school, the nation-state, the economy, as a consumer or producer, institutionalized work, and all the rest. In that light, the Critical Literacy Project is about exploring, interrupting, and maybe rewriting these process of activation and engagement in order to destabilize its apparent naturalness, to explicate its normative features, and to name and critique its ideological consequences.

The variety of ways in which proponents do this work of interrupting can be drawn together (not completely comfortably) under the heading of an over-arching aim: to challenge constantly the singularity of public projects—the family, the school, the nation-state, the economy, and so on—by fashioning a consciousness that aggressively explores, through literacy practices, a multiplicity of normative options for individuals and communities. These challenges are based on a realization that literate representations cannot be neutral; what is seen to be at stake is an appreciation of how thoroughly the objects and practices that are the appurtenances of literacy construct preferred versions of social and economic practice, private and public relationships and moralities, and, in general, ways of being in the world (Gee, 1996).

In this chapter, I draw out and illustrate some family resemblances among the various approaches to critical literacy. I summarize what I take to be the principal ways in which the idea of critical literacy has been developed, I illustrate some of these developments with a quick convenience sample of research (much of it my own), and I attempt to describe some common propositions from which the project of critical literacy might productively proceed.

The chapter is organized into three sections, along the lines of the three aspects of critique just mentioned. The first of these relates to critical attention given to the material products of literacy, *texts*. In this section I briefly summarize accounts of how texts have been analyzed. The second section summarizes some critiques of the acculturational processes of literacy, the *interactional practices* that show how particular kinds of readings and writings are given their form and significance. Here, I take the analysis of classroom talk as an example, and try to show how particular readings of textual materials enhance powerful discourses of generation as an apparently natural interpretive practice. The third section explores the ways in which literacy is deployed as a public fact. I discuss these *discursive materials* using examples from interview materials in which teachers discuss various literacy practices, showing how the interpretations evident in those practices relate to and reinforce prevalent discourses concerning economic class.

CRITIQUING THE PRODUCTS OF LITERACY

I briefly illustrate here some ways of approaching the critique of texts. Gee (1999, this volume) gave a more complete description of linguistic approaches to textual analysis, and Emmison and Smith (2000) described a variety of critical approaches to visual texts. So my goal is not to retrace their steps but rather to supplement their observations through an extended example.

Consider this: How are wealth and poverty represented in high school economics textbooks? In textbook materials, the force of the written mode is to partly to present dense and compact materials about factually complexities topics (Halliday, 1987). This is one of the main attractions of written materials for educational purposes, accounting for the heavy reliance placed on them by modern schooling. This synoptic characteristic, however, can have the non-accidentally effect of pinning the topic down, fixing it in time and space, rather than exploring multiple explanations or perspectives. In general, such a representational mode is tailor-made for describing a complex-world-in-space, not so much how this world got to be like this, or how else it may be accounted for. In exploring high school texts about less developed countries (LDCs), Freebody and Welch (1993) found that such complex, compacted description was common, but that the lack of any historical account left young readers with a limited set of possible explanations of how the economic world came to be like this and what may be done about it. So we asked three questions of these texts:

1. How do texts *describe* global economic inequalities, the gap between first and third world countries, or between rich and poor within a community?
2. How does the text present the fundamental explanations (as opposed to criterial or normative attributes) to be applied to the phenomenon?
3. What, if anything, are presented (explicitly or implicitly) as possible or appropriate personal or communal *responses* to the phenomenon?

One way of looking at the ideological work done in and by texts is to consider how the features of a text, the choices exercised by the author, serve simultaneously to reflect and build answers to these questions. To preview the main features that the texts show in their characterization of this phenomenon, Freebody and Welch found the following: first, the texts describe LDCs—note already the mythical narrative built into modern western economists' choice of that label—in synoptic, "correlational" terms; that is, lists of social, cultural, political, and economic characteristics are presented that are stated as "going with" a country's being "poor." The student-reader's (and for that matter the teacher's) intellectual resources are drawn to the task of assimilating this multiplicity of features, importantly, in isolation, and without any coherent interconnecting argument. The account is clearly synchronic—the LDC is viewed as a complex 'thing' in space, without history.

Second, we found that explanations are also framed correlationally; that is, LDCs are said to be the way they are because of other features they also (happen to) possess, such as large less-educated populations, low personal economic activity rates, and agriculture-based production bases. Finally, we found that the response made available to the reader, and often mentioned in the text, was one of *noblesse-oblige* charity on the part of the developed countries—aid programs and personal "giving." These features, we argued, were directly related to the particular written genres used in these texts, and the ways in which the written presentation of the material was geared to easy learning by students and ready forms of assessment by teachers.

It is worth considering in some detail one attempt at characterizing the phenomenon of the LDC in order to attain an impression of how this "correlational" depiction of inequality presents over a long and detailed stretch of text, and how this characterisation is conveyed as an academic body of knowledge—that is, to get a feeling for the substance of the intellectual task of learning this material as it presents itself to students. Consider the following key sections from a prominent text on economics for upper secondary school (Tisdell, 1979):

Less-developed countries (L.D.C's) tend to be characterised by the following features:

1) Subsistence living and limited use of markets: Most individuals in less-developed countries use their output for their own family . . . and exchange little of their production. . . .

2) A high proportion of the workforce in less-developed countries is engaged in agriculture and in other primary industries. . . . The manufacturing sector and the tertiary sector in underdeveloped countries are also comparatively small.

3) Technical change in less-developed countries is normally slow and producers often cling to traditional methods. In some circumstances, however, traditional methods may be more appropriate than Western capital-intensive methods. . . .

4) Savings are small and the rate of capital accumulation is low. . . . those on high incomes in the L.D.C.'s are reputed to spend most of their income on ostentatious consumption rather than to invest in productive works.

5) Business motivation or entrepreneurship of a productive nature may be lacking. . . . Capitalistic entrepreneurship may be lacking.

6) Unemployment, labour-intensive methods, underemployment. . . .

7) Life expectancy is low, nutrition and health poor. . . .

8) High growth rates of the population and a distorted age distribution of the population add to poverty. The higher rate of (population) increase in the L.D.C.'s may reflect the less frequent use of birth control techniques . . .

9) Urbanization problems but a proportionately low urban population. . . .

10) Lack of social overhead capital. The supply of roads, ports, hospitals, schools, telephone services, water and sewerage facilities is limited. This is a reflection of overall poverty. The ability of the government to raise revenue for public works through taxation is limited . . .

11) Illiteracy is widespread and the technical skills required in modern industry are in short supply.

12) The distribution of income in L.D.C.'s is very uneven . . .

13) Dualism. . . . an urban monetary economy consisting of individuals engaged in Western style industry and a rural traditional barter economy. . . .

14) Export dependency on one or two primary products. . . . The prices of primary products tend to be very unstable and specialization in such a limited range of primary products (lack of diversification) adds to risk as a rule. . . .

(173-179).

One approach here is to document the non-neutral way in which the field is constructed in accounts such as this. In this particular text the nature of human participation and the abstract agencies of poverty are central features. For example, the human participants in this text are as follows:

individuals	9	
the workforce	3	(all engaged in agriculture or equivalent)
family members	3	(all not efficiently employed/employed in inefficient)
populations	2	(not productive. . . ; live in . . .)
producers	1	(cling to traditional methods of . . .)

Of the 87 items in the theme (subject) positions in this account of the characteristics of LDCs, only 18 entail human participants. The remaining 69 themes comprise mainly abstractions and nominalizations, for example: growth rates of populations; high proportion of the population; LDC(s); the rate of capital accumulation; entrepreneurship; technical change; the ability of governments to raise revenue; specialisation in a limited range of primary products; most incomes; and life expectancy. These forces are given agency in the world of this text.

So the thematizing choices of the author display the drive toward abstraction in this description. The human participants who are in the theme positions need to be considered not just in terms of their relative infrequency, but also in terms of how they serve to construct the sociopolitical world of the LDC and how accounts and responses are thus constrained. That is, it is notable that the human participants that appear present the following hierarchical societal composition: Individuals may be producers, combine into families, into workforce, into a population, into a country. That, so to speak, is the human taxonomic tree that this text presents. No descriptive terms for people are given that might afford an explanation or response that relies on subgroups (geographic, economic, ethnic, gender, etc.) within a nation-state contesting or struggling for resources or decision-making power. The "country" is the unit, and the "country" is internally homogeneous on the issues that count in this text.

We can also consider the activities performed by the most common human term, *individuals*: What are the verbs with which this term is associated? The following is the exhaustive list of the verbs accompanied by their attendant predications: individuals, we are told, *use* (their output for their own families); *exchange* (little of their production); *need to consume* (most of their products to survive); *can expect to live* (for shorter periods); *die* (before they reach an economically productive age); *are* (dependent); *(are) engaged in* (Western-style); (those on high incomes) *are reputed to spend* (their income on ostentatious consumption); (those with funds to invest) *have* (a preference for money-lending).

Some individuals, in the world presented in this text, will die at an economically inconvenient age and are dependent. By the same token, some are clearly part if not the whole of the problem—consuming, spending, and lending. Both perpetrator and victim are there in the text, both relentlessly typified, but typified as individuals. It is this individualization that supports the dependence model of development that is built in these texts, but a warning is sounded in the concluding sections of this textbook chapter that this dependence on outside investment will itself become conditional on a satisfactorily stable political system. Thus the final response pattern is established: political reform that is satisfactory in the eyes of the investors. The notion of development in this way is extended beyond economic ethnocentrism to the point of political preference for the nations effecting the necessary economic aid.

Those forms function to de-historicize, de-agentize, and politically neutralize the portrayal of the phenomenon of inequality. They do this through the mutually complementing content and logic of the field (Lee,

1996), and the theoretically unmotivated and nonprogrammatic nature of the individual and communal response options thereby afforded.

It is through this crucial respect that the synoptic work of the text remains difficult to contest, and thus remains capable of pulling off an impressive and creative ideological feat—a subject-reader who can stay mute and ineffectual in the face of learning about gross, dangerous, and patterned inequalities. These choices in part effect this work through the following logic: how the phenomenon is characterized, that is, what is taken to be a legitimate, scientific, educationally appropriate description, affords certain explanations of how it and its context came to be as they are, and (usually) tacitly excludes other possible forms of explanation; the afforded explanation in turn opens the way for some responses, some positions with respect to what a person might/should (and, again, by necessary inference, might/should not) do in the light of the existence of the phenomenon, in this case, of economic disparity.

CRITIQUING ACCULTURATION INTO LITERACY

Perhaps more than any other research community, researchers interested in critical literacy education have taken seriously the proposition that experience with what literacy is and why it matters is mediated and built through everyday interactions between people and with texts. This proposition has guided much of the work that has focused on equity issues, and has led to a spate of research activity, particularly since about the 1980s, on everyday literacy practices. Baker (1991), for instance, outlined the various ways in which the study of classroom interaction, particularly to do with language and literacy, can be approached. Baker outlined general sets of assumptions, and the interrogations they each lead to, under three headings, arguing that literacy lessons can be "read" as: (a) ways of introducing students to texts, books, and stories; (b) ways of connecting students to culture; and (c) ways of connecting students to the preferred procedures and subjectivities of schooling, subjectivities that are informed by discourses about class, ethnicity, gender, and generation and authority.

As an illustration of the latter point, (Gilbert, 1988a, 1988b) showed how the use of certain generic forms in classroom work constrained and constructed gendered subjectivity. Gilbert's work posed questions about the ideological construction and function of children's narratives, and of the generally unremarked pedagogical practices associated with classroom story writing. Such a focus on the role of storytelling and story hearing in the legitimation of dominant cultural values, particularly as they install a naturalized role for narration as part of classroom pedagogical practice, has become a research focus within critically oriented literacy research. A distinctive feature of this work has been its attention to the complex interplay between ethnicity, sexuality, race, generation, class and gender: the multiply positioned social subject. The gendered practices of narrative, and the role of cultural story and storying in the construction and reconstruction of gendered subjectivities have been particularly identified by Davies (1989) and Gilbert and Taylor (1991) as significant issues for educational research.

Austin, Freebody, and Dwyer (2002) addressed the question of how discourses concerning generation—being a grown-up and being a child—become both topics and interactional resources in classroom lessons for children. They documented, for instance, how teachers and students in a Year 5 classroom discussed the sadness of the ending of a novel (about a stranded magpie, *Magpie Island*, Thiele, 1974) that the class group was working on:

Example 7.7: "What's he actually telling you?"

96	T	. . . Umm - do you think the author does that with a purpose what's he trying, he he knows his story is very sad, what do you think he <u>leaves</u> - his readers with a feeling of what. Anita?
97	An	Well so they can work out what happens the way, what they want to happen?
98	T	Yes, there's a feeling there I, I think, Justine.
99	Ju	Suspension? About//
100	T	//Yes?
101	S	Look what they have done to the magpie kind of thing?
102	T	Y:yes? (.) Ok? Joshua? What do you think there's a feeling of at the end? I'd like you to really concentrate and try and think. Carol?
103	Ca	Sorrow.//
104	T	//Sorrow? Is there another feeling other than sorrow, Toni?
105	To	Well at the end how it says BUT IT WAS DARK OUTSIDE and he said it was going to be a bright new day tomorrow, well it was gonna like sort of begin all again? The next day?
106	T	Right. Does anyone feel that the author has left the reader
107	S	( )

108 T   Does the author feel, do <u>you</u> think at least, does anyone feel that he's left you with perhaps a feeling of hope?

109 St   Yeah.

110 T   Why, Amy?

111 Am   Beca:ause well umm he says that bit about all the fisher-men?//

112 T   //The fishermen going past and seeing Magpie. So he is going to survive and perhaps [just

113 Am   [Yeah], kind of think that//

114 T   //Yeah, I think perhaps there's a slight feeling of hope there, I think the author's also trying to tell us something else, that people? (3.0) as well as Magpie but I think he's really giving us a message about ourselves. That we are able to do (1.0) what? What are people capable of doing. (4) I think he really tries to give us this message through (3) the magpie. What do you think, even though, I'll phrase it in another way. Even though people have losses, and hardships, and dreadful periods of sorrow, what's he actually telling you at the end, Colin?

115 Col That it doesn't really matter that there are people that do, I mean, that do//

116 T   //I'd like you to pay a bit more attention

((and later))

119 Am   Like you shouldn't, I think he might be trying to say that you shouldn't feel sorry for yourself you should just try and get on with everything?

120 T   I think that you do survive and life goes on, even though at the time it seems as black as black. Do you think? Yeah.

There had been a discussion earlier in this lesson that hinged on the notion that novels, especially for children, usually have happy endings. Here, we see the teacher working to achieve a happy ending in the talk. Magpie's being stranded and alone was brought off as a happy ending using an allegorical interpretation that reads the magpie as a symbol of hope and survival: Toni's restatement of the final words of the novel (turn 105) was reformulated by the teacher into a "feeling of hope" (turn 108); she then explained this in allegorical terms (turn 114); a few turns later, a student rendered a version of the "moral" of the story and again the teacher confirmed this allegorical rendering.

Later in the lesson, the teacher and students discussed the "feeling" that the "images" in the text evoke. The students talked of the emotional tenor of the conclusion of the novel in terms of sadness, sorrow, disappointment, and depression. The teacher asked for more feelings:

159   T   there's also a tremendous feeling of something else at the
            end I felt.

A few turns later, Toni provided 'hope' (turn 164) which the teacher had suggested at earlier in the lesson (turn 108).

164   To   Hope? So that it might happen maybe he'll//

165   T   //Maybe he'll be
            happy and survive. Yes.

The teacher interrupted Toni's answer at turn 164 to state her own version at turn 165 "Maybe he'll be happy and survive," explicitly stating her preferred allegorical interpretation of the novel. So the teacher worked hard in the talk to establish a "hopeful" reading of the text in the face of the students' insistence on more negative, or at least different, readings. This working toward a particular construction of "the child" as character and reader, Austin and others showed, is consequential for the teacher's assessment of the students' work on the novel. A significant feature of what the students needed to display was some form of compliance with adult-preferred notions of what they, as children, could "read" off from the story, in particular the teacher's installation of a happy ending. As Baker and Freebody (1989) put it, the text to which the students needed to attend most diligently was the "text" of the teacher's reading.

In their study of how picture books were used in the first year of the school in reading lessons, Baker and Freebody (1989, p. 182) drew the following conclusion, which applies equally well to the points just made:

> While the apparent source of an answer lies in the student's background knowledge, in personal preferences, or in the illustrations in the book, the reformulative and evaluative utterances of the teacher can be seen to reveal that virtually all of the retrospectively correct or adequate answers are so found in relation to the teacher's ongoing construction of a reading of the story. . . . We are drawn to the conclusion that it is the teacher's reading and the teachers 'thinking' that are the targets of the students' guesses. It is in this important sense that reading as an organised activity cannot be separated from the relation of teachers and students.

It is therefore in two senses that the study of literacy events in class-rooms, homes, churches, workplaces, and elsewhere can be seen to call for a critical perspective: First, as resolutely social, literacy learning events are embedded in particular relations and these relations come to embody the authority of interpretation for the learner (see, e.g., J. Green, Weade, & Graham, 1988). Second, the social, cultural, and ideological dimensions that texts can be shown variously to draw on become the interpretive resources for both teachers and learners. Students are thus acculturated into ways of reading and ways of interpreting and talking about what they read through the structures of the interactions that make up literacy events, ways they are accountable for displaying (Baker & Freebody, 1993). They are thereby shown and held to ways of activating a form of engagement that is tailored to the social, cultural, and ideological sense-making procedures of the texts they encounter.

CRITIQUING THE DEPLOYMENT OF "LITERACY"

Most critical approaches alert us to the ways in which literacy has itself been made a social, cultural, and ideological fact. Indeed, literacy is some-thing of a superstar, with frequent media appearances, and with the capaci-ty to energize and disturb a community. Often, this amounts to uniting a community in a concern for (usually falling) educational, and thus social, cultural, and moral standards. It seems almost the hallmark of an earnest and forward-looking society that it acknowledge the newsworthiness of lit-eracy—its falling standards, its state of crisis/scandal/disgrace, and all the rest (Freebody, 2001; Freebody & Welch, 1993). It is hard to imagine such superlatives applied to other domains of sociocultural practice, other than perhaps sexuality and drug abuse, and it is unimaginable that any other domain of education could attract such superlatives from media critics—a *geography crisis?*—a *history scandal?* Unlikely.

Asserting that you are not concerned about literacy brings with it seri-ous moral accountability, the equivalent perhaps of mentioning in public that you never brush your teeth. It is, therefore, entirely predictable that in the recent US presidential election, literacy made a cameo appearance: In one of the conservative candidate's campaign advertisements, three terms that floated across the screen while the well-modulated voice extolled the candidate's position were *law and order, prosperity,* and *phonics.* So a criti-cal approach to literacy entails consideration of how the idea of literacy is cast in media events alongside other celebrity values such as cultural cohe-sion, economic development, and a wholesome moral outlook.

In that respect, we can see that public debates about literacy are actually about its absence—illiteracy. The concern in much debate is not to explore how literacy practices are conducted in a society and what implications these may have for economic practice, cultural cohesion, or ideological transformation; it is rather to produce the blame cycles that are a major part of any half decent effort to legitimate the social order by teaching certain groups how to self-marginalize and self-oppress.

At a finer level, we can see that various literacy practices are themselves more valued as indicators of general intellectual, cultural, and, at times, moral well-being than others. In their study of the ways in which elementary school teachers in disadvantaged and affluent schools discussed literacy activities of their students, Gunn, Forrest, and Freebody (1995; see also Freebody, Forrest, & Gunn, 2001) found that the value attached to any particular literacy practice was not fixed, but that it varied according to a the socioeconomic level of the people under discussion. This the researchers termed *value switching*. The observation recalls Bourdieu's (1974) point that the same personal attribute (e.g., attention to detail) can be evaluated positively for some students (as, e.g., meticulousness) and negatively for others (as, e.g., workman-like plodding), depending on the location of the students in disadvantaged versus 'advantaged' circumstances. Specifically, Gunn et al., found that although a certain attribute was valued when displayed by one socioeconomic category of person, the same attribute was devalued when displayed by the contrasting or supplementary category.

Gunn and others found a number of instances of this phenomenon, two of which are described and illustrated briefly here: environmental/functional reading, and the degree of parental caring. Regarding nvironmental/functional reading, the following statements were made by a teacher in a disadvantaged school:

1. r The characteristics of the student's backgrounds that have an influence upon their learning at the school. Now you've mentioned a little bit already, like Thursday nights (shopping), socioeconomic background you mentioned a little bit, what do you mean by that, as far as the influence on their learning?

2. t Well the socioeconomic background of course, there isn't the money to be spent on what you would call a normal upbringing such as, so that the children have enough clothes, food. Books tend to be a luxury item that some families just cannot afford. So that the level of reading material at home, before they come to school, is impoverished, I mean it is probably existent but not to any great abundance. There doesn't seem to be like, mum and dad don't sit down and read a book, is a good idea to do. Or write, is a good idea to do, they do basic functional reading and writing.

3. r What do you mean by functional?

4. t Enough to get them through the day. <u>They can read the street signs</u>. <u>They can read the Kmart sign</u>, they can read, ahh, well they can identify the signs.

5. r What about junk mail, catalogues?

6. t Well they can identify those because they are presented in a predictable text. So that they would probably understand them more than say a novel or that mixed structure of reading and then of course you know the children don't see that at home so they come to school wondering what all the hooha is about books. (emphasis added)

This can be contrasted with:

r So what about similarities and differences between some of your students' home and school contexts, from the amount of literacy, like the home situation and the school situation, do you see similarities and differences?

s Well, I guess the similarities are in the middle class homes where reading is valued, it's modelled, stories are read to them, the parents read, there are books around the house, <u>the kids are, you know I think of the little ones who try to read the street signs and the labels at the Supermarket and things like that know what writing is</u>, whereas some of them will come to school with, they really have not got that conception it's, that's a similarity and differences there I guess. Umm, value on reading and writing, some of them may have stories or books or whatever but um there's no value placed on having the book or caring for a book or whatever, a pad, a book, a pencil, you know, whatever. So I've got that to contend with. (emphasis added)

In the first extract, a category of normality is established. Normal upbringing means money to buy books and presumably middle socioeconomic status (SES). It also involves the attribute of an interest in books. For this category of person, reading street or K-Mart signs is described as functional, identification of predictable text rather than a valued reading skill. In the second extract the category of "middle-class homes" is set up and within this category the attribute of reading street signs and labels is valued. It is seen as part of the modeling and learning process that enables these children to come to school with some "conception" of what reading and writ-

ing are about. In one extract, being able to perform functional or environmental reading is not viewed as a proper reading skill but as a low-level
identification of text, whereas in the second extract the same behavior or
attribute is not "identification" but a worthwhile part of the reading
process and real reading. The amount of value the same practice is accorded
appears to directly relate to, in this case, the SES category to which the
attribute is attached.

With respect to the degree of caring, the following example demonstrates a similar shift in value for the same or similar attribute depending on
the category to which the attribute is being attached. The category of parents is attributed with a "caring" disposition for children. For the teachers
interviewed here, caring is taken to be indicated by protecting children,
teaching them to look after their appearance and possessions, ensuring they
make an effort to do their tasks well, and taking the time to be with children. However, in the following extracts, caring is valued differently
depending on which parent category is doing the caring. The first statements were made by a Grade 1/2 teacher in a disadvantaged school:

r   . . . in the class group itself is there any other information about
    their backgrounds or attitudes?

t   Within this class, *a couple of ESL children have very caring par-
    ents, and the care sometimes gets in the way of giving the chil-
    dren responsibilities.* Because they come from traumatic back-
    grounds, they tend to protect and overprotect the children.
    Ahh, which means that, when you are trying to teach them
    responsibility, it's umm, they are being responsible in the
    class, but at home they are still being very much umm, a
    young child which tends to give the child a fair bit of conflict.
    (italics added)

From a Grade 3 teacher in a disadvantaged school:

r   Children from socioeconomically disadvantaged backgrounds
    are often not motivated to do well in school. (Comment?)

t   Yes strongly agree. I don't think it's so much because it's a lack
    of, caring—though in some cases I think it is—but I think it's
    a case of, because they might be a single parent, just being too
    busy to—*not that they don't love their kids, but—the case of
    just struggling to get ahead. The time, that quality time spent
    with the kids,* because they're working constantly and um . . .
    And maybe even a lot of, I suppose it's the vicious cycle isn't
    it? (italics added)

From a Grade 3 teacher in the nondisadvantaged school:

r   What would you say about the characteristics of your classroom
     and how these characteristics impact on their learning in liter-
     acy development?

t   There's an interweaving all the time with what we're doing in
     the room and what we're doing at home. You know, it's
     reflected, <u>the families just naturally and implicitly support
     their children</u> in their learning and I suppose that's that is
     umm, a factor of most middle class families. (italics added)

English as a second language (ESL) parents in the first extract are stated
to care for their children, but this caring was seen as counterproductive
overprotection. The teacher used the anecdote of a "couple" of ESL children to demonstrate that not all caring is appropriate. In the second
extract, the teacher acknowledged that children from the category of disadvantaged backgrounds probably have caring parents ("I don't think it's
so much because it's a lack of caring") if not in all cases, but even this caring is lacking in some form. Disadvantaged parents are stated not to have
the time to care properly ("that quality of time spent with the kids because
they're working constantly"). Disadvantaged parents are taken to be constantly working, and therefore the quality of care is less. "Middle-class"
parents, according to the third extract, are able to "naturally and implicitly
support their children," a caring disposition that is said to relate directly to
the comparability of helping activity in homes and schools. Thus, how caring is valued and talked into relevance to the pedagogy, is based largely on
the category used by the teachers to describe the parents doing the
caring.
     Along with the more familiar uses of literacy—in the media to deplore
falling standards in schools, and in public political discourse to protest
workers' irresponsibility with respect to economic productivity—we find
that this collection of practices called *literacy* is put to various kinds of
work among educators and community members. But, as with other transcendent terms, the meanings and even the valuations of literacy do not
remain static or fixed from occasion to occasion. As Blackledge (2000)
showed in the case of Bangladeshi women living in England, literacy is a
powerful discursive instrument. Its ready attachment to some groups and
not to others, the ways in which some groups are shown to measure up
against a benchmark that is labeled *literacy*, carrying with it broader deno-
tations to do with cultural level and appropriate motivations and aspira-
tions, all attest to its significant symbolic status in the politics of educational debate. In such debates, the uses of literacy, in the light of its actual uses
in actual sites (Prinsloo & Breier, 1996), and the discourses that are brought

to bear on schooling and training, are all significant focal points for a critical approach to literacy and to education and more broadly.

CONCLUSIONS

Stated most generically, the goal of critical approaches is to interrupt the processes of representation, of showing how the seamless construction of ways of representing human experience is not disinterested, that interests are at work through the privileged forms of representation, and that these in turn are visible in the following phases:

- *Production*: The products of representational practices, that is that texts.
- *Distribution and exchange*: The interactional processes of acculturation by which people are brought into ways of knowing what these representations mean for their practices and for their accounts of social experience (teaching, assessing, and all the rest).
- *Enforced consumption*: The discursive mechanisms through which literacy itself, as a notion and as a social fact, is politically deployed in community, media, and political accounts as a commodity and as a preferred quality of social practice.

It is important to point out as well that, at its most general, the Critical Literacy Project is centrally about producing, distributing and exchanging a particular vocabulary for describing and debating literacy and literacy education. These varying vocabularies, and the norms they represent and reinstall have been documented by, for example, B. Green, Hodgens, and Luke (1994). They documented what they saw to be four distinguishable but overlapping versions of *the literate person* in media accounts and public debates during the decades after World War II. The decade of the 1950s, they argued, was characterized by traditional literary discipline and a concomitant elite literacy. Tertiary attendance was comparatively low, and issues of cultural and linguistic diversity did not figure prominently in any educational discourse. The focus for language and literacy education for the 1960s, they claimed, was firmly on technical skill with a scientific emphasis, and motivated by a strong sense of global competition in science and technology, with the equally strong overtones from the United States of the Cold War consequences of falling behind. In the popular press, the progressivist movements influencing language and literacy education in the 1970s did not figure as prominently as the need to accommodate to apparently nonelitist educational needs occasioned by the rapid expansion of access to education, including tertiary education. Green and others concluded that in the 1970s educators increasingly looked toward psychological, diagnostic approaches to *remediating* the literacy-deficient student, whereas in the 1980s, the urgency of economic issues placed language and literacy in the centerstage as a key competence in the enhancement of economic performance, legitimating the rhetoric of accountability for teachers and educational systems. Green and others concluded that all four versions of the literate person outlined are male and monocultural and that each serves a distinctive set of ideological and economic interests. Each reflects a distinct method of entering a notion of literacy, and a logic concerning its enhancement and its consequences into public debate.

Among researchers interested in theorizing literacy, the literate-skilled citizen was critiqued by Freireans (e.g., Freire, 1985), who pointed to the necessarily political readings and writings that constitute public experience, and by humanists-constructivists, who used post-behavorist learning theories to deplore the teacher-centeredness of a skills definition of reading and writing. The literate-humanist citizen, in turn, was critiqued by cross-culturalists who pointed to the monoculturalism of constructivist approaches to learning and to the vast variability of literacy practices in out-of-school experience (e.g., Street, 1995), and by post-structuralists and critical theorists of the left, who drew attention to the ideological work done by school literacy in the production, distribution and exchange of social goods and services (e.g., de Castell, Luke, & Luke, 1989; A. Luke, 1988; C. Luke, 1989). What Green and others showed is that these developments were not just the outcomes of academic and professional exchange about literacy. These debates themselves have been shaped by the economic, political and demographic changes that characterized northern nations since the 1950s.

We can consider a number of key propositions concerning the nature of literacy (adapted from Barton & Hamilton, 2000). I state these as a set of bald assertions, recognizing their essentially heuristic value:

- *Literacy* is most productively understood as an open-textured category of sociocultural practice. That is, other than some involvement of printed, electronic and iconic-visual representations, literacy practices cannot be strictly defined in terms of criterial and associated features, precisely because the range of sociocultural practices in which these representations play some part can be studied, but not prespecified.
- Social institutions develop a selective tradition of literacy practices, giving heavy duty to some, and less to others, according to their practical, organizational, and ideological purposes. That is, over time, in vocational, civic and domestic domains of life, some literacy practices become more visible and influential than others. In that respect, literacy practices can be interpreted as reflections,

adaptations or modifications of the relations of power that are continuously being rebuilt in the sites of their use.

- In any given setting, being a literate participant necessarily and simultaneously means being able to orient to and manage not only the immediate demands of managing the text, and the sociocultural demands of the practices the text calls for, but also the power relations relevant to the event. It is central to most accounts of critical literacy that these three orientations are seen as mutually embedded.

Critical approaches to literacy view the distribution and exchange of valued literacy practices as centrally implicated in the maintenance of social, economic, and political order. Critical literacy is characterized by a commitment to examine and restore particular forms of literacy education as a key interest of marginalized groups of learners, those who been excluded from access to the discourses and texts of dominant economies and cultures.

Literacy practices are probably the most significant cultural technology through which public interests are conjoined to personal interests—they bring together the procedures called on by public participation and the platforms for identities (dispositions, social positions, cultural affordances, etc.) from which functional reading and writing activities can be both constructed and evaluated. At the same time, literacy practices provide practice in the preferred procedures of citizenship—public and domestic—and thus are a major means of acculturation, of making the personal relevant to the public, and vice-versa. The often brutal pragmatism of current globalized economic rationalism and postmodernists' insistence on the death of grand narratives notwithstanding, modern nation states seem to need to search for transcendent values. Literacy plays in this game. Its use aims to connect personal subjectivities with public programs—economic prosperity, informed citizenry, stable nuclear families, and so on. It is one device that aims to make seamless the conjoining of personal and collective programs of well-being, individual and public activities aimed at the development and building of capacities. In the ways we conventionally acculturate younger people and novice readers and writers, literacy education provides a set of single-line interpretive rituals that connect conceptions of the globally good society to the ways in which we conduct our everyday communications.

Literacy, as an object in public debates, thus renders individuals into collectives in theory and practice. It is given a self-evident moral standing that allows the expansionist commercial and linguistic interests of some social groups to be set aside. It provides an apparently straightforward benchmark that applies, again apparently equally, to entire collectives—the managerial and intellectual elite, workers of all collar colors, the disenfranchised, and the outsiders—connecting them and legitimating their respective positions via the interval that they inhabit on the benchmark. As with other secular religious ideas—nationalism, family, prosperity, and so on—people are conjoined through the ritualized institutional practices of teaching and assessing literacy in a common commitment to a personal and collective attribute and a common fear and disdain for its absence. Literacy is indeed "everybody's business" in all the possible senses of that expression.

The central message from researchers in critical literacy seems to be this: All the workings and trappings of literacy have histories. The materials of literacy, right down to the alphabet and the ways in which sounds are pronounced, the language we read and write in the standard forms of that language, the interpretive practices modeled through schooling, workplace training programs, religious reading lessons, and the rest, and the accounts of domestic, civic, economic, and cultural life that are made available through acculturation into institutionalized reading and writing practices— all these are the traces of the struggles, victories and defeats of certain ideas, groups, communities and language groups. To adopt a critical approach to teaching and researching literacy is to know that this work necessarily figures in those struggles, victories and defeats, one way or the other, no matter how innocent the goals of improving reading and writing appear at first sight.

REFERENCES

Austin, H., Freebody, P., & Dwyer, B. (2002). Methodological issues in analysing talk and text: The case of childhood in and for school. In A. McHoul & M. Rapley (Eds.), *Analysing talk in institutional settings* (pp. 183-195). London: Continuum International.

Baker, C.D. (1991). Reading the text of reading lessons. *Australian Journal of Reading, 14,* 5-20.

Baker, C.D., & Freebody, P. (1989). Talk around text: Constructions of textual and teacher authority in classroom discourse. In S. de Castell, A. Luke, & C. Luke (Eds.), *Language, authority and criticism: Readings on the school textbook* (pp. 263-283). London & Philadelphia, PA: Falmer Press.

Baker, C.D., & Freebody, P. (1993). The crediting of literate competence. *Australian Journal of Language and Literacy, 16,* 279-294.

Barton, D., & Hamilton, M. (2000). *Local literacies.* London: Routledge.

Blackledge, A. (2000). Power relations and the social construction of "literacy" and "'iteracy": The experience of Bangladeshi women in Birmingham. In M. Martin-Jones & K. Jones (Eds.), *Multilingual literacies: Reading and writing different worlds* (pp. 55-70). Amsterdam & Philadelphia, PA: John Benjamins.

Bourdieu, P. (1974). The school as a conservative force. In J. Eggleton (Ed.), *Contemporary research in the sociology of education* (pp. 32-46). London: Methuen.

Clark, R., & Ivanic, R. (1997). *The politics of writing*. London: Routledge.

Davies, B. (1989). *Frogs and snails and feminist tales: Preschool children and gender*. Sydney: Allen & Unwin.

de Castell, S., Luke, A., & Luke, C. (1989). *Language, authority and criticism: Readings on the school textbook*. London: Falmer Press.

Emmison, M., & Smith, P. (2000). *Researching the visual: Images, objects, contexts and interactions in social and cultural inquiry*. London: Sage.

Freebody, P. (2001). Theorising new literacies in and out of school. *Language and Education: An International Journal, 15*, 105-117.

Freebody, P., Forrest, T., & Gunn, G. (2001). Accounting and silencing in interviews: Smooth running through the "problem of schooling the disadvantaged." In P. Freebody, S. Muspratt, & B. Dwyer (Eds.), *Difference, silence, and textual practice: Studies in critical literacy* (pp. 119-152). Cresskill, NJ: Hampton Press.

Freebody, P., & Welch, A.R. (Eds.). (1993). *Knowledge, culture, and power: International perspectives on literacy policies and practices*. London: Falmer Press & Pittsburgh, PA: University of Pittsburgh Press

Freire, P. (1985). *The politics of education*. London: MacMillan.

Gee, J.P. (1996). *Social linguistics and literacies: Ideology in discourses* (2nd ed.). London: Taylor & Francis.

Gee, J.P. (1999). *An introduction to discourse analysis: Theory and method*. London: Routledge.

Gilbert, P. (1988a). Stoning the romance: Girls as resistant readers and writers. *Curriculum Perspectives, 8*(2), 13-19.

Gilbert, P. (1988b). Student text as pedagogical text. In S. De Castell, A. Luke, & C. Luke (Eds.), *Language, authority and criticism: Readings on the school textbook*. London: Falmer Press.

Gilbert, P., & Taylor, S. (1991). *Fashioning the feminine: Girls, popular culture and schooling*. Sydney: Allen & Unwin.

Graff, H.J. (2001). Literacy's myths and legacies: From lessons from the history of literacy, to the question of critical literacy. In P. Freebody, S. Muspratt, & B. Dwyer (Eds.), *Difference, silence, and textual practice: Studies in critical literacy* (pp. 1-29). Cresskill, NJ: Hampton Press.

Green, B., Hodgens, J., & Luke, A. (1994). *Debating literacy in Australia: A documentary history, 1945-1994*. Canberra: Australian Literacy Federation.

Green, J.L., Weade, R., & Graham, K. (1988). Lesson construction and student participation: A sociolinguistic analysis. In J.L. Green & J.O. Harker (Eds.), *Multiple perspective analyses of classroom discourse* (pp. 11-47). Norwwod, NJ: Ablex.

Gunn, S., Forrest, T., & Freebody, P. (1995). Perspectives on poverty, schooling, and literacy. In P. Freebody, C. Ludwig, & S. Gunn, (Eds.), *Everyday literacy practices in and out of schools in low socio-economic urban communities*. Canberra: Report to the Commonwealth Department of Employment, Education and Training, Curriculum Corporation.

Janks, H. (2000). Domination, access, diversity and design: A synthesis for critical literacy education. *Educational Review, 52*, 175-186.

Lankshear, C., & Lawler, M. (1987). *Literacy, schooling and revolution*. London: Falmer Press.

Lee, A. (1996). *Gender, literacy and curriculum: Re-writing school geography.* London: Taylor & Francis.

Lemke, J.L. (1995). *Textual politics: Discourse and social dynamics.* London: Taylor & Francis.

Luke, A. (1988). *Literacy, textbooks and ideology: Postwar literacy instruction and the mythology of Dick and Jane.* London: Falmer Press.

Luke, C. (1989). *Pedagogy, printing and protestantism: The discourse on childhood.* Albany: State University of New York Press.

Martin, J.R. (1992). *English text: System and structure.* Amsterdam: John Benjamins.

Prinsloo, M., & Breier, M. (1996). *The social uses of literacy.* Amsterdam & Philadelphia, PA: John Benjamins.

Smith, D.E. (1999). *Writing the social: Critique, theory and investigations.* Toronto: University of Toronto Press.

Street, B.V. (1995). *Social literacies: Critical approaches to literacy in development, ethnography and education.* London: Longman.

Thiele, C. (1974). *Magpie Island.* Ringwood, Victoria: Puffin Books.

Threadgold, T. (2001). Making theories for different worlds: Making critical differences. In P. Freebody, S. Muspratt, & B. Dwyer (Eds.), *Difference, silence, and textual practice: Studies in critical literacy* (pp. 209-242). Cresskill, NJ: Hampton Press.

Tisdell, C.A. (1979). *Economics in our society: Principles and applications.* Milton, Qld: Jacaranda.

17

Critical Literacy

Theory, Pedagogy and the Historical Imperative

Bronwyn Mellor
Chalkface Press

Annette Patterson
James Cook University

Critical literacy has become a focus of attention in English and literature education in the United Kingdom, South Africa, Canada, the United States, Australia and New Zealand during the past decade. Working in high school and university classrooms from the mid-1970s to the late 1990s gave us the opportunity to combine empirical research with explorations of theoretical issues related to literature education during a period encompassing often far-reaching curricula changes. Our work addressed the interface between theory and practice through a combination of library-based research, classroom observation, and curriculum development.

Initially, with reader-response theory as our informing paradigm, we investigated the responses of secondary and tertiary students to short fiction texts using qualitative and quantitative methodologies (Green & Harker, 1988; Green & Wallat, 1981). Our aim was to understand the reading practices of our students better and, in the light of this knowledge, to devise specific critical literacy approaches to literature study in the classroom and to develop our theory of English education. Qualitative analyses of students' written responses to selected short stories were undertaken as well as statistical analysis of several hundred student interpretations of short fiction texts (Patterson, 1989). Findings gained from the intersection of teaching, research, and curriculum development experiences informed this work in productive but not always predictable ways. Our research did enable the production of more explicitly theorized curriculum materials with which to explore issues of textuality and diversity with our students. However, it also drew attention to contradictions in the field and led to the development of a historical framework within which to reconsider subject English (Mellor & Patterson, 1994; Patterson, 1997; Peel, Patterson, & Gerlach, 2000).

During the past century, a number of different perspectives on English as a subject of study has emerged. Each new perspective has shaped a particular view of English, which it has achieved primarily through a critique of earlier work. Assumptions about the contours of each perspective inform curriculum development in almost every English-speaking country, and the implications for practice of these different perspectives have been widely canvassed through the research literature (Cambourne, Hendy, & Scown, 1988; Dixon, 1967/1975; Graves, 1986; Green & Beavis, 1996; Peel et al., 2000).

A common approach to describing these successive perspectives on subject English is to use some now familiar terms such as *Heritage, New Criticism, Personal Growth, Poststructuralist English,* and *Critical Literacy.* In each case, the new perspective critiqued the previous one and attempted to establish itself as being different to or in opposition to it. Thus, advocates of Personal Growth English critiqued Heritage practices and promoted an alternative perspective on what should constitute English; a perspective later found wanting by educators working from a theoretical base informed by poststructuralism. This process of "change through critique" is an important aspect of English curricula theory.

Broadly speaking, Heritage and New Critical approaches to texts dominated the study of English during the first five decades of the 20th century. During this period, syllabus and curricula tended to focus on the inculcation of grammatical knowledge through formal study of grammar, recitation exercises by which students were taught correct pronunciation, and mastery of particular forms of writing, such as the essay. Students were expected to be familiar with "great works of literature" and with the lives of their authors while younger students were introduced to "classical" literary forms through the study of myths and legends.

During the 1960s, a shift in emphasis occurred with the introduction of "popular texts" and a trend toward encouraging students to explore their lived experiences (Britton, 1970) through process approaches to writing (Graves, 1986). Instead of copying or following an exemplary model, students were expected to conference draft versions of their written texts with teachers or other adults. Students' own choice of text type and form of expression was a feature of the approach and young writers were encouraged to use writing as a means of exploring their developing identities. Students also were encouraged to explore different poetic and narrative forms through wide-reading programs. Personal responses to texts took prominence as teachers began to shun formal critical views of literature and to focus on what the text meant for their own students. Divergent approaches to expressing one's self through writing were encouraged in many classrooms. What became known as Personal Growth English was further developed through the decades of the 1970s and 1980s and was famously encapsulated for British and Australian educators through John Dixon's *Growth Through English* (1967/1975).

The late 1980s and the 1990s witnessed a shift in thinking about English, as the work of French structuralists and poststructuralists began to influence curriculum and syllabus development in England and Australia, in particular. Critiques of process writing (Christie, 1990; Gilbert, 1989; Martin, Christie, & Rothery, 1987) and of reader-response (Corcoran, 1987; Freebody, Luke, & Gilbert, 1991; Gilbert, 1987; Luke, 1988) and curricular theorists whose work was informed by Derrida (Cherryholmes, 1988; Green, 1993) and neo-Marxist approaches (Ball & Goodson, 1984; Goodson, 1983; Street, 1984) were highly influential. These particular theoretical orientations resulted in a new perspective on English as a subject of study. Australian syllabus documents began to focus on texts, including the texts of cinema and television. Furthermore, English as a field of study increasingly incorporated a broad range of interpretative practices that relocated meaning from the words on the page and from the interaction between text and reader (Rosenblatt, 1978) and text and writer (Graves, 1986) to the social, cultural, and historical location of reading and writing practices (Belsey, 1980; Derrida, 1981; Eagleton, 1985; Kristeva & Moi, 1986; Scholes, 1985).

As experienced classroom teachers and beginning researchers at the end of the 1980s, we entered a field that was preparing to reinvent itself in terms of poststructural approaches to the study of texts. We were excited by the work of French theorists such as Derrida, Foucault, Kristeva, and by British literary critics, such as Belsey and Eagleton, and by the contributors to the British journal *Screen* who were politicizing English in ways that would allow students greater access to a wide range of understandings about how texts worked in the world.

As classroom teachers, we had experience of working with students from diverse social and cultural backgrounds. We had been confronted by students' frustration with what they saw as the representation of elitist political and social views. We had stood in classrooms in different countries and been confronted by student hostility when, respectively, we had attempted to teach *The Merchant of Venice* in a Jewish neighbourhood school and *Othello* in a London comprehensive with a high proportion of London-Jamaican students. The need to respond to such situations with some subtlety made research into a wide range of theoretical positions on representation, textuality, and diversity necessary. We focussed in the main on poststructural theory, using the work of such writers as Barthes, Belsey, Davies, Eagleton, Gilbert, and Kristeva and Moi, applying it to the pedagogical problems we were experiencing at that time.

This research informed the next stage of our work. We realized that rather than objecting to the literature we were required to teach that a better approach might be to develop materials that would help students to deconstruct the text, to unpack the oppressive ways in which its meanings were produced and disseminated. We hoped that by doing, this we would provide our students with skills that would carry beyond the classroom to the wider community, skills that would assist them to question and combat the racist, sexist texts they would continue to encounter through the media, in the workplace, and on the street.

Similar to work being undertaken elsewhere, our project of trying to develop an approach to teaching against intolerance, and of providing teachers with materials and techniques to assist students to deconstruct texts, was a collaborative effort. Instructional materials were workshopped in our own high school classrooms and in the classrooms of our obliging colleagues at schools in Perth, Australia and London, England and with university students who were studying to become teachers. It was a team project that included writers, students, classroom teachers, and university academics and it resulted in a range of texts for classrooms (Martino & Mellor, 1994; Mellor, 1989; Mellor, O'Neill, & Patterson, 1987; Mellor & Patterson, 1996; Mellor, Patterson, & O'Neill, 1991; Moon, 1992/2001a; Moon & Mellor; 2001).

AN INSTANCE OF PRACTICE: THE READING OF "ELSA WERTMAN" AND POSTSTRUCTURALISM

The following account of the study of a poem with high school English students traces the intellectual path we were taking at this time. It delineates the type of practice we were attempting to develop in response to both practical and theoretical concerns and demonstrates how we drew on both our reading of research and theory and on our and others' experiences in the classroom.

Reading the poem "Elsa Wertman" by Edgar Lee Masters (1962) with our students[1] in the 1980s brought into focus for us many of the issues we increasingly wanted to address in English lessons; in particular, our desire to analyze textual representations of gender, race, and class. Also highlighted were the practical classroom uses that we hoped poststructuralist theory, with its attention to connections between systems of meaning and power, could be put—specifically, in investigating how texts could have particular meanings that supported the interests of certain groups (Corcoran, 1987; Crowley, 1989; Davies, 1989, 1992, 1994; Morgan, 1997).

The narrative voice used in the poem is that of Elsa Wertman, a young servant girl in the household of a prosperous, but childless couple. She speaks of becoming pregnant to the husband who, with his wife, conceals her role and adopts the baby. Very little textual detail is given about any of the characters involved; the wife, for example, is mentioned only in the following terms:

> One day Mrs. Greene said she understood,
> And would make no trouble for me,
> And, being childless, would adopt it.
> (He had given her a farm to be still.)
> So she hid in the house and sent out rumours,
> As if it were going to happen to her.

Yet the students reading and discussing the poem produced remarkably detailed readings of Mrs. Greene and the kind of person she was. Much of their discussion centered round her role in Elsa Wertman's pregnancy and the subsequent management of it and the child. Their readings of the character of the wife were largely negative and some were decidedly hostile, seeing her as a scheming woman who, behind the scenes, had engineered the birth of the child she could not have. "Why employ such a good-looking girl? She must have known something would happen," was one student's comment. Mrs. Greene's inability to conceive was generally not read sympathetically; on the contrary, some students cited it in support of her husband's infidelity.

The husband's actions, however, were read very differently by different groups of readers. On the one hand, Thomas Greene was argued to be a heartless seducer. On the other, and this was the more frequent reading, he was read as an "ordinary man" (with a "frigid wife") who simply had been tempted by an attractive young woman and had succumbed. In both of these readings it was the wife who was blamed, both for being "cold" and driving her husband to find consolation elsewhere, and for taking the child. In fact, it was her role in the events of the poem—in terms primarily of the extent to which she was culpable in Elsa's situation—that was most fully debated in our students' discussions.

Most interesting to us was the fact that these readings were constructed out of minimal textual information and were clearly highly gendered (Batsleer, Davies, O'Rouke, & Weedon, 1985; Felski, 1989; Fetterley, 1978; Gilbert, 1990.) Having drawn the attention of the students to the minimal textual information provided by the text from which their readings were constructed (by asking them to underline the textual references in the poem to each character), we asked them where their readings had "come from." The students began to re-state their readings, prefacing many of their comments with such phrases as, "It's obvious that, . . ." "You can see that she would, . . ." "It's typical of bored, rich women to, . . ." and so on. When pressed further to account for the production of such readings from so little textual information they offered general explanations such as "expectations formed by other similar stories," "from experience of life," "personal experience," and "reading between the lines" and even, in a confident denial of the validity of readings other than their own, "it's obvious from the clues that are given."

It appeared to us that the students had learned a reading practice that 'naturalised' the reading process so completely that they were unaware of their operation as readers (Belsey, 1980, 1982; Gilbert, 1987). Although impressive in their ability to produce rich and detailed readings from minimal textual information,[2] they were unaware of the ways in which they operated to construct meanings and thus were unable to "read" not only the terms of their own readings but those of others as well. Indeed, the students, all of them successful English students, seemed unable to account for any divergence of interpretation from their own, or for the construction of their readings from minimal textual evidence, beyond appeals to personal opinion.

When pressed to account for their readings, several students argued, "It's reading between the lines," whereas others were keen to see their readings as the result of logical inferences made from the textual detail given. When asked about the existence of divergent readings, one boy quickly answered, "Well, the others aren't logical interpretations"! But most students took a more laissez faire line, arguing again in terms of personal opinion and what readers brought to the reading.

The possible bases for deciding between the different readings constructed of "Elsa Wertman," however, caused unease. "If there wasn't an exam it wouldn't really matter, would it?" one girl asked. "Everyone must read books differently all the time but they don't have to write an answer or essay about it and so it doesn't matter." However, the proposition that one reading was as valid as another and that there were no grounds for raising objections to particular interpretations other than on the basis of personal opinion caused unresolved dissent. Some students had felt strongly that Mr. Greene's behaviour was indefensible and were particularly vehement that it was "wrong" to read him as simply "a typical guy," as some students suggested. They were unable, however, beyond increasingly vehement insistence that they were right, to offer convincing textual evidence to support their views, let alone an analysis of their own interpretations.

THEORISING PRACTICE?

Recent literary theoretical criticism (of which, of course, there were competing strands), including poststructuralist theory, was attractive to us in that it appeared to offer ways of addressing these issues. Initially we drew on three principles:

1. The conception of texts and readings as "made" or constructed.
2. The idea that literature emerges not from a timeless, placeless zone but from a particular social context and is read in another context
3. The argument that texts and readings are never neutral (Bennett, 1987).

We were also aware of the debate among theorists, teachers, librarians, and others about representations of ethnicity, race, genderm and class in texts, and shared this concern and the desire to analyze such representations (Appleman, 1993; Gee, 1996; Janks, 1993a, 1993b; Janks & Ivanic, 1992; Klein, 1985; Morgan, 1997). It was not, we felt, along with Freebody, Luke, and Gilbert (1991) that it was necessary to decide whether a particular text should be "used or 'banned' as a school text because of 'sexist content'" but rather whether it was "to be read blind, and thus vulnerable to that content—or under a critical scrutiny that affords multiple reading positions" (p. 450). Theory, thus, seemed to offer not only a textual practice but also a political agenda, with which we sympathized.

Working from broadly post-structuralist literary critical positions, we saw our aims in general terms as being to teach that "the text is a text," that it is a construction and not a slice or reflection of life (Barthes, 1981). We wanted to make possible a greater consciousness of the processes involved in reading and writing, and of the ideological nature of texts and readings. To summarize, we wanted students to be able to do the following:

• Analyze the construction of readings.
• "Read" other readings or interpretations.
• Consider what is at stake in the disagreement between readings.
• Make visible the gaps and silences of texts and readings.

- Analyze what readings support in terms of the values they affirm.
- Challenge other, especially dominant, readings.
- Construct new readings.

Thus, to be more specific with regard to the reading of "Elsa Wertman," some of the issues that we felt theory enabled us to address were: How are such full character readings constructed out of minimal textual information? How is gender represented? How are the gaps in the text filled? Where are the readings "coming from"? Why are textual gaps filled in specific ways? For what purposes? How else might the text be read? These were questions that not only had we felt unable to answer before, they also were questions that we felt we had not been able to *ask* before in the naturalised space of the "pre-theoretical" classroom.

Theory in the English classroom, it can be argued, resulted in Australia in what is now called Critical Literacy—and thus "theory" was part of the journey we both undertook as English teachers. It led to a conversion from Personal Growth practices to those of Critical Literacy. But, we have to confess, it was not the first conversion we had undergone.

AN EXAMINATION OF WHAT COUNTS AS ENGLISH AS A SUBJECT OR DISCIPLINE

It had seemed to us, teaching in English classrooms in Australia and the United Kingdom a decade or so earlier in the late 1960s and 1970s, that the emphasis on personal response, advocated by an increasing number of theorists, represented an exciting advance in thinking about the ways we formerly had asked our students to engage with texts. Such an emphasis, we thought, might encourage an engagement with texts that not only involved students in close reading but also allowed their role in the meaning-making process to be acknowledged. In pedagogical terms, we saw ourselves as rejecting what, increasingly in progressive English teaching circles, were perceived as the arid and elitist practices of Heritage English and its New Critical approaches to texts and embracing an amalgam of Personal Growth pedagogy and Reader Response theory made popular by such writers as Britton (1970), Barnes (1971), Dixon (1967/1975), Moffett (1968), and Rosenblatt (1970). As teachers, we saw in Personal Growth approaches the possibility of a democratic venture that would create an inclusive environment in which the responses of all students could be valued. We embraced this new Personal Growth perspective on English as enthusiastically as we criticised the Heritage perspective, from which it had taken over.

However, by the 1980s there was criticism that although the rhetoric of Personal Growth was that of enabling personal expression, the pressure for assessment of students' literary understanding in classrooms, meant that in practice it was the text, rather than the reader, that was seen as the repository of a largely singular meaning. Teaching, it was suggested, was more likely to involve a covert modification of minority responses towards a reading that was claimed to be the result of the reader's personal response but was in fact the result of careful direction. Sinfield (1985) noted, "[examination] candidates are invited to interrogate their experience to discover a response which has in actuality been learnt" (p. 132). Such a criticism, it seemed to us at the time, did more than simply point to "bad practice"; there was also a strong suggestion of bad faith.

There were also increasingly powerful challenges to traditional approaches to literature and schools of criticism from theorists working in the fields of semiology, psychoanalysis, Marxism, feminism, poststructuralism and British Cultural Studies. They questioned not simply the institutional practices that apparently prevented the expression of the full personal response, but challenged "Personal Growth" English for its a-historicism and for its severing of all connections between language and power. Eagleton (1985) made this charge quite explicitly: He suggested that literature was typically used in schools to develop "a richly subjective interiority" that legitimized the failure to commit, to act in society: "The task of the moral technology of Literature is to produce an historically peculiar form of human subject who is sensitive, receptive, imaginative and so on . . . about nothing in particular" (p. 5). This, he argued, was not only a dishonest use of literature but also a blocking of "true" English, which he saw as having been distorted in favour of conserving the present social order with its inequalities and injustices.[3] Writing of the origins of English, he argued:

> English emerged . . . as a result of a certain class struggle; and it emerged equally because of a conflict of interests between the sexes. . . . English began, in short, as the inscription of a certain kind of difference and otherness, in terms of both class and gender, at the very heart of the academic institution—and to say that is to claim that it operated as a kind of deconstruction all in itself. (Eagleton, 1991, p. 7)

Repression by the academic institution of this moment of birth resulted, Eagleton argued, in the "erasure of this unnameable difference" and a reconstitution of English into a force to divert attention away from the social and the political into the personal and the "pre-theoretical" and "uncritical."

Eagleton's alternative view of English again seemed to us to offer the possibility of a truly democratic venture—as opposed to an only *apparently*

democratic venture offered by Personal Growth English—that would create an inclusive environment in which the responses of all students could be
valued. Eagleton's lament about English seemed to offer a convincing criticism not only of Heritage model English but also of Personal Growth. It
was one of the arguments that informed our move to the kinds of concerns
explicated previously in our work with students reading "Elsa Wertman."
But there were elements of this conversion from Personal Growth to
Critical Literacy that seemed disconcertingly similar to our earlier disavow-
al of Heritage English in favor of Personal Growth: for example, the belief
in a true English distorted by misleading agencies, the practice of achieving
change through critique and the promise of a breakthrough to a state of
higher awareness.

CHANGE THROUGH CRITIQUE?

More recently, however, we have become interested in the continuities that
are readable across apparently opposed models of English. Present in both
Eagleton's complaint of the "erasure of unnameable difference" and in
Dixon's (1967/1975) much earlier criticism of a "betrayal of . . . vision" by
Heritage English (which he asserted had distorted the "map" of English in
ignoring the personal culture of pupils)—is an underlying belief in a 'true'
English which is blocked or distorted by previous perspectives on English
and about to be re-discovered in a new one. Eagleton is quite explicit about
this: "Our latest theoretical categories of class, race and gender are merely
catching up with the historical forces which brought the subject into being"
(Eagleton, 1991, p. 7).

   It seems to us now that this vision of a true English has not only
informed a continuity of resilient concerns and practices of the subject, but
also defined boundaries of what actually might count as English—again,
across time and apparently opposed perspectives on, or models of, subject
English. In Ball's (1985) historical account of the subject, for example, he
wrote that prior to 1904, English was studied by most children aged 8 and
above in the form of "orthography, etymology and syntax." He also
referred to the examination of English literature as a "specific subject,"
quoting requirements for the third year from the 1876 syllabus: "Three
hundred lines of poetry, not before brought up; repeated with knowledge
of meanings and allusions. Writing a letter or statement . . . the topics to be
given by the Inspector" (p. 54). Neither subject, although termed "English"
and "Literature" was adequate, according to Ball, to be described as gen-
uine English: "To state the position boldly, before the turn of the century
English as a school subject, in the sense that we would understand it today,

simply did not exist" (p. 65). It is not just the absence of literary study from what could be termed a language skills model—"orthography, etymology and syntax"—that disqualifies the subject from being judged to be true English since the kind of study undertaken of literary texts—memorization and recitation, and etymological and semantic knowledge—is also found inadequate.

This judgment has not been challenged in most histories of the subject (Baldick, 1983; Ball, Kenny, & Gardiner, 1990; Dixon, 1967). But, given the differing views of what constitutes the true English and the frequent assertions of its undefinability and ineffability (Light, 1989), Ball's dismissal of the subjects called English and Literature before 1900 has made us curious about just *how* the boundaries of English and Literature are being set here and elsewhere. After all, although both Heritage and Personal Growth have been criticized as distortions of all that English might (and should) be, neither model has been excluded from the designation, "English." And Critical Literacy, despite it being characterised as a radical, even dangerous,[4] alternative to these previous models, is also accepted as a version of English.

Hunter (1988a) suggested continuity across these apparently opposed models of English by arguing that what is common to them all—and, we suggest, what allows them to "qualify" as English—are techniques of moral and ethical improvement[5] adopted from Protestant pastoralism. He traced the adoption by the public education system and by English, in particular, of methods of critical reflection on self and society originally enacted in Protestant Sunday schools. This was possible, he argued, because:

> the literary work lost the autonomy it possessed [in earlier times] as a model for rhetorical imitation and as the object of philological description. It acquired instead . . . the status of a functional device within a particular critical practice; one which focused on the text only as a means of revealing the ethical shortcomings of its reader. (Hunter, 1990, p. 9)

Although Critical Literacy often is characterized as opposed to previous nonpolitical and pretheoretical models of English, we now would suggest that rather than it being a radical break with the past, it is part of a historically based tradition that sees English as a morally formative subject at the heart of the curriculum (Hunter, 1988a, 1991, 1997; Moon, 2001b; Patterson, 1992, 1997). That is, it is the goal of moral and ethical formation (to be achieved through a nondirective pedagogy), common to these apparently very different models of English, which appears to have allowed their acceptance at different times as possible contenders for the title of "true English."

MORAL FORMATION THROUGH ENGLISH

It is interesting to note the similarities between the following statements about the goals and purposes of English, made from what appear to be very different positions from different periods:

> We claim that no personality can be complete, can see life steadily and see it whole, without that unifying influence, that purifying of the emotions which art and literature can alone bestow. It follows then from what we've said above that the bulk of our people, of whatever class, are unconsciously living starved existences, that one of the richest fields of our spiritual being is left uncultivated—not indeed barren, for the weeds of literature have never been so prolific as in our day. (The Newbolt Report, 1921, p. 257)

> Those who in school are offered (perhaps) the beginnings of education in taste are exposed, out of school, to the competing exploitation of the cheapest emotional responses. . . . We cannot, as we might in a healthy culture, leave the citizen to be formed unconsciously by his environment; if anything like a worthy idea of satisfactory living is to be saved, he must be trained to discriminate and resist. (Leavis & Thompson, 1948, p. 3)

> In the Heritage model the stress was on culture as a given. There was a constant temptation to ignore culture as the pupil knows it, a network of attitudes to experience and personal evaluations that he develops in a living response to his family and neighbourhood. But this personal culture is what he brings to literature; in the light of it he reads the linguistic symbols (giving his own precious life-blood!). What is vital is the interplay between his personal world and the world of the writer: the teacher of English must acknowledge both sides of the experience, and know both of them intimately if he is to help bring the two into a fruitful relationship. (Dixon, 1967/1975, p. 3)

Here we have a rehearsal of some of the familiar tenets of English: Literature makes one a better person; works to the general good of society; "un-blinds" and empowers people; trains people to resist a range of social evils; helps to develop the whole person; should be nondirectively introduced to students, and so on. What is surprising, here, is that these tenets are articulated by representatives of opposed positions: Heritage and Personal Growth English. Nevertheless, we found it easier to accept the continuities of these positions—which we thought of as pretheoretical and, therefore, unconscious and uncritical—than to entertain the possibility that

Cultural Studies and Critical Literacy might also articulate these concerns, albeit in a different register. But, consider the following extract:

> Cultural Studies is concerned with the complicity of cultural processes, including the most "innocent" and pleasurable ones (like reading "literature"), in relationships of inequality and power. Cultural processes are viewed in relation to "primary social relations": those social relationships that really make a difference to the kind of lives people can lead, that empower or disempower them in particular ways. . . . A key endeavour . . . is to try and make different and often antagonistic points of view explicit, in order to struggle over them more consciously, more productively, in order to learn from them. (Johnson, 1989, 11)

Johnson's warning about the dangers of "complicity of cultural processes" in relationships of inequality and power provides an echo of Leavis' and Thompson's warning of the dangers of an unhealthy culture with its exploitation of the cheapest emotional responses, and Dixon's warnings of an imposed or artificial culture. Leavis and Thompson find a solution in training students to be able to resist and discriminate, whereas Johnson advocated making antagonistic viewpoints explicit in order to struggle over them more consciously. For Dixon, the untutored world of the student is not deficient—indeed he praised it—nevertheless it requires intervention in order to realise the student's full potential. All extracts, it would seem, see students at risk from varying but powerful deceptions, and in need of empowerment to resist them.

PLUS CA CHANGE?

We are not suggesting, however, that English has never changed. The elitism detectable in the quote by Leavis and Thompson is a long way from the inclusive social visions of both Dixon and Johnson and yet there are similarities that prompted us to re-consider our belief in a complete break between so-called pretheoretical models of English, and Critical Literacy. What these extracts suggest to us is that English has always had a morally formative goal although this has been presented in different ways. English has always seen itself on the side of "good" and despite claims to radically different and oppositional models, it can be argued to maintain a continuity through a teaching practice that seeks to enlighten the student, morally and ethically: that is, English in *all* of its models is perceived as having a cultural and social mission (Baldick, 1983; Leavis, 1972). Both conservative and radical versions appear to offer the promise of an expansion of consciousness to be achieved either through aesthetic fulfillment or theoretical clarification. All of the quotes just presented, we suggest, provide a view of English that is remarkably consistent in its attention to the production of a complete person; one who can see clearly, or who sees things as they really are, or is not deceived by ideology. Interestingly, an expression similar to "seeing things as they really are" is used by theorists as far apart as Matthew Arnold, John Dixon, and Terry Eagleton. What differs according to these writers is what stops us from seeing clearly. For Arnold it was sin. For Leavis it was "mass culture." For Dixon it is the division between feeling and thought and for Eagleton it is ruling class ideology.

The traditional criticism of Heritage and Personal Growth as pretheoretical and naively empiricist—and therefore radically different from Critical Literacy—no longer seems to us to be entirely convincing. Although access to "reality" is desired, it is not assumed by these earlier models of English that reality is a given nor that a greater awareness of life is easily achieved. Effort and struggle are repeatedly emphasised in Arnold's (1869/1950) account of seeing things clearly. He wrote, "the very desire to see things as they are, implies a balance and regulation of mind which is not often attained without fruitful effort" (p. 44). Similarly, Dixon (1967/1975) commented on "the *effort* to find in experience more than we thought we knew, or valued" (p. 55; italics added). He similarly emphasises the struggle involved in seeing "life as it really is" (p. 114), which are the concluding words to his influential book, *Growth through English*. They provide an echo of the Newbolt Report's (1921) much earlier stated ideal to "see life steadily and see it whole" (p. 257). Viewed from this position, the emphasis by Marxist theorist, Eagleton, on the varying ideological impediments to seeing clearly, although in a different register, seems almost traditional; for Eagleton, *and* for Arnold, Newbolt, and Dixon seeing things clearly is not unproblematic nor is "reality" a given. Rather, to see with understanding or consciousness, or to see critically, relies on the development of human capacities, which is achieved by enabling students to see through what is blocking their perceptions.

PEDAGOGY FOR FREEDOM?

Related to the view of English as a morally formative subject is a pedagogy or way of teaching that relies on nondirective methods to bring students to self-understanding and to a point where they can see through the deceptions of the text. In the Critical Literacy classroom, these are ideological deceptions: Rather than coercing students, we enable students to see society as it really is—which is unfair, inequitable, unjust, and in need of change.

Encouraging students to problematize their initial responses to texts (through questioning, textual commentaries, and activities), we invite them to take up multiple reading positions through activities that disrupt the taken-for-granted nature of textual representation, hoping that in the process they will become aware of the power of dominant ideologies. Thus, in an echo of Arnold (1869/1950), who wrote of the need for "a transformative moment" (p. 139), Johnson (1989) called for "changes in person and in the disposition of power . . . in a really deep and transformative sense" (p. 11).

In our earlier practice, we did not question our status as nondirective "guides" to personal transformation. In fact, we prided ourselves on our making clear the bases of our readings, unlike the *deceptively* free reading regimes of Heritage and Personal Growth models of English. Library research (Hunter, 1988a; Michael, 1987) and classroom observations (Mellor & Patterson, 2000), however, pointed to a long-established, although rarely acknowledged, pedagogy that invites students to problematise and adjust their initial readings toward more acceptable interpretations. This, we argue, operates in Critical Literacy as it did in earlier models albeit with different "targets": in support of tolerance of diversity and difference, critical literacy practices attempt to challenge and adjust social norms around issues of gender, race and ethnicity, social class, and sexuality.

Literary theory seemed to offer a means of disrupting taken-for-granted readings of texts in terms of these issues through its concepts of the "forever imperceptible" text that "hides from the first comer" (Derrida, 1981, p. 63) and the "ideologically-directed" reading (Belsey, 1980; Eagleton, 1985; Scholes, 1985). It also appeared to provide techniques by which we could deconstruct the ways in which ideology produced "false consciousness." This, in terms of teaching, however, was usually characterized as resisting and removing impediments to "seeing clearly" rather than attempting to impose new readings and more tolerant norms of belief. But to teach tolerance is not actually to offer freedom. Tolerance, after all, is itself a norm. Critical Literacy does not define tolerance as the acceptance of complete plurality, but rather as respect for *particular* differences. If we were truly happy with complete plurality in the interpretation of texts then why would we intervene in our students' initial readings?[6]

The fact is there *are* readings that are not acceptable in the Critical Literacy classroom: racist or sexist readings, for example. Despite the emphasis in post-structuralist theory on multiple subject positions, the Critical Literacy classroom requires the production of specific readings, it seems to us now, no less than the Heritage or Personal Growth classroom. Although alternative reading practices and multiple subject positions are encouraged, these generally do not include racist or sexist practices or positions—unless for the express purpose of problematizing and deconstructing them.

Because of the history of our subject as nondirective, we tended, like most English teachers, however, to be much happier with the concept of *resisting* power than using power. English proposes the realization of good social and ethical purposes in the inner being or consciousness of the student—depending on the model of English—via practices that promise to un-blind and empower the student. These practices are assumed to free students to recognize the distortions of sin, mass culture, and dominant ideologies and to produce good readings of their own, as opposed to those produced under the power of various distorting agencies—or those that have been imposed by the teacher.

PRACTICES IN THE CLASSROOM: FREE OR NORMATIVE, AND SO WHAT?

As Foucault (1983) suggested, when investigating a particular problem researchers could benefit by focusing not on the easy differences but on the difficult similarities. We have discussed above how research has tended to focus on what appear to be the oppositional aspects of Heritage, Personal Growth, and Critical Literacy perspectives on English—with particular results for the way in which discourses around the subject are framed. Changes in English, we have suggested, are framed in terms of a quest for the "true English" in which the removal of mistaken (if differing) aspects of the previous perspective on the subject will result in *freeing* students to read the text more discriminatingly, consciously or critically. The evidence in the Critical Literacy classroom of this having occurred will be in the students' production of multiple readings—which will include feminist and antiracist readings of texts.

These readings, we have argued, are commonly characterised as not imposed by the teacher, but as realised by the students themselves. Thus, Smith and Mason (1961), working out of a Heritage paradigm, offered a characteristic defence of their teaching that "is not intended to supply packaged judgements [*sic*]—God forbid—but to offer the necessary background and equipment for *independent* inquiry" (pp. 7–8, italics added). So, similar to all versions of English, although the teacher will have offered guidance in the form of question and answer sessions, or general discussion, textual activities or commentary, the students are theorised as having produced "their own readings" as opposed to those imposed by the teacher (Dixon, 1967/1975; Scholes, 1985).

We now think, however, that this opposition—of the freedom to produce one's own readings versus the normative requirement to produce an
imposed reading—is a false one. All classrooms are inescapably normative;
we teach and learn things there. However, simply to acknowledge our nor-
mativity as an inevitable part of an ideological battle for enlightenment
doesn't really do. Nor does arguing that Critical Literacy practices be
taught simply as skills or competencies. In the name of plurality and difference, the Critical Literacy classroom *may* require students to demonstrate
that they can produce a feminist, or antiracist or New Critical or Marxist
reading, or *all* four readings in turn of a text. The aim, however, we now
believe, of such a requirement—however apparently "open-ended" it is—is,
still, "transformation." Rather than students displaying critical consciousness "about nothing in particular," as Eagleton wrote about an earlier paradigm of English, the hope of teaching multiple reading practices is, surely,
that it will produce real changes in students' subjectivities.

It is possible to test this proposition by considering an alternative: make
it a requirement that students produce overtly racist readings as simply a
competence. The problems spring into focus. In our experience, the
encouragement of racist or sexist readings in the classroom has hardly been
necessary. However, some questions—perhaps those implying that the
expression of all personal responses is acceptable—may be used by teachers
in order to get issues "out into the open." Generally, we have found that a
high level of skill is required by the teacher to manage such situations in
order not to offend students who may be targeted or hurt by such discourses. Furthermore, we suggest, the aim of such discussions is not usually
located simply at the level of encouraging personal expression. The aim is
to adjust or modify those racist or sexist views. Similarly, an approach that
encourages playful plurality in relation to a text, we suspect, actually
assumes that through adopting multiple reading positions (usually of a pro-
scribed kind) the ideology of a text and of its "dominant" readings will be
revealed *and* rejected.

While we still try to show students that issues related to gender, race,
ethnicity, and class are not simply personal—they are social and cultural—
we would argue now that this knowledge is *positively* formed; it is not the
result of a generalized enlightenment or consciousness brought about by
the removal of ideological blockages to critical awareness. We now see our
practice as part of a piecemeal attempt to adjust social norms. Schools, we
argue, are one institution among others attempting to make changes in the
direction of equity and social justice in the interests of social harmony. Of
course, these attempts are uneven, imperfect and sometimes may be just
wrong.

We wonder now whether the multiplicity of subject positions promised
by poststructuralism is simply not compatible with a subject that has long

perceived itself as morally formative. This could explain, we suggest, the use of post-structuralist concepts such as "multiple readings, "multiple subject positions" and "resistance" as devices that facilitate the adjustment of students' initial responses (possibly sexist or racist ones) to those required by the Critical Literacy classroom—but that only can be acknowledged as taught within a particular framework of raised consciousness and freedom of choice. These concepts justify teachers' interventions into students' responses by characterizing them as *freeing* students to produce their "own readings"—and they leave teachers more or less safe from charges of imposing readings upon students.

Using poststructuralist techniques in the service of critical practice, we now suspect, perhaps cannot fail to produce contradictions, any more than the techniques used in Heritage and Personal Growth models of English in pursuit of aesthetic and personal fulfillment. Scholes' (1985) comment below, however, appears to make a comforting distinction for teachers: "Our job is not to produce 'readings' for our students but to give them the tools for producing their own" (p. 24).

There are reasons though to think that there are problems with this specification. First, students' "own readings" have to operate as a measure of the success or failure of the degree to which a critical reading—defined in quite specific terms—has been achieved. That is, students' readings have to be *recognizable* as critical readings, according to specific, if usually unstated, criteria. Second, modes of analysis (including deconstructive techniques) or ways of looking at texts are not neutral. As Hunter (1982) pointed out, it is not possible to look at the text and then read it. Reading the text is *how* one looks at the text. Conversely, looking at the text is reading the text. Giving students "tools" or post-structuralist deconstructive techniques does not free them to look at the text "critically" and consequently produce their own readings (which happen to be antiracist, feminist and so on, and thus conforming to the requirements of the Critical Literacy classroom). It is teaching students how to look at the text in particular ways, which is teaching students how to *read* in particular ways.

If the readings produced by students in the Critical Literacy classroom are not latent in the text or reader waiting to be realized when released from the twin deceptions of the slippery text and the ideologically dominant reading, then where do they come from? Missed or overlooked by such a question is the secondary set of texts (A. Luke, 1988; C. Luke, de Castell, & Luke, 1989), such as the teaching activities and commentaries we provide, which outline and teach the procedures, or give the "tools"—the ways of looking—which result in the readings produced. Hunter (1982) called these "the meaning effect." That is, meaning is seen as an effect of using particular ways of looking—that is particular ways of reading— which are taught.

Critical Literacy puts at the heart of its practice social justice issues. Surely, therefore, it is not possible to argue that it is non-normative, any more than any previous version of English, with its particular emphasis on moral and ethical formation, can. Good, whether defined as "discrimination," "sensitivity," "the full personal response" or "critical consciousness," does not emerge from the shadow of deceitful (and variously defined) Evil: It is positively constructed. The teacher's task then can be seen in different terms. It is not to reveal, or allow to be produced meanings that are distorted, blocked, or hidden but, instead, to alter the use of the text and to teach specific ways of looking (reading) that produce particular readings. The aim is to construct the reader as a social agent with particular capacities—such as that of producing feminist or anti-racist or plural or critical readings of a text (Mellor et al., 1991).

WHY BOTHER?

But if, as we have suggested, the explicitly theorized approaches of Critical Literacy are similar to those of earlier models of English—and still beset by many of the same troubling questions—it might be tempting to ask what the advantage is of taking a critical approach to literature rather than a traditional Heritage or Personal Growth one; that is, if the different models of English are all doing the same thing why would we want to change? After all, critical practice seems to promise an awareness, or consciousness, of the forces that influence our thoughts and actions. To move away from this position is not easy for many English teachers—and why would we want to having been trained in a tradition dedicated to moral and ethical improvement? However, as Moon (2001a) notesd, although recent theory has questioned whether we can stand outside our particular historical context and "see through" the distortions of ideology, what we perhaps "can achieve from a social-historical perspective . . . are some partial, strategic reorientations; not a total transformation in consciousness but a degree of movement in thinking about particular problems surrounding representation and meaning" (p. vii).

Thus, despite what may seem like a disengagement from many of the grander, emancipatory promises that "theory," and in particular post-structuralism, seemed to offer, we would still say that it has had significant effects on our thinking and on our practical work over the past 15 years or so. The emphases on textuality, on the construction of meaning, on analysis of the social determinants of reading (Bennett, 1987) and on deconstruction led us to adopt a more explicitly critical practice. It also led to a more analytical and questioning stance in relation to English "itself." That is, not only did poststructuralist reading practices enable us to devise activities to "defamiliarise" classroom texts and students' reading of them, they also opened up English to a scrutiny that previously we had not entertained.

Prior to our engagement with poststructuralism we had not ever wondered why we encouraged students to adopt "a critical, reflective relation to self and society" (Moon, 2001a, p. xx). Now, however, rather than simply accepting that English is an inherently morally formative subject that encompasses the inculcation of a range of aesthetic and ethical abilities via a nondirective pedagogy, we have begun to research how and why these particular characteristics of English emerged. We also have started investigating what "counts" as English and how activities and knowledges not dependent on the presence of critical goals—at present "idealised as *the* mark of good teaching" (Moon, 2001b, p. 6)—might be included in our subject. This need not mean that readings or indeed English itself cannot be changed or challenged on political grounds, but it does mean that such challenges cannot make claims to non-normative modes of critique or to an inherent higher mission that promises inclusivity while excluding other useful methods of interacting with texts.

FUTURE DIRECTIONS

Working from a historical base, Moon (2001b) offered some cautionary comments in his important paper, "History, Research and the X-Files." He argued that subject English has become "increasingly enthralled by a narrow set of reading practices assembled around the figure of the critically reflective reader" (p. 5). This might seem to be the kind of criticism of "progressive" English teaching that we have become all too familiar with. Commonly mounted from the Right in favour of Skills and Shakespeare, such criticism characteristically rejects "theory" while operating itself from unexamined theoretical bases. Moon's position, however, is very different. First, he pointed to the logical emergence of critical practices given the history of the subject. Second, he did not claim that there is anything inherently wrong with critical and reflective reading practices. Indeed, he argued that they are "useful for promoting active learning, and for developing habits of introspection and self-correction" and "as such they have a perfectly legitimate place in the repertoire of teaching practices" (p. 6). What Moon was concerned about is the "over-extension" of reflective and critical reading practices so that they become the only way of interacting with texts and are seen as the apotheosis of the "true" English. Of further concern, he suggested, of the idealisation of such practices is that what he terms "technical skills and knowledges"—including factual knowledge about texts— may be neglected:

For students of English, the neglect of empirical knowledges can prove disabling as they struggle to cope with the burdens of constant interpretation and critique. In the absence of adequate empirical input, students can simply run out of resources with which to construct their readings of texts. For although we may be encouraged to think that those resources lie "within" the student, any interpretive or analytical reading depends in part upon the accumulation of certain facts about texts and their histories, and on the acquisition of particular skills for working with those facts. Unfortunately, empirical knowledges have long been viewed with disdain or suspicion in English, on the grounds that they are "merely" functional, or on the basis that they are instrumental to the maintenance of a *status quo* that English should critique and subvert. Teachers of English are often reluctant to see their classrooms as places where information is traded, preferring instead to see the classroom as primarily an interrogative space. But as anyone will know who has written seriously about works of literature or popular culture, a body of factual knowledge about the text, its production, circulation, and reception, is essential. (p. 6)

Moon referred to English's misgivings about imposing readings on students but argued that the concern to allow students to produce their own readings—which, as noted previously, is not recent but has a long history across opposed models of English—can lead to textual analysis remaining primarily personal despite Critical Literacy's assertions "about the 'social' dimension of meaning" (p. 6). Moon suggested not an alternative approach to Critical Literacy but, rather, an addition to critical analysis and personal response. His proposals—not mortgaged to a view of the "true English"—may allow a reconsideration of the content and practices of English to take place in a more temperate climate.

Our comments here do not constitute yet another conversion: We are not critiquing Critical Literacy in the belief that it is another failed realisation of all that English should be. On the contrary, we claim that the practices associated with moral and ethical formation are an important, historically based part of our subject. However, there are advantages to seeing Critical Literacy not in terms of a theoretical breakthrough or overcoming but, instead, as a manifestation of English as a *construction*. It allows an acknowledgment of its historically imparted tasks of forming a range of literate and ethical capacities and also permits us to respond to the varying requirements of increasingly diverse societies. It would be ironic if the inclusive goals of Critical Literacy did not allow a critical analysis of what counts as English and why, and if its practices were expanded and idealised to the exclusion of all other ways of interacting with texts.

ENDNOTES

1. The students, aged from 15 to 18 years, attended two secondary schools in an Australian capital city, one a co-educational comprehensive high school and one a single-sex girls' school.
2. Stanley Fish's (1980) account of an incident in one of his classes, in which his students produced a reading of a list of linguists' names that they had been told was a poem, is interesting on this point.
3. See also Doyle (1982). Widdowson's (1982) own article from the same collection of essays is also relevant.
4. Comments warning of "classroom brainwashers" and "barbarians [who] are no longer at the gates, but . . . safely ensconced in the citadels" are not difficult to find in newspaper discussions of Critical Literacy approaches. The first quotation is from the *Daily Express* (UK), "Ban Classroom Brainwashers!" June 10, 1988, p. 13; the second is from *The Sydney Morning Herald* (Australia), "Revolution in the English Classroom," Kevin Donnelly, September 6, 1994, p.19.
5. See also Foucault (1988) and Rose (1990).
6. As English teachers, we might well give a Derridean answer to this question, however, Ian Hunter (1988b), in response to Derrida's description of the text as opaque and potentially deceitful, asked whether this is always so—at all times and under all circumstances. He argued that the phrases, "hiding from the first comer" and "forever imperceptible" far from being definitive of textuality at all times and on all occasions are characteristic simply of the way in which texts are *used* in the English lesson. Elsewhere, he writes, "We *make* certain texts ultimately inscrutable as a condition of performing a certain kind of work [on them] . . . " (Hunter, 1991, p. 50). Furthermore, he suggested that readers have to be *taught* to doubt their initial readings—that is, trained to see them as insufficiently sensitive or as distorted by ideology.

REFERENCES

Appleman, D. (1993). Looking through critical lenses: Teaching literary theory to secondary students. In S. Straw & D. Bogdan (Eds.), *Constructive reading: Teaching beyond communication* (pp. 155–171). Portsmouth, NH: Boynton Cook.

Arnold, M. (1950). *Culture and anarchy.* Cambridge, UK: Cambridge University Press. (Original work published in 1869)

Baldick, C. (1983). *The social mission of English criticism: 1848–1932.* Oxford, UK: Clarendon Press.

Ball, S., & Goodson, I. (1984). *Defining the curriculum: Histories and ethnographies.* London: Falmer

Ball, S. J. (1985). English for the English since 1906. In I. Goodson (Ed.), *Social histories of the secondary curriculum: Subjects for study* (pp. 53–88). Lewes: Falmer Press.

Ball, S. J., Kenny, A., & Gardiner, D. (1990). Literacy, politics and the teaching of English. In I. Goodson & P. Medway (Eds.), *Bring English to order* (pp. 47–87). Lewes: Falmer Press.

Barnes, D. (1971). *Language, the learner and the school* (Rev. ed.). Harmondsworth, UK: Penguin Books.

Barthes, R. (1981). Theory of the text. (I. McLeod, Transl.). In R. Young (Ed.), *Untying the text: A poststructuralist reader* (pp. 31–47). London: Routledge.

Batsleer, J., Davies, T., O'Rourke, R., & Weedon, C. (1985). *Rewriting English: Cultural politics of gender and class.* London: Methuen.

Belsey, C. (1980). *Critical practice.* London, UK: Methuen.

Belsey, C. (1982). A space in the syllabus. *Literature, Teaching, Politics, 1,* 58–65.

Bennett, T. (1987). Texts in history: The determinations of readings and their texts. In D. Attridge, G. Bennington, & R. Young (Eds.), *Poststructuralism and the question of history* (pp. 63–81). Cambridge, UK: Cambridge University Press.

Britton, J. (1970). *Language and learning.* Harmondsworth: Penguin.

Cambourne, B., Hendy, L., & Scown, P. (1988). *The whole story: Natural learning and the acquisition of literacy in the classroom.* Auckland, New Zealand: Ashton Scholastic.

Cherryholmes, C. (1988). *Power and criticism: Poststructural investigations in education.* New York: Teachers College Press.

Christie, F. (Ed.). (1990). *Literacy for a changing world.* Hawthorne, Victoria: Australian Council for Educational Research.

Corcoran, B. (1987). Teachers creating readers. In B. Corcoran & E. Evans. (Eds.), *Readers, texts, teachers.* Montclair, NJ: Boynton Cook.

Crowley, S. (1989). *A teachers guide to deconstruction.* Urbana, IL: NCTE.

Davies, B. (1989). *Frogs and snails and feminist tales: Preschool children and gender.* Sydney, Australia: Allen & Unwin.

Davies, B. (1992). Beyond dualism and towards multiple subjectivities. In L. Christian-Smith (Ed.). *Texts of desire* (145-173). Lewes: Falmer Press.

Davies, B. (1994). *Poststructuralist theory and classroom practice.* Geelong, Victoria: Deakin University Press.

Dixon, J. (1975). *Growth through English.* Oxford, UK: Oxford University Press. (Original work published 1967)

Derrida, J. (1981). *Dissemination.* (B. Johnson, Trans.) Chicago: University of Chicago Press.

Doyle, B. (1982). The hidden history of English studies. In P. Widdowson (Ed.), *Re-reading English* (pp. 17–31). London: Methuen.

Eagleton, T. (1985). The subject of literature. *The English Magazine, 15,* 4–7.

Eagleton, T. (1991). The Enemy within. Sheffield: National Association of Teachers of English.

Felski, R. (1989). *Beyond feminist aesthetics: feminist literature and social change.* Cambridge, MA: Harvard University Press.

Fetterley, J. (1978). *The resisting reader: A feminist approach to American fiction.* Bloomington and London, UK: Indiana University Press.

Fish, S. (1980). *Is there a text in this class? The authority of interpretive communities.* Cambridge, Mass: Harvard University Press.

Foucault, M. (1983). *This is not a pipe.* Berkeley: University of California Press.

Foucault, M. (1988). Technologies of the self. In L. H. Martin, H. Gutman, & P. H. Hutton (Eds.), *Technologies of the self: A seminar with Michel Foucault* (pp. 16–49). London, UK: Tavistock.

Freebody, P., Luke, A., & Gilbert, P. (1991). Reading positions and practices in the classroom. *Curriculum Inquiry, 21*(4), 435–457.

Gee, J.P. (1996). *Social linguistics and literacies: ideology in discourses* (2nd ed.). London, UK: Taylor and Francis.

Gilbert, P. (1987). Post reader-response: The deconstructive critique. In B. Corcoran & E. Evans (Eds.), *Readers, texts, teachers* (pp. 234–250). Montclair, NJ: Boynton Cook.

Gilbert, P. (1989). *Writing, schooling, and deconstruction: From voice to text in the classroom.* London, UK and New York: Routledge.

Gilbert, P. (1990). Student text as pedagogical text. In I. Goodson & P. Medway (Eds.), *Bringing English to order* (pp.195–202). Lewes, UK: Falmer Press.

Goodson, I. (1983). *School subjects and curriculum change.* London, UK: Croom Helm.

Graves, D. (1986). *Children writing: process-conference writing.* Balckburn, Victoria: Dove Communications.

Green, B. (Ed.). (1993). *The insistence of the letter: Literacy studies and curriculum theorizing.* London, UK: Pittsburgh: Falmer; University of Pittsburgh Press.

Green, B. & Beavis, C. (1996). *Teaching the English subjects: Essays on English curriculum history and Australian schooling.* Geelong, Vic.: Deakin University Press.

Green, J.L., & Harker, J.O. (Eds.). (1988). *Multiple perspective analyses of classroom discourse.* Norwood, NJ: Ablex.

Green, J.L., & Wallat, C. (1981). *Ethnography and language in educational settings.* Norwood, NJ: Ablex.

Hunter, I. (1982). The concept of context and the problem of reading. *Southern Review,* 15, 1, 80–91.

Hunter, I. (1988a). *Culture and government: The emergence of literary education.* London, UK: Macmillan.

Hunter, I. (1988b). The occasion of criticism. *Poetics, 17,* 159–84.

Hunter, I. (1990). Criticism as a way of life. *Typereader, 4,* 5–20.

Hunter, I. (1991). Learning the literature lesson: The limits of the aesthetic personality. In C. D. Baker, & A. Luke (Eds.). *Towards a critical sociology of reading pedagogy* (pp. 49–82). Amsterdam & Philadelphia, PA: John Benjamins.

Hunter, I. (1997). After English: toward a less critical literacy. In S. Muspratt, A. Luke, & P. Freebody (Eds.). *Constructing critical literacies* (pp. 315–334). Sydney, Australia: Allen & Unwin.

Janks, H. (1993a). *Language and position* (Critical Language Awareness Series). Johannesburg: Hodder and Stoughton in conjunction with Witwatersrand University Press.

Janks, H. (1993b). *Language, identity, and power* (Critical Language Awareness Series). Johannesburg: Hodder and Stoughton in conjunction with Witwatersrand University Press.

Janks, H., & Ivanic, R. (1992). Critical language awareness and emancipatory discourse. In N. Fairclough (Ed.), *Critical language awareness.* London: Longman.

Johnson, R. (1989). Cultural studies in a strong state. *The English Magazine, 22,* 10–14.

Klein, G. (1985). *Reading into racism: Bias in children's literature and learning materials.* London, UK: Routledge & Kegan Paul.

Kristeva, J., & Moi, T. (1986). *The Kristeva Reader.* Oxford, UK: Basil Blackwell.

Leavis, F. R., & Thompson, D. (1948). Culture and environment: The training of critical awareness. London: Chatto & Windus.

Leavis, F.R. (1972). *Nor shall my sword: Discourses on pluralism, compassion and social hope.* London: Chatto & Windus.

Light, A. (1989). Two cheers for liberal education. In P. Brooker & P. Humm (Eds.), *Dialogue and difference* (pp. 31–42). London & New York: Routledge.

Luke, A. (1988). *Literacy, textbooks and ideology.* Lewes: Falmer Press.

Luke, C., de Castell, S., & Luke, A. (1989). Beyond criticism: The authority of the school textbook In S. de Castell, A. Luke & C. Luke (Eds.), *Language, authority and criticism: Readings on the school textbook* (pp. 245–261). Lewes, UK: Falmer Press.

Martin, J.R., Christie, F., & Rothery, J. (1987). Social processes in Education. *Journal of the English Teachers Association of New South Wales, 53,* 3-22.

Martino, W.J., & Mellor, B. (1994). *Gendered fictions.* Cottesloe, W. Australia: Chalkface Press; Urbana, IL: National Council of Teachers of English.

Masters, E. L. (1962). Elsa Wertman. *Spoon River Anthology,* New York: Collier.

Mellor, B. (1989). *Reading Hamlet.* Scarborough, W. Australia: Chalkface Press; Urbana, IL: NCTE.

Mellor, B., O'Neill, M., & Patterson, A. (1987). *Reading stories.* Scarborough, W. Australia: Chalkface Press; Urbana, IL: National Council of Teachers of English.

Mellor, B., & Patterson, A. (1994). The reading lesson. *Interpretations, 27*(3), 20-48.

Mellor, B., & Patterson, A. (1996). *Investigating texts.* Cottesloe, W. Australia: Chalkface Press; Urbana, IL: NCTE.

Mellor, B., & Patterson, A. (2000). Critical practice: Teaching 'Shakespeare'. *Journal of Adult and Adolescent Literacy, 43*(6), 508–518.

Mellor, B., Patterson, A., & O'Neill, M. (1991). *Reading fictions.* Scarborough, W. Australia: Chalkface Press; Urbana, IL: National Council of Teachers of English.

Michael, I. (1987). *The teaching of English: From the sixteenth century to 1870.* Cambridge, UK: Cambridge University Press.

Moffett, J. (1968). *Teaching the universe of discourse.* Boston, MA: Houghton Mifflin.

Moon, B. (2001a). *Literary terms: A practical glossary.* Cottesloe, W. Australia: Chalkface Press; Urbana, IL: NCTE. (Original work published 1992)

Moon, B. (2001b). "The text is out there": History, research and The X Files. *English in Australia, 138,* 5–16

Moon, B., & Mellor, B. (2001). *Writing critical essays: A practical guide.* Cottesloe, W. Australia: Chalkface Press.

Morgan, W. (1997). *Critical literacy in the classroom: The art of the possible.* London, UK & New York: Routledge.

Newbolt Report (1921). *The teaching of English in England.* London: Government Printer.

Patterson, A. (1989). *Reading response: An analysis of the gendered construction of adolescents' written responses to short fiction.* Unpublished doctoral thesis. Perth: University of Western Australia.

Patterson, A. (1992, October). Individualism in English: from personal growth to discursive construction. *English Education*, 131–146.

Patterson, A. (1997). A technique for living: some thoughts on beginning reading pedagogy in sixteenth century England. *UTS Review, 3*(2), 67–90.

Peel, R., Patterson, A., & Gerlach, J. (2000). *Questions of English: Ethics, aesthetics, rhetoric, and the formation of the subject in England, Australia, and the United States.* London, UK: Routledge.

Rose, N. (1990). *Governing the soul: Technologies of human subjectivity.* London, UK: Routledge.

Rosenblatt, L. (1970). *Literature as exploration.* London: Heinemann Educational.

Rosenblatt, L. (1978). *The reader, the text, the poem: The transactional theory of the literacy work.* Carbondale: Southern Illinois University Press.

Scholes, R. (1985). *Textual power: Literary theory and the teaching of English.* New Haven, CT: Yale University Press.

Sinfield, A. (1985). Give an account of Shakespeare and education, showing why you think they are effective and what you have appreciated about them. Support your comments with precise references. In J. Dollimore, & A. Sinfield (Eds.), *Political Shakespeare: New essays in cultural materialism* (pp. 134–157). Manchester, UK: Manchester University Press.

Smith, A. J., & Mason, W. H. (Eds.). (1961). *Short story study: A critical anthology.* London, UK: Edward Arnold.

Street, B. (1984). *Literacy in theory and practice.* Cambridge, UK: Cambridge University Press.

Widdowson, P. (1982). The crisis in English studies. In P. Widdowson (Ed.), *Re-reading English* (pp. 1–14). London, UK & New York: Methuen.

Author Index

Subject Index

Printed in the United States
27512LVS00002BC/1-15